STATES OF GRACE

STATES
OF
GRACE
EIGHT PLAYS
BY PHILIP BARRY

Edited and with a Biographical Essay
by
BRENDAN GILL

Harcourt Brace Jovanovich
New York and London

Printed in the United States of America

The introduction is an expanded version of a Profile that appeared originally in *The New Yorker*.

Library of Congress Cataloging in Publication Data

Barry, Philip, 1896-1949.
States of grace.

CONTENTS: You and I.—White wings.—Holiday. [etc.]
I. Title.
PS3503.A648A6 1975 812'.5'2 75-12532
ISBN 0-15-184910-2

First edition

B C D E

CONTENTS

I am gratefully in debt to Ellen Barry, Philip Barry, Jr., Adèle and Robert Lovett, Fannie and Francis Brennan, Alfred de Liagre, Jr., Donald Oenslager, Archibald MacLeish, and Charles Addams for help in the preparation of this book. I owe thanks as well to Joseph Patrick Roppolo for facts taken from his treatise *Philip Barry* (Twayne) and to Robert N. Schancupp for information in his unpublished dissertation on Barry's early life, entitled "The Thing He Wanted to Do." David Jackson's editorial assistance in the preparation of this book has been invaluable.

STATES OF GRACE

■ THE DARK ADVANTAGE ■

I

Even in a palace life can be lived well. Marcus Aurelius's stoic witticism offers a clue to the fortunate life of the American playwright Philip Barry. He was partial to palaces and to the people who dwelt in them, especially if the palaces were small and sunny and the people smiling. He was still more partial to people who might have lived in palaces and who chose instead to live in pavilions and pleasances, accepting with light hearts the responsibilities that their good luck imposed on them. Barry liked to be around lucky people and he set lofty standards of conduct for them. He wished them to be every bit as disciplined in their happiness as unlucky people are obliged to be in their misery. For both sorts of people the goal must be the same—grace of the body, grace of the spirit. Grace is whatever is fitting, whatever flourishes within bounds. Barry was a lucky man and very hard on himself; sooner than most he achieved the grace he sought and, the price proving greater than he found it easy to pay, sooner than most he died.

Barry's sense of the appropriate manifested itself in his work as it did in his life: nothing bigger than need be. No matter how ambitious the intentions of his plays, he kept them modest in scale. He wrote often in the now little-favored genre of high comedy, but his comedies strove to be deeper than they were high, and he could write a tragedy low enough, bleak enough, coarse enough, to take place in a saloon. He wrote, among other plays, *Holiday, The Animal Kingdom,* and *The Philadelphia Story,* but he also wrote *White Wings, Hotel Universe,* and *Here Come the Clowns.* He had many hits and many flops, and little as he enjoyed the drudgery of putting on plays, he mightily enjoyed the drudgery of writing them. As far as he could tell, it was the task he had been born into the world to perform, and it was agreeable to be well rewarded for what he was almost helpless not to do.

The characters that Barry invented for his so-called drawing-room comedies have tastes that run to simple, costly things. His heroes and heroines state and resolve their problems as best they can over drinks in de-luxe farmhouses, villas, and seaside cottages. Barry shared the tastes of his characters, as he shared their appetites and pursuits. One has only to glance down a list of the places where Barry and his family chose to live over the years—Mount Kisco, Cannes, Hobe Sound, East Hampton, and the like—to see where his preference lay. He was born, in 1896, in a plain wooden house on a humdrum side street in Rochester, New York, and he died, in 1949, in a big apartment high above Park Avenue, in the most fashionable section of New York City. (On his desk at the time was the typescript of his latest play, called *Second Threshold*. Typically, its setting is the library of an elegant old town house on West Tenth Street.) On any map that one can buy, the distance traveled between the points of Barry's birth and death is not very great; on maps of the sort one cannot buy, it is very great indeed. Given the light that it throws on the unexpectedly ample body of his work—twenty-one plays on Broadway in less than thirty years—it is a distance well worth taking the measure of.

More than most American writers of his day, Barry was drawn to the rich and well-born. To their astonishment, he found them interesting and therefore to be cultivated. They were seductive in their good looks and good manners, and so he was careful to remain unseduced by them. They might take him up, those charming insiders, but they couldn't take him in. He had been born an outsider, and that gave him a certain dark advantage. He stood his ground among them, sometimes at moments when they were unaware that he felt any need to do so. He would eat with them and drink with them and at parties and on other social occasions he would give what they spoke of as excellent value—civilities of attentiveness, of badinage, of flattery—but he watched them warily. Some of them he loved, a few of them he admired without love; as for the rest, he might have been content to echo Twain, who on being asked his opinion of the Jews replied with asperity, "They are members of the human race; worse than that I cannot say of them."

Twain was like Barry in being fascinated by the rich and in being somewhat uneasy over the degree of that fascination. He liked the excellent whiskey and cigars of Carnegie, Rogers, and the other new, brigandly millionaires, and he stepped with relish into their carriages and onto their steam yachts, but he kept himself on sentry alert. Eager to amuse them and avid for their admiration, he was yet ineradicably of Hannibal; he never made the mistake of supposing that he was one of the moguls. His white suits and his mop of preposterously unruly white hair served as the credentials that established his separateness from them. He called attention to himself in a way that "nice" people shrank from and could find acceptable only in a mountebank. Though Barry and Twain shared the same temptations in regard to money, fame, and social position, Barry was of a temperament markedly at odds with Twain's; his credentials of separateness were inward and therefore not to be detected by eye or ear, and "nice" people approved of him whether he sought their approval or not.

Barry's wife, Ellen, an able artist, once painted a portrait of him as a birthday present. Thanking her for it, Barry said, "I see you have caught my fox's eye." And so she had. Nearsighted from birth, Barry habitually wore steel-rimmed round spectacles, behind which his eyes shone with an exceptional intensity. Their blue irises seemed to gather up brightness like a burning glass. His scrutiny was so sharp that, standing before him for the first time, you suspected that he was not only seeing you but also seeing into you and perhaps seeing through you. That was a chance you were prepared to take, in the hope that you deserved to be his friend. What that fox's eye observed, the writer's mind never failed to make sufficient note of; in mental equivalents of the neat little brown-paper-covered schoolboy pads in which he jotted down ideas for possible plays, Barry tucked away names, slang phrases, and physical resemblances, to be pondered on and found room for sooner or later, transformed and illuminated.

In his comedies, Barry was an accurate chronicler of a tiny but important fraction of the American population. One of the curious attributes of that fraction is that it has no desire either to be chronicled by others or to chronicle itself. The rich and well-born produce few historians and even fewer novelists, dramatists, and poets, and perhaps this is less curious than it looks at first glance. The fact is that they have little reason to go to the trouble of telling us who they are, or where they came from, or where they may be going. In the most serious sense, they have got past having to know *any*thing about themselves. It is the middle-class stranger on sufferance among them who has something to gain by a close examination of their ways. For him they are instructive; the more he learns about their class, the better able he will be to pass over into it, if that is what he intends to do, or to behave correctly in their presence, if for some reason he should wish to remain outside the pale. When the stranger is also, like Barry, a writer of what are sometimes called drawing-room comedies, then his surroundings become doubly precious to him; he will immerse himself in them in part because he finds them agreeable and in part because they contain the material out of which he will be able to fashion his works. He remains ignorant of even the smallest social details at his peril: care must be taken to distinguish one club tie from another, one rosette from another, and upon inventing as a character an old lady on the Main Line he will see to it that she says "go to bank" and not "go to the bank" and that she "posts" a letter instead of "mailing" it. To a certain kind of writer, and especially to a certain kind of playwright, milieu and métier are one.

Barry was of Irish-Catholic descent, and it would be hard to exaggerate the degree to which, in the period during which he was growing up (that is, in the first years of the twentieth century) his ancestry served to mark him as an outsider. On his father's side, he was a first-generation American; on his mother's side, he was perhaps of the third or fourth generation, but her family—Quinns, long resident in Philadelphia—had remained devout Catholics and so had failed to assimilate themselves into the dominant Protestant culture. Not that their chosen isolation would have struck them as a sign of failure; on the contrary, it was proof of their success in having preserved a precious religious heritage. For it was religion rather than race that encapsulated the Catholics from the south of Ireland upon their arrival in this country. The Protestant Irish of the north were quickly swallowed up in the indiscriminate mass of Presbyterians, Congregationalists, Baptists, and Episcopalians; they fell almost at once into the American vernacular, while the devout Catholics living beside them remained generation after generation Irish and therefore foreign, a minority conspicuously and perhaps dangerously at odds with the majority.

The injustice of the situation was especially painful to the descendants of the tens of thousands of Irish who had settled in this country in the eighteenth century and who had fought as patriots in the Revolution. By an irony of history, these descendants, being still Irish and Catholic, felt obliged to identify themselves with the millions of immigrants who swarmed here from Ireland in the years immediately following the Great

Famine of the eighteen-forties and who established a stereotype of rude manners, boisterous humor, alcoholic belligerence, and political chicanery to which all Irish were assumed to conform. (A few decades later, a similar irony of history played a similarly unfair trick upon the long-settled American Jews of Portuguese and German descent; the waves of Jewish immigrants arriving from Poland and Russia around the turn of the century soon came to stand for all Jews. In both cases, it was a matter of pride for the long-since-established early comers not to deny fraternity with the latecomers, though little or no fraternity existed.)

Of the post-famine Irish, many of the women went into domestic service; many of the men dug ditches, built railroads and subways, and worked their way up to being firemen, policemen, and, with an extra pinch of ambition, saloonkeepers. For a long time, the bulk of the Irish were thought to belong by nature to the servant and laboring classes; the white Protestant upper middle class that was later to be succinctly categorized as WASP looked with amusement on the efforts of these gross underlings to better themselves socially. As late as 1920, in "help wanted" advertisements in newspapers, it was a commonplace to encounter the phrase "No Irish need apply." If they were not to be welcomed even as employees, how likely was it that they would ever be welcomed in WASP homes, clubs, and other self-perpetuating, self-aggrandizing organizations? There was but one way to achieve such a reversal of fate, and it was the oldest way in the world—a way that no WASP had ever jibbed at. The way was simply to get more money than other people. For money always talks and sometimes money shouts, and even when it whispers the deafest of the deaf can hear it and make obeisance to it.

The first rule for achieving what sociologists call "upward mobility" is to acquire as much money as possible. The second rule is to acquire it as quickly as possible, and the third rule is to pretend that one has always had it. In Barry's case, both sides of the family made good remarkably soon after their arrival in this country. His grandfather Quinn, who died long before Barry was born, had prospered in the lumber business in Philadelphia. His father, James Corbett Barry, having been born in Ireland in 1855, came to America as a child, grew up in Philadelphia, left school in his early teens, and went to work as an apprentice stonecutter. He soon developed unusual skills in working tile and in carving the elaborate marble mantels that were then the rage. He fell in love with and, after a long courtship characteristic of the period, married Mary Agnes Quinn. Almost a decade later, he set off from Philadelphia with Mary Agnes and the two children that had so far been born to them—Edmund Henry Barry and James Corbett Barry, Jr.—for Rochester, New York, where he was hired by a local marble-and-granite works. Within a couple of years he had been made foreman of the works and soon thereafter he struck out on his own.

By the early nineties, Jim Barry was being described as a man who had taken his place "among Rochester's most energetic and progressive businessmen"—no small compliment in a go-getting industrial city notable for its ready accommodation to change. (Ready, indeed, to the point of taking advantage even of lucky homophones: in its early days, the presence of many grain mills in Rochester had prompted it to call itself "The Flour City." With the opening of the West, much of the local grain-milling went west as well; at about the same time, a large nursery business sprang up in Rochester, which thereupon dubbed itself "The Flower City.") The two Barry sons had been joined by a daughter, Agnes, and the family lived in a comfortable house on Amherst Street, in a respectable neighborhood of doctors, lawyers, and businessmen. Three years after Agnes's birth came the birth of the Barrys' fourth and last child, who was christened Philip Jerome Quinn Barry. In the fall of 1897, when Philip was just over a year old, his father was stricken with appendicitis, a disease much more dangerous in the days before antibiotics than it is today; Barry's appendix burst and, following an unsuccessful operation, he died. He was only forty-five. A local newspaper published a lengthy obituary, which read in part:

> Many of the dead man's friends recalled how he started in business for himself only a decade ago. He was not rich in this world's goods but he was possessed of indomitable pluck, sterling integrity, and a firm determination that his work would be of the best. He had just achieved a comfortable competence and was on the road to wealth and deserved prosperity when death marked him.

Edmund Barry, then sixteen, had been planning upon graduation from high school to attend Holy Cross College, at which he had already been accepted; instead, he felt obliged to share with his mother the burden of running both the business and the household. For the growing Philip, Edmund came to serve as a surrogate father, and it was a role that neither of them found it pleasing for him to have assumed. The Barry children were all highly intelligent, and Edmund not least; however bravely he may have accepted the blighting of his opportunity to move up in the world by way of college and a profession, it must often have been galling for him to observe his brothers enjoying the fruits of his deprivation. (James Corbett Barry, Jr., like Philip, went off to Yale, which he entered at the exceptionally early age of sixteen. Socially, Yale was a great many notches higher than Holy Cross.) Edmund's fate was not made kinder by the fact that, as things turned out, he presided over a business that was in a state of continuous decline; from the turn of the twentieth century on, fancy marble mantelpieces and the like were going out of fashion, and James C. Barry & Company had to fall back more and more upon the commonplace task of supplying grates and tombstones.

Given the family circumstances, Philip was brought up largely by his mother and sister. Agnes was a delicate, appealing child, drawn early to books. Devout daughter of a devout mother, in her late teens she took her vows as a nun in the Order of the Sacred Heart, rose to a high place in the Order, and today, at eighty-two, is still ardently teaching near Washington, D.C. Alert and humorous-minded, Mother Agnes is full of memories of her beloved family and especially of her "baby" brother. She recalls that flowers would hold Philip's attention for what seemed like hours and that he was also fascinated by butterflies and soap bubbles. Philip attended a Catholic grammar school, Nazareth Hall, where he did well in his studies and badly in deportment—the nuns found it necessary to punish him often for his pranks and unruly ways, and he came to see that representatives of the Church could be harsh and even vindictive as well as holy. The nuns would summon his mother to the school to complain of him, and it appears that Mrs. Barry, distressed by the contrast between the uniformly good behavior of her other children and the deviltries of little Phil, would inquire in mingled love and shame, "Where did I get him?"

Perhaps in part because of his defective eyesight and perhaps also in part because of the exceptional number of childhood diseases that he fell victim to, Philip was never an athlete, never a "joiner." When the young folk on Amherst Street got together to play one-a-cat and other games, Philip was likely to be either on the outskirts of the gang, observing and tossing off an occasional taunting wisecrack, or at play alone in the back yard of the Barry house. Instead of a bodily prowess, he developed a mental prowess that caused him to become known for his quick wit and sharp tongue. He made jokes and, as he grew into adolescence, developed a "line" that girls found delightful and that boys envied. He also became an excellent dancer: it was in him to wish to shine before women more than before men, though, like most Irish-Americans, he always preferred flirtation to commitment.

From early childhood, he was preoccupied with books. They were the chief reward offered in the Barry household for good conduct and an expected gift at Christmas and on birthdays. In the aspiring middle class of those days, books stood for culture and culture for prestige; as soon as possible, one put together what could be spoken of as a library, which would contain, among other staples, many-volumed sets of Ridpath's *History of the World,* John L. Stoddard's *Illustrated Lectures,* and *Selections from the World's Greatest Literature.* Agnes and Philip were especially fond of poetry. With his sister's encouragement, Philip memorized scores of poems; he and Agnes would recite them antiphonally, stanza after stanza. By then, like almost all writers, he had long since provided the obligatory evidence for his literary bent; at nine, he had written a little story called "Tab the Cat," which was published in the *Junior Post-Express,* a children's supplement of the Rochester *Post-Express.* (Every year thousands of diligent tots write and publish in local journals stories on the order of "Tab the Cat," but unless they grow up to be a Philip Barry, history finds no reason to record the fact.) Trifling as the story was, it had the effect that all such precocious debuts have on all born writers: Philip burned to be published again.

The most important event of Philip's life in Rochester may well have been his enrollment in a public high school. The accident of there being no Catholic high school for him to enter upon graduating from Nazareth Hall caused him to move at a single stride away from a narrow religiosity that was threatening to suffocate him into the ample, sunny-seeming air of those well-born, well-to-do Protestants among whom, as it turned out, he was to spend the rest of his life. Unlike the other Barrys, Philip had never been an exceptionally devout Catholic, though he had been a dutiful one; it was characteristic of him that he had objected to Agnes's becoming a nun and that he had resented serving as an altar boy at Mass—one day, taking advantage of the sticky misery he felt on an unusually hot Sunday morning, he cast aside his churchly garments and swore that he would never wear them again. "Where," said his mother, "did I get that boy?"

East High was a welcome revelation to Philip. The boys and girls that he met there—especially the girls—were so good-looking, so easy of manner, so clever at his kind of repartee, and so easy a match for him in scholarship that he was at once enchanted by them. He was enchanted by their surroundings as well. He had chafed at the effortful, lace-curtain gentility of Amherst Street; he felt himself coming into his own on East Avenue, the grand residential boulevard of Rochester, where the big houses sat ranged in self-congratulating propinquity on their level green lawns, like so many stout matrons seated elbow to elbow, implacably chaperoning a ball; soon he was being invited to tea dances and birthday parties in those houses. He was carefully dressed, he had excellent manners, he was eager to please—oh, yes, in spite of the fact that he was Irish and Catholic and without money and without connections, he was worthy of a conditional acceptance; he would be given a chance to see whether, on further testing, he might not, after all, do!

II

The milieu into which Barry slipped with such grace and alacrity—the upper middle class of a prosperous small provincial city—was one that was proving of much interest to a number of other Irish-American young men who would one day be writers. Prominent among them were Eugene O'Neill, in New London, and F. Scott Fitzgerald, in St. Paul; a little later, there would be John O'Hara, in Pottsville. Like Barry, they were all outsiders and they were all intent upon acquiring the perquisites, both outward and inward, of their Protestant betters, with their country clubs and their cars and chauffeurs and, above all, their assurance. In the degree to which these people thought they knew who they were and took pleasure in that knowledge, they deserved to be emulated. One might affect to despise them, as O'Neill did, but no sooner did he begin to have their kind of money than he began to build their kind of houses, in Sea Island, in Danville, in Marblehead; he took care to drive a Cadillac like their Cadillacs and he rented in the Ile de France a château on a scale of splendor that would have struck most of them as being, in their accustomed phrase, "too rich for our blood."

O'Neill had felt snubbed by the not very lofty aristocracy of New London—old families with old money, who were almost certainly unaware of any slight that they had administered to the extremely good-looking if often drunken young man who was to be seen mooning about the streets and beaches of the seaside town. They liked his father, the celebrated actor James O'Neill, who was glad to encounter them at the bar of the Crocker House and who never supposed that because of a drink or two and a few pleasantries exchanged he would become a friend of theirs and frequent their houses. As an Irishman born and an actor, Jim O'Neill knew his place and was comfortable in it; little Monte Cristo Cottage was good enough for him. Besides, he admired the rich and was determined to become rich himself. Though his son Eugene, the parlor radical, railed against the injustice of capitalism, he was not averse to going to Princeton and he would have liked still better to go to Yale—institutions not often cited as champions of social justice. Moreover, when he proclaimed his fraternity with sailors, roustabouts, and the boozy, homeless losers of the world, he was careful to forget (and wished later for his biographers to forget) that he had shipped before the mast not as a sailor but as a passenger—Pa had paid a considerable sum to see to it that his boy had a cozy cabin to himself. Young Gene studied the rough comradeship of the fo'c'sle from a fastidious distance, soiling his hands only with ink. Even as a drunken down-and-outer, he was a self-conscious imitator of the real thing; whenever he and his ne'er-do-well cronies ran out of funds for liquor, Pa could be reached backstage for a quick touch. James O'Neill was by no means the compulsive miser he is depicted as being under the name of James Tyrone in *A Long Day's Journey into Night;* an indulgent, much put-upon man, he was a hundred times more generous as a parent than his son would eventually prove to be.

Resenting the WASP elect, O'Neill pretended to embrace its opposite. The pretense was unconvincing in the actuality of his daily life but it led to valuable consequences in his work; one never doubts the sincerity of O'Neill's sympathy for the penniless failures who people his plays. As for the rich in his plays, they are flimsy caricatures. One guesses that he may have lifted their lineaments and their utterance out of cheap novels (he was an addict of trashy detective stories and murder mysteries); he certainly never studied them at first hand, as, living among them, he might easily have done. In this respect, the outsider O'Neill was wholly unlike the outsiders Barry, O'Hara, and Fitzgerald. Fitzgerald in particular doted upon the rich and sought them out and stared hard at them. They were a delectable puzzle to him, well worth the effort of solving. When he commented to Hemingway that "the rich are different from you and me," he felt that he was saying something profound; Hemingway's wisecrack in reply, "Yes, they have more money," must have struck Fitzgerald as simple-mindedly missing the point. Money, and especially "old" money, alters the nature of the possessor of it; he is set apart from birth, precisely as the possessor of noble blood is set apart. Besides, in wealth as in so many things a difference of degree, if great enough, becomes a difference in kind. The very rich are far more different from the ordinary rich than the ordinary rich are from the rest of us; they are a mysterious species and therefore to be pursued and explained, and it may have been to this point that Fitzgerald was getting ready to address himself when Hemingway obtusely cut him off. No American writer of importance has yet made the superrich the subject of a novel. Fitzgerald would have liked to try his hand at it, but he had so little knowledge of how wealth works that even the disposition of the financial resources of his friends the Gerald Murphys, who were merely well-to-do, appears to have baffled him.

Growing up on Summit Avenue in St. Paul, Fitzgerald began higher on the social ladder than O'Neill, Barry, or O'Hara. For a couple of generations, there had been a certain amount of money in the family, and there was even a distinguished, if collateral, ancestor: the Francis Scott Key after whom Fitzgerald was named was not so close a relative as Fitzgerald liked to pretend, but the relationship was authentic and could be trafficked in. Fitzgerald had a sufficient entrée to the right houses and country clubs and, home on vacation, he would be asked to the right winter dances and summer picnics. If he believed himself to be an outsider and drew much of the energy for his writing from this belief, it was less because he was Irish and Catholic than because, having gained acceptance inside the WASP pale, he wished to rise there. He reached out and he reached up, not always wisely. He was brave and reckless, and no doubt it was to increase his bravery that he fell back upon alcohol, though what it chiefly increased was his recklessness and bad manners. (Janet Flanner, looking back in old age upon life in Paris in the twenties: "Scott could be very tiresome when he drank.")

As Fitzgerald came later to see, it was his fate to be always over-extended, emotionally as well as financially. He would have liked to possess the unassertive security of place and family manifested by Nick Carraway, the narrator of *The Great Gatsby*—Nick, who was able to repeat without irony his father's genteel aphorism, "Just remember that all the people in this world haven't had the advantages that you've had." The fact was that Fitzgerald much more nearly resembled Gatsby, with his "extraordinary gift for hope" and his "romantic readiness," than he did Carraway. Gatsby was the quintessential outsider, who made the mistake of supposing that money would serve to win his heart's desire; Fitzgerald knew better than that, but there were other things he didn't know. His ignorance was profound, and his curiosity, though keen, was short-lived. He was like Henry James in having a first-class mind and therefore first-class intuitions and in having at the same time very little practical information on which to bring his intuitions to bear. James, for example, adored motoring and hadn't the slightest idea what made an automobile run; Fitzgerald was fascinated by Hollywood as an industry, but he never did the donkey work of discovering how that industry operated. For that matter, how did Gatsby operate? Fitzgerald didn't trouble to find out, simple as it would have been to do so, but, oh, how brilliantly that huge hollow place in the heart of the novel is patted over and concealed!

Fitzgerald saw himself as an outsider in terms of geography as well as in terms of wealth and social position. St. Paul was Middle Western, and Fitzgerald's idea of an earthly Paradise was the East Coast: Princeton, New York, the golden scimitar of Long Island. The Alleghanies were not only a mountain range, a thousand-mile-long continental divide—they were the grim heights that divided people as readily as they did water, and into categories not necessarily sympathetic to them. Fitzgerald would have liked to come from that ancestral Maryland which had been the birthplace of Francis Scott Key; he would have liked to own a name—Taft, Saltonstall, Baker—immediately recognizable in the remotest cranny of the Ivy League. He was confident of his intelligence, of his talent, of his exceptional good looks; still, there were barriers that appeared insuperable, and the older he grew (not that he was ever to grow truly old: he was dead at forty-four), the more bitterly he resented them. He worked so hard, against such high odds, to make a lot of money, and then the money trickled away—*rushed* away, leaving him penniless, with his energy diminished and his talent in jeopardy. He could even make heartbreaking jokes about his plight: "It grows harder to write, because there is much less weather than when I was a boy and practically no men and women at all." Though his income was at times torrential, he never possessed any capital: that prize which others possessed without effort, by a trifling, gorgeous accident of birth. More and more he found it necessary to blame his vain attempt to escape financial pressure—for once to manage his talent well instead of badly—upon the elegant enemy beyond the barriers. "That was always my experience," he wrote, in his last years. "A poor boy in a rich town; a poor boy in a rich boy's school; a poor boy in a rich man's club at Princeton. . . . I have never been able to forgive the rich for being rich, and it has colored my entire life and works." A statement all the more touching because the rich in question wouldn't have had the slightest notion that they were in need of being forgiven for anything, by anyone: certainly not for the fact of being rich and certainly not by a poor little failed writer the most celebrated of whose peers—Hemingway—had long since publicly dismissed him and who would gain a just appraisal of his place in letters many years after his death.

John O'Hara, the last of our quartet of Irish-Catholic writer-outsiders, early cultivated the rich and throughout a much longer lifetime than Fitzgerald's—O'Hara died in 1970, at the age of sixty-five—made them the objects of an intense, ice-cold scrutiny. Unlike Fitzgerald, he had a curiosity that never flagged and was never satisfied. He took care to know where everybody's money came from and where it went. He prided himself on measuring with precision every infinitesimal gradation of wealth and social status that he came in contact with, from Pottsville in childhood to Princeton in maturity. (Being an outsider, of course he ended up residing in Princeton, as, for much briefer periods, O'Neill and Fitzgerald had done. Princeton in the twentieth century has been the nirvana of the discerning *arriviste.*) The range of O'Hara's knowledge of how Americans live was incomparably greater than that of any other fiction writer of his time; one would have to go back to Norris, Stephen Crane, and Dreiser to find even the intention on the part of a novelist of acquiring knowledge on the scale that O'Hara acquired it, and with his degree of particularity.

The world both high and low fascinated O'Hara and revolted him; no doubt correctly, he assumed that there had never been a time when it wouldn't have fascinated and revolted him. He was a Jansenist in spite of himself, loathing his body for committing sins that he no longer believed in but that cost him remorse. (Like many people who loathe their bodies, in age he let his body grow coarse with fat; his face came to resemble an uncooked side of beef.) Though not a practicing Catholic, he continued to believe, straight out of the penny catechism, that man was a fallen creature, subject to the most fearsome carnal temptations; to resist these temptations was to love God and not to resist them was somehow to hurt God's feelings and delight the Devil.

Few of O'Hara's female characters are able to remain chaste for long; indeed, he wrote about women and their sexual failings so often and with such relish that many reviewers accused him of seeing all women as nymphomaniacs. The truth was that his dark view of their weakness was but a manifestation of a profound and typically Irish-Catholic disappointment. Almost without exception in O'Hara's day, the puritan Irish, brought up by nuns and priests, wished that every woman, even every mother, could remain a virgin; the fact that women made love, and especially that one's own mother made love, or had once made love, was intolerable. (Surely it was unpleasant enough that we had to be born, in Saint Augustine's words, *"inter faeces et urinam"*—couldn't nature, so extravagant in other respects, have spared us the humiliation of that extreme economy of means?) O'Hara's male characters are less to blame for their sins than his female ones, for the reason that man in his simplicity is never a match for a woman and her wiles. It is Adam and Eve all over again; the bitch is a betrayer, who cannot leave well enough alone. Far better if she had remained a rib!

O'Hara trusted his eye and ear only to the extent that he could keep them free of admiration and pity. In this he was like O'Neill and radically unlike Fitzgerald and Barry, who found much to admire and pity in their fellows. Barry in particular was pained by the evident malignity of the world and sought with increasing despair some reasonable explanation for it. The more troubled he became, the less he was able to write and the less confidence he had in what he wrote. To his friend O'Hara, no explanation of the malignity of the world was necessary: mankind was vile by nature and without surprises. His grim view, far from paralyzing him, seemed to give him extra energy. Following an operation and a warning from his physicians that if he didn't give up alcohol he would die, he stopped drinking and turned himself into a machine for writing. He was obsessed with composing what he believed to be an accurate record of the social structure of his time. He faced the ugliness of the record with equanimity, in story after story, novel after novel. The items of the indictment were many and he was confident that they would last him as long as he lived, and they did.

As for the rich, in O'Hara's view they were no better and no worse than the poor—he would never have been so sentimental as to speak, as Fitzgerald did, of not being able to forgive them. For O'Hara the question of forgiveness didn't arise; there they were, such as they were, and he would tell us honestly everything he had found out about them. He would be honest, too, in admitting that he wanted to be one of them. By the time of his death, he had long been a millionaire. It pleased him that by a tireless, forty-year-long flogging of his remarkable talent he had become one of the richest writers who ever lived. Still, he would have preferred to be born rich, and he was given to pretending that his father, a doctor in Pottsville, had been far richer than he actually was. It was true that Dr. O'Hara had lived well and, if he had not died comparatively young, might have achieved moderate wealth, as Barry's father had been on the way to doing when *he* died; but neither the senior O'Hara nor the senior Barry would ever have become rich in their sons' ambitious interpretation of the word. To the sons, the really rich were the Whitneys, the Morgans, the Goelets, and the Johnny-come-lately Mellons and Rockefellers.

Much has been made of O'Hara's yearning to attend Yale. He blamed his failure to do so on his father's death and the family's subsequent impoverishment and it may be so, but there is evidence that O'Hara, an indifferent student, might not have succeeded in entering the university even under the best of circumstances. All his life, he was so boyishly eager to fulfill that early fantasy that his close friend Wolcott Gibbs spoke of raising a purse to send him to New Haven. Other friends pleaded seriously with the university to bestow an honorary degree on O'Hara, always in vain. The members of the faculty who had it in their power to recommend candidates for degrees to the Yale Corporation thought of him as a dirty writer, preoccupied with sex; they felt safer recommending honorary degrees for people like Walt Disney, whose *Snow White and the Seven Dwarfs* contained no dirty words and gave offense sexually to no one.

O'Hara was haunted by the mystery of Skull and Bones, the oldest and most distinguished of the secret societies at Yale. He accepted it as an indisputable fact of life that the fifteen men elected every year to Bones became a part of the tiny, never openly acknowledged power structure that ran the country. He believed, too, that being a Bones man guaranteed you certain privileges throughout your life—for example, that you would never be allowed to experience total financial failure. There was ample evidence to disprove this hypothesis, but O'Hara, in most such matters so scrupulous a reporter, in the matter of Skull and Bones always chose make-believe over reality. Statistically, it was the case that there were only a few hundred Bones men alive at any given moment; nevertheless, O'Hara saw them as forming an intricate network of elite operators throughout both hemispheres. How many Bones men were openly exercising power in Washington and New York! How many more, O'Hara reasoned, must be wielding power behind the scenes! He would speak with reverence the names of the great men who had been tapped for Bones—the innumerable Tafts, Bundys, and Binghams—and he would take pride in mentioning as well the names of several personal friends of his in Bones. They were names that resounded on Wall Street and in Locust Valley and on Fishers Island and at Kennebunkport: bell-like names, which gave off a formidable hum for a long time after they were dropped.

Throughout its long history, Skull and Bones has kept what it considers to be the barbarian world from acquiring any substantial knowledge of the rituals practiced inside its immense, windowless, brownstone tomb on High Street, in the heart of New Haven. (The tomb itself, vaguely Egyptian in style, is held to be so sacred that, according to undergraduate legend, a plumber or electrician entering it in order to make some necessary repairs must first become a member of the society.) Over the years, O'Hara contrived to accumulate a startling amount of Bones lore, which he would reveal only to Bones men; sharing with them his little scraps and samples of their secrets made him, in a fashion and for the time being, one of them. It was the most cherished of all O'Hara's daydreams that if he had gone to Yale he would have been tapped for Bones. The touching truth of the matter is otherwise. Of the four Irish-Catholic outsider-writers—Barry, O'Neill, Fitzgerald, and O'Hara—O'Hara was the crudest and most contentious. He lacked the good manners and sunny flights of fancy of Fitzgerald and Barry; he was less amiable and therefore less "nice" than even the mordant O'Neill. He was a grudge bearer—a master, as it was later to be said, of the fancied slight. Acrimoniously at odds with the world, though the world could not be sure why, he was the last person likely to be tapped for Bones. He would have stood waiting in vain on Tap Day, and afterward he would have found reason to believe that unknown enemies had ruthlessly conspired to deprive him of the honor he so richly deserved. But there would have been no enemy, no conspiracy; there would have been only his nature.

III

Barry shared O'Hara's preoccupation with Yale and, although the family had met with financial reverses, he could afford to go there. The difficulty was in gaining acceptance. Barry had made an unimpressive record in high school, for in spite of the fact that he was, as he once wrote, "bright in spots," the spots were fewer in number than they ought to have been. He took the entrance examinations for Yale in June, 1913, and failed; after spending another year at East High, he took the examinations a second time and was accepted with four entrance conditions. He spent the summer of 1914 being tutored, was tested a third time, and was allowed to enter Yale in October, with conditions in Latin and grammar. Barry was delighted to find himself in New Haven at last. He was only eighteen, but he felt that his escape from the schoolboy restrictions of Rochester and the stifling protectiveness of a close-knit family had been long overdue.

Never was a young man from the provinces more eager to enter the great world and be transformed by it, and Yale was the ideal place in which to affect the transformation. It would have occurred to few undergraduates, most of whom were looking forward to going into business after graduation, that success was, in William James's contemporary epithet, a "bitch-goddess." What had one been put into the world for if not to succeed? And one succeeded by competing fiercely in every available activity. The competition of the classroom mattered less than competition in extracurricular activities and in sports. A "Y" in baseball or football was well worth fighting for, and even half-dying for, but a Phi Beta Kappa key was supposed to befall one almost by inadvertence; one mumbled an apology for possessing it. Because of his faulty eyesight and perhaps also because of his temperament, Barry was unable to become a star athlete, but he did his best to star in other fields. He studied hard, worked off his entrance conditions, and began to earn grades high enough to permit him to engage in the extracurricular activities that he hoped would make him, shy and modest-seeming though he was, a big man on campus.

The most important extracurricular activities at Yale in Barry's time were the Dramat and *The Yale Daily News,* "The Oldest College Daily." Somewhat less important but of value in opening doors to other honors was *The Yale Literary Magazine,* which described itself as the oldest monthly magazine in America—a superlative that, like the *News*'s, wisely called attention to the magazine's longevity rather than to its merits. Barry twice went out for the Dramat and was turned down; later he heeled the *News* and wrote for the *Lit* and was elected to both boards. He was also elected to a fraternity, Alpha Delta Phi, where he became a close friend of John Farrar, the leader of the literary set at Yale. A trifle tardily—shyness? outsiderness?—Barry was elected to the Elizabethan Club, which came as close as any single institution could to being the intellectual center of Yale. The club occupied a pleasant old white clapboard house on College Street, and in the late afternoons book-loving undergraduates and members of the faculty would foregather there for tea and cakes and conversation. As its name implied, the "Lizzie" contained an extraordinary collection of ancient volumes; one sniffed

Marlowe and Shakespeare in the very air and was perhaps infected by them. The infection was strengthened when living writers—in Barry's day, John Masefield, Vachel Lindsay, Sir Rabindranath Tagore—stopped by for a quiet chat. The literary life was bathed in a romantic glow, to which Barry responded; the outsider in him was quick to note how attractively it paved the way into the heart of the Yale establishment.

The supreme mark of one's having made good at Yale was how one fared on Tap Day. There were several secret societies, and one could hope that if one weren't among the fifteen men tapped for Bones, one might be tapped for Scroll and Key or Wolf's Head. To Barry's profound disappointment, he failed to be tapped at all (though he was later invited to join the secret Elihu Club). His disappointment was all the keener because some of the men he admired then and continued to admire throughout his life—Donald Ogden Stewart, Archibald MacLeish, John Farrar, Robert Lovett, Gerald Murphy, Artemus L. Gates, F. Trubee Davison—were Bones men. Long after college, he remained aware that they had something in common with each other that they would never have in common with him.

Barry's failure on Tap Day was a humiliation especially galling to him because it was so public; it was also, in his eyes, mysterious. Unlike O'Hara, Barry was not paranoid and could draw no easy comfort from imagining a conspiracy against him. He was a practical idealist, who had worked his way up to the top of the class, or close to the top, and he had been flagrantly passed by. The injustice of his fate puzzled him. A sense of being unfairly dealt with by life was to afflict him often in later years, when those of his plays that he most believed in would prove, on opening night, to be the ones that the critics least respected. Perhaps for the first time, he felt that sense of unfairness, in respect to Tap Day, though it may be that the fault lay in part with him, for having taken an unduly optimistic view of his chances. His classmate Wilmarth S. Lewis has said of Barry that he wasn't "terrifically one of the boys" and that "nobody would have been surprised if he had been [tapped], but then nobody was surprised that he hadn't been." Lewis's testimony contains a tiny mystery of its own. An elegant, handsome young man and later a gentleman-scholar of immense erudition, Lewis himself was very far indeed from being "terrifically one of the boys" and was nevertheless tapped for Scroll and Key. Plainly there was more to Tap Day than was permitted to meet the eye. Lewis was a well-connected WASP, who had come east to Yale from the fashionable Thatcher School, in California, and Barry was an unknown Irish-Catholic from a public high school in upstate New York. No wonder that Barry came to be partial to palaces and to the lucky people who lived in them! More clearly than in Rochester, he saw how much harder than the rich and well-born one had to run, simply to catch up with them. Passing them was out of the question.

The First World War had been raging throughout all of Barry's time at Yale. By 1917, when the United States entered the war, many members of the class of '18 had already left New Haven to enlist; within months, a number of them, including one or two friends of Barry, had died on European battlefields. Barry volunteered for service in vain—his weak eyes caused him to be rejected by the Army and Navy and by the Red Cross Ambulance Service as well. He remained at Yale, valiantly doing double duty on the *News* and *Lit* for the sake of his colleagues in uniform and cursing the ill luck that made him seem, to himself if not to the world, a slacker. In April, 1918, he succeeded in wangling a job in the Communications Office of the State Department; within a month, he had arrived in London and was hard at work deciphering cables in the U.S. Embassy offices on Grosvenor Square.

His day was a long drudgery, but no harm in that; Barry was enchanted with London. He had never been abroad, never roamed the length and breadth of a great city, never sought to take in the number and variety of its resources. (In New Haven, he had remained largely ignorant of nearby New York, about which he was soon to write with such authority.) Barry's inherited Irish prejudice against perfidious Albion quickly gave way to Anglophilia. How pleasing the English were and how grateful he was that they should find *him* pleasing as well! He was, so they told him, a "nice" American—the highest compliment that Englishmen are capable of paying a native of their former colonies. Through a Yale friend, he arranged to share a comfortable flat with an English major of impeccable pedigree and all but incomprehensible clipped speech. Barry spent long weekends in the country, in houses bigger than any he had yet encountered in America. The customs that distinguished one social class from another became a subject for study as well as for amusement. Despite the innumerable physical inconveniences of wartime, to say nothing of the mounting toll of dead and seriously wounded on the far side of the Channel, life in England was full of delightful surprises, and Barry, assuming an air of sophistication that he had not yet earned, hurried about in pursuit of them.

Barry had always liked going to parties, and well-mannered young men who could dance and who had a witty "line" were much in demand in London at a time when most young men, witty or not, were otherwise employed. And for the first time Barry became an impassioned theatregoer. Back at Yale, he had about made up his mind to seek his fortune as a writer—a decision that he knew would cause considerable alarm to his family in Rochester. Now his thoughts began to run toward the writing of plays instead of his accustomed verse and prose fiction. It was certainly a fact, observable in the West End even in wartime, that there was money to be made in the theatre and little or none to be made in verse; and money mattered. (Said his sister, Mother Agnes, long after Barry's death, "Phil would never have starved in a garret." And it was true; he was an excellent businessman, who became not only a successful playwright but also a wealthy one.) In his spare time, he set to work on a play called *No Thoroughfare,* prompted by his discovery of Freud. Whatever *No Thoroughfare* may have amounted to as a work of art—Barry himself described it as "a terrible first play"—it is historically of interest as one of the earliest American plays to make dramatic use of the principles of psychoanalysis. He also began work on a short story, "Meadow's End," which appeared several years later, much revised, in *Scribner's Magazine.* Aside from *War in Heaven,* a version in the form of a novel of his play *Here Come the Clowns,* "Meadow's End" was the only prose fiction that Barry published after leaving Yale.

The war ended in November, 1918, and Barry drifted back to New Haven in the early winter of 1919. All the members of his class who had resigned from Yale in order to take part in the war effort were being automatically readmitted to the university and would graduate in June with members of the class of '19. No matter how well or badly they might do in their studies, as returned heroes they were sure to receive their degrees. New Haven seemed to them more than ever a very small town, but it was agreeable being looked up to and made much of. Polished by his stay abroad, Barry became a notable adornment of the

Lizzie Club. Had he not made the acquaintance in London of H. G. Wells, Rebecca West, and other literary lions and lionesses? Had he not written a play, which Thornton Wilder, meeting him for the first time, heard him read aloud at the Lizzie? Was he not already an announced man of letters? Nevertheless, he buckled down to his classes with an unabated puritan diligence; in the short time left to him before graduation, he would get as much out of Yale as Yale was able to give him, and by good luck that happened to be a great deal.

For Barry attended Yale at a time when its English faculty boasted a number of remarkable men, among them William Lyon Phelps, John Milton Berdan, Chauncey Brewster Tinker, and Robert Dudley French. It was characteristic of a certain racy vigor in the Yale of that day that these eminences should invariably have been called (though not quite to their faces until after one had graduated) "Billy," "Johnnie," "Tink," and "Bob." It was also characteristic that Billy Phelps, the oldest of them, in a lecture purportedly devoted to Tennyson could offer as a cheerful aside that he had once been "close enough to Queen Victoria to grab her by the tit." As teachers, Phelps, Berdan, and the rest were rightly proud of the gifted undergraduates in their charge; at the Lizzie, they mingled with them not as teachers but as friends, seeming all of one age and one purpose. Yale was notoriously a forcing house for stockbrokers and bankers, but for the happy teatakers facing an open fire on dark winter afternoons at the Lizzie the chase they were about to embark on had a different beast in view: whether in or out of Academe, they would devote themselves to the high calling of literature.

During the winter of 1919, the Dramat announced a competition for new one-act plays by undergraduates, the incentive being that winners of the competition would have their plays publicly performed and would be elected members of the Dramat. Barry was engaged in roughing out plays in Professor Henry Seidel Canby's course in advanced writing, and he was no less eager to make the Dramat as a senior than he had been as a freshman. The competition was won by Barry and his close friends Stephen Vincent Benét and John Farrar. Barry's play was called *Autonomy,* and he subsequently described it as "a fearful farce," but when it was performed in the Grand Ballroom of the Hotel Taft, in late April, it was very well received. Reviewing the play, Johnnie Berdan said of it that it was "a political satire which depends rather on cleverness of the lines and upon contemporary hits than upon any dramatic situation . . . the total effect was one of delightful cleverness."

Because there was then no drama school at Yale—agitation for the founding of one and for the erection of a suitable theatre for the Dramat was just getting under way—Professors Berdan, Canby, and Phelps all advised Barry to apply for entrance to the famous 47 Workshop presided over at Harvard by George Pierce Baker. This was advice that Barry was eager to accept; the only difficulty lay in persuading his family to go on financing him as he marched in a direction of which they didn't approve. Upon graduating from Yale in June, he returned to Rochester and got a job for the summer as a reporter on the *Post-Express*. The job provided him with enough pocket money for the boxes of candy, flowers, and other gifts with which to pursue his vocation as the suave, natty, but not very dangerous Don Juan of the country-club set in Rochester. Throughout the summer, he flirted with a number of what he always called "sweet young things"—abbreviated to "s.y.t."s in his letters and notebooks—and they were suitably awestruck. How well he danced and how witty he was, this Yale man with the romance of gray London behind him and the prospect of no telling what artistic heights about to be conquered! They had to breathe deep, those s.y.t.s, to keep from fainting.

Barry's two older brothers vehemently made it clear that they wished him to settle down in Rochester, in either the family business or some other business. With equal vehemence Barry made it clear that he would be doing no such thing. His mother wished only for her little family not to be broken up by quarreling—"Where did I get that boy?" Barry held a single trump card, and in the end it proved enough to give him his way. Because his father had died without making provision in his will for his latest child, by law the infant Philip, as one of four children, was entitled to the share in his father's estate that would have come to him if there had been no will—that is, to a fourth of two-thirds of the father's estate, according to its value at the time of the father's death. The quarter share, with accrued interest, would be collectible when the infant reached the age of twenty-one. Nobody had been aware of this quirky legal situation until, when Philip was fourteen, his mother went to court to ask permission to sell certain property belonging to her husband's estate. The value of the estate continued to decline, and it was soon obvious that by the time Philip was twenty-one and entitled to ask for a settling of accounts, his fixed share would amount to the entire estate, leaving the rest of the family penniless. As he was later to note, "When I was fourteen, my brothers began to look at me with respect. I gave my oldest brother a tough fifteen minutes before I signed the property back to my mother when I was twenty-one—though I had always intended to sign the property over to her." (This highly explosive family situation furnished the plot for Barry's second Broadway play, *The Youngest.*) Barry's having behaved handsomely in regard to his inheritance forced his family to behave handsomely in regard to his career; when he got word during the course of the summer that he had been accepted for the 47 Workshop at Harvard, his mother and brothers with grave misgivings allowed him to follow his bent: for the time being, he would put off being a businessman and would try to become that most unreliable thing a writer.

Barry arrived in Cambridge in September, 1919, and took up residence in a rooming house on Brattle Street. The 47 Workshop—in the Harvard catalogue known as "English 47: for Graduates; Lectures and Practice in the Technique of Drama"—met in cramped quarters in Lower Massachusetts Hall and acted out plays on a makeshift stage in the little Agassiz Theatre at Radcliffe. The Workshop's first purpose was to teach prospective playrights the down-to-earth mechanics of composing and staging plays; its second purpose was to see that the students learned as much as possible, in lectures and by reading, about their great predecessors. Once a student had written a play, it was read aloud by Professor Baker and subjected to a lively, unsparing fusillade of criticism from his fellows. (Thomas Wolfe was enrolled in the Workshop in Barry's day and has furnished a characteristically overheated description of it in his novel *Of Time and the River.*)

Barry settled down to work with his accustomed seriousness and discipline. It had cost him a great effort to reach the Workshop and he was determined not to fail there. He and Baker got on admirably from the start, not least because each was so much in need of the other. It was Baker, if anyone, who could make Barry's hope of a career in writing come true; and though Barry may not have been aware of it at the time, it was Barry who could serve Baker well by providing a demonstration of how the Workshop fostered talent and taught it to become productive. For some years the Workshop had been without a playwright of conspicuous promise, and its standing in the always skeptical Harvard community was such that most of Baker's associates on the English faculty regarded him as an amiable crank, who had given up the rigors of scholarship for the mere muddle of "creativity." Baker encouraged Barry to write on American themes. In Baker's words, he should "try to write [about] conditions in the life of the present time which shall be amusing, and at the same time amuse in such a way that one finds one is thinking about the play afterwards—not exactly in amusement, but thoughtfully and pleasantly." This prescription comes close to summing up Barry's intentions in at least a dozen of the twenty-odd plays he was to write.

Another lasting influence on Barry was a Workshop colleague who lived in the same rooming house on Brattle Street and who bore the extravagant name of Kenneth Romauer-Ron Raisbeck. Though he came from the Middle West, Raisbeck liked to convey the impression that he had certain lofty family connections in Europe. His contemporaries saw him as an exotic pre-Raphaelite idealist, mingling attributes of both Oscar Wilde and Bernard Berenson. In contrast to Raisbeck, Barry was assumed to represent "a healthy, pink-cheeked Philistinism." Such an assumption was unjust; at Raisbeck's urging, Barry was quick to champion the superior claims of art over conventional American money-grubbing. The Raisbeck influence is strong in Barry's early plays; later, it shows sign of strain, for Barry, wishing to remain as pure in his aesthetic aspirations as Raisbeck was, wished also to enjoy the greatest possible material success. Throughout his professional life he marched in perilous balance upon that razor's edge; the feat produced a tension that greatly enhances his best work.

Barry's first attempt at a play for the Workshop had to do with a wealthy family on Long Island. The setting no doubt owed a good deal to the fact that one of Barry's closest friends, Ted Babbitt, with whom he had roomed during his last year at Yale, was attending the Harvard Law School. The two young men not only saw each other in Cambridge but also undertook frequent weekend forays to New York, where they attended the theatre and made the rounds of coming-out parties and tea dances. They would stay with the Babbitts either in New York or at their country place at Southampton, and much that Barry heard and saw on those merry, strenuous weekends was useful to him as source material for his play. Following a practice of his *Lit* days in New Haven, he kept a card-index file, and among the headings in the new file were "Comedy Dialogue," "Notes on Plays Seen," "Detached Scenes," and "Words and Phrases." Professor Baker adjured Barry to "write about what you know about." Baker may not have guessed it, but there were occasions when what Barry appeared to know was information that had been acquired only a few hours before he was boldly setting it down on paper.

IV

The most fortunate event in Barry's exceptionally fortunate life was his marriage. It is rare to be able to speak with confidence of the place a man's marriage occupies in the scheme of his life; still more rarely can one speak with confidence of the degree to which a marriage is fortunate, but in Barry's case the evidence is overwhelming: he married the woman best suited to him in every way. From the start, their relationship was in a manner that playgoers would come to think of as Barryesque. The very circumstances of their meeting, of their courtship, and of their marriage and honeymoon, with its unexpected, happy windfall of an ending, were all authentic Barry scenes—charming, intelligent, amusing, concerned.

They met on Fifth Avenue in the Sixties, on a pleasant Sunday afternoon in October, 1919. Barry and Babbitt were strolling along the avenue when Babbitt stopped to speak to a pretty girl of his acquaintance. Barry was introduced. "Ellen Semple, Philip Barry." Miss Semple was tall and slender, brown-eyed and brown-haired, with a delightful smile. Her voice was low and thrilling, with an unusually warm timbre. Within a few days, Barry had telephoned her and had made a date to meet her at the Plaza. He was late in arriving, but she forgave him; and after that they were in love. How different she was from him, in how many enviable ways! Her nature was joyous and unguarded; she was at ease with strangers and it seemed to cost her no effort to give back more to the world than she took from it. She liked parties even more than he did; she would stay up all night dancing. (Over fifty years later, Ellen Barry, living in an elegant small red-brick house in Washington, still likes parties and will happily dance until three, if not until morning, and after a few hours' sleep will be hard at work in her studio.) She was a natural athlete, who swam and rode and played excellent golf and tennis. She was well-born and carefully reared, and she was also—and startlingly—a Catholic. Whether the young Philip Barry would have married a non-Catholic there is no way of knowing; Ellen rendered the question academic. Friends recall Barry's astonishment and pleasure at encountering a fellow-Catholic snugly at home in the very heart of the WASP establishment. He was a lucky man, and Ellen's background, like Ellen's affectionate nature, was a part of his luck.

In 1919 Ellen's peppery, capable, and highly successful little Irish grandfather, John McAnerney, was still alive. In the Civil War, he had fought so gallantly in the defense of Richmond that he had been commissioned a full colonel on the field of battle. After the war, he had come north and grown rich as a banker and entrepreneur. He lived in a big brownstone house on West Forty-ninth Street, just off Fifth Avenue, and he was a figure to be reckoned with in the diocesan powerhouse that centered on St. Patrick's. One of his nine children was Ellen's mother, who had married a brilliant young lawyer from the South, Lorenzo Semple. And he, too, the saints be praised! was a Catholic. There were four Semple children—Ellen had three brothers—and they grew up in the high-ceilinged old house on West Eleventh Street, not far from Washington Square, in which Ellen was born, but the place that the whole family liked best and came to think of as home was Ellistoun Farm, in Mount Kisco. The property consisted of some eighty acres of woods, fields, orchards, and streams, and to the children's delight it was amply furnished with cows, pigs, ponies, dogs, cats, and other creatures.

The Semples kept adding ad lib to the original farmhouse, first room by room and then wing by wing. The stage directions that Barry wrote for his first Broadway play, *You and I*—probably the most romantic stage directions ever written—spring from the emotions he felt on first coming to know the Semple family. The directions, filled with details unneeded by any stage designer, amount to a pleasant short story and are worth quoting in part:

Here you are, in the library of the Whites' country home in Mount Kisco, Westchester County, New York.

The Whites' home is one of those rambling white houses that began as a farmhouse and has been added to year by year as the family grew, and the family's fortunes prospered. In architecture, it is nearer Colonial than anything else. There was always plenty of land, but the orchard, of which Maitland White is so proud, he planted himself.

When you come for your first week-end, he will delight in telling you that when Nancy and he bought the place twenty years ago, the room in which you now stand was, with the exception of a tiny kitchen, the entire lower floor. The second beam from the left in the ceiling will show you where the partition came between living and dining rooms.

The big hall, by which you entered, is the west wing—that came first—and the spacious dining room and study are the east wing, which was built four years later. The servants' wing was added at the same time. The little cottage down by the swimming-pool is of course quite new. That is to be Jean's, when she grows up and is ready to be married—fancy Jeanie married!

You will be awfully surprised and say What!—this enormous place grown out of a little old farmhouse? And Maitland will chuckle and say Oh, Nanny and I have had no end of fun out of it, haven't we, Nanny? And like as not, the next time you come (as you will, if they like you) he will begin to tell you about it all over again. But Nancy will stop him, without in the least hurting his feelings.

The Library—which is also the main living-room—is a huge, uneven, motherly sort of a room that pats your hand as you come into it, and tells you to sit down and be comfortable with the rest of us. Out here we don't even know there *is* such a place as the City!

Farther along in these singular stage directions (what on earth was any designer intended to make of Maitland's chuckles?) we come upon a description of a girl who can only be Ellen: "She is about nineteen, slim, of medium height, with a decidedly pretty, high-bred face, lovely hair, lovely hands, and a soft, low-pitched voice—whatever she may be saying. Heredity, careful up-bringing, education and travel have combined to invest her with a poise far in advance of her years. She has attained the impossible—complete sophistication without the loss of bloom. Her self-confidence is, you will be happy to know, free from any taint of youthful cocksureness."

That was Ellen as Barry first saw her and fell in love with her. During the winter of 1920, he worked hard on his Workshop play, called *Oh*

Promise Me. In March, Professor Baker having gone off to Europe for a lengthy stay, Barry retired from the Workshop, rented a furnished room in New York, and found a job with an advertising agency at twenty-five dollars a week. Writing advertising copy for such products as Pears Soap and Grinnell fire sprinklers was tiresome but unimportant; small as his salary was, he hoped to save some of it and return to the Workshop in the fall. Meanwhile, he was able to see Ellen often, both in town and at Ellistoun Farm. It was a courtship diffident and prolonged only because of his financial situation. He wanted to become engaged to her, but he could not afford to marry her. (It is a vivid indication of how radically courting and marriage customs have altered over the past half-century that Barry considered it out of the question to accept monetary assistance from Ellen's family—once he even refused the offer by Ellen's mother of a railroad ticket from Cambridge to New York, and this *after* Ellen and he had become engaged! Lorenzo Semple was a generous man, but Barry was a proud one; gifts could be accepted in marriage but not before. Nowadays a young couple in love gladly accepts gifts of any kind from any source at any time, without regard to whether they plan to marry; which is very sensible of them.) If Barry were to give up hope of making his name as a playwright and buckle down instead to a career in advertising, he would be certain to have plenty of money and he would have Ellen as well, but he would have betrayed himself and his aesthetic ideals. The dilemma, if by no means novel, was real and he experienced it passionately. With gifted people, nothing goes to waste, and soon Barry came to see that there might be a play in his dilemma; he started working up a scenario for it under the provisional title of *The Thing He Wanted to Do.*

Before this second play could be roughed out on paper, Barry had to busy himself, though at a disconcerting distance, with a Workshop production of his first finished play, *Oh Promise Me.* (The title having recently been made use of by another playwright, Barry eventually named the play *A Punch for Judy*—a title that smacked more of the Hasty Pudding Club than of the Workshop.) When the play went into rehearsal in Cambridge, Barry began firing off daily letters of advice to the cast. From his desk in the advertising agency in New York, he told them far more about the characters in the play than the actors can have wished to hear: for example, the brand of toothpaste the characters used and the brand of cigarettes they smoked. Toward the end of the rehearsal period,

Barry journeyed up to Cambridge and made a few final adjustments to the text. After a successful opening in Cambridge, *A Punch for Judy* went on the road, playing in Worcester, Utica, Buffalo, and Cleveland. It gave a single performance at the Morosco Theatre, in New York, where the local reviewers gave it an amiable salute. It then played in Boston, at a benefit for the Radcliffe Club, and was again praised as a thoroughly professional accomplishment.

Professor Baker wrote to Barry in New York that he must "push the play all you can." Barry gave it to an author's agent to do the pushing for him, but few producers appeared interested in putting it on. Meanwhile, Barry was striving to find a better-paying job. Through his friend John Farrar, he was offered an editor's job on a magazine, at a salary of four thousand dollars a year. When Barry apprised the advertising agency of this offer, it countered with the not quite equivalent offer of a salary of sixty-five dollars a week. That sum struck Barry as sufficiently handsome to justify his proposing to Ellen, and on June 8, 1921, their engagement was formally announced by her parents. By September, when *A Punch for Judy* had not yet found a producer, Barry's dilemma became extreme: money or art? marriage or lonely struggle? One day he solemnly informed Ellen that he felt obliged to break off their engagement; he would never be able to forgive himself if he failed to return to the Workshop, but he considered it unfair to ask her to remain bound to him while he took his long chance on making good. Oh, earnest, idealistic, passionate young man! The following morning he was on the telephone to Ellen, begging that their engagement be allowed to continue; and of course Ellen, confident of Philip's talent and touched by his need, at once consented. Off he went to Cambridge, to the hard work of writing the play that was to make their virtuous dreams come true—the play that was at first called *The Thing He Wanted to Do,* and then *The Jilts* and at last *You and I.*

Barry had a room in a rooming house on Gorham Street, for which he paid twenty-five dollars a month in rent. He ate most of his meals and spent much of his time at the Signet Club, to which, as a graduate student, he had recently been admitted. For reasons of economy, he lived almost entirely on Shredded Wheat at the Signet and made good use of the Signet stationery. Daily he sent off letters to Ellen in New York and Mount Kisco and Ellen faithfully replied. She was taking classes at

Barnard, she was playing golf, she was planning soon to visit a ninety-four-year-old great-grandmother in Montgomery; her days were reassuring to him in their conventional Junior League busyness, since plainly nothing in them mattered as much to Ellen as he did. In his letters to her he recounted his arduous bouts of writing and rewriting. *The Jilts* being well advanced, he was starting another play, which he called *Poor Richard*. (It later became *The Youngest.*) One of his letters goes, in part:

> This, my dear, at the end of a long Sunday. Early Mass, and much hard prayer for Matey and his family. [*The Jilts.*] Work until five. Into town with Ken [Raisbeck] and Beau-Roderick, the most sportive of all Irish terriers. . . . A lecture at the Workshop by Mr. Pope of the Fine Arts Department . . . and home through the moonlight to you. . . . I'm growing more and more confident that this new play can be a good 'un. It's curious how an idea develops in the sun and rain of a little thought. I have the characters named—at least tentatively—and the action divided into acts. I was afraid it would be a four-acter, but I believe now it can be done in three. I also have my climaxes in hand. Properly managed, the material should shape into a very interesting and moving piece. More power to my elbow!

A few weeks later, Barry was evidently aware that he might appear overly preoccupied with his own concerns. He wrote to Ellen:

> How do you do, my dear? It has been a braw day, and I have done a fair amount of work. Don't you get just a little bored with my accounts of it? Angry protests? . . .

Nevertheless, he was soon back on his main topic:

> I hope that I can have the first draft of *Poor Richard* finished by the end of the month, so that I may get down to see you then. Mustn't come before . . .

In the late spring of 1922, *The Jilts* was being offered to producers in New York. Both the Theatre Guild and Brock Pemberton, having given it respectful attention, turned it down. (Barry later recounted how he had gone to Pemberton's office and said, " 'Make up your mind about this play, because it is going to be a hit.' Of course I was scared pink when I said it.") Barry now entered *The Jilts* in the Belmont Repertoire Company competition. By the terms of the competition, the winning play would be given a five-hundred-dollar prize by Richard Herndon, manager of the Belmont Theatre, and would be guaranteed a professional production within six months. Barry worked feverishly on *Poor Richard* and was able to finish it in time to submit it to the Belmont judges along with *The Jilts*. The Herndon Prize, as it was commonly known, had great prestige; nothing would serve a young playwright so well in gaining immediate recognition, and at that moment nobody was more impatient for recognition—and money, needful for marriage—than Philip Barry.

Ellen and Philip had been planning to marry in September, but with uncharacteristic boldness they advanced the date of the wedding to July. Since Philip had hitherto proved on occasion impetuous but never improvident, it must have been Ellen's spirited optimism—for generations, the Semples and the McAnerneys had been lucky people, and it was in their blood to expect good things of the future—that pushed him toward the taking of chances. He had had his year at the Workshop, but so far there was nothing to show for it except two plays that nobody appeared to want; he could not even be sure that, after the honeymoon, a job would be waiting for him in the advertising world that he had been so eager to escape from. He was a born worrier, but for once he stopping worrying. The young man in love had triumphed over the young man bent upon making good.

Ellen and Philip were married on July 15, 1922, at the Church of St. Francis, in Mount Kisco, and the wedding reception was held in the garden at Ellistoun Farm. Lorenzo Semple was a partner in the celebrated international law firm of Coudert Brothers, which had a prosperous office in Paris; among its many French clients was the film company Pathé, which then furnished weekly newsreels to movie theatres all over the world. Semple saw to it that a Pathé movie crew was on hand to record the wedding day. The film is in Mrs. Barry's possession, at her house in Washington; in 1975 one is able to watch the handsome young couple of over fifty years ago leaving the church and posing with self-conscious pride and much laughter in the summery garden of Ellistoun Farm, while Ellen's grandfather Colonel McAnerney, white-mustached and smoking a cigar, holds court in the midst of admirers.

Among the hundreds of presents received by the newlyweds was a pretty cottage on the Ellistoun Farm property and a wedding trip abroad. A few days after the wedding, the Barrys sailed for Europe. They spent the rest of the summer traveling in England, France, Switzerland, and Italy and were westward bound across the Atlantic in late September when a wireless message was slipped under their cabin door. The message was brief and very welcome—three words from Ellen's father, and they read: "CONGRATULATIONS PRIZE PLAY."

V

The Jilts, newly renamed *You and I,* went into rehearsal in January, 1923, with an exceptionally strong cast: Frieda Inescort, Geoffrey Kerr, Lucile Watson, H. B. Warner, Ferdinand Gottschalk, and Reginald Mason. Barry was continuously on hand to make revisions; it was the beginning of his custom of relying on much rewriting in rehearsal and out of town in the preparation of a final text for a play. (In the case of *The Philadelphia Story,* the play went into rehearsal when only the first and second of its three acts had been written.) After a week's tryout in Stamford, *You and I* opened at the Belmont Theatre, in New York, on February 19. The reviewers were unanimous in their praise and the play at once became a hit. Thomas Wolfe, Barry's colleague at the Workshop, was understandably impressed. To his mother in Asheville he wrote:

> Herndon told Baker last week that the play ought to run through the hot weather. [Hot weather was a constant threat to Broadway in the days before air-conditioning.] That is, to September or later. This means over thirty weeks for Philip Barry . . . and his royalties are at present about $700 a week. The contract reads that the movie rights are to be split equally between producer and author; they average around $15,000, so young Barry—he is three or four years older than I—stands to make a tidy little fortune.

The play gave one hundred and seventy-four performances in New York, played most of the major cities in the country, and enjoyed a long vogue among stock companies and nonprofessional acting groups. It had a successful production in London and the movie rights were sold to First National Studios for eleven thousand dollars—less than the envious Wolfe had predicted. After many delays, the movie version of the play was finally released in 1931; it starred Lewis Stone and Doris Kenyon and caused no great stir at the box office.

Professor Baker had urged Barry to write about what he knew at first hand. *You and I* dealt with the choice between fulfilling oneself at no matter what cost and failing to do so because, having fallen in love and married, one must provide for one's wife and family. Barry said that in writing the play he had imagined himself as a middle-aged man who had made the wrong choice; it was a pleasing irony that a heartfelt play about making the wrong choice was the first consequence of Barry's having made the right choice and that this play should then have given him the financial means to go on making right choices ever after.

Impetuousness and improvidence had richly rewarded the young Barrys, and further good fortune was in store for them. One evening Semple, returning by train from New York to Mount Kisco, stopped off at the Barry cottage, handed them a set of blueprints of a villa in Cannes that he was in a position to acquire at a good price, and in his usual affectionately playful fashion said to them, "This house is for you, if you'd like it. Let me know before I catch the 8:32 tomorrow morning." Let him know tomorrow morning, indeed! The Barrys moved into the villa in the summer of 1923, naming it the Villa Lorenzo after the generous donor, and it remained in the family until 1951.

Barry worked on a revision of the second of his Workshop plays, *Poor Richard,* during their first season at Cannes. The play had been optioned by Richard Herndon, who, finding himself unable to deal with it, had turned it over to Robert Milton, the director of *You and I*. After trying out in Atlantic City and Baltimore and undergoing two or three changes of name, the play opened on December 22, 1924, at the Gaiety Theatre, in New York, under the title of *The Youngest*. The reviews were mixed, but audiences liked the play and especially admired Henry Hull as Richard, the youngest of the Winslow sons. The play dramatized a young man's rebellion against the Philistinism of his middle-class, money-grubbing family, whom he outwits when he discovers—as Barry had—that he has accidentally come into possession of the entire family fortune. The play gave one hundred and four performances. With his usual coolness of self-appraisal, Barry said later of his two first Broadway plays, "*You and I* was a success and I liked it. *The Youngest* was a moderate success and I didn't like it."

So began a career that was to last for almost thirty years. By the conventional standards of fame and wealth, over that long period Barry became one of the most successful playwrights in America. He was proud to find himself achieving a permanent place in the history of our theatre and he was grateful for the monetary rewards that that place assured him. It was important to him to be able to feel on a comfortable financial footing with those worldly and well-read insiders—the elect of the elect, like the Bob Lovetts and the Charlie Paysons—who enjoyed the company of playwrights, novelists, and poets. One had to have money enough to share the give-and-take of pleasant social occasions without strain. The Barrys and their close friends the Gerald Murphys learned to use their money wisely; the outward grace with which they lived was the sign of an inner grace that they never stopped seeking to possess in greater abundance. Living well was nothing so simple as "the best revenge" (revenge upon what? upon whom?); it was a quest. The Barrys at the Villa Lorenzo, in Cannes, and the Murphys at the Villa America, a few miles along the coast at Cap d'Antibes, were known for their exquisite manners and exquisite taste; important as these attributes were, they concealed as much as they made plain. The paradox faced by Murphy the painter and Barry the writer was that good fortune already bestowed could yet require to be earned, and not once but many times. The means of earning it was the fulfillment of their talent in daily hard work. Murphy mysteriously broke off painting at what amounted to the beginning of his career; Barry never stopped writing, though with every passing year the task grew more difficult, the self-doubt more grave.

And with reason, for an oddity was invisibly present inside his success, and the oddity was failure. Of the twenty-one plays that Barry had on Broadway, the majority enjoyed short, unprofitable runs. His fame and his wealth came from the drawing-room comedy hits, like *Paris Bound, Holiday, The Animal Kingdom,* and, above all, *The Philadelphia Story,* but no less important to Barry, and often more interesting to his admirers, were the plays in which doggedly, year after year, working outside the traditional drawing-room setting, he struggled to express his ever-darkening view of life. What these plays sought to state was often hard, if not impossible, to dramatize; moreover, they were the very plays in which Barry was at his most experimental, and the new forms he essayed were often as intractable as the ideas they were intended to embody. Barry found himself committed to a contest that he was both too brave to withdraw from and too weak to win. To the degree to which he chose to go on experimenting, one might say that, whether consciously or no, he was choosing to fail. The defeats he suffered were galling to him and yet he never gave up.

Like most authors, Barry wrote too much. The difficulty and self-doubt that he suffered were not only burdens to him but goads as well: they forced him to drive himself to the limit in play after play—too many plays! Still, for students of Barry the number of plays is a boon, and the so-called flops are in certain respects more worth examining than the hits. In the work of art that succeeds, problems that the artist may have been sorely pressed to resolve resist detection, simply *because* the artist has resolved them so well; in the failed work of art, the problems, being unresolved, remain highly visible and what one learns from them may offer valuable clues to the artist's successes.

The play with which Barry followed *The Youngest* was called *In a Garden,* and it marked the first time that Barry attempted what he thought of as high comedy. The play, which starred the celebrated Laurette Taylor, got mixed to poor notices—Barry was accused, among other things, of having filled it with too many ill-sorted-out ideas—and gave but seventy-three performances. Barry afterward consoled himself with the boast that he had proven that he "wasn't just another playwright . . . by writing the most sophisticated high comedy that ever came from a native-born American." It is a measure of his disappointment that, modest man that he was, he should have been provoked into boasting of anything. The unexpected phrase "native-born American" is also perhaps a sign of resentment: the uneasy outsider in Barry is stating a claim before a host of insiders on Broadway, not all of them native-born.

The failure of *In a Garden* might have led a less ambitious man than Barry to repeat the formula of the earnest comedies *You and I* and *The Youngest.* Instead, Barry announced that he was writing a comedy that "would probably ruin the man who produced it." The play turned out to be a fantasy called *White Wings.* Reckless enough of Barry to risk a fantasy in the hard-boiled, bootlegging twenties; still more reckless to make it a fantasy laid in the period of the not-yet-romanticized turn of the century, with, of all people, a manure-shoveling street cleaner as a hero and the inventor of the automobile as a villain. *White Wings* was the first of Barry's plays to contain no overt autobiographical material; it was inspired by a passage in a humorous book written by his friend Donald Ogden Stewart, *Mr. and Mrs. Haddock Abroad.* (Barry later based a character in *Holiday*—Nick Potter—on Stewart and got Stewart to play the part. Stewart received much praise for his skill at depicting himself.)

White Wings opened in New York in December, 1926, slightly more than a year after the opening of *In a Garden.* The producer for whom Barry had cheerfully predicted ruin was Winthrop Ames, a man of intelligence, taste, and large private means, who had built two of the most attractive theatres on Broadway—the Booth and the Little Theatre, both still standing in 1975—and who told Barry that, while he was aware that *White Wings* would almost certainly lose money, he liked it so much that he felt duty-bound to produce it. As things turned out, the play was admired by a number of reviewers, Robert Benchley among them, but it appeared to baffle the public. Unfortunately, Ames had a theory that if business at a play was worse the second week than it had been the first, the play was doomed and must be abandoned. In the case of *White Wings,* business was indeed worse the second week than it had been the first, and although Barry argued that business would pick up in the third week—as, in fact, it did—Ames had made his usual decision and had already promised the theatre to another producer. Playing toward the end to full houses, *White Wings* closed after twenty-seven performances. It is one of the handful of Barry plays that is constantly spoken of for revival, possibly in the form of a musical.

After *White Wings* came the Biblical curiosity *John.* While Barry was writing it, Professor Baker triumphantly transferred his base of operations from grudging Harvard to hospitable Yale. Thanks in part to Barry's undercover activities as a go-between, Yale had been given a fully equipped professional theatre for the use of the Dramat and the Baker Workshop by the philanthropist Edward S. Harkness. (Coincidentally, Harkness was one of the rich Connecticut "summer" people whom O'Neill despised without knowing them and who served in part as a model for the prissy plutocrat T. Stedman Harder in *A Moon for the Misbegotten.* In life, Harkness was a harmless, pleasant man; the most vivid thing about him was the fact that he gave innumerable millions of dollars to Yale. O'Neill was Baker's most famous student, and at Baker's urging O'Neill had accepted an honorary degree from Yale the previous June. Little guessing that O'Neill would one day bestow on him an odious immortality, Harkness was among those who applauded the award.) Barry spoke at a conference organized by Baker shortly after the opening of the new theatre. Baker had suggested that Barry should address himself to the question of what, as a working dramatist, "you have felt is ill-adjusted, or might be better or more helpful in the relations between the professional and non-professional worlds of the theatre."

Barry began his speech by noting that "Mr. Baker could not have come to a better man. I know both worlds and I know them intimately." He reviewed his career, beginning with the happy six-month run of *You and I,* then went on to say:

> With that production behind me, and armed with the invaluable professional experience I had gained in the course of it, I set to work with a will. I determined to write plays at once better and more successful. The results of that determination are now history. I tell you, industry and experience are what count in the theatre. My next play [*The Youngest*] ran three months, my next [*In a Garden*] two months, and my last one [*White Wings*] three weeks. I am now busy on a manuscript which will, I hope, contain enough that is of promise to decide Mr. Baker to readmit me to the Workshop.

Witty remarks, much enjoyed by the audience, but there was a dark Irish bitterness in them, and a foreboding. For the manuscript he mentioned was *John,* which he worked on the following summer in Cannes, along with the comedy that was to become *Paris Bound* and a murder mystery, written in collaboration with Elmer Rice, called *Cock Robin. John* was a tragedy in five acts, and its plot had to do with events in the life of John the Baptist as he awaited the arrival of the Messiah. The play opened in November, 1927, and gave only eleven performances. Reviewers said of it that it was too long, that the subject matter was often at odds with itself, that the dialogue was too colloquial, and that the actors had been poorly chosen. The last criticism was one that Barry himself heartily concurred in. The play had proved more Biblical than he had intended by virtue of the fact that the cast amounted to a chittering-chattering Tower of Babel. John, for example, was played by Jacob

Ben-Ami, a Yiddish actor who was said to be "without the gift of speaking English that can be understood," while Herodias was played with an extreme Oxford accent by the English actress Constance Collier.

Barry's chagrin over the failure of his first "serious" work—one that was obviously an attempt to write in a classic vein and on a classic scale—was soon tempered by the success of the comedy *Paris Bound,* which opened a few weeks later and was an immediate hit. In theme, the play was scarcely less serious than *John,* being a study of the perplexing place of sexual fidelity in marriage. Barry was in dead earnest in making a case for the irrelevance of fidelity; surely there are things in marriage more important than this abashing proof of our membership in the animal kingdom. The play is a charmer from start to finish; one smiles continuously in the reading of it and one longs to see it on a stage again. It gave a total of two hundred and thirty-four performances in New York, went on tour, was sold to the movies, and continued to provide handsome royalties for many years.

Barry and Rice, meeting daily in the bar of a steamer on their way to Europe, had cobbled up the murderous shenanigans of the plot of *Cock Robin* in malicious cold blood; they thought of it as a potboiling prank—a means of rebuking critics and theatregoers by giving them precisely what they wanted. The play was written largely by mail, with Rice forwarding prolix first drafts to Barry and Barry tightening them up and polishing them. The play opened a couple of weeks after *Paris Bound,* was as well received as its authors had cynically anticipated it would be, and ran for a hundred performances. Money was now pelting in upon Barry in reassuring abundance. His circumstances, both professional and personal, were perhaps never to be happier. In the cycle of seasons, the Barrys touched down at Cannes, Paris, London, New York, and Mount Kisco; they gave amusing parties and went to amusing parties; and they took pride in two sons, Philip and Jonathan. (Philip is now a movie and TV producer, living in California; Jonathan is a physician and also lives in California. Philip has two daughters, Miranda and Stephanie Ann Thankful, both named after characters in Barry's last play.) The Barrys were enviable in their youth, good looks, wealth, and increasing celebrity, and they knew it; what could they do but be grateful and knock wood?

Holiday opened on Broadway in the fall of 1928. It starred the

Barrys' friend Hope Williams, who had made a name for herself in *Paris Bound,* and amounted to an emblem of the happiness of that period in the Barrys' life. It is a kindly comedy, whose precepts are Barry's own. Written at the height of the boom, at a time when America had never been more grossly materialistic, the play argues that wealth and convention suffocate the soul; a man must take radical chances in order to find out who he is capable of becoming. Money is good only as a weapon for cutting oneself free of trammels. The hero of *Holiday,* Johnny Case, is an embodiment of Barry's continued preoccupation with the relations between outsiders and insiders. Like Barry himself, Johnny has unexpectedly made good at an early age. He has fallen in love with a member of the aristocratic Seton family, and because of his financial success the family is willing to accept him and make him over into one of them. Johnny senses that life holds a greater promise for him than a mere comfortable place among the insiders; he will remain an outsider, going his own way at no matter what cost. *Holiday* was an immediate hit. It ran on Broadway for two hundred and twenty-nine performances, grossed over half a million dollars, and was sold to the movies for thirty-five thousand dollars.

Given the ease and agreeableness of Barry's life at the time, it is at least superficially ironic that he spent the summer of 1929 in Cannes writing the somber *Hotel Universe.* It is a play beautiful as well as somber; many students of Barry consider it his best work. The setting, borrowed from the Murphys' Villa America, is a terrace overlooking the Mediterranean. On the terrace are gathered half a dozen attractive men and women of varied backgrounds; at first glance, they would seem to be among the most fortunate people alive, but one perceives that something dreadful has happened: a malignancy no more palpable than air has put them in jeopardy. Death hovers all around them, not so much a threat as a temptation. Only recently death has seduced a delightful young acquaintance of theirs, who smilingly dove into the sea and committed suicide.

Barry has given the play the appearance of a drawing-room comedy, and it is no such thing. On the contrary, it is a fantasy, whose theme is existential despair and whose subject matter concerns the grim fact that people's lives often come to an end before they die. All those nice people on the terrace in *Hotel Universe*—like all those nice people on the Murphys' terrace at Cap d'Antibes; the Scott Fitzgeralds, the Robert Benchleys, the Ring Lardners, Dorothy Parker?—are engaged in a desperate struggle to find themselves by finding meaning in their lives, or, failing that, by finding meaning in the universe. This was a struggle that Barry remained a party to until his death. Despite the skepticism that he felt in regard to the Church and its conduct in the world, he was never not a Catholic; he was bound to the Church by emotional ties that no reasoning could loose. Once, he told Katharine Hepburn that he would be unable to get up out of the chair in which he was sitting if he weren't able to believe in some sort of God—some divine principle, however little aware of man—at work somewhere beyond us. *Hotel Universe* was one of the several attempts he made to give philosophical speculations a dramatic form; that he was able to provide the play with a happy ending is a tribute not only to his ingenuity as a playwright but also to his courage as a man: he would live with his doubts as other men live with an incurable malady.

Hotel Universe was treated respectfully by the reviewers, though many claimed to find it baffling. It failed to catch on with the public and closed after eighty-one performances. *Hotel Universe* contains several novelties of historic interest, among them Barry's use of psychodramas as an integral part of the plot and his insistence that the play be acted without an intermission. Nobody appears to have found this objectionable except Barry himself; a chain-smoker, he soon learned that at least once during the course of the play he would have to go sneaking up the aisle for a quick smoke in the lobby.

Less than a year after *Hotel Universe*, Barry was back on Broadway with still another serious play, *Tomorrow and Tomorrow*. Knowing that people expected comedies from him, he predicted that the play would have a run of eight weeks. To his astonishment, it ran for two hundred and six performances and was sold to the movies for eighty-five thousand dollars. Reviewers described it as Barry's *Strange Interlude,* and it is true that certain incidents in the plot echo O'Neill. Marriage, adultery, the responsibilities of parenthood, both licit and illicit—these characteristic Barry concerns are dealt with in Barry's characteristically conversational tone of voice. The play attempts too much, and one of the main characters (whom Barry himself subsequently called a fake) comes only intermittently to life.

Tomorrow and Tomorrow was followed by *The Animal Kingdom,* which opened in January, 1932, to general praise, and ran for a hundred and eighty-three performances. It is a comedy simple in theme and economic in plot. Barry argues that a man may be more truly married to his mistress than to his wife, and in that case an adulterous relation is more honorable than monogamy. The point is proved without a line or a gesture too many, and the dialogue is at once the wittiest and most natural-seeming that Barry had yet achieved.

The Animal Kingdom was the last success that Barry was to enjoy for some time. A long period of professional failure was ushered in by a family tragedy. The Barrys had always hoped for a daughter; one was born to them in 1933 and died of an undiagnosed infection at the age of a year and a half. It was the most sorrowful event in their twenty-seven years of married life, and one can observe in Barry's plays the degree to which he never fully recovered from it. Indeed, it is not too much to say that he was haunted thereafter by the idea of a perfect daughter—one who mingled aspects of his mother, his sister, and his wife. In his notes for possible plays, a constant subject is the father saved from loneliness and death by a daughter's love. This is in part the subject of *Second Threshold,* the play that Barry was working on when he died.

In 1934 came *The Joyous Season* and in 1935 *Bright Star*. In a speech given the following year, Barry said that he had decided after *Bright Star* to get out of the theatre. "I had had two utter and complete failures, one after the other: *The Joyous Season,* which ran joylessly for two weeks, and *Bright Star,* which flickered and went out after one. I meant those plays. I respected those plays. Each was presumably well and competently presented under honorable auspices and at a strategic time of year: mid-season and early season, respectively, in clean, well-lighted theatres. Each boasted a star, with, presumably, a following. They were my eleventh and twelfth plays to reach Broadway and each represented at least a full year of work on my part, I'm that slow and serious. . . . Well, both plays died the death, and I expect you have heard just how dead a dead play is: a thimble would have held the ashes of both of them."

For a while, Barry toyed with writing a novel (and later did write the novel *War in Heaven*), but the lure of the theatre proved too much for him. The producer Jed Harris talked him into preparing an adaptation of a comedy that a couple of Smith College girls had written several years earlier. Barry entitled the adaptation *Spring Dance* and appears not to have been very much surprised when it closed after twenty-four performances. "Jed Harris is a spellbinder," he said, and let the failure go at that. In 1938, *Here Come the Clowns* opened to mixed reviews. It was easily the most ambitious play that Barry had written, as well as the most serious. Its theme was the nature of good and evil; its subject matter was the confrontation sought by Clancy, an ex-stagehand, with God. Clancy, well played by Eddie Dowling, was determined to seek God out and put certain simple and terrible questions to Him. Why did He allow so much misery and wickedness in the world? Had He perhaps long since lost the battle with Satan? Or had He simply turned His back on man? Barry was accused, as usual, of being too profound for his own good. He was told, as usual, that his symbolism was obscure. Indignantly, he took to the papers to explain how very explicit his symbols were: the Globe Theatre stood for the world, the dwarfs and transvestites in Ma Speedy's Café des Artistes stood for all "forms of human wretchedness, congenital and imposed." In spite of Barry's public efforts, the play closed after a run of eighty-eight performances.

In the following year came Barry's greatest success, *The Philadelphia Story*. Starring Katharine Hepburn, for whom Barry had written it, the play ran for over four hundred performances in New York and grossed a total of over two million dollars. Miss Hepburn, who had taken the precaution to acquire the movie rights before the play opened, later sold them to M-G-M for a hundred and fifty thousand dollars. "Phil and I were both box-office poison at the time," Miss Hepburn has said. "Moreover, our producer, the Theatre Guild, was on the verge of bankruptcy. It was very pleasant indeed for the three of us to make our comebacks together." *The Philadelphia Story* admirably illustrates the fact that all Barry's plays, whether serious or comic, share precisely the same moral concerns. The characters say funny things and have funny things befall them, but they are natives of the same Barry country as the troubled characters moving through the twilight in *Hotel Universe*. Tracy Lord and Clancy would not be likely to meet, but if they were to do so they would have something substantial to say to each other.

Barry was to experience nothing as gratifying as the triumph of *The Philadelphia Story* throughout the rest of his career. During the forties he had a couple of extreme failures—*Liberty Jones* and *My Name Is Aquilon* (an adaptation of a play by Jeän Pierre Aumont) and a couple of mild successes—*Without Love,* which starred Katharine Hepburn and gave a hundred and thirteen performances on Broadway, and *Foolish Notion,* which starred Tallulah Bankhead and gave a hundred and four performances on Broadway. Both shows did well on the road, and it was unquestionably their stars that carried them. This was satisfactory to Barry in the case of Hepburn and unsatisfactory to him in the case of Bankhead; in or out of the theatre, it would be hard to imagine two people with less in common than the mannerly, soft-spoken Barry and the joyfully foul-mouthed Tallulah.

Barry worked intermittently for many years on the play that was to become *Second Threshold.* From his notebooks, it appears that at some point it was to have been a play about his friend Benchley, who died in 1945. Little by little, the play altered and darkened in tone as Barry grew older. By the spring of 1949, its central character was a wealthy man in middle age who, after a distinguished career in government, finds so little of interest left to him in life that he contemplates doing away with himself in the guise of a hunting accident. Barry's friend James Forrestal committed suicide that spring, and Barry feared that his play might be thought to be based on that event. The play underwent further revisions, always with the purpose of emphasizing the man's relationship to his daughter. In one of his notebooks, Barry wrote, "Two people whom life has treated badly. Maybe she has been jilted by a married man. Companions in adversity. The perfect combination: mature wisdom with youthful freshness . . . Love without the complications."

After Barry's death, *Second Threshold* was completed from Barry's latest revisions and notes by his friend and colleague Robert E. Sherwood. The play opened in New York in January, 1951, at the Morosco Theatre, the very theatre in which, thirty years earlier, Barry's first play had been performed. It was directed by his old friend Alfred de Liagre, Jr., and had a handsome setting by still another old friend, Donald Oenslager. (De Liagre's production assistant was a young man named Philip Barry, Jr.) The play starred the well-known English actor Clive Brook and marked the debut of a pretty actress named Betsy von Furstenberg. It received the now all but obligatory mixed reviews, in which Barry was praised for his witty dialogue and damned for his bleak thoughts. Even posthumously, he was expected to embrace the sunny views of the young man who wrote *Paris Bound*. Grace of the body, grace of the spirit—they had been goals far harder to achieve than that eager and diligent young man had supposed. With luck, over the long years of one's life the cost of achieving them would be only just bearable, and no man could bear the cost alone. That was the theme of *Second Threshold*—a fitting one for a playwright in his middle years to dramatize. And the title of the play was charged with promise. Barry had weighed both words with care.

Barry himself was never to cross that second threshold. He died of a massive heart attack on Saturday, December 3, 1949, in the family apartment on Park Avenue. A Requiem Mass was celebrated on December 5th at the Church of St. Vincent Ferrer. Among the honorary pallbearers were Robert Lovett, Artemus L. Gates, John O'Hara, John P. Marquand, Robert E. Sherwood, Gerald Murphy, Arthur Hopkins, Lawrence Langner, Dana Atchley, and Charles Addams. Barry was buried in the Catholic cemetery in East Hampton. Later, Ellen Barry arranged to have placed above his grave a small white marble monument in the shape of an open playscript. On the left-hand page are carved his name and the dates of his birth and death. On the right-hand page, as if in Barry's own hand, are two lines from *Hotel Universe:* "All things are turned to a roundness. Wherever there is an end, from it springs the beginning."

YOU AND I

YOU AND I

was first produced by Richard G. Herndon
at the Belmont Theatre, New York City,
on February 19, 1923.
It was directed by Robert Milton;
the setting for Act I was designed by Raymond Sovey;
for Act II by J. L. Shute and Robert Goode,
of the 47 Workshop, Harvard University.

CAST

MAITLAND WHITE • H. B. Warner
NANCY WHITE • Lucile Watson
RODERICK WHITE • Geoffrey Kerr
VERONICA DUANE • Frieda Inescort
GEOFFREY NICHOLS • Reginald Mason
G. T. WARREN • Ferdinand Gottschalk
ETTA • Beatrice Miles

■ SCENES ■

ACT I

The library of the Whites' country home in Mount Kisco, Westchester County, New York. A late September evening.

ACT II

"The Studio" in the attic, an afternoon the following May.

ACT III

"The Studio" later the same evening.

■ ACT I ■

Here you are, in the library of the Whites' country home in Mount Kisco, Westchester County, New York.

The Whites' home is one of those rambling white houses that began as a farm house and has been added to year by year as the family grew, and the family's fortunes prospered. In architecture, it is nearer colonial than anything else. There was always plenty of land, but the orchard, of which MAITLAND WHITE *is so proud, he planted himself.*

When you come for your first weekend, he will delight in telling you that when NANCY *and he bought the place twenty years ago, the room in which you now stand was, with the exception of a tiny kitchen, the entire lower floor. The second beam from the left in the ceiling will show you where the partition came between living and dining rooms.*

The big hall, by which you entered, is the west wing—that came first—and the spacious dining room and study are the east wing, which was built four years later. The servants' wing was added at the same time. The little cottage down by the swimming pool is of course quite new. That is to be Jean's, when she grows up and is ready to be married—fancy Jeanie married!

You will be awfully surprised and say What!—this enormous place grown out of a little old farm house? And MAITLAND *will chuckle and say Oh, Nanny and I have had no end of fun out of it, haven't we, Nanny? And like as not, the next time you come (as you will, if they like you) he will begin to tell you about it all over again. But* NANCY *will stop him, without in the least hurting his feelings.*

The library—which is also the main living room—is a huge, uneven, motherly sort of a room that pats your hand as you come into it, and tells you to sit down and be comfortable with the rest of us. Out here we don't even know that there is *such a place as the City!*

There is a large white fireplace, with two ample chairs flanking it. A long table stands just away from the center of the room. There are a few more easy chairs, and a writing desk. A great sofa invites you to abandon yourself to its lethal depths. Wherever there is not a window or a door, there are built-in bookcases, filled with books.

MAITLAND *will show you, among the really fine etchings upon the wall, two rare Whistlers, in which he takes a just pride. You enter—through glass doors at the right—a kind of sunroom, from which, if you are sufficiently enterprising, you may proceed through the garden into the orchard. The woodwork of the library is a soft ivory. There is no scheme of decoration, but the whole effect is one of warmth and light and color. It is what you would call, not a beautiful, but a charming room.*

The time is about seven o'clock of a late September evening and someone, someone whom you must wait a moment to see, is playing a frivolous tune on the piano in the sunroom. In the middle of a measure, the music stops abruptly. There is a short silence, followed by the bang of a discord. Then, with her head high, thoroughly angry, VERONICA DUANE *enters and traverses the library, nearly to the hall.*

She is about 19, slim, of medium height, with a decidedly pretty, high-bred face, lovely hair, lovely hands, and a soft, low-pitched voice—whatever she may be saying. Heredity, careful up-bringing, education and travel have combined to invest her with a poise far in advance of her years. She has attained the impossible—complete sophistication without the loss of bloom. Her self-confidence is, you will be happy to know, free from any taint of youthful cock-sureness.

RONNY [*as she is fortunately called*] *was made to wear clothes well, and she wears her present out-of-door ones superlatively so. There is something in the ensemble—it may be a scarf, the marking of a sweater, or the tongue of a shoe—that everyone will have next summer:* RONNY *adopted it at Deauville last spring.*

Following her comes RODERICK WHITE, *with the fireplace as his objective. There he stands leaning back against a chair, stuffing a pipe with tobacco, and looking just a little bit scared.*

He is a well set-up, thoroughly nice boy about 21, with high color, hair carefully brushed, a disarming smile. Although his expression is bright and animated, his countenance appears to be totally without guile. Only RICKY *knows the multitude of scrapes that has got him out of.*

If you come near enough, particularly on a rainy day, you will catch, as it hovers about his golf clothes, a thoroughly satisfactory aroma of peat smoke. RICKY *has a proper regard for old clo'. His poloshirt, though it may be a little frayed, has the merit of being clean. His brown-and-white shoes—genuine antiques—have not.*

RONNY [*With a rigid back to him*]: I think I'll be—going home.

RICKY [*Amiability itself*]: Good idea—if you expect to dress and be back here in time for dinner. [*A pause*] Well—you needn't be so darn snootey about it. [RONNY *wheels about and faces him.*]

RONNY: Ricky—I could kill you for doing that.

RICKY [*Puffing on his pipe*]: I've been resisting the impulse all summer—and when you turned your head and looked up that way—well—it was rather pleasant.

RONNY: I don't see how you dared!

RICKY: Oh, come on, Ronny—you can't get away with that. You loved it.

RONNY: Who said I didn't! For months you've had me literally quaking in my boots. Because I knew that if ever you did, I'd—I'd—

RICKY [*Bearing in her direction*]: Ronny! Did you know that, too . . . ? [*She nods her head, dumbly.*]—And *do* you now—as much as I do . . . ?

RONNY: Hang it—of course I do!—On the fifteenth of October you're going abroad for three years. For the love of Pete, why couldn't you have held out just two weeks more?—Then you'd have gone, and I'd have forgotten you.—And that would have been all there was to it.

RICKY: —In a pig's eye.

RONNY: I tell you it would! And now—after this—[*She flings a magazine from table to sofa.*] Oh—a sweet winter I'll put in, getting over you!

RICKY [*Genuinely dismayed*]: Getting *over* me . . . ? Gosh, I don't want you to do *that!*

RONNY: No—I'll sit around doing basketwork, while you and your little playmates at the Beaux-Arts scamper up and down Paris.

RICKY [*Grandly*]: I am going abroad to study architecture—not to go on parties.

RONNY: Show *me* a student on the Left Bank who doesn't study life! Thanks, Rick. By spring you will be but a memory.

RICKY: But—but Ronny—can't you get it into your silly head that I'm *really* in love with you? I'm—you've—oh damn it—*won't* you marry me?

[RONNY'*s hand, in a quick gesture, covers his. For one breathless moment their eyes hold them together.*]

RONNY: Ricky! [*Then she removes her hand, and shakes her head with conviction.*] Uh-uh. It's awfully nice of you—but I couldn't wait three years for the Prince of Wales.

RICKY [*Moodily*]: Fat lot you love me.

RONNY: Oh—don't think I'm an absolute dud—[*With a trace of em-*

barrassment] You—know how it is—with Father and Mother, don't you?

RICKY: Why—they don't hit it off too well, do they?

RONNY: Mother's never said a word to me—but of course she's simply sticking it out till I'm what-they-call "settled." I had it all planned to marry the next person I was honestly fond of. But now you—you egg —you've ruined it. I'll have to forget *you* first. It would be such a filthy trick—when I—when there was someone I actually—[*She shudders.*] Oh—I couldn't stand it!

RICKY: I can't imagine being—to anyone but you, really I can't.

RONNY [*Softly*]: It would be too delightful, to be—to you. [*There is a pause.*]

RICKY [*A sudden idea*]: Listen, Ronny: there's no reason why we *shouldn't* be—I'll go into Father's factory, instead. Mr. Warren said he'd start me at two thousand a year, and if I was any good—

RONNY: But Rick—you've *always* meant to be an architect. I won't have you wash out on it for me.

RICKY: Oh—will you listen?—I'm not washing out on anything. I'll study on the side—and drift into it gradually. I can go to night school—

RONNY: " 'Whom are you?' said Cyril."

RICKY: But why not? Other people have. Life shouldn't be all gravy, anyway. After ten years of school and college I feel like a burglar at the prospect of riding Dad for three years more. I know I could swing it every bit as well, right here on my own.

RONNY: But that sounds like such a makeshift. And supposing once you got into business you had to stay put?

RICKY: Well, that's no calamity. Father dished painting in order to marry Nanny. And do you suppose he's ever regretted it? Look at them!

RONNY: I know—they're so happy, it's painful. But—

RICKY: Ronny, it's simply that I want *you*—so much more than anything else, that it's silly even to talk about it.

RONNY: Are you sure you'll keep *on* wanting me more?

RICKY: Damn right, I will!

RONNY [*Thoughtfully*]: There's a kink in it somewhere. . . .

RICKY: Oh—you're full of cold tea. Listen: I'll work like the very devil, and next summer we'll be married. What do you say?

RONNY [*After a troubled pause*]: Why—I've no really strong objections. . . .

RICKY [*In embarrassed delight*]: Oh Lord—this is wonderful. . . . [*She rises and faces him. They stand looking at each other, silently.* RICKY *finally ventures it.*] Dearest. . . .

RONNY: Angel. . . .

RICKY: Darling. . . .

RONNY: Lover. . . .

RICKY [*Groping for it*]: Uh—uh—*Precious.*

RONNY [*Dramatically*]: My tr-r-r-easure. [RICKY *presents a cheek, but* RONNY *edges away.*] Not on your life. . . . [RICKY *intrepidly kisses her on the cheek. She laughs.*] Gosh, Rick—you're poor!

RICKY: How do you know?

RONNY: I read a book.

[*At which* RICKY *takes her in his arms, as if she were made of spun-glass.*]

RICKY: "To Veronica from Roderick, with love."

[*He kisses her lightly, but unmistakably.*]

RONNY [*Softly*]: Oh—how diverting.

RICKY: I'm going to tell Mother!

RONNY [*In consternation*]: She'll crown me!

RICKY: Rot, my child. She'll think what a clever lad her son is.

RONNY: I'm scared of her. . . .

RICKY [*Pooh-poohing*]: Scared of Nanny?—Why, she's nothing but a kid.

RONNY: She appalls me. She knows so much. . . .

RICKY: She'll be all for it. Just you see—[*He starts toward the door, but comes back.*] Ronny—honestly—I simply adore you. . . .

RONNY [*With a faint smile*]: Dear—you've got nothing on me.

[*On this second expedition he reaches the door, and calls upstairs.*]

RICKY: Mother! [*Where can she be?*] Dearest! [*Can she have gone out?*] Oh, Nanny—stick out your neck!

NANCY [*An enchanting voice from above*]: What is it, you simpleton?

RICKY: What do you think?

NANCY: I think it's time you changed for dinner.

RICKY: Ronny and I are engaged. Can you beat it?

NANCY: Wh-a-a-t—?

RICKY: We have plighted our troth. Big news. C'mon down! [*He returns to* RONNY.] Beau'ful—I feel awfully sacred all of a sudden. Tell you what I'll do; I'll go to church with you in the morning.

RONNY: Check. The Maiden's Prayer.

RICKY: Then I'll take you on for nine fast holes before luncheon. Give you a stroke a hole—two, on the sixth—and beat the shoes off you!

RONNY: You lie, Dumbell, you won't.

RICKY: A dollar a hole. Are you on?

RONNY [*Scornfully*]: Am I on! For nine dollars, I'd—

[NANCY WHITE *appears in the hall doorway, carrying a half-written letter in her hand. She is a young forty, not-so-short, not-so-tall, but anyway with a slim, girlish figure, lively, humorous brown eyes, dark brown hair, and a manner as charming as her appearance. Despite her poise, one feels that her age is merely put on—youth dwells in her spirit, and no mere calendar can oust it.* RICKY *meets her at the door, and they enter together, his arm about her shoulder.*]

RICKY [*With a gesture toward* RONNY]: Behold!—My willing slave.

NANCY [*A brave attempt at severity*]: Veronica—is what Roderick tells me true?

RONNY: All but the "slave," Mrs. White.

[NANCY *looks from one to the other, goes to* RONNY, *takes her hand, gazes into her eyes for a moment, and then kisses her on the cheek.*]

NANCY [*Emotionally*]: My dear! [*She brushes away a hypothetical tear, and reaches one hand out behind her, to* RICKY.] My first-born child!

RICKY [*For* RONNY*'s information*]: Nanny wanted to go on the stage once. She just eats a thing like this.

NANCY [*Pointing an imperious finger toward the sofa*]: Ricky—sit down there! [RICKY *obeys, grinning.* NANCY *designates a place beside him.*] Veronica—[RONNY *sits at his side, a little frightened.* NANCY *pulls a large chair around, and sits facing them.*] Now, you two precious idiots, we'll talk this over.

RICKY [*To* RONNY]: Isn't she immense?

[*He affects a most solemn expression, and leans forward attentively, resting his chin upon his hand.*]

NANCY: I thought the fact of your living next door to each other for twelve summers would act as an antitoxin.

RONNY: You could have knocked me over with a feather, Mrs. White.

NANCY: I dare say. But of course it's quite out of the question. You're nothing but children.

RICKY [*Shaking his head reprovingly*]: Gosh, Nanny—that's awfully old stuff. . . .

NANCY [*With some acerbity*]: Roderick—be kind enough to reserve your infantile comments. [RICKY *subsides. She leans back with sigh.*]—Nothing but children. It is beautiful, my dears, but quite, quite ridiculous.

RICKY: Pardon the interruption—but how old were you, when *you* became a Married Maiden?

NANCY: That has nothing to do with it!

RICKY [*Indulgently*]: I know—but just as a matter of record. . . .

NANCY [*The dignified mother of two children*]: I was—nineteen. But—

RICKY: You mean a couple of weeks past eighteen. What're you, Ronny?

RONNY: I'll be twenty in December. Big girl.

RICKY: Check. And how about Dad?

NANCY: He was a great deal older than you are!

RICKY: Your memory's failing! He had me just four months.

NANCY [*Ironically*]: I don't want to be sordid—but what *do* you expect to live on?

RICKY: Query: What did *you* live on, Darling?

NANCY: Why—I had a little of my own, and your Father worked.

RICKY [*With a gesture*]: 'S a perfect equation!

RONNY: I've about two thousand a year from Aunt Isabel's estate. Dad's promised me a house. . . .

NANCY [*To* RICKY]: And may I ask what you intend doing about your architecture?

RONNY [*Leaning forward*]: You and me both, Mrs. White. . . .

RICKY: Quiet, Child—let me manage this. I'm going like a breeze. [*To* NANCY] Well, you see, I'm going to pass that up, and—

NANCY [*Really troubled*]: But—

RICKY: Oh—maybe not for good. Maybe, by and by, when we get on our feet—

NANCY: "By and by!" Somehow, that sounds vaguely reminiscent to me. Unless you do it now, you'll never do it!—That's certain as death and my hay fever.

RICKY: Well, really—what if I don't? I mean, you told me that Father wanted to paint, or something—but you and he were married at 21 and 18 respectively, and he went into business, and stayed there. What I mean is, it seems to me that you two have made a pretty good go of it.

NANCY [*Proudly*]: We have made an uncommonly good go of it. But—[*She scrutinizes* RICKY'*s ankles in despair.*] Oh—your stockings again! Ronny—can't *you* make him wear garters?

RONNY: Isn't it awful?—Slippety-slop. . . .

NANCY: What you find attractive in him, I'm sure I can't see.—I was saying . . . ? Ah yes—my reminiscences—[*She hesitates. Then to* RONNY] Of course, you look very charming as you are. But we dine at a quarter before eight. . . .

[RONNY *rises and moves toward the hall.*]

RONNY: Then I'd better shove off.

NANCY [*Just as she is about to go out*]: Oh—uh—Veronica—

RONNY [*Turning*]: Yes . . . ?

NANCY: Do you think you really love my Ricky?

[*A short pause.* RONNY *looks straight at* NANCY.]

RONNY [*Simply*]: I've—never given a happy hang for anyone else. I'd—simply—lie down and die for him.

[RICKY *rises and makes for her, but a sweep of* NANCY'*s arm intercepts him.*]

NANCY: —A quarter before eight. And—I think it will be all right—somehow—

RONNY: Oh—you *are* a dear. . . .

RICKY [*Calling after her*]: Make it seven-thirty, if you can. President of Dad's company's coming, and we may rate a cocktail!

RONNY [*A voice from the hall*]: Right-o!

[NANCY *goes to the desk, with her unfinished letter.*]

NANCY: I'm writing to your sister. Your love . . . ?

RICKY: Sure. But don't say anything about Ronny and I—

NANCY [*Automatically*]: "—about Ronny and *me*."

RICKY [*Grammar is an affectation*]: —about Ronny and I. You know Jean—she'd have it all over the school in six minutes.

NANCY: Now—I want to talk to you sensibly.

RICKY: Shoot, Darling—

[NANCY *opens a drawer of the desk. It is filled to overflowing with small pieces of paper. Two fall upon the floor.* RICKY *picks them up and looks at them.*]

NANCY: You see these?

RICKY: Sketches—Father's . . . ?

NANCY: Yes. Before I give Roberts his clothes to press, I always go through the pockets. Not more than twenty times in twenty years have I failed to find one or two of these, all nicely folded up and tucked away. He does murals, too. That's why the wall beside the telephone is repapered so often. . . . [*Looking at sketches, which* RICKY *gives her*] Charming, aren't they . . . ?

[*She puts them back and closes the drawer. Taking* RICKY'*s arm, they return together to the sofa.*]

RICKY: But what's Dad's foolishness got to do with my—?

NANCY: There's something very sad in that folly, Rick. It's like the beating of clipped wings . . . longing for flight. . . .

[*Ricky stares at her.*]

RICKY [*Disgustedly*]: Oh—if you're going to get deep on me—

NANCY: You've no idea how deep it goes. . . . [*She studies his face for a moment and then continues, matter-of-factly*] Now Ronny is a sweet, lovable girl. And if the truth must be known, I heartily approve of early marriages, when—

[*Ricky leans over and pecks her cheek.*]

RICKY: Great!

NANCY: Behave yourself, and listen to me!—*When* they are possible without too great sacrifices. Ricky—from the time you began to play with blocks, you've wanted to study architecture. Don't you still . . . ?

RICKY: Why of course I do. But I can't have both—and I want Ronny more.

NANCY: We might arrange—

RICKY: —To carry the two of us?—That's like you, Dear—but no thanks. When I'm married, I've got to be on my own. Maybe I'm in the same place Father was. Well—I know what I want most, just the way he did. It's a simple question of values. . . .

NANCY: Your values may shift a little, later on.

RICKY [*By way of refutation*]: Did Father's?

NANCY: —And when you're forty or so, you may look on love as a kind of captivating robber—who chatted so sweetly, as he plucked your destiny out of your pocket. . . .

RICKY: There you go again! Ask Dad—*he* knows!

[*From the hall is heard a whistled refrain which, possibly, you will recognize as Rodolfo's Narrative from "La Bohème."*]

NANCY [*Rapidly*]: —You may suddenly feel choked-off—thwarted—in the one really big thing you could have done. Then—though you love her dearly—you'll resent Ronny. You'll try not to let her see. If she loves you, she can't avoid it. Or even you yourself may not know quite what's wrong. You may simply find, all at once, that you are very empty, very unhappy. . . .

RICKY: But Nanny—look how happy Father is!

[*The whistle draws closer.*]

NANCY: You can't tell much by a whistle, son. . . .

[MAITLAND WHITE *comes in. He is 43, about five feet ten, and golf and squash have kept him in the pink of trim. He is not particularly handsome, but with a face and smile that—unless you be an incurable misanthrope—win you immediately. There are a few gray hairs, which* NANCY *or the barber will pull out at his next sitting. To look at him you might think him any one of a number of things. You guess that it is business, and you know that he is successful. His hands—long, slender and restless—and a kind of boyish whimsicality in him, are all that betray the artist. He wears a dinner coat, and wears it well. He is unwrapping a large, flat package as he enters. He places it upon the center table, and carelessly drops the paper to the floor.*]

MATEY [*To* NANCY]: Do come here and see this Watteau print I've got for your room—

[*He sets it up against some books, and stands off to look at it, continuing his low whistling.* NANCY *goes to his side, picking up the paper en route, and slips her arm through his.*]

NANCY: Matey—you lamb—it's too enchanting!

MATEY: —How pensive, how reluctant, it is. The way that man combines grace and abandon is a miraculous thing. . . .

RICKY: Father—I'm going to marry Ronny Duane—

MATEY [*Quite unimpressed by this momentous announcement*]: —I call it at once a bubble, and a monument. See this lady, with her head turned, so. You know, my dear—I think she's extraordinarily like you. . . .

NANCY: Imbecile!—Look at her nose . . .

[MATEY *does so. Then lifts* NANCY'*s chin and studies her face for a moment.*]

MATEY: I could fix that with one line.

[*Being so accessible, he kisses her.* NANCY *steals a furtive look at* RICKY, *who does not attempt to conceal his disgust.*]

RICKY: Aw—cut it out!—I say, Father, that I'm going to—

MATEY: —It's called "The Embarkation for Cythera"—hangs in the Louvre. [*Chuckles reminiscently*]—Remember that night the summer before we were married—when *we* embarked for Greenwich in the sailboat from Long Island?—And got becalmed half way across? Lord! I'll never forget your Mother's face, as we tiptoed in at five-thirty!

RICKY [*Compassionately*]: Poor Dad—middle age at last.

MATEY: What *is* that infant babbling about?

RICKY: It's the first time I've ever heard you brag of what a cutup you were as a lad. Unmistakably, Dad—you're *done*. . . .

MATEY: Done, eh—? Who beat you 6-love, 6-3, 6-2 this morning?

RICKY: Oh—you're *fit* enough. It's the mind that goes first.

MATEY [*Scornfully*]: Middle age!

[*Nonetheless, he does look a little worried.*]

RICKY: I don't want to bore you—but I was breaking the news of my approaching nuptials with one Veronica Duane. . . .

MATEY: —And didn't I felicitate you? How careless. Congratulations, my boy—and upon the inheritance, too.

RICKY: The—what . . . ?

MATEY [*With a gesture*]: The—uh—legacy. . . .

RICKY: What do you mean?

MATEY: Why—er—haven't you come into a large fortune, as well?

RICKY: I haven't been advised of the fact.

MATEY: Then how do you expect to marry Ronny?

RICKY: She's got her own running expenses, and I'm going to work.

MATEY: I sincerely trust that eventually you will.

RICKY: I want to begin right away. I'm not going abroad, Father.

[MATEY *looks to* NANCY *for an explanation. She makes a helpless gesture, as if to say, "I've done all I can." A pause.* MATEY *is dumbfounded. He turns to* RICKY, *drops his bantering air, and speaks kindly and sympathetically.*]

MATEY: Look here, old fellow, this is a little confusing. Would you mind telling me more about it?

RICKY: Why—there isn't a great deal to tell, Sir. It's just that we're—very much in love, and want to be married as soon as we possibly can. I figure that if I go to work now, by spring everything will be rosy.

MATEY: What do you plan to do?

RICKY: Same as you—the Warren Company.—Caught you, Sir—you thought I'd say "sell bonds."

MATEY: And your architecture goes by the boards, eh?

RICKY: Why should it? I can study evenings, and Sundays, and finally—[*At this patent absurdity,* MATEY *laughs.* RICKY *is injured.*] Well—I can. . . .

MATEY [*Gravely*]: Ricky—our method of upbringing for you and Jean has allowed room for very few "Thou-shalt-nots." I'm not going to start ordering you about now, but there are a few things, that—as an older man—I want to remind you of—

[NANCY *proceeds to examine the Watteau print more closely.*]

RICKY: Yes, Dad. . . .

MATEY: I have my own eyes, and the word of your masters at school and college, to tell me that you have a considerable gift for building design. You love the work, and you're unusually well-suited to it. You need technique, and a background—and you need them badly. Three years at the Beaux-Arts will give you the best there are. . . .

RICKY: But Ronny—

MATEY [*A little exasperated*]: If Ronny won't wait for you, there'll be another girl just as charming, later on. . . .

[NANCY *puts down the picture and looks at them.*]

MATEY: I want to tell you, Son, that the most important thing in a man's life is his work—particularly when he has equipment such as yours. It's hard to get going; for a while you need absolute independence—freedom to think only "I—I—I—I and my work"—After marriage that is no longer possible. From then on it's "You and I"—with the "You" first, every time. "*You* and I"—

RICKY: Sound grammar, anyway.

MATEY [*Swiftly*]: I'm not speaking idly!—And don't underestimate, either, the suffering a flouted destiny can send you. There's a course you feel cut out to take—step off it now, and you'll regret it as long as you live.

[NANCY *aimlessly picks up a magazine.*]

RICKY: But—I simply can't give up Ronny—

[MATEY *stares at him, and then rises abruptly from his chair.*]

MATEY [*Brutally*]: In my opinion, any man who sacrifices his career for the sake of a girl, hasn't the backbone of—a cup custard. [NANCY*'s head drops a little, over her magazine.* RICKY *glances at her apprehensively.*]—And any girl selfish enough to permit—

RICKY: Dad—isn't this a bit rough on Mother?

MATEY: Rough on—? What do you mean . . . ?

NANCY [*Very quietly*]: Don't be silly, Ricky.

[MATEY *looks from one to the other.*]

MATEY: But . . . ?

NANCY: I must go and dress. . . . [*To* RICKY] You'd better come too.

[*She starts to cross, toward the hall.*]

MATEY: Just a moment, dear—[*Again to* RICKY] It's sheer nonsense to think you can manage two occupations—. One or the other must go. You—

RICKY: I'm afraid it's no use, Father. I've thought it all out, and my mind's made up.

[MATEY *shakes his head sadly—pityingly, perhaps. Before* NANCY *reaches the door,* ETTA, *in maid's costume, enters. The kindest of all laws—that of compensations—has endowed her with lustrous hair, perfect coloring, a charming figure, and eyes to which the Blue Grot is a dirty gray. Who cares at what age the psychological tests will place her?*]

ETTA: Mr. Warren has arrived.

[*Yes, here is* G. T. WARREN *himself. He is about 55, and partially bald—a short, plump, gusty little man, with a ready smile. He has the conceit of most self-made men, but in his case, it is made amusing by his naïveté. He is, in the business vernacular, always "on his toes," and literally exudes prosperity and good nature. He speaks rapidly, and with conviction.* NANCY, MATEY *and* RICKY *rise to greet him.*]

MATEY: "—and seizing his golf-clubs, and the latest 'Cosmopolitan,' our Captain of Industry determined to relax."

WARREN [*Briskly, as always*]: Hello, White. Relax, is the word. Never felt stiffer. [*Taking* NANCY'*s hand, and beaming upon her*] And how's the little woman?

NANCY: Growing up, Mr. Warren. Delightful, having you here. I'd concluded you thought rest only for the dead. [*To* ETTA] Have Mr. Warren's chauffeur take his car to the garage. He will stay in William's quarters. [*To* WARREN] Do sit down. Would you like a pick-me-up?

WARREN [ETTA *is in the corner of his eye*]: I'll wait—. What a pretty girl! [*The pretty one goes out.*]

NANCY: Better than that, she's one of the few mortals who can get on with my old Katie. She came as a temporary, but I think I'll perpetuate her.

[WARREN *advances deeper into the room, mopping his brow and adjusting his cuffs.*]

WARREN: Miserable trip, coming up. Brought that advertising man Davis, far as White Plains with me. He talked saturated markets and customer resistance till I had to ask him if he handled a hot-air furnace account!

[*At which he chuckles. And if you were one of his clerks, you may be certain you would roar with laughter. But*—]

NANCY [*With a grimace to* MATEY]: Mr. Warren says the quaintest things.

WARREN: Well—as I told that reporter fellow who interviewed me last week—"Smile through to success"—that's been my motto ever since I was a kid. [*To* RICKY] Hello, Son—all through with college?

RICKY: —The youngest living graduate. . . .

WARREN: I must mind my who's and whom's. Let's see—it was Harvard, wasn't it?

RICKY [*A gentle reproof*]: Mr. Warren—*please*—

WARREN: My mistake! Well—I got *my* education at the University of Hard Knocks, and—

RICKY [*An end to these wall mottoes!*]: "—and began business without a nickel in my pocket—and look at me now!"

[WARREN *stares at him for a moment and then laughs.*]

WARREN: White—this is a fresh youngster of yours, but I like his spirit. Can't stand men who're afraid of me.

RICKY: You know—I like you, too. You look exactly like our old baseball trainer. If you don't mind, I think I'll come and work for you. I won't be like this in the office. At toil, I'll be very reserved. But *here*—? Well—both good fellows, wot?

WARREN [*I can be a hale fellow, as well met as any*]: Both good fellows! When can you start?

RICKY: A week from Monday. Are you on?

WARREN: Suits me. Given up your other plans?

MATEY [*Quickly*]: I don't think he's quite decided, G. T.

NANCY: He's not himself today, Mr. Warren.

RICKY [*Scowling at them*]: As a matter of fact, Sir, they're full of red ants. I have *quite* decided, and I've never been more myself.

WARREN: He couldn't do better than to come with us. This is an age of business. [*He picks up the Watteau print and glances at it.*] H'm—pretty. . . . [*Replaces it and turns again to* RICKY] I'll put you through the production end in six months. Then the sales department. Then the—you see, we're entirely departmentalized. [*Takes pencil and paper from pocket, and sits beside* RICKY] Look here. It's arranged like this. Here's the top: "G. T. Warren"—

RICKY: Himself!

WARREN: Then the vice-president—you know old Lawson. Then your father. Beneath us, come the—

[*Then—as people will—they all talk together. But unless you have an inordinate interest in business, you would better listen to* NANCY *and* MATEY.]

MATEY [*To* NANCY]: I nearly forgot. Who do you think is staying with the Carharts?

[WARREN *is saying, "I'll draw it like a line of descent, showing the complete unit."* RICKY, *for want of something better, replies, "—The Warren genealogy, h'm?"*]

NANCY: —Someone swanky.—Who?

MATEY: Geoff Nichols. He just phoned me.—Got back from China last week.

NANCY [*Puzzled*]: Nichols . . . ?

[WARREN *says, "—Might call it that. First—Administration; then Sales; next—Distribution—with that little arrow indicating our foreign business"—at which* RICKY *appreciatively murmurs, "Europe too!"*]

MATEY: You remember Geoffrey—he was one of our ushers.

NANCY: The writer person!

MATEY: Of course.—Haven't laid eyes on him for years. He's going to stop in for a moment before dinner.

[WARREN *has informed* RICKY *that "We cover the entire world" and gone on to explain: "Then Production—then finally the Purchasing Department—raw materials. There—you have it all—a three-million-dollar business. Simple, isn't it?"*]

NANCY: Must we talk literature to him?

MATEY [*Laughing*]: Heavens—*no!*

[RICKY, *having told his future employer that "It depends on what you call simple," brings the competitive conversation to a conclusion.*]

RICKY: You can count on young Roderick for the literary stuff. I've just gone another two inches on my Five-Foot-Shelf of Books.

WARREN [*Giving* RICKY *the diagram*]: I'll leave this with you. And if you're half the man your father is—

RICKY [*Laconically*]: Oh—I'll draw circles around Dad.

NANCY: Would you like to go to your room, Mr. Warren?—The gray room, Ricky. And remember—a *stiff* shirt!

RICKY: What! Is the dear Duchess coming? [*To* WARREN] The gray room's usually reserved for ambassadors and bishops, Sir, but—[*With a deprecating gesture*]—You see how you stand with us.

[WARREN *laughs, and puts his hand on* RICKY*'s shoulder, preparatory to going out.*]

WARREN [*To* MATEY]: White, you've been looking completely worn out. Why not pack up and forget business for a month or two?

MATEY: The Company would crack to pieces!

RICKY: Not with you and me there, would it, Chief?

WARREN: No indeed! We've got youth on our side. It's your poor old father, who's aging so fast. [*Slips his arm through* RICKY*'s as they cross Left*]—Both good fellows, eh?

RICKY [*Solemnly*]: The best there are! [*They go out, and their voices die away on the favorite theme.*] You know—I think I'm going to like business.

WARREN: We *need* young blood. I've always said—

MATEY [*A little annoyed*]: That amazing child!

NANCY: He's cleverer than you think. G. T. was pleased as Punch. [MATEY *seats himself in a chair.*] Oh—I've gone flat, from standing so long. [*She sinks down on the arm of* MATEY*'s chair.*] Why don't you make me go up and dress?

MATEY [*Sternly*]: Go up and dress!

NANCY: I won't!

MATEY [*Comfortably*]: You're an obstinate baggage.

NANCY: I am the wife of your bosom, and you adore me.

MATEY: —Which makes you none the less obstinate, and none the less a baggage.

NANCY: Matey—you're a grand old thing—do you know it?

MATEY: I do.

NANCY: —But it doesn't become you to admit it—[*A slight pause*] I believe I'm in love with you.

MATEY [*Impressively*]: It is my fatal fascination. [*Suddenly troubled*] Nanny—have I been looking done in, lately—or done up—or done anyway?

NANCY: Why—*no!* [*She turns his head around and scrutinizes his face.*] —A little tired, perhaps. [*She finds a gray hair, and with squinting eye and set mouth, proceeds to separate it from the others.*] Here's another gray one. Out you come, false prophet! [MATEY *submits to the operation. The offending member is held up for his inspection.*] *Voilà!*—As the driven snow. . . . [MATEY *laughs, a little nervously.*]

MATEY: Any other signs?

NANCY: Of what?

MATEY: Senility.

NANCY: None but the fact that you are being unusually childish.

MATEY: Well—G. T. and the infant both spoke of it.

NANCY: Of what?

MATEY: My premature decline.

NANCY [*Lovingly*]: Matey—you idiot!

MATEY: Well, after all—here I am, forty odd—life's half over. . . .

NANCY: I never heard such nonsense! You're in the very prime of life. . . .

MATEY [*With a grimace*]: "Prime"—wretched word. Soon I'll be "spry." —What a week it's been! Went to the mat with G. T. again yesterday. He can't seem to get it into his head that if we're to keep up our expansion, we've got to advertise in a big way—like Colgate's. . . .

NANCY: Of course we have—

MATEY: I've been at him for years. Our appropriation is fifty thousand, where it ought to be five hundred. And he says he won't increase it a nickel until he finds a way to advertise the entire line as a unit. Which is simple rot.

NANCY: He's a tightfisted old fool.

MATEY: No, he's not. He's merely obtuse.

NANCY: You put things so beautifully, my dear.

MATEY: Honestly, Nanny—I get so fed-up at times, I could throw over the whole works.

NANCY [*With genuine sympathy*]: Poor lamb. Seriously—what about a holiday? It's years since we've been abroad.

MATEY: The market's shot to pieces. We can't afford it—not if we're to send Ricky.

NANCY: But—you know—he's not going.

MATEY: You think he's actually in earnest about the factory?

NANCY: I'm almost certain he is. But perhaps—on the side—he can—

MATEY: "On the side"!—Heaven save him from it! His one hope for peace is to forget it entirely—[*Shaking his head sadly*] Oh—it's criminal for that boy to give up his career. [*A slight pause*]

NANCY: Was it—criminal—for *you* to, Matey?

[*Another pause. Then* MATEY *laughs easily.*]

MATEY: So *that's* what he meant! [*Reassuringly*] It's quite different with us—quite.

NANCY: *Is* it?

MATEY [*With spirit*]: Of course!

NANCY [*Dubiously*]: Well—I'm glad to know *that*. [*From the hall is heard a man's voice saying, "Well—if people* will *leave their doors open they can expect other people to walk in without ringing—so here I am!"*] I wonder if that's—

[*Quite right—it is* GEOFFREY NICHOLS. *He is* MATEY'*s age, taller, very slight and with a most engaging manner. In comparison with the other successful literary men of your acquaintance, his affectations are very few.*]

MATEY: Geoff! By Gad—this is fine!

NICHOLS [*Taking his hand delightedly*]: Matey—you pig! If you don't look prosperous! And this is—Mrs. Matey—[*Crooking a speculative finger at* NANCY] Your name is—don't tell me, now—your name is—Nancy! And you were the prettiest bride ever I saw. What a wedding! I was frightfully sorry about that punch bowl—I should have known that I couldn't balance it on my nose. By Jove, you seem *two* years older, instead of—[*He covers his eyes with his hands, in mock dismay.*] Oh—I mustn't say it—I can feel my shroud as I do. . . .

NANCY: You delightful man.

NICHOLS [*To* MATEY]: I begged you not to marry. I eat my words. I behold the ideal wife.

NANCY: Can nothing induce you to stay and dine?

NICHOLS: It would be writing my doom with the Carharts.

NANCY: Then do come to us for next weekend.

NICHOLS: I'm so sorry. I sail Wednesday on the *Majestic*.

NANCY: Pity us.

NICHOLS: But Monday—join me in town for dinner and the theater—I've seats for the *Chauve-Souris.*

NANCY [*To* MATEY]: Are you free?

MATEY: As these United States.

NANCY [*To* NICHOLS]: We should be charmed. Now I simply must re-drape myself for dinner. You want to talk, anyway. Don't go till I come down, will you?

[NICHOLS *bows, and with her most gracious smile* NANCY *goes out.* MATEY *offers* NICHOLS *a cigarette, which he accepts.*]

NICHOLS: Well—"home is the sailor, home from the sea"—and all that jolly rot.

MATEY: Geoff—it's been twenty years at least.

NICHOLS: I demand a recount!

MATEY: I last broke bread with you in the Spring of '99. . . .

NICHOLS: My Victorian Memoirs.

[*They seat themselves.*]

MATEY: Where *have* you been?

NICHOLS: Everywhere! I'm a veritable flea for travel. London is my old lady—Paris, my mistress—and Rome—ah, Rome—my saint in décolleté! [MATEY *laughs, a little enviously, and begins sketching, absently, on the back of a magazine.*] —And what have the long years held for you, as they say?

MATEY: Oh—here and New York—business as usual.

NICHOLS: What different lives we've had.

MATEY: Haven't we?

NICHOLS [*Reflectively*]: —And yet at twenty we were much the same. Twenty—the incendiary age, Matey.—I was going to set the world on fire with my novels—your match was a paint brush.

MATEY: And I gave up my painting to marry Nancy Lyon. . . .

NICHOLS: —While I forsook sweet Kitty Nash, to wed with an inkpot! A pair of jilts, we two! Well—what do you think of *your* bargain?

MATEY: I've come out the winner, Geoff.

NICHOLS: And so have I!

MATEY: Impossible!—I've a happy home—sufficient leisure—a regular income—two fine, spoiled children—and a wife that's a simple miracle. Trump them, if you can!

NICHOLS [*Gaily, with the gesture of laying cards on the table, one by one*]: The world's my home—every hour of my time is my own—I'll match my income with yours any day!—And as for your last three items, I say what Bacon said: "A man with wife and children has given hostages to Fortune!"

MATEY: But old lady Fortune has done me rather well.

NICHOLS: Oh—she has her favorite slaves. But freedom's the thing! As Shaw said to me one day last April—dash it—what *was* it he said?—At any rate, it was simply convulsing.

MATEY: But how on earth have you done any work?

NICHOLS: Work? Why, every new experience is material. Wherever I go, my typewriter follows. No worries, no responsibilities—just *life*—the one life I have—spiced and succulent.

MATEY: While I—day after day—"Nine to five—nine to five."

NICHOLS: Those words are the businessman's epitaph.

MATEY [*Determined to be sprightly*]: Oh—one has one's moments. Even a businessman.

[NICHOLS *glances at* MATEY'*s sketch.*]

NICHOLS: But as I remember, you showed amazing promise. I've known artists with wives—with children, even. Why didn't you go on with it?

[MATEY *returns the magazine to the table, and pockets the pencil.*]

MATEY: Well, you see, Nancy and I married ridiculously young—neither of us rich, but both accustomed to a certain standard of living.—A regular income became pretty much of a necessity.

NICHOLS: —And you put it off. Tsch—what a shame—

MATEY [*Reluctantly*]: Perhaps—I don't know. Sometimes—when I think that I haven't yet done the thing I wanted to do—my forty-three years do seem rather futile and misspent. It's been particularly salty today. My boy Roderick, for whom I've expected great things—[*He shifts uneasily in his chair.*] Oh, well—it's the old story over again: Expediency's heel, on the neck of inclination.

NICHOLS: But some phases of your life must be very interesting. Now business is not without its—

MATEY: Geoff, business is a dump for dreams. I believe every fourth man in it has something shut down in him. You can see it in their faces. Some of them wanted to paint, like me—some to write, to sing—to be doctors, lawyers—God bless me, even preachers! But expediency ordered it otherwise. And now most of them will die in the traces, poor devils . . . die of market reports—Babsonitis—hardening of the soul—

NICHOLS: Ah yes—as someone says, "Most men lead lives of quiet desperation."

MATEY [*Softly*]: "Quiet desperation." [*He rises, sharply.*] By God—here's one who's fed up with it! I've a good mind to chuck business *now*—and go to painting!

[NICHOLS *looks somewhat alarmed; this is being taken too literally.*]

NICHOLS: —You're not serious . . . ?

MATEY: So serious, that the turn of a hair would decide it.

NICHOLS [*Rising after a helpless pause*]: You must realize that the—uh —artistic life—has its *dis*advantages, too. One's laurels are so insecure. Popularity is such a fickle thing . . .

MATEY: Who said anything about popularity?

NICHOLS [*Shrugging*]: One might as well live, as not.

MATEY: If you do good work, you make quite enough.

NICHOLS: But my income isn't half what it's reputed to be! And the irregular hours! Lord, Matey—my nerves are chaos.

MATEY: Mine are paralyzed.

NICHOLS: —And look at me!—My age—and still flitting about from pillar to post like a gouty bumblebee . . .

MATEY: In motion, at any rate. I never leave the ground. [NICHOLS, *with a profound sigh, sinks into a comfortable chair.*]

NICHOLS [*The fraud*]: What I wouldn't give for a home like this—and children—and a wife like your Nancy!

MATEY: You have your Art . . .

NICHOLS: She's not so sweet as Kitty Nash!—And if it weren't for her and her importunities, I might have Kitty now—and a home that *is* a home.

MATEY: You've compensations. . . .

NICHOLS: No, Matey. I suppose I should have, if I could honestly feel that art—true art—was the gainer for my sacrifice. But a popular novelist! Oh—don't you suppose *I* know what my stuff is worth? [*He continues with deep feeling.*] I give you my word—there's no such hell on earth as that of the man who knows himself doomed to mediocrity in the work he loves—whatever it may be. You love painting—you think you could paint great pictures.—Well—go on thinking—but don't try it. No! No!—You've done well in business—be wise, and stick to it.

MATEY: I am stuck.

NICHOLS: What are you, anyway?

MATEY: Why—uh—I'm a manufacturer . . .

NICHOLS: What do you make?

MATEY [*This is painful*]: Oh—uh—various things . . .

NICHOLS: But what's the—*pièce de résistance,* so to speak?

MATEY [*Very painful indeed*]: Well—uh—I suppose one would say—uh —*soap*. . . .

NICHOLS: Soap! God!—You can get your *teeth* into soap!

MATEY [*Cynically*]: You can into *ours*. It proclaims itself made of only the purest edible fats.

NICHOLS: Believe me, I envy you—

MATEY: But you've no idea of the—*hunger* I have, to be painting.

NICHOLS: Can't you find time to daub a bit on the side?

MATEY: Business life has no side. It's one dimension. Try it and see. Ah—if only I could get free of it—altogether free of it, for a while. To feel a brush in my hand again—to see a picture grow under my eyes—to create—good God!—something other than a cake of soap.

NICHOLS: By Jove—if it's *good* soap . . .

MATEY [*Interrupting*]: —But this house—and the apartment in town—and the servants—and the children to educate! Of course it's impossible—plainly impossible.

NICHOLS: And lucky for you that it is. Forget it, Matey, forget it—

MATEY: I wish to heaven I could!

[NANCY*'s entrance—a vision in evening dress—brings the men to their feet.*]

NICHOLS: Ah—*vous êtes adorable!*

NANCY: *Mille fois merci, cher Monsieur.*

NICHOLS [*Glancing at his watch*]: I'd no idea it was so late. [*Going to the door, followed by* MATEY] I shall look forward to Monday night. Sherry's at 7:30?

NANCY: Me, and my man Matey; prompt, as always.

NICHOLS [*At door*]: *Dieu soit béni d'avoir conçu une aussi ravissante personne—*

NANCY [*Which serves him right*]: The new slippers of my old grandmother are red. [NICHOLS *laughs, and he and* MATEY *go out.* NANCY *moves toward the desk, humming—and stops halfway with a perplexed frown. Continues to desk, again humming. Seats herself and begins to finish letter.* MATEY *reënters, and, going to the table, stands there with his fingers resting upon it, staring down at the Watteau print, rapt in thought.* NANCY *speaks, without turning.*]—Enjoy your talk?

MATEY [*Absently*]: What—?—Oh—uh—*yes*—very much . . . [*His voice trails off*] . . . very much . . . [*A pause*] What a fascinating time Nichols has had of it!

NANCY [*A few more lines, and Jean's letter will be finished*]: M-m-m—I must read something of his. . . .

MATEY [*Half to himself*]: "Hostages to Fortune." [*A pause; lower*] "Most men lead lives of quiet desperation."

NANCY: What, dear . . . ?

[MATEY *looks a little startled.*]

MATEY: I said, "Most men lead lives of quiet desperation."

[NANCY, *puzzled, glances over her shoulder at him. Turns again, reflectively biting the end of her pen. Then cheerfully continues her writing.*]

NANCY: Well—so long as they're quiet about it—let's—let them go right ahead—shall we . . . ? [MATEY, *deep in thought, does not answer.* NANCY *seals the note, addresses it, stamps it with a bang, and goes to him. She puts her hands upon his shoulders, and faces him about.*] Matey—you sweet old thing—what *is* the matter?

MATEY [*With an attempt at a smile*]: Oh—nothing. . . .

[*He cups her elbows in the palms of his hands for an instant and then leaves her.*]

NANCY [*After a thoughtful pause*]: Dear—it seems to me that you've about everything that a person could desire. We've—most of the good things of life—health—position—enough money—a happy family. [*She hesitates.*]—And we've—each other. Nor is ours the tame, settled love most people have at forty. Some blessed good fortune has kept the keen edge on it. I love my children—but compared to you—oh, Matey! [*A little laugh*] I fancy—there's more woman in me, than mother. . . . [*A pause;* MATEY *says nothing.* NANCY *is chilled.*]—You have been unusually successful in your work. What more could any man ask—than *you have* . . . ?

MATEY [*Impatiently, but with intense suffering*]: Nanny—*Nanny*—what *do you* know about it!

[NANCY *catches her breath sharply, holds it a moment, and then lets it go.*]

NANCY [*Almost in a whisper*]: I suppose—you know—it—just about knocks the heart out of me, to hear you say that. . . . [*She waits for a response. None comes. She clenches her fists, half raises her arms, and throws back her head, in pain.*] Oh—this *can't* be you and I. [*Her arms drop again, lifelessly. A moment's silence. She regains her composure, and going to* MATEY, *speaks to him in a matter-of-fact voice.*] Maitland—as you love me—there's something I want you to do.

MATEY: What is it?

NANCY [*Directly*]: —Leave business for a year. Get leave of absence, if possible. Otherwise, resign. . . .

MATEY [*Affecting to be puzzled*]: But—my dear—*why* . . . ?

NANCY [*With an impatient gesture*]: Oh—*please!* Do you think I've had all these years of you—to be fooled by pretense now? I've known for a *long* time that you weren't happy—and why you weren't. But I've *not* known—quite how much it meant to you. I want you to devote the year to painting.

MATEY [*Indulgently*]: It's a nice idea, Nanny, but—

[*His gesture includes the house, the cars, the servants.*]

NANCY [*Rapidly*]: We'll give up the apartment. We'll stay out here over the winter. One car—and run it ourselves. We'll keep Katie and Etta—and let the others go. I'll do the upstairs myself. Ricky will be in business—no longer an expense. My own income will be enough to dress Jean and pay her school bills.

MATEY: You understand—I've very little outside of my salary?

NANCY: Little—but plenty for us. We'll economize in everything—[*She looks at the three lighted lamps with a smile.*]—We'll—begin with the electric lights. The front attic can be made into a studio. . . .

MATEY: People would think I'd lost my mind.

NANCY [*Scornfully*]: People!

MATEY: I suppose they wouldn't have to know. But G. T.—

NANCY [*Quickly*]: Tell him it's—personal research work.

MATEY: —And if the research finds nothing?

NANCY: Matey—if you don't still think the bird in the bush worth any two in the hand, you might as well die.

MATEY [*Smiling*]: That's very deft, indeed. But I'm *not* going to be bullied into—

NANCY: Nobody's bullying you.

MATEY: Well—we'll think it over. Perhaps—by-and-by . . .

NANCY: We'll do nothing of the sort. You must tell G. T. tonight. How long would it take you to wind up your affairs?

MATEY: Why, I always keep them arranged, so that if anything should happen to me—

NANCY: Splendid! Something *has* happened to you: You've decided to start painting the first of the month.

MATEY [*After a thoughtful pause*]: Nope. It's no use—the whole thing's too absurd.

NANCY: This isn't a whim. If you won't do it for your own happiness, perhaps you will for mine. . . . [MATEY *glances at her quickly.*]

MATEY [*In spite of himself*]: By Gad, Nanny—you *are* a brick!

NANCY [*Enigmatically*]: Maybe I'm not a brick at all. Maybe I'm—just fighting for something I thought I had.

MATEY [*Scoffing*]: *Thought* you had!

NANCY: At any rate, you've got to do it. . . . [*This should settle it.*]

MATEY [*But it doesn't*]: No, Nanny, *no.*—Think of the practical side—the expense.

NANCY: I did. My plans for economy quite astonished me!

MATEY: They might apply out here. Not in town.

NANCY: *Town* . . . ?

MATEY [*Lamely*]: I'd—uh—I'd naturally do portraits, wouldn't I?—And that necessitates models, doesn't it?

NANCY: Well?

MATEY: Well—the countryside's not precisely dotted with them. [NANCY *amusedly shakes her head over him.*]—And that's only one objection.

NANCY: I've seldom heard a lamer one. If I can get servants to come to the country, why can't you get models?

MATEY: You don't realize that—

[NANCY *presses a button in the wall.*]

NANCY: Matey, I realize that the thing of main importance is for you to begin your painting at once.

MATEY: I never saw such a devil for speed.

NANCY: —Give yourself time to think up objections, and you won't start at all. If I can manage with a temporary maid, you can with a temporary model.

MATEY: Some pinched, painted relic, I suppose—

NANCY: Not at all.

[ETTA *enters, the apotheosis of young, fresh beauty.*]

MATEY: It's impossible, Nanny. It's—

ETTA: You rang?

NANCY: Yes.—Etta—I—uh—I presume you never posed as a model?

[ETTA'*s mouth opens in astonishment. She looks from one to the other.*]

ETTA: Why, *Ma'am!* Of *course* I didn't! Who said that I—?

NANCY: There, Etta—no one. I merely—

ETTA [*Is a pretty girl never safe from scandal?*]: Didn't I not bring the best of references? Wasn't I not three years in my last place?—And two in the—a *model!* Why I—

[MATEY *is studying her, crimson lake in his eye.*]

NANCY: You know—a model may be a model, and still be—er—*model. . . .*

ETTA [*Desperately*]: But Mrs. White—really—I tell you that—

NANCY: Yes—I comprehend. You have never been a model—never, in the *slightest* degree. Now, what I am attempting to tell you, is that Mr. White expects to spend the next year painting in the attic . . . [ETTA *regards* MATEY *as if he had gone insane. He is most uncomfortable under her scrutiny*] . . . which will be made over into a studio. [*To* MATEY] Do you think Etta would serve your purpose?

MATEY [*Off his guard*]: Why, you know—it's quite extraordinary—[*Then, with attempted nonchalance*] Oh—I dare say she might do to start with.

NANCY [*To* ETTA]: If you will consent to remain here in the country with us this winter, and pose for a few hours each day—

ETTA [*Gently*]: I am sorry, Ma'am—

NANCY: Just a moment!—I shall increase your wages, and help you with your work.

ETTA [*Firmly*]: No, Ma'am—I could not consider it. Not for all the money in the world.

NANCY [*Frankly puzzled*]: But—I don't understand. Would you mind telling us why? [ETTA *hesitates, peering at* MATEY]—You may be quite frank.

ETTA: Well—I do not like to say nothing, but the man of the house in the third last place I was in, made advances that was—advances that *were*—most unwelcome. You know how careful a girl has got to be—specially when Nature has blessed her with looks like mine. I can usually tell by their eyes— [*She tries to get a look at* MATEY'*s, but the clever man outwits her*.] I am not saying nothing against Mr. White. So far, he has behaved like a real gennulmun. But if I should ferget myself to the extent of—oh, you know what artists are—they, and sailors—

MATEY: I think I can practically assure you that my admirable conduct will continue indefinitely.

ETTA [*Cannily*]: You cannot tell what'll happen, if you take to paintin'. I know all about artists; women to them are as tinders to the flames. . . .

NANCY: There's the Hearst of it, Matey! [*To* ETTA] I shall vouch for Mr. White. He is not at all—combustible. Come now, will you—or will you not?

ETTA: No Ma'am—I cannot do it. I would like to help you, but I simply dassent—do not dare to—do it.

NANCY: Very well. You are an extremely silly girl. That's all—[ETTA *turns to go out*] Oh—by the way—in the morning please pack that old foulard of mine, and the gray crêpe de chine. I wish them sent to the C. O. S.

ETTA [*Heartbroken at having to wear something less becoming next Thursday*]: But—didn't you say—?

NANCY: I was mistaken. I thought you were more obliging.

ETTA: But I *am* obliging—

NANCY: You have given me no indication of it.

[ETTA *looks searchingly at* MATEY. *He shifts uneasily in his chair.*]

ETTA: But Ma'am—I want to *improve* myself. I want to be a lady, Mrs. White. In all my spare time I read books. I study you and your friends, and seek to em-ulate you. . . .

NANCY [*Kindly, after a disconcerted pause*]: Thank you, Etta. But surely every lady should know something about art. Now Mr. White is a very charming, cultivated man—[MATEY *rises abruptly.*]—Your hours with him would be a great opportunity for you.

ETTA [*With difficulty*]: Well—well, there is one thing we would have to have an understanding on: none of his gennulmun friends could come in while I—while I was—was—[*She is unable to go on.*]

NANCY [*Puzzled*]: —While you were—? [*It suddenly dawns upon her, but she controls her mirth.*] But I cannot see your objection. I should think you would look very charming in your—[*To* MATEY] Do you think one of my *dresses* will do—or shall we have one made?

[ETTA *looks first surprised, then considerably relieved as she echoes the wonderful word "dresses."*]

MATEY: Better have it made—[ETTA*'s face lights up.*]

NANCY [*Smiling*]: Well, Etta—?

ETTA [*Beaming*]: Oh, *yes,* Ma'am—I didn't understand. Yes, Ma'am—with pleasure.—And any of his friends that want to look on—

NANCY: Well—that's better.—You may bring the tray in now—five glasses. Mr. White will give you more explicit directions later. [ETTA *fixes* MATEY *with an appraising stare, borne with difficulty by him. She finally goes out.* NANCY *now laughs without constraint.*] Oh—Matey—I couldn't have stood it a minute longer! Virtue in jeopardy! What a brave fight she put up!

MATEY [*Shaking himself*]: Whew!—I feel like the Seven Deadlies! I could do with a cocktail. . . .

NANCY: They're coming.—You know, I don't think she's at all certain about you yet.

MATEY: I hope she understands that I'm going to paint, and not conduct a finishing school. Seriously though, Nanny—we're insane to rush into this thing as if—

NANCY [*Her merriment gone at once*]: *Rush?*—After twenty *years?* My *dear!* [WARREN*'s voice is heard from the hall.*]

WARREN [*Expounding it*]: —So you see, the entire organization is composed of interlocking units—

MATEY [*Opening his hand to release them*]: All right! There they go—the two-in-the-hand! We're off for the bird-in-the-bush! [NANCY *exclaims in joy.*]

RICKY [*Seriously*]: I think that cost-accounting system is a knock-out, Sir. [*He and* WARREN *come in, dressed for dinner.*]

NANCY: Mr. Warren, Maitland has something important to tell you— [ETTA *enters, wth a tray of glasses and a cocktail shaker.*]

WARREN [*To* MATEY]: What about? No business, I hope.

[ETTA *places the tray on the table.* MATEY *begins to shake the shaker.* ETTA *watches him like a hawk. He tries to cover his embarrassment.*]

MATEY [*Giving shaker a final shake*]: I'll tell you later. Prepare for the worst! [*To* ETTA] I'll serve them. . . . [*Still she watches him, transfixed. He loses patience.*] I say *I* will *serve* them!

[ETTA *goes out.* MATEY *fills glasses, and gives one to* NANCY *and one to* WARREN. RONNY *appears in hall. She is in evening dress and leaves her wrap in* ETTA*'s hands as she sails past her.*]

NANCY: We must hurry through these. The birds will be ruined. [*Nobody notices* RONNY.]

RONNY [*In self-defense*]: Good evening, Ronny—[RICKY *rapidly reaches her side.*]

NANCY: My dear—how sweet you look!

RONNY [*Why not be honest?*]: I think I look pretty well, myself. . . .

RICKY: Plain face, but a nifty dresser.

RONNY: Hellow, Handsome—I hardly knew you. Aren't you clean!

RICKY: Dad's in the business.

NANCY: This is our friend Miss Duane, Mr. Warren.

WARREN: Very glad to meet you, Miss Duane.

RONNY [*In her cool manner with strangers*]: How do you do? [RICKY *quickly whispers something to her. She goes to* WARREN, *smiling graciously. Extending a slim hand to him, she speaks as if she had not heard the name.*] Oh—Mr. *Warren!* How delightful! I hear you're to have a new laborer next week. . . .

WARREN: Indeed I am—*Rocky!* [RICKY *scowls at the name.*] He begins in what we call "The Kitchen."

RONNY: How amusing! I should think he'd be simply priceless, mixing cold cream. He's such an oilcan as it is, that—

RICKY: Dad! Give her a cocktail—quick!

[*He takes one from* MATEY *and gives it to her.*]

RONNY [*Accepting it*]: Good dog. . . .

[MATEY *gives* RICKY *another, and takes one for himself.*]

NANCY [*To* WARREN]: Will he need an apron?

WARREN: White overalls!

RONNY [*Slowly sipping her cocktail*]: Little Purity—with a lily in his hair. . . .

RICKY [*Disregarding her and raising his glass*]: Here's to bigger and better soap!

WARREN [*To* RONNY]: Never you mind—Rocky and I—

[RONNY *all but chokes at the repetition of the name.*]

RICKY [*Politely*]: The name is "Ricky," Sir.

WARREN: Ricky and I are going to smile through to success—aren't we, old fellow?

RICKY: Chief—we're going to laugh out loud!

MATEY [*From table*]: Here, G. T.—give me your glass.

[WARREN *shakes his head, and he and* NANCY *place their empty glasses upon the tray.*]

RICKY [*To* RONNY]: —That's Mr. Warren's motto: "Use our Pearly Paste, and Smile with Confidence."

RONNY [*Over her cocktail*]: Gosh, you're coarse. . . .

RICKY [*Aggrieved*]: I *must* say, I fail to see anything coarse about—

NANCY: Never mind, Ricky. [*To* WARREN *and* MATEY] Are we ready . . . ?

[NANCY, WARREN *and* MATEY *go to the door.* RONNY *is finishing her cocktail.*]

RICKY: C'mon, Beau'ful—lap it up!

RONNY [*Putting down her glass*]: M-m-m-m—I shall be charming at dinner.

[MATEY *stands at the door to let them all pass, and turns to follow.* NANCY *reënters hurriedly, and in reply to his questioning glance says, "I'll come in a minute." He goes out and* NANCY *tours the room, turning out the lamps one by one.* RICKY *calls from the dining room*]:

RICKY [*Imperatively*]: Dear-r-r-r-r-est—!

NANCY [*Singing it out, with a falling inflection*]: Com-m-m-m-m-m-ing—!

[*She turns out the last lamp, and is rapidly crossing the darkened room to the lighted hall, as*

THE CURTAIN FALLS.

■ ACT II ■

You may be a little out of breath when you come into MATEY'S *Studio, for it is in the attic, and you must climb a flight of steep steps to get there. The stairway is in a small recess at the back, and we shall see your head first. The small door at the left—as you enter—is the entrance to the playroom.*

The Studio is a spacious, rectangular room with a large dormer window cut in the back wall, and in the right wall two smaller windows through which may be seen the tip of an apple branch, in bloom. The curtains at the windows show NANCY'S *touch—this room has been great fun for her, and she has been very successful in keeping out of it any suggestion of the "arty."*

At one side, there is a long refectory table, covered with a "runner" and bearing two wrought-iron sconces, each containing six white candles. By the large window there are bookshelves and a comfortable sofa. Chairs ad lib.—but space is the thing.

Being essentially a workroom, there is a dais with a throne chair for the model, an easel (turned away from the front), a small worktable with brushes, paints, etc., and a life-sized lay-figure (a great family joke, by the way) which sprawls upon the floor in a thoroughly gauche manner.

With the exception of a bearskin and a small rug, the floor is uncovered. On the walls you will see Hokusai's "Fujiyama" and "The Wave"—and very good prints they are. There are also two mounted heads of wild goats, upon the smaller of which a red Spanish beret is set at a rakish angle.

The fact that the studio was once an attic is still apparent, to the close observer, through the medium of only partially hidden trunks, and a dappled-gray hobbyhorse.

It is late the following May—about four in the afternoon. MATEY, *in a smock, with a small daub of paint on his cheek, is busily painting at his easel.* ETTA *poses in the throne chair. She wears a simple, exquisite afternoon dress, and a small string of pearls at her throat. Her hands rest in her lap. Her hair is dressed most becomingly, and the transformation into a charming lady of unusual grace and beauty is quite complete. For a few moments* MATEY *paints silently. Gradually* ETTA'S *features lose their repose. An expression of acute suffering grows in her eyes. She wrinkles her nose and sets her teeth. Finally:*

ETTA [*At the end of her tether, poor dear*]: Mr. White—I have jest *got* to do it. . . .

MATEY [*Patiently ceasing his work*]: All right, Etta—go ahead—[ETTA, *with a great sigh of relief, vigorously scratches her nose.*] Would you like to rest for a moment?

ETTA: Oh—may I . . . ? [MATEY *gestures acquiescence, lays brushes on worktable, and goes to the open windows, where the bees are humming among the apple blossoms.*] *Sech* a relief! [MATEY *picks a small sprig of blossoms and presents it to her.*]

MATEY: Here—this will refresh you.

[*For his own refreshment, he lights a cigarette.* ETTA *inhales the fragrance of the blossoms and regards the twig lovingly.*]

ETTA: Oh—thank you. M-m-m-m—I jest simply love apple blossoms.

MATEY: You have an unhappy knack of pronouncing "just" and "such" as if they were spelled with "e"s instead of "u"s.

ETTA: "Just"—"Such."

MATEY: That's better. . . .

ETTA [*Diffidently*]: It's nice, being a lady, Mr. White—[*Lest he misunderstand her*]—Of course, I *am* a lady. But—[*Looking down at her dress and fingering her pearls*]—I mean a de luxe one—like those that come to see Mrs. White. How I'd love to be like they are—and talk the way they do!

MATEY [*Absently, as he studies the portrait*]: You should practice—in private.—It's only the mouth that bothers me now.—" 'The Portrait of a Lady,' by an Unknown Artist"—[*Reflectively*] When we've sold it to some great lover of art, *then* perhaps I'll sign it—[*Softly*] *When*—[*He extinguishes his cigarette and picks up his brush and palette.*] Come on—are you ready?

ETTA: Jest—*just* a minute. . . . [*Once more she strikes her pose, and* MATEY *silently continues his painting.*] Is it really almost done?

MATEY [*Engrossed*]: It may be two minutes—it may be two days.

ETTA: I could jest cry, I could—

MATEY: Please don't—I'm no good at marines. [*He paints rapidly for a few moments. Then stands off and regards her quizzically from several positions.*] Softer lines around the mouth—[*Just to make it sure, she grins.*] No! No!—You know better than that! *Soft,* I said. [*He studies her attempt.*] Bring your eyes into it. . . . [*He shakes his head hopelessly, but continues to paint. Suddenly a little laugh escapes her.*] What are you laughing at?

ETTA: It just struck me funny—here you've been trying for months to make that look like me, when with a camera you could get it perfect in a jiffy.

[MATEY *stares at her speechless.*]

MATEY [*Softly*]: Oh my God. . . . [*With increased vehemence*] You sit there prattling of cameras, when you ought to be thanking heaven for the dignity that's done you! Don't you see the chance you've got? Who was Helen of Troy, but a pretty thing with convenient morals? Who was—La Gioconda, but a woman with a smile? If there'd been no Homer to sing of Helen, no Leonardo to fix that smile forever with his brush, they'd both be dead and forgotten as—[*He picks up the twig of apple blossoms*]—as this will be tomorrow! And—[*She is staring at him without a trace of comprehension in her face*]—and you haven't the faintest idea what I'm talking about. [*He throws the twig out of the window, falls into thought for a moment, and then speaks again, with restrained but poignant feeling.*] Is there nothing that will make you understand what this means? [*He indicates the portrait.*] Can't you realize that what is here is more than merely you and my work? That in it, there's a—spirit that can strike life into—[*He holds the prostrate lay-figure up to view*]—a lump of sawdust, like this? You?—Why it can immortalize you! Let me see in your face—joy—wonder—consecration! [*A big order: Etta bites her lip anxiously.*]

ETTA: All at once, or—one at a time?

[MATEY *shakes his head, as if to say "No use," and placing the lay-figure at the foot of the easel, again ponders a means whereby he may instill into his subject's spirit a something that will show in her face. Finally an idea strikes him, and bringing a high stool to a position directly in front of* ETTA, *he sits upon it, and proceeds to draw for her as alluring a verbal picture as he can.*]

MATEY: Now listen! You want to be a lady, don't you?—Well—I'll make you one. Think—up on Fifth Avenue, there's a palatial white edifice. There, in a long, high room lavishly embellished with palms and other potted plants, *you* sit, *you,* Etta—the hostess at a most de luxe reception. The room is filled with fashionable ladies in their jewels and furs and orchids. Their stylish escorts stand about with silk hats in their white-gloved hands. From everywhere, they've come thronging to pay you homage—earls and dukes and duchesses—ambassadors and their wives . . . [*Can it be that he, too, has read "The Earl's Revenge"?*] . . . And for all time, you will live in their memories. In the far capitals of the world exquisite women will sit before their glasses in costly boudoirs, and whisper sadly, "Ah—if I were as lovely as she!" Handsome men, on whose word the fates of empires hang, will pause in the middle of an important stroke of diplomacy, and sigh to themselves, "Ah—what would I not do, for the love of such a lady!" You will be with them at their rich dinners—their gorgeous balls. Books will be written about you, and elegantly bound in leather. And you will hold your queenly sway, not for a season or two, like other fine ladies—but for a hundred years, *two* hundred! You, Etta, *you*—the finest lady of them all! [*His voice sinks*] Can you—see it?—*feel* it—? [*A look of wonderment has grown in her eyes. She sits entranced, her face transfigured with a kind of gracious, queenly joy.* MATEY *draws a deep and grateful breath and rising goes slowly to the easel, with his eyes still upon her, repeating softly:*] The—finest—lady—of—them—all—! [*He paints rapidly, but with infinite care, looking from her to the portrait and back again. A few more strokes—and tossing his brush in the air, he exclaims jubilantly:*] There! By the Lord Harry, we've got it! Etta—you *Love*—we've *got* it! [ETTA *comes out of her trance and starts forward.* MATEY *seizes her hand and drags her to the portrait.*] Look—it's done! [*She gazes at the marvel with widening eyes, while* MATEY *gleefully daubs a sign "Fresh Paint" on a piece of cardboard.*]

ETTA: Oh—if that isn't simply the grandest thing!—And to think that it's me—a lady like that! Oh, *isn't* she lovely! [MATEY *places the sign on the corner of the easel, thereby eliciting a giggle from Etta—not a difficult achievement.*]—Jest as if it was a park bench! Mr. White—you do the *cutest* things. . . . [*In sheer jubilance,* MATEY *takes her hands and dances her around.*]

MATEY [*To the tune of "Round and Round the Mulberry Bush"*]: It's done! It's done! It's done—done—done—so early in the morning!

ETTA [*Breathlessly*]: But it's *afternoon!*

MATEY: —So early in the *morning*—!

[ETTA, *at first a reluctant partner, at length abandons herself to the celebration.*]

MATEY and ETTA [*As they dance around*]: It's done! It's done, done, done—so early in the morning!

[NANCY *enters, attired—heaven save us!—in a short black housedress, and a white apron.*]

NANCY: The ceilings may hold out downstairs. But the odds are against it. What is it all about?

MATEY [*Ten years off his age*]:—History, my dear!—I've finished the portrait! We were celebrating the dawn of a new epoch in American Art—[*He performs a pirouette.*]—So early in the morning!

NANCY: Finished . . . ? Oh—wonderful—! [*She goes swiftly to the *portrait and regards it with shining eyes.*] Matey—I could go on my knees to it. . . .

MATEY [*Huskily*]: I'm—glad it pleases you, dear—

NANCY: *Pleases* me!—Can't you see what's in my silly eyes? [*She blinks back the tears, and laughs joyfully.*] There—I'm a fool. Oh!—Those pearls might be alive! You know, one feels awfully cocky, with a husband who can—[*She sees* ETTA *staring at her and trying to control her laughter.*]—What is it you find so diverting?

ETTA [*With the air of the lady* MATEY *has painted*]: Your appearance. It amuses one.—Chawming, though—really *quate* chawming. . . .

NANCY: You'd better go finish cleaning the silver. [ETTA, *somewhat diminished, goes out.*] Matey—you've simply ruined her. She'll serve the children's dinner guests tonight like a queen throwing pence to the poor.

MATEY [*Amused*]: Why not have a buffet supper up here, instead? [NANCY *is struck by the idea.*]

NANCY: May we?—Splendid! They'd love it.—And incidentally, with all this—atmosphere, we can figure on less food.

MATEY: —How many are they?

NANCY: Sixteen, counting you and me—the prospective ushers and bridesmaids, you know. They've hit on rather a sweet way of announcing it at Ronny's dance. Ricky's to be a troubadour, and Ronny a seventeenth-century lady. I've a costume for you. . . .

MATEY [*As he scrapes paint from the palette*]: Good.—How *are* the funds, dear?

NANCY: They haven't been lower since the day after our wedding trip.

MATEY: Thank God there's a picture for sale—and a dividend due.

NANCY [*Regarding the pile of mail on the table*]: You haven't touched your mail since Tuesday!

MATEY: Me and the Goddess has been talkin' confidential.

NANCY [*Looking over the mail*]: Perhaps it's in this lot—no. . . .

MATEY: It'll come Monday.

NANCY: Here's one from your broker, dated May 24th. . . .

MATEY: A circular, probably. [*He takes the mail from* NANCY, *slitting the envelopes with his scalpel.*]

NANCY: Oh, I meant to ask you—are these of any use? [*She takes two square slips of paper from the pocket of her apron.*] They were in the pocket of that smock you wanted washed. [*Giving him one of them, she studies the other.*] They're not sketches, are they?—I had one fearful moment when I thought you'd gone in for cubism.

MATEY: Not I!—This is merely a demonstration proving that if a National Advertising Campaign increased our sales—I mean Warren's sales—only four per cent, it would more than pay for itself.

NANCY [*Dryly*]: What could be fairer than that? [*Proffering the second bit of paper*] And this—?

MATEY [*More reluctantly*]: —It's a diagram showing that by running the raw mix from the vats direct to the ripeners by pipe, we'd save at least two and one-half per cent on our production costs. . . .

NANCY: Most ingenious of you. I suppose I'd best reserve a *separate* drawer for these.

[*She holds out her hand for them.* MATEY *stares at them dumbly for a moment, then tears them up and jams the pieces into his pocket.*]

MATEY: Habit again!—Must I ride two horses my whole life long?

NANCY [*Calmly*]: That, I presume, is the question.

[MATEY *begins to read his mail.*]

MATEY: Remind me to pay my insurance policy Tuesday, will you? Here's another notice from them. And the infernal income tax on the fifteenth. Otherwise, they'll double it. Hope the dividend's not late. . . .

[NANCY *takes a bill from his hands.*]

NANCY: Here—I'll take that. It's a bill for Jean's mumps.—Whew! They've gone up—fifty dollars a mump!

MATEY [*Giving her another*]: What do you want done about this?

NANCY [*Which she returns promptly*]: Nothing. By now those Armenians must be living on caviar.

MATEY [*Reading a letter*]: Good Lord!

NANCY: What's the matter?

MATEY [*As he goes to the sofa*]: Is this a morning paper?

NANCY: —"The Times." Dear—what *is* it? [*She reads the letter which* MATEY *extends to her.*] Oh—how awful. . . . [MATEY *opens the newspaper to the financial page.*]

MATEY: It may have been a false alarm. I don't see anything. Yes—here it is—. Here it is, all right—and worse than they prophesied, too.

NANCY [*In spite of herself*]: If you'd only got this letter in time!

MATEY [*Ironically*]: Ah, no!—I was too busy with my brushes to watch the market, and read my mail. [*He scans the letter again.*] Well—I've got to have cash by Tuesday, loss or no loss. You'd better take Hubbard's advice, and hold on to your stock. I'll go to town and see him right away. A fine mess I've got us into!—Matey and his money—they were soon parted, weren't they?

NANCY [*Her comforting arms about him*]: Dear—*don't* say things bitterly, like that. We didn't expect this to be a bed of roses. . . .

[*Up from the stairs comes* RICKY, *golf trousers—linen; coat—homespun, and over one ear a troubadour cap, with flowing feather. He has a guitar tied around his neck by two long silk stockings, and thrums a chord as he enters.*]

RICKY: Say, Nanny—where's the rest of my costu—[*He discovers his parents once more unmindful of their dignity.*] Will you two *never* grow up? [NANCY *and* MATEY *part, looking a little sheepish, and* MATEY *goes to a chair at the window—reading the paper.*] I feel more like Chanticleer than a troubadour. Don't mind my freezing on to a pair of your stockings, do you? Lord! You must have long legs!

NANCY [*Primly*]: I mind very much. There's a ribbon with the rest of it downstairs.

RICKY: I cannot relinquish the socks. [*He crosses to* MATEY, *thrumming and singing.*] "List to me, Lady Love, heark to my plea—" [*But stops suddenly at the sight of* MATEY'*s face*] What's the matter, old Lad?—You look as though a mule had kicked you.

MATEY: *Two* mules, Rick—

NANCY: Your father has had bad news from his broker.

RICKY [*All bantering aside*]: Gosh, Dad—that's a rotten shame. I've got four hundred and sixty saved up, if that'll help any—

MATEY: The money for your wedding trip?

RICKY [*Chamber of Commerce, please note*]: What's Bermuda—compared to our own Niagara Falls?

MATEY: Thanks, Son—but I don't think I'll need it. [*With an attempt at jocosity*] I may sell my picture over the weekend.

NANCY: It's finished. You haven't seen it yet. . . . [*Ricky examines the portrait admiringly.*]

RICKY: I call this painting! Say, how about my buying it?

MATEY: You haven't enough.

RICKY: I'll take it on installments. Listen, lady—[*He prepares to sing to the picture.*] "List to me, Lady Love—" [*But* MATEY *brings the serenade to a deservedly abrupt conclusion.*]

NANCY: What have you children been doing?

[RICKY *finds a comfortable place on the window seat.*]

RICKY: Ronny's had the nag out—went home to change— coming right over. I've been shooting clay pigeons— only got twelve out of twenty-five—but I gave the others a nasty scare. [NANCY *laughs.*] Say, Dad, G. T.'s up here with the Thompsons over Sunday. Said he might drop in to see you.

MATEY: I hope he does. Is he still handling most of my work?

RICKY: No—didn't I tell you?—new man came in three weeks ago. Name's Chadwick—

MATEY [*Sharply*]: T. L. Chadwick—?

RICKY: Think so. He's famous as the Battle of the Marne—and acts it. They say he's dragging down forty-five thousand a year. He's taken over your job—*I* thought G. T.'d keep it open for a year, anyway.

[*This has all been a considerable shock for* MATEY. *For a moment he stares speechlessly at* RICKY, *then turns to* NANCY, *speaking in a changed voice.*]

MATEY: What time do you expect Geoff?

NANCY: About four-thirty.

MATEY: Good—I'll have time to see him before I leave.

[*He goes out by stairs.* RICKY *rises, and with a gesture of disgust with himself, goes to a chair near* NANCY.]

NANCY: Rick—you must learn tact. You couldn't have chosen a worse moment to speak of that new man at Warren's.

RICKY [*Shamefacedly*]: I knew it as soon as I opened my face. I ought to be shot. But after all, Nancy, I can't say that I blame G. T. . . .

NANCY [*Suddenly*]: Are you really happy there?

RICKY [*Offhand*]: Sure. Why not?

NANCY: Tell me honestly!

RICKY [*Confidentially*]: Well—you see it's this way: When I look at the men higher up in the office—men of about forty or so—and realize that if I barge through in really noble style that that's where *I'll* land at forty—I don't exactly jump up and down and clap my hands at the prospect. But after all—that's life, isn't it, darling?—You get some things, and some things you don't. And I've packed a *couple* of hearts full in Ronny and you—[*To prove it, he kisses her cheek*] You're a wench after my own heart.

NANCY [*Persisting*]: But *don't* you miss your architecture?

RICKY [*Strumming*]: Rarely think of it.

[RONNY *comes in, very fresh and sprightly, as the result of a ride, a tub and a pretty new dress.*]

RONNY [*However*]: I don't expect to sit down for several centuries.

RICKY: Serves you right for jumping that green mare. If I were her—

NANCY: "—if I were *she*."

RICKY [*A proper rebuke to the purist*]: . . . If I were her—I'd have bounced you off on your nose.

RONNY [*So sweetly*]: No, precious one—if you'd been the mare, I'd have taken you over the roof. [*She sees the portrait, which occasions a deep breath of admiration.*] Oh, this is too beautiful.

NANCY [*Who is putting* MATEY'*s paint table in order*]: I'm inclined to agree with you, Ronny.

[*But there is a sudden new interest, for* RONNY *sees the mannikin. She picks it up and hugs it passionately.*]

RONNY: Oh—I want her! I want her!

RICKY: —Name's "Genevieve." She's Dad's mistress.

NANCY: Ricky!

RICKY [*With a gesture*]: Art's his mistress. Genevieve is Art.

[RONNY *takes from a chair a piece of the same stuff as* ETTA'*s dress, and wraps it about the figure's shoulders. Henceforward, "Genevieve" remains gratefully near her.*]

NANCY [*As she moves toward the stairs*]: I'll be back in a few minutes. If Mr. Nichols comes, you entertain him, will you?

RICKY: Certainly shall! [NANCY *goes out, and* RICKY *turns to his* RONNY.] As studios go—not so nasty—wot? [*He lights a cigarette for her and one for himself.*]

RONNY: I love it.

RICKY: Nanny calls it the Zoo. [*He takes her hand and conducts her across the room.*] Here you see a mountain goat, at the age of seven months. And here—[*Indicating another specimen on the opposite wall*]—the same goat, several years later.

[RONNY *nods gravely.* RICKY, *before letting her hand go, raises it to his lips and kisses it. For a silent moment life's infinite fulfillment looks out to each, from the other's eyes.* RONNY *speaks softly.*]

RONNY: You dear—[*But, after all, one must be practical*] Not *very* stiff! —Chuck us a cushion, will you, Dreadful?

[RICKY *procures a cushion from the window seat and another from the sofa.*]

RICKY [*Preparing a place for them on the floor*]: Lord—three sets of tennis—and I'm fit for the ash can! This working indoors all week takes it out of you, do you know it?

[*They seat themselves, back to back on the cushions.*]

RONNY [*Sleepily*]: Um—. Now do you *really* like it there, Stupe?

RICKY: Child, I'm engrossed!

RONNY: Sure?

RICKY: Absolutely! I'd no idea soap and toothpaste could hand me such a thrill. Had a talk with G. T. this morning. Told me I'd rate three thousand as soon's I marched back down the aisle.

RONNY: He's a sweet old thing. We'll be filthy rich. [*Yawns*] Umph!

RICKY: I regard that as a deliberately unfriendly act.

RONNY: I'm a dead bunny.

RICKY: Not too sprightly myself. Let's play shut-eye for a while.

RONNY [*Closing her eyes*]: You're on. Night-O. . . .

RICKY [*Hunching his shoulders*]: Move over. . . .

RONNY: Great Oaf!

[*They close their eyes, and there is a short pause.*]

RICKY: ". . . and God bless everybody in this house." [*Another short pause*]

RONNY: —Two minds without a single thought. . . . [—*And still another. Then* RONNY *begins to wriggle.*] Hell's bells—I'm being prodded in the spine. What is it?—something in your pocket, or just—anatomy . . . ? [RICKY *is wide-awake in a moment.*]

RICKY [*Eagerly*]: Oh—I forgot. [*Rising, he puts out his cigarette, and extracting an old book from his pocket, again seats himself.*] Look here, Beau'ful—I picked this up in a bookstore this noon. Sixteen dollars. It's a first edition of Mossgrave's "Architecture, and ye Associated Artes"—published in 1611—illustrated with woodcuts—rare as hell.

RONNY [*Regarding it sleepily*]: Priceless!

RICKY: You said it. And look—[*He opens the book to the flyleaf and proudly points to the signature thereon.*]

RONNY: "I. Jones—His Book."—Should I be impressed?

RICKY [*Ironically*]: A little. Do you know who it is?

RONNY: I bite: Who?

RICKY [*Impressively*]: This book belonged to—Inigo Jones!

RONNY: What a screaming name. [*To "Genevieve"*] Did you hear that, Genevieve?—"In-again Jones" [*To* RICKY] She wants to know who he was?

RICKY [*Witheringly*]: —Just one of the greatest architects that ever lived, that's all. Designed Whitehall, and Queen's House, and a few miserable little things like that. Not *very* famous.

RONNY [*Somewhat abashed*]: I am the Indian Club among Dumbells.

RICKY [*Studying the pages*]: —And look at this—isn't it great? [*He becomes engrossed in the book.* RONNY *watches him closely.*] Honestly if I could design a façade like that, I'd die happy.—And this gargoyle—you see the vine motif has been carried—

RONNY [*Quietly*]: Put your arm around me, Ricky. [*Absently he does so.*]

RICKY [*Going right on*]: —The vine motif has been carried out even here.

And I'll be blowed—this must be one of the very earliest developments of the rose window—

RONNY [*Experimentally*]: Rick—I want to be kissed—[RICKY *kisses her. A piece of paper falls from the book to the floor.* RONNY *sighs.*] Oh—that's rather delightful. . . .

RICKY [*For the moment, genuinely moved*]: Damn right! [*But only for the moment, for he turns back to the book, almost immediately*]—The facing shows that it's at a very primitive stage—

RONNY [*A certain heartbreaking realization is slowly tightening about her*]: Does it . . . ?

RICKY: Um. . . . [*He sees that she has picked up the piece of paper, and is studying it listlessly.*] Here—lay off!—That's not finished yet!

RONNY: What is it?

RICKY: It's a plan I was making for our new diggings. Now you know what made me late for your dinner last night. [RONNY'*s face lights up; here is hope.*]

RONNY [*Eagerly—handing it to him*]: Tell me about it!

RICKY [*Explaining*]: You see—I wanted something we could add on to—the way Dad and Nancy did to this. First comes the cellar—for the furnace and things. Downstairs: hall, living room, dining room—that little hole in the library, kitchen—out back, servants' quarters above it. Upstairs: four bedrooms—yours and mine, and two guests' rooms. Three baths. Top floor: small storeroom and playroom. . . .

RONNY: . . . For us . . . ?

RICKY [*Solemnly*]: For our progeny.

RONNY: Isn't it big! How many do you think there ought to be?

RICKY: Oh—conservatively—three or four. . . .

RONNY [*Thoughtfully*]: Well—I'll see what I can do. . . . [*She leans over to examine the plans more closely.*] What are these?

RICKY [*With additional enthusiasm*]: Ah—here's the real work! Look, Beau'ful—the stables—miniature reproduction of Charles the Second's at Windsor. And this is the kennels—just like some I once saw for St. Bernards at a monastery near St. Moritz.

RONNY [*Regarding him oddly*]: They're more interesting than the house, aren't they?

RICKY: Ever so much!—You see it's one of my pet convictions that you can make any building beautiful—even a cowshed—without in the least contradicting its original charac—[*He regards her in surprise.*] Dearest!—What is the matter with you?—You look like the very devil—

RONNY [*Confused*]: I—? Why—I—Don't be a fool, Rick—[*Her hand brushes across her eyes. She sighs, shakes her head, and laughs shortly.*] I'm—just simply in a fog over tonight. . . .

[RICKY *regards her dubiously, then becomes matter-of-fact once more.*]

RICKY: Oh say—I don't want to muff that troubadour stunt. Slip me the dope again, will you . . . ?

RONNY [*Lifelessly*]: It's—not my idea, you know. It's Mother's: We're to have supper on the south terrace at twelve. When they're all seated, you amble up below the second story window, and begin—

[RICKY *begins thrumming and singing gaily. As he does so,* RONNY *frowns over the revelatory little slip of paper.*]

RICKY [*Singing and strumming*]:

"List to me, Lady Love, heark to my plea:
Love holdeth no bounty so precious as thee,
Flown my heart's gayety, lovelorn my life,
Sad and desolate I, save I have thee to wife."

—and then you press a red, red rose to your lips, and toss it lightly to me, and I catch it in my teeth, or something, and *voilà*—[*He strikes a chord.*] The kitty is out of the bag!

RONNY [*Slowly*]: And—suppose—instead—I just—turned away—and shut the window—*would* you be sad and desolate—?

RICKY: On the contrary I should execute a few choice clog steps and sing:

"Be she fairer than the day
Or the flow'ry meads in May—
What care I how fair she be
If she be not so to me?"

[*During the song* RONNY *has rolled the plans together into a small roll.*]

RONNY [*Rising*]: Is that the way you'd really feel—do you think?

RICKY [*Gaily*]: Sure!

RONNY [*Quietly*]: I'm glad.—Because I—don't—

RICKY: Don't what . . . ?

[*His soft strumming continues, an ominous accompaniment to the words that follow.*]

RONNY: . . . Don't love you, Rick.

[*The mannikin is permitted to topple to the floor.* RICKY *looks at* RONNY, *appalled—and then laughs.*]

RICKY [*Scoffing*]: No—that's why you're marrying me!

RONNY: It's—why I'm *not*. . . .

RICKY [*Not to be taken in*]: Too late now.

RONNY: It's—just this side of—too late. . . . [*Pause,* RICKY *is trying bravely to smile.*] I—*mean* it, you know.

RICKY [*With difficulty; his smile comes and goes. He stands the guitar against a chair and goes to her*]: Ronny—please find some other way to—ride me. I'm—you're—I—you see, I'm such a fool about you, that I can't—play up to this.

RONNY [*Speaking in a small voice*]: It—breaks me into little pieces—but I mean it.

[*He takes her hand.*]

RICKY [*Dazed and incredulous*]: Ronny—you—you simply *can't.* . . .

[RONNY *withdraws her hand.*]

RONNY: Do—you remember that day last autumn—what I told you about Father and Mother—? [RICKY *tries to speak, but nods, instead.*] —How I said I was going to marry the next nice person I was—fond of?—You were the nice person, Ricky—[*Shakes her head, sorrowfully*] Oh—the nicest one!—And I thought surely I'd love you. But—I don't. And I can't—just *can't* go through with it, without—

RICKY [*With effort*]: I—don't know what to do. I don't know what's expected of me. I—don't quite understand it. Nearly—but not quite. I can't believe that you—you've simply got to tell me some more about it. . . . [*There is a sound at the stairs.* RICKY *glances over his shoulder. His voice lowers.*] Hell—Nichols, I suppose. . . . The playroom—quick!

[*He holds the playroom door open and follows her through, closing it after them.* ETTA *comes up the stairs, dressed as a lady still, but carrying a sobering dustcloth. She places the guitar upon a trunk and begins aimlessly to dust. Goes to the portrait, looks at it adoringly, turns about, as though posing before a mirror, the better to see her profile, then suddenly pirouettes to her first position. She picks up "Genevieve," and looking about to see that she is alone, places her upon a chair facing the dais. Then, draping herself in the throne chair, she touches her hair lightly with the arched tips of her fingers, assumes a rather weary expression, and begins to talk to her inanimate companion:*]

ETTA [*Affectedly*]: Yes—*such* weather! Just *too* dreadful! I've had no gulf for weeks. . . . [*Lowly, to herself*] Gulf—golf—galf—gowf—guff—[*This satisfies her. Aloud*]—I have had no guff for weeks. [*A pause. Then she smiles, and extends a properly limp hand to the air*] Oh—ah—how-do-you-do?—So good of you to come. [*She waits for the inaudible answer.*] *No!* What a piddy! [*Lowly, to herself*] Piddy—pity—pitt-ty—[*This is quite satisfactory, so she tries it aloud:*] *What* a pitt-ty! [*Pause. To "Genevieve"*] But my deah—my bridge is *simply* deplorable! [*Pause. This has been a good one, and she is well pleased with herself. There is more than one person at this most de luxe of receptions, so she greets another:*] Oh—ah—how-do-you-do? [*The response is audible this time, for* GEOFFREY NICHOLS *has quietly mounted the stairs to the studio.*]

NICHOLS: How do you do?

[ETTA *has one very bad moment, but fortunately regains composure in time.*]

ETTA [*What's good for one, is good for another*]: So—good of you to come—

NICHOLS [*A little surprised*]: Thanks. Permit me to present myself: I am Geoffrey Nichols.

ETTA [*This, with effort*]: How do you do? I am—Miss—Henrietta Hone—[*With a gracious gesture*] Won't you sit down?

NICHOLS: Thanks—[*He finds "Genevieve," however, the occupant of the logical chair. Tenderly, he places her upon the floor, and takes her place, facing* ETTA.] An extraordinary person at the door told me that Mrs. White would be up here—

ETTA: Oh, yes—that was Katie. What a piddy—[*Oh! She has muffed it!*]

NICHOLS: Not at all! I consider myself very fortunate. Are you staying with the Whites?

ETTA: Yes.

NICHOLS: Charming, aren't they?

ETTA [*A little less securely*]: Yes. [*Pause.* NICHOLS *is rather taken aback by her apparent aloofness.*]

NICHOLS [*At a loss*]: Er—

[ETTA *turns quickly.*]

ETTA: My deah—my bridge is *simply* deplorable.

NICHOLS [*Sympathetically*]: I'm *so* sorry. Mine is, too. Will they expect us to play? [ETTA *looks away, not answering.*] I hope not. I've just gone two rounds of goff, and—

ETTA: Of *what* . . . ?

NICHOLS: —Of goff—and lost six balls, and most of my mind. [ETTA, *unnoticed by him, forms the word "goff" several times with her lips.*] I've been chanting the "Götterdämmerung," with variations, most of the afternoon—

[*It is not a distaste for Wagner that causes* ETTA *to flinch.*]

ETTA: Mr. Nichols—I do not consider such language at all refined.

[*For one appalled moment,* NICHOLS *stares at her. Then he realizes that she is, of course, purposely burlesquing. This guest of the*

Whites' has, indeed, both originality and charm! He laughs delightedly.]

NICHOLS: Delicious! [*He settles himself more comfortably, and speaks with amused gravity:*] Of course, I ain't exactly what you'd call a *gent* —but I gotta hearta gold. . . . [ETTA *never changes expression.*] How long have you been here with the Whites?

ETTA: Oh—quite a while—

NICHOLS: I must take Nancy to task for this. I'm a native now, you know. I've taken the Burton place for the summer. I can't think why I haven't see you. . . .

ETTA: Do you attend the dances at the Odd Fellows Hall?

NICHOLS [*Not to be outdone*]: No—I'm of the Loyal Order of Moose. But I hear they're real tasty affairs.

ETTA [*Soulfully*]: They are grand.

NICHOLS [*We are getting on*]: What a delightful person you are! Won't you lunch with me tomorrow?

ETTA [*Slowly*]: Why—I *can't*—

NICHOLS: Then when *may* I see you?

ETTA [*Hesitatingly*]: Uh—uh—Thursday afternoon?

NICHOLS: Splendid! We'll motor out to Waukubuc.

ETTA: That would be elegant.

NICHOLS [*Mockingly*]: "Excuse our dust!" [*A silence; he finds nothing to top that mental image of a red and white pennant on the back of his car.*] Do you suppose Nancy knows I'm here?

[ETTA, *who has had enough practice for the present, rises and goes quickly to the stairs.*]

ETTA: I'll go tell her. . . .

NICHOLS [*Protesting*]: Oh, please—I didn't mean—I'm enjoying myself so much, really. . . .

[ETTA *continues straight on, regardless. At the top of the stairs, she meets, coming up,* NANCY, *who has changed to an afternoon dress.*]

NANCY [*Hastily to* ETTA]: The flowers for tonight have come. Bring them up here now. And you must change—*at once!* [ETTA *goes out.*] Geoffrey—do forgive me. I simply had to scrub up. Did you just arrive? [*She moves toward portrait.*] Look! The *chef d'œuvre* is finished! Now please tell me honestly what you think of it. Isn't it enchanting? Would you believe my Matey could do it?

[NICHOLS *is more than a little puzzled. He glances toward the stairs and proceeds to play safe.*]

NICHOLS [*Enthusiastically*]: Such grace of line! What a flair for color! The flesh tints are exquisite. It's simply incredible!

NANCY: Yes. . . . There—we've done our duty! Now tell me what you *really* think.

[NICHOLS *permits himself the steadying influence of a cigarette.*]

NICHOLS: Well—upon my word, I don't know. It's such an extraordinary fine likeness, I suspect it's not great work. He may be merely—clever with a brush—as I'm clever with a typewriter.

NANCY [*Feelingly*]: Oh—I *hope* it's not that! [*Realizes what she has said, and laughs.*] Geoffrey—you know what I mean—

NICHOLS: No—I am completely mashed.

[*They seat themselves upon the sofa.*]

NANCY [*In a businesslike manner*]: Our really pressing problem now is how to sell it.

NICHOLS [*Reflectively*]: If I only had a stationary home—

NANCY: That's very kind. But he wouldn't hear of it, anyway. How *does* one market pictures—do you know?

NICHOLS: Why—I suppose you get them exhibited. . . .

NANCY: You've a nice broad back. Will you walk up and down Fifth Avenue?

NICHOLS: That *was* helpful, wasn't it?

NANCY: If only someone would want it at once.

NICHOLS: Has he done anything else?

NANCY: Just a few sketches. It was difficult, getting under way.

NICHOLS: Such a different life—quite natural. Last autumn, I did my best to dissuade him. Frankly—how do you think he likes it?

NANCY: Oh, underneath, I think he's been very—I think he's been *happier*—

NICHOLS: Good! You know, apart from my personal interest—to me Matey is Everyman.

NANCY: How do you mean, precisely?

NICHOLS: My gardener kept me occupied for twenty minutes this morning telling me what a splendid carpenter he would have made—and means to make still. [*He laughs shortly.*] He's sixty-three.

NANCY [*Thoughtfully*]: I see. But is it the same?

NICHOLS: Maybe not.—How have you weathered the change?

NANCY: I've tried—Oh, I've tried so hard! [*With a little shudder*] It's shameful, the way prosperity softens one.

NICHOLS [*Incredulously*]: You—?

NANCY [*Nodding*]: It's a little pathetic, you know, to find you're the sort of person whose conception of a real sacrifice consists in managing with two servants, instead of five.

NICHOLS [*Nothing truer, you know*]: Nonsense! Sacrifice is relative. You suffer as much from lack of luxuries as another woman from lack of meat.

NANCY: Maybe—but it's rather disconcerting, to reach down into your—depths, and touch bottom so quickly.

NICHOLS: Matey's not faltering, is he?

NANCY [*Rising*]: No—only a trifle worried. The family budget does it—it's not precisely bulging. And today—poor dear—he's had such upsetting news—[*with a wry smile*]—Someone at a directors' table said, "Please pass the dividends."

NICHOLS: What a bore. [*Thoughtfully*] I wonder if I couldn't—

NANCY [*With a grateful smile*]: No—he wouldn't let you. When it comes to taking help, he's the rankest of egotists!

NICHOLS: But—[*A thoughtful pause. He rises and looks at the portrait. His face lights up*] Nancy—I've an idea! This portrait—it's really charming. Now Mrs. Carhart is having her usual drove of twenty or so up for the weekend. There are certain to be a few wealthy patrons of art among them, and—

NANCY [*Excitedly*]: Geoffrey!

NICHOLS: —I'm sure that if I asked her, she'd hang it in her drawing room. One of them might want to buy it. At any rate, they'd talk—and it would be a fair test of its worth. The only difficulty is, that if they damned it, Matey would be so cast down that—

NANCY: You darling! Listen: he won't have to know anything about it! He's going into town on the 4:51—coming out again later in the evening. . . .

NICHOLS: Yes?

NANCY: Yes.—Can't we take it over right after he goes—and have it back before 9:30? They'd have plenty of time to see it. . . .

NICHOLS: I don't know why not. But—if it wasn't a go, some one of them might speak about it afterwards. . . .

NANCY: But they won't know who did it! You see—it isn't signed! Say it's the work of an unknown painter—a protégé of Matey's—just in case—[*Turns to portrait*] Oh, it isn't dry yet. Suppose we had an accident with it?

NICHOLS: That's not likely—wrap it carefully. I'll drive over now and see her—come back for you about 5:30. Then we'll—

[*There is a sound on the stairs.* NANCY *murmurs "Sh-h-h!" and nods an excited assent.* MATEY *enters.*]

MATEY: What's to happen at 5:30? I shan't be here.

NICHOLS: That's just the point. Nancy and I are going to run away together.

MATEY: Good! She needs a change. [*He indicates the portrait.*] Have you seen the—uh—"White" . . . ?

NICHOLS: Rather!—I'm delighted with it.

MATEY: Isn't he nice, Nanny?

NANCY: No one has ever so endeared himself to me.

MATEY: I'm going to let the Metropolitan and the Luxembourg fight it out. Look here, Balzac—what do you think of this left arm?

NICHOLS: But my good Gainsborough—I find it a bit muscular!

MATEY: That, my dear Hawthorne, is light—not muscle.

NICHOLS: But I tell you, Sargent, that I know a muscle when I see one!

MATEY: The thing I want really to know, Chambers, is just how well *do* you see?

NICHOLS: Quite well enough, Mr. Christy, to know a tendon from a sunbeam.

MATEY: Harold Bell, I find you a very stuffy person. . . .

NICHOLS: Oh, Briggs!—Think what you'll suffer when the critics start to bark! [MATEY *throws up his hands in surrender.* NICHOLS *becomes serious*] By the way, Matey—I've five or ten thousand that's simply mouldering away. Do you know of any trustworthy individual who'd be willing to take it on for a year or so at, say, six per cent . . . ?

MATEY: Why—[*He looks suspiciously to* NANCY, *who brazens it out.*] —There must be any number of them, old son. But I can't think of one just at the moment.

NICHOLS: If you hear of one, let me know. I'd consider it a favor.

MATEY [*Slowly*]: Yes—I'll let you know. . . .

NICHOLS: Well—I must be rolling along. The Duanes' dance ahead of me—and I haven't done a line all day.

MATEY [*Amiably*]: We artists must think of posterity, mustn't we?—See you later, anyway!

NICHOLS: Right-O. . . .

NANCY: I'll go down with you. . . .

[NICHOLS *stands aside to let her pass, and is about to follow when* MATEY *stops him.*]

MATEY: Oh—Geoff—

NICHOLS: Yes?

MATEY: Thanks very much—but I really think I can manage without it. . . .

NICHOLS: Without what?

MATEY [*Smiling*]: The five or ten thousand at six per cent.

NICHOLS [*Impatiently*]: *Damn* the interest, Matey.

MATEY: It's bully of you—but I don't think I'll need it.

NICHOLS: Well—in case you do—

[*He turns to go.* MATEY *goes to the far window and stands there, looking out. Just as* NICHOLS *reaches the stairs,* ETTA *comes in. She is in her simple gray working dress once more, and carries a box of flowers and a water-filled vase.* NICHOLS *stares at her—his incredible suspicion confirmed.*]

ETTA: Good-bye, Mr. Nichols—

NICHOLS [*Genially*]: *Good*-bye! [*He glances at* MATEY, *who is apparently oblivious, and continues lowly:*] Oh—uh—in case I can't come myself on Thursday, I'll send my chauffeur. He's a delightful chap—Odd Fellow, I believe—

[*With a gracious bow, he goes out.* ETTA *begins to arrange the flowers in the vases.* MATEY *comes over to the portrait.*]

MATEY [*Absently*]: What did Mr. Nichols say?

ETTA: I'm going riding in his auto Thursday afternoon. It'll be wonderful practice. He's the funniest man!—I had a perfectly *lovely* talk with him before Mrs. White came in. [MATEY *looks at her in frank amazement. Then his brow puckers reminiscently, and he suddenly sees the joke on* NICHOLS. *He laughs silently to himself, but* ETTA *is aware of nothing amiss.*] I can't imagine how anyone *could* be much pleasanter'n Mr. Nichols.

MATEY [*Genuinely*]: Nor I! Friends are very nice things—and sons—and wives.—And money's a nice thing, too—you know that, when you haven't any. . . . [RICKY *enters from the playroom, looking very white and sick. He carries the roll of white paper—his "plans"—upon which he nervously twirls the engagement ring. At first* MATEY *does not see him.*] Job gone—income gone—Art's a hard mistress, Etta—she picks your bones dry—

ETTA [*The Champion*]: Oh, *no,* Mr. White! Art is lovely—jest lovely.

MATEY [*Seeing* RICKY]: Hello, Rick!—Where did *you* blow from?

RICKY: Playroom. . . . [*There is a short pause.*] Father—you might as well know—it's all off between Ronny and me.

MATEY [*Astounded*]: What's this?

RICKY [*With an attempt at a smile*]: Over—done—*fini*—. We aren't going to be married.

MATEY: But I don't understand. . . .

RICKY: It took *me* a long while too. It was all—bogus. She wants to see you—don't know why. Please don't cross-examine her—I think I've asked about all the questions there are—

MATEY [*Impotently*]: But—tonight—?

RICKY [*Turns to him*]: Too late to call off the dance, of course. We're going right ahead with it—just as if it were an—ordinary party. [*He laughs ironically.*] Not *very* different! [*He sees* ETTA, *who, you may be sure, is not missing a word.*] C'mon, Etta—finish those later. [ETTA *goes out and* RICKY *turns again to* MATEY.] Be decent to her, won't you?—She's feeling pretty sunk.

[*He picks up the guitar, but as he does so, a string twangs. With a scarcely perceptible shudder, he carefully replaces it upon the trunk.* RONNY *appears in the playroom doorway. Her color is high, and her eyes very bright. She holds her chin up, as if by effort. For a moment their eyes meet, and* RICKY *contrives to smile, before he goes out, leaving her with* MATEY.]

RONNY: Mr. White—

MATEY: Yes, Ronny. . . .

RONNY: Ricky—told you?

[MATEY *nods, unable completely to hide his scorn for this little jilt.*]

MATEY: You don't love him, h'm—?

RONNY [*Passionately*]: Love him! Oh—if a year ago someone had told me that I'd ever love anyone as I love Rick now, I'd have—I'd have— [*She cannot go on.*]

MATEY: Then I fail to see why you've—

RONNY: I'll tell you why!—If I told *him,* he'd just laugh me out of it. Give me your word no one else shall know—no one at all. . . .

MATEY [*After a pause*]: Very well—my word.

RONNY: I'm between Ricky and the thing he wants to do. That's plain. If I don't marry him, he'll go abroad and study as he should. [*Her hand falls upon his arm.*] *You* know what it means to him. *You* know he *must* be what he's cut *out* to be!

MATEY: You dear child. . . .

[*He picks up her hand and touches his lips to it. She takes it from him at once.*]

RONNY [*In pain*]: Oh—please—that's Ricky's trick!

MATEY: You're very brave, Ronny, and very fine—[*She shakes her head violently.*]—but we can't afford to send him abroad, now.

[RONNY *straightens up, puzzled and shocked.*]

RONNY: Wha-a-a-t . . . ?

MATEY: I am not a rich man. I depended largely upon my salary. It stopped when I left business.

RONNY: But you've *something*—and I only need half of what I have a year. Take the other half—put it with whatever *you* can. I'd be happier—*much.*

MATEY: My dear. . . . But there's been bad news, you see. I've almost nothing, now—not even enough for Nancy and me.

RONNY [*Cruelly*]: Then why don't you go back to business? [MATEY *flinches, in spite of himself.*]

MATEY: One has—certain obligations to oneself—you know. [RONNY *squares off—a cold fury.*]

RONNY: I've just taken my heart and [*With a gesture of breaking it between her hands*] done *that* with it. For him—for my Ricky! And you can stand there talking about yourself! Aren't you his father? Aren't you responsible for him?

MATEY [*Genuinely moved, but smiling a little*]: You are telling me I've—given hostages to Fortune?

RONNY [*Impatiently*]: I don't know anything about "hostages." I just know that there's something big in Ricky, that's got to come out. You can help him—and because you *can,* you *must.* He's your son—you've let yourself in for it!

[*This is too much;* MATEY'*s spirit is up at last.*]

MATEY: Listen to me: your reasoning's very bad. You say I'm responsible for Ricky. All right—I'm responsible for bringing him out of nowhere into a very lively, very interesting world—for giving him twenty-one years of every advantage a boy can have. Now why shouldn't I think of myself for a while?

RONNY: When all that time you've been teaching him to love something, aren't you bound to stick by him till he shows what he can make of it?

MATEY: He had his chance.

RONNY: And now that it's gone, must he wait till he's—forty, or so—for another? [*This shot tells.*]

MATEY [*Doggedly*]: Why not?—That's what *I* did.

RONNY: So—you want everything to be for him—just as it's been for you—

MATEY [*Sharply*]: Please! Please!

RONNY: —Only *you* had Mrs. White in its place. He'd have nothing: I'd feel like a thief. You're *used* to doing what you don't want to do. He's not. He'd be just—empty. . . .

MATEY: He can quit now, and do what he wants on his own.

RONNY: —And so he would! But could he go abroad? Could he be all that he *might* be?

MATEY: That's up to him.

RONNY: It's up to—! Oh, we *can't* argue, can we? What makes my reasons right for me is just what makes them wrong for you.

MATEY: That's the old and the young of it, Ronny.

RONNY [*Swiftly*]: But there's one thing we jibe on! Both of us love Ricky. What you won't do for duty, you *will* do for love!

MATEY [*With a gesture toward his painting*]: Do you know how I love this?

RONNY: Not half so much as Ricky! He's your *son*. He'll come first!

MATEY [*Whimsically*]: You haven't convinced me, Ronny. But you've reminded me that there's a very cruel law that rules most men's destinies.

RONNY [*An avalanche*]: Not only *men's!*

[*She shuts her eyes in pain, swallows hard, shakes her hand as if to shake something out of it, and then raises her chin sharply.* NANCY *appears at the top of the stairs, carrying a large piece of brown wrapping paper and a ball of cord.*]

NANCY: Matey—your train . . .

[RONNY *wheels about and confronts* NANCY. *For a moment, you feel that she is about to attack her as she attacked* MATEY. *But when her voice is heard it is the voice of a broken-hearted little girl, trying her best to be spunky to the end.*]

RONNY: Doing anything special Monday morning?

NANCY [*Puzzled*]: Why, no.

RONNY: If I may, I want to come over—

NANCY: Do . . .

RONNY: —and cry on your shoulder.

NANCY: But what has happened?

[RONNY *flings her last words over her shoulder as she goes down the stairs.*]

RONNY: I'll be in about eleven! [NANCY, *bewildered, looks after her for a moment and then turns to* MATEY.] Matey—what *is* it?

MATEY [*Grimly*]: A joke on me—one of fate's funniest. [*He crosses toward the stairs, shaking his head and laughing softly and bitterly.*] Laugh, my dear—laugh at me. [NANCY *is gazing after him intently, as*

THE CURTAIN FALLS.

■ ACT III ■

It is shortly after nine, the same evening, and the studio is unlighted, save for the bright moonlight which flows through the great dormer window upon the empty easel. Through this window a string of Japanese lanterns is seen, glowing in the dim distance.

There is a sound at the stairs. NANCY *enters, and crosses quickly to the long table, fumbles for a match, scratches it, and begins to light the half-burned candles in the sconces.*

The increasing light shows that the fifteen chairs at the table have been hastily pulled back, and that the table has not yet been entirely cleared. The dappled-gray hobbyhorse has been brought from its hiding place, and upon it sits "Genevieve," a paper cap upon her head.

NANCY *is dressed as a Spanish Lady. She wears a black dress, a lace mantilla of black shot through with jade green, earrings, beads, bracelets, and a jade comb in her hair, which is worn high, in the Spanish fashion.*

As she lights the candles, a heavy, halting step is heard upon the stairs. She seizes one of the sconces, and crossing to the stairway, holds it high above her head, to light the entrance.

NANCY: Geoff—do hurry. . . . [*Still the very slow, heavy steps continue.* NANCY *becomes impatient.*] . . . Do you want him to come in and *find* us? [*The steps continue at the same speed.*] Be careful at the corner! [*A silence. Then the steps begin again, slower than before.* NANCY *is vexed.*] Oh—I *know* you'll rip it to shreds! [*Pause. Then suddenly the steps begin to race.* NANCY *leaps back, and the tip of the portrait, wrapped in brown paper, appears, and behind it* NICHOLS, *who enters as if he had been hurled by a catapult. He wears a Pierrot costume of black and silver, a black skullcap, and an enormous white ruff at his neck.*] Useless person—utterly . . .

NICHOLS: Useless! Three flights of stairs without a mishap—and she calls me useless!

[*Together, they remove the paper and a protecting frame from the portrait, which* NICHOLS *replaces upon the easel.* NANCY *folds the paper, ties string around it, and conceals it and the frame.*]

NANCY: Do you really think there's a chance?

[NICHOLS *extracts a watch with great difficulty from somewhere within his clothes.*]

NICHOLS: Mrs. Carhart sent word that she'd phone me here before 9:30. [*He looks at the watch.*] Sixteen past. By a lightning calculation, fourteen minutes left.

NANCY [*Seating herself at the table*]: I wonder who it could be.

NICHOLS: *I* haven't the slightest idee.

NANCY: But whom was she having up?

NICHOLS: She expected the Graysons, and the Hoyts—

NANCY: Wait a minute!

[*She takes down the names, writing with a crayon upon a piece of* MATEY'*s sketching paper.*]

NICHOLS: —And the Crams, and Reggie de Courcy—

NANCY: Wretched little worm. Tony Cram must be blind.

NICHOLS: And the Webbs, and Gregory Kendall—

NANCY: It might be Kendall! Wouldn't that be luck?

NICHOLS: —Doubt if it's Greg. He once dined with Whistler.—And the Warrens—

NANCY: The G. T.'s—?

NICHOLS: Yes—not staying there. Just came in with some other people for dinner.

NANCY: Well—we can cross *them* out. Go on.

NICHOLS: And Mrs.—what's her name—Parkerson—

NANCY: The front-page Parkerson?

NICHOLS: Herself.

NANCY [*With a grimace*]: Me-aow! Who else?

NICHOLS: Burke McAllister, and the David Ewings. . . .

NANCY: Precious, fat old things! *They* might—

NICHOLS: It'd be a great feather for Matey, if he made their November Loan Exhibition.

NANCY: They're the ones!—It's come to me in a vision!—That all—?

NICHOLS: So far as I remember.

NANCY: Perhaps three or four of them will simply battle for it. You referee, Geoff—[*Thoughtfully*]—And perhaps no one will want it at all. And what will my Matey do then, poor thing . . . ? [*Dropping her head upon her hand*] Oh—I'm too old to be as excited as this over anything! What *can* be keeping him? [*She goes to the window and looks out.*] See the lanterns strung through the orchard at the Duanes'. They look like plums and oranges, come suddenly to life. . . . Ricky

—the lamb—he was such a corker at dinner. Kept them in perfect gales of laughter—just as if nothing had happened at all. Oh—that wretched girl.

NICHOLS: Odd—her tacking about this way, at the last minute. Simple funk, perhaps. . . .

NANCY: Nonsense! She dives twenty feet, without turning a hair!

NICHOLS: I could dive forty—before I could marry.

NANCY: What time is it now?—Come here—let's go over this again—

[NICHOLS *makes a movement to take out his watch. Then remembers what a task it is, and desists.*]

NICHOLS [*Glibly*]: Just 9:21.

[MATEY *comes in.* NANCY *conceals the list.*]

NANCY: Hello, Matey. Thought you'd never come.

MATEY: So did I. That train was more than usually local. My dear—how charming you look.

NANCY: I am a product of southern Spain, where men are men—and women, minxes.

NICHOLS: Three guesses what I am.

[ETTA *comes in.*]

ETTA [*To* NICHOLS]: There's a telephone call for you.

[NANCY *starts, and then sets about concealing her excitement.*]

NICHOLS: Thank you, Etta. . . .

ETTA [*Shyly*]: You're welcome, Geoffrey. . . .

[NICHOLS *accelerates his exit, and* ETTA *turns to follow him.* NANCY, *with an effort, avoids the laughter that has overcome* MATEY, *and calls to her.*]

NANCY: Etta—

ETTA [*Turning*]: Yes, Ma'am—

NANCY [*After a pause*]: Ah—never mind. . . . [ETTA *goes out.* NANCY *and* MATEY *seat themselves upon the sofa.* MATEY *still laughs.*] I can't rebuke the girl. Matey—you *shouldn't* fool with people's souls, that way. She's miles above domestic service now. We must do something about her.

MATEY [*Seriously*]: Um. I know we must—

NANCY: It's a nice idea, though—

MATEY: What?

NANCY: —That in creating the portrait of a lady, you may have created a lady as well. [*She glances toward the stairs and continues nervously.*] How did you find things in town?

MATEY: Pretty bad. It took another slump today. I told Hubbard to sell four hundred shares at ten o'clock Monday. No use grousing over it, I suppose.

NANCY: Not the slightest. Let's forget it till we *have* to think—

MATEY: That's been our method with most disagreeable things, hasn't it?

NANCY: Um.

MATEY: —And we've marched along pretty damn splendidly, haven't we?

NANCY [*Nodding*]: I'm so glad contentment hasn't caught us—and wrapped us in cotton wool. We'll never be quite content, you and I.—So we'll never be dead until they shut our eyes and fold our hands.

MATEY: And even then I dare say our spirits will go on poking about the heavenly shrubbery—looking for birds that may be there!

NANCY: Darling—it's the way to live—[*Another furtive glance at the stairs*]—But it plays simple havoc with your nerves. . . . [*Suddenly*] Matey—tell me you love me.

MATEY: Child! I abominate you.

NANCY: Ah—very satisfactory.

MATEY: I particularly like you in earrings.

[NANCY *taps one of the pendant earrings with her forefinger.*]

NANCY: "Waggle-waggle!"

[*They laugh at their absurdity.*]

MATEY: I phoned Greg Kendall from the Club, but they said he was in the country. I've concluded that the thing to do with the portrait, is to get an exhibition.

NANCY [*Keeping her voice steady*]: Kendall might even want it himself.

MATEY: I doubt it. But he often acts as an agent, you know.

NANCY [*Airily*]: Would you like Mr. Ewing to have it?

MATEY: Oh, no—not at all! Be hung along with Goya and El Greco? My dear—such ignominy!—How did the supper go?

NANCY: Delightfully—for all but the three of us who knew. [*She shakes her head sadly.*] Ricky would have broken your heart.

MATEY: He didn't sulk?

NANCY: Matey!—Our boy *sulk?* He was splendid!

MATEY: I was certain of it.

NANCY: That girl! I don't see how she dares—

MATEY: Nanny—if only I could tell you.—Ronny—

[*He is interrupted by* NICHOLS' *entrance.* NANCY *goes to him quickly, and in the recess of the stairway they whisper together excitedly.*]

NICHOLS: Ssss-s-s-s—pss-sssh—pscpssch—

NANCY: Not *really!?*—But I never *heard* of anything so remarkable!

MATEY [*Approaching them*]: Here—what's this?—Why not include the smaller nations in the conference?

NANCY [*Motioning to him behind her back*]: Go away!

[*They whisper more earnestly.* MATEY *returns to the sofa.*]

MATEY: What *have* you two got up your sleeves?

NICHOLS [*Over* NANCY'*s shoulder*]: A white rabbit, now. It *was* a white elephant. [MATEY *picks up a magazine and begins to look it over.* NANCY *and* NICHOLS *join hands and keeping perfect step, march over to a position in front of* MATEY. MATEY *speaks to them indulgently:*] Yes, my little ones—what can I do for you?

NANCY [*At once timid and exultant*]: Maitland—Geoff and I have something to tell you. . . .

MATEY [*Quite unimpressed*]: Fancy that, now.

[NANCY *turns imploringly to* NICHOLS.]

NANCY: I *won't* have my biggest moment ruined by such crass stupidity.

NICHOLS: Really, old son—we've three columns of news.

MATEY: Um.—Newspapers bore me.

NANCY [*In desperation*]: Matey—we've sold your picture.

NICHOLS: Not quite *sold,* but—

NANCY: At any rate, we've got an offer for it.

MATEY: Well, well—isn't that nice? [*He sighs.*] Come on—we might as well get it over with: Who has made the offer?

[NANCY *appeals to* NICHOLS. *He laughs.*]

NICHOLS: The truth is that we don't *know* who!

MATEY: I shouldn't have spoiled it. Make it a good one: The—uh—Corcoran gallery—or the Vatican—[*Yawning and settling back*] What tiresome people . . . [NANCY *determinedly takes him by both ears, shakes his head, and literally lifts him to his feet.*] Here!—Let go!

NANCY: Matey! Will you listen? I tell you we're serious!

[MATEY *looks at* NICHOLS, *who solemnly raises his right hand.*]

NICHOLS: By the bones of my ancestors!

[MATEY, *dumbfounded, looks from one to the other.*]

MATEY: Well, of—I'll be—*Tell* me about it—quick!

NANCY [*Eagerly*]: It was Geoff's plan. He gets the credit.

NICHOLS: It was just as much yours as mine.

NANCY: But *Geoffrey*—you *know* you—

MATEY [*Impatiently*]: Honors are even! Come *on—what* . . . ?

NANCY [*Very rapidly*]: Well—we took the portrait over to Mrs. Carhart's. Geoff had arranged with her to hang it in her drawing room, and show it to everyone before dinner—said it was by a protégé of yours. Then, just before you arrived, her chauffeur brought it back, and with it a message saying that she'd phone before nine-thirty. That was Geoff's call, and—

MATEY [*Confused*]: But—who—?

NICHOLS: That's what we don't know. It was her butler who phoned. Said she was sending the—prospective purchaser here to see me now.

NANCY: —And it's probably either Kendall or the Ewings! They were both there. And it's an out-and-out offer—

NICHOLS: A handsome one, Matey—four thousand dollars.

MATEY: Four thousand dollars—for the work of an unknown modern?

NICHOLS: I made him repeat it three times. Not, of course, that I doubted its worth. . . .

MATEY: Oh, no—certainly not—of course not. But—[*In sudden buoyancy*] I say!—He must have *liked* it, h'm . . . ? [*He gathers* NANCY *to his side with one sweep of his arm, and grasps* NICHOLS' *hand.*] Oh—you bully good people! I wouldn't trade you for any other two on earth! [*He goes to the portrait.*] Geoff—bring those candles over, will you?

NANCY: No—let me!

[*She picks up the sconce, and holds it up to light the portrait.* MATEY *dips his brush.*]

MATEY: Now for the great ceremony. Anonymity—farewell!

NANCY [*Reluctantly*]: I wonder if we aren't being—a little—previous . . . ?

MATEY [*With his brush poised*]: Why . . . ? [*To* NICHOLS] Didn't you say it was definite?

NICHOLS: It seemed so to me.

NANCY: But—there might be a slip—'twixt the offer—and the check.

MATEY [*Hesitating*]: I wonder—What do you think, Geoff?

NICHOLS: He'll be here in a moment. Why not wait?

MATEY: I bow to your good judgment. I'll sign it under his very nose.

NICHOLS [*Suddenly*]: I'm going to give up my popular writing, and see if I can't do one thing I'm not ashamed of—

MATEY: Fine!—Of *course* you can. . . .

NICHOLS: I don't know. You jilted your art, but I did worse. I sent mine on the streets. She's not a forgiving lady.

MATEY [*In high spirits*]: Not forgiving?—When she came back to me after years of neglect? Try her! Try her!—Now tell me: who else saw it?

NANCY: I have a list right here—

NICHOLS: I cling doggedly to a belief that it may be Mrs. Parkerson.

MATEY: I hear she has some beautiful things.

NICHOLS: —And she likes new people.

NANCY: Matey—I *won't* let that woman have it!

MATEY [*Good-humoredly*]: Not even for four thousand dollars?

NANCY: Not for twenty! [MATEY *draws a line and wafts a kiss to the dreadful woman.*]

MATEY: *Au 'voir,* Mrs. Parkerson. We thank you for your kindly interest—but our prig of a wife objects to you. [*He reads over the names.*] Of course—it might be any one of these—with two or three exceptions. . . .

NANCY: How I do hope that—[*She hesitates, troubled.*] It's almost too ideal, to be altogether true.

MATEY: Nanny—you haven't been—pulling my leg?

NANCY: As if I could—in a thing like this! [*Again, apprehensively*] But—I mean—it seems so adventitious—so—pat to our needs.

[*Enter* RICKY *in a troubadour costume, but without the guitar.*]

MATEY: Still—if he definitely said—. Well, Rick, you look positively dashing.

RICKY: Keep your seats; the chorus will be right in. [*He sees "Genevieve" on the hobbyhorse.*] I see the Lady Godiva still rides. Hi, Mr. Nichols!

NICHOLS: Hello, Ricky. [*To* MATEY] Don't you think I'd better go down and wait for—whoever it is?

NANCY: By all means. I'll go with you.

RICKY: Stick around a minute, will you, Nanny?

NANCY: I'll be with you presently, Geoff.

NICHOLS [*Going out*]: Right.

RICKY [*To* NANCY]: Ronny is downstairs. She wants to talk to you.

NANCY: I—don't think I care to see her now. . . .

RICKY: Off that, Dearest. If Ronny wants to change her mind, why that's her privilege. I'll expect you to be just as nice to her as you possibly can be. And by that, I don't mean any of your well-known politeness at ten below zero. . . .

MATEY: I haven't yet told you how sorry I am about this.

RICKY [*Smiling*]: Oh—it's not every one has *your* luck getting married.

NANCY: Come here, Rick—[*He goes to her and she takes his face between her hands and kisses him.*] Tell Ronny to come up—

[RICKY *hugs her, drops his head upon her shoulder for a moment, and then looks up, smiling brightly.*]

RICKY: Thanks, old Precious—thanks. [*He goes out.*]

NANCY: Matey—he makes me ache all over.

MATEY: Our own good fortune seems nothing when I think of it.

NANCY: He'll get over it, of course—they always do. But a thing like this takes the sweetness out of a boy. It hardens him—makes him shrewd—metallic—[*Flaming into anger against* RONNY]—And all along I've thought that Ronny's air of inconsequence was—merely an overlay—to many things fine, and true—

MATEY: My dear—it *is*—

NANCY: This looks it, doesn't it—this parody of love!

MATEY: —It's hardly that, Nanny.—And you must be very careful with her.

NANCY [*Coldly*]: —And why should I be?

[RONNY *enters by the stairs. She wears a long dress of peacock-blue satin, brocaded with silver, a silver girdle and silver slippers. Binding her hair is a slim bandeau of pearls. It is the costume of a seventeenth-century court. She looks considerably older—a charming woman of, say, 26. She crosses a few steps from the top of the stairs, and stops.*]

MATEY: Van Dyck might have painted you.

RONNY: I wish he had. I'd like it better—if I were—just stuck up somewhere. . . . [*To* NANCY] I hadn't a chance at dinner—I wanted to be sure that—you weren't hating me too much—

NANCY: I'm afraid I am very old-fashioned. Forgive me—but I find it difficult to regard jilting with anything but—distaste.

MATEY [*An entreaty*]: *Ronny—?*

RONNY: All right—only Ricky mustn't know.

MATEY [*To* NANCY]: Ronny told me something this afternoon—she told me a number of things. One of them was the motive for what she has done. She loves him very much. Rightly or wrongly, she felt that she was keeping him from the thing—from a perhaps notable career. So she broke her engagement, and gave him a trumped-up reason for it.

NANCY [*Incredulously*]: *She* could do *that?!*—When I—? Oh—

[*She stands with her head bowed, one hand resting upon the table.*]

MATEY [*He must say something*]: No doubt she's placed too much importance upon it. She's—[NANCY *turns to* RONNY.]

NANCY: Ronny—I think I am one of the few mothers who consider the girl their son loves, really good enough for him.

RONNY [*Barely audible*]: You're very kind. But—

NANCY [*With a gesture asking her to come to her*]: Please—[RONNY *crosses, and* NANCY *takes her hand.*] You make me feel very little. You are doing something that I, years ago, hadn't the courage to do.

[RONNY *looks from her to* MATEY. *Then realizes what she means.*]

RONNY: Oh—it's not at all the same, you know.

NANCY: I think it is very much the same—[*Pause*] But—I don't know what to advise you. I've—had a happy life, my dear. . . .

MATEY: —And so have I, Ronny—a very happy one.

[NANCY *glances at him, gratefully.*]

NANCY: It's—doubtful now, whether we *could* send Ricky abroad. . . . [RONNY *looks at* MATEY, *who looks away.*] . . . even if he would consent to go. And it may be that you and your love could mean—

MATEY: —Could mean—much more than anything else could, without them.

RONNY [*Quietly*]: —As I see it, that's not the point—

MATEY: But the more I think of it, the more certain I am that—

RONNY: It's no good arguing, Mr. White. I'm sure I'm right.—And you know what a stubborn little mule I am. . . .

NANCY: You've told your mother?

RONNY: —That it was off? Yes. Told both of them. Father won't speak to me, and I left Mother eating aspirin tablets. [*She laughs shortly.*] It's a great life.

NANCY: I only hope you're not making a mistake.

RONNY: It's not a mistake. Not if Ricky is started right.

[*Again* MATEY *looks away.*]

NANCY: I'm afraid we couldn't afford—what do you think, Maitland?

[RONNY *holds* MATEY'*s eyes for a long instant. Slowly he shifts his gaze to* NANCY.]

MATEY [*With difficulty*]: It—doesn't seem likely—no.

RONNY [*After a pause*]: Then at least he can go into an architects' office —you must insist on that.

NANCY: —And perhaps turn out to be merely—clever with a ruler? No—he might better stay in business.

RONNY: Then—[*Almost breaking*] Oh—just because last autumn I was a selfish, shortsighted little fool, is this all to be useless now?

[*She looks at* MATEY, *and after a moment he turns and meets her gaze without flinching.*]

MATEY: —One thing's certain: If Ricky is to do it at all, he must have the best training possible.

RONNY [*With a wan, grateful smile*]: I knew you'd think that.

MATEY [*After a short pause*]: Happily, I've just had some rather good news about—my painting. And—

RONNY: Oh—I'm *so* glad!

[MATEY *smiles his thanks.*]

MATEY: —And it is possible that the success of this particular piece may make my future work even more profitable.

RONNY [*Her eyes shining*]: Then—everything's all right for *both* of you, isn't it?

MATEY: That's what I'm hoping.—So I think you may be confident, that your very fine and generous sacrif—

RONNY [*Swiftly*]: Please don't say "sacrifice." It's not one—not if Ricky comes through as I know he will.

MATEY: —At any rate, what you have done will not—go for nothing.

RONNY [*Lowly*]: That's good of you. Thanks—I'm—satisfied now. [*She turns.*] I'd better go back—the people have started to dribble in.

MATEY: Will you tell Ricky I should like to see him here in about half an hour?

RONNY [*Lifelessly*]: I'll tell him. [*She begins to move toward the stairs. Reaching* NANCY, *she turns impulsively, and buries her head in her shoulder.*]—And I thought love all just a happy lark!

NANCY [*Tenderly, as she pats her head*]: Not all, Dear.

[RONNY *smiles much as* RICKY *did and straightens up quickly.*]

RONNY: Not—*any*—

[*There is a sound from the stairs and* WARREN*'s voice is heard.*]

WARREN [*With difficulty*]: *Is* there any top?—Or—do we—just—keep going—?

NICHOLS [*Cheerily*]: Push on, Brave Heart—push on!

MATEY [*Lowly, to* NANCY]: Lord—I forgot Rick said G. T. was up here. I'll take him downstairs. Geoff should have known. [*He quickly moves the easel back into the shadow, and covers the paint table with a silk scarf, which he snatches from a chair. The sound draws closer, and* RONNY *steps back to let* WARREN *and* NICHOLS *enter.* WARREN *wears a dinner coat, and looks quite exhausted.*] Hello, G. T. I heard you were somewhere in the neighborhood.

[*They shake hands, blocking* RONNY*'s exit.*]

WARREN [*Breathlessly*]: H'lo—White—[*Looks around for a chair, and finding none near by, sits upon a trunk*] I'd—no idea—your house—was so tall.

NANCY: How do you do, Mr. Warren? So long since we've had this pleasure.

WARREN: How-do-do, Mrs. White? I expected—Saint Peter.

MATEY: I think we'd be more comfortable downstairs.

WARREN: Maybe we would. But—now that—I'm up—here—[*Taking a deep breath*]—I'm going—to sit down—long enough—to—make it pay.

[*He sees* RONNY, *and rises.*]

RONNY: How do you do?

[WARREN *looks puzzled at first, then beams and shakes hands with her.*]

WARREN: Why—bless my soul—it's Miss—Miss Duane, isn't it? My, how pretty you look—just like a picture. Your young man is doing very well for me. I—uh—understand the secret's coming out tonight. Let me be among the first to congratulate you—he's a fine boy.

RONNY [*Glancing furtively at the stairs*]: Thank you very much.

MATEY [*To save the situation*]: G. T.—

WARREN [*Going right on*]: —Yes, a wife's the best thing in the world for a young man, if he can afford one—[*He chuckles*]—and I'll see to it that *you* two don't starve right away. [*and continues talking to her, while looking at* MATEY. RONNY *quietly slips out.*] Expect big things of Ricky. Don't doubt that someday he'll be more valuable to me than his father ever thought of being. And I once thought White indispensable! Well—I mustn't keep you too long. I wish you every happiness—[*Turning about slowly*]—my dear. And I'm sure—[*He sees that she is not there, and laughs.*] Humph—that's one on me!

MATEY: G. T.—there are two or three things I'd like to mull over with you. Let's go down to the library. We can talk better there. I'm expecting a caller—but he won't keep me long.

[WARREN *goes to the sofa,* MATEY *watching him anxiously.* NICHOLS *goes to the window and stands there silently looking out, weaving his fingers in and out behind him.*]

WARREN: Don't see anything wrong with this. [*He seats himself and his long pent-up curiosity finally breaks through.*] White—what on earth've you been doing with yourself?

MATEY: Oh—resting—and indulging a few neglected tastes.

[WARREN *looks to* NANCY *for corroboration.*]

NANCY: You said he needed a rest, you know.

WARREN: Eight months of it?—It's not resting after the first six weeks. It's rotting. . . . Well, I'm not here to talk vacations.

[NANCY'*s hand flies to her mouth. She bites her knuckle, drops her hand, turns quickly and looks at* NICHOLS. *He crosses to them.*]

NICHOLS: Oh, yes—Mr. Warren saw the portrait, Matey—

[*Dance music begins to be heard faintly, from the Duanes'.*]

MATEY [*Easily*]: That's right—you were at the Carharts', weren't you? Amusing chap—this protégé of mine. A bit erratic, of course—you know painters. . . .

WARREN: Um.

MATEY: Oh—by the way—did you hear Ewing or Kendall say anything about coming over?

WARREN: —Here?—No. And listen—those fellows make me tired. You should have heard them pulling your friend's picture to pieces. All about "dim cherry-askuro" and "flat composition"—and all that highbrow rot. Blind as bats—both of 'em! Missing the greatest thing about it! [*Leaning forward, and tapping* MATEY*'s knee confidentially with his forefinger*] White—I want to tell you that that picture has Human Interest Appeal!

MATEY [*Bravely*]: You—found it interesting?

WARREN [*Settling back*]: Enough to pay four thousand dollars for it!

NANCY [*Quietly*]: You are the prospective purchaser, Mr. Warren?

[NICHOLS *returns to the window.* MATEY *nods his head reflectively, staring at the floor.*]

MATEY: H'm—very generous offer, very—

WARREN: You bet I am!—Why, it's the sweetest face I ever saw! [*He rises and crosses to the easel.*] This it?—Ah—if that doesn't give trumps to all the Old Masters *I've* ever seen—

[*He gazes at the portrait with a rapt expression.* MATEY *brings himself heavily to his feet.* NANCY *edges closer to him, watching him.*]

MATEY: You say—Kendall and Ewing and the others—didn't think so much of it? [NANCY *is at his side.*]

WARREN [*Snorting*]: Bah—they make me sick!

MATEY [*Very softly*]: They make *me*—a little sick. . . .

[NANCY *grasps his hand behind his back, and presses it as tightly as she can, as* WARREN *moves the easel around to get the full light upon the face.*]

WARREN: But that didn't change *my* opinion. If you discovered this, I'm tremendously indebted to you.

MATEY [*Dully*]: Oh—not at all—

WARREN: But I tell you it's just what I've been after for years! It's the most perfect type you could ask for!

MATEY: Type—? Perfect—? What *for?*

WARREN [*Triumphantly*]: Why—to personify the Warren Line, of course!

NANCY: Oh—this is unthinkable!

[WARREN *looks at her, surprised. He has not caught the words, but the tone was unmistakable.* MATEY *drops his hand upon her shoulder, removing it in an instant.*]

MATEY: Just a minute, Dear. [*To* WARREN] Let me get this straight.—Precisely why is it that you want the picture?

WARREN: Advertising, man, advertising.—What did you think?
[MATEY'*s head sinks.*]

MATEY: I—*didn't*—

WARREN: Why—you ought to be delighted. Haven't you been howling for years for a big national campaign? And haven't I been holding out till I could find a way of putting the whole line over as a unit? Well, your dream's coming true—'n so's mine—[*Tapping the shoulder of the portrait*]—And we owe it all to this little lady right here.

MATEY: Ah—this is Fame!

WARREN: You're right it is!

NICHOLS [*To* MATEY]: Millais once did a painting for Pears' Soap, you know. . . .

MATEY: Thanks, Geoff.

WARREN: Look!—Can't you just *see* it with "The Warren Line Is Purity Itself" written in 9-point script across the bottom?

MATEY: —Instead of the painter's signature. Yes—I can see it. [*He turns and regards* WARREN *speculatively.*] G. T.—you're not aware of it—but in a way you're—uncannily like God.

[NANCY'*s head drops upon her breast.* NICHOLS *abruptly returns to the window. The music at the Duanes' stops, and the faint sound of laughter is heard.*]

WARREN [*After a pause. Surprised, then amused*]: Me—? God—? Ho! Ho!—Thanks for the compliment. [*Again contemplating the picture*] Wonder if it wouldn't be better to put something in her hand. Art Department could retouch it in—a bunch of flowers . . . or a can of talcum—

NANCY [*Quietly*]: I think, Mr. Warren, that its great charm is its—refreshing freedom from artifice—

WARREN: Well—you ought to know. You're a woman—and it's women we want to reach. [*To* MATEY] Make the check out to you?

MATEY: You'd better wait. The—artist may not care to have it used for advertising purposes. I'll—let you know Monday. . . .

WARREN [*Laughing*]: What? Temperament? [*He goes to the table and writes a check.*] Wave this under his nose. If he's as poor as most artists, he'll soon forget his highty-tighty notions.—And tell him I want to see him about doing two or three more, in different poses. Same price. . . .

MATEY [*Directly*]: That, I am certain he will not consent to.

NANCY [*Softly*]: Ah—you *brick!*

NICHOLS [*Simultaneously*]: Bravo!

WARREN [*To* NANCY]: What's that?

NANCY: I was speaking to my husband.

WARREN: Oh. [ETTA *enters with a note for* MATEY. WARREN *leaves the check on the table, and rises.*] You watch—he'll come around. He'll—

MATEY: It is—the *face* you like, isn't it?

WARREN: Certainly. I don't know anything about the technique, or whatever you call it.

[ETTA *passes* WARREN, *unnoticed by him.*]

MATEY: I think perhaps we—can find the model—and some proficient—commercial artist can do her in other poses.

WARREN: Suits me.—Say now—before I go—there's one more thing—

ETTA [*Giving* MATEY *the envelope*]: A message for you, sir—and thank you, sir.

MATEY [*Gravely*]: All right, Etta.

[ETTA *joyfully turns to go out.*]

WARREN [*Continuing*]: I'm not too well pleased with the way the Chicago—[*As she passes* WARREN, ETTA *looks up at him. He stops speaking abruptly, and his mouth drops open in amazement. He turns and watches her as she goes out. He looks again at the portrait, then wheels about quickly, and explodes.*] White—there's something damn queer about this whole thing. Did *you* paint this picture?

MATEY [*Smiling*]: G. T.!—Imagine me an artist!

WARREN [*Suddenly* WARREN'*s face lights up in complete understanding*]: *Now* I see it! *That's* why you left! You knew we had to advertise. You knew I couldn't find what I wanted. So you got a big idea—worked it out by yourself—and then sprang it on me! What a fellow you are!

MATEY: It's a pretty explanation—but quite erroneous, quite—

NICHOLS: Oh, agree with him, Matey—what's the odds?

MATEY: You're quite wrong—

WARREN: Dammit, right *or* wrong, I want you back. And now that I've O.K.'d your advertising plans, you ought to be on hand to manage 'em.—Well, what do you say?

MATEY: I don't know. I'll—tell you that on Monday, too. [*Thoughtfully*] If I should come back—would you agree to my having Fridays and Saturdays free the entire year round—to devote to a—hobby of mine?

WARREN: Absolutely!

MATEY: I'll think it over, and let you know.

WARREN [*Tapping the portrait*]: Have this sent to me, will you?

MATEY: If the artist agrees. Your house?

WARREN: No—right to the office.—And you ought to shake up that Chicago crowd, and shake 'em up good! You could leave Wednesday and be back by the first of the week. . . .

MATEY [*Reflectively*]: I'd have a lot to tell those fellows.

WARREN: I bet you would!

NANCY [*Alarmed*]: —But didn't you say that weekends were to be free?

WARREN: Oh, occasionally it may be necessary to—[*With a gesture*] Business is business, you know.

NANCY [*Softly*]: So it is. . . .

WARREN: Well—I'll be going along. Good night, Mrs. White.

NANCY: Good night.

WARREN [*To* MATEY]: Expect to hear from you Monday. No need to come down with me.

NICHOLS [*Crossing from window*]: No—let me—[*As he passes* MATEY, *he stops and looks at him searchingly.*]

WARREN [*On the stairs*]: Good-bye! Good-bye, Mr.—uh—uh—*Good*-bye! [*He goes out.*]

MATEY [*With a smile*]: No, Geoff—not done yet!

NICHOLS: It's a rotten shame—*I* know what it's like—

[*He follows* WARREN *down the stairs.* MATEY *tears open the envelope and extracts the note.* NANCY *crosses to him.*]

MATEY: Something of a facer, isn't it?

NANCY: Oh, Matey—be careful, be careful! Don't do anything till you're sure that you're right.

MATEY: No, dear. . . . [*Turning to the signature of the note*] H'm—from Greg Kendall—

NANCY [*Eagerly*]: Oh—what does he say?

[MATEY *frowns over the writing.*]

MATEY: "Ewing and I—home—a lovely—" [*He gives it to her.*] Can you make it out?

NANCY [*Reading slowly*]: "Ewing and I have had a lively discussion concerning the portrait painted by your protégé. Ewing insists that—" [*She stops and looks at him fearfully.*]

MATEY [*Grimly*]: Let's have it.

NANCY: "Ewing insists that it is of no consequence, but I cannot bring myself wholly to agree with him. . . ." [*Delightedly*] Matey!

MATEY: Crumbs are good.

NANCY [*Continuing*]: "I find the technique above average, and the brushwork distinctly promising. My main objections hang upon a certain inflexibility in treatment. We do not expect a painter's early work to be individual, but such rigidity is as ominous as it is uncommon. [*She turns the page.*] . . . Unless your young friend is content with a place in the ranks of the agreeably mediocre, he should devote the next three or four years to the most painstaking study under a good European master. This may, or may not, be his salvation."

MATEY [*Staring straight in front of him*]: —And there's not a better judge than Kendall!

NANCY: No . . . ?

MATEY: —Nor a fairer one.—But it doesn't convince me—do you understand? Not by half! Ah—how I'd like to show them!

NANCY: You will—I'm sure you will.

MATEY [*Grasping at the straw*]: —He did like my brushwork. You see?—That's very important.—Now if I should get someone in town to tutor me—

NANCY: You—who have just said "If he's to do it at all, he must have the best training possible"—?

[*He looks at her oddly.*]

MATEY [*Half to himself*]: Which of us—

NANCY: You're not one to do things by halves. Why not go abroad, as Kendall advises? *I* shan't mind—and it's no one else's business. Rick can support himself. I've still enough for Jean and me. And—[*She hesitates*]—for *you*—why, we can sell the place, you know. It ought to bring enough—land's valuable up here.

MATEY: But Nanny—you love it so.

NANCY: So do I—love you.

MATEY: But it's yours—it's your own—

NANCY [*Softly*]: Have I—anything—my *own* . . . ?

[MATEY *draws her to him.*]

MATEY: Ah—my dear—[*A pause*] I don't know what to do. I don't know—This afternoon—I'll never admit that all Ronny said was right. But on one thing we were agreed—on a weakness of mine—[*There is a tinge of harshness in his forced gaiety*]—A *weakness,* Nanny—that's what love is, in an artist! [*From the stairs comes the sound of whistling.*]

NANCY: What was it she said?

[RICKY *comes in, softly continuing the tune the orchestra at the Duanes' has been playing.*]

MATEY [*With a gesture toward him*]: This—

RICKY: I am informed, O King, that you command my presence. Let the royal tongue wag—[*He sits on a trunk and begins to whistle again, lowly.* MATEY *looks at him speculatively*]—or, in the vulgar parlance, shoot—

MATEY: Ricky—how do you feel?

RICKY [*With a short laugh*]: Well, Dad, if you really want to know, I feel like holy hell.

MATEY: I thought so.

RICKY: But I promised to act like a little soldier. And when a fellow lets himself in for something, he's got to see it through, hasn't he? So—[*He whistles a bar*]—Cheero! [*and goes on whistling moodily.*]

MATEY: When—a fellow does *what?*

RICKY: Lets himself in for something—

[*He returns again to his whistling.* MATEY *is in a study. Suddenly his brow clears, and he speaks spiritedly.*]

MATEY: Rick, how'd you like to go abroad—as you planned?

[RICKY *glances at him quickly.*]

RICKY: What? [*A thoughtful pause*]—Take the wherewithal from you? No—thanks a lot—but it can't be done. I'll manage all right in some New York office.

NANCY: That's the *you* in him speaking, Matey.

[MATEY *thinks rapidly for a moment.*]

MATEY: —But I've good news for you.—When you were born, your grandfather took out an endowment policy in your name. You're supposed to get it when you're thirty—a yearly income of about two thousand, for a term of five years.

RICKY: But—I'm only—

MATEY: —Hubbard's the executor. This afternoon he told me that it can come to you now—provided I consider you old enough to expend it properly.

RICKY: Gosh, Dad—that's knockout news—

MATEY: —And if you and Ronny are careful, it's enough to take her with you. Together, you'll have four thousand a year. You'll do better work than you would if you had more—

RICKY: But Ronny doesn't—

MATEY: Let me finish! Son—the happiness of a man's family can mean a lot to him—a tremendous lot. So if you've something you feel it's your destiny to do—something out of the beaten track—unusual—difficult—you'd better begin your married life doing it.

NANCY [*Quietly*]: And if you don't?

MATEY: The chances are it will never be done.

[RICKY *looks from one to the other, bewildered.*]

RICKY: But listen—

NANCY [*To* MATEY]: Then what—?

[*For a moment* MATEY'*s head sinks. He lifts it again, smiling.*]

MATEY: Why—then I suppose—you turn philosopher.

NANCY: —Philosophy—to fill an empty heart. It must be rather dreadful. . . .

MATEY: . . . It *would* be—if one's heart *were* empty. But when it's full already—well—habit has a way of changing destinies, don't you think? [*He laughs lightly.*] How's that—for philosophy? [NANCY *turns away.*]

RICKY: Wait a minute, Dad—I'm in a perfect fog.—You're sure you don't need that money yourself?—It's yours, you know—[MATEY *shakes his head decisively.*] Then it—oh, it'd be—I mean, you simply couldn't beat it. Gosh, how I'd work—But as for Ronny—[*He looks up, smiling.*]—She doesn't want me. . . .

MATEY: Tell her what I've told you—and see what she says.

[RICKY *looks at him searchingly.*]

RICKY: Dad—*what do you know—?*

MATEY [*With sudden sharpness*]: Never mind what I know! Stop arguing, and try it—quickly—before your luck changes!

[RICKY *turns and starts for the stairs as fast as he can.* NANCY *picks up the guitar from the trunk.*]

NANCY: Ricky—! [*He stops, and she holds it out to him*] Here—[*He comes back, and takes it.*]

RICKY [*Breathlessly*]: Thanks, Dearest. . . . [*He kisses her, hastily.*] I love you. . . . [*He makes the stairs in record time and goes out.*]

NANCY: His grandfather did nothing of the sort.

MATEY: I know he didn't. But he wouldn't have taken it from me—not for both of them.

NANCY: Are you certain—you're acting wisely?

MATEY: Wisdom has nothing to do with love, my dear.

NANCY [*A stilled voice*]: Matey—if this is failure, it's a kind I've never seen before.

MATEY [*Brightly*]: Why—you talk as though I'd given it up entirely! Didn't you hear me arrange with G. T. for time to—

NANCY [*With a hopeless gesture*]: Weekends . . . ?

MATEY: Um.—And by and by when Ricky's on his feet, and Jean is married—

[NANCY *buries her head in his shoulder.*]

NANCY [*Pitying him with her whole heart*]: Oh—*Matey*—you'll be nearly fifty!

MATEY: You call that old!?

NANCY [*Clinging to him*]: I don't like the look of this—at all. . . .

[MATEY *holds her to him, staring fixedly into space over her shoulder. The orchestra at the Duanes' begins to play a waltz. His face brightens.*]

MATEY [*As briskly as he can*]: Well—if we're going to the dance, I'd better get into costume. [*He blows out the candles, and* NANCY *turns out the lamps, leaving the room lighted only by the moonlight, which faintly illuminates the small windows, and flows strongly through the great dormer upon the portrait, and upon* NANCY. *A shaft of pale light lights the stairs from below.* MATEY *takes one last look at the portrait and then goes to* NANCY.]—What hideous disguise have you got for me?

NANCY: The usual—a matador.

MATEY: No!—Tonight I shall be something different.

NANCY: But there isn't anything!

MATEY: Yes, there is—[*He picks up his smock and holds it out for her to see.*] I am going, my love—[*The smock envelops him now, and he turns to give* NANCY *the full picture as he stands there, a parody of himself and his hopes*]—as an artist!

[NANCY*'s hand goes out to him in a little vain protest. He takes the red Spanish beret from the animal's head on the wall and sets it jauntily upon his own. He lifts "Genevieve" from the hobbyhorse, and takes* NANCY*'s arm through his. The three cross toward the stairs,* MATEY *with his head high—"Genevieve" on one arm,* NANCY *a tragic figure on the other—whistling the waltz with the orchestra, as*

THE CURTAIN FALLS.

WHITE WINGS

WHITE WINGS

was first produced by Winthrop Ames
at the Booth Theatre, New York City,
on October 15, 1926.
It was directed by Winthrop Ames;
the settings were designed by Woodman Thompson.

CAST

JOSEPH, *a Horse*	George Ali
MARY TODD	Winifred Lenihan
ARCHIE INCH	Tom Powers
MR. ERNEST INCH	William Norris
HERBERT, *a Cabby*	J. M. Kerrigan
PAUL PILLSBURY (*White Wings*)	Donald McKee
RALPH OTIS (*White Wings*)	Earl McDonald
CLYDE SIMS, III (*White Wings*)	Ben Lackland
KIT CANARI	Donald Macdonald
MRS. FANNY K. INCH	Jessie Graham
MAJOR PHILIP E. INCH	Albert Tavernier
CHARLIE TODD	Arthur Allen
DR. BOWLES	Donald McKee
DR. DERBY	Earl McDonald
TAXI-DRIVER	Ben Lackland
CITY EMPLOYEE	Phil Sheridan

■ ACTION AND SCENES ■

The action of the play takes place in the streets of an American city at varying intervals between 1895 and 1915.

ACT I
The Boulevard

ACT II
Scene 1—The Parkway
Scene 2—The Parkway

ACT III
The Parkway

NOTE: The settings for the three acts should be so designed as to key the action of the play just out of reality. This may be accomplished by means of a realistic foreground and backgrounds painted "in the "flat to give a poster-effect.

■ ACT I ■

A section of the Boulevard, backed by a long wall which supports the Parkway. This wall must be low enough to show, in the setting for Act II (which is the reverse of this setting), the head and shoulders of the Cabby, who sits upon the box of his cab in the Boulevard.

On the wall, obliterating part of a "Post No Bills" sign, are several of the advertising posters of the period. Among them "Doctor Munyon" with his finger upraised and his reassuring "There is Hope."

A narrow, curbed sidewalk runs along the back wall and follows the line of a two-storied brick building, which juts out at Right. At the angle of the wall a brief flight of stone steps leads up to the Parkway. Above the main entrance to the building is a sign "The Elite. Sea Food. Family Entrance," the mica surface of which is illuminated by a Welsbach-burner enclosed in a glass globe. Below it the picture of a goat's head simply announces "Bock." The second story of the building (which rises above the Parkway wall) is seen to be brightly lighted, although the window blinds are drawn. From off left, a gas streetlight adds a little more illumination to the scene. There is a moon in the sky and a mass of clouds framing it. Dimly in the background past the Parkway the outlines of a few buildings may be seen.

Backed against the curbstone beside the restaurant stands an old-fashioned open cab. The cabby is absent from the box, and the absurd figure of a horse, his sides bulging, is nodding in his traces. He is held by an iron weight, fastened to his bit, and wears a bunch of leaves over one ear. This is JOSEPH, *and there are two men in him.*

The time is about two o'clock on a spring morning in the late nineties.

At rise, piano and violin music is heard from the upper story of the restaurant. The horse flips an ear, turns his head and listens for the music. Nods again, then turns his head toward the wall, listens. Then shakes his head, lets himself down upon the pavement, and goes to sleep.

The door of the restaurant is opened, and MARY TODD *comes out, on the arm of* ARCHIE INCH, *who is a nice-looking boy of about twenty.* MARY *is eighteen, gay, pretty, attractive. She carries a stiff little bouquet of flowers.* ARCHIE, *in white duck trousers and short blue coat, and* MARY, *in a party dress, with a broad sash and a ribbon at the back of her hair, are dressed in the fashion of the period. In the middle of the street* MARY *stops, takes her arm from* ARCHIE'S, *and goes back to the step of the restaurant.*

ARCHIE: What's the matter?

MARY: My slipper—I've got to fix it.

[*She takes it off, fusses at the heel and replaces it.*]

ARCHIE: I suppose it'll go on all night.

MARY: It'll—? What'll—?

[ARCHIE *glances toward the lighted windows.*]

ARCHIE: —That'll—[*The music stops. He explains.*]—Kit's party.

[MARY *yawns.*]

MARY: It was fun, wasn't it?

ARCHIE [*Gallantly*]: I met *you,* Miss Todd.

MARY: Still—it was fun. . . . [*A moment, then she starts toward left.*] But gracious—when I saw that clock!

ARCHIE: Where are you going?

MARY: Home, of course.

[*He offers his arm. She takes it. They smile at each other.*]

ARCHIE: Where's "home"?

MARY: Poplar Street.

ARCHIE [*Indicating the cab*]: Let's take this.

[*Mary laughs.*]

MARY: Six blocks? Don't be silly.

ARCHIE [*Shyly*]: It's—always been a—sort of an ambition of mine to take a girl home in a cab—a—an *open* cab. [*She stares at him. He smiles engagingly.*] You'd—I'd appreciate it ever so much, if you would.

MARY: But there's no one to—[*The horse drags himself to his feet.*] Please don't get up. [*To* ARCHIE] But there's no one to drive the beast.

ARCHIE [*Eagerly*]: I know the cabby. He's a friend of mine. He's probably just stepped into a saloon. *I* can find him.

[MARY *eyes the horse distrustfully.*]

MARY: —And leave me alone with that monster? Not on your life. —Have you got a watch?

ARCHIE: Yes.

MARY: We'll wait ten minutes for the cabby to come. Then we'll walk. [*She seats herself upon a beer box against the restaurant wall.*] Um—this is pleasant. I like gutters. I was practically raised in one. We'll wait eleven minutes. Here—[*She indicates a place upon another box at her side.* ARCHIE *looks at the horse, and hesitates.*] What's the matter?

ARCHIE: I suppose it's kind of foolish, but I never like to sit while a horse is standing. Sort of—you know—sign of respect.

[MARY *laughs delightedly. The horse gestures graciously for* ARCHIE *to sit down.*]

MARY: You're a great jollier, aren't you?

ARCHIE: "Jollier"—?

[*He seats himself beside* MARY.]

MARY: I've never been out this late. I hope sleep finally overcomes Father.

[*The horse settles himself again and goes to sleep.*]

ARCHIE: My father's always up late. Mother says he's a prowler.

MARY: A what?

ARCHIE: A night prowler. Even after being on duty all day long, he'll prowl the streets till nearly morning. It's as if he was looking for something—something he'd lost.

MARY: Poor man.

ARCHIE: I don't think he's very happy.

MARY: Mine's terribly happy. He's a mechanical genius. I am, too, in a smaller way. I don't suppose I ought to tell you, but we're going to revolutionize the world.

ARCHIE: When, especially?

MARY: Tomorrow afternoon. [ARCHIE *laughs.*] You can laugh!—But just you stand around the streets a little tomorrow.

ARCHIE: That's my job—Any street in particular?

MARY: Up there on the Parkway. You'll see history made tomorrow.

ARCHIE: That ought to be—[*He yawns.*]—More fun than reading it.

[MARY *yawns also. The piano and violin begin another tune.*]

MARY: You sleepy, too?

ARCHIE: I am, a little.

MARY: All of a sudden.

ARCHIE: Um.

MARY: Rather pleasant sensation.

ARCHIE: 'Tis, isn't it?

MARY: Like—being—just a little bit drunk, I suppose.

ARCHIE: I don't know.

MARY: I feel it first in the back of my neck. Sleep, I mean.

ARCHIE: It's awful pretty.

MARY: What is?

ARCHIE: The back of your neck.

MARY: Is it? I've never seen it. [*A pause*] It's my ears *I* like. Look— [*She raises her hand to brush the hair back from an ear, but is too sleepy to complete the motion and lets it fall again.*]—Some other time.

ARCHIE: I'll bet they're peacherinos—Don't forget.

MARY: Remind me—[*They begin to breathe regularly, in unison.* MARY *leans against him.*] Funny—even with my eyes shut, I can see your face. [*Another pause*]—It's a funny face, even for a man. *I* like it. And I like the way you sit down—You sit down with a will.

ARCHIE: I try to do everything that way.

MARY: It must be a strain at times.

ARCHIE: I've got the constitution of the United States.

MARY: Some day you must tell me all about it.

ARCHIE: Tomorrow—may I call?

MARY: I'll be too tired. I told you I've got the world to revolutionize.

ARCHIE: The day after?

MARY: I promised to pitch quoits with friends.

ARCHIE: Thursday.

MARY: My Sunday-school class meets Thursday. [*A pause. In a far-away voice.*] Oh—I'm going under. I'm slipping—slipping. It's—ver' pleasant—verrr' pleas-ant—[*Faintly*] Cabby! Cabby!

[*A long pause. Their breathing becomes more and more regular. The music stops. Gradually* MARY'S *head sinks down upon his shoulder and his arm goes about her, as she settles against him. His other hand gropes for hers and finds it. He bends his head and rests his cheek against her brow. Then, prowling furtively along from Left, the Parkway above them, comes the figure of a sad, nervous little man of about forty, in a white duck uniform and white helmet. This is* MR. ERNEST INCH. *He stops at a point directly above them, leans on his arms upon the wall and sadly contemplates the space before his eyes.*]

MR. INCH [*Softly*]: Where's it gone to—my pretty life? Oh, what's become of it? [*A pause. Then he glances down and sees* ARCHIE *and* MARY. *He looks closely at* ARCHIE, *fumbles for his watch, brings it forth, examines it, returns it to his pocket, leans over the wall and whispers.*] Archie! [*There is no response.* ARCHIE *glances upwards, then shuts his eyes tighter.*] Son! [*Still no response. He waits an instant and whispers a little louder:*] Archie! Go home to bed.

[*Again no response. Then, after a moment,* MARY *speaks, as if from a dream:*]

MARY: "Archie," did you say your name was?

ARCHIE: Archie.

[MR. INCH *leans back from the wall and cups his chin thoughtfully in his hand.*]

MARY: Darling Archie. . . .

ARCHIE [*Rousing himself*]: What—? What's that you say?

[*The horse wakes up.*]

MARY: Never mind. Let's sleep awhile. Darling . . . darling. . . .

ARCHIE: I heard you that time! Listen! There's something I want to ask you—

MARY: Shhh! Later. Go to sleep, now. . . . [*For a long time they do not speak.* MR. INCH *stands regarding them with a troubled expression, biting his nails.* ARCHIE*'s arm brings* MARY *closer and closer to him. Except for this barely perceptible motion, they might be asleep. The horse cocks his head in their direction, and begins to roll his eyes savagely from them to* MR. INCH. MR. INCH *nervously gestures to the horse to be quiet, and the horse becomes quieter.* ARCHIE *slowly bends his head and kisses* MARY *upon the cheek. After an instant she averts her face murmuring:*] As—that was nice. . . . [*Again* ARCHIE*'s arm tightens about her, and this time she lifts her face to his.* MR. INCH *is gazing at them, spellbound.* ARCHIE *is about to kiss* MARY *for the second time, when suddenly the horse whinnies sharply.* MARY *starts, in alarm.* MR. INCH *covers his eyes with his hand, and goes off, Right.* MARY *grasps* ARCHIE*'s arm and looks fearfully behind her.*] What was it?

ARCHIE: Just the horse. [*The horse begins to paw the ground.*] He must have heard something. They hear things we don't. [*Unseen by* ARCHIE, MARY *makes a threatening gesture toward the animal.* ARCHIE*'s face is shining with joy.*] Darling—isn't it wonderful?

MARY: Oh, I don't know. Dogs smell things we don't.

ARCHIE: I mean—that we *love* each other.

MARY [*Aghast*]: That we *what* each other?

ARCHIE [*Happily*]: Love!

MARY: Well, for jumping to conclusions.

ARCHIE: What's your name? Your whole name?

MARY: Mary Todd. But—

[ARCHIE *repeats the name, as if tasting it.*]

ARCHIE: "Mary Todd." I like that—We must be married soon—When shall we be married, Mary?

MARY: How would, say, nineteen-ten or twenty do?

ARCHIE: Don't joke.

MARY [*Indulgently*]: Now, listen, child—

ARCHIE: We're engaged to be married!

MARY [*Gently*]: —And you wanted me to be the first to know. I do appreciate that. [ARCHIE *turns from her, miserably. She laughs.*] So just because two people want to kiss each other, they get married!

[ARCHIE'*s honest eyes meet hers again without wavering.*]

ARCHIE: They'll never find a better reason.

MARY: Of all the—[*Suddenly she becomes grave.*] You know, that sounds quite wise.

ARCHIE: It *is* quite wise.

MARY: You're a funny boy.

ARCHIE: I love *you,* Mary.

MARY: Tomorrow you won't.

ARCHIE: Tomorrow ten years, I shall. I'm as funny as that.

[MARY *ponders.*]

MARY: You *are* nice. And I *would* like to get married some day to a really *nice* man. [*A pause. Then, suddenly*] Listen—do you like engines?

ARCHIE: I'm afraid not. What have engines got to do with—

MARY: You don't know anything about them! I know everything about them! They're the most thrilling, exciting—

ARCHIE: I'm afraid I wouldn't care for them. It's horses I like. I love horses.

[MARY *regards him for a moment quizzically.*]

MARY: —In fact you worship the ground they walk on.

ARCHIE: Well—yes—in a way.

MARY: And in addition to worshipping it, you sweep it.

ARCHIE: That's—a form of worship, I suppose.

MARY: You *are* a great jollier, aren't you?

ARCHIE: Why?

MARY: —Telling me you're a street cleaner, and all that—

ARCHIE [*With dignity*]: —A White Wing, if you please.

MARY: Well then, a White Wing.

ARCHIE: 'Tisn't very surprising, is it?—We Inches have been White Wings for generations.

[MARY *turns quickly and grasps his arm.*]

MARY: Your name isn't Inch?

ARCHIE: Yes, it is. "Archibald Inch." My friends call me "Archie."

MARY: "A-A-Archie Inch"—

ARCHIE [*Pleased*]: That's right.

MARY: —But "Mary Todd"! Think!—"Todd." [*He looks at her wonderingly.*] My father's name's Charlie Todd.—Remember?

ARCHIE: I know a Charles Doremus—that wouldn't be him?

MARY: No, no! Father used to be your furnace man—years ago—[ARCHIE *frowns.*]—Your Mother discharged him on account of the engines he kept building in the cellar. They used to smell a little. He told me all about you once—remember your seventh birthday?

ARCHIE: I don't remember anything that happened before I was ten.

[MARY *gazes at him intently.*]

MARY: —He said that you—[*She stops abruptly, then concludes.*]—Well, something must have changed you. I don't see how you could have grown into this, from that.—Have you been a White Wing long?

ARCHIE [*With pride*]: Two years.

MARY: —But aren't you awfully young?

ARCHIE: I'm over twenty.

MARY: Dear me.

ARCHIE: I'm Chief of one of the Boulevard divisions. My cart's up there—[*He points over his shoulder to the Parkway.*] On a clear day you can see it from here. [*He ponders.*] "Charlie Todd"—[*And shakes his head.*] Nope.

MARY: He's practically the greatest man in the world.

ARCHIE: I admire greatness. Amongst us Inches it is a family tradition to be content with nothing short of genuine public achievement. Do you know anything about horses?

[MR. INCH *re-enters from Right on the Parkway, stops and listens.*]

MARY: Only the usual gossip, I'm afraid.

ARCHIE [*Obviously quoting someone*]: I hope you appreciate the important part Horse has played in the advance of Civilization. From an obscure beginning in the army and upon the farm, he has gradually become the very axis about which our social and economic life revolves.

MARY: You don't say.

ARCHIE: Yes, I do.—And directly, Mary—directly upon the heels of generations of horses, have come generations of Inches.

MARY: Good for them—

ARCHIE: —Of course the *first* Inches came over on the *Mayflower*—

MARY: But the horses—they were here already.

ARCHIE: Yes.

MARY: Father says *our* ancestors ran for the *Mayflower* and missed it.

ARCHIE: Look—here's a tintype of us taken in uniform last summer at the Lake. See?—Three generations of White Wings.

MARY: The second one must have moved.

ARCHIE: That's Papa. Cameras make him nervous. Anything that clicks suddenly.

[MR. INCH *begins to bite his nails.*]

MARY: I'll bet nothing scares Grandpa. Is he as fierce as his whiskers?

ARCHIE: He more or less founded the family.

MARY: I can easily believe it.

ARCHIE: For the second time, that is. *Re*-founded it, you might say. Yes, even after the final failure of the Inch-by-Inch Community Idea in '63—even then the old Inch Idealism still burned true. Grandfather—but probably you've heard of *him,* in connection with General Boocock's march upon Antietam.

MARY: I'm a little weak on the Civil War.

ARCHIE: For the fact that a thousand horses rode two hundred miles without leaving a single clue, one man was responsible. And that man was my grandfather—Major Philip Inch—at that time Corporal Inch.

MARY: I like Papa best. He looks sweet.

[MR. INCH *smiles faintly.*]

ARCHIE: It's a pity he's so unhappy.

[*The smile leaves* MR. INCH*'s face.*]

MARY: Is he always?

[ARCHIE *nods.*]

ARCHIE: I don't know why, exactly. Maybe it's because—Well—you see, they had hoped for a large family, but I'm an only child, Mary. I'm the last of our line.

MARY: But that's not *his* fault!

[MR. INCH*'s lip begins to quiver.*]

ARCHIE: No, maybe not. [MR. INCH *rests his head upon his arms and begins to cry softly over the wall.*] Still, he's inclined to take things personally—so we've made it a rule never to mention big families in his presence.

MARY: That's considerate, I'm sure.

ARCHIE: It avoids scenes. I hate scenes.

MARY: Do you like olives?

ARCHIE: Olives?—

MARY: I just thought I'd change the subject. [*One of* MR. INCH'*s tears splashes down upon her hand.*] Why! It's raining.

[MR. INCH *fades into the background and goes out, Right.*]

ARCHIE: No, it's not.

MARY: I felt a drop on my hand. Look—[ARCHIE *examines her hand, then gazes, puzzled, into the air. A little river of tears is now running down the Parkway wall. They rise and look at it.*] It's certainly raining up there. See there!

ARCHIE: Maybe we're just on the edge of a storm.

MARY: I wish friend cabby would come.

ARCHIE: He will.

[*She looks at him closely.*]

MARY: —A White Wing. [*Then, with decision*] Never mind—I like you anyway.

ARCHIE [*Puzzled*]: —"Anyway"—?

[*She nods, then raises her finger hopefully, in imitation of the finger of "Dr. Munyon" in the poster.*]

MARY: Look, Archie; Doctor Munyon: "There is hope!" I can save you! Come with my father and me; we've put the cart before the horse.

ARCHIE: You've done what?

MARY: Literally—cart before the horse. In fact, no horse whatever. We've dispensed with him.

ARCHIE: You know, I can't make you out at all.

[MARY *gazes for a moment full into his eyes. Then she picks up one of his hands, looks at it intently, lifts it to her lips, kisses it, and drops it again.*]

MARY: Nor can I you.

ARCHIE [*Lowly*]: Why did you do that?

MARY: —Dunno. I never know why I do things. I just do them.

[*She walks away from him toward the horse.*]

ARCHIE: I've never known a girl like you. I've never even imagined one.

[MARY *laughs.*]

MARY: Maybe I'm something new. I am!—A speed-engine on wheels! You—you're just a handsome horse, with winning ways. [*The horse stamps.*] Everything about you's as back-number as—[*She eyes the horse.*]—As your fat friend here will be when Dad and I get through with him. [*She pulls a face at the animal.*] Oh, you don't know what's coming to *you,* my Black Beauty! [*Suddenly the horse bares his teeth and makes a lunge at her. She ducks, then turns angrily and gives him a sharp blow upon the nose with her fist.*] Get away, you fool! [*She examines her knuckles.*] Well, of all the nerve.

ARCHIE [*Advancing*]: You dare hit that horse!

MARY: Did you see what he did? [*To the horse*]—Know your natural enemy, don't you? Well, here's one for Father—

[*She squares off again.* ARCHIE *leaps between her and the horse.*]

ARCHIE: Stop it! You—you suffragette—

[MARY *regards him curiously.*]

MARY: I beg your pardon. I forgot how close you were. [ARCHIE *strokes the horse.* MARY*'s irony melts into genuine pity.*] Poor you—poor Inches everywhere. Father and I—we never thought of what it will mean to *you.*

ARCHIE: What what will mean? [*The horse nuzzles against his shoulders.*] There, old fellow—it's all right. There—there—

MARY: Do you really adore them so?

ARCHIE: They're my life, Mary. [*He smiles uncertainly.*] I *might* manage to make friends with engines, if *you* would with *them.*

MARY: I don't say they're not all right in their place, you know—to make pets of, or ride on for pleasure, if you can *call* it pleasure. But they've certainly no business in the city.

ARCHIE: The city's business depends on them.

MARY: The city's for men. Father says men shouldn't depend on anything they can't make for themselves. What if all the horses in the world should get hives, or heaves, or whatever it *is* they get, and die tomorrow? Where'd we be then? We can't make horses. "Beasts of burden," your grandmother. They're the masters now. And they know it. Not much longer, though.

ARCHIE: They're terribly nice, really they are. You don't know them—[*He reaches into his pocket and brings forth a cube of sugar and hands it to her.*] Here—Please—Don't be narrow. Try it—

MARY: Sugar.

ARCHIE: Give him one.

[MARY *looks from the sugar to the horse.*]

MARY: How do you do it?

ARCHIE: —In the flat of your hand—like this—[*He feeds a piece to the horse.*] Bend your fingers back.

[MARY *thrusts the sugar under the horse's nose.*]

MARY: Here, you—sweets to the—[*The horse turns his face to her.*] Heavens! What an outlook! [*The horse stiffens.*] Niiiice Horsie—[*The horse ceases his purring.*] Here, stupid—[*The horse rolls his eyes.*] It isn't poisoned, you know. I hadn't time to poison it. [*Impatiently, she thrusts the sugar against his muzzle.*] Oh, *take* it, you ass!

[*The horse throws his head up.*]

ARCHIE: Don't call him an ass! They don't like that.

[*And indeed the horse looks very angry.* MARY *looks from him to* ARCHIE, *scornfully.*]

MARY: No—? Well he's lucky to get off that easily. My *real* opinion is that he's neither horse nor ass: he's a combination. In fact, he's—*ouch!* [*For the horse has taken advantage of this unguarded moment to seize the sugar in his mouth, and with it,* MARY*'s hand.*] Ouch! Ouch! *Ouch!* [*She beats the beast's head with her free hand. The orchestra begins to play another tune.*] Archie! Archie!

ARCHIE [*Somewhat alarmed*]: It's—it's just horseplay.

MARY [*Shrieking*]: You *chump,* you!

ARCHIE: P-please don't, Joseph. P-please don't play so roughly!

MARY: Oh! His teeth! Let go! Let *go!*

[ARCHIE *seizes the horse's jaws and tries to coax them open.*]

ARCHIE: Open! You don't know your strength, Josie. [*Still the beast holds.*] *Open,* do you hear me?

MARY: Ohhh! What *good* are you?

[*At this,* ARCHIE *throws all reverence to the winds, seizes the animal's ear, pulls his head down and fetches him a brutal kick in the stomach. The horse doubles up, stamps, relinquishes his hold upon* MARY*'s hand and lunges at* ARCHIE, *receiving a blow upon the nose, which finally stills him. He stands panting, rolling his bloodshot eyes wildly.* ARCHIE *takes* MARY *in his arms.*]

ARCHIE: Darling! Darling—

MARY [*Faintly, against his shoulder*]: It's—it's all right. Didn't hurt much.

ARCHIE: Mary—I love you so. You're my life, Mary. Your poor hand—let me see—

[*He takes the wrong hand and kisses it.*]

MARY: Here—[*She gives him the right one, he kisses it.*] His teeth are all loose. I could feel them giving. It was horrible.

[ARCHIE *binds her hand with his pocket handkerchief.*]

ARCHIE: Of course I don't want to make excuses for him. He acted unpardonably. But—but—[*Suddenly he stops, in blank horror.*] Mary!

MARY: What?

ARCHIE [*Slowly, awfully*]: I've—beaten—a horse—

MARY: Well, I should hope you had. [*Overcome with remorse,* ARCHIE *feeds a handful of sugar to* JOSEPH, *who devours it eagerly and belches his satisfaction.* MARY *moves Right.*] *I'm* going to walk home.

ARCHIE: You can't walk with that hand.

MARY: I've got feet, thanks.

[*From off Left comes the sound of a husky bass voice singing "White Wings, They Never Grow Weary."* ARCHIE *urges* MARY *into the cab.*]

ARCHIE: Get in, dear. Here's the cabby.

MARY: Ride behind *that* monster *now?*

ARCHIE: He's sorry. He'll behave. Won't you, Joseph? [*The horse turns his head from them haughtily, nose in the air. The singing draws nearer; "They carry me cheerily over the sea. Night comes, I long for my dearie—"*] Oh, *please,* dear. You must—[*She shakes her head.*] Not afraid, are you? [*She looks at him scornfully, and steps into the cab.*] There. There, *that's* right. Oh, this'll be *peachy!* [*He mounts the steps and bends over her.*] Kiss me, Mary. [*She looks at him, startled, then rises, to leave the cab.*] I said *kiss* me. [*Suddenly she throws her arms about his neck and kisses him. He laughs joyfully.*] There! You *had* to. You wanted to! You'll keep on wanting to—then you'll marry me!

MARY: No—*no!*

ARCHIE: Yes—*yes.* I can't ever lose you, now. You may think I can, but I can't. Remember what I said: "They'll never find a better reason!" Oh, Mary—*say* you'll marry me!

MARY: How can I? I don't love you.

ARCHIE: Then—tell me the kind of fellow you think you *might* love.

[*She regards him thoughtfully.*]

MARY: Tomorrow—-where'll you be about six?

ARCHIE: We're going to take in a new member tomorrow. After work we'll meet up there on the Parkway for the ceremony.

MARY: Look for me at six.

ARCHIE: Yes, yes! But tell me what I asked you: the kind of fellow—

MARY: —Maybe somebody who would drop everything and—follow my father. I think I might grow very fond of *him*.

ARCHIE: Where's your father going?

MARY: I told you! To put the cart before the horse. [*Impulsively*] Oh, *Archie,* what a chance! What a chance for any one!

ARCHIE [*Bewildered*]: But—

MARY: Tomorrow.

[HERBERT, *the cabby, enters along the Parkway, from Left, in a long coat and a brilliant papier-mâché topper. Extremely rosy of complexion and teetering slightly, he continues to roar his song: "I sppppreead out my White Wings, and—"*]

ARCHIE: Herbert, is that you?

[HERBERT *stops dead in his tracks and focuses.*]

HERBERT: Well, if 'tisn't the Chief!

[*The horse begins to wag its tail joyfully.*]

ARCHIE [*Severely*]: Are you the worse for liquor?

[HERBERT *descends the steps into the Boulevard.*]

HERBERT: The worse? Hunnerpercen the better, if you ask me. [*He does a brief clog step, then whips off his topper.*] Seen my new hat? [*He shows it, proudly.*]—Made of chewed-up paper, varnished. New 'nvention. Sheds the wet. [*With great deliberation he spits upon the hat, wipes it with his sleeve and shows it again.*] See? Couldn't do that with a *silk* hat.

MARY: Let's *start!*

HERBERT: Presently, Miss. [*To* ARCHIE] I said to your grandpa this morning: "Major," I said—

ARCHIE: We're in a hurry!

HERBERT: This modern generation! Where will you stop?

MARY: *When* will we *start?*

HERBERT: Presently, Miss, presently—with the help of God.

[*He unfastens the horse's weight, places it upon the floor below his seat and disdaining* ARCHIE'*s help, with difficulty mounts the box and takes the reins.* ARCHIE *seats himself beside* MARY. *The horse cranes his neck wildly toward them.*]

HERBERT: Cllck—cllck—Giddap! [*The horse does not move.* HERBERT *flaps the reins against his back.*] Giddap, I say!

[*The horse plants his feet, snorting.*]

MARY: Ninny! What's your whip for?

HERBERT: Hush, lady. Don't mention whips. That's Mr. Inch with you.

ARCHIE [*Coldly*]: Well?

HERBERT [*Whispering*]: 'S a ver' spirited animal, sir. Got pure stallion blood in 'im. [*Coaxingly*] C'mon now, Josie-boy. Don't make Herbert speak to you again. Cllck! [*The horse stamps, again craning his neck in* MARY'*s direction.* HERBERT *whispers, this time to* JOSEPH.]—This is really embarrassing. What will our fares think of you? Giddap, Josie!

[*The horse plants his feet more firmly.* HERBERT *turns to* ARCHIE.]—He acted like this once before, when I had a murderer inside 'n didn't know it. *He* knew, though.

MARY: —And he knows now.

[*She rises but* ARCHIE *forces her into the seat again.*]

ARCHIE: Please—[*He swings himself over the dashboard onto the box.*] Give me the reins. [*He takes the reins from* HERBERT *and pulls them taut.*] Cllck, cllck!

[*No result.* ARCHIE, *in growing anger, saws the bit back and forth.*]

ARCHIE: Now gittap! *Gittap,* I say! [*The horse neighs cynically.* ARCHIE *rises furiously, seizing the whip.*] Will you *move!*

[*He gives the beast one savage lash across the back and he begins to move slowly Left, trembling and snorting.*]

HERBERT [*Shocked*]: Why, *Mr.* Inch!—after all he's done for you—

ARCHIE: Shut your trap, or I'll kick you out. [*Between his teeth, to* MARY] Poplar Street, did you say?

MARY: A hundred and one.

[ARCHIE *flaps the reins and the horse begins to move faster.* MARY *sits forward on the seat, straight as a ramrod.* HERBERT *lifts his head and bawls his song, as they drive off.*]

HERBERT:

"Whiiiite Wings, they nevvur grow weeeary,
They carry me cheerilee ovvur theee sea—
Night comes, I long for my dearieeeeee,
I spprreead out my whiiiite wingssss
An' fly-ee 'ome t' theeeee."

CURTAIN

■ ACT II ■

Scene One

The Parkway, just before six o'clock the following evening. The scene is the reverse of the scene of Act I. In the background are the buildings of a placid, rather attractive little city. In the sky, a pattern of clouds.

The Parkway is a continuous asphalt pavement from Left to Right, with a two-foot stone wall at back. At Left, against this wall, is the rear of the second-story of "The Elite." Also at Left, is a short flight of stone steps, leading down to the Boulevard.

The Parkway is empty, although the head and shoulders of HERBERT *are visible above the Parkway wall, as he dozes upon his box in the Boulevard.*

After a moment the sound of wheels is heard approaching from off Right, and MR. INCH *comes in, pushing his little red cart ahead of him, biting his lip and staring into space. He wears a white duck uniform and a white helmet. Up and down the left sleeve of his jacket runs an entire column of service stripes. The cart is marked in white with a large D.S.C. and his number "2." It contains broom, brush and shovel.* MR. INCH *runs the cart absently into the curb, leans back against it, takes off his helmet and disconsolately mops his brow.*

MR. INCH: Oh, dear—

[*He stands there staring at the pavement, shaking his head sadly. The sound of rapid feet is heard from off Left, and* MARY *comes running in, hatless, and carrying a can of oil. She passes* MR. INCH, *then stops, turns and faces him. For a moment they gaze at each other silently.* MARY *smiles.* MR. INCH *returns her smile uncertainly.*]

MARY: Hello.

MR. INCH: Hello.

MARY: You're Mr. Inch, aren't you?

MR. INCH: Yes.

MARY: That's nice.

[MR. INCH *points to the oilcan.*]

MR. INCH: What you got there?

MARY: Here?

MR. INCH: Yes.

MARY: Oil.

MR. INCH: What for?

MARY: Oh—oiling things.

MR. INCH: That's nice.

[*They gaze at each other for another moment, smiling. Then:*]

MARY [*Singsong*]: Well, good-bye—

[MR. INCH *makes a stiff little gesture.* MARY *turns and runs off Right. Gradually the smile leaves* MR. INCH'*s face. He seats himself upon the curbstone, takes from a bag attached to his cart a cake of sapolio, a can of water, a small brush and a cloth, and begins listlessly to polish his shovel. After a moment he stops, and sits staring in front of him again, a picture of misery.* ARCHIE *comes pushing his cart in hastily from Right. He is dressed as his father, but with an insignia upon his helmet, and only two service stripes upon his sleeve.*]

ARCHIE: Hello, sir! You're ahead of time. I suppose you've heard it's practically settled about Clyde.

MR. INCH: We're really going to take Clyde Sims on the Force?

ARCHIE: This afternoon—provided, of course, there's no hitch in the final proceedings. I don't look for any. He wrote an excellent paper and has qualified perfectly both in straightaway sweeping, and going around lampposts.

MR. INCH: Oh, dear, oh, dear.

ARCHIE: What's the matter, sir? You aren't worried about *him?*

MR. INCH: Yes, I am!—Aw, Archie—we'd oughtn't to take on a new man, really we'd oughtn't. And Clyde's too young—he doesn't know his own mind yet—a boy just out of college.

ARCHIE: But his name has been up for years!

MR. INCH: He'd ought to have stuck to the Law, like his father and grandfather.

ARCHIE: The professions are hardly to be compared, Papa.

MR. INCH: He'll never make a White Wing—never in this world.

ARCHIE: On the contrary, he has a genuine talent for it.

MR. INCH: Well, I hope he fails in his test, that's what I hope!

ARCHIE [*Reprovingly*]: Why, Father—

MR. INCH: I do!—Oh, I know the glamor our life has for outsiders—but I'm talking from the inside—the way way in inside. [*A brief pause*] I can't face him. I wish I was some place miles away from here.—I wish I was in Madeira, there's where I wish I was.

[ARCHIE *frowns, puzzled.*]

ARCHIE: Madeira?

MR. INCH: I was reading my Baedeker last night in bed. Baedeker, bed—[*He smiles, foolishly.*] Beddie—bye, Baedeker—

ARCHIE: Don't be silly, Papa—Has anyone been along here looking for me?

MR. INCH: No—One thing about Madeira struck me particularly.

ARCHIE: What?

MR. INCH: There—there aren't any horses there. Archie, I think I'd rather work in Madeira.

ARCHIE: It must be a primitive place. They use oxen, don't they?

MR. INCH: Well, it would be a little change.

ARCHIE [*Good-humoredly*]: Change, change! You're forever talking about change.

MR. INCH: Horses, horses—I'm forever following horses—twenty years. You get sort of sick of 'em after twenty years—And all day today they've been acting so queerly. It's enough to drive a man crazy.

ARCHIE: You're just tired and nervous. Come, sir—brace up!

MR. INCH: It's them that are nervous about something. Twice I was nearly stepped on, and three of 'em bit at me.

ARCHIE: Maybe there's a thunderstorm coming. They get them hours before we do.

MR. INCH: There's *something* in the air. *That's* sure—And I think it's more than a thunderstorm. [*A brief pause*] I know the boy's father. Cornelius Sims was a fine man. I can't see Clyde do it—I can't! I can't!

ARCHIE: Shh! The cabby will hear you.

MR. INCH: I don't care!—Anyway, he's asleep.

ARCHIE: I don't pretend to understand your attitude, but if you don't like your vocation, why not leave it?

MR. INCH: Your mother—Archie, since she married me, that woman's been more of a White Wing than the White Wings.—And your grandfather—you know how the Major feels—Nope—I can't do it.

ARCHIE: At least you *can* stop criticizing the Service in public. Coming from you—an Inch—think of the effect on the man in the street.

MR. INCH: Listen, Son; when you were a little chap of seven I heard you say to your mother and the Major that sooner than be a White Wing, you'd—

ARCHIE: I am quite content with *my* lot, thank you.

MR. INCH: I don't know what became of that little boy. *He* wasn't content with anything. I had high hopes for that little boy. Life's funny—

ARCHIE: Life's *great!*

MR. INCH: You mean you think it's going to be.

ARCHIE: I *know* it will be.

MR. INCH: The picture man says "See the pretty birdie!—Hear him peep!"—But there isn't ever any pretty birdie—it's a lie, to keep you quiet—You look, though—and you listen—

ARCHIE: Well—?

MR. INCH: —What you see, is a black cloth and a round eye. What you hear is a click, and a sliding sound.

ARCHIE: It won't be that way for me, nor for Clyde, either.

MR. INCH: Oh, I hope not! [*He sighs.*]—I thought I'd find pretty birdies all through my life—[*He turns away.*]—I've found sparrows.

ARCHIE [*Shocked*]: Father!

MR. INCH: —But I look! I keep looking—

ARCHIE: Yes, and you'll find them yet.

[MR. INCH *shakes his head.*]

MR. INCH: —They're never in the same place twice. I'm always in the same place.

ARCHIE [*Cheerfully*]: The world's moving, sir. You move with it.

MR. INCH: No, Son—nor do you. We run backwards, we Inches. It slides under our feet. We're always just where we started. [*He grasps* ARCHIE*'s arm.*] Oh, if ever you get a chance to turn round, take it, Son! Don't wait till your old legs won't run but one way. [*He shakes the arm.*]—Pretty birdies, ahead, Archie! Behind—sparrows, sparrows—

[ARCHIE *laughs nervously.*]

ARCHIE: Really, Papa, you're—

[MR. INCH *suddenly becomes furious.*]

MR. INCH: Don't you "really" me! [*He softens again as suddenly.*] Aw, Archie—you're just a child.—So is Clyde. Why don't you see things as they are, like children do? Why don't you call 'em their right names? [*He pronounces deliberately.*] "Street cleaners."

ARCHIE: White Wings!

[MR. INCH *stamps his foot.*]

MR. INCH: Street cleaners! Street cleaners!

[*From off Right comes the sound of approaching voices and cartwheels.* ARCHIE *takes his father's arm.*]

ARCHIE: Come along with me. The men mustn't see you like this.

MR. INCH: I don't care.—Street cleaners!

ARCHIE: Come now—come—

[*He hurries him off Left, stopping for a moment to place the cart beside his own. From Left, in single file, enter the* THREE WHITE WINGS. *They are dressed as* ARCHIE *and his father, but with varying numbers of service stripes, two of them with no insignia upon their helmets, and the third with a black derby hat in place of a helmet, and no number badge. The little red carts each contain a broom, brush and shovel, are marked with the white "D.S.C.," and numbered "51," "114," and "9."* PAUL PILLSBURY *comes first, whistling a popular song of the period. He is 35,* RALPH OTIS *is 30, and* CLYDE SIMS, III, *is 22.* PAUL *bumps his cart into place beside* ARCHIE'*s and* MR. INCH'*s.* RALPH *and* CLYDE *do the same.* CLYDE'*s cart and implements have seen very little use.*]

PAUL: Ooomph!

RALPH: What a day.

CLYDE: Gracious, it's hot.

PAUL: Do you suppose it's the heat that's started them off?

RALPH: —The horses?—Can't tell, when they get spells like this. One of 'em goes funny for some reason of his own, and the rest of 'em catch it.

[PAUL *and* RALPH *take sapolio, cloths and brushes from the bags attached to their carts, seat themselves and begin industriously polishing their shovels.* CLYDE *leans over the wall, watching the crowds pass in the street below.*]

PAUL: There was a ring around the moon last night.

RALPH: I knew a man once, and a meteor fell in his backyard. Three weeks later his grandmother died in Duluth.

[HERBERT *suddenly starts up from his box and calls to an unseen individual:*]

HERBERT: Cab? Cab, sir? [*A brief pause. Hope dies in his face. He reseats himself.*] All right. Walk.

[*Another pause.* CLYDE *leans further out over the wall, raises his derby, waves his hand, then turns to* PAUL *and* RALPH.]

CLYDE: —Mrs. Mendlessohn—My, she's got fat.

PAUL: Rubberneck.

RALPH: Stretch it.

PAUL: Throw it up and catch it.

[CLYDE *looks a little hurt.*]

RALPH: You'd better quit mashing and fix your cart. The Major's due in five minutes.

PAUL: You're not *on* the Force yet, you know.

CLYDE: I shall be this afternoon.

RALPH: Maybe.

CLYDE: I guess I got a B-plus on my paper.

PAUL: The written test is pie, compared to the oral.

RALPH: I'll never forget the day *I* came up against the Major. I thought it was back to the Bank for me.

PAUL: Better not be overconfident, Sims—or you may have to find another way to land that rich wife you're after.

CLYDE: I don't know what you mean.

RALPH: Oh, we're on to you!—You're in this job for the runaways you can stop, and nothing else.

CLYDE: That's a lie!

[RALPH *and* PAUL *laugh.*]

RALPH: —Anyway, take my advice and don't let the Chief see the way you use your instruments.

PAUL: —Shoveling against the broom—lah-dee-dah, lah-dee-dah—

CLYDE: But it's the proper way! I know it is.

PAUL: You amateurs have grand theories.

RALPH: Listen, Candidates: you may shovel against the broom in the laboratory, but in the street you brush into the shovel.

CLYDE: You're just trying to confuse me! [RALPH *shrugs.* CLYDE *becomes anxious.*] Look here: isn't this right? Broom—shovel—[*He makes a gesture of sweeping and emptying*]—dump.

[RALPH *goes through his motions.*]

RALPH: —Shovel—*broom*—dump. [*And* PAUL *through his, by way of confirmation.* CLYDE *looks off Left, then sounds a low, intense warning.*]

CLYDE: Cheese it! Cheese it, the Chief!

[PAUL *and* RALPH *throw startled glances off Left, then all quickly seat themselves upon the curbstone and begin polishing their shovels furiously.*]

HERBERT: Cab? Cab, sir? Here you are, sir—*open* cab!

[*A tense moment, then* HERBERT *smiles, leans forward, takes the blanket from his horse's back, folds it up, seizes the reins and whip and moves off Left, to the accompaniment of rumbling wheels.* ARCHIE *comes in Left, followed by* MR. INCH. ARCHIE *watches the* WHITE WINGS *silently for a moment. Then:*]

ARCHIE: Sims—

[CLYDE *looks up, inquiringly.*]

—Rub with the grain. You'll find it easier.

CLYDE: Yes, sir.

ARCHIE [*Going to him*]: You have all my best wishes, Sims.

[CLYDE *takes his hand, gratefully.*]

CLYDE: Th-thank you, sir.

[MR. INCH, *with broom and shovel, removes odds and ends from the pavement.* ARCHIE *looks out over the wall, glances at his watch, then turns to* RALPH.]

ARCHIE: Major Inch has already left Headquarters. We may expect him at any moment. Oh, Ralph—

RALPH: Yes, Chief?

ARCHIE: Has anyone inquired for me?

RALPH: I don't think so.

[*He looks to* PAUL.]

PAUL: —No. No one's been by at all.

[KIT CANARI *enters from Right, on a bicycle. He is a little older than* ARCHIE, *well-dressed, attractively homely, and with an air of being much amused with life.*]

Well—get on to the scorcher!

KIT: Hello, Archie.

ARCHIE: Hello, Kit.

KIT: How's the Spick-and-Span Brigade?

[*He dismounts, rests his bicycle against the wall, removes his trousers-guards and puts them in his pocket.*]

ARCHIE: —Men, this is my friend, Mr. Christopher Canari.

KIT: Hello, boys.

PAUL: How do you do.

RALPH [*Simultaneously*]: Glad to meet you.

CLYDE [*Simultaneously*]: Charmed, I'm sure.

[KIT *flips a cigarette butt to the pavement.* MR. INCH *sweeps it up, protesting:*]

MR. INCH: Hey! Hey!

KIT [*To* ARCHIE]: I just saw that little What's-her-name you took home last night.

[MR. INCH *prods the bicycle with his shovel.*]

ARCHIE [*Very casually*]: Oh—Nice child. Where was she?

KIT: —Hurrying down Poplar Street with a can of oil—Shouted something over her shoulder about being up here at six, to see history made.—Through with work, are you?

[*He glances into the carts.* ARCHIE *looks over the wall.*]

ARCHIE: —Afraid not—I never saw so many gigs out. It looks like a little overtime tonight!—Lord!—Is that Mother? [*He turns anxiously to* CLYDE.] Sims, I'll never forgive myself: when a final candidate receives his helmet, it is customary to—

CLYDE: —The flowers for Mrs. Inch. I know, sir. I have them.

[ARCHIE *sighs in relief.*]

ARCHIE: Thank heaven! Up, men—up!

[*Up the stairs from the Boulevard comes* MRS. FANNY INCH, *a plain and forceful woman of about forty. She is dressed in her finest and carries a parasol and a large net bag containing a new* WHITE WING*'s helmet, wrapped in tissue paper. The* WHITE WINGS *rise, uncover, and stand stiffly at attention.* MRS. INCH *goes to* ARCHIE *and kisses him on both cheeks.*]

MRS. INCH: Dear boy—

ARCHIE: This is Kit Canari, Mother.

MRS. INCH: One of the Boston Canaris?

KIT: I'm afraid not.

MRS. INCH: Never mind. Family isn't everything. [*She turns to the* WHITE WINGS, *smiling her most social smile and working her eyebrows slightly.*] Won't you sit down? [*All sit and continue their polishing except* CLYDE. MRS. INCH *turns to him.*] Well, Clyde—how does it feel?

CLYDE [*Overcome*]: Mrs. Inch—I—

MRS. INCH [*Tenderly*]: I know. I know. Don't try to say it. What a day this is for all of us. How happy your dear father and mother would be. But they know—you may be sure they know, Clyde.—Now we must see that everything about you is just letter-perfect. [*She fusses over him.*] The Major is most punctilious about details. I often say, no woman was ever more finicky. If he—[CLYDE *is staring anxiously off Left. Suddenly he starts and gasps.*]

CLYDE: —The Major! He's here!—And I've forgotten everything!

MRS. INCH: It will come back. Be calm—just be calm.

ARCHIE: Fall in!

[*The* WHITE WINGS *form themselves into a line facing front, each beside his cart, each with his broom upon his shoulder.* MR. INCH *is at the Left end of the line, with his broom against the wrong shoulder.* ARCHIE *is at the Right end, a step in advance of the others. From Left, enters* MAJOR PHILIP INCH *in a resplendent white uniform, with many service chevrons, a Phi Beta Kappa Key, and a Carnegie Medal or so. He is about seventy, distinguished in appearance, and very much impressed with himself. He carries a thin copybook with blue covers, of the sort used in college *examinations. The line of* WHITE WINGS *stiffens.* ARCHIE *gives the command.*]

'Ten-shun! [*The line becomes even more rigid. A salute is given, and returned by the* MAJOR. ARCHIE *speaks in a stilted voice, eyes straight ahead.*] Good afternoon, Grandfather.

MAJOR INCH: Afternoon. [*He bows to* MRS. INCH, *who returns his bow.*] —Fanny. [*She takes the new helmet from her bag and unwraps it. The* MAJOR *goes to* MR. INCH *and murmurs softly:*] Will you never learn? [*He changes the broom to the right shoulder, pokes* MR. INCH'*s stomach in, grunts and centers his attention upon* CLYDE.] Is this the new man?

ARCHIE: Yes, sir. Clyde Sims, Third, sir.

MAJOR INCH [*To* CLYDE]: Do you know who I am?

CLYDE: Yes, sir. Major Philip Inch, sir. I have heard of you in connection with the march upon Antietam.

MAJOR INCH [*Softening*]: It was nothing. [*To* ARCHIE] Did you tell him about my wounds?

ARCHIE: No, sir.

[MAJOR INCH *removes his helmet, advances to* CLYDE, *bows his head and parts the hair upon his scalp.*]

CLYDE [*Sympathetically*]: Tsch—tsch—tsch—

[MAJOR INCH *steps back and replaces the helmet upon his head.*]

MAJOR INCH: It was nothing. [*He opens the blue book and glances over it.*] Hum . . . hum. . . . Your paper is not bad, not at all bad. But as to the derivation of my name, "Philip," you say merely that it is from the Greek. That is hardly adequate. Well?

CLYDE: "Philos" and " 'ippos." . . .

MAJOR INCH: Meaning?

CLYDE: "The lover of a horse."

[MAJOR INCH *looks suspiciously to* ARCHIE.]

MAJOR INCH: You told him.

ARCHIE: No, sir. Really.

[*The blue book is handed to him, and is passed down the line to* MR. INCH, *who drops it into his cart.*]

MAJOR INCH [*To* MRS. INCH]: The helmet—

MRS. INCH [*In a whisper, to* CLYDE]: The flowers—

[*She gives* MAJOR INCH *the new helmet.* CLYDE *reaches into the depths of his cart, brings forth a bouquet of flowers with trailing ribbons and presents it to* MRS. INCH.]

MRS. INCH: Oh, thank you—thank you, Clyde.

[MAJOR INCH *sets the helmet upon* CLYDE*'s head.*]

MAJOR INCH: This is merely for size. You are prepared for the oral test?

CLYDE: I am, sir.

[MAJOR INCH *advances, opens* CLYDE*'s mouth and peers into it.*]

MAJOR INCH: Say "Ah." . . .

CLYDE: Ahhhhh.

[MAJOR INCH *releases him.*]

MAJOR INCH: Hum. [*He bends over, picks up* CLYDE*'s foot, gazes at the sole of his shoe, then drops it again.*] Hum. [*A brief pause*] And cough. [CLYDE *coughs.*] Any pain?

CLYDE: Not a bit, sir.

MAJOR INCH [*Suddenly*]: Who is your favorite poet?

CLYDE: Horace.

MAJOR INCH: —Character in history?

CLYDE: Paul Revere.

MAJOR INCH: —Regular Know-it-all, aren't you? Well, answer me this, if you can: If a farmer has a stud farm which produces two crops of studs per season, how many—

[*He is interrupted by the wild entrance from Left, in the street below, of* HERBERT, *in head-and-shoulders.* JOSEPH *is apparently running away with him. He is hatless, tugging at the reins, and bawling breathlessly:*]

HERBERT: Whoa! Whoa! Damn you! Whoa! *Whoa!* You crazy coot—

ARCHIE: Fall out!

[ARCHIE *and the* WHITE WINGS *fly to the wall.* KIT *follows.* JOSEPH, *crazed with fright, is doing his best to climb over the wall into the Parkway.*]

MRS. INCH: Joseph! Stop that! What are you thinking of?

HERBERT: Git down, you! Hey! Git *down!*

MAJOR INCH: Drop that whip!

[JOSEPH *is finally quieted without further recourse to the whip.*]

PAUL: What happened?

HERBERT: —There on Elm Street—red buckboard—someone's unhitched the horse—it was coasting along by itself.

[PAUL *grunts.*]

KIT: No wonder your plug was scared.

HERBERT [*In an awestruck voice*]: —And they was people in it—man and young woman.

MRS. INCH: —No one we know, I hope.

CLYDE: Gracious—weren't they simply panicky?

HERBERT [*More awesomely still*]: They was laughing—[*Then, vindictively*] But maybe by this time—[*With relish*]—Maybe that laugh's stilled forever.

ARCHIE [*Sharply*]: How could—how could a carriage coast on *Elm* Street? It's flat as your hand.

HERBERT: Then somebody 'gin it one hell of a shove.

KIT: Elm near Poplar?

HERBERT: Just round the corner. [*Suddenly* KIT *snaps his fingers excitedly and runs off Left.*]—An' Josie wasn't the only one it scared, neither. Altogether, I saw six bolt.

CLYDE: Six! That's a *lot*. Someone ought to—

MAJOR INCH: Fall in! [*The* WHITE WINGS *obey. But suddenly something in the Boulevard below catches the* MAJOR*'s eye. He freezes in his tracks, his eyes bulging. Distant shouts are heard off Right. The* MAJOR *gasps:*] Oh, my God!

[*The shouts and general confusion come nearer. The* WHITE WINGS *stand at attention, all eyes forward.*]

ARCHIE [*In measured tones*]: What—is—it—Grandfather—?

[*The* MAJOR *does not answer. Instead, he braces himself against the wall and gazes down into the street. Dogs bark, women scream, the pandemonium increases.* HERBERT *is having a difficult time holding his horse, for at least three runaways are taking place.*]

MAJOR INCH: My God. My God.

[MR. INCH *passes a nervous hand across his forehead. He is breathing hard. Suddenly, through the uproar, a steady "chug-chug" makes itself heard. Then*]

ARCHIE [*Sharply*]: Fall out!

[*In an instant the line breaks and the* WHITE WINGS *are staring over the wall,* MR. INCH *endeavoring to push through them into a place.*]

MR. INCH: What is it? What is it?

RALPH: Heavens alive!

[PAUL *whistles his astonishment.*]

MRS. INCH [*Simultaneously*]: Mercy! Mercy on us!

MRS. INCH: I want to see! I want to see! [ARCHIE *turns and he and* RALPH *lift him up on their shoulders.*] Why—why, it's coasting *up hill!*

MAJOR INCH: Don't be ridiculous.

MR. INCH: But look, Papa, look!

MRS. INCH: I've seen that man before.

MR. INCH: Why, it's Charlie Todd! [*He pulls his hat off and waves it excitedly.*] Hi, there! Hello, Charlie!

[*The* MAJOR *reaches up and drags him to the ground.* ARCHIE *stands like a statue, staring fixedly into the street.* MR. INCH *endeavors again to get through the line to the wall, but without success.*]

MRS. INCH: He's got a young girl with him.

[*All eyes are now turned toward the Right.*]

MAJOR INCH: It's—it's turning up here!

[ARCHIE *wheels about suddenly.*]

ARCHIE: Men—fall in!

CLYDE: There's a runaway nobody's paying any attention to!

[*He's about to vault the wall.*]

ARCHIE: Sims!—Did you hear me? [CLYDE *reluctantly falls in.* MR. INCH *springs into his place at the wall.*] Inch!

MAJOR INCH: I'm in command. You forget yourself.

ARCHIE: Fall in, I say! [*The* MAJOR *falls in.* ARCHIE *turns to* MR. INCH.] Inch! [MR. INCH *falls in. The line is now complete.*] Left wheel! [*The line wheels and forms a cordon across the road.*] Still pond! [*The line halts.*] No more moving!

[*There is an anxious pause.*]

MR. INCH: I—I'm not happy here.

CLYDE: We'll die like rats.

ARCHIE: Shut up!

MR. INCH: My heart's going like anything.

[*The uproar from below diminishes, but the steady "chug-chug" increases ominously in volume from the Right.*]

ARCHIE: Steady, men. Keep your line! Stand your ground! Don't budge!

[*The line stands firm. At last, from Right, in chugs the first horseless carriage, with* MR. CHARLIE TODD, *a cheery individual of about forty-six, smiling his elation at the steering-bar. Beside him sits* MARY, *her head proudly in the air.* MAJOR INCH *pipes out:*]

MAJOR INCH: Stop!

MR. TODD: Oh, I can, easily. All you do is this—[*He reaches for a lever, and with a grinding of brakes the buggy halts.* MRS. INCH *screams in alarm, and the line of* WHITE WINGS *breaks.* MR. TODD *smiles indulgently upon* MRS. INCH.]—Keep your shirt on, Mrs. Inch. I warned you of this years ago.

MRS. INCH: Then it is Charlie Todd—Todd, the furnaceman!

[MR. TODD *rises from his seat and bows.*]

MR. TODD: Clinkers painlessly removed. [*He claps his hands together and begins a spiel in the manner of a circus barker.*] *Now* then, Ladies and Gents, gather right around. Step right up, Ladies and Gents, Gents and Ladies—view the horseless buggy—the automatic buckboard—see the wunnerful, maaahhh-veelous, in-cred-i-ble, mee-rackelous manner 'n' wich this modern little gig skips along without a hoss. Hear her snort an' snap an' stutter! Watch her skip an' scat an' scutter! Someone asks what makes her go? Well, 'neath the seat, upon a treadmill walk ten thousand young red ants! In my hand I hold a pepper pot of Potter's Best Red Pepper! The more pepper I give 'em, the faster they go! The more—

MRS. INCH: Charlie Todd, you aren't being open with us.

MR. TODD: Why, Mrs. Inch, I'd no more try to deceive a lady like you, than I'd slit my own mother's throat. Why, I'd sooner—

[*He touches something and the buggy jumps forward.*]

KIT: That's the ticket!

MRS. INCH [*Simultaneously*]: Heavens save us, Jefferson Davis!

[*She retreats.*]

MR. TODD: Pardon me, ma'am, but your placket's open.

[*She clutches at it.*]

MR. INCH [*Admiringly*]: Is it your own invention, Charlie?

MR. TODD: A fellow in Rochester—he got his patent in first.

MARY: Wouldn't that jar you?

MR. TODD: Yes— but mine *runs.* So patents be damned!

MARY: Look and wonder, People, 'cause we can't stay long.

MR. TODD: Nope—can't stay long. Restless little buggy, this—

MARY: —Won't stand still.

MR. TODD: Won't stand still.

MAJOR INCH: "Horseless"? Horseless hell, sir! *We* know the horse is somewhere!

MR. TODD: —Just the point, Major—

MARY: —From now on, the horse is nowhere!

[*She is looking at* ARCHIE, *who stands like a graven image.*]

KIT [*To* ARCHIE]: Right!—Horse is nowhere from now on.

MARY: —And a good thing, too.

MR. INCH: You don't like horses?

MARY: I hate horses!

[*An awful pause, Then*]

MAJOR INCH [*Heavily*]: God forgive you, child.

PAUL: It's a crazy-looking little dingus.

CLYDE: Horrid color.

RALPH: Umph! Smells to heaven!

MRS. INCH: *I* noticed that, too.

MR. TODD: You didn't!

MRS. INCH: I've got a nose. It's an affront.

MR. TODD: —Just the place for it. [*She turns from him, insulted.*] Oh, Mrs. Inch—[*She glances over her shoulder.*]—Placket. [*She arranges it once more.*]—Still living in the same place, Mr. Inch?

MR. INCH: Same old place, Charlie.

[PAUL, RALPH *and* CLYDE *are examining the vehicle curiously.*]

MR. TODD: —I can see it now—the iron deer in the front yard—that back parlor, where Mrs. Inch used to call down the register: "Oh, Mr. Todd! Mr. Toh-od! Will you send up a little more heat?"—And those ancestors on the walls, all in uniform. The biggest of the lot was the Major himself—and on horseback, at that—where'd you get that horse, Major?

MAJOR INCH: I rented it.

MR. TODD [*To* MARY]: —The portrait is entitled "Philip E. Inch, on his Favorite Mount, 'Esquire.' "

MAJOR INCH [*Stiffly*]: I was founding a family. I knew what was proper.

MR. TODD [*To* MARY]: —A speaking likeness—he has a *beautiful* seat.

MAJOR INCH: I have heard it said that one would think I was part of the horse.

[MARY *laughs suddenly.*]

MR. TODD: Hush, my dear—this is no time for fooling. [*He descends from his perch to the pavement.*]—Nice job, eh, Mr. Inch?

MR. INCH: D—Does it go fast?

MARY: Well, I *started* with a hat on.

[*She gets out of the auto-buggy and faces* ARCHIE, *triumphantly.*]

MR. TODD: —Speed? [*Gloating*] We passed Willie Tittman's mare!

MARY: Well, what do you think of it, Archie?

ARCHIE: I—It's—

[*He cannot go on.*]

MR. INCH: —But what does make it go?

MR. TODD: —Not oats. *That's* sure. No—nor red pepper. Gasoline, that's what—gasoline and erl—

MARY: Oil.

MR. TODD: Erl.

MARY: Oil.

MR. TODD: Erl.

KIT [*Echoing*]: —Gasoline and erl.

[*There is an awful silence, as the import of this sinks in. Then the* MAJOR *demands hoarsely:*]

MAJOR INCH: Men—if this thing succeeds, do you know what it means for us? [*The* WHITE WINGS' *faces become very grave. He concludes.*] —It means extinction.

[MR. INCH *is endeavoring to keep his feet from dancing.*]

ARCHIE: But it won't succeed!

MARY [*Flaring up*]: Who says it won't?

ARCHIE: —An impersonal machine—it can never in this world supplant a noble creature like the horse.

MR. TODD: Can't, eh?

MARY: Watch it!

MR. TODD: Good-bye, you fine sorrels! Good-bye, you sleek roan mares! You hacks, you plugs, you pacers!

MARY: Charlie Todd's done for you!

MR. TODD: God be with you in the boneyard!

MRS. INCH: Take your blasphemies out of our sight!

MR. TODD: Why, Mrs. Inch!—You wouldn't let a mere economic revolution come between *us?* [*She turns away. He continues gleefully.*] Oh, we'll build 'em little and we'll build 'em big! The streets'll be full of 'em! We'll build palaces on wheels, and we'll build cottages! By God, we'll build tin shacks for the men who lug dinner pails!

KIT [*To* ARCHIE]: You know, it's so crazy it must be true.

ARCHIE: But it isn't true. It can't be true.

MR. TODD: Archie, I can't understand you at all. Of course, I do remember that as a kid no bigger than that, you did use to run around the back parlor in a white-duck suit, after a wooden horse named Dobbin your papa pulled on a string—

MR. INCH: Easy there, Charlie.

MR. TODD: —With a big pair of paper wings hitched onto your shoulders. But that was before you'd ever seen the real White Wings at work. You thought they were marvelous beings that soared up and down the Boulevard, over the horses' heads, beating up a breeze that kept the city spick and span.

MR. INCH: —Fanny and the Major. They let him think it.

MR. TODD: —But that was only until your seventh birthday, when as a great treat, your grandpa took you out to see them actually at it.

MR. INCH: Charlie—

MRS. INCH: As if a child's mistake mattered now.

MR. TODD: —When I saw you streaking back down the street with the Major hot after you, I came upstairs. There was your mother waiting for you with a lovely birthday present—a shiny little cart, and a tiny broom and shovel. Well, you didn't say much when you saw 'em. You couldn't, you were crying so hard. But the Major got the pieces of that shovel straight in the stomach and Dobbin you kicked clear across the room into a bowl of goldfish. You seem to have changed, Archie.

MR. INCH: It's education did it. Fanny and the Major.

[ARCHIE *looks at them.*]

MRS. INCH: We gave him the best there was in us. He learned once more to respect tradition and love horses.

MAJOR INCH: We spared no effort to make him every inch an Inch.

MRS. INCH: Yes, and we succeeded!

MR. TODD: Wonderful thing, education. [HERBERT *spits deliberately over the wall into one of the carts.*] Listen, Archie, I'm going to manufacture these buggies on a big scale; eventually I aim to turn out two a month. That'll take capital. Tomorrow morning early we leave on a tour to find it. I want someone to go along—someone who looks so far ahead he can't see the horizon. Mary says you're my man. Will you come with us?

ARCHIE: Thank you. Thank you very much. But I can't.

[MRS. INCH *and* MAJOR INCH *draw breaths of relief.* MR. INCH *shakes his head, sadly.* MARY *shuts her eyes.*]

KIT: Can't? Well, of all the poor lobsters! *Why* can't you?

ARCHIE [*After a moment*]: —Because I don't believe in it.

[MR. TODD *glances at* MARY. *She averts her head.* ARCHIE *looks at his feet.*]

MR. TODD: I'm sorry you don't, Archie. I'm very sorry. I hoped you would.

ARCHIE: It's the horse I believe in.

[KIT *advances eagerly.*]

KIT: Will you take me, sir? I'm Kit Canari. I'd go to hell in that gig.

[MR. TODD *hesitates.*]

RALPH [*Growling*]: Bet you would. Damned cigarette smoker.

MARY [*Sharply, painfully*]: Take him!

MR. TODD [*To* KIT]: Five-thirty in the morning. Hundred and one Poplar.

MARY: Let him come along now.

KIT: Bye-bye, Archie. You can have my bicycle. [*To* MR. TODD] All right, sir. Any time you're ready.

[MR. TODD *cranks. The auto-buggy starts feebly, then stalls dead.*]

MR. TODD: Hum.

PAUL [*Without a smile*]: Ha-ha.

[MR. TODD *scratches his head.*]

MR. TODD: Perhaps the gasoline. [*He peers into the gasoline tank.*] Plenty of gasoline. [*He begins to crank again.*] Oh, yes! The erl—

[*He crawls under the car.*]

CLYDE: Isn't he agile!

[MR. TODD *re-emerges from beneath the car, his face smudged and unhappy.*]

MR. TODD: Lots of erl.

MRS. INCH: Apparently.

MR. INCH [*Reflectively*]: No waste products.

MAJOR INCH: Oh—Herbert—

HERBERT: —A little towin' job? Sure! *I* ain't proud.

[*He takes the reins and prepares to come to the rescue.* MR. TODD *cranks again, without results.* MAJOR INCH, MRS. INCH *and the* WHITE WINGS *look intensely pleased.*]

RALPH: It's simply shot its bolt.

MR. TODD: Probably needs a new mainspring.

PAUL: Drag it off.

HERBERT: Horseless wagon! That's good, that is! [*He laughs.*]—Only you better get a horse.

PAUL: Yea! Get a horse!

RALPH *and* CLYDE: Get a horse!

[HERBERT *and his cab move off Right in the Boulevard below.*]

ARCHIE: Here, Mr. Todd—let me.

MARY [*Sharply*]: No! No! He shan't touch it!

[KIT *advances.*]

KIT: Give me a try, sir.

[*He spins the crank. There is a faint chug-chug.*]

MR. TODD: That's it! Now we've got it. [*But the chugging dies.*] That—that sounded final.

MARY: Oh, hell.

MAJOR INCH: Oh, Todd—

MR. TODD [*Impatiently*]: What? What?

MAJOR INCH: I've called a cab. Just in case.

KIT: Don't be discouraged, sir. As big a thing as this, you know—it's bound to take time.

MR. TODD: Yes—yes, of course.

[MARY *has taken a coil of rope from the front of the auto-buggy. She turns contemptuously to* ARCHIE.]

MARY: Good-bye, you—

ARCHIE: Mary—Oh, this can't make any *real* difference!

MARY: I hope you'll be comfortable, in your casket. [*She turns away.*] Sympathy from a friend.—Get in, Father. Canari and I will tie it.

[MR. TODD *mounts the buggy and takes the steering bar.* MARY *and* KIT *tie one end of the rope to the back axle. The cab backs in from Left, and is brought to a halt in the proper position.*]

HERBERT [*To the horse*]: That's right. Now just hold that.

[KIT *and* MARY *fasten the other end of the rope to the cab axle.*]

MAJOR INCH: Can you take us, as well, Herbert?

HERBERT: Get right in, Major—you'll give Josie confidence.

MAJOR INCH: Fanny—

[*He hands* MRS. INCH *in and takes his seat beside her.*]

MRS. INCH: I could see at once it wasn't practical.

MAJOR INCH: Supplant the horse, indeed!

HERBERT: Ready there?

KIT: Go ahead.

[*With a great flourish,* HERBERT *cracks his whip, the cab starts, and slowly the entire caravan begins to move off Left,* HERBERT *upon the box, the* MAJOR *and* MRS. INCH *in the cab, the auto-buggy, with* MR. TODD *sitting grimly at the steering bar, and on foot behind it,* MARY *and* KIT. ARCHIE *watches the departure sadly, the* WHITE WINGS *with delight—*CLYDE *shouts after them:*]

CLYDE: Come again, some day!

PAUL: Only bring your own horse!

RALPH: Yea! Get a horse!

[*Only* KIT *and* MARY *are now left in view.* KIT *takes* MARY*'s arm comfortingly through his. She turns and confronts the* WHITE WINGS.]

MARY: You!—You *sparrows*—

[*A brief silence. Then*]

CLYDE [*Gently*]: Get a horse?

[MARY *and* KIT *follow the auto-buggy off, and the* WHITE WINGS *follow them, calling in louder and louder chorus:*]

WHITE WINGS: Get a horse! Get a horse! Get a horse!

[ARCHIE *and* MR. INCH *are left alone in the street, looking after them.*]

CURTAIN

■ ACT II ■

SCENE TWO

The Parkway about seven o'clock of an autumn evening several years later. The city in the background has undergone several changes and taken on something of the appearance of a manufacturing town, but the pattern of clouds in the sky has not changed. A long window has been cut in the back wall of "The Elite." As it grows darker in the course of the scene, this window is illuminated by a bluish light, from a mercury lamp within the building, which is now a garage. The Parkway is illuminated by a segment of light cast by an offstage arc light, nearby, at Left. Against the Parkway wall stand three little red carts, each with its broom, brush and shovel. HERBERT'*s cab stands in its old place in the Boulevard, but* HERBERT, *now somewhat dilapidated, is seated upon the wall, whip in hand.*

At Right, directly in the middle of the Parkway, a square has been roped off around what appears to be the unfinished foundation for a monument of some sort. A lighted red lantern warns of danger here.

HERBERT *is telling a story to* JOSEPH, *who listens sympathetically, his head lifted into full view from behind the wall.*

HERBERT: "—An' have you got a ca-ar?" asks Mike. "Shure!" says Pat. "What make is it?" asks Mike. "I ca-al it 'Teddy'," says Pat. "Why 'Teddy'?" asks Mike. [*He leans over the side of the cab, spits into the street, wipes his mouth with the back of his hand, and chuckles.*] "Because," says Pat, "because it's the Roughest Rider ivver was ma-ade!" [*From* JOSEPH *comes a long-drawn gurgling whinny of pleasure, a horselaugh, in which* HERBERT *joins. Then* JOSEPH *makes an interrogation, to which* HERBERT *responds.*]Yeah-eh—I know *your* parlor-stories! [*A narrative neighing begins, with pauses and inflections.* HERBERT *listens attentively.*] *Yea-eh*—[*More neighing.* HERBERT *nods.*] Yea-eh—[*More neighing.* HERBERT *interrupts.*]—In a band, you mean?—Or with a line o' goods? [*An explanatory neigh, then a narrative one.* HERBERT *interrupts again.*]—Springfield, *Massachusetts?* [*A short neigh, then the narrative continues, with many suggestive inflections.*] *With* a bath? [JOSEPH *replies in the affirmative.*]

—And what did *she* say? [JOSEPH *concludes his story.*] Oh, Josie! Josie! [*Both* HERBERT *and* JOSEPH *laugh with great relish.*] Well, you certainly get the brass ring, Josie. [*He pushes* JOSEPH*'s head down, controls his mirth and wipes his eyes.*] My oh me. My oh me. Times has changed, Josie—changed cruel. [*He becomes a little sad.*] Yea-eh —we got plenty o' time to sit around crackin' jokes now. Six fares in two days. Six fares. [*He sighs.*] My oh me. My oh me. Remember when—? Oh, well—[*A pause. He begins listlessly to play with his whip, finally attempting, with a weak gesture, to crack it. It does not crack. He tries again—and again. It does not crack. He lets the end drag forlornly over the side, drops his head upon his breast, and sighs again.*] My oh me. [*A pause, then*] What's o'clock?

[*A hoof is heard to tap seven times upon the pavement.*]

HERBERT: —Seven. Yep—there's the lights—[*The arc light comes on, off Left.*] We'll wait awhile longer. Nights like this brings 'em out. [*He takes the butt of a cigar from his hat and lights it. From Left,* MR. INCH *enters, bearing a block of marble in his arms. He crosses with it to the foundation and rests it there, panting.* HERBERT *speaks.*] Could I help you, sir?

[MR. INCH *starts and gasps. Then*]

MR. INCH: Oh—it's only you.

HERBERT: Could I be of any help, sir?

MR. INCH: Shhh! Not so loud!—Come here—[HERBERT *descends from the wall and goes to him.*] We've got to be careful, Herbert, I'm sure they've got wind of it.

HERBERT: Who? Wind o' what? What's this place roped off for, Mr. Inch? What was you and Mr. Archie doin' here this mornin'?

MR. INCH: Shhh!

HERBERT: There's no one about, sir.

MR. INCH: You can't tell—we think they've been watching. *You're* with us, aren't you, Herbert?

HERBERT: Now as always, sir.

MR. INCH: Then help me set this in place. [*He and* HERBERT *set the block into the corner of the foundation.*] There—! Does it look straight to you?

HERBERT: Straight's a die, sir. But what is it?

MR. INCH: It's the cornerstone.

HERBERT: Cornerstone!—For what, Mr. Inch?

MR. INCH: This—[*He looks about him furtively.*]—The Major Philip E. Inch Memorial White Marble Drinking-Fountain for Horses.

HERBERT [*In awe*]: No! So that's it! Ah, what a noble notion! And right here at the very gates of the Park! What a grand situation, sir.

MR. INCH: Will it keep them out, do you think?

HERBERT: The autos? Sure, sir! Sure it will! Better than any City Ordinance ever could!

MR. INCH: The Park is our last stronghold, Herbert—we can't give up the Park without a struggle.

HERBERT: It's the real Inch spirit you have, sir.

MR. INCH: I'm so afraid they'll try to stop it some way. I hope not. This unveiling—it—it means a great deal to us, Herbert, or—or should. We've suffered reverses here lately, and the—the outlook's not favorable.

HERBERT: Oh, things'll take a turn for the better!

MR. INCH: Well, it's uncertain, at best. November oats are up four points.

HERBERT: Ah, that's terrible, terrible—

MR. INCH: We are not rich in this girl's woods—I—I—mean vice versa —and my son's last dollar—a shining new silver dollar—it went into this cornerstone, with other mementos of the Age.—And the marble columns—we couldn't afford to buy them—they're dreadfully expensive—so—so—we just took them from the family vault in Mt. Hope. I don't think they'll mind—the people who are there, I mean.

HERBERT [*Stoutly*]: It's what they would wish, sir.

MR. INCH: —And finally there was the question of the bronze horse to settle—we planned to have one to put on top, you know, but—well —ever try to buy a bronze horse?

HERBERT: No, sir—I can't say I did.

MR. INCH: You've no idea what they come to—even used ones. So—so we had to fall back on the deer in our front yard. It had a lot of antlers and things but they unscrewed and we thought that maybe with it 'way high up there—

HERBERT: You'd never know it from a horse!

MR. INCH: Wouldn't you?

HERBERT: Never in this world!

[MR. INCH *presses his arm gratefully.*]

MR. INCH: Herbert—

HERBERT: Yes, sir?

MR. INCH: Perhaps you'd like to stand with us, at the unveiling—

HERBERT: *Me,* sir?

MR. INCH: Yes.

HERBERT: Ah, 'twould be the crownin' glory of my life!

MR. INCH: Then we'll expect you here in ten minutes.

[*He moves Right.*]

HERBERT: I won't budge from the spot, sir!—And, oh, thank you, thank you, sir!

[MR. INCH *goes out.* HERBERT *cracks his whip.* KIT *enters up the steps from the Boulevard.*]

KIT: Oh, Herbert—

HERBERT: Yes, sir? Where to, sir?

KIT: How long have you been here?

HERBERT: Mr. Canari, is it?—Quite awhile, sir.

KIT: Have you seen a young lady come up, in the last few minutes?

HERBERT [*Carefully*]: On foot, would she be?

KIT: —In a car—a car with a Michigan license.

HERBERT: Nope—no Michigans today. [*Then cheerfully*] But she'll be along sir.—And wouldn't she like a nice carriage ride, later on, when the moon comes up? [KIT *is again examining the roped enclosure, and does not answer.*]—Ummm—don't it smell good, there on the river road. Ain't it still an' nice! [*Still no answer from* KIT.]—Can't drive autos in the Park, you know—City Ordinance.

KIT: Not this evening, thanks.

[HERBERT *smiles bravely.*]

HERBERT: As you like, sir.

KIT: If I were you, I'd keep off the Boulevard tonight.

HERBERT: Why's that?

KIT: It may be dangerous.

HERBERT: They can splutter all they like. Thy don't scare *us,* no more.

KIT: I'd get off it, and keep off.

HERBERT: Go hide in the Park, maybe. Cover ourselves with leaves, eh?

KIT: I particularly wouldn't go into the Park. I'd just go right home, stable my horse, and go to bed.

HERBERT: I guess *we're* all right.

KIT: Well, it's your own life.

[*A pause. Then a nervous pawing from below as a motorcar approaches with cutout wide open.*]

HERBERT: This is our reg'lar stand. We stay put. [*But* JOSEPH *retires in a panic down the street.*] Hey! stop that horse! [*He runs down the steps. The motorcar comes to a stop in the Boulevard below, and* MARY*'s voice is heard.*]

MARY: Kit?

KIT: Come on up! Quick! [MARY, *completely enveloped in a linen duster and a veil, mounts the steps.*] Mary! [*He laughs.*] It *is* you, isn't it? [*She removes the veil.*]

MARY: I've been driving since dawn. Fourteen hours. Broke my back. *I* know the sight I am.

KIT: A sight for sore eyes, that's what you are.

MARY: Sweet Kit.—But don't mention eyes. Mine won't focus. I see everything in the flat. Since Buffalo I've gone down hill rapidly. Every milestone I passed was a tombstone. Prop me up somewhere and tell me why you wired.

KIT: How does Spotless Town look to you?

[*She gazes at "The Elite."*]

MARY: There's the old Elite. Anyway, *that's* the same.

KIT: Stung! It's the Elite Garage now. *My* Elite Garage. [*She stares. He nods.*] Nothing's the same, Mary.

MARY: I feel a thousand.

KIT: Except the Inches. They remain constant.

[*A brief pause*]

MARY [*Lowly*]: Why am I here, Kit? Why did you wire?

KIT: Have you had any dinner?

MARY: No—nor lunch—hadn't time. And I need food. Kit—I'm the sort that needs her food. And I could sleep, too—[*She slumps wearily against the wall.*] Oh, *I could sleep!*

KIT: You can eat and sleep to your heart's content, when it's over.

MARY [*Impatiently*]: When what's over? *What's* over—that's what I'm asking you.

KIT: I want you to wait and see for yourself.

MARY: Your voice sounds funny. I've a feeling I should have stayed in Detroit.

KIT: To keep on dying by degrees, eh?

[MARY *laughs shortly.*]

MARY: By inches, don't you mean?

KIT: Yes, that's just what I mean, Mary.

MARY: Tell me—tell me quickly—

[KIT *indicates the roped enclosure.*]

KIT: See that?

MARY: What's it for?

KIT: On that spot, in a few moments, there'll be something decided; whether Archie quits the horses, or whether he follows 'em to the end.

MARY: Then he's still at it—

KIT: Still at it. But look—[*She looks at him. He strikes* DR. MUNYON*'s posture and raises a hopeful finger.*] "There is hope!"—You can save him. [MARY *starts and gasps.*]

MARY: Don't do that! [*She drops her face into her hands.*] I'm going dippy—

KIT: Um—for love of a man in a uniform—a white uniform. *I* know. Can't fool Kit.

MARY: But what can I do?

KIT: Wait and see what they're up to. Watch, and decide. Then if you want to stop it, I'm ready.

MARY: You didn't tell him I was coming—

KIT: Nope.

MARY: He's—never even asked for me?

KIT: Nope.

MARY: How—how does he seem?

KIT: Thin—and white. White as his uniform. They're in a desperate state, Kiddo, desperate. You can't dodge autos for ten hours a day, and—[MARY*'s exclamation of pain cuts him short.*] Sorry.

MARY: What holds him?—Is it just stubbornness, do you think?

KIT: Deeper than that. Family stuff. Faith. [*A pause.*] Mary, in the front yard of that man's mind, there stands an iron deer. [MARY *laughs bitterly.*]

MARY: Deer? Oh, no! Horse!

KIT: Anyway, if you want to get it out, you've got to blast. Tonight's the night. Now or never. Hence my telegram.

MARY [*Thoughtfully*]: —Got to blast.

[KIT *goes to the roped enclosure and takes two small rocks from the pile.*]

KIT: You'll see a ceremony here the like of which—well, I'll tell you just one thing about it: if it goes through, then at last the Inches' dream of glory is going to jell.

MARY: Jell?

KIT: Jell. Distill into a symbol. If you know Archie at all, you know that'll be the end of him.

MARY: But what can I do—? Oh, *Kit—?*

[KIT *returns to her with the rocks.*]

KIT: Just don't let it happen. Stop it. Here—[*He gives her the rocks.*] —If you think you need help, crock that arc light—[*He points to the arc light.*]—I'll be waiting in the garage for the signal—got my troops all lined up—[*He consults a slip of paper.*]—Nine Ramblers, eleven Stanley-Steamers, six Pope-Toledos, eight Wintons, three Americans—

MARY: That's plenty, plenty—

KIT: They'll pour out down below there, close ranks, and charge up around into the Parkway, along here into the Park. Once I turn 'em loose, nothing can stop 'em. They'll smash this to bits, Mary—what's left, Archie can put into his hat. So there you are—You press the button and I'll do the rest.

[MARY *glances off Left.*]

MARY: The arc light—

KIT: Just keep plugging till you hit it.

MARY: I won't miss but once—Then throw myself at his head, eh?

[KIT *grins.*]

KIT: Sure!—And rebound, maybe. [*A brief pause*]—I'll catch you if you do, Mary. [*She looks at him. He grins again.*]

MARY: Kit, you fool, you.

KIT: There should have been two of you, you know. One for me.

MARY: Oh, I *like* you so *much. Twice* as much as him.

KIT: "But"—?

[MARY *gestures helplessly.*]

MARY: But.

KIT: That's all right. I have my stamp collection. [*There is a noise of someone coming from off Right. He draws her into the shadows.*] Here they are.—I warn you now. They'll just about break your heart. Mind you don't get touched, and go soft. He's a drowning man—may struggle—brutal, kiddo, be brutal!

MARY: —Iron deer—got to blast—

KIT: —White Wings' last stand—your last chance. Well—don't cry on your dynamite.

[*He goes out, down the steps to the Boulevard.* MARY *leans back against the wall, and places the two rocks within reach at her side. A moment of silence, then* ARCHIE *hurries in from Right, carrying a folded American flag, which he places on the foundation without unfolding it. Nervously, furtively, he examines the structure to see that everything is ready. He wears his White Wing uniform, and his face is nearly as white as it.* MARY *watches him for a moment, then steps out of the shadow, and faces him. At the sound of her footstep, he turns and sees her. For an instant their eyes hold them rigid, speechless. Then, all at once, they rush together, and* MARY *buries herself in his arms, with a cry.*]

MARY: Archie!

ARCHIE: You've *come*—

MARY: Tight, you—*tight!* Oh, break my back—*break* it!

[*They kiss.*]

ARCHIE: Dear, oh, my dear—

[*She stands off from him a little, and runs her hand up and down the front of his jacket.*]

MARY: You're thin. You're so thin. Poor, poor darling—what have they done to you?

ARCHIE: Awful—it's been awful.

MARY: I know! All day long—[*In recitative*]—Nine Ramblers, 'leven Stanley-Steamers, six Pope-Toledos—

[ARCHIE *lowers his head and begins to dodge.*]

ARCHIE [*Agonized*]: Don't—don't—

[MARY *gathers him into her arms.*]

MARY: Never mind—never mind.—Mary's with you, Archie—

ARCHIE: You had to come—you missed me so—

MARY: *I* won't miss but once.

ARCHIE: It's as good as a mile.

MARY: It's a sight for sore eyes.—Dippy, I am—quite dippy.—You're so white.

ARCHIE: White's my color.

MARY: —Spotless of Spotless Town. Oh, I'm in love with a man in a uniform, me—you press the button, I'll do the rest—

[*He draws her closer to him.*]

ARCHIE: Mary—

MARY: Listen, Archie Inch: years are inches. Year by year we die by inches, inch by inch, year by year—

ARCHIE: Then let's together—it takes longer.

MARY: I don't know, I don't know.

ARCHIE: *Marry* me, Mary.

MARY: —He said you were a drowning man, Kit did—are you drowned, my dear?

ARCHIE [*Wretchedly*]: I don't know what I am.

MARY: You're a White Wing.

[ARCHIE *attempts to lift his head proudly.*]

ARCHIE: A White Wing!

MARY [*Bitterly*]: Horse power, that's what—and stalled dead.

ARCHIE: Then start me—start me!

MARY: Look, Archie—[*She raises her finger:* DOCTOR MUNYON *in the poster.*] "I can save you!"—You'll start—I can start you! [*She works his arms once, with a cranking motion, then puts her mouth against his.*] Breathe again—breathe—I'll prime you—breathe—*breathe!*

ARCHIE: Oh, marry me, Mary—marry me!

MARY [*Against his breast*]: —And you'll quit 'em, you'll quit 'em, won't you—

ARCHIE: What?

MARY: —The horses, quit the horses.

ARCHIE: How could I, dear?

MARY: Easy! Easy!

ARCHIE: But they're beautiful—you don't know! All our traditions, our—

MARY: No more of that! Hear me? [*A motorcar roars past in the Boulevard.*] There's *our* music!

[*In a blind fury* ARCHIE *wheels about from her in the direction of the noise.*]

ARCHIE: Bastards! We'll fix 'em—*we'll* show *them,* we will! [*Then, in a careful, plotting voice*] —Tonight, Mary—great event—my last dollar goes into it—make history—history! See here—Construction on Eastern Parkway—Major Philip Inch Dedicates—"Old Things Are Best," says Archie Inch in Special Interview.

MARY: New things are best!

ARCHIE: —Something old, something new—oh, *when* will you marry me, Mary?

MARY: When will you quit 'em?

ARCHIE: I can't—ever—

MARY: Then watch out—I'll rebound! [*She flings herself against him. He stands firm. She drops her face in her hands, murmuring:*]—Dippy, quite dippy—oh, catch me, catch me, someone! [*From off Right comes the murmur of voices and the sound of wheels. She looks up, suddenly.*] What's that?

ARCHIE: It's my family.

MARY [*Sharply*]: And it's me!

ARCHIE: But they're old—

MARY: —And I'm new!—I'm new and bright and shiny! [*She faces him with her hands out, offering herself, asking him to choose.*] Well?

ARCHIE: Dear, there are some things—once they're explained to you—

MARY: "Explained"!?—Oh, my poor boy—[*A brief pause*]—It's true, then, I've got to blast.

[*The sound from off Right draws nearer.*]

ARCHIE: After this ceremony's over, I'll—[CLYDE SIMS *comes in, Right, in White Wing uniform. On a wheelbarrow in front of him he wheels a large object loosely covered with a strip of burlap.* ARCHIE *points to the shadows, back Left.*]—Wait a moment back there—it won't take long.

CLYDE: All ready, Archie—here they come.

[*He stops the wheelbarrow near the foundation, removes the burlap and reveals a battered and rusty iron deer. He and* ARCHIE *lift it from the wheelbarrow, set it in place on top of the foundation and cover it with the old American flag. A procession begins to enter from Right. First come two men,* DR. BOWLES *and* DR. DERBY, *the one in clerical garb, with Roman collar, the other in cap and gown. Their faces are expressionless as masks.* CLYDE *gives them programs for the ceremony.*]

DR. DERBY [*To* DR. BOWLES]: These affairs are always late.

[DR. BOWLES *consults his watch.*]

DR. BOWLES: Shocking!

DR. DERBY: I know this costume's not suitable for the evening, but I've been so busy all day with meetings and what-not—you understand?

DR. BOWLES: Trust in God and no one will notice.

[MR. INCH *comes in and greets them quietly. Following him, in an invalid chair made from a segment of one of the little red carts, comes the old Major, in full White Wing dress-uniform, with Decorations. The chair is propelled by* MRS. INCH, *now of the shabby-genteel.* HERBERT *comes last, carrying his hat. All receive programs from* CLYDE *and group themselves near the foundation.* MR. INCH *whispers to* MRS. INCH:]

MR. INCH: I think I'm against this—it's been so dreadfully expensive, and—[MRS. INCH *glares at him.*] I've got a right to my opinion, Fanny.

ARCHIE: Are you ready, Dr. Bowles?

[DR. BOWLES *nods, advances and bows his head. All become quiet and all heads are bowed. With great unction, and a marked clerical intonation,* DR. BOWLES *begins:*]

DR. BOWLES: Jabber, jabber, jabber, jab—jabber, jabber. Jabber, jabber, jabber, jab, jab, jabberjab. [*He takes a long breath.*] Jaaaaaaaaber, jab, jabber. Jaaaaber jab—jabber. [*And concludes very impressively:*] Jabber, jabber, jabber.

[*All respond in chorus.*]

ALL: Jabber.

[*All raise their heads again.* DR. BOWLES *retires.*]

ARCHIE: The speech of acceptance is to be made by a gentleman whose reputation is known to us all: Dr. Derby—Horace Peabody Proctor, Professor of Veterinary Science and Associated Arts and Crafts. Dr. Derby!

[*He bows to* DR. DERBY, *who advances pompously.*]

MR. INCH [*To* MRS. INCH, *in a whisper*]: Isn't it in the wrong order?

[*She shakes her head vigorously.*]

MRS. INCH: Hush!

MR. INCH: —But something must have upset Archie. Archie—[ARCHIE *looks at him.*]—Upset?

[ARCHIE *shakes his head.* DR. DERBY *clears his throat.*]

DR. DERBY: Good evening all—The subject of my address was to be "Has the Horse a Soul, Like Myself"—Has he a soul?—But the fact is I hadn't time to prepare it. So I can merely thank you from—[*All find places and seat themselves. He proceeds.*] —My heart, Mr.—er —Inch—

MRS. INCH [*Whispering*]: —*Major* Inch.

DR. DERBY: —*Major* Inch—for myself, for the City, for the University, and for all lovers of the Horse, whose name is Legion.—I may say that the conclusion of my address was to be "Indeed He Has!"

[*He bows. All applaud. He retires.*]

ARCHIE: Now I have the honor to present Major Philip E. Inch, who will preside over the formal unveiling of the Major Philip E. Inch Memorial White Marble Drinking-Fountain for Horses—

[*Assisted by* MR. *and* MRS. INCH, MAJOR INCH *rises.*]

MAJOR INCH: It is nothing. As a young man with General Boocock, I was wounded in the service of the horse. In that instant I foresaw his future and determined to found a family which would follow him to the end. But I take myself no credit whatsoever for the Major Philip E. Inch Memorial White Marble Drinking-Fountain for Horses—the idea originated with my grandson Archibald, upon whose shoulders now rests the entire burden of our tradition—

MARY [*From the shadows*]: —And what a load.

DR. BOWLES: Quiet there, please.

MARY: After you, Alphonse.

DR. DERBY: Look out now, I have influence.

MARY: I've had it.

DR. DERBY: I mean I can have you arrested.

MARY: Chestnuts.

MRS. INCH: Plainly a case of the wrong training in childhood.

MARY: Chestnuts. Horse chestnuts.

ARCHIE: Go on, Grandfather.

MAJOR INCH: —My grandson conceived this Fountain as a means of shaming speed demons into the abandonment of their fiendish engines for return to the great God-given means of conveyance, Holy Horse. [*All, except* MARY, *uncover,* MRS. INCH *unpinning her hat. The* MAJOR *proceeds:*]—For our destinies are welded—Horse and Inch, Inch and Horse. The motorcar is our common enemy—it attacks all our time-honored customs and traditions—

MARY: If they can't stand, let them fall!

MAJOR INCH: Ernest, speak to the woman.

MR. INCH [*To* MARY]: How do you do?

MRS. INCH: Speak to her!

MR. INCH: I did.

ARCHIE: Go on, Grandfather!

MAJOR INCH: —While we recognize the motorcar as the merest passing fad, the aim and purpose of the Major Philip E. Inch Memorial White Marble—

MARY: —Monument to the horse!

ARCHIE: Mary!

MARY: A fountain?—Soon there won't be a horse left to drink from it!

ARCHIE: Mary!

MRS. INCH: You know this person?

MARY: Can seven people hold the world back with a water trough? Can they, Archie? Oh, *make* it a monument, do!—And top it with a Winged Defeat, for children of old White Wings to come and weep at.

MAJOR INCH: She-devil! Slut! Take her off!

MARY: Yes—and move it to one side—quick!—it's blocking traffic!

MRS. INCH: Who is this woman?

ARCHIE: I'm sure I don't know.

MARY: You—? [*She closes her eyes, sways slightly, makes a half-gesture toward him and murmurs:*] Oh—

ARCHIE: Go on, Grandfather!

[*The* MAJOR *gathers himself to proceed. Suddenly* MARY *takes a stone from the wall and throws it at the arc light. It misses. The* MAJOR *proceeds:*]

MAJOR INCH: Beneath the accusing finger of this white marble edifice, the roaring, shrieking, crazy rush will cease. . . . [MARY *throws another stone with more deliberation. There is a crash, and the sound of shattered glass as the arc light is extinguished. All start in alarm, but the* MAJOR *plunges on:*] Farewell, this Juggernaut hell-bent on destruction—[*From the garage below, in swelling volume, comes the sound of many motors starting. He raises his voice.*] Welcome again, peace and tranquillity. . . . [*He turns right.*] Stop that noise!—Welcome, quiet streets, calm countryside—[*His voice cracks. He wheels savagely about, mounts his wheelchair and calls over the wall:*] Have that noise stopped, I say! Have it stopped! [*The noise continues. He gathers himself for a final shriek.*] Have it stopped or—or I withdraw my gift!

[*The noise grows louder.* MAJOR INCH *draws himself up threateningly, then all at once crumples into his chair.* ARCHIE *and* MRS. INCH *fly to him. The noise of the motors has become a steady, low roar.*]

MR. INCH: Maybe—maybe we'd better go home.

[MRS. INCH *begins to trundle the* MAJOR *off, Right.* MR. INCH *and the others follow.* ARCHIE *and* MARY *are left alone. The door of the garage is opened, the noise of the motorcars increases for a moment, then diminishes into a steady roaring bass as they pass along the Boulevard. Gradually, to this bass, bulb horns add a treble in minor key, similar to the opening phrase of "White Wings, They Never Grow Weary."*]

MARY: Archie—

ARCHIE: This—all of this—it's what *you* stand for, is it?

MARY: All of it!

ARCHIE: Noise and speed. . . .

MARY: Music! Flight!

[ARCHIE *turns from her.*]

ARCHIE: Agh!

MARY: Oh, they caught you young—Devils! Grew whiskers on *you* in the cradle, poor dear. . . .

ARCHIE: God, this racket!

[*Their voices begin to synchronize with the beat of the motors.*]

MARY: Archie—you hear the world move—you'll move with it!

ARCHIE: I've heard Grandfather's heart crack in two—I've heard *that*—

MARY: But Grandpa's day's done. He's *had* his day, Grandpa. Move, Archie—*move!* Else you'll rot on your feet.

ARCHIE: Move?

MARY: Quit the horses!

ARCHIE: Not so long as I live!

MARY: Live? Die! That's all history—finished!

ARCHIE: They're my life—I'm a White Wing!

[*She takes him by the arms and wheels him about into the light, searching his face for some ray of hope.*]

MARY: Deep roots, iron deer have. [*She clings to him suddenly, desperately.*] Oh, *Archie*—help me save you!

[*The noise of the motors falls into a faster staccato, of definite pattern. Their voices coincide in speed and emphasis.*]

ARCHIE: You're not for me. I see that. [*With a gesture*] Better go. I stay put.

MARY: But we *love*—you and me—We two *love!* What of that?

ARCHIE: Go! I don't want to see you! I'm through with you! Go!

MARY [*Rapidly*]: Quit, quit, quit, quit, quit—quit the horses, quit the horses—

ARCHIE [*More rapidly still*]: Go! I don't want you! I'm through with you! Go!

[MARY *strains against him, her face lifted to his.*]

MARY: Quit! Will you quit? Will you quit? Will you quit?

ARCHIE: No! Never! Will you go? Will you *go?*

[*She drags his hand to her lips and kisses it.*]

MARY [*Sobbing*]: *Good*-bye, Archie boy—

[ARCHIE *looks away, his face contorted.*]

ARCHIE: Good-bye—good-*bye*—

MARY [*Through her tears*]: Mind your step in the street. Cars come quick. Don't get hit.

[*He shakes his head, unable to speak. The motors are still racing past in a steady stream below. The different-toned bulb horns keep reiterating in minor key variations on the eight notes of the opening phrase of "White Wings, They Never Grow Weary."* MARY *goes swiftly to the steps, and out. A moment, then* CLYDE *comes running on from Left, a white streak through the darkness.*]

CLYDE [*Gasping*]: Archie! They're turning up here! Headed for the Park! The Park—Archie! Get out of the way! Driving like demons—knock the Fountain to bits! [*He tries to drag* ARCHIE *off Right.*] Come on—quick!

ARCHIE: No!

[CLYDE *runs out.* MR. INCH *hurries in from Left, glancing fearfully back over his shoulder. He is frightened out of his wits.*]

MR. INCH: Archie! Look out, Son. Get out of here!

[ARCHIE *seizes his father's wrist and brings him to one of the little red carts. He uncovers it and takes the shovel and broom from it.* MR. INCH *looks at* ARCHIE *in despair.* ARCHIE *holds the shovel out to him.*]

MR. INCH [*In a panic*]: But why, Archie, why?

[ARCHIE *thrusts the shovel into* MR. INCH'*s trembling hands and himself takes the broom. A faint light from the distant approaching headlights begins to play over the monument.* ARCHIE *leads* MR. INCH *to the foundation, and they mount it together. The sound of the approaching motors again swells into a roaring bass for the shrill treble of the horns' insistent phrase.* ARCHIE *whips the flag off the iron deer. The headlights now blaze from off Left, and break over the two figures upon the monument.*]

ARCHIE: —For the Horse, Father!

[ARCHIE *stiffens and faces the onrushing motors, broom upraised in one hand, while the other supports his drooping father.*]

CURTAIN

■ ACT III ■

The Parkway at dawn on a winter morning, several years later. The city has prospered. There is now an office building several stories high in the background, and a higher one under construction near it. The pattern of clouds, however, is unchanged.

The foundation for the Memorial Drinking-Fountain has been removed. Against the wall at Left stands a green park bench. In the Boulevard below stand JOSEPH *and the cab, but* HERBERT *is absent from the box. At Right, against the Parkway curb, stands a small galvanized-iron can, and near it, in the old position, one sadly dilapidated little red cart. Occasionally in the course of the act, motorcars are heard passing in the Boulevard.*

The sparrows are chattering noisily and MR. INCH, *who appears to have aged considerably, is seated upon the bench at back, poring over a notebook. He wears a rusty black overcoat over his white uniform. Bright light still comes from electric street lamps, off Left and Right. For a moment* MR. INCH *stares moodily into space, biting his lip. Gradually his hand steals into his coat pocket and brings forth a large revolver, of the sort known as "horse-pistol." He holds it away from him, his hand trembling while he once more hopelessly examines the notebook. Gradually, reluctantly, his eyes turn to the pistol. He gasps and shudders. Then he takes a deep breath, rises and places the barrel of the pistol against his stomach, waits an instant, looks down at it, then shakes his head, and puts it into his mouth. He removes it with a grimace and spits disgustedly into his cart. Then he seats himself upon the bench, reverses his hold upon the weapon so that his thumb is upon the trigger, and presses the barrel against his helmet. His poor little face wrinkles in horrible anticipation. Suddenly from the Boulevard below comes a sharp whinny, from* JOSEPH, *the Horse.* MR. INCH*'s hand closes convulsively, and the pistol slips up against his helmet and is discharged. From above a dead sparrow drops at* MR. INCH*'s feet. He picks it up, regards it in bewilderment, murmurs "A sparrow" and chucks it into his cart. A step is heard from off Right.* MR. INCH *glances anxiously in that direction, then quickly hides the pistol beneath his helmet upon the bench, reseats himself upon the curbstone and begins once more to pore over the* *notebook.* ARCHIE, *dragging his broom behind him, enters from Right, in uniform, with a mourning band about his sleeve. He, too, appears older, and there are bitter lines about his eyes and mouth. He stops, and looks suspiciously at* MR. INCH.

ARCHIE: I thought I heard a report.

MR. INCH: There—there wasn't a bit of truth in it.

ARCHIE: I smell smoke.

MR. INCH: That factory's burning soft coal, on the sly.

[ARCHIE *goes to his side.*]

ARCHIE: There's a hole in your hat.

MR. INCH: A—a moth got into it. [*Pettishly*] Can't a moth get into a man's hat without all these questions?

[ARCHIE *indicates the notebook.*]

ARCHIE: What's that?

MR. INCH: It's awful—last month's accounts.

ARCHIE: As bad as ever?

MR. INCH: Worse. [ARCHIE *seats himself beside him.*] Just listen, Archie: "Rent, for one nasty little drafty bedroom for A. Inch, E. Inch and Major P. E. Inch, eighteen dollars; very indifferent food, thirty-one dollars; laundry, nineteen-twenty-five; final installment undertaker's bill, interment Mrs. Fanny K. Inch, fifty-four-forty—

ARCHIE: That pomp was ridiculous.

MR. INCH: No pomp was too ridiculous for Fanny.—Oh, and Archie—what *can* we do about Grandpa's goings-on?

ARCHIE: Poor old fellow.

MR. INCH: But it's such an item: "Fine, Major Inch, vagrancy, ten dollars; fine, Major Inch, sassing traffic-cop, five dollars; fine, Major Inch, committing nuisance in Packard salesrooms, twenty dollars—" Where's it coming from? Where's it coming from?

ARCHIE: Lord only knows.

MR. INCH: —Then there were all sorts of divers sundries, what-nots and unaccounted-fors—and when I got all through I had to spend another ten cents for red ink, to write down the deficit.

ARCHIE: I'll keep the accounts after this.

MR. INCH: I wish you would! Well—I suppose we'd ought to get started again.

ARCHIE: It isn't four yet. Let's wait till the café crowd goes home.

MR. INCH: This night work'll kill me some day—Or some night. I miss my sleep. Sleep's nice. I *like* to sleep—[*A pause*]—it's lonely, Archie—just the two of us left, this way.

ARCHIE: Two?

MR. INCH: Of the *real* ones, I mean. [*He sniffs contemptuously.*] They *call* themselves White Wings.

ARCHIE: There are hosemen enough.

[MR. INCH *sniffs again.*]

MR. INCH: Hosemen!

ARCHIE: Oh, don't play the snob! It only makes us more ridiculous than we are.

MR. INCH: You can say what you like—it *hasn't* the quality of the old handwork.

ARCHIE: Damn the quality.

MR. INCH: What I *don't* see, is where the City gets the right to expect us to help with the ashes.

ARCHIE: Don't you? Well, take my word for it, it'll be garbage next.

[*He kicks the galvanized can by way of emphasis.* MR. INCH *rises.*]

MR. INCH: When that comes, I quit!

ARCHIE: Come along—

[MR. INCH *turns suddenly and grasps his arm.*]

MR. INCH: Son, why don't you get out of it?

ARCHIE: You know why. [*With intense hate*] Mother—she knows why, too!

MR. INCH: You've turned bitter, Son.

ARCHIE: Have I?

MR. INCH: I—I don't believe in death-bed promises. She oughtn't to have asked it.

ARCHIE: But she did, didn't she? And I promised.

MR. INCH: Break it!

ARCHIE: You didn't teach me to break promises, as a child. You taught me to keep them, regardless. [*With sudden venom*] Oh, you taught me a lot of fine things!

MR. INCH: —"So long as there's a horse left in town—" That was like Fanny. She was a great girl for plugging loopholes. [*A pause. Then softly insinuatingly*]—But maybe—maybe if there were a few more fires like last night's at Potts' Livery Stables—if a few of them were to happen *together,* say—

ARCHIE: Don't talk rot, Father. Come on—

[*He moves Left.*]

MR. INCH: Archie, you'd ought to have married that nice crazy Todd girl.

ARCHIE: Let's get going, shall we?

MR. INCH: I—I wrote her a letter, the other day.

ARCHIE: You—? [*Sharply*] What do you mean?!

MR. INCH: It—it was just a friendly sort of letter: "H-how are you?" and "Hope your father's still doing well," and—and—well, I had some ink left over, and—

ARCHIE: Take your cart and come along. [MR. INCH *makes a half-hearted attempt to push his cart into action.*] Come along, old fellow.

MR. INCH: I—just—can't. I can't do it tonight. Don't ask me to go on again tonight. I'm tired, Son.

[*He goes back to the bench and sinks down upon it.*]

ARCHIE: Oh, I know!

MR. INCH: No, you don't. No one knows. Forty-two years I've been at it, Archie. Forty-two years—

ARCHIE: Come on, old chap.—That won't help any.

MR. INCH: —From eight in the morning till six at night—every day—sweep and shovel, shovel and sweep. And now, these last two years, from midnight till seven, shovel and sweep, sweep and shovel. I can't go on any longer, Archie.

[*He begins to cry softly. Archie comforts him.*]

ARCHIE: There, there, old man—never mind. We'll arrange something for you.

MR. INCH: F-f-forty-two years I've been at it. I've done my best—no one can say I haven't done my best. I've been gay—I've whistled at my work—[*He makes a pitiful attempt to whistle now.*]—But I can't whistle any more. It won't come. My heart's gone out of it, Archie—my heart's gone out of my work.

[ARCHIE *puts his arm about his shoulders.*]

ARCHIE: *I* tell you!—There's a drugstore open—we'll have a Coca-Cola first.

[MR. INCH *brightens.*]

MR. INCH: C-Coca-Cola? [*He brushes away his tears.*] G-got any money?

ARCHIE: A little—

[*He leads him Right. It is now apparent that* ARCHIE *walks with a limp.*]

MR. INCH: Wait a minute—my hat—I can't go without my hat. [*He takes his hat from the bench, leaving the revolver covered with a handkerchief, and rejoins* ARCHIE.] I'm not the complaining sort, as a rule, am I?

ARCHIE: Indeed you're not!

MR. INCH: It's just that lately it's come over me—the realization—[*He stops, leans for a moment on his cart and looks despairingly at* ARCHIE.] Archie—my life—I—I don't feel that I'm *getting* anywhere. [ARCHIE *coaxes him off Right.*]

ARCHIE: Shhh, Father! Just don't think about it. [MR. INCH *stumbles along at his side.*] Don't think about anything—thinking's bad—just don't think—

[*They go out. A moment's silence, then* HERBERT *mounts his cab in the Boulevard, turns and cranes his neck after them.*]

HERBERT: It's sad, Josie—it's real sad. Poor Mr. Inch. He ain't the man he was, as a boy. [*The horse neighs suggestively.* HERBERT *gives him a lash with the whip.*]—But none o' *your* wisecracks—hear? You're no stallion yourself.

[*He settles down again. The noise of an approaching motorcar is heard from off Left, on the Parkway.* HERBERT *peers in its direction, then drops his head upon his chest and feigns sleep. Finally a battered little taxicab comes on from Right, and comes to a halt at Left, in response to its occupant's imperative tapping upon the window. The* TAXI-DRIVER, *himself a most urbane gentleman in an immaculate uniform, leaps to the pavement and opens the door for* MARY *to alight. She is smartly dressed in a modern suit of some dark material, but otherwise appears to have changed very little.*]

MARY: One moment, please—[*She goes to the end of the Parkway wall, Right, and calls down into the street.*] Hello, there!

[*The garage window is opened.*]

A VOICE: Canari Motor Works. Night Watchman speaking.

MARY: Is Mr. Kit Canari there?

THE VOICE: Who is it wants him, please?

MARY: Miss Todd—Mary Todd.

THE VOICE: Afraid I can't disturb him now. He's in bed.

MARY: Then get him up. It's important! [*She returns to the* TAXI-DRIVER.] How much?

TAXI-DRIVER: Two hundred and twenty-nine seventy.

MARY: That's a lot.

TAXI-DRIVER: It's my regular rate, Miss. Quite a run from Detroit, you know. Still, if you feel it's exorbitant—

MARY: Oh, no—that's for you to decide.

TAXI-DRIVER: —Or the taximeter, let us say!

MARY: I beg your pardon.

TAXI-DRIVER: Not at all.

MARY: Here you are—that's two hundred and fifty.

TAXI-DRIVER: Thanks loads. And a thousand apologies for those annoying brake bands.

MARY: Not at all—how much is the car itself worth?

TAXI-DRIVER: —To sell, you mean?

MARY [*Quickly*]: Would you sell it?

TAXI-DRIVER: With pleasure, if you'd care to have it.—Shall we say a hundred and fifty?

MARY: I'll take it for that.

TAXI-DRIVER: Splendid! Let me see now; a hundred and fifty from two fifty—one hundred dollars.

[*He returns a number of the bills she has given him.*]

MARY: Thank you.

TAXI-DRIVER: Thank *you.*

[*He goes to the cab and returns with a walking stick.*]

MARY: Good-bye.

[*He smiles, engagingly.*]

TAXI-DRIVER: Let us say "Au revoir"?

MARY: All right.

TAXI-DRIVER: Au revoir.

MARY: Au revoir.

[*He smiles, doffs his cap, bows slightly and goes off, Right, in the direction of Detroit, contentedly swinging his stick.* KIT *comes up the steps from the Boulevard.*]

KIT: Mary—is it really you?

[*She laughs.*]

MARY: So far as I know, Kit.

[*He goes to her quickly.*]

KIT: May I?

MARY: Will you?

[*She puts her face up. He kisses her hand.*]

KIT: But you said you'd never come back.

MARY: That was silly of me.

KIT: Tell me what brought you.

MARY: The Rolls, there—[*She takes a letter from her bag.*]—And this. Listen—it's from Archie's father: [*She reads the letter.*] "Dear Miss Mary Todd: Well, how are things going with you? Things are not going so well here. I wish you could do something about my boy Archie. We're obliged now to live three in one room and we go to bed at 8 A.M., but all morning long he keeps calling in his sleep 'Mary! Mary! Oh, Mary! Mary! Mary!' And it is really rather difficult for me, as I work hard all night, am nearly sixty-three, and need my rest. I am afraid that it is a matter of life or death, possibly both, and trust that you will take immediate steps, and no joke about it. Well, good-bye for the present, from your friend and well-wisher, Ernest Inch." [*She returns the letter to her bag.*]—And it's in red ink.

KIT: What about it?

MARY: I've come to marry him, Kit.

KIT: Are you crazy?

MARY: Probably.

KIT: —Still really in *love* with him?

MARY: I want to kiss him.

KIT: Then do, for God's sake, and get it over with.

MARY: I did—but it didn't. I keep on wanting to.

KIT: —So because a woman wants to kiss a man, she marries him!

MARY: Do you know a better reason?

KIT: Pardon me, while I get out my ear trumpet.

MARY: I'm wiser than you in lots of ways, old son. I've learned that some things don't change.

KIT: —And Archie's job is one of them.

MARY: No—I've come to take him away from it.

KIT: What if he won't go?

[MARY *smiles.*]

MARY: In that case, I may have to marry you, after all.

KIT: Do you mean it?

MARY: Yes, if you like. [*A brief pause*] You're sweet, Kit—and long-suffering. [*With decision*] Yes, if you like!

KIT: Careful!—You'll never marry Archie—never in this world. It's too crazy.

[*She moves Right.*]

MARY: —I'll look for him along here. You wait.

KIT: —I've told you, Mary: the Inches will follow 'em so long as there's one left to follow.

[MARY *stops and turns.*]

MARY: —You might find out, if you can, just how many there *are* left to follow.

[*She goes out.* KIT *mounts the bench to look over the wall, stepping on the revolver as he does so. He picks it up in surprise, and examines it.*]

HERBERT [*Opening his eyes again*]: —That wouldn't be hard to answer, sir.

[KIT *hastily puts the pistol in his pocket and turns in surprise.*]

KIT: What wouldn't?

HERBERT: —"How many horses."

KIT: You haven't been listening, or anything like that, have you?

HERBERT: What else've I got to do, I'd like to know?

KIT: Maybe *you* agree with me that the Inches will stay at it till they die—

HERBERT: Well—Mr. *Archie's* apt to. Promised his ma—that so long's there's a plug left in town—

KIT [*Quickly*]: Are you sure of that?

HERBERT: —Heard 'im say so with 'is own lips. [*He chuckles.*]—Touchin', ain't it? But as for that question of your lady friend's—

KIT: Well, what about it?

HERBERT [*Cautiously*]: —How many left—just at this moment?

KIT: Yes.

HERBERT: An.

KIT: What's that?

HERBERT: An horse.—This half-paralyzed ruin 'at stands before you now.

KIT: You're talking through your hat.

HERBERT: Oh, I am, am I? Listen here, Mister: I don't doubt but there'll always be horses in the provincial cities—I suppose you can find a number of 'em right this minute in such places as N'York an' Boston. But please to remember that this town *makes* autos. Ain't been a *private*-owned horse here since Mrs. Prentice's bays went under the hammer to George Major, in Amityville.

KIT: There are plenty of others.

HERBERT: Yeah-ah? Well, last September, the Quality Dairy moved out to Brighton. On January first, the Upton Chain stores went on a strictly cash-an'-carry basis. An' so on an' so forth till last night, when Potts' Livery burned to the ground. All was lost except Josie: he got out down a fire escape.—So when I say "an horse left" I mean *an horse left*—Don't I, Josie?

[*The horse whinnies asthmatically.*]

KIT: But confound it, this is serious! How old is the brute?

HERBERT: Mister, you wouldn't believe me. I might tell you he was born the same day as Major Inch—but what's the use?

[*A short, strangled whinny from Josie*]

KIT: I don't like the sound of that throat.—And paralyzed too, you say?

HERBERT: Sure! Practically completely paralyzed. But he don't mind. It's the charley-horses he minds. He suffers terrible with charley-horses.

[*A heartrending whinny from* JOSIE. KIT *becomes more nervous.*]

KIT: May prove too much for him at almost any time, eh?

HERBERT: Oh, don't you worry your head over Josie!

KIT: —But I'm agonized over Josie!—If there weren't any horses, how could there be White Wings?

HERBERT: There couldn't.—Not the genuine.

KIT: Archie'd be let out in spite of himself—well, he mustn't be!

HERBERT: He won't, sir—Joseph here—he's good for years yet.

KIT: I wouldn't give him five minutes, in a fog. Listen, Herbert—

HERBERT: Yes, sir?

KIT: Archie's job is as important to me as to him, now. So you and I have got to arrange somehow to have at least three horses kept in the city right along, day and night. Do you know anyone with any, in the country hereabouts?

HERBERT: Well, there's my Aunt Eunice. She keeps a string o' polo ponies out near Honeoye.

[KIT *hurries down the steps and out into the Boulevard.*]

KIT'S VOICE: Take me to the Western Union.

HERBERT: Sure.—But don't you give yourself one moment's concern over Josie.

KIT'S VOICE: Get a move on, will you?

HERBERT: Clllck! Clllck! [*His head and shoulders are seen to turn slowly, and the sound of slow wheels and faltering hoofbeats is heard as they move off Right.*]—Joseph lives a sort of charmed life, might say. Why, Mister, sometimes I think this horse is immortal. You'd be surprised if I was to tell you the real name o' the winner o' the Kentucky Derby back in '84—Yes, sir! Why, you wouldn't believe me! Cllck—cllck!—Take it easy, Josie—

[*The Parkway is empty for a moment, then* MAJOR INCH *steals on from Left, shrunken and dishevelled in an old Union uniform and campaign hat. In his hand he carries a small tack hammer. He looks about him furtively, then takes two pins from his coat lapel, crouches down beside the taxicab and drives them into a rear tire. This done, he rises again and peers down the Parkway, Left, where he spies another quarry. His old eyes light up expectantly, he takes another pin from his lapel, raises his hammer and runs stealthily off Right.* MARY *reënters slowly up the steps, goes to the bench, and gazes moodily down the street.* ARCHIE *enters from Left, goes to the cart, and places his broom in it.* MARY *senses rather than sees him. They turn simultaneously and meet each other's eyes.*]

MARY [*In a whisper*]: Archie—[*He stares at her, speechless.*] Hello, Archie.

ARCHIE [*Without moving*]: Hello, Mary.

MARY: "Hello-hello"—is that all?

ARCHIE: What else?

MARY: There must be a thousand things.

ARCHIE: I don't know them. [*For another moment they gaze at each other, transfixed, then he turns his cart about.*] If you'll excuse me—I must go to work.

MARY: No!

ARCHIE: I'm sorry. It's been—nice to see you.

[*He begins slowly to wheel the cart off Right.*]

MARY: Oh, my dear—you're lame—

[ARCHIE *laughs harshly.*]

ARCHIE: So I am.

MARY: How did it happen?

ARCHIE: —I was trying to hold the world back, if you'll remember. [*He laughs again.*]—It rolled over on my foot. [*With an exclamation, she starts toward him.*] Stay where you are, Mary! [*She stops dead. A pause. Then*] Now, listen: It's no use. I'm a White Wing. I was born one. I'll die one.

MARY: I don't care!

ARCHIE [*Ironically*]: You'd like to share my brilliant life?—Join me in the Gentle Art of Sweeping Up?

MARY [*Eagerly*]: —That's—that's all you call it now?

ARCHIE: I call it manure. [*His voice rises.*] I call most things manure!

MARY [*Softly*]: The great Inch tradition—

ARCHIE: Manure.

MARY: The faith of your fathers—

ARCHIE: Manure.

MARY [*Sharply*]: Then get out of it!

ARCHIE: Why?

[*She looks at him a moment. Then falters.*]

MARY: Love—

ARCHIE: Manure. [*She gasps, stiffens, then goes to him swiftly and strikes him across the face with her open hand. He seizes her wrists and drags her against him.*] You—! [*For a moment they stand rigid, glaring savagely at one another. Then all at once she slumps into his arms.*]

MARY: Oh, marry me—

ARCHIE: No.

MARY: Marry me, Archie—marry me!

ARCHIE: I can't.

MARY: Come with me, Archie—come, dear—we'll go—[*He shakes his head.*] I've bought you a taxicab—see? I'll teach you to run it.

ARCHIE: I must stay as I am.

MARY: Now—? When you know what it is? When you feel as you do?

ARCHIE: I can't help myself. [*She stands off from him and looks at him, uncomprehendingly.*] I promised my mother on her deathbed.

MARY: But the dead can't hold the living!

ARCHIE: Oh—*can't* they!

MARY: It's wicked! It's sinful!

ARCHIE: It was part of the scheme for me.

MARY: —A promise like that—

ARCHIE: A promise is a promise.

MARY: Oh, my poor boy—

ARCHIE: And I'll keep it. There's always someone who gets caught between two ages. I'll keep it—it will round out my life. Good-bye—[*He gropes for her.*] Darling—darling—

MARY: No, no! I don't! I'm sick of saying good-bye to you!

ARCHIE: We're not for each other. Good-bye, dear—good-bye.

MARY: Oh, I love you!

ARCHIE: —And I you.

MARY: Come with me.

ARCHIE: Good-bye—

MARY [*Wildly*]: Then I'll stay! We'll face it out together. I'll put starch in your uniforms. I'll keep your shoes shined bright!

[*The cab returns to its stand in the Boulevard.* KIT *is now beside* HERBERT *upon the box, and so close to the Parkway wall that he can touch it. He looks at* ARCHIE *and* MARY, *who are still in each other's arms, with an expression of mixed wonder and resignation.*]

ARCHIE: You can't. I won't let you. Good-bye—good-bye—

[*He holds her closer, kissing her tear-stained face. She keeps murmuring.*]

MARY: —A promise like that—and I can't save you—can't save you—a promise like that—

[*But they take leave of each other.* KIT *watches them. His features set.*]

KIT [*To* HERBERT]: I suppose this is what's called love.

HERBERT: Looks like it. [*He spits contemptuously over the side of the cab.*] Nobody seems to enjoy it much.

KIT: —Well, it's enough for me.—Tell your Aunt Eunice her ponies won't help me—our horse deal is off.

James Corbett Barry (1855-1897) and Mary Agnes Quinn Barry (1858-1927), Philip Barry's father and mother

Philip Barry at sixteen months and as an altar boy at seven

Barry as an undergraduate at Yale. He was then writing romantic love poems for the *Lit.*

You stopped and turned your head
And threw a little laugh across your shoulder to me.
Then I knew
That you must love me someday
—As you do.

He signed his verse "P. J. Q. Barry," a fine name for a romantic poet.

Barry employed two sizes of writing—a bold, exuberant-looking hand for personal letters, like this one to Ellen, and a constrained, neat hand for professional purposes. In December, 1921, Philip at Harvard was firing off love letters to Ellen in Mount Kisco at the rate of at least one a day. The letter shown had to do with his labors over his play *The Jilts,* later to be renamed *You and I.*

the case in a first draft.

This last three weeks before Christmas is going to contain some of the hardest sledding I've ever been through. But, conceited little fool that I am, I look forward to the grand an' glorious feeling when it's over.

Forgive me my abstracted air. It doesn't mean anything except that

Mr. and Mrs. Lorenzo Semple of New York, Mount Kisco, London and Paris, announce the marriage of their daughter, Ellen Marshall Semple, to Mr. Philip Barry, son of Mrs. James Corbett Barry, of Rochester, New York. Miss Semple is a carefully brought-up young girl, whose education at divers and sundry convents and Mrs. MacIver's School, has turned exceedingly raw material into a damsel of no mean charm. She was originally a member of the Junior League, but was asked to resign on account of the unremitting jealousy of the other members of that august institution. Mr. Barry is a graduate of Sing-Sing, class of '92, of Yale College, Class of 1918, and of Harvard, class of IG., where he is at present ekeing out a humble existence writing plays of doubtful import. His clubs are the Putter, Mashie, and Ribbed-Face Stymie. The wedding, with luck, will take place in the Autumn. Any small or large gifts that you may care to send, will be acknowledged with thanks.

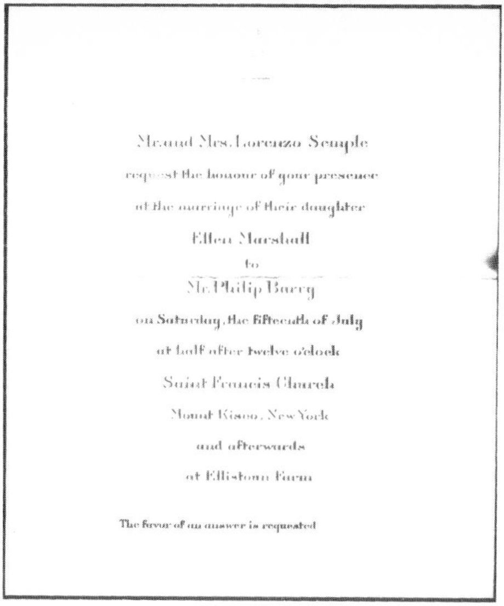

Mr. and Mrs. Lorenzo Semple
request the honour of your presence
at the marriage of their daughter
Ellen Marshall
to
Mr. Philip Barry
on Saturday, the fifteenth of July
at half after twelve o'clock
Saint Francis Church
Mount Kisco, New York
and afterwards
at Ellistown Farm

The favor of an answer is requested

Far left, Barry's parody announcement of Ellen's and his engagement. The wedding took place earlier than they had at first dared to hope, and the gifts proved gratifyingly on the large side; among them was a wedding trip abroad and a pretty cottage on the grounds of the Semple farm.

The wedding reception was held in the Semple garden in Mount Kisco. On Ellen's right is Edmund Barry, Philip's oldest brother, who served as best man.

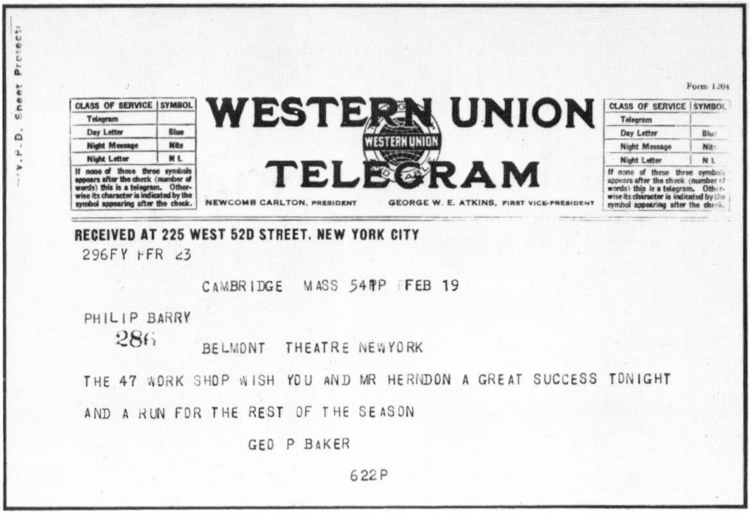

Form 1204

CLASS OF SERVICE	SYMBOL
Telegram	
Day Letter	Blue
Night Message	Nite
Night Letter	N L

If none of these three symbols appears after the check (number of words) this is a telegram. Otherwise its character is indicated by the symbol appearing after the check.

WESTERN UNION TELEGRAM

NEWCOMB CARLTON, PRESIDENT   GEORGE W. E. ATKINS, FIRST VICE-PRESIDENT

RECEIVED AT 225 WEST 52D STREET, NEW YORK CITY

296FY FFR 23

CAMBRIDGE MASS 541P FEB 19

PHILIP BARRY

286

BELMONT THEATRE NEWYORK

THE 47 WORK SHOP WISH YOU AND MR HERNDON A GREAT SUCCESS TONIGHT AND A RUN FOR THE REST OF THE SEASON

GEO P BAKER

622P

Telegram received on opening night of Barry's first Broadway play, *You and I*. The sender was Professor George Baker, head of the 47 Workshop at Harvard. In those days a telegram dispatched from Cambridge at 5:41 P.M. would be delivered by hand at the stage door in New York well before curtain time.

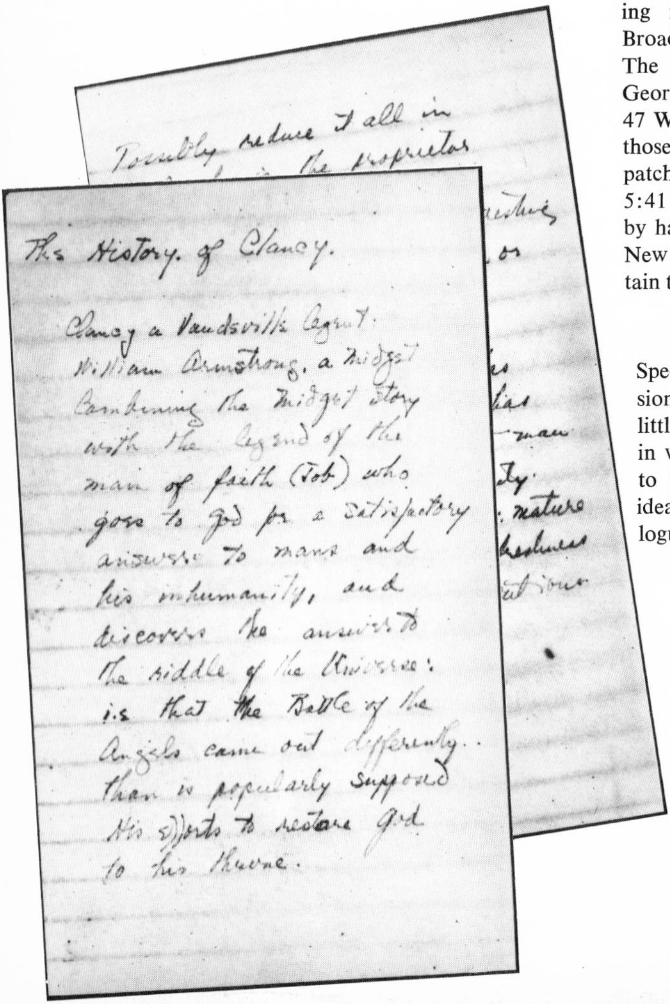

The History of Clancy.

Clancy a Vaudeville agent:
William Armstrong, a midget
Combining the midget story
with the legend of the
man of faith (Job) who
goes to God for a satisfactory
answer to man's and
his inhumanity, and
discovers the answer to
the riddle of the Universe:
is that the Battle of the
Angels came out differently
than is popularly supposed
His efforts to restore God
to his throne.

Specimens of Barry's professional handwriting, from the little brown pocket notebooks in which he was accustomed to jotting down, in pencil, ideas for plays, scraps of dialogue, and the like.

Above, a picture-postcard of the Hôtel du Cap, on the French Riviera, circa 1922. In those days it was a favorite wintering place of the British and Russians; in summer it slumbered.

Below, the Barrys' villa at Cannes, a present to them from Ellen's father, Lorenzo Semple. Here Barry wrote much of *Hotel Universe,* the setting for which was the terrace of the Gerald Murphys' house, Villa America, at Cap d'Antibes.

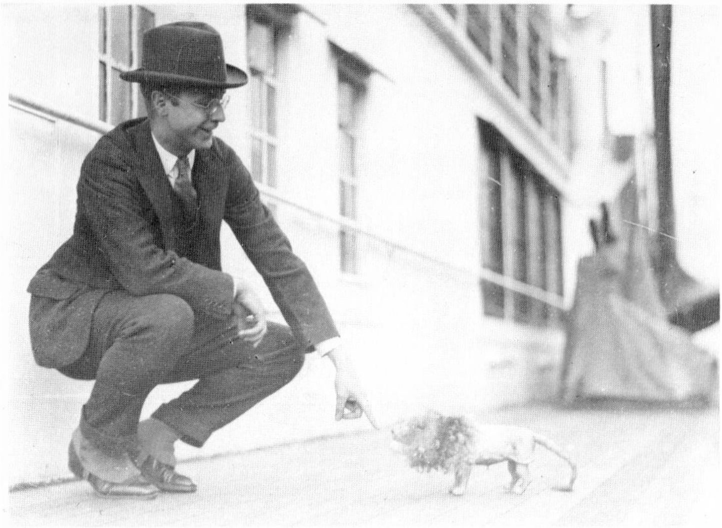

The Barrys' friend Donald Ogden Stewart, aboard the *Paris,* 1924. The lion that he is so bravely making friends with was a *bon voyage* gift from the Barrys. Stewart was something of a dude: note the suave Homburg, the natty spats.

The writer John Dos Passos at La Plage de la Garoupe, at Antibes. The Gerald Murphys' son Patrick is on his shoulders. It is the summer of 1927.

Barry at Antibes

HERBERT: What's that?

[KIT *springs from the box over the wall, onto the bench.* ARCHIE *and* MARY *are oblivious.*]

KIT: All off!—Here's where I turn philanthropist. [*He turns and looks down over the wall at the horse.*] Pull your nag's head up! [*He takes the pistol from his pocket and conceals it against his side.*] Hear me? Pull it up! Now grab the lines! Tight!

[MR. INCH *wanders in from Left wiping his brow.* MARY *and* ARCHIE *hear nothing, see nothing. Slowly* KIT *raises the pistol and takes aim.*]

MR. INCH: Hey! Watch out there! That's loaded!

KIT: It's for a suffering horse—[*With fine malice*]—the last god-damn suffering horse in the city.

[MARY *leaves* ARCHIE'*s arms and stares in amazement at* KIT.]

MR. INCH: Honest? Honest, is it?

HERBERT: It's true, Mr. Inch. Oh, stop 'im—quick—stop 'im!

[MR. INCH *drops his helmet behind the garbage can, darts at* KIT *and snatches the pistol from his hand.*]

MR. INCH: Then let me!

KIT: Get out, you, or I'll—[*Suddenly he realizes* MR. INCH'*s purpose and relinquishes the pistol.*] Go to it.

[MR. INCH *takes trembling aim at the horse, but his wrist droops and his hand finally drops nervelessly to his side as he himself collapses upon the bench, murmuring:*]

MR. INCH: —Hadn't the guts. Just hadn't the guts.

[*But in a swift movement* MARY *takes the pistol from him, goes to the wall and fires twice. After each shot a gong sounds. The horse is seen to rear up, and disappear again.* MAJOR INCH, *with a curious, long-drawn-out cry, very like a whinny, staggers on from Right, and pitches forward upon his face near the taxicab.* HERBERT *clambers down from his box, and out of view.*]

HERBERT'S VOICE: Josie! Josie!

[ARCHIE, KIT *and* MR. INCH *hasten to the spot where the* MAJOR *lies.*]

KIT: It's the Major, all right.

HERBERT'S VOICE [*From below*]: Hold on a minute, Josie. Herbert'll unhitch you.

MR. INCH: Oh dear, oh dear—

HERBERT'S VOICE [*Joyfully*]: He's still breathin'! He's still breathin'!

[ARCHIE *and* MR. INCH *bend over the prostrate form of the* MAJOR.]

MR. INCH: Has—has anyone a pocket-mirror?

MARY: Here—

[*She goes to them and gives* ARCHIE *a small mirror from her handbag.*]

MR. INCH: Ho-hold it in front of his mouth, Archie.

[ARCHIE *does so.*]

MARY: Poor old man.

[MAJOR INCH *sits up in the street, gazes into the mirror, adjusts his necktie, strokes his mustache and murmurs feebly:*]

MAJOR INCH: It was nothing.

HERBERT'S VOICE: There, dearie—Why, you're nothin' but a bag o' bones. I can lift you myself.

MAJOR INCH [*Barely audibly*]: Ernest—

MR. INCH: Yes, Father?

MAJOR INCH: There is—still work to be done.

[MR. INCH *gulps.*]

MR. INCH: Yes, Father.

[*The* MAJOR *slumps back into* ARCHIE'*s arms.* MR. INCH *clears his throat and begins to sing in a quavering voice:*]

MR. INCH: "White Wings, they never grow weary—" [*A peaceful smile settles upon the* MAJOR'*s countenance.*] "They carry me tenderly over the sea—" [*From Right,* HERBERT *enters, dragging his cab behind him. Upon the back seat of the cab, in a semi-recumbent posture, sits* JOSEPH, *the dying horse, with a large handkerchief bound about his brow.* HERBERT *is singing dolefully; one measure behind* MR. INCH.]

HERBERT: "White Wings, they never grow weary. They carry me cheerily over the sea—"

MR. INCH [*Simultaneously*]: "Night comes, I long for my dearie—" [HERBERT *halts just behind the taxicab and mounts the seat beside* JOSEPH.] "I spread out my White Wings and fly home to thee." [HERBERT *feels for* JOSEPH'*s heartbeat, then suddenly cries out:*]

HERBERT: He's gone! Oh me, poor Josie—he's gone!

[ARCHIE *and* MR. INCH *abruptly stop singing,* MARY *gazes intently at* HERBERT *and* JOSEPH, *then slowly and apprehensively turns to look at the* MAJOR.]

MARY: —And the Major's gone with him, Archie.

[ARCHIE *and* MR. INCH *stare incredulously at the still face of the* MAJOR. *Then* ARCHIE *lifts the body by the shoulders.*]

MR. INCH: Now we can take him home.

[*He takes the* MAJOR'*s feet, and he and* ARCHIE *lift him from the ground.* KIT *starts the taxicab, and backs it nearer to them.*]

ARCHIE: Oh, no—not in that.

MR. INCH: He'd never forgive us.

HERBERT: There was a horse.

[*A motor-truck is heard approaching from off Right in the Boulevard, and above it. The voice of the* CITY EMPLOYEE *calling lustily:*]

THE CITY EMPLOYEE: Sloppo! Sloppo!

[ARCHIE *indicates the cab, with his head.*]

ARCHIE: Here, Father—

[*As he and his father carry the* MAJOR'*s body Right to the cab, a heavy garbage truck, partially loaded, backs in Left in the Boulevard and stops at the base of the Parkway steps. Upon the driver's seat is the* CITY EMPLOYEE, *a robust individual with a dirty face and a decided manner. He interrupts his song, and stares in wonder over the wall at the group on the Parkway. With the assistance of* KIT, *the* MAJOR *is propped up on the cab seat beside* JOSEPH. KIT *has found a rope in the taxi, and he and* MARY *begin to tie the shafts of the horse-cab to the rear axle of the taxicab.* HERBERT *is crooning sadly:*]

HERBERT: —Poor Josie—poor Josie—Where'll I lay my Josie—where'll I lay 'im to rest?

KIT: Archie—[ARCHIE *turns to him. He nods in the direction of* MARY.] *I'll* tie it.

[ARCHIE *goes to* MARY. *She takes his hand and leads him to the taxicab.*]

MARY: Come, dear—I'll show you how—

[ARCHIE *mounts the driver's seat and takes the wheel.* MARY *stands on the running board beside him.*]

MR. INCH: My hat—where's my hat?

[*He begins to search for it.* KIT *finishes hitching the taxicab to the horse-cab.*]

MARY [*To* ARCHIE]: Push that out with your foot. [ARCHIE *throws out the clutch.*] Now pull this in. There! [ARCHIE *sets the gears.*]

MR. INCH: My hat! I can't go without my hat! Has anybody seen my hat?

MARY: Now let go with your foot—very gently—[ARCHIE *releases the clutch and the taxi starts forward, very slowly.*] That's it!

ARCHIE: I like the feel of it.

MARY: Do you, Archie?

[*The procession begins to move slowly off Left.* ARCHIE *is at the wheel,* MARY *beside him.* MAJOR INCH *and* JOSEPH *sit silent and stiff side by side on the seat of the open cab.* HERBERT *marches on foot behind them, wiping his eyes.* KIT *lights a cigarette and casually follows.*]

MR. INCH: Wait a minute!—My hat!

[*He looks under the bench.* HERBERT *begins to sing, slowly and mournfully.*]

HERBERT: "Wiiite Wingssss, they nevurrr grow wee-ery. They carrrry mee cherrilee ovurrr thee seeeee—"

[*The procession goes out, Left.* MR. INCH *finds his hat behind the garbage can and claps it on his head.*]

HERBERT [*Off Left*]: "Night comes, I long forrr my dee-reeee, I sprread out my Wiiite Wingsss, an' fly 'ome to theeeee—"

MR. INCH: Wait! Wait! Here I come! Here I come!

[HERBERT *has recommenced his dirge, which continues, in diminishing volume, throughout the following scene, to the final curtain.*]

THE CITY EMPLOYEE: Hey, you—! [MR. INCH *turns to him.*]—My buddy's sick.

MR. INCH: I—I'm sorry. Nausea?

[THE CITY EMPLOYEE *indicates the galvanized can, Right.*]

THE CITY EMPLOYEE: They give me orders to grab on to one o' you White Wings. Heave me that can o' dainties, will yuh? [MR. INCH *glances furtively at the can, then off Left, hesitates, and begins to bite his nails.*] What's a matter? Too good for it?

MR. INCH: I—I didn't say that.

THE CITY EMPLOYEE: C'mon, heave!

[MR. INCH *bears the can to the wall.*]

MR. INCH: I—I'm not employed f-for this sort of work.

THE CITY EMPLOYEE: Get under it!

[*With difficulty* MR. INCH *hands the can up to him.*]

MR. INCH: I—I'll report you! I'll—

THE CITY EMPLOYEE: Don't let it throw you! [*He takes the can, dumps it and hands it back.*] Throw it away!—Now hop aboard an' we'll finish the rounds.

MR. INCH: I—I can't, I've got an engagement.

[*The man's huge hand shoots out and grasps him by the collar.*]

THE CITY EMPLOYEE: —Not today, you ain't. [*He drags* MR. INCH *over the wall onto the driver's seat, and grinds in the gears of the truck.*] We'll see how yuh do. Maybe getcha job permanent. [MR. INCH, *his face contorted, looks over his shoulder, Left, from whence come the last dying strains of* HERBERT'*s song.* THE CITY EMPLOYEE *again begins his own call.*] Slopppoooo-o! Slopppooo-o! [*The truck begins to move off Right.* MR. INCH *receives a sharp nudge in the side.*] Hey, you! Sing out! [MR. INCH *lifts up his poor, suffering little face and bravely sings out.*]

MR. INCH: Straw-berries! Straw-*berries!* Nice—fresh—straw-*berries!*

CURTAIN

HOLIDAY

HOLIDAY

was first produced by Arthur Hopkins
at the Plymouth Theatre, New York City,
on November 26, 1928.
It was directed by Mr. Hopkins;
the settings were designed by Robert Edmond Jones.

CAST

LINDA SETON	Hope Williams
JOHNNY CASE	Ben Smith
JULIA SETON	Dorothy Tree
NED SETON	Monroe Owsley
SUSAN POTTER	Barbara White
NICK POTTER	Donald Ogden Stewart
EDWARD SETON	Walter Walker
LAURA CRAM	Rosalie Norman
SETON CRAM	Thaddeus Clancy
HENRY	Cameron Clemens
CHARLES	J. Ascher Smith
DELIA	Beatrice Ames

■ SCENES ■

ACT I

A room on the third floor of Edward Seton's house in New York.

ACT II

A room on the top floor.

ACT III

A room on the third floor.

■ ACT I ■

SCENE: *A room on the third floor of* EDWARD SETON'*s house in New York. The only entrance is at Left. It is a very large rectangular room of the Stanford White period. The panelling is heavy, the mouldings are heavy, the three long windows looking out over the park at Back are hung with heavy curtains. The portrait of* SETON'*s father, by a contemporary English master, hangs over the fireplace, at the right. It is a handsome room, and quite a comfortable room, but rich, very rich. At Right and Left are two comfortable sofas, a table behind each. On one table are two telephones, one for the house, the second for outside. On the other table, magazines and newspapers, and a cigarette box. This side of the sofa, near Center, are two upholstered benches, and at Right and Left of each a large chair. In the corners of the room, at Back, stand two more chairs, a table and lamp beside each.*

TIME: *It is about twelve o'clock on a bright, cold Sunday morning in mid-December, this year.*

AT RISE: *A fire is burning in the fireplace. Sunday papers are strewn upon a low table and beside a chair near it.*

JULIA SETON *is seated at a desk, Right, writing a note. She is twenty-eight, and quite beautiful. She writes in silence for a few minutes, then calls, in response to a knock at the door:*

JULIA: Yes? [HENRY *enters from Left.* HENRY *is the butler. He is fifty, of pleasant appearance, of pleasant manner.*] Oh, hello, Henry. How have you been? [*She seals the note.*]

HENRY: Well, thank you, Miss. We're very glad to have you back again.

JULIA: It was a lovely trip.

HENRY: A Mr. Case to see you, Miss. He said you expected him, so Charles is bringing him up.

JULIA: That's right. How many are we for lunch?

HENRY: Six, I believe. Only Mr. and Mrs. Cram are expected.

JULIA: Hasn't Miss Linda friends, too?

HENRY: Not as we've been told, Miss.

JULIA: Have an extra place set, will you?

HENRY: Yes, Miss. [HENRY *collects the newspapers from the floor and chairs, and piles them in a neat pile upon a table. After a moment* CHARLES, *a younger manservant, appears in the doorway.*]

CHARLES: Mr. Case, Miss.

JULIA [*Rises from the desk and calls in the direction of the hall*] Come in Johnny! Quick!—Of all slow people. [CHARLES *stands aside to admit* JOHNNY CASE, *and enters after him.* JOHNNY *is thirty, medium-tall, slight, attractive-looking, luckily not quite handsome. He goes at once to* JULIA.]

JOHNNY: There was a traffic jam. Men were dying like flies.—Did you really go to church?

JULIA: Yes, but I ducked the sermon. I was sure you'd get here before me. You're staying for lunch, you know.

JOHNNY: Thanks, I'd love to. [*Both look warily at the two men tidying up the room.*] I'm actually hungry again. Those same old shooting pains.

JULIA: Isn't it extraordinary the appetite that place gives you? You should have seen the breakfast I ate on the train.

JOHNNY: Why wouldn't you join me? You were invited.

JULIA: Miss Talcott would have swooned away. She's the world's worriedest chaperon as it is. [HENRY *goes out.* CHARLES *has begun to gather ashtrays upon a larger tray.*]—You can leave the trays till later, Charles.

CHARLES: Very well, Miss. [*He moves toward the door.* JULIA *talks against his exit.*]

JULIA [*To* JOHNNY]: Have you ever known such cold?

JOHNNY: Never.

JULIA: It's hard to believe it was twenty degrees lower at Placid.

JOHNNY: You don't feel it, there.

JULIA: That's what they say.—And you can close the door, Charles. It makes a draught.

CHARLES: Yes, Miss.

JULIA: When Mr. Seton comes in, would you ring this room from the door? Two short ones.

CHARLES: Very good, Miss. [*He goes out, closing the door after him. For a moment* JULIA *and* JOHNNY *stand transfixed, looking at each other. Then* JULIA *smiles slightly and says:*]

JULIA: Hello, Sweet—[*In an instant* JOHNNY *is beside her and she is in his arms, being kissed. At length she stands off from him, murmuring:*] Johnny—Johnny—mind your manners.

JOHNNY: But dear, where are we?

JULIA: We're here, all right. [JOHNNY *moves away from her and looks about him.*]

JOHNNY: But where's "here"?

JULIA: Where I live. Don't you like it?

JOHNNY: But Julia, seriously, what *is* all this?

JULIA: All what?

JOHNNY: All this house—and armies of men underfoot picking up newspapers, and—

JULIA: Aren't you silly, Johnny. I told you where I lived. [*She seats herself upon a sofa.*]—I wrote it on the back of an envelope for you.

JOHNNY: But it's enormous. I'm overcome. It's the Grand Central. How can you stand it?

JULIA: I seem to manage.

JOHNNY: Don't you find you rattle around a good deal in it?

JULIA: I hadn't noticed that I did.

JOHNNY [*Cups his hands and calls through them*]: Hoo! [*Then*] There's a bad echo.

JULIA: You stop criticizing this house, or I'll call the bouncer.

JOHNNY: But you must all be so *rich,* Julia!

JULIA: Well, we aren't poor.

JOHNNY: You should have told me, you really should.

JULIA: Would it have made any difference?

JOHNNY [*Laughs*]: Lord, yes! I'd have asked you to marry me in two day, instead of ten.

JULIA [*A pause. Then*]: How do you mean?

JOHNNY: I went through an awful struggle. You've no idea. I had very definite plans for the next few years, and at first a wife looked like quite a complication.

JULIA: What were the plans?

JOHNNY: For one thing, I was worried about having enough for both of us. If I'd known, I'd have spared myself. It's simply swell now. Good Julia.

JULIA: Aren't you funny, Johnny.

JOHNNY: Why?

JULIA: To talk about it.

JOHNNY: It? Money? Why? Is it so sacred?

JULIA: Of course not. But—

JOHNNY: I'm simply delighted, that's all.

JULIA: —That I have—uh—money?

JOHNNY: Yes. Sure. [*She laughs.*]

JULIA: You're amazing.

JOHNNY: But why not?—If I'd suddenly discovered you could play the piano I'd be delighted, wouldn't I?

JULIA: Is it like knowing how to play the piano?

JOHNNY: Well, they're both very pleasant accomplishments in a girl.

JULIA: But, my dear, you're going to make millions, yourself!

JOHNNY: Oh, no, I'm not.

JULIA: You are too!

JOHNNY: —Am not.

JULIA: Are too. [*A brief pause*]

JOHNNY: How did you happen to decide I'd do, Julia?

JULIA: I fell in love with you, silly.

JOHNNY: You might have done that, and still not have wanted to marry me.

JULIA: I do, though.

JOHNNY: You know awfully little about me.

JULIA: *I* know enough.—You aren't trying to get out of anything, are you, Johnny?

JOHNNY: Watch me.

JULIA: Because you haven't a chance, you know.

[*She rises and goes to the window at Back.*]

JOHNNY: But what's there different about me? What did it?

JULIA: You're utterly, utterly different.

JOHNNY: —I am a man of the pee-pul—

JULIA: That might be one reason.

JOHNNY: I began life with these two bare hands.

JULIA: —So did the gentleman over the fireplace. [JOHNNY *looks at the portrait above the mantel.*]—Take heart from Grandfather.

JOHNNY: You wouldn't tell me you're *those* Setons!

JULIA: Forgive us, Johnny, but we are.

JOHNNY [*Overwhelmed, lowers his head*]: It's too much.

JULIA [*Lightly*]: —What man has done, man can do—or words to that effect. [*She is looking out the window, down into the street.*]

JOHNNY: See here, child—if you think I'm a budding young Captain of Industry, or—

JULIA: Sh—wait a minute.

JOHNNY: What's the matter?

JULIA: It's the motor. At least I think—yes, it is.

JOHNNY: Him?

JULIA: Wait a minute—No—it's only Linda. Father must have decided to walk home with Ned.

JOHNNY: Did you tell him, as you planned to?

JULIA [*Again moves toward the sofa*]: Father? Just exactly as I planned to.

JOHNNY: I'm still not sure that church was a good place.

JULIA: I wanted to give him a chance to think, before he started talking. He never talks in church.

JOHNNY: What did you say?

JULIA: I said, "Look here, Father: I'm going to marry Johnny Case." And he said, "What's that?" And I said, "I said, I'm going to marry Johnny Case."

JOHNNY: And he never even peeped?

JULIA: Oh, yes.—"And who may Johnny Chase be?" "Case," I said. "Not Chase." "Well, Case, then?"—I told him I'd met you at Placid, that he'd meet you at luncheon and that you were with Sloan, Hobson, Hunt and Sloan.—That was right, wasn't it?

JOHNNY: Sloan, Hobson, *Hunter* and Sloan.

JULIA: It was near enough. He said, "I know Sam Hobson," and began to pray rapidly—and that was all there was to it.

JOHNNY: But probably there'll be more.

JULIA: Yes, probably a lot more—I hope you're feeling strong.

[*They seat themselves together upon the sofa at Right.*]

JOHNNY: Seriously, how do you think he'll take it?

JULIA [*Laughs*]: —Seriously! [*Then*] You'll have one big thing in your favor, Johnny.

JOHNNY: What?

JULIA: You'll see.

JOHNNY: I know: It's this necktie.

JULIA: Johnny—

JOHNNY: Julia—

JULIA: Don't jest, boy.

JOHNNY: Oh, darling, let's not let the fun go out of it!

JULIA: Is it likely to?

JOHNNY: No, but—

JULIA: Say it.

JOHNNY: What was the point of spilling it so quickly?

JULIA: I had to tell Father. It would be different if Mother were alive. I could have broken it gently through her, I suppose. But as it is—

JOHNNY: —Eventually, I know. But why the rush?

JULIA: I had to tell him. He'd never have forgiven me.

JOHNNY: It could have been such a swell guilty secret for a while.

JULIA: I can't see what particular fun a secret would have been.

JOHNNY: Can't you, dear?
JULIA: No.
JOHNNY: All right.
JULIA: Oh, don't say "all right" that way! You don't mean "all right."
JOHNNY [*Smiles*]: All right.
JULIA: You're the most outspoken, direct man I've ever known, and you sit there, sobbing over—
JOHNNY: It's all right, dear. Really it is.
JULIA: I thought you wanted us to be married as soon as possible.
JOHNNY: I do.
JULIA: Well, then.
JOHNNY: When shall we?
JULIA: There's another place Father comes in.
JOHNNY: I should think it would be pretty much up to you.
JULIA: You don't know Father.
JOHNNY: But let's not have an elaborate one—wedding, I mean.
JULIA: I doubt if we can avoid it. We've got to think of Father.
JOHNNY: It's getting pretty complicated.
JULIA: You didn't think it would be simple, did you?
JOHNNY: I suppose I just didn't think.
JULIA: You couldn't have. [*In sudden exasperation*] Oh, Johnny, *Johnny* —what's the matter with you?
JOHNNY: I just hate the thought of sitting down with a man and being practical about you—so soon, I mean. [JULIA *softens.*]
JULIA: —Angel. [*She kisses him, lightly.*] It's got to be done, though.
JOHNNY: All right. I'll gird up my loins.—You know, I'll bet he'll hate this necktie. It doesn't look substantial.
JULIA: You might sit like this—covering it with your hand.
JOHNNY: I love you, Julia.
JULIA: I love you, Johnny.
JOHNNY: That's the main thing, isn't it?
JULIA: Darling, that's everything—
JOHNNY: Kiss?
JULIA: With pleasure—[*They kiss.*]
JOHNNY: —Don't go.
JULIA: I wouldn't think of it.
JOHNNY: It'd be swell to have this whole day free with no ordeals to face.
JULIA: It'll be over soon.—I think we'll have Ned and Linda on our side.
JOHNNY: Lord, do they have to mix in, too?
JULIA: Well, they're my brother and sister.

JOHNNY: Are they good guys?

JULIA: —Dears. Ned's a little inclined to drink too much, but I think he'll outgrow it. You ought to be able to help him, I think. Linda's a curious girl. She's developed the queerest—I don't know—attitude toward life. I can't make her out. She doesn't think as we do at all, any more.

JOHNNY: We?

JULIA: —The family. Father's worried sick about her. I think *we* can help her a lot, though—I hope we can.

JOHNNY [*Rises and goes to the fireplace*]: She might prefer to work it out for herself. So might Ned.

JULIA: You *are* strange this morning, Johnny.

JOHNNY: How?

JULIA: You seem—not to like things quite as much as you might.

JOHNNY: Oh, yes, I do!

JULIA: We can't just wander forever up snowy mountains through pine woods with never a care, you know.

JOHNNY: Come here, darling. [*He goes to her, she to him. They meet.*]—We can do better than that.

JULIA: Do you suppose?

JOHNNY: I know.

[JULIA*'s head drops.*]

JULIA: Oh, I feel so awfully sad all at once.

JOHNNY: Don't—*don't.* Don't ever—[*His grasp tightens upon her shoulders.*] Look up here—! [*With an effort, she looks up.*]—Now please kiss me several times. [*She kisses him, once, twice, lightly.*]

JULIA: Is that all right?

JOHNNY: All right, hell. It's perfect. [*He bends to kiss her again, when the door suddenly opens and* LINDA SETON *enters, in hat and fur coat.* LINDA *is twenty-seven, and looks about twenty-two. She is slim, rather boyish, exceedingly fresh. She is smart, she is pretty, but beside* JULIA*'s grace,* JULIA*'s beauty, she seems a trifle gauche, and almost plain. She is pulling off her hat.*]

LINDA: I must say, that of all the boring—[*She stops at the sight of* JULIA *and* JOHNNY.] Why, Julia. For shame, Julia. [JULIA *and* JOHNNY *part.* LINDA *throws her hat and gloves upon a chair.*] Is this a way to spend Sunday morning? Who's your partner? Anyone I know?

JULIA: It's—[*She recovers her composure.*]—This is Mr. Case—my sister, Linda.

JOHNNY: How do you do?

LINDA: Well, thanks.—And you?

JOHNNY: I couldn't be better.

LINDA: Good.

JULIA [*With dignity*]: —*Johnny* Case, his name is. I'm going to marry him.

LINDA: That makes it all right, then. [*She takes off her coat.*] Who's coming to lunch? Susan and Nick didn't telephone, did they?

JULIA: —In just about one month I'm going to marry him.

LINDA: Stand over here in the light, will you, Case? [JOHNNY *turns to her scrutiny.*]—But I've never even seen you before.

JULIA: Neither had I, until ten days ago at Placid.

LINDA [*To* JOHNNY, *with hope*]: You aren't a guide, are you?

JOHNNY: No. I'm a lawyer.

LINDA: Wouldn't you know it.

JULIA [*Seats herself upon a chair at Right*]: I want you to be maid-of-honor, Linda.

LINDA: I accept. What'll we wear? [*She sits upon the bench at Left, and* JOHNNY *upon the sofa facing her.*] Listen: is this what came over Father in church?

JULIA: I imagine so.

LINDA: Then you've told him already.

JULIA: Yes.

LINDA: Tsch-tsch, this modern generation. [*To* JOHNNY] Well, young man, I hope you realize what you're getting in for.

[DELIA, *a housemaid of about thirty-five, comes in, takes* LINDA*'s coat, hat and gloves, and goes out with them.*]

JULIA: That's pleasant.

LINDA: I don't mean you. You're divine. I mean Father—and Cousin Seton Cram and Laura and the rest of the outlying Setons—and the general atmosphere of plenty, with the top riveted down on the cornucopia—

JULIA: Johnny will try to bear up, won't you, Johnny?

JOHNNY: I'll do my best.

LINDA [*Goes to* JULIA *and seats herself upon the bench facing her*]: But how *did* you happen to get together? Tell Linda everything.

JULIA: Well, I was walking along the road with Miss Talcott one morning on the way to the rink and who should I see but—

LINDA: —*Whom* should I see but—

JULIA: —And who should I see but this man coming along, carrying skis.

LINDA: Fancy that. A downright romance. Go on, dear—

JULIA: Do you really want to know?

LINDA: I'm hungry for romance, Sister. If you knew the way my little heart is beating against its bars right this minute.

JULIA: He had a queer look on his face.

LINDA: I can believe that. His eyes must have been burning.

JULIA: As a matter of fact, the trouble was with his nose. So I stopped him and said, "I suppose you don't realize it, but your nose is frozen." And he said, "Thanks, I hadn't realized it." And I said: "Well, it is." And he said, "I don't suppose there's anything you personally could do about it."

LINDA: Fresh.

JULIA: I thought so too.

JOHNNY: She was fresh to mention it. It looked to me like an out-and-out pickup.

LINDA: Obviously.

JULIA: I know a good thing when I see it.

LINDA [*To* JOHNNY]: —So you swept her off her snowshoes?

JOHNNY: It was touch-and-go with us.

LINDA [*To* JULIA]: I think I like this man.

JULIA: I was sure you would.

LINDA: Well, my dears, take your happiness while you may.

JOHNNY: Watch us.

JULIA [*Laughs*]: No—*don't* watch us! Hello, Ned—

[NED SETON *enters from the hall. He is twenty-six. He is as handsome in his way as* JULIA *is in hers. His features are fine, a little too fine. He displaces very little, but no one minds: he is a nice boy.* JOHNNY *rises.* NED *goes to* JULIA.]

NED: Oh, *you're* back.—Then it was you who took that shaker out of my room.

JULIA: This is Mr. Case—my brother Ned. [JOHNNY *moves to* NED. *They shake hands briefly.*]

NED: How do you do?—It was you who took it, Julia, and I'm getting sick of your meddling in my affairs.

JULIA: I'm going to marry him. [NED *turns slowly, as* JULIA*'s words penetrate, and regards* JOHNNY.]

NED: You've got a familiar look about you.

JOHNNY: That's good.

NED: Is your name Johnny Case?

JOHNNY: Johnny Case.

NED: —One Saturday, quite a while ago, I went down to New Haven for a game. Afterwards, you took me all the way home from the Field, and put me to bed somewhere.

LINDA: How sweet.

JOHNNY: Call me Nana. [*He goes to the sofa at Right.*]

NED: I never got a chance to thank you. Thanks.

JOHNNY: It's all right.—Anytime.

NED [*Settles down with a newspaper on the sofa at Left*]: He's a good man, this Case fellow.

LINDA: The point is, there's no moss apparent, nor yet the slightest touch of decay.

NED: I expect Father'll be a job. When do they come to grips?

JULIA: Before luncheon, I suppose.

LINDA [*Rises*]: That soon? See here, Case, *I* think you need some coaching.

JOHNNY: I'd be grateful for anything in this trouble.

LINDA: Have you anything at all but your winning way to your credit?

JOHNNY: Not a thing.

JULIA: Oh, hasn't he, though!

LINDA: The first thing Father will want to know is, how are you fixed?

JOHNNY: Fixed?

LINDA [*Firmly*]: —Fixed.—Are you a man of means, and if so, how much?

JULIA: Linda!

LINDA: Be still, Beauty. [*To* JOHNNY] I know you wouldn't expect that of a man in Father's position, but the fact is, money is our god here.

JULIA: Linda, I'll—! —Johnny, it isn't true at all.

NED [*Looks up from his paper*]: No?—What is, then?

LINDA: Well, young man?

JOHNNY [*Goes to her*]: I have in my pocket now, thirty-four dollars, and a package of Lucky Strikes. Will you have one?

LINDA: Thanks. [*She takes a cigarette from him.*]—But no gilt-edged securities? No rolling woodlands?

JOHNNY: I've got a few shares of common stock tucked away in a warm place.

LINDA: —Common? Don't say the word. [*She accepts a light from him.*] I'm afraid it won't do, Julia.—He's a comely boy, but probably just another of the vast army of clock-watchers. [*She moves toward the window.* JOHNNY *laughs and seats himself on the sofa at Right.*]

NED [*From behind his newspaper*]: How are you socially?

JOHNNY: Nothing there, either.

LINDA [*Turning*]: You mean to say your mother wasn't even a Whoozis?

JOHNNY: Not even that.

JULIA: Linda, I do wish you'd shut up.

NED: Maybe he's got a judge somewhere in the family.

LINDA: Yes, that might help. Old Judge Case's boy. White pillars. Guitars a-strummin'. Evenin', Massa.

NED: You must know some prominent people. Drop a few names.

LINDA: —Just casually, you know: "When I was to Mrs. Onderdonk's cock fight last Tuesday, whom should I see but Mrs. Marble. Well, sir, I thought we'd die laughing—"

JULIA [*To* JOHNNY]: This is a lot of rot, you know.

JOHNNY: I'm having a grand time.

LINDA: " 'Johnny,' she says to me—she calls me 'Johnny'—"

JULIA: Oh, will you be *quiet!* What on earth has set you off this time?

LINDA: But it's dreadful, Sister. [*To* JOHNNY]—Just what do you think you're going to prove with Edward Seton, financier and cotillion-leader?

JOHNNY: Well, I'll tell you: when I find myself in a position like this, I ask myself: What would General Motors do? Then I do the opposite.

LINDA [*Laughs and reseats herself. To* JULIA]: It'll be a pity, if it doesn't come off. It'll be a real pity.

JULIA: It will come off. [*To* JOHNNY] Father isn't at all as they say he is.

JOHNNY: No?

JULIA: Not in the least.—Ned, where is he? Didn't he come in with you?

JOHNNY: Don't hurry him. There's no hurry.

NED: He said he had to stop to see Sam Hobson about something.

JULIA [*To* JOHNNY]: You.

JOHNNY: That's nice. I hope I get a good character.

LINDA: If it does go through all right, are you really going to make it quick?

JULIA: The second week in January. The tenth.

LINDA: —Announcing when?

JULIA: Right away—next Saturday, say.

LINDA [*Eagerly*]: Oh, darling, let me give a party for it!

JULIA [*Puzzled*]: Do you want to? I thought you hated the thought of—

LINDA: *I* want to! Not Father. *I* want to.

JULIA: Why, of course, dear. We'd love it.

NED: Who'd like a drink? [*No one bothers with him.*]

LINDA: —Father's to have nothing to do with it. And we *won't* send out cards. I'll telephone people.—Saturday's New Year's Eve, do you know it? Oh, Lord, Lord—let's have some fun in this house before you leave it!

JULIA: Why, Linda—

LINDA: I mean it! Let me, won't you?

JULIA: If Father doesn't mind.

LINDA: No "ifs" at all!—And just a few people—very few. Not a single bank of pink roses and no string quartet during supper. All I want by way of entertainment is just one good tap dancer. Let me plan it. Let me give it. Julia, let *me* do something for you once—*me,* Julia.

JULIA: I'd love it, dear. I really would.

LINDA: It won't be a ball, it'll be a simple sit-down supper—and you know where?—The old playroom.

JULIA: Why, not the—

LINDA: —Because the playroom's the one room in this house anyone's ever had fun in!

NED: I haven't been up there for ten years.

LINDA: That's your loss, Neddy. I've installed a new-fangled gramophone, and I sit and play to myself by the hour. Come up some time. It's worth the trip. [*She turns suddenly to* JOHNNY.]—Do you know any living people, Case? That's a cry from the heart.

JOHNNY: One or two.

LINDA: Give me a list. [*To* JULIA]—Seton and Laura can't have a look-in —is that understood? [*To* JOHNNY]—A terrible cousin and his wife— the Seton Crams. They're coming for lunch today. I hope your digestion's good. [*To* JULIA]—Not a look-in, remember.

JULIA: I don't know how you'll keep them out.

LINDA [*Rises abruptly*]: Oh, Julia—this is important to me!—No one must touch my party but me, do you hear?

JULIA: All right, darling.

LINDA: If anyone does, I won't come to it.

NED: —At that, you might have a better time. [*He rises.*] Look here, Case—

JOHNNY: Yes?

NED: Cocktails aren't allowed at midday, so just before luncheon's announced I'll ask you if you care to brush up.

JOHNNY: And guess what I'll say.

JULIA: There'll be wine with lunch, Ned.

NED: You have to give it something to build on, don't you? [*A buzzer sounds twice.* JULIA *and* JOHNNY *rise.*]

JULIA: —It's Father! He's home.

LINDA: He'll go up to his sitting room first.

JULIA [*Moves toward the door*]: I know. Come on with me, Ned.

NED: I don't want to see him.

JULIA: Please come with me. [NED *goes out. She turns to* JOHNNY.] You wait here with Linda a moment. I'll either come down again or send word. Just talk a while. [*She follows* NED *out. A brief pause. Then* LINDA *goes to the bench at Left, and* JOHNNY *to the one at Right.*]

LINDA: How ever do you do, Mr. Case?

JOHNNY: —And you, Miss—uh—?

LINDA: Seton is the name.

JOHNNY: Not one of the bank Setons!

LINDA: The same.

JOHNNY: Fancy!—I hear a shipment of earmarked gold is due in on Monday. [*Now they are seated.*]

LINDA [*In her most social manner*]: Have you been to the Opera much lately?

JOHNNY: Only in fits and starts, I'm afraid.

LINDA: But, my dear, we must do *something* for them! They entertained us in Rome.

JOHNNY: —And you *really* saw Mount Everest?

LINDA: Chit.

JOHNNY: Chat.

LINDA: Chit-chat.

JOHNNY: Chit-chat.

LINDA: Will that go for the preliminaries?

JOHNNY: It's all right with me.

LINDA: I love my sister Julia more than anything else in this world.

JOHNNY: I don't blame you. So do I.

LINDA: She's so sweet, you don't know.

JOHNNY: Yes, I do.

LINDA: She's beautiful.

JOHNNY: She's all of that.

LINDA: —And exciting, too—don't you think?

JOHNNY: —Don't. I'll start gittering.

LINDA: It's terribly important that she should marry the right person.

JOHNNY: That's important for everyone.

LINDA: It's particularly so for Julia.—I suppose you realize you're a rather strange bird in these parts.

JOHNNY: How's that?

LINDA: You don't know the kind of men we see as a rule.—Where have you been?

JOHNNY: Oh—working hard.

LINDA: Nights?

JOHNNY: Nights too.

LINDA: What about these little jaunts to Placid? Come clean, Case.

JOHNNY: That's the first holiday I've ever had.

LINDA [*Unconvinced*]: Yes.

JOHNNY: You heard what I said.

LINDA: Then you can't have been working long.

JOHNNY: Just since I was ten. [*She frowns, puzzled.*]

LINDA: —Ten. At what?

JOHNNY: —Anything I could get. Law, the last few years.

LINDA: —Must be ambitious.

JOHNNY [*Expels his breath in a long, tired jet*]: I am. Not for that, though.

LINDA: For what, then?

JOHNNY: Oh—to live. Do you mind? [*There is a pause.*]

LINDA: What is it you've been doing?

JOHNNY: I don't call what I've been doing, living.

LINDA: No? [*He shakes his head.*]

JOHNNY: —A while ago you asked me if I knew any living people. I know damn few.

LINDA: There aren't but damn few.

JOHNNY: Well, I mean to be one of them some day. Johnny's dream.

LINDA: So do I. Linda's longing.

JOHNNY: There's a pair called Nick and Susan Potter—

LINDA: So you know Nick and Susan?

JOHNNY: I should say I do.

LINDA: So that's where I've heard your name. Aren't they grand?

JOHNNY: It seems to me they know just about everything. Maybe I'm wrong.

LINDA: You're not, though.

JOHNNY: Life must be swell when you have some idea of what goes on, the way they do.

LINDA: They get more fun out of nothing than anyone I know.

JOHNNY: You don't have such a bad time yourself, do you?

LINDA [*Leaning forward*]: Case, are you drawing me out? [JOHNNY *laughs.*]

JOHNNY: Sure! Come on!

LINDA: Well, compared to the time I have, the last man in a chain gang thoroughly enjoys himself.

JOHNNY: But how does that happen?

LINDA: You tell me, and I'll give you a rosy red apple.

JOHNNY: It seems to me you've got everything.

LINDA: Oh, it does, does it?

JOHNNY: What's the matter? Are you fed up?

LINDA: —To the neck.—Now tell me about *your* operation.

JOHNNY: I had been ailing for years—I don't know—life seemed to have lost its savor—

LINDA: Couldn't you do your housework?

JOHNNY: Every time I ran upstairs I got all rundown. [LINDA *laughs.* JOHNNY *leans forward.*] You'd better come on a party with Julia and me.

LINDA: Anytime you need an extra girl, give me a ring.—When?

JOHNNY: How's Tuesday?

LINDA: Splendid, thanks.—And how's Thursday?

JOHNNY: Blooming.

LINDA [*Reflectively*]: —Looked badly the last time we met.

JOHNNY: —Just nerves, nothing but nerves.

LINDA [*A moment's pause. Then*]: —Do I seem to you to complain a good deal?

JOHNNY: I hadn't noticed it.

LINDA: Then I can let myself go a little: this is a hell of a life, Case.

JOHNNY [*Looks about him*]: What do you mean? All this luxe? All this—?

LINDA: You took the words right out of my mouth.

JOHNNY: Well, for that matter, so's mine.

LINDA: What's the answer?

JOHNNY: Maybe you need some time off, too—I mean from what you're doing, day in, day out—

LINDA: *Days* out, please—*years* out—

JOHNNY: All right: take it. Take the time—

LINDA: —And of course *that's* so easy.

JOHNNY: —It can be done. *I* intend to do it. I intend to take quite a lot of it—when I'm not so busy just making the wherewithal.

LINDA: Case, you astonish me. I thought you were a Willing Worker.

JOHNNY: I am, if I can get what I'm working for.

LINDA: And what would that be?

JOHNNY: Mine is a simple story: I just want to save part of my life for myself. There's a catch to it, though. It's got to be part of the young part.

LINDA: You'll never get on and up that way.

JOHNNY: All right, but I want *my* time while I'm young. And let me tell you, the minute I get hold of just about twenty nice round thousands, I'm going to knock off for as long as they last, and—

LINDA: Quit?

JOHNNY: Quit. Retire young, and work old. That's what I want to do.

LINDA: —Grand. Does Julia know about it?

JOHNNY: No—there's no use getting her hopes up until it happens.—Don't tell her, will you?

LINDA: She has enough of her own for two right now—or ten, for that matter. Mother and Grandfather did us pretty pretty.

JOHNNY [*Shakes his head*]: Thanks, but I've got to do myself—only just pretty enough.

LINDA: I see. That's foolish—but you're all right, Case. You haven't been bitten with it yet—you haven't been caught by it.

JOHNNY: By what?

LINDA [*So reverently*]: The reverence for riches.

JOHNNY [*Laughs*]: You *are* a funny girl.

LINDA: —Funny, am I? And what about you, you big stiff?

JOHNNY [*Laughs, and rises*]: —Just take Johnny's hand, and come into the Light, sister. [JULIA *enters.* JOHNNY *turns to her.*] Did you see him?

JULIA: I saw him.

LINDA: Julia! How was he?

JULIA: I don't know yet.—Johnny, you go up to Ned's room. You haven't arrived yet. Take the elevator—Father's coming down the stairs. Quick, will you?

JOHNNY: When do I arrive?

JULIA: One o'clock. It's quarter to.

JOHNNY: This is getting a little complicated, if you ask me.

JULIA: Nobody asked you. Go on! Do as you're told.

JOHNNY [*Turns*]: See here, you saucy—

LINDA [*Goes to the fireplace*]: Go on, Case. Don't expect simplicity here—just think of our Fifth Avenue frontage. [JOHNNY *laughs and goes out.* LINDA *turns to* JULIA.] Tell me: was Father awful?

JULIA: —The same old story, of course: I'm being married for my money.

LINDA: That's always flattering.—But Case didn't know our foul secret, did he?

JULIA: No.

LINDA: Even if he had, what of it?—And what good's all this jack we've got, anyway—unless to get us a superior type of husband?

JULIA: I hate you to talk like that! I hate it!

LINDA: Listen to me, Julia: I'm sore all the way through. I've been sore for a long time now, ever since I really saw how it—oh, never mind. Anyway, I don't doubt that if Case *had* known he'd still be running. You're in luck there.

JULIA: You do like him, don't you?

LINDA: She asks me if I like him!—My dear girl, do you realize that *life* walked into this house this morning? Marry him quick. Don't let him get away. And if Father starts the usual—where *is* Big Business, anyhow?

JULIA: He said he'd be right down.

LINDA: Stand your ground, Julia. If you don't know your own mind by now, you haven't got a mind. Name your date and stick to it. I'm telling you.

JULIA [*Slowly*]: I want Father to see that Johnny has the selfsame qualities Grandfather had—and that there's no reason why he shouldn't arrive just where he did.

LINDA: —If he wants to.

JULIA: Wants to! You don't know Johnny. You don't know how far he's come already—and from what—

LINDA: —Or where he's going.

JULIA: *I* do! *I* know! I can see it clear as day! [*A moment. Then*] Linda—

LINDA: What?

JULIA: It'll be awful to leave you.

LINDA: I don't know exactly what I'll do, when you go. I've got to do something—get out—quit on it—change somehow, or I'll go mad. I could curl up and die right now.

JULIA [*Touched*]: Why, darling—

LINDA: Why, my foot. I don't look sick, do I? [*She moves to the fireplace*] Oh, Lord, if I could only get *warm* in this barn! [*She crouches before the fire and holds her hands to it.*]—Never mind about me. I'll be all right. Look out for yourself. When Big Business comes down, just watch you don't let him—[*The door opens. She looks over her shoulder and sees her Father.*]—But by a strange coincidence, here he is now.

JULIA: Did you see Mr. Hobson, Father?

[EDWARD SETON *enters. He is fifty-eight, large, nervous, distinguished. He wears a black morning coat, a white carnation in the buttonhole, and gray striped trousers. He takes nose glasses from his nose and folds them away in a silver case.*]

EDWARD: Yes.—Of course, my dear, there is another thing to be considered: What is the young man's background? Is he the sort of person that—? Ah, good morning, Linda.

LINDA: You saw me in church, Father. What's on your mind? You look worried.

EDWARD: I presume Julia has told you her story?

LINDA: Story? She's told me the facts.

EDWARD: But we mustn't rush into things, must we? [*A glance passes between* JULIA *and* LINDA.]

JULIA [*Goes to him*]: I want to be married on January tenth, Father. That's—that's just two weeks from Tuesday.

EDWARD [*Moves to the table behind the sofa at Right, and begins to search through the newspapers*]: Quite impossible.

LINDA: Why?

JULIA: Yes, why? I—I'm sure I couldn't stand a long engagement.

EDWARD: As yet, there is no engagement to stand.

LINDA: The boy has loads of charm, Father.

EDWARD [*Quickly*]: You know him?

LINDA: I've heard tell of him.

EDWARD [*Tastes the word*]: Charm.

LINDA: —I suppose it's solid merit you're after. Well, the rumor is he's got that, too. Sterling chap, on the whole. A catch, in fact. [NED *wanders in and seats himself upon the sofa at Left, with a newspaper.*]

JULIA: What did Mr. Hobson say, Father?

EDWARD: We must find out about the young man's background.

JULIA: What did he say?

EDWARD: Have you the financial section of the *Times,* Ned?

NED: No, I try to take Sundays off, when I can.

EDWARD: —Which reminds me: I should like you to make a practice of remaining in the office until six o'clock.

NED: Six!—What for?

EDWARD: As an example to the other men.

NED: But there's nothing for me to do after three.

EDWARD: You will find something.

NED: Look here, Father—if you think I'm going to fake a lot of—

EDWARD: Did you understand me, Ned? [*A moment:* NED *loses.*]

NED: —Oh, all right.

JULIA: What did Mr. Hobson say about Johnny, Father?

EDWARD [*Settles himself upon the sofa with the financial section, now happily found*]: His report was not at all unfavorable.

LINDA: That must have been a blow.

JULIA: —But what did he *say?*

EDWARD: We must find out more about the young man, Julia. He seems to have some business ability—he has put through what looks like a successful reorganization of Seaboard Utilities. He holds some of the stock.

NED: Seaboard! Poor fellow—

EDWARD: —Shrewd fellow, perhaps. Hobson says signs are not unfavorable for Seaboard.—We'll buy some in the morning, Ned.

LINDA: Just another ill wind blowing money to Da-Da.

EDWARD: But we *must* know more about Mr. Chase's background.

JULIA: Case, Father, Case.

LINDA: Let it go. Chase has such a sweet banking sound.

JULIA: He's from Baltimore.

LINDA: Fine old prewar stock, I imagine.

NED: Wasn't there a Judge Case somewhere?

EDWARD: We shall see. We shall take steps to—

LINDA: Father, if you reach for a Social Register, I'll cry out with pain.

EDWARD [*With decision*]: Well, I most certainly intend to know more about the young man than his name and his birthplace.—He does not, of course, realize that you have spoken to me, as yet?

NED: Of course not.

LINDA: Julia works fast, but not *that* fast, do you, Julia? [JULIA *does not answer.*]

EDWARD: I propose not to allow the subject of an engagement to come up in my first talk with him. I believe I am competent to direct the conversation.—You and Ned, Julia, may excuse yourselves on one pretext or another. I should like you to stay, Linda.

LINDA: I *knew* I should have learned shorthand. [EDWARD *smiles.* HENRY *enters.*]

EDWARD: I shall trust your memory.—Yes, Henry?

HENRY: Mr. Case wishes to be announced, sir.

EDWARD: Yes. [HENRY *goes out, closing the door after him.* EDWARD *arranges his cuffs and takes a firmer seat in his chair.*]

LINDA: —So does Mr. Case's engagement. I want to give a party for it New Year's Eve, Father.

JULIA: Wait a minute, dear—

EDWARD [*Watching the doorway*]: You may give a party if you like, Linda, but whether to announce an engagement, we shall see——

LINDA: —Another point about my party is that it's *my* party—mine.

EDWARD: Yes?

LINDA: Yes—and as such, I'd like to run it. I can do quite well without your secretary this time, darling—and without Seton's and Laura's helpful hints, I can do brilliantly.—There's someone at the door.

NED: Keep a stiff upper lip, Father. No doubt the fellow is an impostor.

EDWARD [*Laughs*]: Oh, we shall learn many things this morning! He is not the first young man to be interviewed by me.

JULIA: Father—

EDWARD: Yes, daughter?

JULIA: Remember: I know what I want. [JOHNNY *enters.*] Oh, here you are!

JOHNNY: Here I am.

JULIA: Father, this is—Mr. Case. [JOHNNY *goes to* EDWARD. *They shake hands.* NED *rises.*]

EDWARD: How do you do, Mr. Case?

JOHNNY: How do you do, sir?

EDWARD: —My daughter, Linda.

LINDA: How do you do?

JOHNNY: How do you do?

EDWARD: And my son, Ned.

JOHNNY: How do you do?

NED: I recall your face, but your figure puzzles me.

EDWARD: Julia, if you and Ned will do the telephoning I spoke of, Linda and I will try to entertain Mr. Case until the others come—won't we, Linda?

LINDA: Sure. I'm game.

JULIA [*Moves toward the door*]: —Coming, Ned?

NED [*Following her*]: I wonder what we'd do without the telephone. [*They go out.*]

EDWARD: Sit down, Mr. Case.

JOHNNY: Thank you. [*He seats himself upon the bench, Left, and* LINDA *sits on a small stool at the fireplace.*]

EDWARD: I presume, like all young people, you have the bad habit of smoking before luncheon?

JOHNNY: I'm afraid I have.

EDWARD: —A cigar?

JOHNNY: Not right now, thank you.

EDWARD [*Lets himself down into a sofa*]: We've been quite at the mercy of the snow these days, haven't we?

JOHNNY: It doesn't seem much after Placid.

EDWARD: Placid—ah, yes! My daughter Julia has just come from there.

JOHNNY: I know.

EDWARD [*A brief pause. Then*]: —You are in business in New York, Mr. Case?

JOHNNY: Yes, I'm in the Law. I'm with Sloan, Hobson.

EDWARD: An excellent firm.—And a born New Yorker?

JOHNNY: No. I was born in Baltimore.—In eighteen ninety-seven. July sixth. I'm thirty.

EDWARD: Baltimore—I used to have many friends in Baltimore.—The Whites—the Clarence Whites—Possibly you knew them.

JOHNNY: No, I don't believe I ever did.

EDWARD: —And then there was Archie Fuller's family—

JOHNNY: I'm afraid not.

EDWARD: —And let me see now—Colonel Evans—old Philip Evans—

JOHNNY: Nope. [*There is a silence. Then*] I haven't been there in some years. And I shouldn't be likely to know them, anyway. My mother and father died when I was quite young. My father had a small grocery store in Baltimore, which he was never able to make a go of. He left a number of debts which my mother worked very hard to clear up. I was the only child, and I wasn't in a position to help very much. She died the May before my sixteenth birthday. [LINDA *is listening with growing interest.*]

EDWARD: But how sad.

JOHNNY: It *was* pretty sad.—I hadn't any connections, except for an uncle who's in the roofing business in Wilmington. He wasn't much good, though—he was inclined to get drunk—still is—

LINDA: We have an uncle like that, but he keeps off roofs.

JOHNNY [*Smiles at her, and continues*]: —But I was what's called a bright boy, and I managed to wangle a couple of scholarships. They helped a good deal in school and college, and there were always plenty of ways to make up the difference. In term time I usually ran eating-joints and typed lecture notes. In summers I sold aluminum pots and pans—

EDWARD: [*Weakly*]: Linda! Are you there, Linda?

LINDA: Yes, Father.

JOHNNY:—Or worked in a factory or on a newspaper. Once I got myself engaged as a tutor. That was pretty unpleasant. Then there were department stores at Christmas and florists at Easter. During law school I slept all night on a couch in a doctor's office, and got fifteen a week for it. That was soft.

EDWARD [*It is all he can say*]: Admirable!

JOHNNY: No—it simply happened to be the only way to get through. [*A brief pause. Then*] Anything else, sir?

EDWARD: I beg your pardon?

LINDA [*Rises*]: I should think you would.

JOHNNY: —Is there anything more I can tell you about myself?

EDWARD: Why, uh—that is to say, uh—[*He flounders and stops. A moment, then* JOHNNY *moves toward him.*]

JOHNNY: Well, Mr. Seton, how about it?

EDWARD: About it? About what?

JOHNNY: Julia and me.

EDWARD: You and Julia? I'm afraid I—

JOHNNY: —About our getting married.

EDWARD [*There is a silence. Then*]: This is a complete surprise, Mr. Case. I don't know quite what to say to you.

JOHNNY [*Smiles*]: "Yes" would be pleasant.

EDWARD: I am sure it would. However, we must go into it rather more carefully, I am afraid.

JOHNNY: The only difficulty is the time. Julia's idea is January tenth. It's mine, too.

EDWARD: We shall see about that.

JOHNNY: May I ask *how* we shall see, sir?

EDWARD: Mr. Case, I do not know you at all.

JOHNNY: I'll give you every opportunity you permit me. How's lunch tomorrow?

EDWARD: Tomorrow I have several—

JOHNNY: —Tuesday?

EDWARD [*Hesitates*]: Will you meet me at the Bankers' Club at one on Friday?

JOHNNY: I'm terribly sorry, but Friday's out. I've got to go to Boston on business.—Better make it tomorrow. [*A moment.* NED *and* JULIA *re-enter. Then* EDWARD *speaks, hastily:*]

EDWARD: —Very well. I shall arrange my appointments.—Ah, Ned, Julia—and what do you suppose can be keeping the Crams? [*But* JOHNNY *cuts in before they can reply:*]

JOHNNY: —Thank you. In the meantime, I think Mr. Hobson or Mr.

Sloan might say a good word for me. I'm nobody at all, as things go. But I'm quite decent and fairly civilized, and I love your daughter very much—which isn't a bit hard. She seems to like me quite a lot too, and that's about all that can be said for me—except that I think we've a simply grand chance to be awfully happy.—What do *you* say, Julia?

JULIA: Oh, so do I!

LINDA: Come on, Father, be an angel. *I* think he's a very good number.

EDWARD: I am afraid it is too important a matter to be decided off-hand.

JULIA: But I want to be married on the—

EDWARD [*With sudden sharpness*]: You will be married, Julia, when I have reached a favorable decision—and upon a day which I will name.

JULIA: I—our plan was—the tenth, and sail that night on—

EDWARD: The tenth is out of the question.

JULIA: Oh, but Father—! I—

EDWARD: —And we shall let it rest at that, for the moment.

LINDA: But you'll come round, Father! I have a swell hunch you'll come round. Oh, Lordy, Lordy, what fun! Let's all join hands and—[*Voices are heard from the hall.*]

EDWARD: Seton?—Laura?—Is that you I hear?

LINDA: You bet it is.—Let's *not* join hands.

[SETON CRAM *and his wife,* LAURA, *enter.* SETON *is thirty-six, somewhat bald, inclined to a waistline, but well turned out in a morning coat, striped trousers and spats.* LAURA *is thirty-two, a shade taller than* SETON, *with a rather handsome, rather disagreeable face. She is as smartly dressed as a poor figure will allow.*]

SETON: Hello, hello!

EDWARD: —How are you, young man?

SETON: Blooming, thanks. We walked all the way up. [*They shake hands with* EDWARD.]

LAURA: I do hope we're not late, Uncle Ned.

EDWARD: No, indeed!

LINDA: You're early.

LAURA: Julia, my dear, you're back. [*She kisses her and then bears down upon* LINDA.]—And Linda! How simply stunning!

LINDA [*Wards off the impending kiss*]: Careful, Laura—I've got the most terrible cold.

LAURA [*Returning*]: But I never saw you looking better!—Hello, Ned.

NED: Hello.

EDWARD: This is—uh—Mr. Case—my nephew, Mr. Cram, and Mrs. Cram. [LAURA *inclines her head.*]

SETON: How do you do?

JOHNNY: How do you do? [NED *edges away from* LAURA. EDWARD, *still stunned, stares in front of himself.*]

LAURA: —Isn't it horrid how chapped one's hands get this weather? I don't know *what* to do. How was Placid, Julia?—You must have had *such* a divine time. Were there loads of amusing people there?—And lots of beaux, too— Oh, you needn't deny it!—We know Julia, don't we, Seton?—And you, Linda—we haven't seen *you* for ages—[*She seats herself upon the bench at Right*]—Now sit right down and tell us *everything* you've been doing—

LINDA: Well, take the average day: I get up about eighty-thirty, bathe, dress, and have my coffee.—Aren't you going to brush up before lunch, Ned?

NED: —Would you care to brush up before lunch, Case?

JOHNNY: I think I shall, if I may. [*He follows* NED *to the door.*]

LINDA: —Julia?

JULIA: I'm all right, thanks.

LINDA: But look me *me,* will you! [*She moves quickly across the room after* NED *and* JOHNNY, *flecking imaginary dust from her dress as she goes.*]—Simply *covered* with dust!—Wait, boys!

CURTAIN

■ ACT II ■

SCENE: *The playroom on the top floor is a long and spacious low-ceilinged room with white woodwork and pale blue walls upon which are lightly traced storybook designs in silver, white and green.*

At Right and Left there are two windows with window seats below them, curtained in a white-starred cretonne of a deeper blue than the walls.

The only entrance is from the hall at Back.

At Right there is a low platform for horizontal bars and a punching bag, above which a pair of trapezes swing from the ceiling. At present they are tied up. Against the back wall behind them is a glass cabinet containing a collection of old toys, arranged on shelves in orderly rows.

Also at Right is a table, with tablecloth spread, and four small chairs. Against the back wall at Left is an old-fashioned music box, and in the corner near it a small electric gramophone. Also at Left is a low couch and a table, a miniature easy chair and a folding cushion.

TIME: *New Year's Eve, this year.*

AT RISE: *The playroom is empty, and lit only by a pale night glow from the windows. A moment, then* JULIA *opens the door, and calls:*

JULIA: Linda! [*There is no answer. Dance music is heard from downstairs.*] She isn't here.

NED [*Reaches past her to an electric button and lights the room*]: I didn't say she was. All I said was it's where she comes, as a rule, when she finds herself in a jam. [*They come into the room. Both are in evening clothes. In one hand* NED *carries two whisky and sodas. He puts one glass on the table and retains the other.*]

JULIA: I don't believe she's in the house.

NED [*Takes a swallow of his drink*]: Maybe not.

JULIA: I told them all at dinner that she had a blinding headache, but expected to come down later.

NED: That's as good as anything—[*And another swallow*] Let's get out of here. This room gives me a funny feeling.

JULIA: Wait a minute.—You know how furious Father was when she wasn't there for dinner—[*She goes and shuts the door, closing out the music.*] What can we do, Ned?

NED: Search me.

JULIA [*She moves to a chair and seats herself*]: But it's her party!

NED: Don't make me laugh, Julia. It was, maybe, until you and Father took it over.

JULIA: *I* did?

NED: You stood by and saw it done. Then the Crams got hold of it. Among you, you asked the whole list—which was just what Linda didn't want. You threw out the team of dancers she'd engaged for supper, and got in that troupe of Scotch Songbirds. You let Farley, with his Flower Fancies, turn it into a house of mourning. Among you, you made Linda's funny little bust into a first-class funeral. I can't say I blame her, no. However—[*He raises his glass.*]—drink to Linda.

JULIA: Well, I do! She should have realized that Father couldn't announce my engagement without *some* fuss.

NED: She should have, yes. But unlike me, Linda always hopes. [*Again his glass is raised.*] Bottoms up to Linda.

JULIA: Don't, Ned.

NED: Don't what?

JULIA: You've been drinking steadily since eight o'clock.

NED: Yes?—Funny old Ned. On New Year's Eve, too. [*He drains his glass and takes up the other.*]

JULIA: Will you kindly stop it?

NED: Darling sister, I shall drink as much as I like at any party I agree to attend. [*She turns from him with an exclamation.*]—And as much as I like is as much as I can hold. It's my protection against your tiresome friends. Linda's out of luck, she hasn't one.

JOHNNY [*Comes in. Music and Voices are heard from downstairs*]: —Believe it or not, I've been talking politics with an Admiral. [*He looks about him.*]—What a nice room!

NED: It's too full of ghosts for me. It gives me the creeps.

JULIA: She isn't here, Johnny.

JOHNNY: Linda?

JULIA: Yes, of course.

JOHNNY: Did you expect she would be?

JULIA: Ned thought so.

NED: Ned was wrong.

[HENRY *and* CHARLES *enter.* HENRY *carries table linen and silver and a tray of plates and glasses;* CHARLES *a pail of ice containing two bottles of champagne and a plate of sandwiches. They go to the table.*]

JULIA: Isn't there room for everyone downstairs, Henry?

HENRY: Miss Linda telephoned to serve supper here for six at half-past eleven, Miss.

NED: Ned was right.

JULIA: From where did she telephone, do you know?

HENRY: She didn't say, Miss. [*There is a pause.* HENRY *and* CHARLES *proceed to set the table.*]

JOHNNY [*To* JULIA]: I think I know where she is, if that's any help.

JULIA: You? Where—?

JOHNNY: With Nick and Susan Potter.

JULIA: What's she doing with them?

JOHNNY: Dining, I imagine.

NED: It's eleven-twenty now.

JULIA: Where did you get your information, Johnny?

JOHNNY: I met her coming in this afternoon. She said she wouldn't stay in the house tonight. Apparently it meant more to her than anyone thought.

NED: Not than I thought. I warned Father.

JOHNNY: It was no use talking to her. She was going out to dine somewhere by herself. I knew that Nick and Susan were having Pete Jessup and Mary Hedges, so I telephoned Susan and asked her to ask Linda, too.

JULIA: I wish you had spoken to me first.

JOHNNY: Why?

JULIA: People like that aren't good for Linda.

JOHNNY [*Looks at her for a moment, puzzled, and then laughs*]: What are you talking about, Julia?

JULIA: They make her even more discontented than she is. Heavens knows why, but they do.

NED: Apparently she's bringing them back with her. [HENRY *and* CHARLES *go out, closing the door after them.*]

JULIA: Well, they certainly can't expect to have supper up here by themselves.

NED: No? Why not?

JULIA: They simply can't, that's all.

NED: What is this conspiracy against Linda, anyway? Are you all afraid she might cause a good time here, for once—and if she did, the walls might fall down? Is that it? [JULIA *does not reply.* JOHNNY *seats himself near her.*]

JOHNNY: I do love this room, don't you, Julia?

JULIA [*Briefly*]: Yes.—It was Mother's idea for us.

JOHNNY: She must have been sweet.

JULIA: She was.

NED: —Father wanted a big family, you know. So she had Julia straight off, to oblige him. But Julia was a girl, so she promptly had Linda. But Linda was a girl—it looked hopeless. [*His voice rises.*]—So the next year she had me, and there was much joy in the land.—It was a boy, and the fair name of Seton would flourish. [JULIA *looks at him in alarm.*]—It must have been a great consolation to Father. Drink to Mother, Johnny—she tried to be a Seton for a while, then gave up and died.—Drink to Mother—

JOHNNY [*Laughs uneasily*]: You're talking through your hat, Ned.

NED: But I'm not.

JULIA [*To* JOHNNY]: Can't you possibly persuade him that he's had enough?

NED: It's all right, Julia: you heard what I said.—There's a bar in my room, if you want anything, Johnny. Tell as many of the men as you think need it. It's all very pleasant and hole-in-the-wall like everything else that's any relief in this house.—Drink to Father. [*He drains his glass, sets it down upon a table, turns on his heel and goes out, closing the door after him.*]

JULIA: We must do something about them—we *must,* Johnny!

JOHNNY: —Him and Linda.

JULIA: Yes, yes!

JOHNNY: I don't see what.—It seems a lot more goes on inside them than we've any idea of. Linda must be at the end of some rope or other. As for Ned—

JULIA: He always does this—always—

JOHNNY [*Rises*]: He began some time.—I'll keep an eye on him, though, and if he stops making sense I'll get him to bed somehow.

JULIA: —And Linda's got to bring her friends downstairs.—People know there's something wrong, now—they must know.—She's simply *got* to!

JOHNNY: All right, darling. Only—

JULIA: Only what—

JOHNNY: —Do try to enjoy tonight, won't you?

JULIA: But I am, Johnny. I think it's a lovely party!

JOHNNY: Then how about getting that frown from between your eyes and not feeling personally responsible for three hundred guests, and a brother and sister?

JULIA: —Someone's got to be.

JOHNNY: —Let your Father, then.

JULIA: Poor man. Reporters have been after him all day long.

JOHNNY: Me, too. I've never felt so important.

JULIA: I hope you didn't talk.

JOHNNY: I just asked for offers for the story of how I wooed and won you. Farm Boy Weds Heiress as Blizzard Grips City.

JULIA [*Laughs*]: What *did* you say?

JOHNNY: I didn't see them.

JULIA: That's right. Father was awfully anxious that nothing be added to what he sent in—except, of course, what they're bound to add themselves.

JOHNNY: Evidently it's a good deal.

JULIA: Well, that we can't help.

JOHNNY: The French Line wrote me. They want to give us a suite, in place of the cabin.

JULIA: I doubt if we ought to accept it.

JOHNNY: No? Why not?

JULIA: I think it might not look so well. I'll ask Father.

JOHNNY [*A brief pause. Then*]: Perhaps we oughtn't to go abroad at all. Perhaps *that's* too great an evidence of wealth.

JULIA: Now, Johnny—

JOHNNY: —But we're going, my dear, and in the most comfortable quarters they choose to provide.

JULIA: What a curious tone for you to take. [*He looks at her in amazement, then laughs genuinely.*]

JOHNNY: Julia, don't be ridiculous! "Tone to take." [*She turns from him.*]—We may be suddenly and unexpectedly important to the world, but I don't see that we're quite important enough to bend over backwards.

JULIA [*A silence. Then*]: Of course, I'll do whatever you like about it.

JOHNNY: It would be nice if you'd like it too.

JULIA [*She returns to him*]: And I'll like it too, Johnny. [*He bends and kisses her lightly.*]

JOHNNY: —Sweet. [*He takes her by the hand and draws her toward the door.*]—Come on, let's go below and break into a gavotte.

JULIA [*Stops*]: —Do something for me, will you?

JOHNNY: Sure.

JULIA: —Stay here till Linda arrives, then make her come down. I can't wait. *Some* female member of the household's got to be around, if it's only the cook.

JOHNNY: —I'll *ask* her to come down.

JULIA: Insist on it!

JOHNNY: Well, I'll do whatever a gent can in the circumstances.

JULIA: You're *so* irritating! Honestly, I hate the sight of you.

JOHNNY: Julia—

JULIA: What?

JOHNNY: Like hell you do.

JULIA: I know. It's hopeless. [*She goes to the door, opens it, then turns to him again. Laughter is heard from downstairs.*] Do as you like—I love you very much.

JOHNNY: —You get through that door quick and close it after you, or you won't get out at all.

JULIA: —Just to look at you makes my spine feel like—feel like— [*He moves swiftly toward her, but finds the door closed. He stands for a moment staring at it, transfixed, then pulls it open, calling "Darling!"—But instead of* JULIA, *he finds* NICK POTTER.]

NICK: Hey! What is this?

JOHNNY: Nick! [NICK *moves away from him, scowling, and straightening his coat. He is about thirty-four, with an attractive, amusing face.*]

NICK: —Get fresh with me, and I'll knock your block off. [*He sees the champagne and goes to it.*] What have we here—some kind of a grape beverage?

JOHNNY: Mumm's the word.—Where's Susan?

NICK: Coming.—I hear you're engaged. Many happy returns. Is it announced yet?

JOHNNY: Thanks.—No, it's to come with a roll of drums at midnight—"A lady has lost a diamond and platinum wristwatch."

NICK: —With that gifted entertainer, Mr. Edward Seton, at the microphone—

JOHNNY: That's the plan.

NICK: I heard about his work with this party.—He has the true ashman's touch, that man.

JOHNNY: He's been all right to me.

NICK: Oh, sure—he believes you're a comer. That's what won him over so quickly—the same stuff as Grandpa Seton himself—up-from-nothing—hew to the line—eat yeast. Me—of course I'm God's great social menace because I never got out and did Big Things.

JOHNNY: I really like him. I like him a lot.

NICK: Keep your men on him, though. Don't relax your vigilance. [*He is opening the bottles and filling the glasses. Music and voices are heard through the open door.*]

JOHNNY: —You think, for instance, that if *I* should quit business—

NICK: Just try it once. Why, he'd come down on you like Grant took Bourbon.

JOHNNY: You've got him all wrong, Nick.

NICK: Maybe.—Anyhow, you're not really thinking of it, are you?

JOHNNY [*Goes to the couch*]: I am, you know!

NICK: On what, may I ask?

JOHNNY: Well, I've got a nice little mess of common stock that's begun to move about two years before I thought it would. And if it goes where I think it will—

NICK: —Haven't you and Julia a pretty good life ahead as it is, Johnny?

JOHNNY: You and Susan have a better one.

NICK: Listen, baby—I don't think I'd try any enlightened living stuff on this family. They wouldn't know what you were talking about.

JOHNNY: Julia would.

NICK: —Might. But the old man's a terror, Johnny. Honestly—you don't *know*.

JOHNNY: Enough of your jibes, Potter. You answer to me for your slurs on a Seton.

NICK [*Moves toward him*]: —Seats on a Slurton—I want to get three seats on a Slurton for Tuesday night [*—and confronts him with an empty bottle*] Go on, hit me, why don't you? Just hit me. Take off your glasses—[*and returns to the table.*]—I was dragged against my will to this function. And somehow I don't seem to so well.

JOHNNY: What?

NICK: —Function.

[LINDA *and* SUSAN *enter.* SUSAN *is thirty, smart and attractive. She goes straight to* JOHNNY *and kisses him.*]

SUSAN: Cheers from me, Johnny.

JOHNNY: Thanks, Susan.

SUSAN *and* NICK [*Together*]: We only hope that you will be as happy as we have been. [LINDA *closes the door. Voices and music cease to be heard.* NICK *continues to fill the glasses.*]

JOHNNY [*To* LINDA]: What did you do with Pete and Mary?

LINDA: They're coming in a heated barouche.

JOHNNY: Linda, I'm to inform you that there's another party going on in the house.

LINDA: You mean that low-class dance hall downstairs? [*She moves toward* NICK.] Don't speak of it. [NICK *gives her a glass of wine, and then one to* SUSAN.]

NICK: Here, Pearl, wet your pretty whistle with this. [NICK *and* JOHNNY *take glasses.* SUSAN *raises hers.*]

SUSAN: —To Johnny and his Julia.

JOHNNY: Julia—[*They drink.* LINDA *seats herself in a chair near the table.*]

SUSAN: —Merry Christmas, from Dan to Beersheba.

NICK [*Examining the table*]: —Only sandwiches? What a house!

LINDA: There's solid food on the way.

NICK: I'll trade twenty marbles and a jacknife for the carcass of one chicken, in good repair.

LINDA: You should have been with us, Johnny. Not one word of sense was spoken from eight to eleven.

SUSAN: —When Linda got homesick.

LINDA: I'm a die-hard about this evening and this room. I only hope nobody else wanders in. [JOHNNY *seats himself near* LINDA.]

NICK: I tell you who'd be fun.

LINDA: Who?

NICK: Seton and Laura.

LINDA: They wouldn't stay long.—You see those trapezes?

NICK: Yes?

LINDA: Time was when Seton and I used to swing from them by our knees, and spit at each other.

NICK: Great!

LINDA: I'm happy to say now, I rarely missed.

JOHNNY: But aren't we going downstairs?

LINDA: No, Angel, we're not.

NICK: It's grand here. It takes sixty years off these old shoulders. [*He looks at his watch.*] Eleven-forty.—Doctor Stork's on the way, dears, with Little Baby New Year. [*He goes and seats himself with* JOHNNY *and* LINDA.]

LINDA: I wish someone would tell me what *I'm* to do next year—and the year after—and the year after that—

SUSAN: What you need is a husband, Linda. [*She joins the group.*]

LINDA: Have you got any addresses?

SUSAN: He'll arrive. I only hope you'll know how to act when he does.

LINDA: Well, I won't take No for an answer.

NICK: Don't you do it.

LINDA: And in the meanwhile what? Hotfoot it around the world with a maid and a dog? Lie on one beach after another, getting brown?

NICK: Oo, I *love* to play in the sand.

SUSAN [*To* LINDA]: —You just won't stay put, will you, child?

LINDA: And grow up to be a committee-woman and sit on Boards? Excuse me, Susan, but from now on any charity work *I* do will be for the rich. They need it more. [NICK, SUSAN *and* JOHNNY *are eating sandwiches and sipping their wine.*]

NICK: Now look, Linda—let me tell you about yourself, will you?

LINDA: Go ahead.

NICK: There's more of your grandfather in you than you think.

LINDA: Boo.

NICK: There is, though. He wasn't satisfied with the life he was born into, so he made one for himself. Now, you don't like *his* five-story log cabin so you're out in the woods again with your own little hatchet.

SUSAN: The Little Pioneer, with Linda Seton.

JOHNNY: —Linda's off on the wrong foot, though. She's headed up the fun alley. She thinks having fun is the whole answer to life.

LINDA: *I* do?

JOHNNY: You do.—Me—it's not just entertainment *I'm* after—oh, no —I want all of it—inside, outside—smooth and rough—let 'er come!

NICK: You're right, too.—Life's a grand little ride, if you take it yourself.

JOHNNY: —And no good at all if someone else takes you on it. Damn it, there's *no* life any good but the one you make for yourself.

SUSAN [*A protest*]: Hey, hey—

JOHNNY: —Except yours and Nick's, maybe.

LINDA: But they *have* made theirs!—Haven't you, Susan?

SUSAN: About half-and-half, I should say. I don't know quite what we'd do if we had to earn our own living.

NICK: Earn it.—Is it settled about the wedding, Johnny?

JOHNNY: The twelfth—a week from Friday.

LINDA: Why not the tenth?

JOHNNY: Your father had a corporation meeting.—Ushers' dinner on Monday, Nick.

NICK [*To* SUSAN]: Don't wait lunch for me Tuesday.

SUSAN: Just come as you are.—Oh, I gave a scream.

LINDA: What's the matter?

SUSAN [*To* JOHNNY]: —Then you've put off your sailing, too?

JOHNNY: We had to.

SUSAN: Don't tell me it's the *Paris* now?

JOHNNY: Yes. Why?

SUSAN: But we changed ours from the tenth to the *Paris* so as not to bump into your wedding trip!

NICK: Well, we'll change back again.

JOHNNY: Don't think of it. It'll be great fun.

LINDA: Guess what *I* did in a wild moment this morning—

NICK: What?

LINDA: —Had my passport renewed—and Ned's. I want to get him away.

SUSAN: You're sailing then too?—It's a field day!

LINDA: No—not till a week or so after.

JOHNNY: Come along with us, Linda. It'd be grand. We'd own the boat.

LINDA: You'll have had plenty of family by then, little man. We'll join up later.

JOHNNY: How long do you plan to stay over, Nick?

NICK: Oh—June—August—September—like the dirty loafers we are.

LINDA: Loafers nothing!

JOHNNY: You've got the life, you two.

LINDA: Haven't they? [*To* SUSAN] You know, you've always seemed to me the rightest, wisest, happiest people ever I've known.

SUSAN: Why, Linda, thanks!

LINDA: You're my one real hope in the world.

JOHNNY: Mine, too.

SUSAN: Well, when we're with a pair like you—shall I say it, Nick?

NICK: Just let them look at us: Beam, darling—

SUSAN [*Beams*]: —The Beaming Potters.

NICK: —In ten minutes of clean fun—

NICK *and* SUSAN [*Together*]: We hope you'll like us! [*Then*]

NICK: —And what about you, Johnny? How long will you and Julia be there? [*A moment.* JOHNNY *smiles. Then*]

JOHNNY: Well—maybe indefinitely.

LINDA: How do you mean? Julia said March.

JOHNNY: Julia doesn't know yet.

LINDA: Johnny, what *is* this? !

JOHNNY: Well, some stock that I got at about eight was kind enough to touch fifteen today. And if a deal I think's going through does go through, it'll do twice that.

SUSAN [*Puzzled*]: I must be dumb, but—

JOHNNY: Friends, there's a very fair chance I'll quit business next Saturday.

LINDA: Johnny!

NICK: For good?

JOHNNY: —For as long as it lasts.

SUSAN: As what lasts? Have you made some money?

JOHNNY: I think I shall have, by Saturday.

SUSAN: Good boy!

LINDA: Oh, very good boy!

NICK: —And Julia doesn't know your little plan?

JOHNNY: I haven't breathed a word of it to her. I wanted to be sure first. It all depends on what a Boston crowd called Bay State Power does about it. I'll know that Monday.

LINDA: They'll do it! I don't know what it is, but I know they'll do it! Oh, Lord, am I happy! [*A moment. Then*] But, Johnny—

JOHNNY: What?

LINDA: I'm scared.

JOHNNY: Of what?

LINDA: Listen to me a moment: Father and Julia— [*She stops, as* SETON *and* LAURA *appear in the doorway, and exclaims in disgust*:] My God, it's Winnie-the-Pooh! [JOHNNY *and* NICK *rise.* LAURA *gazes about her.*]

LAURA: But isn't this lovely!

SETON: Well, well, so here you are! [*He comes into the room.* LAURA *follows.*]

NICK: So we are.

SETON: Hello, Nick.—Hello, Susan!

NICK: How are you?

LAURA [*To* SUSAN]: My dear, what fun! We simply never meet any more.

SUSAN: —Just a pair of parallel lines, I expect.

LAURA: I must say you're a picture, Susan.

SUSAN [*Rises and goes to the couch*]: —Madame is in a thin bed-jacket, by Hammacher Schlemmer.

LAURA: May we sit down a minute? [*She seats herself in* NICK*'s chair.*]

LINDA: Why not?

LAURA: I've never been up here. It's awfully pleasant.

LINDA: We like it.

NICK: Of course, it's rather far from the carline—

SUSAN: And the water isn't all it might be—

NICK *and* SUSAN [*Together*]: But *we* like it!

JOHNNY: Don't change it, friends. It's the poor man's club.

LAURA: What on earth are you all talking about?

LINDA [*Rises and goes to the table*]: Oh, just banter—airy nothings—give and take—

NICK: It's our defense against the ashman's touch.

LAURA: I *love* the decorations.

LINDA: They *love* to be loved.

LAURA: I'm afraid I don't follow you.—You're not all tight, are you?

LINDA: On the continent, dear, on the continent.

NICK: We have a very high boiling point.

SETON [*Leans over and plucks* JOHNNY*'s sleeve*]: You old fox, you.

JOHNNY: Yes? How's that?

SETON: Sam Hobson's downstairs. He's just been telling me about your little haul in Seaboard. You might have let your friends in on it.

JOHNNY: There's still time. Climb aboard if you like.

SETON: I have already.—Do you know there's an order in our office to buy sixty thousand shares for Ross, of Bay State Power, all the way up to thirty?

JOHNNY [*Quickly*]: Are you sure of that?

SETON: I took the order myself.

JOHNNY: Then that cinches it.

SUSAN: Is it a real killing, Johnny?

JOHNNY: For me it is!

SETON [*Impressively*]: —Just thirty or forty thousand, that's all.

SUSAN: —No odds cents?

LINDA: Johnny—Johnny—

NICK: Let this be a lesson to you, young man.

SETON: —Anyone mind if I talk a little business?—The impression in our part of town is, it's you who put Seaboard on the map.

JOHNNY: I wouldn't go so far as that.

SETON: Ross said so himself.—Look here: we'd damn well like to have you with us, in Pritchard, Ames.

JOHNNY: Thanks, I've heard about that.

SETON: The Chief's told you already?

JOHNNY: I saw him this afternoon.

SETON [*To* NICK]: —To begin at twice what he gets now—and probably a directorship in Seaboard, to boot.

NICK: Well, well—to boot, eh?

SETON [*To* JOHNNY]: I hope you said yes.

JOHNNY: I told him I'd let him know.

SETON: Believe me when I tell you the first fifty thousand is the hardest. —It's plain sailing after that.

LINDA [*Suddenly*]: Look out, Johnny!

SETON: —In two years we'll make your forty thousand, eighty—in five, two hundred.

NICK [*Edges over to* JOHNNY]: —Lend a fellow a dime for a cup of coffee, mister? [JOHNNY *laughs.*]

SETON: Well, how about it?

JOHNNY: I'll let him know.

SETON: You couldn't do better than to come with us—not possibly.

JOHNNY [*Rises and puts his glass on the table*]: It's awfully nice of you, it really is.

LINDA: Look out, look *out!*

JOHNNY: Don't worry, Linda.

SETON: —Just let me give you a brief outline of the possibilities—

LINDA: That will do for business tonight, Seton.

SETON: I just want to tell Johnny—

LINDA: It's enough, really.

SETON [*Laughs, and rises*]: You're the hostess!—Then let's all go downstairs and celebrate, shall we?

LAURA [*Rises*]: Yes, let's.—It's such a wonderful party.

LINDA: I'm not going downstairs.

SETON: Oh, come along, Linda—don't be foolish.

LAURA: Do come, dear. Your father said to tell you he—

LINDA: Yes—I thought so.—But I'm not going downstairs.

NICK [*Moves away from them to the other side of the room*]: Where's the old music box we used to play, Linda?

LINDA: Over there—but I've got something better—[*She goes to the gramophone in the corner.*] Listen—it's electric—it'll melt your heart with its—

NICK: Take it away. [SUSAN *rises.* SETON *and* LAURA *move toward the door.*]

SUSAN: Nick—you wouldn't go whimsical on us!

NICK: Oh, God, for the old scenes—the old times—

SETON: It's a quarter to twelve now, you know—

NICK [*Examining the music box*]: Welcome, little New Year—

LAURA: Linda, I really think that—

LINDA: I know, Laura.

NICK [*Reads the music-box's repertory from a card*]: "Sweet Marie"— "Fatal Wedding"—"Southern Roses"—

SUSAN: —And *this* is the way they used to dance when Grandmamma was a girl.

NICK [*Covers his eyes and gulps*]: Don't. My old eyes can scarcely see for the tears.

LAURA: You're all absolutely mad.

[HENRY *and* CHARLES *enter, with a chafing-dish and a platter of cold meats. A chorus of male voices is heard from downstairs.*]

SUSAN: Heavens, what would that be?

LINDA: It's the Scottish Singers, the little dears—[*She is watching* JOHNNY.]

NICK: I wouldn't have come if I'd known the Campbells were coming—[CHARLES *closes the door.* LINDA *starts a loud new dance-record on the gramophone.*]

SETON [*Angrily*]: What do you think this gets you, anyway?

LINDA: Peace and quiet!

NICK [*Huddles himself in his arms*]: What a night! What a night!

SUSAN: What Nick really wants is some nice beer to cry into.

LINDA: Will everybody please stop sobbing! Stop it!—Take some wine, will you, Case?

JOHNNY: Thanks.

LINDA [*Intensely*]: If you weaken now—!

JOHNNY: I never felt stronger.

LINDA [*Turns to* SUSAN]: Peter and Mary—they couldn't have ditched us, could they?

SUSAN: Oh, no, they'll be along—

NICK: Eleven forty-seven—what *can* be keeping old Doctor Stork? [HENRY *and* CHARLES, *having placed the platter and chafing-dish upon the table, go out.*]

LAURA [*At the door*]: Linda—really—people are beginning to wonder a little—

LINDA: I am *not going downstairs.*

LAURA [*Laughs unpleasantly*]: Well, of course, if—

LINDA: But I wouldn't dream of keeping anyone who wants to—

LAURA [*Stares a moment, then turns to* SETON]: Apparently we aren't welcome here.

SETON: I gathered that some time ago.—Linda, I think your conduct toward your guests tonight is outrageous.

LAURA: And so do I.

LINDA: I imagined that was what brought you up, you sweet things.

SETON: If you ask me, it's one of the worst cases of downright rudeness I've ever seen.

LINDA: And has someone asked you?

LAURA: —When a girl invites three hundred people to her house, and then proceeds to—

LINDA: I invited six people—three of whom you see before you. The others came on someone else's say-so—yours and Father's, I believe.

LAURA: Perhaps we'd better go home, Seton.

LINDA: Oh, you're here now. Stay, if you like. I'd prefer it, however, if you'd do your commenting on my behavior not to my face, but behind my back as usual—

LAURA [*Opens the door*]: Come, Seton—[*She goes out, with all the hauteur she can command.*]

SETON [*To* LINDA]: When I think of the—

LINDA: —Before you go, you wouldn't care to swing on the old trapeze a while, would you—? [*He stares. She turns away.*] I suppose not [SETON *goes out, closing the door after him.* LINDA *moves toward the table.*] Oh, the cheek, the cheek!

NICK: Someday they'll draw themselves up like that and won't be able to get down again. [*He goes to* JOHNNY.] Well, Johnny—!

JOHNNY [*At the table*]: Lord, it's the grandest feeling—Oh, wait till Julia hears! On tonight of all nights, too! What a break that is!

LINDA: I've never been so happy for anyone in my life.

NICK: Go to it, boy!

JOHNNY: Oh, won't I? Watch me! [*Then*]—Where'll we spend the spring?—Let's all spend the spring together!

NICK: What do you say, Susan? Do you think we could stand them?

SUSAN: There'll always be a curse and a blow for you with us, Johnny.

LINDA: Can I come? Please, can I come, too—? [*She trots in among them.*]

NICK: Don't leave us, darling. We want you. We need you. [SUSAN *joins them. She sits at the end of the table, opposite* NICK, *and* JOHNNY *and* LINDA *behind it, facing the front.* JOHNNY *refills the glasses and* SUSAN *and* LINDA *serve the food.*]

SUSAN: How about the south of France?

JOHNNY: Why not?

LINDA: No, no—the air reeks of roses and the nightingales make the nights hideous.

JOHNNY [*Overcome*]: Don't—don't—[*He gives each of them a glass of wine.*]

NICK [*A suggestion*]: If we went to Norway, we could all paint a house at midnight.

JOHNNY: —Norway's out. It's got to be some place you can swim all day long.—You know, it's just dawned on me that I've never swum enough. That's one of the things I want to do: *swim.*

NICK [*Rises and leans upon the table*]: Young man, in the bright lexicon of youth there is no such word. Swimming is for idlers.

SUSAN: —And Hawaiians.

LINDA: —And fish.

NICK: Are you a fish? Answer me that.—Can you look yourself squarely in the eye and say "I am a fish"? No. You cannot.

JOHNNY: You are a hard man, sir.

NICK: It is life that has made me hard, son.

JOHNNY: —But I want only to be like you, Daddy—how can I be like you?

NICK: You ask me for the story of my success?—Well, I'll tell you—

LINDA: Come—gather close, children. [*They turn their chairs and face him.*]

NICK: —I arrived in this country at the age of three months, with nothing in my pockets but five cents and an old hatcheck. I had no friends, little or no education, and sex to me was still the Great Mystery. But when I came down the gangplank of that little sailing vessel—steam was then unknown, except to the very rich—Friends, can you picture that manly little figure without a tug at your heartstrings, and a faint wave of nausea? But I just pulled my belt a little tighter, and told myself, "Don't forget you're a Potter, Nick"—I called myself "Nick"—and so I found myself at my first job, in the glassworks. Glass was in its infancy then—we had barely scratched the surface—but I have never shirked work—and if there was an errand to be run, I ran five errands. If someone wanted to get off at the third floor, I took him to the tenth floor.—Then one day came my big chance. I was in the glass-blowing department then—now Miss Murphy's department—and a very capable little woman she is—

LINDA: Why, Mr. Potter, I'm no such thing.

NICK: Oh, yes, you are, Miss Murphy! Well, sir, I was blowing glass like a two-year-old, whistling as I blew. Suddenly I looked down and found in my hand—*a bottle*—or what we now know as a bottle. I rushed to my employer, a Mr. Grandgent, and said, "Look, Mr. Grandgent—I think I've got something here. Mr. Grandgent looked —and laughed—*laughed,* do you understand?—I went from city to city like some hunted thing, that laugh still in my ears. But with me went my bottle. They called it Potter's Folly. They said it would never work. Well, time has shown how right they were. Now the bottle is in every home. I have made the bottle a National Institution!—And that, my dears, is how I met your grandmother. [*He bows.*]

LINDA [*Rises, champagne glass in hand*]: —To one who, in the face of every difficulty, has proved himself a Christian gentleman.—Music, music! [*She goes to the gramophone and starts a record.*]

SUSAN [*Rises*]: —To one who has been friend to rich and poor alike—

JOHNNY [*Rises*]: —To one who, as soldier—

LINDA: —As statesman—

SUSAN: —As navigator—

JOHNNY: —As man about town—

LINDA: —As scout-leader—

NICK: —As Third Vice-President of the second largest spat factory in East St. Louis—

JOHNNY: On behalf of the hook-and-ladder company of the First Reformed Church, I want to say a few words about our brave Fire Laddies. Has it occurred to you—[*The door opens and* JULIA *and* EDWARD *enter.*]

EDWARD: Linda!

LINDA: Yes?

EDWARD: Please turn that machine off. [SUSAN *goes to* NICK.]

LINDA: You know Mr. and Mrs. Potter, Father—

EDWARD [*Curtly*]: How do you do? [*Then to* LINDA] Turn it off, Linda— [LINDA *stops the record.*]

NICK [*To* SUSAN]: —Fell, or was pushed.

JOHNNY [*Moves eagerly toward* JULIA]: Julia! Listen, darling! I've got a grand surprise for you—

EDWARD: Just a moment!—You must all come down, now. It's nearly twelve, and we want the entire party together to see the New Year in.

LINDA: But there are two parties, Father—the one down there and mine—*here.*

EDWARD: Please do as I say, Linda.

LINDA: I asked for permission to have a few of my friends here to-night. You said I might. I've got some of them, now, and—

EDWARD: —I noticed you had.

LINDA: —And more are coming.

JULIA: They've come, haven't they?

LINDA: How do you mean?

JULIA: Peter Jessup and What's-her-name—Mary Hedges—

LINDA: What about them?

JULIA: They're downstairs.

LINDA: They—?—How long have they been there?

JULIA: Twenty minutes or so. I said you'd be down.

LINDA: Oh, you did, did you?

JULIA: —They're being very amusing. I said we expected them to be. Jessup has done his trained-seal act to perfection, and now I think Mary Hedges is about to give her imitations. [*There is a silence.* LINDA *stares at her, speechless.*] They're a great success, really.

LINDA [*Without turning*]: Nick—will you and Susan bring them up to my sitting room? I'll be there in a minute.

SUSAN: All right, Linda. [*She moves toward the door.* NICK *follows, gazing anxiously at the ceiling as he goes.*]

NICK: —The New Year ought to be just about passing over Stamford. [*They go out, closing the door after them.*]

JOHNNY [*Goes to* JULIA]: Julia! Big news, dear—guess what's happened?

LINDA [*To* EDWARD *and* JULIA, *before* JULIA *can reply*]: Oh, this is so humiliating.—Peter and Mary are my guests, do you understand? Not paid entertainers—[*She moves away from them.*]

JULIA: I'm sorry. I simply couldn't imagine mixing in people like that to no purpose.

LINDA: Couldn't you?

JULIA: No.—But of course I can't follow your reasoning these days, Linda. I can't follow it at all.

EDWARD [*To* LINDA]: There's no cause for temper, child. Just run along now, and we'll follow. Julia and I want to talk to Johnny for a moment.

JULIA [*Turns again to* JOHNNY]: What is it, Johnny? Quick, tell me!

LINDA: —Listen to me, Father: tonight means a good deal to me—I don't know what, precisely—and I don't know how. Something is trying to take it away from me, and I can't let it go. I'll put in an appearance downstairs, if you like. Then I want to bring a few people up here—the few people in the world I can talk to, and feel something for. And I want to sit with them and have supper with them, and we won't disturb anyone. That's all right with you, isn't it?

EDWARD: Your place is downstairs.

LINDA: Once more, Father: this is important to me. Don't ask me why. I don't know. It has something to do with—when I was a child here—and this room—and good times in it—and—

EDWARD: What special virtue this room has, I'm sure I don't see.

LINDA: You don't, do you—no—you can't. Well, I'll tell you this room's my home. It's the only home I've got. There's something here that I understand, and that understands me. Maybe it's Mother.

EDWARD: Please do as I have told you, Linda.

LINDA: I suppose you know it's the end of us, then.

EDWARD: Don't talk nonsense. Do as I say.

LINDA: It *is* the end. But all the same, I'm going to have supper here tonight in my home with my friends.

EDWARD: I have told you—

LINDA: —You thought I'd come around, didn't you? You always think people will come around. Not me: not tonight. And I shan't be bothered here, either. Because if there's one thing you can't stand it's a scene. I can promise you one, if you interfere. I can promise you a beauty. [EDWARD *turns from her.* LINDA *looks about her, at the room.*]

EDWARD: —Well, Johnny, so there's good news, is there?

LINDA [*Suddenly*]: Was Mother a sweet soul, Father? Was she exciting?

EDWARD [*To* JOHNNY]: —A happy day all around, eh? An engagement to be announced, New Year's to celebrate—and now—

LINDA: Was Mother a sweet soul, Father? Was she exciting?

EDWARD: Your mother was a very beautiful and distinguished woman. [*To* JOHNNY]: Naturally, I am delighted that—

LINDA: Was she a sweet soul, Father? Was she exciting? [*For an instant* EDWARD *loses control of himself.*]

EDWARD: Linda, if you are not happy here, why don't you go away? I should be glad if next month you would take your maid and Miss Talcott and go on a trip somewhere. You distress me. You cause nothing but trouble and upsets. You—

LINDA: All right, Father. That's just what I'm going to do, after the wedding. No maid and no Miss Talcott, though. Just me—Linda—the kid herself—

EDWARD: As you wish.

LINDA: I've wanted to get out for years. I've never known it so well as tonight. I can't bear it here any longer. It's doing terrible things to me.

EDWARD: —And will you leave this room now, please?

LINDA: This room—this room—I don't think you'll be able to stand it long. I'll come back when you've left it—[*She goes out. There is a silence. Then*]

JULIA: She's dreadful tonight. She's made one situation after another.

EDWARD: Never mind, my dear. Things will settle themselves. [*He seats himself in a chair at Right.*] Well, Johnny—I don't think I need worry about the way *you'll* take care of Julia, need I?

JOHNNY [*Laughs, uncertainly*]: We'll try to manage!

EDWARD: I consider what you've done a fine piece of work. I congratulate you.

JULIA: Oh, and so do I—so do *I,* dear! [*She sits near her father.*]

JOHNNY: —But you don't know yet, do you?

EDWARD: The fact is, Seton has just now told us.

JULIA: Isn't it marvelous?—Oh, what a New Year!

EDWARD: —Your stock is going up with a rush, it seems. It's time to make hay, I think.

JOHNNY: Hay?

EDWARD [*With relish*]: Money! Money!

JULIA: *Now* all those years you worked so hard—they'll pay interest now, Johnny! [*The frown grows between* JOHNNY*'s eyes.*]

EDWARD: Of course, I could put you into the Bank tomorrow—but I am not sure that that would be advisable at present.

JULIA: —That will come, won't it, Johnny? [*To* EDWARD] You'd better not wait *too* long, though—he may cost you too much!

EDWARD [*Smiles*]: We'll have to risk that. People always do. [*Then seriously*]: Pritchard, Ames is an excellent house. In my opinion, you could not do better than to go with them. Then, in five or six years, you come to us on your own merit. After that, as the children put it, "the sky's the limit." You're in a fair way to be a man of means at forty-five. I'm proud of you.

JOHNNY [*There is a pause. Finally*]: But—I'd made up my mind not to take the Pritchard, Ames offer.

EDWARD: What? And why not?

JOHNNY: I don't want to get tied up for life quite so soon. You see, I'm a kind of a queer duck, in a way. I'm afraid I'm not as anxious as I might be for the things most people work toward. I don't *want* too much money.

EDWARD: Too *much* money?

JOHNNY: Well, more than I need to live by. [*He seats himself facing them and begins eagerly, hopefully, to tell them his plan.*]—You see, it's always been my plan to make a few thousands early in the game, if I could, and then quit for as long as they last, and try to find out who I am and what I am and what goes on and what about it—now, while I'm young, and feel good all the time.—I'm sure Julia understands what I'm getting at—don't you, Julia?

JULIA [*Laughs, uncertainly*]: I'm not sure I do, Johnny!

EDWARD: You wish to occupy yourself otherwise, is that it?—with some —er—art or other, say—

JOHNNY: Oh, no, I've got no abilities that way. I'm not one of the frail ones with a longing to get away from it all and indulge a few tastes, either. I haven't any tastes. Old china and first editions and gate-legged tables don't do a thing to me. I don't want to live any way or in any time but my own—now—in New York—and Detroit—and Chicago—and Phoenix—any place here—but I do want to live!

EDWARD: —As a gentleman of leisure.

JOHNNY: —As a man whose time, for a while at least, is his own. That's what I've been plugging for ever since I was ten. Please don't make me feel guilty about it, sir. Whether I'm right or wrong, it's more important to me than anything in the world but Julia. Even if it turns out to be just one of those fool ideas that people dream about and then go flat on—even if I find I've had enough of it in three months, still I want it. I've got a feeling that if I let this chance go by, there'll never be another for me. So I don't think anyone will mind if I—just have a go at it—will they, Julia? [JULIA *is silent.*]—Will they, dear? [JULIA *rises.* JOHNNY *rises with her.*]

JULIA [*After a moment*]: Father—will you let Johnny and me talk a while?

EDWARD: —Just a moment—[*He rises and turns to* JOHNNY.] As I understand it, you have some objection, perhaps, to our manner of living—

JOHNNY: Not for you, sir. I haven't the slightest doubt it's all right for you—or that it's the answer for a lot of people. But for me—well, you see I don't *want* to live in what they call "a certain way." In the first place I'd be no good at it and besides that I don't want to be identified with any one class of people. I want to live every whichway, among all kinds—and know them—and understand them—and love them—*that's* what I want!—Don't you, Julia?

JULIA: Why, I—It sounds—

EDWARD: In all my experience, I have never heard such a—

JOHNNY: I want these years now, sir.

JULIA: Father—please—[*He turns to her. Their eyes meet.*]—It will be all right, I promise you.

EDWARD [*Moves toward the door, where he turns once more to* JOHNNY]: Case, it strikes me that you chose a strange time to tell us this, a very strange time.

JOHNNY [*Puzzled*]: I don't quite—

EDWARD: —In fact, if I had not already sent the announcement to the newspapers—asked a number of our friends here tonight to—

JULIA: Father!

JOHNNY [*Very quietly*]: Oh, I see.

JULIA: Father—please go down. We'll come in a minute. [EDWARD *hesitates an instant, then goes out.*]

JOHNNY [*Still hopeful, turns to* JULIA]: —Darling, he didn't get what I'm driving at, at all! My plan is—

JULIA: Oh, Johnny, Johnny, why did you do it?

JOHNNY: Do what?

JULIA: You knew how all that talk would antagonize him.

JOHNNY [*A moment*]: You think talk is all it was?

JULIA: I think it was less than that! I'm furious with you.

JOHNNY: It wasn't just talk, Julia.

JULIA: Well, if you think you can persuade me that a man of your energy and your ability possibly *could* quit at thirty for *any* length of time, you're mistaken.

JOHNNY: I'd like a try at it.

JULIA: It's ridiculous—and why you chose tonight of all nights to go on that way to Father—

JOHNNY: Wait a minute, dear: we'd better get clear on this—

JULIA: I'm clear on it now! If you're tired, and need a holiday, we'll have it. We'll take two months instead of one, if you like. We'll—

JOHNNY: That wouldn't settle anything.

JULIA: Johnny, I've known quite a few men who don't work—and of all the footling, unhappy existences—it's inconceivable that you could stand it—it's unthinkable you could!

JOHNNY: —I might do it differently.

JULIA: Differently!

JOHNNY [*A moment. Then*]: Julia, do you love me? [*She looks at him swiftly, then looks away.*]

JULIA [*Lowly*]: You—you have a great time standing me against a wall and throwing knives around me, don't you? [*In an instant he was taken her in his arms.*]

JOHNNY: Oh, sweet—

JULIA [*Against his shoulder*]: What do you do things like that for? What's the matter with you, anyway?

JOHNNY [*He stands off and looks at her*]: Haven't you the remotest idea of what I'm after? [*She looks at him, startled.*] I'm after—all that's in me, all I am. I want to get it out—where I can look at it, know it. That takes time.—Can't you understand that?

JULIA: But you haven't an idea yet of how exciting *business* can be—you're just beginning! Oh, Johnny, see it through! You'll love it. I know you will. There's no such thrill in the world as making money. It's the most—what are you staring at?

JOHNNY: Your face.

JULIA [*She turns away*]: Oh—you won't listen to me—you won't hear me—

JOHNNY: Yes, I will.

JULIA [*A pause. Then* JULIA *speaks in another voice*]: And you'd expect me to live on—this money you've made, too, would you?

JOHNNY: Why, of course not. You have all you'll ever need for anything you'd want, haven't you?

JULIA [*Another pause, then*]: —I suppose it doesn't occur to you how badly it would *look* for you to stop now, does it—?

JOHNNY: Look? How? [*She does not answer.*]—Oh—you mean there'd be those who'd think I'd married money and called it a day—

JULIA: There would be. There'd be plenty of them.

JOHNNY: —And you'd mind that, would you?

JULIA: Well, I'm not precisely anxious to have it thought of you.

JOHNNY: —Because *I* shouldn't mind it—and I think that lookout's mine. Oh, darling, you don't see what I'm aiming at, either—but try a little blind faith for a while, won't you? Come along with me—

JULIA: Johnny—[*She reaches for his hand.*]

JOHNNY: —The whole way, dear.

JULIA: —Wait till next year—or two years, and we'll think about it again. If it's right, it can be done, then as well as now.—You can do that for me—for us—can't you? [*A moment. Then he slowly brings her around and looks into her eyes.*]

JOHNNY: You think by then I'd have "come around." That's what you think, isn't it?—I'd have "come around"—

JULIA: But surely you can at least see that if—! [*She stops, as* LINDA *re-enters.*]

LINDA: It lacks six minutes of the New Year, if anyone's interested. [*A moment, then* JULIA *moves toward the door.*]

JULIA: Come on, Johnny.

JOHNNY [*To* LINDA]: Where are the others?

LINDA: My pretty new friends? Well, it seems they've ditched me. [*She starts a tune on the music box.*]—*This* won't make too much noise, do you think?

JOHNNY: How do you mean, Linda?

LINDA: I imagine Peter and Mary got tired of being put through their tricks, and slid out when they could. Nick and Susan left a message upstairs with Delia saying that they had to go after them. I'm supposed to follow, but I don't think I will, somehow.

JULIA: Oh, I *am* sorry.

LINDA: Are you, Julia? That's a help. [*She goes to the supper table.*]—Anyone care for a few cold cuts before the fun starts?

JOHNNY: You're not going to stay up here all alone—

LINDA: Why not? I'm just full of resources. I crack all kinds of jokes with myself—and they say the food's good. [*She takes a bite of a sandwich and puts it down again.*] Ugh! Kiki—

JULIA: Linda, this is plain stubbornness, and you know it.

LINDA [*Wheels about sharply*]: Listen, Julia—! [*She stops, and turns away.*] No—that gets you nowhere, does it?

JULIA [*To* JOHNNY]: Are you coming?

JOHNNY: I think I'll wait a moment with Linda, if you don't mind.

JULIA: But I do mind!—Will you come, please?

JOHNNY: —In a moment, Julia. [JULIA *looks at him. He meets her gaze steadily. She turns and goes out. There is a pause. Then*]

LINDA: You'd better run on down, don't you think?

JOHNNY: Not right away. [*Another pause*]

LINDA: I'm afraid I don't know how to entertain you. I've done all my stuff.

JOHNNY: I don't need entertaining.

LINDA [*Another pause, a very long one.* LINDA *looks uncertainly toward the music box. Finally*]—You wouldn't care to step into a waltz, Mr. Case?

JOHNNY: I'd love it. [*She extends her arms. He takes her in his. They begin to waltz slowly to the music box.*]—There's a conspiracy against you and me, child.

LINDA: What's that?

JOHNNY: The Vested Interests—

LINDA: I know.

JOHNNY: —They won't let you have any fun, and they won't give me time to think.

LINDA: I suppose, like the great fathead you are, you told them all your little hopes and dreams.

JOHNNY: Um.

LINDA: —Pretty disappointing?

JOHNNY: Bad enough.

LINDA: Poor boy.

JOHNNY: How about your own evening?

LINDA: Not so good, either.

JOHNNY: Poor girl.

LINDA: But we won't mind, will we?

JOHNNY: Hell, no, we won't mind.

LINDA: We'll get there—

JOHNNY: We'll get there! [*She stops in the dance and looks up at him for a moment, curiously. Then he smiles at her and she smiles back.*]

JOHNNY: —Place head, A, against cheek, B, and proceed as before—[*They begin to dance again.*]—Of course they may be right.

LINDA: Don't you believe it!

JOHNNY: They seem—awfully sure.

LINDA: It's your ride still, isn't it? You know where you want to go, don't you?

JOHNNY: Well, I thought I did.

LINDA: So did I.—Pathetic, wasn't it—all my fuss and fury over anything so unimportant as this party.

JOHNNY: Maybe it was important.

LINDA: Well, if it was, I'm not. And I guess that's the answer.

JOHNNY: Not quite.

LINDA: —Me and my little what-do-you-call-it—defense mechanism—so pathetic. Yes, I'm just chock-full of pathos, I am.

JOHNNY: You're a brick, Linda.

LINDA: Oh, shut your silly face—[*Then*] You're right, you know—there *is* nothing up the fun alley.

JOHNNY: Fun-alley?

LINDA: I had a nice little seven-word motto for my life, but I guess she don't work—

JOHNNY: What was it?

LINDA: "Not very important—but pretty good entertainment."

JOHNNY: H'm—

LINDA: For "pretty good" read "rotten." [*They dance for a few moments, silently. Then* LINDA *stops.*] There. That's enough. I'm getting excited.

JOHNNY: —What?

LINDA: —It was grand. Thanks. You can go now. [*She has not yet left his arms. Suddenly from outside comes the sound of bells tolling. Her grasp tightens upon his arm*] Listen! [*She looks over her shoulder toward the window. Horns begin to be heard from the distance, long-drawn-out, insistent.*]

JOHNNY: It's it, all right.

LINDA [*Again she turns her face to his*]: Happy New Year, Johnny.

JOHNNY [*He bends and kisses her*]: Happy New Year, dear. [*For an instant she clings to him, then averts her face.*]

LINDA [*In a breath*]: Oh, Johnny, you're so attractive—

JOHNNY [*With difficulty*]: You're—you're all right yourself—[*There is a dead silence. Then she leaves his arms, turns and smiles to him.*]

LINDA: —You can count on Sister Linda.—Run on down now—quick! They'll be waiting.

JOHNNY [*Hesitates*]: Linda—

LINDA: What?

JOHNNY: They've—your father—I've been put in a position that—

LINDA: Do you love Julia, Johnny? [*He turns away.*]

JOHNNY: Of course I do.

[NED *enters silently, another glass in hand. He stands in the shadow at Left, watching them, swaying almost imperceptibly.*]

LINDA: —Well, if ever she needed you, she needs you now. Once it's announced she'll go through with it. Then you can help her. I can't do anything any more. I've tried for twenty years. You're all that's left. Go on, Johnny—[*He goes to the door. From downstairs a swelling chorus of male voices begins "Auld Lang Syne."*]—And tell those choirboys for me that I'll be in Scotland before them.

[JOHNNY *goes out, closing the door after him.* LINDA *stops the music box, then moves slowly to the window, Right, where she stands silently for a moment, looking out.* NED *is still watching her, immobile. At length she turns to him:*]

LINDA: —Just take any place, Ned. [*He goes to the couch and sits there.*]

NED: —Rum party down there, isn't it?

LINDA: A hundred million dollars knocking together never made many sparks that I could see. [*She takes a glass of wine from the table*] What's it like to get drunk, Ned?

NED: It's—How drunk?

LINDA: Good and drunk.

NED: Grand.

LINDA [*She seats herself near the table, facing him*]: *How* is it?

NED: Well, to begin with, it brings you to life.

LINDA: Does it?

NED: Yes.—And after a little while you begin to know all about it. You feel—I don't know—important—

LINDA: That must be good.

NED: It is.—Then pretty soon the game starts.

LINDA: What game?

NED: —That you play with yourself. It's a swell game—there's not a sweller game on this earth, really—

LINDA [*Sips her wine*]: How does it go?

NED: Well, you think clear as crystal, but every move, every sentence is a problem. That—gets pretty interesting.

LINDA: I see.

NED: Swell game. Most terribly exciting game.

LINDA: You—get beaten, though, don't you?

NED: Sure. But that's good, too. Then you don't mind anything—not anything at all. Then you sleep.

LINDA [*She is watching him, fascinated*]: How—long can you keep it up?

NED: A long while. As long as you last.

LINDA: Oh, Ned—that's awful!

NED: Think so?—Other things are worse.

LINDA: But—but where do you end up?

NED: Where does everybody end up? You die.—And that's all right, too.

LINDA [*A pause. Then*]: Ned, can you do it on champagne?

NED: Why—[*He stops and looks at her, intently.*]—What's the matter, Linda?

LINDA [*She finishes her glass and sets it down*]: Nothing.

NED: I know.

LINDA: Yes?

NED: Johnny.

LINDA: Give me some more wine, Ned—

NED [*Rises and goes over to her*]: He's a funny guy, isn't he?

LINDA: Give me some, Ned—

NED [*He goes to the table, refills her glass, returns, and gives it to her*]—You can tell me about it, dear.

LINDA [*Looks up at him. A moment, then*]: I love the boy, Neddy.

NED: I thought so.—Hell, isn't it?

LINDA: I guess it will be.

NED [*Raises his glass*]: Here's luck to you—

LINDA [*Stares at her glass*]: I don't want any luck. [NED *moves away from her to the table near the couch. He finishes his drink, leaves it there and sinks down upon the couch.* LINDA *carefully sets her glass of wine, untouched, upon the supper table, and rises.*] I think what I'd better do is—[*She moves slowly to the door, and opens it. The song is just finishing. It is applauded.* LINDA *hesitates at the door.*]

Ned—[*He does not answer. Suddenly, from downstairs, comes a long roll of drums.* LINDA *stiffens. She starts to close the door, but is held there, her hand upon the knob.* EDWARD*'s voice begins to be heard:*]

EDWARD: Ladies and gentlemen—my very good friends: I have the honor to announce to you the engagement of my daughter, Julia, to Mr. John Case—an event which doubles the pleasure I take in wishing you—and them—a most happy and prosperous New Year. [*There is prolonged applause and through it congratulations and laughter. Slowly she closes the door, but still stands with her hand upon it. Finally she speaks, without turning:*]

LINDA: Ned—[*He does not answer.*] Ned—maybe I ought to go down and—I'm not sure I *will* stay up here—do you mind? [*He is silent. She turns and sees him.*] Ned! [*He is asleep. She goes to him swiftly, speaking again, in a low voice:*] Ned—[*A moment. Then*] Poor lamb. [*She bends and kisses him. She goes to the doorway, turns off the lights in the playroom, and opens the door. A confusion of excited voices is heard from downstairs. In the lighted hallway* LINDA *turns to the stairs, raises her head and goes out, calling above the voices*] Hello!—Hello, everyone!

CURTAIN

■ ACT III ■

SCENE: *The same as Act I.*

TIME: *Twelve days later. Ten o'clock at night. The curtains are drawn and the lamps lighted. Coffee service is on a small table near the fireplace.* NICK *and* SUSAN *are taking their coffee.* LINDA*'s cup is on the table. She stands near the sofa at Left Center, frowning at* NICK.

LINDA: No?

NICK [*Shakes his head*]: Not possibly. [*He is behind the sofa at Right, upon which* SUSAN *is seated.*]

SUSAN: Why should Johnny pick a place like that?

LINDA: Why should he go away at all?

NICK: I'd have done the same thing—I'd have just giv' 'er a look, I would, and flounced out.

SUSAN: Hush, Nick. This is no time for fooling.

LINDA [*Thinks a minute, then head down, eyes on the floor, she paces across the room and back, and across again. She stops opposite them and turns.*]—Atlantic City.

SUSAN: You don't go to Atlantic City for six days to think.

NICK: Old Chinese proverb.

LINDA: But where can he be, then?—*Where?*

SUSAN: Don't worry, Linda. I'm sure he's all right.

NICK: Susan and I parted forever at least forty times. [*To* SUSAN]—Or was it forty-seven?

SUSAN: Of course.—And they haven't even done that. They've just put off the wedding a while.

LINDA: I know, but—[*She looks away, anxiously.*] Oh, Lordy, Lordy—

NICK: Johnny will come around, Linda. He's up against the old fight between spirit and matter—anyone want to take a hundred on spirit?

LINDA: I will! I'll take two hundred!

NICK: It's a bet, Madam. [*He looks at his watch.*]

SUSAN: Don't forget we have to go back to the house for our bags, Nick.

NICK: There's lot of time. She doesn't sail until midnight. "She"—a boat that size, "she"—the big nance. [*To* LINDA]—You don't really want to see us off, do you?

LINDA: Oh, yes! But can you stop back for me on your way down?

SUSAN: If you like.

LINDA: I don't want to leave here till the last minute. I keep feeling that something may happen.

SUSAN: Where's Julia now?

LINDA: She went to dine some place with Father. He won't let her out of his sight—or into mine.

NICK: No wonder Johnny took to the woods.

LINDA [*Quickly*]: —The woods?

NICK: —Or wherever he did take to.

LINDA: Now I know!

SUSAN: Yes?

LINDA: It was at Placid they met. It was at Placid they—of course! [*She goes to the telephone behind the sofa, at Left.*]

NICK [*To* SUSAN]: It may be. They say they always return to the scene of the crime.

LINDA: Long distance, please.

SUSAN: —In which case, I suppose Julia wins.

NICK: I don't know. It's pretty cold at Placid. There's nothing for a rapid pulse like a little wet snow up the sleeve.

LINDA: Long distance, please—

SUSAN [*To* NICK]: Would you mind telling me how a man like Johnny is attracted to a girl like that, in the first place?

NICK [*To* SUSAN]: You're too young to know, Susan.

LINDA [*At the telephone*]—Long distance?

SUSAN: I can think of several people who'd be better for Johnny than Julia.

LINDA: I want to speak with Lake Placid, New York—

NICK: I can think of one, anyway.

LINDA: —Placid—the Lake Placid Club.

SUSAN: Do you suppose she's in love with him?

NICK: Suppose? I know. Look at her.

LINDA: "P-l-a-c-i-d"—

NICK: Tiger, Tiger, Tiger.

LINDA: Quiet a minute, will you? [*To the telephone*]—Placid—calm—peaceful. Yes. And I'd like to speak with Mr. John Case.

SUSAN: If I could grab you the way I did, she can—

NICK: But there's more in this than meets the ear, darling—Julia.

LINDA: Quiet! [*Then, to the telephone*]—Miss Seton. *Linda* Seton. [*To* SUSAN]—I don't want to give him heart failure, thinking it's—[*To the telephone*]—John Case—Lake Placid Club—Linda Seton. Thanks. [*She replaces the receiver and returns to* NICK *and* SUSAN.] I'm sure he's there. I feel it in my bones.

NICK [*A pause. Then*]: Linda, Johnny asked me not to tell anyone, but I think you ought to know something: the fact is, he's got a single cabin on the *Paris* for himself tonight.

LINDA: He—? How do you know?

NICK: Because I got it for him.

LINDA: You don't seriously think he'd do it?

NICK: No—I can't say I do.

LINDA: Well, *I* do! Oh, Lord—then he's in New York now!

NICK: Maybe so.

LINDA: He can't be, or he'd be here.—Where did he go to, Nick?

NICK: —Of that, I wasn't informed.

LINDA: You know, this is aging me.

SUSAN: We know something else you don't know, Linda.

LINDA: Oh! What is it?

NICK: —Look out, Susan. Steady, girl.

LINDA [*Glances at them quickly, then lights a cigarette*]: What is it?

SUSAN: How did you happen to decide not to come abroad, as you planned?

LINDA: Why, I—well, I thought probably Johnny and Julia—they'd rather not have any family tagging along, and besides that, I want to get Ned off on a trip with me—out West, if I can.

SUSAN: I know. But—

NICK [*Again* NICK *cuts across her*]: —I saw Ned in Jimmy's last night. He was—well, if I may use the word—

SUSAN: Look here, Linda—

LINDA [*To* NICK]: —I think he's all right tonight. He went to a show with the Wheelers.

NICK [*Reflects*]: I wonder if they're really in love with each other.

LINDA: They're terribly in love.

SUSAN: What makes you think so?

LINDA: I know it. Johnny couldn't help but be, and Julia—

SUSAN [*Glances at* NICK]: You meant the Wheelers, didn't you?

NICK: Why, I—yes, I did.

LINDA: I don't know about them. [*She moves away from them, then back again.*]

SUSAN: Can't *you* do anything with her, Linda?

LINDA: Who—Julia?

SUSAN: Yes.

LINDA: I've talked myself blue in the face. It's no good. She won't listen. I've had the cold shoulder and the deaf ear so long now I'm all hoarse and half frozen.

SUSAN: I thought she's always depended on you.

LINDA: Well, she doesn't any more.

SUSAN: You love her a great deal, don't you?

LINDA [*Laughs shortly*]: I expect I do!

SUSAN: —But my dear child, don't you see that if she thinks just as your father does—

LINDA: Johnny'll fix that. Johnny'll fix everything.

SUSAN: He'll never change *them,* Linda.

LINDA: Susan, you don't know that man.

NICK: —It'd be a pity to deprive your father of the pleasure he'd take in putting him over on the town.

LINDA: Don't speak of it. That's one thing Johnny's been spared so far. I don't think he's had an inkling of *it* yet.

NICK: It will come: Mr. and Mrs. John Sebastian Case have closed their Sixty-fourth Street house and gone to Coney Island for the hunting. Mrs. Case will be remembered as Julia Seton, of Seton Pretty.

SUSAN: I'd like a picture of him, when it happens.

NICK: I wouldn't.

LINDA: —If they'd only listen to me—I've got to make them listen!— And he's so sweet, he's so attractive. What's the matter with the girl, anyway? She ought to know by now that men like Johnny don't grow on every bush.

SUSAN: —But you see, the things you like in him are just what she can't stand, Linda. And the fate you say he'll save her from is the one fate in this whole world she wants.

LINDA: I don't believe it.—Even so, she loves him—and there's been a break—and wouldn't you think she'd at least be woman enough to hang on—*hang on!*

SUSAN: I don't know. There's another who isn't woman enough to grab.

LINDA [*There is a silence. Finally* LINDA *speaks*]: —I don't quite get you, Susan.

SUSAN: Well, to make it plain, no man's lost this side of the altar.

NICK: She's talking a lot of—[*Then, to* SUSAN] Come on, Pearl—ups-a-daisy.

LINDA: Susan—

SUSAN: Yes, dear?

LINDA: Julia has never in her life loved anyone but Johnny.

SUSAN: —And you.

LINDA: And me.

NICK [*In spite of himself*]: —And herself.

LINDA [*Turns on him sharply*]: That's not true!—Even in this it's of him she's thinking—she may be mistaken, but it *is* of him!

SUSAN: I've no doubt she believes that.

LINDA: Well, I believe it too!

NICK: —Come on, will you, Susan?

LINDA: I think it's rotten of you to suspect things of Julia that aren't Julia at all, and I think it's worse of you to—

NICK: We're sorry, Linda, really we are.

LINDA: You aren't sorry! You're—[*Suddenly she covers her face with her hands.*] Oh, what's the matter with me?

SUSAN: Linda, I could shake you.

LINDA: I wish you would.—I wish someone would, till there was nothing left to shake.

SUSAN: —And there's not a thing to do about it?

LINDA: What there is to do, I'm doing. [*She goes to the window at Back. A silence. Then*]

SUSAN: —And if you did anything else, I expect you wouldn't be Linda.

NICK: Linda, I think you're just about the—[*But that is as close as he can get to a declaration of faith.*]—Oh, hell—[*He turns to* SUSAN.] Will you come, dear? It's ten-thirty.

SUSAN [*Rises and moves toward* LINDA. NICK *follows*]: But if Johnny should—[LINDA *faces her.*]—Promise us one thing, Linda.

LINDA: What?

SUSAN [*After a moment*]: Nothing.

LINDA: I love you two.

SUSAN: —And so do we love you.

LINDA: —Call back for me when?

SUSAN: In half an hour.

NICK: Less.

LINDA: —Then could your car possibly take me out to Mary Hedges'?

SUSAN: But of course! What a good idea—

LINDA: Mary asked it—I'll have a bag packed. [JULIA *comes in.*] Oh, hello, dear.—Are you back already?

JULIA: Isn't it late? Hello, Susan. Hello, Nick. I thought you were sailing. [*She leaves her evening wrap on the sofa, Left, and moves toward the writing table at Right.*]

SUSAN: We are.

NICK: At the crack of twelve. On the way now, in fact.

JULIA: I hope you have a grand trip.

SUSAN: Thanks. [DELIA *enters and takes* JULIA*'s wrap from the sofa.*]

LINDA: —Delia, will you pack a bag for me, please? I'm going to Mrs. Hedges until Tuesday.

DELIA: Yes, Miss. [*She goes out.* NICK *and* SUSAN *stand at Center, facing* JULIA.]

SUSAN: I'm sorry we won't be here for the wedding, Julia.

JULIA: I'm sorry too, Susan.

NICK: When's it to be?

JULIA: We haven't quite—set a date, yet.

SUSAN: —In the spring, some time?

JULIA: Possibly before.

NICK: Let us know, won't you?

JULIA: Of course.

NICK [*A brief pause. Then*]: —Then you're not coming down to the boat tonight?

JULIA: I'm afraid I can't. Bon voyage, though.

NICK [*Thinks rapidly*]: Thanks. Can we take any word to Johnny for you?

JULIA: To Johnny?

NICK: Yes.—Or a basket of fruit, maybe?

JULIA: He'll be there, will he?

NICK [*This, at any rate,* NICK *can do*]: I should imagine so, if he's sailing.

JULIA: Sailing!

NICK: Isn't he?

JULIA: I wasn't aware of it.

NICK: Well, all I know is that the morning he left for wherever he went to, he telephoned me to get him a single cabin through Andrews, of the French Line. I don't believe it's been given up, or I'd have heard from them. I thought of course you knew, or I—

JULIA: I think I should—if he were going.

NICK: Yes, I suppose so. [*To* SUSAN] We won't expect him, then.

SUSAN: No.—Goodbye, Julia. [*They move together toward the door.*]

NICK: Look us up, when you arrive. Immigrant's Bank.—We'll see you later, Linda.

LINDA: I'll be ready.

SUSAN: Thanks. Lovely evening—

NICK *and* SUSAN [*Together*]: —And you must come and see *us* some time! [*They go out. There is a silence.* JULIA *looks for a cigarette.*]

LINDA: It may be true, Julia. I think the chances are it is.

JULIA: What?

LINDA: —That Johnny's going with them.

JULIA [*Laughs*]: Not possibly, darling!—Why don't they keep these cigarette boxes filled—

LINDA: Stop it, Julia!

JULIA: Stop it?

LINDA: —Pretending you don't give a damn.

JULIA [*Finds and lights a cigarette*]: You seem to be taking my little difficulty more seriously than I am. [*She moves toward the sofa at Left.*]

LINDA: If you don't want Johnny to go off tonight and make a hash of both your lives, you'd better send him some word to the boat.

JULIA [*Smiles*]: Somehow, I don't think that's necessary.

LINDA: Why not?

JULIA: Well, for one reason, because he won't be there. He's no more sailing tonight than I am.

LINDA: You don't know that he's not!

JULIA: I don't know that he is, so I think I'm safe in assuming it.—Do you want to go to the Todds' dinner on Wednesday? They telephoned—

LINDA: —Julia, why do you want to shut me out in the cold like this?

JULIA: I wasn't aware that I was.

LINDA: —But won't you just *talk* to me! Oh, please, Julia—

JULIA: I don't know what there is to say.

LINDA: Never so long as I remember has there been anything we couldn't—

JULIA: If there's been any shutting out done, it's you who've done it, Linda.

LINDA: Me?!

JULIA: Johnny and I have had a difference of opinion, and you're siding with him, aren't you?

LINDA: But he's right! He's right for you as well as for himself—

JULIA: I think that's for me to decide.

LINDA: Not Father?

JULIA: Father has nothing to do with it—

LINDA: Oh, no!

JULIA: He happens to agree with me where you don't, that's all.

LINDA: We've always agreed before—always.

JULIA: No—I think quite often I've given in, in order to avoid scenes and upsets and—oh, well—

LINDA [*A silence. Then*]: —Is that true, Julia?

JULIA: You've always been the "stronger character," haven't you? At least people have always thought so. You've made all the decisions, you've always had the ideas—

LINDA: —And you've been resenting me right from the very—[*She moves away from her, toward the fireplace.*] Oh—I can't believe it—

JULIA: It's nothing to get in a state about—and I didn't say I resented you. You've been an immense help, often. But when it comes to determining my future, and the future of the man I'm going to marry—

LINDA [*Turns on her sharply*]: —Your future! What do you want, Julia —just security? Sit back in your feather boa among the Worthies of the World?

JULIA: Well, I'm certain that one thing I *don't* want is to start this endless, aimless discussion all over again.

LINDA: But I tell you you can't *stand* this sort of life forever—not if you're the person I think you are. And when it starts going thin on you, what'll you have to hold on to?—Lois Evans shot herself—why? Franny Grant's up the Hudson in a sanitarium—why?

JULIA: I'm sure I don't know.

LINDA: —Nothing left to do or have or want—that's why—and no insides! There's not a poor girl in town who isn't happier than we are— at least they still *want* what we've got—*they* think it's good. [*She turns away.*]—If they knew!

JULIA: —And *I* think it's good.

LINDA: Lord, Julia, don't tell me that you *want* it!

JULIA: I want it, and it's all I want.

LINDA [*There is a silence. Then*]: —Then it's good-bye, Julia.

JULIA: Oh, Linda, for heaven's sake don't be so ridiculous! If you're so damn set on being violent, get a few Russians in and talk life with a great big "L" to them.

EDWARD [*Comes in, an admonishing finger raised*]: Ah—ah—ah!

LINDA [*Turns to him*]: —Father, I think you're both giving Johnny the rottenest kind of a deal.

EDWARD: In what way?

LINDA: Every way! Why do you do it? It can't be that you think he's out to marry for money. You must realize how simple it would have been for him—to conform to specifications now, and then just not get up some fine morning.

EDWARD [*Moves to the table behind the sofa at Right*]: I don't regard the young man as a fortune hunter, Linda.

LINDA: Well, what is it, then?

EDWARD [*Finds a cigarette and comes forward with it*]—I think his outlook has merely become—somewhat confused, shall we say, and—

LINDA: —And you'll straighten it out for him.

EDWARD [*To* JULIA]: We shall try, shan't we, daughter?

LINDA: Why hasn't he a right to spend some part of his life as he wants to? He can afford it. What's he got to do? Pile up so much that he can be comfortable on the income of his income?

EDWARD [*Seats himself in a chair near the sofa*]: —That would be an excellent aim, but I think we shall hardly require it of him.

LINDA: I'd like to hear the requirements.

EDWARD: Any self-respecting young man wishes to earn enough to support his wife and his family.

LINDA: Even when his wife already has—? Even when there's no possible need of it?

EDWARD: Even then.

LINDA: Oh, Father, what a fake idea that is!

EDWARD: I don't think so. Nor does Julia.—In addition, he has somehow developed a very curious attitude toward work—

LINDA: It seems to me saner than most. He wants his leisure at this end—good sense, I call it.—Which is harder to do, anyway—? Go to an office and rustle papers about or sit under a tree and look at your own soul?

JULIA [*Contemptuously*]: Heavens!—The office, I should say.

LINDA: Then you've never looked, Julia.

JULIA: You can't talk to her, Father.

EDWARD: I should like to understand what he—and you—are aiming at, Linda, but I must confess I cannot. [NED *comes in.*]—I consider his whole attitude deliberately un-American.

LINDA [*Stares at* EDWARD]: Are you serious?

EDWARD: Entirely.

LINDA [*She stares for a moment more*]: —You're right. I believe it is.

NED [*Seats himself on the sofa, at Left*]: I've always said the Americans were a great little people.

LINDA: —Then he's a bad one, and will go to hell when he dies. Because apparently he can't quite believe that a life devoted to piling up money is all it's cracked up to be.—That's strange, isn't it—when he has us, right before his eyes, for such a shining example?

JULIA: I thought *you* were the one who found leisure so empty.

LINDA: —You think I call this, leisure? A life sentence to *this?*—Or that he does?

JULIA: I think any variety of it he'd find quite as empty.

LINDA: —Even if it should be, he's got a right to discover it for himself! Can't you see that?

JULIA: I can see the discovery would come, quick enough.

LINDA: —And you don't want to be with him to lend a hand, if it should? [JULIA *is silent.*]

EDWARD: Linda, I listened most attentively to our young dreamer the other day. I have listened quite as attentively to you this evening. I am not entirely without intelligence, but I must still confess that most of your talk seems to me to be of the seventeen-year-old variety.

LINDA: I'm glad if it is! We're all grand at seventeen. It's after that that the—sickness sets in.

EDWARD [*Chuckles, shakes his head and rises*]: —I feel very well, myself—and you look in perfect health, my dear. [*He moves toward the door.*]

LINDA: —You both think he'll come around, Father—compromise, any-way. You'll get fooled. He won't give way one little inch.

EDWARD [*At the door* EDWARD *turns, smiling*]: Stubborn—?

LINDA: Right! And sure he's right!

EDWARD: We shall see—[*He goes out, victor.*]

JULIA: —Is that all, Linda?

LINDA: Where are you going?

JULIA: To bed.

LINDA: Now?

JULIA: Yes. Have you any objections?

LINDA: You actually won't lift a finger to keep him off that boat tonight?

JULIA: He has no idea of taking it.

LINDA: You don't know him!

JULIA: Well, I think I know him a little better than you. I happen to be engaged to him.

[HENRY *has entered with a tray containing a decanter of whisky, ice, a bottle of soda, and one glass.*]

NED: Thanks, Henry. [HENRY *bows and goes out.*]

JULIA: Ned, I thought you went to the theatre with the Wheelers—

NED: I did, but it was so bad I left. [*He rises, goes behind the table and makes himself a drink.*]

JULIA: Wasn't that just a trifle rude?

NED: I don't know, Julia. Look it up under R in the book of etiquette, will you?

JULIA: I can't imagine what you're thinking of these days.—Drinking alone—that's pretty too, isn't it?

NED: I never thought of the aesthetic side, but I see what you mean. [*He takes a long swallow of his drink.*]

JULIA [*Regards him contemptuously, then, to* LINDA]: If there's any message of any sort, I wish you'd ring my room.

LINDA: All right. [JULIA *goes out.* LINDA *seats herself and stares moodily in front of her.*]

NED: —Like a drink?

LINDA: No, thanks.

NED [*Again settles down upon the sofa*]: —You know, most people, including Johnny and yourself, make a big mistake about Julia.

LINDA: What's that?

NED: They're taken in by her looks. At bottom she's a very dull girl, and the life she pictures for herself is the life she belongs in. [*The telephone rings.* LINDA *goes to it.*]

LINDA: —You've never hit it off, that's all. [*At the telephone*] Hello.—Yes.—Yes.—What? When, do you know?—Well, ask, will you? [*To* NED] He *was* there.

NED: Who and where?

LINDA: Johnny—Placid. [*To the telephone*] Yes? This—? I see. No. No. That's right. Thanks. [*She puts down the telephone and turns again to* NED]—And left this noon.

NED: Then he'll be around tonight.

LINDA: You think so? This late?

NED: He'll be around.

LINDA [*A moment. Then*]: Ned—

NED: What?

LINDA: Do you remember what we talked about New Year's Eve?

NED [*A brief pause. Then*]: Sure—I remember.

LINDA: Tell me something—

NED: Sure.

LINDA: Does it stand out all over me?

NED: Why?

LINDA: Nick and Susan—I think they got it.

NED: Anyone who loves you would, Linda.

LINDA: Oh, that's awful. I'm so ashamed—[*Then she raises her head.*] I'm not, though!

NED: Why should you be?

LINDA [*Suddenly*]: Look here, Ned—you're in a jam too, aren't you?

NED: Me?

LINDA: You.

NED: Sure, I suppose so.

LINDA: Is it that you hate this—[*Her gesture includes the house and all it represents.*]—Or that you love that—[*She indicates his drink.*]

NED: H'm—[*He looks about him*] Well, God knows I hate all this—[*and lifts the glass before his eyes.*]—And God knows I'm crazy mad over this—[*He takes a deep swallow and sets the glass down.*] I guess it's both.

LINDA: What are we going to do?

NED: Nothing, that I know of.

LINDA: But we must!

NED [*Hunches down into the sofa*]: I'm all right.

LINDA: You're not—but you'll pull out of it—and *I'll* pull out of it.

NED: I'm all right. I don't mind any more.

LINDA: You've got to mind. We can't just let go, can we?

NED: *I* can. I have.

LINDA: No. No!

NED: Listen, Linda: I've had the whole thing out with myself, see? All of it. A lot of times. And I've developed my what-do-you-call-it—technique. I'm all right. There's no reason for stewing over me. I'm—[*He squints at his glass.*]—Very happy.

LINDA: There must be some sort of life for you—

NED: —But there *is!* Haven't I got the swell Seton name to uphold? [*He laughs shortly.*]—Only that's where I'll fox it. I'll make *it* uphold me.

LINDA: Neddy—listen: After the wedding we'll go out to Boulder, both of us.—We'll live on horseback and in trout streams all day long every day until we're in hand again. We'll get so damn tired that we won't be able to want anything or think of anything but sleep.

NED: You make it too hard. Come on—have a drink—

LINDA: Oh, you're dying, Neddy!

NED [*Very patiently*]: All right, Linda.

LINDA: Won't you do that with me?

NED: Thanks, but uh-uh. Nope.

LINDA [*Moves away from him to the other side of the room*]: Oh, won't anyone ever again do what I *know* they should do?

NED: That's what's the matter with you, Linda. You worry so much over other people's troubles you don't get anywhere with your own. [HENRY *enters.* LINDA *is staring at* NED.]

HENRY: —Mr. Case, Miss.

LINDA [*A silence, then* LINDA *recovers herself*]: Yes?—Have him come up, will you? [HENRY *bows and goes out. A moment.* NED *watches her. Then*]

NED: —Are you sure you *want* to get over him?

LINDA: No. I'm not. And that's what scares me most. I feel alive, and I love it. I feel at last something's happening to me. But it can't get anywhere, so it's like living on—*your* stuff. I've *got* to get over it.

NED: —Because it seems so hopeless, is that it?

LINDA: Seems! What do you mean?

NED: Don't you know? [LINDA *can only look at him. He goes to her.*]—Then let me tell you something: you're twice as attractive as Julia ever thought of being. You've got twice the looks, and twice the mind, and ten times the guts. You've lived in her shade for years now, and there's nothing to it. You could charm a bird off a tree, if you would. And why not? If you were in her way, she'd ride you down like a rabbit.

LINDA [*Softly*]: Oh, you stinker—knowing the way she loves him—you stinker, Ned.

NED [*Shrugs*]: All right. [*He wanders in the direction of the door*]—Tell him hello for me, will you?

LINDA [LINDA*'s voice rises*]: —If there's one thing I'll do in my life, it'll be to let the fresh air back into you again, hear me?—I'll do it if I have to shoot you.

NED [*Turns and smiles back at her*]: —All right. [*He goes out. With an exclamation* LINDA *goes to the window and looks out, huddling herself in her arms.*]

JOHNNY [*Enters. A moment, then*]: Hello, Linda.

LINDA: Hello, Johnny.

JOHNNY: Is—? [LINDA *moves to the telephone.*]

LINDA: I'll send for her.

JOHNNY: Wait a minute. [*A silence. He looks about him.*] I feel as if I'd—been away quite a while.

LINDA: Yes.

JOHNNY: I went to Placid.

LINDA: I see.

JOHNNY: It was horrible there.

LINDA: I can imagine it.

JOHNNY: Oh, Linda, I love her so—

LINDA: Of course you do, Johnny.

JOHNNY: It—makes anything else—any plans—ideas—anything—

LINDA: —Seem so unimportant, of course.

JOHNNY: But I know they are important! I know that!

LINDA [*Smiles*]: Still—

JOHNNY [*Turns away*]: That's it—*still*—

LINDA [*A moment*]: I think it'll come out all right, Johnny.

JOHNNY: Maybe, in the long run.

LINDA: Have you—I suppose you've decided something or other—

JOHNNY: I'm going to stay at my job, if that's what you mean.

LINDA [*After a moment, very quietly*]: I see.

JOHNNY: But only for a while! Only a couple of years, say—just until I can get through to her that—well, it's what she asked, and after all, a couple of years isn't a lifetime.

LINDA: No, of course not.

JOHNNY: I can see the way they look at it—I could hardly expect them suddenly to do a complete about-face, and—but hang it, they ought at least to see what I'm getting at!

LINDA: Perhaps eventually they will.

JOHNNY: That's what I'm counting on.

LINDA [*Another silence. Then*]: The fun's gone out of you, Johnny. That's too bad.

JOHNNY [*Stares at the floor*]: It'll be back.

LINDA: I hope.

JOHNNY [*Looks up suddenly*]: Linda—you agree that there's only the one thing for me to do now—

LINDA [*Smiles again*]: Compromise—

JOHNNY: Yes, damn it! But *you* think that's right, don't you?

LINDA: I don't think it matters a bit what I think—

JOHNNY [*Goes to her suddenly and seizes her wrists*]: It does, though! You think it's right, don't you? Say you think it's right!

LINDA: Shall I send for Julia?

JOHNNY: Say it first!

LINDA [*With difficulty*]: Johnny—when two people love each other as much as you, anything that keeps them apart must be wrong.—Will that do? [JOHNNY *drops her hand and moves away from her.*]—And shall I send for her now?

JOHNNY: Go ahead.

LINDA [*Goes to the telephone and presses a button in the box beside it*]: With luck, we'll manage not to include Father this time.

JOHNNY: Oh, Lord, yes! [LINDA *again presses the button, and again several times.*] Asleep, probably—

LINDA: Of course not. [*She presses it again. Then*] Julia—yes—would you come down a minute? No—but there's no telegram *to* send up. Will you come, Julia? [*Her voice changes.*] Julia, it's terribly important that you come down here at once. [*She replaces the telephone and turns to* JOHNNY.] She'll be right down.

JOHNNY: If she doesn't fall asleep again.

LINDA: Johnny—don't talk like that. I can't stand to hear your voice do that.

JOHNNY: You care more what happens to me than she does.

LINDA [*Startled*]: What? Don't be silly. [*Then, with difficulty*] Maybe I feel things about you that she doesn't because—well, maybe just because *I'm* not in love with you.

JOHNNY: You know what I think of you, don't you?

LINDA [*Smiles*]: I'd be glad to hear.

JOHNNY: I like you better than anyone else in the world.

LINDA: That's very nice, Johnny—because I like you a good deal, too. [*For a long moment their eyes hold them together. Then* EDWARD *comes in and, with a start,* LINDA *sees him.*] Oh, for the love of Pete—

EDWARD [*Advances to* JOHNNY, *hand outstretched*]: Well, well—good evening!

JOHNNY: Good evening, sir. [*They shake hands.*]

LINDA [*Turns away*]: —Both members of this club.

EDWARD: They tell me you've been away. Very pleasant, having you back.

JOHNNY: It's pleasant to be back.

EDWARD: —Quite at the mercy of the snow these days, aren't we?

JOHNNY: Quite.

EDWARD [*Moves toward the fireplace*]: Still, they say Americans need four seasons, so I suppose we oughtn't to complain, eh?

JOHNNY: I suppose not.

LINDA: Father—Johnny came tonight to see Julia—

EDWARD: —That doesn't surprise me a great deal, daughter—not a great deal!

LINDA: —Julia—not you and me.—Come on—let's go byebye.

JULIA [*Enters*]: Linda, what's the idea of—? [*She sees* JOHNNY.] Oh—

JOHNNY [*Goes to her swiftly*]: Get a wrap, will you? We're going out—

JULIA [*Hesitates*]: Father—you won't mind if Johnny and I—

EDWARD: Please close the door. I wish to speak with both of you. [JULIA *gestures helplessly to* JOHNNY *and closes the door.*]—You insist upon putting me in a position that I don't in the least relish—[JULIA *seats herself upon the bench at Left. The door is opened again, tentatively.*] Who's that?—Oh, come in, Ned, come in.

NED [*Enters and moves toward his drink*]: Sorry.—I just wanted—

EDWARD: Sit down, Son— [NED *seats himself upon the sofa Left.* EDWARD *continues to* JULIA *and* JOHNNY.]—Coming between two young people in love is furthest from my wish and intention.—Love, true love, is a very rare and beautiful thing, and—[NED *rises and moves silently toward the door.*] Where are you going? Please sit down! [*He waits until* NED *has returned to his place, then continues.*]—And I believe its path—that is to say, the path of true love, contrary to the adage, *should* run smooth. But in order that it may—I am a man of fifty-eight years, and speak from a long experience and observation—it is of paramount importance that—

JOHNNY: I beg your pardon, sir.

EDWARD: Yes?

JOHNNY: If Pritchard, Ames still want me, I'll go with them when we get back from our wedding trip—about March first, say. [LINDA *turns away. There is a silence. Then*]

JULIA [*Softly*]: Oh, Johnny—[*She goes to him.*]

JOHNNY: I'm still not convinced—I still don't believe in it, but it's what Julia wishes and—and I'm—glad to defer to her wish.

LINDA: And now, in Heaven's name, may they be left alone—or shall we all move over to Madison Square Garden?

EDWARD [*Disregarding her*]: You are not convinced, you say—[LINDA *exclaims impatiently.*]

JOHNNY: Would you like me to lie to you, sir?

JULIA: It's enough for me, Father.

JOHNNY: Julia said a year or two. I'll stay with them three years. I'll work harder than ever I've worked before. I'll do everything I can to make a success of it. I only ask that if at the end of the three years I still feel that it's wise to quit for a while, there won't be any more objections.

EDWARD: I doubt if by that time there'll be reason for any.

JOHNNY: We'll have to see about that, sir.

JULIA: Well, Father?

EDWARD [*A pause. Then*]: When is it you wish to be married?

JULIA: As soon as possible.

JOHNNY: Sooner.

EDWARD: The invitations must be out for ten days at least.—How would two weeks from Wednesday suit you?

JULIA: That would be perfect.

EDWARD: No doubt there will be a sailing later that week.—Well, now, the sun's shining once more, isn't it?—And we're all friends again, eh?

LINDA: Just one big family.

EDWARD: —And what are your plans for your wedding trip, may I ask?

JOHNNY: We haven't any very definite ones. Mostly France, I expect.

EDWARD: It's well to arrange even honeymoons a bit in advance.—Now let me suggest a little itinerary: You'll land at Plymouth or Southampton, and proceed straight to London. I'll cable my sister tomorrow. She and her husband will be delighted to have you stay with them.

LINDA: Good Lord, Father—

EDWARD [*To* JOHNNY]: He is Sir Horace Porter—one of the most important men in British banking circles.

JULIA: Father, I'm not sure—

EDWARD: You can scarcely go abroad and not stop with your Aunt Helen, Julia. In addition, it will save hotel expense and Johnny will be able to learn something of British methods.—Then I shall cable the Bouviers in Paris.—He was expert adviser to the Minister of Finance in the late war—a very good man for you to know. If they aren't already in Cannes, they will be very glad to have you visit them. And if they are, you could not do better than go straight to the South yourself and—

JOHNNY: I had thought of this as more of a lark than a business trip, sir.

EDWARD: —But there's no harm in combining a little business with pleasure, is there? I've never found there was.

JULIA [*To* JOHNNY]: They have a lovely place in Cannes.

EDWARD: A week in London—a week in Paris—

LINDA: An hour in the Louvre—

EDWARD: —Ten days in Cannes—ideal! Then you might sail from Genoa and return by the Southern route. [*To* JULIA] I'll arrange to have your house ready for you to go into March first.

JULIA: —Thanks, dear.

JOHNNY: What house is that, Julia?

JULIA: Father's lending us the sweetest little place on Sixty-fourth Street.

NED [*To* LINDA]: Would you call the Sixty-fourth Street house little?

LINDA [*Watching* JOHNNY]: —By comparison.

EDWARD [*To* JULIA]: And I have also decided to turn the cottage at The Poplars over to you for the summers.

JULIA: Father, you shouldn't—you really should not! [*She goes to him and takes his hand.*]

NED: Now there *is* a small place—hasn't even got a ballroom.

JULIA: Oh, Johnny—wait till you see it!

EDWARD [*Is beaming*]: This is not a deed of gift, you know—not yet. Perhaps when you have occupied them for—er—five years or so, my hard old heart may soften.

JULIA: —Listen to him—*his* hard old heart! [*To* JOHNNY]—Have you ever known of anyone so sweet?

JOHNNY [*After a moment*]: Julia—I'm sorry—but I can't stand it.

JULIA [*A silence. Then*]: Would you—mind telling me what you mean?

JOHNNY: If we begin loaded down with possessions, obligations, responsibilities, how would we ever get out from under them? We never would.

EDWARD: Ah?

JOHNNY: —No. You're extremely generous—and kind—but it's not for me.

EDWARD: And may I ask what *is* for you?

JOHNNY: I don't know yet, but I do know it's not this.

EDWARD [*Very quietly*]: We are to understand, then, that you are *not* returning to work.

JOHNNY: That work? For this? [*He shakes his head.*]—No.

JULIA: But you said—!

JOHNNY: —I'm back where I was, now. I can see now that it's got to be a clean break, it's simply got to.

EDWARD: But the other day, if I remember correctly, you intimated that you might follow some occupation—

JOHNNY: Eventually, yes. I think I may still be fairly active at thirty-five or forty.

EDWARD: —And in the meantime you expect just to lie fallow, is that it?

JOHNNY: Not lie—be! I expect to dig and plow and water for all I'm worth.

EDWARD: Toward the—er—eventual occupation which is to overtake you—

JOHNNY: Exactly.

EDWARD: I see.—Julia, if you marry this young man now, I doubt if he will ever again earn one penny. [*He moves to the table behind the sofa, at Right.*]

JOHNNY [*Advances*]: Julia, if it's important to you, I'll promise you I shall always earn my own living. And what's more, if there's need of it, I'll always earn yours.

JULIA: Thanks.

JOHNNY: Oh, my dear, we've got to make our own life—there's nothing to it if we don't—there's no other way to live it!—Let's forget wedding invitations and two weeks from Wednesday. Let's go now. Let's be married tonight. [EDWARD *turns, in amazement.*]

JULIA: I must decide now, must I?

JOHNNY: Please—

JULIA: —And if I say No—not unless you—?

JOHNNY: —Then I'm going tonight, by myself.

JULIA [*A moment. Then*]: Very well—you can go. Because I don't quite see myself with an idler for a husband.

JOHNNY [*A silence. Then* JOHNNY *speaks slowly*]: I suppose the fact is, I love feeling free inside even better than I love you, Julia.

JULIA: Apparently—or what you call feeling free.

JOHNNY [*Turns to* EDWARD]: Good-bye, sir. I'm sorry we couldn't make a go of it. Thanks for trying, anyhow. [*He goes to* LINDA *and takes both her hands*]—Good-bye to you, Linda. You've been sweet.

LINDA: Good-bye, Johnny. So have you.—I hope you find what you're looking for.

JOHNNY: I hope *you* do.

LINDA: You did want someone along with you on the big search, didn't you?

JOHNNY: I did, you know.

LINDA: Poor boy.

JOHNNY: —But we won't mind, will we?

LINDA: Hell, no—*we* won't mind.

JOHNNY: We'll get there—

LINDA: Sure! *We'll* get there!

JOHNNY: Linda—

LINDA [*She leans toward him*]: Oh, please do—

JOHNNY [*Bends, kisses her briefly, and moves toward the door*]: Good-bye, Ned. [NED *attempts a good-bye, but cannot say it.* JOHNNY *goes out. There is a complete silence for a moment. Then* LINDA *murmurs:*]

LINDA: I'll miss that man. [*Another silence, which* JULIA *finally breaks:*]

JULIA [*Half to herself*]:—He's really gone, then.

EDWARD: Yes.—And in my opinion—

LINDA [*Turns sharply*]: —Good riddance, eh? [EDWARD *nods sagely.*]

JULIA: —Really gone—

LINDA [*Goes to her*]: —Oh, never mind, dear, never mind. If he loves you, he'll be back!

JULIA [*Turns upon her*]: —Be back? Be *back,* did you say? What do you think I am? Do you think all I've got to do with my time is to persuade a—a lightweight like him that there's something to life but having fun and more fun? [LINDA *stares, unable to speak.*]

EDWARD: I hope, Julia, that this experience, hard as it may have been, will teach you that—

JULIA: Oh, don't worry about me! I'm all right. [*She laughs briefly.*]—Even a little more than all right, I should say.

NED [*Rises*]: —Um.—Narrow squeak, wasn't it? [*Suddenly* LINDA *grasps* JULIA*'s arm.*]

JULIA: What's the matter with you?

LINDA: You don't love him.

JULIA: Will you kindly let go my arm?

LINDA: You don't love him!

JULIA: Will you *please*—

LINDA: Answer me! Do you or do you not?

JULIA: And what's that to you, may I ask?

EDWARD: Now, children—

LINDA: What's it to me! Oh, what's it to me! [*Her grasp tightens on* JULIA*'s arm.*] Answer me!

JULIA: Father—what's the matter with her?

LINDA: You don't, do you? I can *see* you don't. It's written all over you. You're relieved he's gone—*relieved!*

JULIA: And suppose I am?

LINDA: —She asks me suppose she is! [*Again she confronts* JULIA.] Are you? Say it!

JULIA [*Wrenches herself free*]: —I'm so relieved I could sing with it.—Is that what you want?

LINDA: Yes!—Thanks! [*She throws back her head and laughs with joy, and moves quickly to the table behind the sofa at Left.*] Oh, Lordy, Lordy—have I got a job now! [*From her handbag on the table she takes two brown envelopes, goes to* NED *and gives him one of them.*]

NED: What is it? [*He sees*] Passport—

LINDA: What do you say?

NED: When?

LINDA: Now. Tonight.

NED: Oh, I couldn't tonight.

LINDA: Of course you could! If I can, you can.

EDWARD [*Advances*]: Linda, where are you off to?

LINDA [*To* NED]: Will you come?

NED: Well, you know I'd like to, but—

LINDA: Then come!

EDWARD: Linda, where are you going? Tell me instantly.

LINDA: —On a trip. On a big ride. Oh, what a ride! Do you mind?

NED: Listen, Father, I'd—

EDWARD: A trip now is out of the question. Please remember you have a position to fill. You are not an idler. [*To* LINDA]—A trip where?

LINDA [*To* NED]: You won't?

NED: I can't.

LINDA: —Caught.

NED: Maybe.

LINDA: —I'll be back for you, Ned.

NED [*Almost inaudibly*]: I'll—be here—

DELIA [*Enters*]: Excuse me, Miss Linda—Mr.and Mrs. Potter are waiting in the car. Your bag has gone down.

LINDA: Bring my fur coat, will you, Delia?—And throw a couple of hats in the hatbox and take it down, too.

DELIA: Very well, Miss. [DELIA *goes out.*]

LINDA [*Turns to* JULIA]: —You've got no faith in Johnny, have you, Julia? His little dream may fall flat, you think—yes! So it may! What about it? What if it should? There'll be another—the point is, he *does* dream! Oh, I've got all the faith in the world in Johnny. Whatever he does is all right with me. If he wants to sit on his tail, he can sit on his tail. If he wants to come back and sell peanuts, Lord how I'll believe in those peanuts!—Good-bye, Julia.—Good-bye, Father. [*She leaves them and goes to* NED.] Good-bye, Neddy—

NED: Good-bye, kid—good luck—[*For a moment they cling together. Then*]

LINDA: Oh, never you fear, I'll be back for you, my fine bucko!

NED: All right, kid. [*She moves toward the door.* NED *is drawn after her.* DELIA *enters with the fur coat.* LINDA *takes it from her.* DELIA *goes out.*]

EDWARD: As yet you have not said where it is you are—

JULIA [*Exclaims suddenly*]: I know!

LINDA [*Going out*]: —And try to stop me, someone! Oh, please—someone try to stop me! [*She is gone.*]

NED [*Stands looking after her, murmuring softly*]: Oh, God, oh, God—

EDWARD: I shall not permit it! I shall—

NED: —Permit it!—Permit Linda?—Don't make me laugh, Father.

JULIA [*Advancing*]: She's going *with* them, isn't she? *Isn't* she?

NED [*Smiles and picks up his glass again*]:—Going to get her Johnny.

JULIA [*Laughs shortly*]: A fine chance she's got!

NED: —Any bets? [*Then savagely*]—Any bets, Julia? [*He raises his glass*]—To Linda— [*The portrait above the fireplace catches his eye.*]—And while we're at it—Grandfather! [*He drinks.*]

CURTAIN

HOTEL UNIVERSE

HOTEL UNIVERSE

was first produced by the Theatre Guild
at the Martin Beck Theatre, New York City,
on April 14, 1930.
It was directed by Philip Moeller;
the setting was designed by Lee Simonson.

CAST

PAT FARLEY • Glenn Anders
TOM AMES • Franchot Tone
HOPE AMES • Phyllis Povah
LILY MALONE • Ruth Gordon
ALICE KENDALL • Ruthelma Stevens
NORMAN ROSE • Earle Larimore
ANN FIELD • Katherine Alexander
FELIX • Gustave Rolland
STEPHEN FIELD • Morris Carnovsky

■ ACTION AND SCENE ■

The action of the play is continuous, and takes place in the course of about two hours, upon the terrace of a house in the south of France, near Toulon.
The time is an evening in early July, last summer.

The terrace is like a spacious, outdoor room, irregularly paved with flags of gray stone. The house itself forms one wall on the left, a wall from which two screened doors open—the first from a hall, the second from a sitting room. Down Left, against this wall a flight of outside stairs, guarded by a slender iron railing, mounts to a balcony.

The other entrance is at Right, down from the garden by stone steps. A three-foot wall follows the back and left sides of the terrace just to where the row of small cypresses, which screens the garden terrace, begins. Over and beyond the wall nothing is visible: sea meets sky without a line to mark the meeting. There, the angle of the terrace is like a wedge into space.

Down Right, a small but ancient fig tree in full leaf rises from the pavement. There is a large fanback chair beneath it. Upon the wall at Back, there are two folding cushions. A small upright piano stands against the wall of the house. Near it, there is a table, upon which stand a carafe of brandy, a bottle of Cointreau, a bottle of champagne, and glasses. A few straw and wicker chairs and a sofa complete the furniture. It is about nine o'clock in the evening, and still quite light.

ANN FIELD *sits at a small table at Left, a silver coffee service before her. She is about twenty-eight, and lovely. Near her, taking their coffee, sit* TOM *and* HOPE AMES, LILY MALONE *and* NORMAN ROSE. *On the other side of the terrace, half asleep upon a cushion with a coffee cup beside her,* ALICE KENDALL *reclines. She is twenty-six, very smart and rather pretty.* PAT FARLEY *is at the piano. He is thirty-two, medium tall, slight, likable-looking.* NORMAN ROSE *is the handsomest of the men, and about thirty-eight.* TOM AMES *is forty, of amiable good looks.* HOPE, *his wife, is four years younger, in full bloom.* LILY MALONE *is small, slight and thirty. Without a feature to remark upon, she is able to impart to her small, impudent face a certain prettiness. All are browned by the sun and wear light summer clothes. The women, except* LILY, *who is in a linen day dress, wear simple evening dresses. The men are in flannels.*)

PAT: —And this is a cheerful number from the heart of Old Provence: "Le Roy a fait battre Tambour." Yvette Guilbert used to do it.

[*He plays and sings the song, with its threatening, repeated refrain "Rat-a-plan, rat-a-plan, rat-a-plan-plan-plan-plan."*]

TOM [*At the conclusion*]: Sad.

HOPE: Oh, isn't it!

LILY: Lovely, though.

ALICE: But Ann said to play something gay.

PAT: Yes? How gay, Ann—very gay? [*He looks at* ANN. *She meets his eyes for a moment, then averts her head sharply.*] Well, here's how the monks tried to be gay at Easter. It's Gregorian—eleventh century—rejoice, rejoice—God, how gay. [*He begins to intone the chant: "Halleluiah! Halleluiah!"*]—Can't you see the lines of them, shuffling along, heads down, hands in sleeves, rejoicing, rejoicing?

[*He continues to sing "Halleluiah! Halleluiah!" Suddenly* ANN *rises.*]

ANN: Pat!

[*But he goes on singing.* ANN *mounts the steps to the balcony and goes into the house.* HOPE *rises and goes to* PAT.]

HOPE: Pat—

PAT: What?

HOPE: Quit it!

PAT: Why?

HOPE: Why must we take our nerves out on Ann?

PAT: "Nerves" did you say?

HOPE: —You heard what I said. And you've been the worst. Knowing what you used to be to her, I suppose the torture's great fun.

PAT: Go away, Hope.

HOPE: —Then why do you suppose she suddenly leaves us this way?

PAT: It's her own house, isn't it?

HOPE: Yes—and a fine time we've been giving her in it! The wonder to me is that she's endured our bad manners as long as she has.

TOM: Oh come now, darling—

HOPE: I mean it! All we've done for three mortal days has been to sit around and make bitter cracks about anything we could put our tongues to.—Don't you realize that we're the first Americans she's seen since she's been here? She begged us to come. It meant so much to her to have us. And now, on our very last night with her, we still behave like—oh, I'm so ashamed.

[*She returns to her chair.*]

TOM: What do you want us to do, Hope?

NORMAN: Yes, what shall we?

HOPE: I don't know—something—anything but what we have been. It must be horrible for her, living here. She had a right to expect we'd bring some breath of life with us. And what have we given her?

PAT: Say it: the breath of death.

LILY [*To* HOPE]: You know the reason for our so-called "nerves," don't you?

TOM [*Quickly*]: Now don't start that, Lily. We agreed when we left Antibes not to speak of that again.

NORMAN: Yes—Ann's got enough to depress her, without adding the sad story of a person she never knew or heard of.

LILY: Nobody's going to burden Ann with it. The point is, what it did to us. Every time I close my eyes I see him: a bright, sweet, utterly unimaginative boy of twenty-six—

HOPE: Don't—

LILY: —Standing up there, brown as a berry in a pair of blue swimming pants on the highest rock over the sea, and—Pat, did you really hear him say that?

PAT: Of course I did. He said: "Look, Farley, I'm off for Africa!"

TOM: It was the most beautiful dive I've ever seen.

ALICE: He couldn't have meant it. I'm sure it was an accident.

PAT: Accident nothing. It was suicide.

LILY: Just five minutes before, I was rubbing his back with oil. He asked me to. He couldn't reach between the shoulders.

PAT: Little mother—

LILY: Shut up.

HOPE: He had a daisy behind his ear, the way a grocer boy wears a pencil—

TOM: And didn't look silly, either.

LILY: Not he!

NORMAN: Of course there must have been some reason for what he did.

HOPE: Please, let's not talk about it any more. It isn't safe to dwell on things like that. It makes you morbid.

TOM: There was something grand about the way he did it.

LILY: He laughed up at me—the way his teeth gleamed from the water! —Did he have unusually white teeth?

PAT: —Brushed them night and morning. Promised nurse he would.

HOPE: Pat—

PAT: Oh, what the hell—you all make me sick. None of us gave a hang for him. We scarcely knew him.

TOM: We do now.

PAT: A neat job, I call it—no body to dispose of. You know, it's the devil getting a body out of France. The export duty's enormous. And I think there's a luxury tax.—Do I offend you? Sorry.

LILY: Why did he do it? Why did he *do* it?

PAT: He'd just had enough, that's all. Eleven o'clock in the morning, up on a rock in the blazing sun—[*He looks away, his eyes narrowing.*] "I'm off for Africa" and that's all. Lord, it's magnificent. It's scored for drums, that. [*He sings again.*] "Rat-a-plan, rat-a-plan, rat-a-plan, plan, plan."

TOM: Look here, if we don't get that boy off our minds—

LILY: I know. There's something contagious about it. It's like having been in a room with a person with—

HOPE: Lily—

LILY: All right.

TOM: No one is to mention it again. We're here on this visit to dispense cheer to Ann, aren't we? Isn't that why we came? Well, then—

LILY: Hopeless, hopeless, hopeless.—As cheer-makers I'd sell the lot of us at a nickel a pound, on the hoof.

TOM: We can keep the ball in the air until we go, at any rate.

HOPE: We've simply go to. Think of her—buried down here for three years in this fake, rootless country, dying of homesickness with a half-mad father—

ALICE: I saw him, you know.

HOPE: *You* did!

NORMAN: When?

TOM: Where, Alice?

ALICE: It must have been him. Last night I woke up and couldn't get back to sleep again. I thought I heard someone down here, so I came out on the balcony. It was a funny light. Everything was—I don't know—awfully pale. For instance, that fig tree didn't seem to have any color.

TOM: But where was he? Here?

ALICE: Yes. At least there was a man—quite a nice-looking man, with gray hair. He was all in white. He was standing here at the wall, looking out over. The lighthouse was lit, and every now and then it would light him all up.

PAT [*Unimpressed*]: Was there a very bright star in the sky?

ALICE: I didn't notice.

LILY: You ought to look out for those things, Alice, you really ought.

ALICE: I can see it all so distinctly, even to the way a button on his coat caught the light and a lace on his shoe that was untied and dragged along after him.

PAT: Then what did he do—ride off on a unicorn?

ALICE: No, he just went up there into the garden, the rooster after him.

HOPE: The what?

ALICE: Didn't I tell you? He had a white rooster with him.—After a while I heard it crow, quite far away.

HOPE: It must have been dawn then—

ALICE: No—it was nowhere near it.

LILY: Well, it must have been dawn somewhere—

PAT: It usually is—

TOM: You dreamed all that, Alice.

ALICE: I saw it.

PAT: —While we're here he's staying down at the what-do-you-call-it—the little house—the bastide. I imagine he's sicker than he thinks. A fine end for one of the foremost electrical experts in the country, eh? A swell finish for the only first-rate physicist we've ever had.

ALICE: But hasn't he always been a little—you-know?

PAT: He never seemed so to me.—Who'll have a drink?

[*He refills his glass.*]

NORMAN: But when was it he began to crack?

PAT: Only about five or six years ago.—This is a noble brandy.

TOM: I heard something about his haranguing a crowd in Central Park once—

PAT: He can't take people casually—that was part of his trouble. He's supposed to have some kind of power over them. Somebody said it's because he always seems so close to death.—It tastes like cucumbers.

LILY: I've never known anyone to seem further from it than that boy standing there on that rock, and—

HOPE: Lily!

LILY: Oh, all right.—Only I never have—not anyone.

PAT: Finally Ann had to bring him here, where he doesn't see anyone but her, and seems to be all right. It's a swell deal for Ann. [*His tone changes.*] So we thought we'd come and put on a show for her, did we? We thought we'd remind her of what a big, gay, exciting life exists outside these walls—rub a little salt in, just so she'd be really content to stay on here—is that it?

TOM: Lord, you can be a louse.

PAT: You bet I can.—If Ann has any illusions about what goes on in the great big wonderful world back home, *I* haven't.

[*He goes to the wall and sits there, looking out.*]

HOPE: Just the same, Pat—

PAT: —Oh, go ahead. Do as you like. Be bright, be merry.

[*A silence.* LILY *looks about her.*]

LILY: I'm not happy in this old place. It's too violent, it's too dramatic. I know I'm an actress but hang it, I'm on a holiday. You get a sense of things being born all the time. They come bursting out of the ground. There's too much raw life about.

TOM: The house used to be a small hotel—the Hôtel de l'Univers, it was called. I heard a tale or two about it down at the port today. It had been deserted for quite awhile before Ann and her father took it.

HOPE: Deserted? Why?

TOM: The boatman said things began to happen.

[PAT *laughs.*]

PAT: The man in 608 had a nightmare, and the lady in 609 rang for ice water.

ALICE: Things! What things?

TOM: The idea seemed to be that people began to resemble other people and the place itself other places. And time went sort of funny. Their pasts kept cropping up.

LILY: —Excuse me, friends, but *I'm* taking the night boat for Albany.

TOM: I'm only telling you what I heard at the port.

NORMAN: There may be something in it.—When *I* stepped out on this terrace the other night, it was for all the world like the Grand Central the first time I saw it, when I was fifteen. I don't mean just the way it looked. I mean—

LILY: I know—and now it's a hilltop in New Hampshire. We played Concord once. I used to climb out my window at night when Father had drunk enough to sleep—and up it, and lie on my back there.

[*She closes her eyes.*]

TOM: Maybe what you call the "raw life" here makes people children again.—Lord, I remember the way Under the Piano became as many places in as many moments: a boat to London, and then London. An airship, and a grocery store. A circus tent, and 'way down cellar.— And it was—for the moment it really was.

[*A silence, Then*]

HOPE: Tom, I wonder how the children are? I'm worried. I think I'll cable.

[*Another silence. Then*]

LILY: Dear, dear Father—how I miss him.

ALICE: Oh, she's got her father on the brain. Every theatre we went to in Paris, she did nothing but talk about how he used to play—

LILY: That's enough, Alice.

ALICE: Of course we're sorry he's dead, but why we should be bored with endless accounts of his—

LILY: I say it's enough!

TOM: This is pleasant.

HOPE: I tell you, you're all in a state.

PAT: I don't doubt that the people who used to come here were, too. Lord knows it's on the edge of the world.

[HOPE *glances toward the house.*]

HOPE: Here she is. Now for heaven's sake—

[ANN *comes in from the house.*]

ANN: —That was foolish of me. Please don't mind. [*She goes to the coffee table.*] More coffee, anyone?

TOM: *I* will.

HOPE: Me too. It's so delicious.

ANN: It took me two years to discover why French coffee was so vile.

HOPE: *I* could have told you. They load it full of chickory.

ANN: But the real trouble is in the roasting. They roast it black, till it looks like shoe buttons.

NORMAN: That was the spirit that won the War.

TOM [*Reflectively*]: —When I was a child, I used to have a pair of button shoes that I wore Sundays.

LILY [*To* NORMAN]: Has there been a war? I've been away—

TOM: I don't think they make them anymore.

ANN: —So what did I do, but buy a roasting machine of my own. It makes a very fine smell of a morning. More, Pat?

[PAT *turns.*]

PAT: Thanks, I'll take another brandy.

TOM: So will Tom. I like my good things together.

[PAT *fills two glasses for them and returns to the wall with his.*]

HOPE: It stays light so late, doesn't it?

ANN: Wasn't the beach a glory today? Wasn't it? Oh, I love that beach! It's my mother.—Why do you go? Why don't you all stay on with me? I'll be good to you—

LILY: If we could—

ANN: You're really splendid, you know. You are so splendid!

LILY: Don't make me cry, Ann.

ANN: You? [*She laughs.*] Imagine! [*And turns to* PAT.] What *are* you doing there, Pat?

PAT: Me? Oh, just looking—

ANN: But I thought you didn't like views.

PAT: This isn't a view. For a view you've got to have a horizon. There's not a sign of one out there. The sea meets the sky without a line to mark the meeting. The dome begins under your feet. The arc's perfect.

ANN: But I want to see your face. I'm fond of your lean, brown face— [*He turns to her.*] That's better!—Pat, you're older. [*He turns away again.*]—But I like you better older!

LILY [*After a slight pause*]: It's fantastic, this terrace. It just hangs here. Someday it'll float off in space—and anchor there, like an island in time.—I'm full of whimsies tonight. I need a good dose at bedtime.

ANN: Lily, why do you spoil everything you say?

LILY: Do I?

ANN: Yes. What are you afraid of?

LILY: Oh—these people's gibes.

ANN: I don't understand it.

LILY: Ah, Ann—come on home with us! We do need you so.

HOPE: Yes, Ann! To Paris tonight—sail with us Wednesday. Just as a farewell present. Oh, do!

ANN: What a grand idea!—Tied up in a box—ribbons! Lovely!

HOPE: Isn't it even possible?

[ANN *laughs.*]

ANN: No dear, it's not—not possibly possible.

[LILY *picks up a book and begins to read it.*]

HOPE: But surely you could leave your father for a month, say. You could get a good nurse in Marseilles or Toulon, and—

ANN: Father doesn't need a nurse.

HOPE: I'm sorry. I'm stupid.

ANN: No you're not. You're sweet. You're all sweet. But I'm like that theoule tree—um, smell it!—I live here.

NORMAN: Three years is quite a while in one place—

ANN: Not here. Ever since we came my sense of time's been confined to music.

[PAT *lights a cigarette.*]

PAT: —Look, everyone: there's nothing travels so fast as light—thirty million miles a minute. But by the time they see this match on Orion we'll all have been dead fifty years, maybe more.

[FELIX, *a French butler of about fifty, in a white summer uniform, comes in from the house.*]

ANN [*Laughing*]: There's a modest man!—He thinks they're hanging out

At quayside, Antibes: the Barrys in their fashionable Mercedes—Ellen at the wheel and Philip obscured by the rear-vision mirror. Perched behind them is Gerald Murphy, skipper of *Weatherbird,* whose masts and rigging are visible in the background.

Lunch at Eden Roc, when it was not yet a favorite meeting place of Hollywood moguls. Ellen Barry is on the left; Barry, on the right, is holding a big Kodak with the gingerliness of the born nonphotographer. Though he was often the subject of snapshots, he rarely took any.

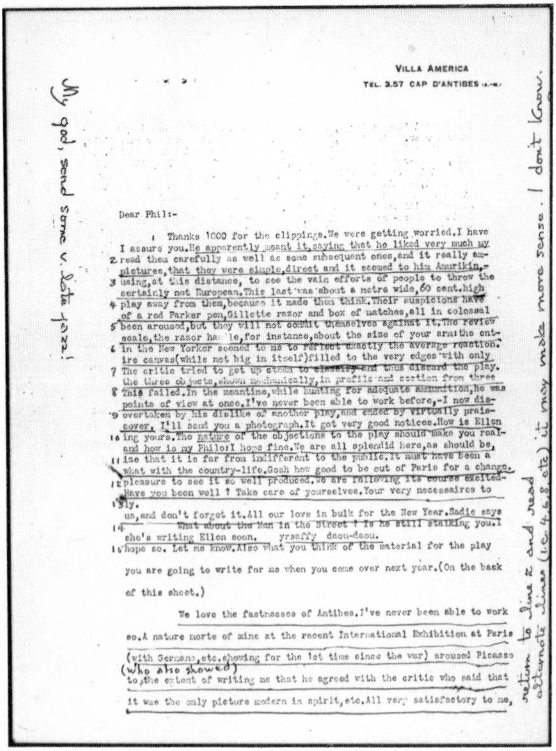

VILLA AMERICA
TÉL. 3.57 CAP D'ANTIBES

Dear Phil:-

1 Thanks 1000 for the clippings. We were getting worried. I have
I assure you. He apparently meant it, saying that he liked very much my
2 read them carefully as well as some subsequent ones, and it really am-
pictures, that they were simple, direct and it seemed to him Amurikin,-
3 using, at this distance, to see the vain efforts of people to throw the
certainly not European. This last was about a metre wide, 60 cent. high
4 play away from them, because it made them think. Their suspicions have
of a red Parker pen, Gillette razor and box of matches, all in colossal
5 been aroused, but they will not commit themselves against it. The review
scale, the razor handle, for instance, about the size of your arm: the ent-
6 in the New Yorker seemed to me to reflect exactly the average reaction.
ire canvas (while not big in itself) filled to the very edges with only
7 The critic tried to get up steam to classify and thus discard the play.
the three objects, shown mechanically, in profile and section from three
8 This failed. In the meantime, while hunting for adequate ammunition, he was
points of view at once. I've never been able to work before, -I now dis-
9 overtaken by his dislike of another play, and ended by virtually prais-
cover. I'll send you a photograph. It got very good notices. How is Ellen
10 ing yours. The nature of the objections to the play should make you real-
and how is my Philo: I hope fine. We are all splendid here, as should be,
11 ize that it is far from indifferent to the public. It must have been a
what with the country-life. Gosh how good to be out of Paris for a change.
12 pleasure to see it so well produced. We are following its course excited-
Have you been well ? Take care of yourselves. Your very necessaires to
13 ly.
us, and don't forget it. All our love in bulk for the New Year. Sadie says
14 What about the Man in the Street ? Is he still stalking you. I
she's writing Ellen soon. yrsaffy daou-daou.
15 hope so. Let me know. Also what you think of the material for the play
you are going to write for me when you come over next year. (On the back
of this sheet.)

We love the fastnesses of Antibes. I've never been able to work
so. A nature morte of mine at the recent International Exhibition at Paris
(with Germans, etc. showing for the 1st time since the war) aroused Picasso
(who also showed)
to the extent of writing me that he agreed with the critic who said that
it was the only picture modern in spirit, etc. All very satisfactory to me,

My god, send some v. late jazz!

return to line 2 and read alternate lines (i.e. 4, 6, 8, etc) it may make more sense. I don't know.

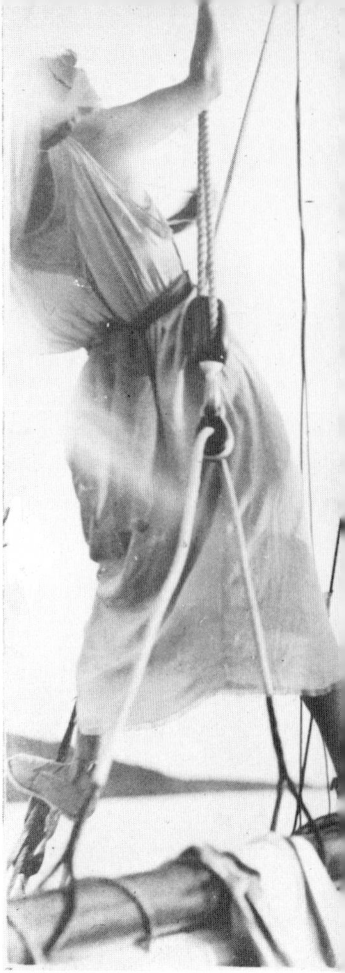

Above, left, a characteristic Gerald Murphy stunt. He is writing a letter to Barry in America from the Villa America in Antibes. (The letter, undated, was probably written in the late fall of 1925.) Having got to the bottom of the page and finding himself with much left to say, he simply goes back to the top of the page and begins typing between the lines. At the end of the letter, he scribbles "return to line 2 and read alternate lines (i.e. 4, 6, 8, etc) it may

make more sense. I don't know." The Barrys subsequently numbered the alternate lines and underscored them in order to simplify the task of reading them. Murphy often wrote letters in longhand which at the bottom of the page would continue marching up the right-hand side of the page, across the top, and then down the left-hand side to a conclusion. Like everything Murphy touched, the letter became an amusing work of art.

Sailing out of St. Tropez aboard the Murphys' hundred-foot-long schooner, *Weatherbird.* Ellen Barry is hoisting sail (or pretending to) at left, Sara Murphy is at rear, and Gerald Murphy is contentedly upside down at right; behind Murphy, a glimpse of Barry.

Opposite, Sara Murphy on *Weatherbird.* She was known for setting styles, but this time she has gone too far; on a rolling deck those high-heeled pumps could be dangerous.

Adèle Lovett (Mrs. Robert Abercrombie Lovett)
merrily rolling along one sunny day in Cannes in 1934

The Barrys and their sons, Jonathan and Philip, Jr., whooping it up in Paris in 1931

A party at the Barrys' house in Hollywood in the thirties. Robert Benchley, with his back to the camera, appears to have brought off an anecdote that pleases Donald Ogden Stewart, Marc Connelly, and Barry, though Connelly has the look of a man who had been waiting for a different, and perhaps better, punch line.

Here Benchley whispers to Connelly what appears to be the better line.

Ellen and Philip Barry and a mild party prank: a duckling is being invited to test Phil's whiskey, apparently without success.

STEPHEN VINCENT BENÉT
220 EAST 69TH STREET
NEW YORK CITY

When homo sapiens raised his head
And walked erect in Eden's vale,
There was a critic there, who said
"I liked him better with a tail."

When people first began to hark
To stories of the fall of Troy,
There was a critic to remark
"Is this obscure? Oh boy, oh boy!"

When Hamlet shook his trammels off
And darkness fell upon the slain,
There was a critic there, to cough
"Why must he write about a Dane?"

"The tale's too old, the tale's too new,
The tale is one my uncle tells.
This, Mr. Keats, will never do.
He should have written something else."

Beauty and workmanship and fire,
All things that lift above the sod,
One works to make these things entire--
And then come critics.
O my God!

Respectfully submitted

SVB

Barry at work on "War in Heaven," which is his play *Here Come the Clowns* in the form of a novel

Barry's friendship with the poet Stephen Vincent Benét (*above*) dated from their days at Yale. In literary matters, he trusted Benét above anyone else. Barry's play *Here Come the Clowns* having been adversely received by the critics, Benét at once mailed off to Barry the verse shown here.

of windows on Orion, to see him light a little match! [*She turns to* FELIX.]—Oui, Felix?

FELIX [*To* PAT]: Pardon, Monsieur—

PAT: Oui?

FELIX: Il est neuf heures juste, Monsieur.

PAT: Bon. Merci.

[FELIX *traverses the terrace and goes out into the garden.*]

ALICE: —And why was that, may I ask?

PAT: We've got to leave before eleven. I told him to let me know every half-hour from nine until then.

ANN: That was perfectly dear of you, Pat. That will help. [*A moment. Then impulsively*] Oh, I don't see why you at least can't stay on! I want you to. Pat—stay—

PAT: I wish I could, but I've got dates with mountains.

[TOM *pours himself a glass of champagne.*]

TOM: If you had any sense at all you'd know you ought to train for mountain climbing.

PAT: I feel pretty good, thanks.—Oh, by the way, would you mail some letters for me in New York?

TOM: Sure.

[PAT, *from a book on the wall takes several small envelopes and one large one and gives them to* TOM.]

TOM: —The big one's got no address.

PAT: There are four or five others inside it. I thought they'd be easier to carry.

[TOM *puts the envelopes in his pocket, the large one with difficulty.*]

TOM: You were wrong.

[LILY *slams her book shut and tosses it upon the sofa.*]

LILY: —Another blonde heroine who won't take her milk, and Mama will throw up.

[*There is a silence, which* ALICE *finally breaks.*]

ALICE: —Did I tell you?—I saw the most amusing boat this afternoon: all white, with sienna sails, and a thin white prow—

[*Another silence.*]

TOM: —Gondolas are built in a rather curious way. You know how they seem to pivot—well—

[*But he relapses into silence.*]

HOPE: The air's so heavy—give me a glass of water, someone.

[TOM *gives her his glass of champagne.* HOPE *takes a swallow, and chokes.*]

HOPE: This isn't water.

TOM: The water in France isn't safe. It's full of Frenchmen.

PAT: —And sometimes an American, who swims out too far.

[LILY *turns on him, angrily.*]

LILY: Oh damn you, Pat! Shut your trap, will you?

NORMAN [*Quickly*]: How long is the drive to Toulon?

TOM: Fifty minutes, Mr. Rose.

HOPE [*Reflectively*]: —Bags to be packed.

ANN: No, no—please—there's all the time in the world!

[*Another brief silence. Then* PAT *speaks:*]

PAT: It was funny motoring over here. We passed the old Hotel Beau-Site in Cannes. Lord, how it took me back. I had an English tutor there, named Briggs, when I was twelve. He fell in love with my mother.

ALICE: What did she do? Fire him?

PAT: Heavens, no.—Mother?

[NORMAN *starts a record on a portable gramophone which stands upon the wall—it is the "Naïla" of Delibes.*]

LILY: Dear God, not that again. If you knew what that tune does to me.

[NORMAN *promptly turns it off and returns to his chair. Silence is again about to descend upon them, but* HOPE *will not have it.*]

HOPE: Seriously, Ann—how did you know we were at Antibes?

ANN: I told you: I had a hunch.

[TOM'*s elbow catches on the bulky envelope protruding from his coat pocket. Unnoticed by* PAT, *he takes it out, opens it and extracts four smaller envelopes from it.*]

HOPE: I know you said that. But seriously—

ANN: I have them, I tell you!—It's not my first one about Pat, is it, Pat? —Do you remember my cable to London once, years ago?

PAT: What? Oh yes—yes, sure.

ANN: I got a feeling that he was in some kind of trouble, so I cabled.—But what the trouble was, I never knew.

[TOM *is distributing the letters in his inside pockets and his wallet.*]

LILY [*To* PAT]: Don't tell me anything's ever gone against *you,* darling. I couldn't bear it.

ANN: —I asked you about it once before, didn't I?

PAT: Did you?

ANN: Yes. Don't you know what you said?

PAT: What?

[*Now* TOM *has but one letter without a place for it. He reads the ad-*

dress upon it, starts slightly, frowns, and looks from it to PAT, *and back again.*]

ANN: You said: "I'll tell you that the day before I die."

PAT: All right. That still goes.

NORMAN: It sounds ominous.

ANN: Doesn't it!

[TOM *taps the letter reflectively. Then*]

TOM [*Suddenly*]: Pat—this letter—

[PAT *turns swiftly, goes to him, and takes it from his hand.*]

PAT: Oh—oh, that—I'll tell you about that later.

TOM: I think you'd better.

[LILY *is watching* ANN.]

LILY: —I wish I was like Ann.—Ann, I do wish I was like you. I feel so inadequate near you.

[ANN *laughs and blows her a kiss.*]

ANN: Darling! You're famous—I'm nobody. I do nothing but read of your triumphs.

LILY: —The triumph of trash. You can have my public, if you'll give me your heart.

ANN: But you have it already!

LILY: I'd like to think that.

TOM: You may.

LILY: I want to play Cordelia in *King Lear*.

NORMAN: Cordelia?! You?

LILY: —And Booth turns a handspring in his grave. All right, but somehow that part fascinates me. Whenever I think of it I go absolutely cold. And still I know that if ever I have the guts to do Cordelia, my life will be a different thing.

PAT: Then why not try it? I'll back you, Lily.

LILY [*In fright*]: No! No! I wouldnt dare. [*Then she laughs.*]—No. I start my farewell tour any day now. I'm going to play the Styx instead.—That's a joke, the *river* Styx.

NORMAN: Everybody laugh.

[LILY *springs up.*]

LILY: Norman, there are times when I can't stand this damned Jewish superiority of yours, and this is one of them.

NORMAN: Really? I'm so sorry.

LILY: —The way you look down from your eminence of three thousand years—honestly, who do you think you are, some Disraeli?

NORMAN: He was later, wasn't he?

LILY [*To the others*]: You see?

NORMAN: Besides, I've always considered him enormously overrated.

LILY: I wouldn't mind so much if it made you happy. But you're one of the most wretched men I know.

TOM: Go on—bankers are always happy.

ALICE: Norman's more than a banker. He's a financial genius. My uncle says so.

[ANN *laughs.*]

ANN: There, Norman! Now are you happy?

[*A moment. Then*]

NORMAN: No.—I'll tell you, Ann: here's how I see my life—

LILY: Tune in on Norman Rose Hour.

NORMAN: —There are several angles to it: When a man decides he wants to accumulate a fortune—

TOM: It's going to be a speech.

PAT: —I can't speak to Mr. Morgan just now. Tell him I'll call him back.

TOM: —Nine-thirty A.M. The great Norman Rose enters his office—

[*He goes to the table.*]

LILY [*In three tones of voice*]: Good morning, Mr. Rose. Good morning, Mr. Rose! Good morning, Mr. Rose!

[TOM *grunts, seats himself at the table and contemplates the bottles and glasses.*]

TOM: I see my desk is piled with work again.

LILY: You must learn to depute the smaller duties to underlings, Mr. Rose.

TOM: I have to think of my stockholders. [LILY *knocks three times upon her book.* TOM *turns.*] Who's there?

LILY: It's me, Mr. Rose. Little Lily Malone. You know *me.*

TOM [*Wearily*]: Come in, come in!

[LILY *enters the great man's office.*]

LILY: —A gentleman to see you, sir.

TOM: I don't like gentlemen. It's ladies I like.—Come closer, Miss Malone.

[LILY *stiffens.*]

LILY: —A Mr. Patrick Farley. Morgan and Company. Sleighs and Violins Mended.

TOM: Show him in.

LILY: —Mr. Rose will see you now, Mr. Farley. [PAT *comes in,* LILY *announces him:*] Mr. Farley, Mr. Rose.—I know you'll like each other.

[LILY *retires.* TOM *indicates a chair.* PAT *seats himself.*]

TOM: Well, Farley, what is it?

PAT: It's—just about everything, Doctor. I feel awful.

TOM: Your Chemistry is down. C-minus.

PAT: Yes, sir.

TOM: Your Physics is down. D.

PAT: Yes, sir.

TOM: Your English is down.

PAT: Yes, sir. I can keep everything down now, sir.

TOM: You were not so good at that last night, Farley.

PAT: I think you are forgetting your place, Rose. Please remember that my grandfather kept slaves, and your grandfather was one of them.

TOM: Yes, and a good one!

PAT [*Sneering*]: —Pride of race, eh?

TOM: If you like.

PAT: And if I don't?

TOM: Farley, I am a busy man.

PAT: —Just so. And that is why I want to ask you a question:—That shipment of earmarked gold for Sweden—

TOM: My God.

PAT: Don't temporize, Mr. Rose. He is my God as well as yours.

TOM: But I must have a moment to myself, to think. [*Suddenly*] I know what! I'll telephone about it!

[*He takes a long spoon from the table and holds the handle to his ear.*]

PAT: —That was the old Norman Rose speaking. That was the Norman Rose we once knew, and loved.

[TOM *speaks into the other end of the spoon.*]

TOM: Get me Equitable Trust. [*Then to* PAT] What ever became of your Aunt Jessie Sprague?

PAT: None of that now! Don't try to get me off on sex.

TOM [*To the telephone*]: Hello?

PAT: Say this to him first: Say "What *is* earmarked gold?" [TOM *nods and waits a moment. Then*]

TOM: Hello, is that you, Trust? Yes. This is Norman Rose speaking—the old Norman Rose. Listen now, Eq—about that gold for Sweden—Sweden, yes.—Look here, old man, maybe you can tell me: what *is* earmarked gold? [PAT *nods approvingly. There is a silence.* TOM *holds his hand over the end of the spoon and turns to* PAT.]—He's bluffing. [*Another moment, then again to the spoon*] Oh it *is,* is it? That's what it is, is it? Well, let me tell *you* something: you're not a big enough man to bluff Norman Rose. No sir!—Well, it's your *business* to know! [*To* PAT]—Still bluffing. [*To the telephone*] All right, all right—that's all right with me! But if you think you can—hello! Hello, are you there? Hello—hello—[*He puts down the spoon and turns to* PAT.] He's gone. He's hung up, the big bluffer.

[PAT *fixes him with his eye.*]

PAT: It's you who are bluffing, Rose. [*He points his finger at him.*] What *is* earmarked gold?

TOM [*Confused*]: I—why, it's—I'm not sure, but I *think* it's—

PAT: We have no place here for men who are not sure.

TOM: Don't be hard on me, boy.

PAT: I'll give you two alternatives.

TOM: Make it three.

PAT: I'll give you three alternatives.

TOM: Four.

PAT: Four and a half.

TOM: Five. Five twenty-five!

[PAT*'s fist descends upon the table.*]

PAT: Sold!—To the gentleman in the straw hat, for five twenty-five!

TOM: But who—who are you?

[PAT *rises, opens his coat, and points to his badge.*]

PAT: The Chairman of your Board of Directors. [TOM *covers his face.* PAT *speaks quietly:*] Good afternoon, Mr. Rose. [TOM *rises, and makes one mute gesture of appeal.*] Good *afternoon,* Mr. Rose.

[TOM *hulks out of his office, a broken man.* PAT *seats himself at the table and pours a drink.*]

NORMAN [*Laughing*]: All right! I'll resign!

HOPE: Silly—they are so silly.

ANN: It was lovely! Do another—

HOPE: No, they mustn't. I'm always afraid they'll slip over the line and turn into the people they're pretending to be.

LILY: It would be grand just to let yourself go sometime. I wonder what would happen?

HOPE: I hate to think.

LILY: It couldn't be any worse than it is. [*She closes her eyes.*] Hopeless, hopeless—

NORMAN: What?

LILY: Hopeless.

PAT [*Humming*]: Rat-a-plan, rat-a-plan, rat-a-plan-plan-plan-plan.

NORMAN [*To* LILY]: But while there's life, my dear—

LILY: —There's the rent to pay.

PAT: —And what's the big premium on life, I'd like to know?

NORMAN: Well, it does look like all we've got.

PAT: There was a great big war, Pet, and we survived it. We're living on borrowed time.

TOM: Lost: one battalion.

PAT: We're not lost. Our schedule is different, that's all.—What I mean is, we'll have had the works at forty instead of eighty.

NORMAN: I've got a theory people expect too much from life.

ANN: But you can't! That's one thing that's not possible!

LILY: Then why is everyone so disappointed in it?

ANN: Because all they concern themselves with are its probabilities. Think of the things that might happen, can happen, do happen! The possibilities!

LILY: There might be a ray of hope in that. Who, for instance, would ever have thought that the little backstage rat I was, would spend a weekend with the King of Spain?—Not that I enjoyed it.

ALICE: —Snob.

ANN [*Laughing*]: You might spend a weekend with yourself sometime, Lily. You just might have a lovely time.

LILY: I'd bore myself stiff. I'd get to showing myself card tricks.

TOM: A person's got to look for disillusionment all the way along. It's the price paid by everyone who uses his head for anything but a hatrack.

ANN: But Tom! What do you want with illusions in the first place?

LILY: Oh—just to make himself feel important. That's why he quit his business with such a great big gesture.

TOM: I quit publishing because it seemed ridiculous to devote my life to bringing out books about life.

LILY: Exactly—and how important the gesture made you feel. Sure. That's what we're all after—and that's all we're after.

ANN: You know, Lily, you're so compeltely debunked, there's very little of you left.

LILY: I tell you, to beat this game you've got to be born rich and healthy, and preferably a Farley—with Pat's private slant that nothing matters a damn anyway.

PAT: Is that my slant?

LILY: Isn't it?

ANN: It wasn't when I knew him.

PAT: People change, they say.

ANN: It breaks my heart to have you change, Pat.

[PAT *glances at her, then looks away.* ALICE *stretches upon her cushion.*]

ALICE: Oh, you all think too much. Why don't you be like me?

LILY: Need you ask, dear?

ALICE: I know that when I die, I die. But in the meantime I hope to keep my days and nights fairly full.

LILY: Of what?

ALICE: I may not be as clever as you, Lily, but I'm a whole lot happier. [*She yawns luxuriously.*]

LILY: I have a cat that is, too.

ALICE: I love cats. Cats have the right idea.

PAT: They also have kittens.

[NORMAN *clears his throat.*]

NORMAN: It all resolves itself into the fundamental problem of the location of Man in the Universe.

PAT: Really? Is that all?

TOM: Oh Lord, how can anyone believe he matters any, when he knows that in a few years he'll be dead and done with?

ANN: You honestly think that *this* is all there is, then?

TOM: This what?

ANN: This life.

TOM: Why, of course. Don't you?

[ANN *laughs.*]

ANN: Oh no, no, *no!* Of course not! Not possibly.

[*They all look at her in astonishment. Even* ALICE *raises herself upon her elbow on the cushion.* LILY *murmurs:*]

LILY: —She's marvellous. She's really marvellous.

TOM: Chemistry is chemistry, Ann.

ANN [*Still laughing*]: Heavens, Tom, is that as far as you've got?

LILY: There's always the next step. Look: you see that nice little white scar there?

[*She holds one hand out for her to see, wrist upward.* ANN *is serious in a moment.*]

ANN: Lily—what do you mean!

HOPE: Lily! You didn't!

LILY: —Didn't I, though.—At last a real use for old razorblades.

HOPE: But when?

LILY: Oh—about a year ago. I forget, exactly.

HOPE: But my dear—*why?*

LILY: I just got sick of myself. [*She apologizes.*]—It wasn't very successful. I know too much. I made the tourniquet myself.

PAT: That's right, Actress, do your stuff. God's out front tonight.

LILY: —Will you tell the Kind Gentleman I enjoyed his little piece, but found no part in it for me?

TOM: Don't talk that way, Lily.

LILY: Why not?

TOM: It's blasphemy. I was born a Catholic, and I don't like it.

[LILY *stares at him, finds him quite serious.*]

LILY: "Blasph—"? I haven't heard that word in years. Say another.

NORMAN: I thought you'd given up your religion?

TOM: So I have. But all the same, the only real dope on life I ever got was from an old priest at school. I'd like to see that old fellow again. He was a nice old fellow. Father Francis, his name was.

ANN: There's been a great space left in you, Tom. It will take some filling.

TOM: And with what?

LILY: They say cyanide is quite satisfactory.

HOPE: Don't, Lily—

LILY: Why? Don't tell me *you've* never thought of it.

[HOPE *is about to reply, but does not.*] Ha-ha! Caught you—

TOM: Darling—you haven't really—

HOPE: Well, haven't you?

TOM: I know, but—

HOPE: Is it anyone's special privilege? Am I not worthy?

[LILY *laughs, and turns to* ALICE.]

LILY: Alice?

[ALICE *sits up.*]

ALICE: Yes, dear?

LILY: No, there'd be no point in it for you—it would be too little change.—But what about you, Norman? Do you ever yearn out windows?

[NORMAN *smiles.*]

NORMAN: I can't say I've ever seriously contemplated it, no.

LILY: Then go on and contemplate it.

[*A brief pause. Then*]

NORMAN: Well, I wouldn't do anything positive—but if I knew I could save my life by changing from this chair to that one, I doubt if I'd move.

[*Again* LILY *laughs.* ANN *is gazing at them in amazement.*]

LILY: This is grand! [*To* ANN] I suppose we can count you out, though.

ANN [*Briefly*]: Yes. I'm out.

LILY: —And as for you, Patrick? How long since *your* last confession?

PAT: I'm sorry to disappoint you, but it's never crossed my mind.

LILY: And if I were you, I'd take precious good care it never did.

PAT: Thanks. You're kind. I'll remember.

LILY: —Because I don't think it would cross yours. I think it would stick there. [*She looks about her. Then, to Ann*] Four out of six. Not a bad average, is it?

TOM: Pat, why was that letter addressed to me?

[PAT *smiles.*]

PAT: Suppose my foot should slip on an Alp?

TOM: Do you expect it to?

PAT: Not particularly, but there's always the hope.

TOM: You're not usually so foresighted.

PAT: But this time I am.

TOM: —I don't like it. May I read it now?

PAT: It would make me feel a little foolish. It's signed "Oceans of love, Patrick."

ANN: What letter are you talking about?

PAT: One that he—

ALICE [*Suddenly*]: Oh, good Lord—

HOPE: What's the matter?

ALICE: Suddenly I had the most abominable chill.

LILY: On a night like this?

ALICE: What a fool I am, really.

[NORMAN *wraps a thin beach blanket about her.*]

LILY [*Sweetly*]: Please dear, let *me* say that.

NORMAN: I wouldn't give two francs for any of our nervous systems.

HOPE: It's probably too much sun and too little sleep for a week.

[PAT *pours himself another brandy.*]

PAT: —And the grape—the grape and the grain.

[*And drains the glass. Again silence descends upon them.* HOPE *finally breaks it.*]

HOPE: Is it always so heavenly here, Ann?

ANN: —Except for some overcast nights in the Autumn with no moon, no stars. Then there's such blackness as you wouldn't believe.—Only the light from the lighthouse on the Ile de Port-Cros, crossing the terrace here—like the finger of God, Father says.

[*It has got darker, but the atmosphere possesses a luminous quality that imparts a strange definiteness of outline to the objects and the people upon the terrace. Again, silence. Then*]

LILY: I'm sad.—I could cry.—I am crying.—Oh, behave yourself.

[*Suddenly* ANN *stands bolt upright, rigid.*]

HOPE: What is it?!

ANN: Wait a minute.

HOPE: Honestly, Ann, I do wish—

ANN: Wait! [*For a moment they wait, silent, tense. Then from the distance is heard one muffled report.*] —There. It's all right. Don't worry.

HOPE: But what on earth *was* it?

ANN: It's Father. He's at the bastide. Sometimes he fires a sunset gun. I get to expect it.

ALICE [*Awed*]: He won't do it again tonight, will he?

ANN: I said a sunset gun. It sets only once a day as a rule. [*There is a silence. She rises, abruptly.*] Well, why shouldn't he, if he likes? I think it's splendid of him! [*A moment. Then she laughs shortly.*] Sorry! [*Waits another moment, and continues.*]—I imagine he'd seem a trifle strange to you, but to me it's a pretty grand sort of strangeness. I believe he is a very wise man.

TOM: I don't doubt it.

ANN: I don't always understand him, but that's my fault. I understand better than I used to, and sometime I hope to understand all. So I just try to follow him wherever his mind leads. I've been beautiful places there with him.

TOM [*After a pause*]: I unearthed a marble tablet in the lower garden today. It was in Latin and said: "To Semptronius who, at age 12, danced here, and pleased."

ANN: But how charming that is!—Can't you see him?—Semptronius—

[TOM *rises. All at once he is as excited as a child.*]

TOM: I'd like to dance here, too. [*To* PAT] Will you play? And would anyone mind?

HOPE: —Now that's what I mean! Really, we're not acting at all sensibly, don't you realize it?

[TOM *looks at her, and returns to the wall.*]

TOM: —Ten years ago I wouldn't even have asked. It's a rotten feeling, knowing your youth's gone—knowing that all the brave things you once dreamed of doing, somehow just won't get done.

PAT [*As a small boy would say it*]: I wanna go out to the South Seas like Father *Da*mien!

TOM [*Soberly*]: I did, at that.

ALICE: Who is Father Damien?

TOM [*Reciting*]: Father Damien was a noble priest who went to the South Seas to help the lepers and got it himself.

HOPE: Sometimes I don't know his voice from little Tommy's.

[*Suddenly* TOM *stands up upon the wall.*]

TOM: Look, Mummy! Look where *I* am!

HOPE: Get down, Tom, you'll fall.

TOM: Don't punish me, Mummy.—Reason with me.

HOPE: —Acting like that! I don't know where you think you are.

[TOM *descends from the wall.*]

TOM: —Under the piano. [*He moves away from them, toward the table.*]—Under the apple tree—[*He seats himself cross-legged beside the table, whistling a tune softly through his teeth and trying to wrench the top from a wooden champagne stick. A moment, then he calls, as a small boy would:*] Hey, Pat! C'mon over!

[PAT *comes forward to him.*]

PAT: Hello, Tom.

TOM: Hello, yourself.

PAT: Where're the other fellows?

TOM: How should I know? I got better things to do than follow *them* all over everywheres.

[*He examines his stick with interest.* PAT *seats himself on the ground beside him.*]

HOPE: Don't, Tom.—Make them stop, Ann. They go too far with it.

[*But* ANN *is silent, watching them intently.*]

PAT: —Gosh, I feel good, don't you?

TOM: I feel all right.

PAT: —But don't you ever feel—gosh, I don't know—*good?*

TOM: You don't feel very good when you've got things the matter with you, like I have.

PAT: What have you got? [*No answer*] Aw, come on, Tom—is it really bad?

[TOM*'s head bends lower over his stick.*]

TOM: It's awful.

PAT: Aw gosh, I'm sorry—tell me, Tom—

[*A moment, then*]

TOM: Will you promise never so long as you live—[PAT *nods eagerly.*] —I think I've got something, Pat.

PAT: What?

TOM: I think I got the leprosy.

PAT [*Appalled*]: You've—? Gosh, Tom, why do you think that?

TOM: I read a book last night about Father Damien in the South Seas and he got the leprosy and I think I've got it.

PAT: How—how do you suppose you ever—

TOM: I gave an old woman a dime the other day, and she went and kissed my hand, and I think it must of been her that gave it to me.

PAT: But didn't you wash or anything?

TOM: I couldn't till I got home. And it takes awful fast. Look at that—[*He shows his wrist.*]

PAT: Where?

[*He almost touches* TOM*'s wrist—but draws his hand back, fearfully.*]

TOM: Doesn't it look sort of—white to you?

PAT: It does, sort of.

TOM: —And scaly. That's the way it starts. My foot's the same way. I could tell for sure by putting it in hot water.

PAT: Hot water!

TOM: If you've got it, you don't feel anything, not even the water, even. Father Damien didn't. That's the way he knew.

[NORMAN *is drawn over to them. He, too, has begun whistling softly. His tune is "Pony Boy."*]

PAT: Oh, he was prob'ly just a crazy ole priest.—H'lo, Norman.

[TOM *scowls.* NORMAN *gestures "Hello," and goes on whistling, hands in pockets.*]

TOM: —A *what,* did you say?

PAT: Well, there *are* crazy priests. Anyways, I bet there have been, sometime.

TOM: Never. Never one. God wouldn't let there be.

NORMAN: What about Theo-philus?

TOM: Who?

NORMAN: Theo-philus.

TOM: I wouldn't either. [*A moment*] *Why* would I?

PAT: I suppose you think we didn't notice you didn't eat that ham sandwich the other day and asked for a sardine.

NORMAN: I wanted a sardine. I like sardines better. I like their taste better.

PAT: Yes, you do!

TOM [*To* PAT]: —Anyone says sardines taste better'n ham says so for some good alterior reason, you bet.

NORMAN: You know what *you* are, don't you?

TOM: What?

NORMAN: Cath'lic! Cath'lic!

TOM [*Soberly*]: I am a Catholic. Yes. I am proud to be a Catholic.

NORMAN: Yes—well, before *I'd* go to confession and things—

TOM: You know why?—You wouldn't get the chance. They wouldn't let you in. See, Mr. Jew?

TOM: What did he do that was so crazy?

NORMAN: Just burnt the library at Alexandria, that's all.

TOM: I never even heard of it.

PAT: I did. Alexander the Great built it, quite a long time ago, to please his vanity.

NORMAN [*Reciting*]: —And Theo-philus was a crazy Christian monk that burnt up the library which was the greatest in the whole world and which history tells us contained over seventy thousand volumes.

TOM: Well, if he did, I bet he had some good reason. I bet they were impure books, or something.

NORMAN: He was crazy.

TOM: I bet he knew they were good and lascivious and he just burnt 'em to the honor and glory of God.

NORMAN: He was crazy.

PAT [*Pointedly*]: Of course, you'd say so, anyway. I guess you'd say any Christian holy man of God was crazy.

TOM: You are a Jew, aren't you?

[NORMAN *raises his head proudly.*]

NORMAN: Of course I am. What about it?

TOM: You crucified our Lord, that's what about it.

NORMAN: Oh, no I didn't.

PAT: Who did, then?

NORMAN: —The Roman soldiers. See?

PAT: Oh, you think you know everything. All you do is sit around and read books, little Ikey.

NORMAN: I'm not an Ikey! Don't you call me that!

TOM [*To* PAT]: —You're just as bad as he is. A heretic's what *you* are—Protestant-dog-sit-on-a-log-and-eat-meat-on-*Friday!*

PAT: I'll eat anything I like any day I like—see? *And* ham.

TOM: It's all right now, only wait'll you die. Just wait'll then.

PAT [*To* NORMAN]: Pooh, "when I die." That's what the priest tells him—

TOM: Well, just let me tell *you:* when I grow up maybe *I'm* going to be a priest. See? Maybe I've got a vacation right this minute. See?

PAT: A what?

TOM: A vacation—a call.

[PAT *looks at him in wonder.*]

PAT: Gosh.

TOM [*Closer to him*]: Just think that over, Mr. Fresh.—And when you hear of me going out to the South Seas and places like Father Dami—

[*Awestruck, he remembers his malady. In fear he peers at his wrist again.*]

PAT: Is it any worse?

TOM: I—I think it's spread a little.

PAT: Listen—

TOM: What—

PAT: I know a fellow's got a doctor book. Only he won't lend it. You go to look at it at his house. Shall we—?

TOM: All right. [*A moment. Then*] Pat—

PAT: What?

TOM: What would you do if *you* had the—the you-know?

PAT [*After thought*]: I'd kill myself.

TOM: You couldn't. You'd go straight to hell. And the tortures of the you-know are as nothing to the tortures of hell.

PAT: Just the same I'd do it, though. I certainly wouldn't go around with the lepr—[TOM *claps his hand over his mouth.*] Let go!

TOM: —You promised! [*To* NORMAN]—You get out. Get out, now!—If you know what's good for you—

[NORMAN *leaves them.* PAT *struggles.*]

PAT: Let go! I'm—I can't breathe. Let go—!

[*Still* TOM *holds him.* PAT *struggles harder. He begins to beat at him with his fists. Finally freeing himself, he goes at him more violently.* TOM *retaliates. They go up and down the terrace, advancing, retreating, clinching, separating, raining blows upon each other in dead earnest.* HOPE *suddenly realizes that they are no longer playing, and cries:*]

HOPE: Stop it! [*But they go on. She begins to strike at* PAT.] Stop! Stop it, do you hear me? [*She turns imploringly to* NORMAN.] Norman!

[NORMAN *goes to* TOM.]

NORMAN: Come on, now—that's enough! [*He holds his arms from behind.*] What's got into you two?

[HOPE *stands between* PAT *and* TOM, *protecting* TOM. *They are gasping for breath, glaring at each other.* TOM *lurches forward once more.*]

HOPE: Stop, Tom!—How often must I tell you—[*Then she takes him in her arms.*] Oh, didn't I beg you not to!

[ANN *goes to* PAT.]

ANN: Pat—Pat, dear—

[PAT *stares at her blankly for a moment, then suddenly slumps down into a chair.*]

PAT: I'm—I don't know—

[NORMAN *releases* TOM, *who stares first at* HOPE, *then at* PAT, *amazement growing in his eyes.*]

ALICE: Well, of all the—

ANN: Wait!—Are you all right, Pat?

PAT [*Weakly*]: Sure.

[HOPE *covers her face.*]

HOPE: Oh, I'm scared—I'm so scared.

ANN: Of what, Hope—of seeing life burst the walls of the little room we try to keep it in?

[*Suddenly* TOM *turns upon her.*]

TOM: Well, Ann—if you know so much, what's the answer to the whole works?

ANN: If I could tell you—

HOPE [*Gently*]: Tom—listen—

TOM [*Suddenly savage*]: I say, what's the answer? I want to know! [*He averts his head, sharply.*] God help me, I've got to know!

ANN: —But I can't tell you!—I don't know how.—Oh my dears—what is to become of you? How can I let you go to rove the world like ghosts this way? You're so pitiful, and I love you so!

[FELIX *comes in from the garden.*]

FELIX [*To* ANN]: Pardon, Mademoiselle—

ANN: Oui? Qu'est-ce que c'est?

FELIX: C'est le père de Mademoiselle qui fait demander si elle a besoin de lui.

ANN: Ou est-il?

FELIX: À la bastide, Mademoiselle.

[*A moment.* ANN *looks about her, at the others. Then*]

ANN: I'll go to him.

[*She turns and goes out, up the garden steps.* FELIX *turns to* PAT.]

FELIX: Paardon, Monsieur—il est neuf heures et demie, Monsieur.

PAT: Merci.

[FELIX *bows and goes out, into the house, taking the coffee service with him. There is a long silence, then* LILY *collects herself and speaks:*]

LILY: What did he say to Ann?

ALICE: Her father sent to ask if she needed him. She's gone to him.

HOPE: Needed him!—For what, I wonder.

[*Another pause.* LILY *ventures hopefully:*]

LILY: It is not generally known that polo was invented by Chinese women.—An interesting fact, is it not? [*No one replies.*]—Nope.

NORMAN [*Reflectively*]: —I'd like to go all alone to Andorra.

ALICE: Where's that?

NORMAN: I don't know.

ALICE: Then what do you want to go for?

NORMAN: No Federal Reserve—no "giant mergers."—Time to think—Lord, time to think!

LILY: About what?

NORMAN: Lily, I'm sorrier for you than for anyone I know.

LILY: I don't want your pity, Mr. Rose. I just want your money.

NORMAN [*Pondering*]: When I was working in that fur shop on Twenty-third Street. I was a free man. [*A moment. Then he rises abruptly.*] I think I'll go in and pack.

[*And goes out into the house*]

TOM: Of course *I* think the trouble with Norman is, he's caught and he knows it. He'd like to retire now, but he can't. Too much depends on him.

[PAT *laughs shortly.*]

PAT: —All looking for the answer, when there isn't any answer. [*A moment*]—Unless maybe it's "Off for Africa."

HOPE: —That will do, Pat. Don't even start it.

ALICE: I still don't see why men like you three can't enjoy life.

LILY: Promise me something, dear—

ALICE: What?

LILY: —When you die, leave your head to the Rockefeller Institute. It's a little gem.

[ALICE *rises and moves toward the house.*]

ALICE: Oh, you're always so bright—

LILY: I know. Isn't it the devil?

ALICE: If you weren't, *au fond,* such a common little piece—

LILY: —N'est-ce pas? [*To the others*]—She thinks in French.

[*At the door* ALICE *turns and contemplates them.*]

ALICE: Honestly, it's all so boring—

[*And goes out*]

LILY: The trouble with that girl is complete lack of vitamins A to Z.

HOPE: Do you suppose Norman is really in love with her?

LILY: I don't know. Anyhow, there's a chink in that fine Semitic pride of his. It would never risk a refusal.

HOPE: But surely if she cared for him—

LILY: She doesn't—too much effort.

[*A pause.* TOM *rises.*]

TOM: Oh Lord, if only I'd died at fifteen.

PAT: Maybe you did.

HOPE: It's been a ghastly week all around. No wonder we're depressed.

[TOM *looks at her.*]

TOM: Hope, sometimes I feel I don't know you at all. [*He mounts the steps to the house.*]—And we're supposed to be the lucky ones! We're the ones who've got the world by the top of the head.—I'll let you know when I'm packed, Hope.

[*And goes out*]

HOPE: I'm coming now. [*To* PAT *and* LILY]—He came abroad this time to study the origins of Ecclesiastical Precedence in Rome. He got as far as Antibes. He gets vaguer all the time. I'm so worried about him I can't see straight.

PAT: Of course *I* think Tom's trouble is having too much time on his hands.

HOPE: But it's his time to himself he always said he wanted! That would solve everything. And now that he's got it, *it's* not enough. I wish to heaven we were home with the children and he was still rushing madly for the 8:22. He cursed it, but it kept him going.

PAT: You're just travel-worn, that's all. Why not let him make his crusades for Truth by himself?

HOPE: —And get sent for the first day he's lonely? That's what's always happened.—Except once, just once, when he did go to Canada for a month. [*She rises.*] He accomplished two things toward his soul's salvation there—two great things.

PAT: What?

HOPE: —He grew a red beard and learned to whistle through his teeth. [*She moves toward the stair*]—Talk about children! He's the worst one I've got. Oh, if you *knew* how I want to stay home with my *real* babies!

[*And goes into the house.*]

LILY: —Which is the answer, of course, to Hope.

PAT: What is?

LILY: She's so peaceful, so normal. She's all home and babies.

PAT: That's not a bad thing to be.

LILY: It's a grand thing to be.—And so is it to be the fine, free, roving soul that Tom might. It's the combination that's wrong. Of course *I* think the real trouble with them both is—[*Suddenly she stops, and laughs.*] Do you realize what we've been doing?

PAT: What?

LILY: —When I go in, what will you say about me?—The trouble with Lily is what? What's wrong with Lily?

PAT: Is there anything?

LILY: Plenty. But Pat—

PAT: What?

LILY: I think we've been good for each other, don't you?

PAT: I suppose so.

LILY: You lie, you don't!

[PAT *looks at her mildly.*]

PAT: Don't be violent, Lily.

[LILY *groans.*]

LILY: —Now he's going to turn gent on me again. That's the catch with you: you were born a gent and you can't get over it.

PAT: I think I've done pretty well.

LILY: Oh you do, do you? Well, listen to me—

PAT: Lily, I'm sunk.—And low, deep, full fathom five.

[*She looks at him curiously. There is a silence. Then she speaks in a different tone:*]

LILY: Have a drink.

PAT: No, thanks.

LILY: Pat, when I first knew you, your spine had turned to jelly—

PAT: Yes?

LILY: Yes. And your slant was all wrong. You'd been expecting too much of something—I don't know what—and hadn't got it. You were a mass of sobs.

PAT: That's a pretty picture.

LILY: It was you.—I'd knocked around enough, man and boy, to know what people really are. I taught you to expect nothing, didn't I?

PAT: Yes.

[*She raises her glass.*]

LILY: —And what a dandy little mother's helper *this* is—

[*She drinks.*]

PAT: Yes.

LILY: —And that there's no de-lousing station big enough to pass the whole world through.

PAT: That's right.

LILY: Well—have a drink.

[*But he decides not to.*]

PAT: —I suppose they're good things to have learned.

LILY: I've changed your slant, haven't I?

PAT: Something has.

LILY: You've done a lot for me, too. How is it I don't fall in love with you, I wonder—

PAT: I don't know. Have you tried very hard?

LILY: Awfully hard.

PAT: I'm sorry. Maybe I'm just not your type.

LILY: Would you like to be?

PAT: I never gave it much thought.

LILY: Don't I attract you at all, Pat?

PAT: You might, if I thought about it.

LILY: Think about it. [*He does so. They look intently into each other's eyes.*] Have you thought?

PAT: Um.

LILY: What's the answer?

PAT: I'm attracted.

LILY: Much?

PAT: Quite a lot.

LILY: Would you mind kissing me, Pat?

PAT: On the contrary.

LILY: Then do, please. [*He kisses her. She clings to him briefly, then turns away.*] Oh, it's so awful—

PAT: Thanks! [*Then*]—What is?

LILY: I don't feel anything. I don't feel anything at all.

PAT: No. I thought not.

[*She turns quickly.*]

LILY: You knew about me?

PAT: I imagined.

LILY: Don't get me wrong, Pat. I'm not one of the girls, either.

PAT: I never supposed you were.

LILY: I just—don't feel anything for anyone.

PAT: Some people have all the luck.

LILY: Oh, no—don't say that! I want to, so much—[*A moment*] It seems to me—dimly—way back somewhere, I loved someone terribly. I don't know who—my father, maybe.

PAT: There you go about your father again.

LILY: —All I know is, that since, there's been nothing.

PAT: Maybe that did the trick, Lily.

LILY: How?

PAT: Maybe that's all you get.

LILY: You're a wise guy, in a way.

PAT: You think?

LILY [*Touching his forehead*]: —The Farley brow, eight months gone with Minerva. Where do you get all your dope?

PAT: The ravens feed me.

LILY: Oh, hell—nothing happens anymore.

PAT: Buck up, Lily. Something will before you know it.

LILY: A broken neck would be welcome.

PAT: Give things a chance. Don't try so hard for them.

LILY: All right, teacher.—Have another drink?

PAT: Later—when the night wears on a bit.

LILY: Yes—and won't it, though—

[ALICE *appears on the balcony.*]

ALICE [*Lowly*]: Listen, you two—

[LILY *puts on her humorless smile.*]

LILY: Yes, Angel? [*To* PAT] Reach me my Winchester, will you?

ALICE: Honestly, I've got the queerest feeling.

LILY: I told you a week ago you swallow too fast.

ALICE: —I don't suppose we could decently leave *before* eleven—

PAT: No, I don't suppose we could.

ALICE: I was afraid we couldn't. [*She moves toward the doorway, but sways against the railing. She exclaims, weakly:*] Oh—come up here a minute, someone—will you? I feel awful.

LILY: Right away, dear.

[ALICE *goes out, into the house again.*]

PAT: You'd better go. She may be ill.

[LILY *is looking off into the garden.*]

LILY: Ann's coming back. One thing, Pat—

PAT: What?

LILY [*As she moves to follow* ALICE]: If I were you, I'd be careful tonight.

PAT: About what?

LILY: About Ann. You may not know it, but you're still the world to that girl.

PAT: You're talking tripe, Lily.

LILY: Just the same, I'd be careful. [PAT *turns abruptly and looks out over the wall.* FELIX *has come out upon the balcony, with three or four small candle lamps, unlighted, which he arranges upon the balcony wall.* ANN *comes in from the garden.*] Ann—do you suppose your maid could give me a hand with my things?

ANN: But of course! She's in my room. Call her.

[LILY *mounts the steps.* FELIX *takes out his watch.*]

LILY: —And it isn't tripe, my Patrick.

[*From far in the distance beyond the wall a small pencil of light is cast. It performs an arc in space, sweeping across the terrace, flooding over the upper wall of the house and disappearing again in the garden above.*]

FELIX: Pardon, Monsieur—il manque dix-sept minutes de dix heures, Monsieur.

PAT [*Without turning*]. Bon.

[FELIX *goes into the house.*]

LILY [*At the top of the steps*]: What happens when you forget to wind him up?

[*She goes into the house by the other door.* ANN *stands silently watching* PAT *until the door has closed behind* LILY. *Then suddenly, swiftly, she goes to him, takes him by the shoulders and turns him about, facing her.*]

PAT: Oh hello, Ann.

[*From the distance piano music begins to be heard.*]

ANN [*Lowly, intensely*]: I won't have it, Pat. I just will not have it!

PAT: It?—What's that you won't have?

ANN: Something's burning you up. Tell me what it is!

PAT: I'm afraid you're imagining things. Where's the music from?

ANN: Réné Mayer has a house up the road. It's always full of musicians. —You've got to listen to me. I—

PAT: Have you heard Sandy Patch's new song? [*He moves toward the piano.*]—It's called "Drunk and Disorderly." It goes like this—

ANN: Don't, Pat—we haven't time—

PAT: Then let's get the others down, shall we?—And enjoy what there is left.

[*He makes a move toward the house. Her hand upon his arm stops him.*]

ANN: Wait!

[*She looks away, to control herself, her hand still upon his arm.*]

PAT: I'm all right, my dear. Really I am.

ANN: We've known each other quite a few years, now—

PAT: We have, haven't we? I feel pretty spry, though, don't you?

ANN: We've always been able to talk.

PAT: They say I could talk when I was only—

[*Her hand tightens upon his arm.*]

ANN: —Which we've always done directly, and honestly.

PAT: Yes?

ANN: Shan't we now?

PAT: If you like. Why not?

ANN: When you leave tonight I shan't see you again for at least a year —maybe more—

PAT: Oh— before I forget—

[*From his pocket, in a fold of tissue paper, he brings a very simple and fine ruby pendant, and gives it to her.*]

ANN: What is it?

PAT: It was Mother's. I'm sure she'd want you to have it. I know I do.

ANN: Beautiful—

PAT: I think so.

ANN: But Pat—it's priceless—

PAT: So was she. So is Ann.

ANN: Oh, thank you for it! Put it on for me—[*He catches it around her throat. She turns again, facing him, then stands for a moment with her forehead against his breast.*] Pat—my dear Pat—

PAT: Things don't go the way we'd like them to, Ann.

[*A moment, then she leaves him.*]

ANN: —You've been dodging around corners, to get away from me.

PAT: I didn't know it.

ANN: I won't bite you, Pat.—What's been happening to you these past three years? I'm still a little interested.

PAT: It's been pretty much the same sort of life, thanks.

ANN: What are you doing with all that money?

PAT: Oh—spending some of it—giving away quite a lot of it. It's an awful pile to make a dent in.

ANN: You never found the job we used to talk so much about—

[PAT *smiles.*]

PAT: How well she knows me.

ANN: There are only two people in this world who are really important to me, you and Father.

PAT: I'm—thanks, Ann. That's good to know.

ANN: I've been able to help him a little—

PAT: I should think you had.

ANN: I'd give the eyes right out of my head, if I could help you. [*He lifts her hand to his lips, kisses it, and turns away.*] Oh Pat, *Pat*—whatever has happened to you?

PAT: Myself.

ANN: —Don't you go telling yourself you're no good! You're the best there is.

PAT: You don't know.

ANN: Oh, yes I do!

PAT: Anyhow, let's not get solemn about—

ANN: —And what do you suppose it means to me to know that a person I love as I love you is breaking up into little pieces over something I've no share in?

PAT: But Ann—you don't love me anymore.

ANN: I do, though. I've never got over it—never. I love you with all my heart. [*A silence. She smiles uncertainly.*]—I don't suppose by any chance you love me back—

PAT [*With difficulty*]: There's something in the way. Nothing can ever come of you and me now. There's something in the—

[*He turns away, with an exclamation.*]

ANN: Tell me.

PAT: I can't.

ANN: —You'll be shocked to hear I'm living with you in my mind. I've taught myself to dream about you nearly every night. That gives me —rights.

PAT: Ah, Ann—let it go—please let it go.

ANN: I can't. I simply can't.—You've always been a life-and-death person. You take things terribly hard. I'm sure it's not as hopeless as it seems. [*But he does not answer.*]—Do you remember the first time we met, on the Westbury Road?—me, lost, with a sprained ankle, and you—

PAT: —When I forget anything about you and me—

ANN: I wish we could get back there. I wish we could start from the Westbury Road again.

PAT: —But we can't.

ANN: —Such a dear, serious boy you were. All the time you were in college you used to come to me with your little troubles—

[*He laughs.*]

PAT: —Would I row on the Crew?—I didn't make the Dramatic Club.—What if they passed me up on Tap Day.—Poor Ann—

ANN: I was important to you then—

PAT: You still are.

ANN: Come to me now with your big trouble, Pat.

PAT: I'm just a flop, darling.

ANN: It's a little soon to decide that, don't you think?

PAT: I told you my schedule was different.

ANN: Pat, whatever happened, happened four years ago. You came back from a year in England, and you were changed. It was a girl, wasn't it? I saw her picture in your study. What was it—wouldn't she have you?

[PAT *smiles.*]

PAT: I forget. What did she look like?

ANN: Very young, quite English, very fair. A lovely face—pretty, oh, so pretty.

PAT: Funny—I've forgotten.

ANN: I haven't.—Then you went over again the next winter—for how long was it?

PAT: I don't know—three weeks—

ANN: That's when I had my hunch about you. It wasn't long after you'd sailed. I was walking up Madison Avenue and in a florist's window I saw a lot of hawthorn blossoms—

[PAT *starts slightly.*]

PAT: Hawthorn—

ANN: Yes. They were lovely, and I was going in to get some when all at once I began to feel terribly queer. It was as if the bottom had dropped out of everything. I knew it had something to do with you, and I love you and I just went on home without them.

PAT: I don't get it at all.

ANN: Nor do I.—But the next morning I passed the same shop and saw that the hawthorn was gone. Somehow, that was terrible. I couldn't get warm again all day. I love you and I had to cable you.

PAT: I don't get it.

ANN: I've never known such a change in a person, as in you when you came back. Suddenly you were as hard as nails, and so bitter. I hated leaving you that way when I came here with Father. But I was sure you'd get through it somehow, back to yourself. Now I see that you haven't. I see that it's worse than it ever was, it's destroying you. Oh, Pat—it can't be just some fool of a girl who wouldn't have you.—What has done it?

PAT: Honestly, Ann—it's all so long ago.

ANN: But I've *got* to know. Tell me!

[PAT *shakes his head.*]

PAT: It's all too ridiculous. Really. I never even think of it anymore.

ANN: Whether you do or not, it's got you still. Something awful's got you. Tell me—it will help to tell me. Ah, *please*—because I love you—

PAT: I would if I could. I want to. I simply can't.

ANN: I'll find out!

PAT: All right, Ann.

ANN: —But can't you *accept* it, somehow? Can't you take life whole—all of it—for what it is, and be glad of it? Why do you have to go at it with a tin box of paints, daubing it up pretty? You're grown-up, now.—Why, my dear! What have I said? What is there in that, to hurt you so?

PAT: Listen: you can have your marvellous life. I'm not taking any.

ANN: What are you talking about?!

PAT: —The lot of you—clutching, grabbing at some little satisfaction that lasts a day or two—a swell business.

ANN: You dare talk to me about my life like that!

PAT: Yours—theirs—anyone's—

ANN: Oh, you're horrible—

[PAT *looks at her intently.*]

PAT: So you're the last to go. You fail me too—

ANN [*A cry*]: —You?—And who are you, that you shouldn't be failed sometime?

PAT: I don't know, Ann. I've often wondered. [*Again he moves to the wall and stands looking out over it, the light from the lighthouse breaking over his head.* ANN *sinks into a corner of the sofa. From the distance, the piano music begins to be heard more clearly. For a long time they are silent. Then* PAT *speaks. His voice is one of wonder, almost of fright.*]—They're right about this place—it *is* so, you know—it's really so—

ANN: What is?

PAT: —Like other places—like another place—

ANN: Where?

PAT: —A house my mother had in Florida, four years ago, when I came back from England—

ANN: That was the second time—

PAT: Yes. It was in March. I came straight down here from New York—I mean straight down there. Mother was in the patio all alone, having coffee—[*Still he looks out over the wall, without turning.*]—I had so much to tell her—I'll never forget it—I thought if only I could talk to someone who—

[ANN *speaks, softly:*]

ANN: Hello, Son. It's good to have you back.

PAT: —Could talk to someone who might, just might, have some little faint idea of what I—

ANN: Hello, Son. It's good to have you back.

[*A moment. Then*]

PAT [*A murmur*]: Hello, Mother. It's good to be back.

[*He comes forward to her, slowly.*]

ANN: I didn't expect you quite so soon.

PAT: I know.

[*He sinks down upon a cushion on the floor beside her. The eyes of both are straight ahead, not looking at each other.*]

ANN: You're looking tired.

PAT: It was a rotten trip. [*He goes on in a low voice, almost mechanically:*]—I think I'll stay a while this time.

ANN: I'm glad.

PAT: It seems like a pleasant place.

ANN: It's peaceful.

PAT: That's good.

ANN: Ah, Pat—what is it, dear? I've worried so about you.

PAT: Yes. I suppose.

ANN: I've wanted to ask, but—

PAT: I know. I just couldn't talk.

ANN: Are you so very much in love?

PAT: Yes.

ANN: Tell me about her. Who is she?

PAT: Oh, it's all over now.

ANN: Over?

PAT: Yes.

ANN: But are you sure?

PAT: I'm certain.

[*A moment. Then*]

ANN: Who was she, then?

PAT: —Mary Carr—the niece of one of my dons at Cambridge. [*A moment. His voice hardens:*]—Cambridge—another of Father's fake ideas. Finish me off, eh? Turn me into the little gentleman. Every inch a Farley—God!

ANN: Hush, Pat—

PAT: —Be good at everything. Shine! Always shine! And if you can't, don't play.—I can still hear his voice.

ANN: —Mary Carr, I've seen her photograph. She's very lovely.

PAT: Yes.

ANN: —And young.

PAT: She was eighteen in November. [*A pause. Then suddenly*] God, that is young. Father was right *there,* at least.

ANN: What happened when he went over to you last year—

PAT: I cabled I wanted to get married. He cabled me to wait, he was coming. I waited. He came. He talked me out of it. [*Bitterly*]—She wasn't suitable.

ANN: But that wasn't *your* reason—

PAT: I tell you I let him talk me out of it!

ANN: You agreed to put it off, that's all.

PAT: Yes—that's what I told myself—and that's what I told Mary.—That's what the little swine I was, grunted at Mary—just put it off a while, that's all. But somehow the point missed Mary—somehow she didn't get me.—She just stopped talking in the middle of a word, and went into the house. And I took a train, and sailed with *him.* He was ill then—or said he was—we couldn't wait a day.

ANN [*Hesitantly, after a pause*]: You—I suppose you and she—you'd been a good deal to each other.

PAT: We'd been everything.

ANN: I see.

PAT: —But there wasn't to be a baby, if that's what you mean—[*Again the bitter voice returns.*] Wise boy, young Farley. *He* knows his way around!

ANN: But you wrote her. Surely you wrote her.

PAT: All the time, but I never had one little word from her. A dozen times I'd have gone over, but how could I with Father dying and then all that tangle settling the estate? [*He concludes, lowly.*]—It was a year and three months since I'd seen her, when I'd sailed. I didn't even wire—I was afraid she'd run away somewhere.

ANN: But she hadn't, had she?

PAT: No.

ANN: She was there—

PAT: She was there.

[*A moment. Then*]

ANN: —And she just won't have you.

[*Her hand reaches to comfort him. He turns to her.*]

PAT: Mother, she just won't have me. [*Suddenly he stares at her.*] You're not—oh, damn you, Ann—

[*He rises, and leaves her. She follows him.*]

ANN: All right! But tell me. You've got to finish now! [*In another voice*] —Surely it isn't hopeless. Surely you can—

PAT: But it is, you see.

ANN: I don't believe it. Where is she now?

PAT: Down in the ground.

ANN: Pat—she isn't—?

PAT: She is, though—as a doornail.

ANN: Oh, my poor boy—

PAT: My poor Mary.

ANN: But listen to me—listen—!

PAT. No. *You* do: [*He points his finger at her, and speaks:*] Three days before I came, she walked out under a tree where—she'd walked out under a hawthorn tree at the end of a very sweet lane we knew, and stood there and shot herself.

ANN: Pat—Pat—

[*He moves away from her.*]

PAT: You wanted to know, didn't you?

[*She looks at him. Then*]

ANN: —So I lose you to a dead girl.

PAT: I've lost myself to her.

ANN: You loved me first!

PAT: But she died—[*He goes to the piano and seats himself, running his fingers silently over the keys.*]—If only I could get back to her somehow. If I could just let her know I did come back.

ANN: How much of it is losing her—and how much the loss of yourself?

PAT: I don't understand that.

ANN: —You used to have a fair opinion of Pat Farley. That was essential to you—that *was* you.

PAT: All I know is that nothing's been any good to me since. I'm licked, Ann.

ANN: Well, what are you going to do about it?

[*Unnoticed by them* STEPHEN FIELD *has appeared at the top of the garden steps, where he stands, a figure in white, watching them. He is about fifty-eight, slight in build, gray-haired, with a face uncommonly strong, fine and sensitive, lined and worn as it is, gray, too, as it is.*]

PAT: What is there to?

ANN [*Suddenly, sharply*]: Pat!

PAT [*Without turning*]: What?

ANN: You said you'd tell me this the day before you died—

[*As she reaches the word, he strikes a chord and drowns it.*]

PAT: —But I changed my mind, didn't I?—And told you now? [*He turns toward the house, and calls:*] What'll I play? Call your tunes, gents—almost closing time!

ANN: —And the letter to Tom—Oh my dear—what is it?

PAT: Don't be a fool.

[*A moment, then* STEPHEN *speaks:*]

STEPHEN: Pat—

PAT [*Without turning*]: What do you want?

[*He is completely unnerved now.*]

STEPHEN: I wouldn't do it, if I were you.

PAT: Do what?

STEPHEN: I really wouldn't. Things may change.

[*He speaks with a clear, incisive strength.*]

PAT: —Change? How? Who wants things changed? [*He turns, stares at him a moment, then rises.*] Oh, how do you do, Mr. Field? How are you?—Everything's fine with me. Everything is—

STEPHEN: —And yet I wouldn't do it. I wouldn't go from here to those high places—to that strange accident. I really wouldn't.

[PAT *laughs shortly.*]

PAT: Honestly!—If you think just because a fellow's planned a trip to climb an Alp or two—

[ANN *takes his shoulders in her hands, turns him about and gazes into his eyes.*]

ANN: Pat!

PAT: I don't know what he's talking about. [*To* STEPHEN] I don't know what you're talking about. You're beyond me. I can't follow all this—

ANN: Oh, my poor Sweet, why do you want to do it? [*She shakes his shoulders.*] *Why?*

PAT: Why not?—Maybe you can tell me that!—Why not?—I should have three years ago, but I was too yellow then. [*Still she stares. Another silence, then he pulls away from her, mumbling:*]—All right. Don't worry about me. It's all right. Small brainstorm, that's all.—Over now—

ANN: Promise it!

[*He gestures vaguely.*]

STEPHEN: It is not so easy. He is in love with death.

[PAT *turns to him and sings, beating time with his finger.*]

PAT: —Rat-a-plan, rat-a-plan, rat-a-plan-plan-plan-plan—[*He stops on the high note, holds out his arms, and cries:*] Yes!

[*And goes to the point of the wall, where he stands with his back to them.*]

ANN: Father—Pat's mine—I can't lose Pat!

[FELIX *comes out upon the balcony, watch in hand.* STEPHEN *descends the steps and comes upon the terrace.*]

STEPHEN: I know, dear. [*He is watching the house.*]—But let us take it quietly. Let us take it very quietly—

FELIX [*To* PAT]: Pardon, Monsieur—il est dix heures, juste.

[PAT *does not reply.* FELIX *goes out.*]

STEPHEN: —Here are your other friends.

[TOM *and* HOPE *enter.*]

TOM [*To* HOPE, *on the balcony*]: —No, no—what's the good of talking?

HOPE: Well maybe if you'd—

[*She sees* STEPHEN *and stops.*]

ANN: This—these are Tom and Hope Ames.—My father, Hope.

HOPE: How do you do, Mr. Field?

TOM: How do you do, Sir?

[STEPHEN *murmurs a greeting.* LILY *enters from the house.*]

LILY: —I gave Alice a bromide, and she's sleeping like a log. She's—

[*She sees* STEPHEN *and stops.*]

STEPHEN: What a beautiful color you all are. You look like savages. People don't realize that the sun here in the Midi is—

TOM: Didn't I meet you once with Father Francis at St. Luke's?

STEPHEN: I'm afraid not.

TOM: Perhaps it's just that your voice reminds me of him.

[LILY, *eyes wide, stands staring at* STEPHEN.]

STEPHEN [*To* HOPE]: What do you think of our little retreat here?

HOPE: It's lovely. The days have gone so quickly.

STEPHEN: —Quickly—so quickly. [*To* LILY]—Why do you stare at me so?

LILY: Why I—I'm terribly sorry. I—

STEPHEN: But what is it?

LILY: It's just that you're so like my own father—

STEPHEN: Yes?

LILY: He was an actor in a touring company. He died years ago in Cleveland. He wanted me to be a dancer. I used to dance for him, often. It was a great pleasure to him. I mean to say—

STEPHEN [*Gently*]: I am sure it was.

[NORMAN *comes in from the house.*]

LILY [*In a burst*]: —He was superb! He was so kind, so loving. He was the most beautiful man I've ever—! [*She stops suddenly, then continues:*]—But he deserted my mother, you know. He was simply foul to her.—Hell, I suppose he was just a ham actor—yes, and a drunkard, to boot. [*Again she stops.*]—What am I spilling all this for? What's biting me now?

[STEPHEN *turns inquiringly to* ANN.]

ANN: —Lily Malone, Father.

STEPHEN: Poor child. [*To* NORMAN]—And this?

NORMAN [*Advancing*]: I'm Norman Rose, sir.

[*They shake hands.*]

STEPHEN: I understand that you must leave us soon.

NORMAN: I'm afraid we must, sir.—At eleven, to be exact.

STEPHEN: That is unfortunate. [*Again he smiles.*] Well—let us set the hourglass on its side, and ask the Old Gentleman to put his sickle by, and sit down with us and rest a moment. [*He seats himself.*] Before you go I want you all to see my bed of white phlox in the lower garden. In the moonlight it is white as white was never. I have banked the petunias near it—

HOPE [*Delightedly*]: But *I* did that at home!

[STEPHEN *is watching the balcony.* ALICE *has appeared upon it.*]

STEPHEN: The odor at night is so sweet, so pungent—cinnamon and gunpowder.—And is this Alice?

[ALICE *comes down the stairway without touching the railing, eyes far away, walking as in a dream.* ANN *rises.*]

ANN: Yes—

LILY: Go back to bed, you foolish girl.

[ALICE *approaches them, unseeing.*]

ANN: —This is my father.—Alice Kendall, Father.

STEPHEN: How do you do, my dear?

[*But she does not regard him.*]

NORMAN: She's—!

ANN: Father, what is it?

STEPHEN: Sh! Be gentle with her—

HOPE: Oh, I don't like it!

LILY: I told you about that time she walked out into the hall, in Paris.

[ANN *goes to* ALICE.]

ANN: —There, dear, it's all right. Just be quiet—quiet—

[PAT *is watching her, fascinated.*]

PAT: Take her back. It's horrible—

[*Swiftly, directly* ALICE *walks to the angle of the wall.*]

HOPE: Norman—don't let her hurt herself!

[NORMAN *and* ANN *have followed her.*]

ANN: Alice—*Alice*—

[ALICE *turns to her. In a moment her eyes uncloud.*]

ALICE: —But hello, my dear. They didn't tell me you were coming down. Divine house, isn't it?

[*She speaks as if she were reading aloud.*]

ANN: Listen to me a moment, dear—

ALICE: They're right. There's nothing like May in England. Who's on the party, do you know?

ANN: Oh—lots of people. But Alice, listen—

ALICE: Any extra men?

ANN: I think so.

[PAT *goes to the wall and stands there with his back to them.*]

ALICE: I like this Norman person—

ANN: Yes, he's very nice. But—

[ALICE *laughs shrilly.*]

ALICE: I know!—But not too nice! [*Her voice lowers, confidentially.*] My dear, he burns me up. He looks so strong—so strong. I'll bet he'd give a girl a roll for her money, don't you? [*A moment. Then to herself, with real feeling:*]—Why can't he tell?—Why doesn't he know the way I ache for him?

PAT: Take her back, take her *back*—

ALICE: —Which one shall I wear?—I think the blue one, with the ruffle down the front—

[*She unfastens a shoulder clasp, and steps out of her dress.*]

HOPE: But she mustn't—!

[ANN *turns to* NORMAN *with a helpless gesture.*]

NORMAN: I'll speak to her.—Alice!

[ALICE *whispers:*]

ALICE: Who's that?—Is that you, Norman?

NORMAN: Hello, Alice—

ALICE: It was naughty of you to bring me here, you know it was—[*She leans toward him.*] What did you tell the clerk at the desk?

NORMAN: Why, I just said that—

ALICE: Oh, I'm a pretty girl! [*She extends her arms.* NORMAN *takes one of her hands in his.*] Why does no one want me? What are they afraid of?

NORMAN: Maybe they do. [*He turns to the others, painfully.*] I love this girl. I've been crazy about her for years.

STEPHEN: Humble yourself before her beauty, sir.

ALICE: Come—there are people in the next room. I can hear them.

They may come in—[*Suddenly she drags her hand from his and cries in terror:*]—Ann—Ann! [ANN *goes to her swiftly.*]—This man's—been following me everywhere—

ANN: It's all right, darling, he won't hurt you. He's a nice man.

[ALICE *begins to whimper.*]

ALICE: Is he? [*She turns to* NORMAN, *fearfully.*] Are you? [*He nods, speechless. She darts a glance at* ANN *and huddles herself in her arms.*] —But look at me—out on the street like this. Where's my little jacket? I want my little jacket—

[NORMAN *wraps a thin beach blanket about her, and gives her her dress.*]

NORMAN: Here you are, dear.

[*He leads her gently to the steps. She looks up at him with a smile of childlike trust.*]

ALICE: You *are* a nice man—

[*They mount the steps. There is a silence until they have gone out, into the house.*]

LILY: She seemed to be so many places all at once.

STEPHEN: Sleep has freed her from time and space. One day sleep's sister will free her further. [*He hums a measure of a song, laughs softly, and concludes:*]—And near the white phlox I have a dappled pink variety which I developed by crossing a strain of crimson—

TOM [*An appeal*]: Mr. Field—What's the—? Mr. Field—!

STEPHEN: —Yes. It does bewilder one at first. I know. I too used to believe life had one aspect only. I was so sure that sleep and dreaming was—well, sleep and dreaming. And of course I knew that with death it was all over—

PAT: Well?

STEPHEN: Well, now I know I was mistaken.

PAT: How?

STEPHEN: I have found out a simple thing: that in existence there are three estates. There is this life of chairs and tables, of getting up and sitting down. There is the life one lives in one's imagining, in which one wishes, dreams, remembers. There is the life past death, which in itself contains the others. The three estates are one. We dwell now in this one, now in that—but in whichever we may be, breezes from the others still blow upon us.

PAT: I'm sorry, I don't follow you.

STEPHEN: There are no words for it. It is a sense, a knowing. It may come upon you in a field one day, or as you turn a corner, or one fine morning, as you stoop to lace your shoe [*A brief pause*]—Or even as it came on me.

TOM: How was that, sir?

STEPHEN: Here on this terrace.

ANN: Father—

STEPHEN: I know, dear.

PAT: —So life does go on, does it?

STEPHEN: Oh, yes. Of course.

PAT: How, for instance?

[STEPHEN *smiles.*]

STEPHEN: —As it was in the beginning, is now, and ever shall be—

PAT: —World without end, eh?

STEPHEN: Without end.

PAT: Hah! That'd be a good joke.

LILY: Look out, Pat.

[NORMAN *comes out again upon the balcony and stands there, watching them.*]

STEPHEN: —Let us be bold and change the "world" to "universe."—A fine night, isn't it? [*His gesture includes the sky.*]—There is the space we one day shall inhabit, with all our memories and all our dreams. I ask you to admire this, gentlemen—

LILY: It's not always so fine, is it?

STEPHEN: But I ask you to admire that, too! [*To* PAT] If one could but once see his life whole, present and past together in one living instant, he would not wish to leave it before his time—oh no!

PAT: I know my time.

STEPHEN: I thought I knew mine once. My mind was quite made up, that night. Nothing was to deter me.—But the light from the Ile de Port-Cros described its arc as it does now. [*He stands erect.*] It stopped me, held me.—How long I stood here, I don't know. But when I was aware again—

ANN: Father—

TOM: —What had happened to you? [HOPE *goes to him and tries to draw him away from the wall, murmuring "Tom—Tom!" but he does not answer and will not come.*] Say what had happened!

[*The terrace, in a brief space, has become flooded with moonlight. There is a silence. Then* STEPHEN *begins to speak again, this time more softly, gently, coaxingly:*]

STEPHEN: I had walked back in time. It is a very interesting excursion. You merely lift your foot, place it so, and there you are—or are you? One thinks one is going forward and one finds instead the remembered touch of water somewhere—the odor of geranium—sight of a blowing curtain—the faint sound of snow—the taste of apples. One finds the pattern of his life, traced with the dreadful clarity of dream. Then he knows that all that comes in remains—nothing is lost—all is important.

ANN [*A small voice*]: Father—

STEPHEN: Are you afraid?

[*A moment. Then*]

ANN: No.

HOPE [*In a whisper*]: But I am, I am! Tom—Tom, listen—

[TOM *does not stir.* HOPE *leaves him.*]

STEPHEN: Here is the moon at last, you see?—Here is our day's reflection, hung in space. [*He hums another measure and again laughs softly.*] Space is an endless sea, and time the waves that swell within it, advancing and retreating. Now and again the waves are still and one may venture any way one wishes. [*A moment*] They seem to be still now—quite still. So which way would you go—where would you travel?

[*A silence. Then* TOM *moves into the angle of the wall.*]

TOM: To what I was—

[*Another silence.* LILY *moves toward* STEPHEN.]

LILY: To him I love—

NORMAN [*After a moment*]: Wherever I should go—

[*He turns and goes into the house again.*]

HOPE: Nowhere. I'm happy as I am—or would be, if Tom were—

[*A silence. Then*]

PAT [*A murmur*]: To Mary—Mary—

ANN [*A cry*]: No, no!— To the Westbury Road!

[PAT *hums softly.*]

PAT: —Rat-a-plan-plan-plan-plan.

STEPHEN [*To* LILY]: Listen: there is a turning. All things are turned to a roundness. Wherever there is an end, from it springs the beginning.

PAT [*Barely audible*]: —Ta-plan-plan-plan-plan.

[LILY *moves to the garden steps and out, following the movement of* STEPHEN'*s hand.* TOM *turns and gazes at* HOPE *with a curious expression.*]

HOPE: What's the matter with you?

STEPHEN: Pat—Ann—it was not so long ago. Was it so long ago?

[ANN *shakes her head hopelessly, and moves toward the garden, mounts the steps and goes out. Slowly* PAT *crosses the terrace in the opposite direction, and enters the house.*]

HOPE [*To* TOM]: What are you staring at?

[TOM *smiles, but does not reply.* STEPHEN *turns to* TOM *and* HOPE.]

STEPHEN: And for us—shall we see my white phlox, first?

HOPE: Oh, Mr. Field—you mustn't let them go on like this! It's so frightening. [*She turns and sees* TOM *still staring at her.*] Tom's looking at me in the queerest way.—It's as if he didn't know me.

STEPHEN: Possibly you have changed.

HOPE: I—?

STEPHEN: —In his eyes. Perhaps you have one child too many.

HOPE: I don't know what you mean.

STEPHEN: It may be that he sees you not as a mother, but as a woman that he loves. I should not discourage that.

[TOM *goes to* HOPE *and gently turns her about, facing him. He looks at her with a curious smile.*]

HOPE: Tom, what's the matter with you, anyhow? [*His answer is to take her in his arms and kiss her. She frees herself.*] Honestly, I don't know what you're thinking of! What on earth has—[*He takes her face in his hands and kisses her again. She averts her head.*] I can't imagine what's come over you. I want to talk to Mr. Field. [*To* STEPHEN] It seems to me that you're all—[TOM *comes to her again, takes both her hands in his and smiles into her eyes.*] I'm not fooling. I really mean it.

PAT [*From the house*]: Mary? *Mary!*

HOPE [*To* STEPHEN]: Who's he calling?—I tell you it isn't good for people to let themselves go that way—[TOM *draws her into his arms, and holds her there.*] It's a form of self-indulgence.—Stop, Tom! It's a—[*Again* TOM *kisses her.*] Tom, will you let me *go!*

[*He opens his arms suddenly and she is freed, almost falling. She recovers herself and turns once more, with dignity, to* STEPHEN.]

PAT [*From the house*]: Mary! Where are you?

HOPE: The things that are happening here to-night aren't natural, and what's not natural must be wrong.

STEPHEN: To me they are more natural than nature.

HOPE: Of course I don't pretend to follow *your* extraordinary—[*From behind her,* TOM *is taking the hair pins from her hair. She stamps her foot in exasperation.*] Honestly! This is *too* much! [*To* STEPHEN] I hope you realize that goings on of this sort are not at all usual with us.

STEPHEN: I think that is a pity.

[*Tenderly, lovingly,* TOM *kisses the back of her neck.*]

HOPE: Tom—don't be an utter fool! [*To* STEPHEN]—To me, life is a very simple thing—

STEPHEN: Is it?

HOPE: One has one's home, one's children and one's husband—

STEPHEN: Or has one home and children only?

[HOPE *looks at him, startled.* TOM *returns to the wall.*]

HOPE: You mean you think that to me, Tom's just another—?

STEPHEN: What do *you* think?

[HOPE *turns to* TOM.]

HOPE: Tom, darling—*surely* you must know that I—

[LILY*'s voice is heard from the garden, calling as a little girl would.*]

LILY: Good-bye, Pa! Good-bye!—Come right home after, won't you, Pa?

HOPE [*To* STEPHEN]: You see? That's Lily. Oh I know she'll hurt herself! [*To* TOM.] Now you stay right here, won't you? Please, Tom—like a good boy. [*She hurries off to the garden, calling:*] Lily! Wait, dear!

[*A moment, then* TOM *speaks from the depths of his wretchedness:*]

TOM: Oh, Father Francis—can't a fellow do anything without it's being sinful?

[STEPHEN *goes to a chair and seats himself.*]

STEPHEN: What have you to tell me?

TOM: —So much. I know it's after hours. I know you're tired, but—

STEPHEN: Come—

[TOM *comes, head down, hands clasped. He kneels beside* STEPHEN*'s chair and makes the Sign of the Cross.*]

TOM: —Bless me, Father, for I have sinned. It is about three months ago since my last confession. Since then, I accuse myself of the following sins: Father, I've cursed and sworn and taken the name of the Lord in vain. I've neglected my morning prayers and missed Mass once, and been distracted during Mass seven times—

STEPHEN: Yes—but what is really wrong?

TOM: I've been drunk, and had immodest thoughts, and eaten meat on an Ember Day, and committed acts of impurity four times—

STEPHEN: But what is really wrong?

[TOM *chokes.*]

TOM: Oh, Father Francis—I don't believe any more! Nothing's got any meaning for me. I look around me, and nothing means anything at all—and I want it to! It must—it's got to—or I'll, or I'll—

STEPHEN: Your childhood faith is gone—

TOM: It wasn't true.

STEPHEN: Are you so sure?

TOM: Yes, and it meant so much to me. I even thought I ought to be a priest, but I lost my faith.

STEPHEN: Perhaps in order that you need not be one.

TOM: I know I've got no soul—nobody has.

STEPHEN: Look closer.

TOM: I have. It isn't there. There isn't any. There never was.

STEPHEN: At some time there is a soul born to every body—and like it, subject to many ills. But the soul's life is the only life there is, so the world is peopled with the living and with the dead. We know the living. Sometimes the dead deceive us.

TOM: You mean that maybe mine is—?

STEPHEN: No. The dead do not deceive me.—I mean that birth is painful. The infant suffers too.

TOM: It's awful—I can't stand it. Let me be damned!

STEPHEN: No.

TOM: But now I'm nothing—let me be *something!*

STEPHEN: Now you begin to be.

TOM: I keep wanting to do great things—too great for what I am—

STEPHEN: There are many men who would go to the ends of the earth for God—

TOM: I would! I keep starting to—

STEPHEN: —And cannot get through their own gardens.

TOM: Oh, don't! I'm such a weak soul—

STEPHEN: —Such a human being.

TOM: Something always stops me, always—

STEPHEN: Your own humanity.—But there are strong souls who never leave their gardens. Their strength is not in the doing, but in the wish to do. There is no strength anywhere, but in the wish. Once realized, it has spent itself, and must be born again.

TOM: But I don't know what I'm here at all for—

STEPHEN: To suffer and to rejoice. To gain, to lose. To love, and to be rejected. To be young and middle-aged and old. To know life as it happens, and then to say, "this is it."

TOM: Yes—but who *am* I? And what shall *I* be when it's over?

STEPHEN: You are the sum of all your possibilities, all your desires—each faint impression, each small experience—

TOM: —But when it's *over?!*

STEPHEN: You will be what your spirit wants and takes of them. Life is a wish. Wishing is never over.

[*A brief silence.* TOM *rises to his feet.*]

TOM: —Then everything about me *has* a meaning!—Everything I see and feel and think and do—dream, even!

[STEPHEN *closes his hand over* TOM'*s.*]

STEPHEN: Great heaven, yes!

TOM: I've got a feeling that I'm dreaming now.

STEPHEN: It may be.

PAT [*From the house*]: Mary!

TOM: —But Father Francis—are you ill?

STEPHEN: Why?

TOM: You look awfully white—and your hand—it was as cold as ice. I'm afraid I've been a strain for you. Good Lord, Father—you do look white. Here—take this—[*He goes to the table and pours a glass of brandy.* STEPHEN *goes to the fanback chair in the shadow in the corner of the terrace.* TOM *turns with the glass.*] This will fix you. This—why, where are you, Father? [*He looks about him.*] Confound it, where's he gone to? He looked sick—[*He calls:*] Father Francis! [STEPHEN *does not answer.* TOM *moves toward the house, with the brandy. As he reaches the steps,* NORMAN *darts out with a small, white fur rug in his hands.*]

NORMAN: One minute, Mister!

TOM: What do you want? Have you seen Father Francis?

NORMAN [*In a moderate Jewish accent*]: How'd you like to buy a nice fur neckpiece?

TOM: Don't be a fool.

NORMAN: —Make a present to your lady-friend, eh? You can have it cheap—

TOM: No, thanks. Let me by—I'm in a hurry.

NORMAN: All right—I resign—I quit!—I'll get a job as runner in a bank. In five years I'll be rich—I'll be the biggest man in Wall Street! [*Again he offers the rug.*] Look—five dollars—it's worth fifty—

[TOM *tries to pass him.*]

TOM: Oh, for God's sake, Norman—Father Francis is ill—

NORMAN: I'll have money, power—that's what makes you happy—that's the life! [*Again, the rug*] Look: It's a bargain. Buy it. An inside tip: the National City's taken half the issue at 91, and Pritchard, Ames is bidding for another hundred thousand at—

TOM [*Suddenly*]: I know—the bastide!

NORMAN: Don't you call me that, you leper!

[TOM *pulls away from him.*]

TOM: Get away, I'm not fooling. Let me by!

[*He crosses the terrace quickly, and goes up the garden steps and out.*]

NORMAN: But what a bargain! [*He shrugs.*] *I* should care. [*Then he turns and speaks to the empty chair in front of him:*] Look, here, Mr. Sterner—I resign—I'm through!

STEPHEN [*From the corner of the terrace, hidden in his chair*]: When I've given you such a fine opportunity, when I have even—?

NORMAN: Oh, I'll pay you back!—But I'm quitting, see? I've got better things to do than this. I'll educate myself. I'll—

STEPHEN: So ambitious, eh? Ah, you're all alike, you young people.—And next you marry a Gentile girl I suppose, and have her despise you—ruin you.

NORMAN: Oh no!—Say, am I such a fool as that? Marry a *shiksa*—me? Whose uncle is a rabbi—? I guess not! But what I'll do is get an honest job—yes! "White fox"—this cat fur! I'm sick of it—I'm through. I'll get up in the world. You watch me! Have educated people for my friends—

STEPHEN: May you be happy with them.

NORMAN: —Happy and strong and rich and honest! Watch me! [*He offers the despised rug to another unseen client, is refused, and shrugs again.*] No?—*I* should care!

[*And re-enters the house, whistling. For a moment* STEPHEN *is alone upon the terrace.* PAT*'s voice is heard from the house, in growing alarm:*]

PAT: —Aren't you here?—It's me—it's Pat, Mary!

[STEPHEN *passes his hand over his brow.*]

STEPHEN: My head—my head. [*A moment. Then*]—But this is very strange. What is this mist that closes in around me? This is a winter mist, and it is summer. Wait a bit, you, I am not ready yet!

[*The distant music changes to "L'Enfant et les Sortilèges" from Ravel's ballet "Five O'clock."* LILY, *her hair flying about her shoulders, runs down the steps from the garden. She is crossing in the direction of the house, when the music stops her. She listens intently for a moment, then with a swift motion slips the belt from her dress and drops it upon a chair. Her appearance has changed to that of a girl of thirteen. She begins to rise up and down upon her toes, in a formal movement of ballet practice. Her breath becomes a little short. Frowning, she bends and feels her instep.* STEPHEN *rises from his chair, and turns to her. She exclaims in joy:*]

LILY: Pa! Oh Pa, you *did* come right home!

[*She runs and kisses him. He strokes her head.*]

STEPHEN: Well, well, well—and how has my little sprite endured her prison?

[*He speaks in the eloquent voice of an old-fashioned actor.*]

LILY: —Prison? Oh, I've been all right. I like it here. I think it's a nice hotel—nicer than the one in Harrisburg was, much nicer, warmer.—Pa, were you good tonight?

STEPHEN: I was splendid.

[*He seats himself in another chair, facing her.*]

LILY: How many curtain calls were there?

STEPHEN: Alas, none. But I was magnificent.

LILY: I wish I'd gone. I wish you'd of let me. Could I maybe come tomorrow aft?

STEPHEN: Say "afternoon," child. Do not clip your words.

LILY: "Afternoon."—But could I?

STEPHEN: We shall see. [*With a gesture*] Fix me my drink—[LILY *goes to the table and makes a brandy-and-soda.*]—And one for yourself.

LILY: I—I don't want any.

STEPHEN: And one for yourself, I said!—'Twill do you good.

LILY: Just a little one, then—it makes me feel so funny.

[STEPHEN'*s manner begins to change.*]

STEPHEN: I like you funny.

LILY: Can I put sugar in it?

STEPHEN: Put anything you like in it. Put salt in it.

LILY: Oh—I wouldn't like that!

[*She brings him the glass, and a small one for herself. He seizes her glass and tastes it.*]

STEPHEN: Water!

LILY [*In fright*]: But Pa, I—

STEPHEN: —Your mother's daughter, eh? Lying, deceiving—

LILY: I'm not! I just didn't want—

STEPHEN [*The actor*]: Whose child are you, eh? Are you my child, at all?

LILY: Oh yes, yes! Pa—I *am* your child! Truly I am!

STEPHEN: Then obey me—without question, without equivocation. [*He drains his glass and gives it to her.*] Fill them both.

LILY: All right. I'll put some in—I'll put a lot in.

[*Again she goes to the table with the glasses, refills them and returns to him.*]

STEPHEN: Let me taste—[*He tastes her glass, and gives it back to her.*] That's better. You are your old man's daughter. Give me a kiss—

[*She kisses his cheek. He takes a swallow from his glass and she does likewise.*]

LILY: —But you aren't an old man! You aren't old at all. And look, Pa: I don't ever lie to you. I love you too much to. I just can't tell you how much I—[*She strikes a posture, and declaims:*] "Then poor Cordelia!—And yet, not so; since, I am sure, my love's more richer than my tongue . . . good, my Lord, you have begot me, bred me, loved me: I return those duties back as are right fit—obey you, love you, and most honor you."

STEPHEN: "Pray, do not mock me: I am a very foolish, fond old man. Fourscore and upward, and, to deal plainly, I fear I am not in my perfect mind. . . . Do not laugh at me: for, as I am a man, I think this lady to be my child, Cordelia."

LILY: "And so I am, I am!"

STEPHEN: —Not bad, not half bad. You get the feeling well enough, but you lack voice. You need filling out everywhere. You're thin all over. I don't like you thin.—What did you do while I was playing?

LILY: Well, you know how it snowed—

STEPHEN: Yes?

[*She is sipping from her glass.*]

LILY: Well, I got a whole shoe box full off the window sill and I was making a little girl out of it, only as fast as I made her she melted.

STEPHEN: What else?

LILY: Well, I did my toe exercises.

STEPHEN: For how long?

LILY: A whole hour.—Well, almost a whole hour.

STEPHEN: You're lying to me.

LILY: Oh no, Pa!

STEPHEN: Don't you ever lie to me.

LILY: Oh, no.

STEPHEN: If you do, I'll treat you the way I did your mother.

LILY: Pa! You wouldn't ever leave me!

STEPHEN: Just let me catch you lying once.

LILY: But I never, never!

STEPHEN: See that you don't.

LILY: I don't know what I'd do if ever you should leave me—

STEPHEN: —Pick up with some cheap tout, most likely, and go off with him.

[LILY *turns her innocent eyes upon him.*]

LILY: What?

STEPHEN: Never mind. [*She passes her hand vaguely over her eyes.*]—What ails you?

LILY: It's—beginning to feel, in my head.

STEPHEN: Drink it down.

LILY: I can't. My throat won't turn over any more. And—and things are going round—

STEPHEN: Then start the music and go around with them.

[*She giggles.*]

LILY: Oh, that's funny! That's so funny. You're such a funny man.

STEPHEN: Stop laughing.

LILY: I—I can't stop.

STEPHEN: Go start the music—[*Struggling hard to control her hysterics,* LILY *starts the gramophone. Again, it is the "Naïla" of Delibes. He follows the introductory bars with his hand, as if conducting an orchestra.*] Now then—

[*With difficulty, she empties her glass, and begins to dance, haltingly.*]

LILY [*An appeal*]: Oh, Pa—

STEPHEN: What?

LILY: I don't want to.

STEPHEN: Why not?

LILY: My foot hurts. I hurt my foot practicing.

STEPHEN: If you'd done it right, you wouldn't have hurt it. Go on and dance.

LILY: I can't, truly I can't.

STEPHEN: Is a man to have no amusement when he comes home of nights after playing his heart out to silly fools who don't know art from turnips? Come on—get going.

LILY [*Almost in tears*]: Pa—this isn't like you. This isn't my you at all. My you tells me stories about queens and palaces and you hold me on your knee and rock me off to sleep and you tuck me in at night and say God love you, little daughter. That's what *you* do.

STEPHEN: Oh I do, do I? And how often? In my tender moments twice a year.—Not like me, is it? I'll show you what's like me. Will you dance?

LILY: Oh yes, yes. See? I'm dancing—

[*Again she begins to dance, this time more haltingly. He stands over her.*]

STEPHEN: Faster!—Wasn't Burbage amused when he came home? Wasn't Barrett and wasn't Booth? Is it too much to ask, eh?

LILY: Oh no, Pa! See me, Pa?

STEPHEN: That's better.

[*She goes on, as well as she is able. At length*]

LILY [*Panting*]: —My hurt foot—it won't go up any more—

STEPHEN: No? Try it.

[HOPE *appears at the top of the garden steps, where she stands unseen by them, watching them in horror.*]

LILY: But I *am* trying!—Is it all right if I just—? [*Again she tries to rise upon her toes, and cannot. She attempts a pitiful* pas seul, *fails in it, falls to the floor. Then, all at once she turns into a raging fury and screams:*] God damn! Hell!

[*He laughs.*]

STEPHEN: Good!

LILY: Oh, I hate you. I hate you. I don't *love* you anymore!

STEPHEN: Splendid! Go on—more!

[*She rises to her feet and confronts him, trembling with rage.*]

LILY: You're a dirty drunk! You left my mother when she was sick. You can't act. You're just a super, that's all you are. You can't act any!

[*Laughing, he holds his arms out to her.*]

STEPHEN: Come here. Give us a kiss.

LILY: No. You smell of whisky and nasty grease paint. You're dirty—I hate you! I won't stay with you any longer—I'll run away, that's what I'll do!

PAT [*From the house*]: Mary! I've come back. Where are you?

[STEPHEN*'s voice changes back to his own voice. Suddenly he seems very tired.*]

STEPHEN: —Then go quickly. Go very quickly. See—there is the door. It is open. Go in, and up the stairs, and to your room.

[*She gazes at him for a moment, then turns and walks directly to the steps and into the house. Again* STEPHEN *sinks into a chair, his hand over his eyes. There is a slight pause, then* HOPE *comes down from the garden.*]

HOPE: Oh, that was terrible! Why did you do it?

STEPHEN: I—? I did nothing. Tell me what happened—

HOPE: You know perfectly well what happened!—And she adored him. She—[*She turns and follows* LILY *into the house, calling:*] Lily!

[STEPHEN *is alone. He rises from his chair with effort, and moves toward the garden steps. He stiffens suddenly, then exclaims in wonder:*]

STEPHEN: What's this? [*Another moment. Then, more sharply*] Come now! What is it?! [*He slumps against the wall, and plucks at his left arm, which has gone limp, then tries to raise his right hand to his head and cannot.*]—Cerebral hemorrhage, is that it? That's very interesting, I'm sure. The left side is quite numb—the lesion must be in the right lobe, in the Area of—God, when we crack we crack, don't we? [*A moment. Then summoning his remaining strength*— But I am not ready, yet! [*He makes his way to the fanback chair in the corner of the terrace and slowly lets himself into it. He calls:*] Pat! Ann! [*Another moment*] There—there's the pulse—it is quite hard, quite stringy—[*Again he calls:*] Ann!—But the breathing is regular, Doctor—difficult, but regular.—I say, not yet! I'll go, but in my proper time.—Curious there is no pain—only a sense of—[*He catches his breath*]—No pain, did I say? [*and collects his strength for a final cry*] Ann!

[*And sinks lower into his chair. From the distance piano-music begins to be heard again. It is a popular waltz of ten years ago. A moment, then* ANN *comes down the steps from the garden. She is limping. As she crosses the terrace she murmurs to herself:*]

ANN: Poor dear—poor darling—what can I do for him? [*As she reaches the sofa her ankle gives way under her and she sinks down upon the floor, exclaiming:*] Ouch—*ouch*—oh, where *is* that road?

[PAT *comes in from the house, calling softly:*]

PAT: Mary! Where are you, Mary?

ANN: Ouch—ouch—

[PAT *hesitates a moment, then comes up to her.*]

PAT: Excuse me. Is there anything the—?

[ANN *starts in alarm.*]

ANN: —Oh!

PAT: I'm all right. I'm harmless.—But I was just wandering around here and I saw you from across the field and I thought something might be the matter, and—

ANN: —There is. Plenty.

PAT: What? Can I help?

ANN: Well, for one thing, I've probably broken my ankle. And for another, I'm lost. And for another—no, I'm not sure you can.

PAT: Does your ankle hurt?

ANN: Oh no, it feels wonderful. They do, you know.—Ouch!

PAT: Maybe if I could get a car up into this field for you—

ANN: Have you got one that climbs fences?

PAT: What are you lost from?

ANN: The Westbury Road.

[*A breeze brings the music closer.*]

PAT: That's easy.

ANN: It hasn't been.

PAT: You're practically on it. It's just over there—

ANN: No!

PAT: Honest.

ANN: Then what's that music I've been hearing? Isn't it the Club?

PAT: No. It's from a party I'm at.

ANN: At?

PAT: Well, one I got away from.

ANN: Whose?

PAT: Mine. At my house.

ANN: I'm impressed. Why wasn't *I* asked?

PAT: You would have been.—Where do you live?

ANN: I'm staying down here with some people named Ames. But I got the wanders and had to walk.

PAT: So did I.—Tom and Hope Ames?

ANN: That's right.

PAT: They said they couldn't come.

ANN: Maybe they don't like parties. Or maybe they didn't want people to see me. In the Spring I get freckled.—Oh, this *damned* ankle!

PAT: Quit talking about your ankle. What's your name?

ANN: Ann Field. What's yours?

PAT: Don't laugh—

ANN: No.

PAT: Patrick—[*She laughs.*] You said you wouldn't.

ANN: But I've always wanted to know one!—What was it you said to Mike?

PAT: That's not very new, you know.—My last name's Farley.

ANN: —Not one of the great, enormous, important, rich ones!

PAT: Well—

ANN: —Please, forget everything I've said. You're beautiful. You'll get me home all right.

PAT: I'm—er—I came down for the spring holidays, and I thought I'd swing a little party, and—

ANN: Why, bless his heart, he's embarrassed! Lovely!

PAT: Oh, go to hell.

ANN: You're sweet. I think you're really sweet.

[PAT *seats himself beside her.*]

PAT: Foolish to stay indoors a night like this. Foolish to sleep even.—You've got awfully pretty hands.

ANN: Thanks. My eyes are nice, too. They don't cross, or anything.

PAT: Say—you come right back at a fellow, don't you?

ANN: Do I?

PAT: —Ever read a poem called "Pale hands I loved beside the Shal-i-mar"?

ANN [*Suspiciously*]: What about it?

PAT: I just wondered. Didn't you like it?

ANN: I thought it was awful.

PAT: Why?

ANN: I don't know. I just did.

PAT: You're a funny girl. Maybe you don't like poetry.

ANN: —Maybe I do! [*He laughs.*] I like the way you laugh.

PAT: I'll hire me a couple of expert ticklers.

[*And then they both laugh.*]

ANN: You have awfully white teeth, haven't you?

[*Suddenly* PAT *frowns.*]

PAT: —What?

ANN: I said, you have—

PAT [*Slowly*]: I know—I'm trying to think: there was someone with white teeth that gleamed from the water—oh, never mind. [*Another moment. Then*]—Funny, our meeting like this. I suppose that's the way good things happen.

ANN: Maybe—I wish you'd brought a crutch, though, or a wheelchair.

[*He eyes her reflectively.*]

PAT: How much do you weigh?

ANN: Something fairly serious—or I did. Tonight I've walked a good deal of it off.

PAT: We've got to do something about moving you.

ANN: I hoped you'd get around to that.

PAT: That is, eventually. There's lots of time.—Say, are you moody?

ANN: Maybe.—Am I?

PAT: Because I am. That's why I got to walking tonight. I had something on my mind.

ANN: So had I.

PAT: Really? What?

ANN: My father.

PAT: Is he—is he sick?

ANN: I don't know.—What is it that worried you?

PAT [*A moment*]: —Well, you see, at Christmas I came down with the Copes—

ANN: Are they like the measles?

[PAT *laughs, and explains:*]

PAT: —Down *here,* with Johnny and Nora Cope. Well, one night we were coming home quite late from somewheres and we stopped in at the dog wagon in the village to get—[*He stops suddenly and stares at her.*] Jee-rusalem! I believe you're her!

ANN: "She," you should say.—Who?

PAT [*Overcome with awe*]: Good Lord Almighty—

ANN: I wonder if it's the same dog wagon I know.

PAT: Of course!—But this is—Gosh! Do you know what this means to me?

ANN: I'm trying awfully hard to follow, but—

PAT [*Still staring*]: I had a Western, with a lot of onions, and we got up to go and there was a girl there sitting at the counter with a couple of other people and a great big glass of milk and she looked up as I went by, and—

[ANN *smiles.*]

ANN: I did, didn't I?

PAT [*Excitedly*]: Yes!—and the milk had made a little white rim along your upper lip and—

ANN [*Distressed*]: Oh dear—

PAT: It was beautiful.—And ever since, I've seen your face the whole time, in my mind, and I could never find you. It's been terrible.—And now—Oh Lord!—Imagine!

[ANN *smiles.*]

ANN: Well—here I am.

PAT: It's just miraculous, that's all, it's miraculous. Gosh, I don't know what to say. You know this isn't like the usual—there's something terribly right about it.—Ever since that night I've been longing to—Jeez, I thought I'd go crazy if I couldn't find you—been longing to take your face in my hands like this, and—

[*He takes her face between his hands.*]

ANN: Wait. Let me look at you.

[*She looks.*]

PAT: I'm not much on looks—

ANN: Shhh! [*She looks a longer time.*] Why—it's the queerest thing. I think I—

PAT: —And to kiss that lovely mouth that had the white rim along the top of it—

ANN: But somehow—I don't think you'd better—yet—

PAT: No, I suppose not.—But I don't see why! [*A moment. Still they gaze at each other. Then*] Look: do you ever get a feeling that you—oh, Lord—that you know all about it?

ANN: Sometimes.

PAT: I do now! I've never felt alive before! Everything's as clear as—[*Suddenly, directly*] Look: I'll be at the Ameses for lunch tomorrow. Tell 'em I like steak.

[ANN *laughs.*]

ANN: I like *you!*

PAT: —As much as I like steak?

ANN: How much do you like steak?

PAT: I'm crazy for it. I dream about it. Well—?

[*Again* ANN *laughs, and rises.*]

ANN: Come on.

[*He catches her hand in his.*]

PAT: Ah, Ann—tell me, Ann!

ANN: No, no! This is ridiculous. It's—

[*She frees herself.*]

PAT: Oh, please! Tell me—do you like me?

[*A moment. Then*]

ANN: Yes.

PAT: Much?

ANN: A lot. Terribly!

[*For* PAT *this is almost too much to bear.*]

PAT: Gosh, I'm glad.

ANN: I hope I'll be.—Come on—shall we?

PAT: Look: You've got to come up to the Spring Dance with me, and the ball games, and the boat races—I row Number Seven—and—oh, Ann—

ANN: What, Pat?

PAT: It's wonderful.

ANN: It is, it is.—Do come—come on—[*They go on another step or two, toward the garden steps, where again her ankle gives way. He catches her in his arms. She recovers herself and, still in his arms, turns and looks at him. For a long moment their eyes hold them to-*

gether. At length they kiss. For an instant ANN *clings to him, then leaves him.*] Pat—Pat—we're crazy.

PAT: No!

ANN [*Breathlessly*]: Come on—We must—

[*She takes his hand. He turns.*]

PAT: First, let's look back at our meadow.

[ANN *frowns, half puzzled, half in alarm. Then*]

ANN [*Suddenly, sharply*]: No! That's wrong!

[*He had not said that. The spell is breaking.*]

PAT: What is? [*He takes a deep breath.*]—Um! Doesn't it smell good, though! What is it? Hawthorn?

ANN: No!

PAT [*Slowly, from very far away*]: But I—I guess they're right. I guess there's nothing like May in England—[*Suddenly he stops, releasing her hand. His face becomes troubled. He looks at the house, frowning.*] What's that house?

ANN [*A sudden cry*]: Don't think, Pat! Don't think at all! Come with me—

PAT: —But there's something I've got to do in this house.

ANN: No!

PAT: Yes. And I can't think what. And it's terribly important. I've waited too long. It's got to be done at once. It's getting late.—I know!—I've got to pack a bag. It's late. I've got to get that bag packed. I've got to pack a bag and catch a boat and go to England.

[ANN *is still at the garden steps. His eyes have not left the house.*]

ANN: Stay with me, Pat! I'll lose you there!

PAT: I tell you she's waiting, and it's getting late.

[*Again he moves toward the house.*]

ANN: Oh, why must I always lose you?

[*She goes up the garden steps and out.* PAT *advances further toward the house, but* STEPHEN *rises*—]

STEPHEN: Pat!

[PAT *halts, turns slowly, looks at him, then goes to him.*]

PAT: Why—why how do you do, Mr. Carr! I feel as if I'd been away for—I came across the fields and down the lane—the hawthorn's early, isn't it? I didn't wire. I thought I'd surprise her. How has she been?

STEPHEN: You cannot surprise her.

PAT: You mean she had a hunch that I was—? But where is she, then? I've been calling her all over everywhere. [STEPHEN *does not reply.*

Suddenly PAT *becomes alarmed.*] Say, what is this—a joke? Because if it is—yes, and what about my letters? Why didn't she answer them? Did you and Father fix it so she wouldn't get them? I've been almost crazy. I've been—where is she? She's here—I know she's here—[*He calls:*] Ann! [*Then feeling something wrong, whispers:*]—Mary. [*Then, more confidently*] It's Pat, Mary! [*He turns again to* STEPHEN.]—And you needn't think we're going to stay on with people who fixed it up to separate us, either. Not for one minute. I'm going to take her with me this very night, and—

STEPHEN: That is too soon.

PAT: It's not. Haven't we waited years already? We'll be wanting to get married right away. Tomorrow, most likely—or the next day—

STEPHEN: —Too soon.

PAT: Look here, Mr. Carr—[*Then correcting himself:*] Mr. Field.—I know you're a sick man. But Ann's got her whole life ahead of her. You can't take it from her. You've taken too much of it already. I don't hold with those old ideas. Ann and I are in love, and if you don't grant that that's the most important thing, it's time you did. I'm sorry to have to put it this way, but I've got to speak as I feel. I'll certainly never expect a child of mine to—to—

STEPHEN: —To what?

PAT: —To give her whole life up to me, and I don't think you should.

STEPHEN: I see.

PAT: You let her bring you here, away from all the—

STEPHEN: —She has needed me as much these last three years as I have needed her.

PAT: That may be. But—

STEPHEN: Wait! [*He looks at* PAT *intently, then speaks with a slow emphasis:*]—But now she does not need me any longer.

PAT: What are you looking like that for? What do you mean? [*Then suddenly, wildly*] She's not! That's not true—you're lying. It's not possible—it can't be! She's here—I know she's here! [*Again he calls:*] Ann! Ann!

STEPHEN: She does not come.

PAT: Ann, dear! It's Pat, Ann!

STEPHEN: And still she does not come.

PAT: Oh, don't keep saying that! She's here—I can feel her all about me. [*He wheels about and looks around him.*] What kind of a deal is this, anyway? What am I doing—dreaming? [*Then one last despairing cry:*] Ann! [*And a long silence. Finally*]—Because she thought I wasn't coming back—[*Another moment. Then, in anguish*]—I can't believe—but how? *How* did she? She couldn't have hurt that sweet place at her temple, that lovely breast. What has death to do with her?

STEPHEN: —With anyone.

PAT: But I did come back! I wasn't the swine she thought me. I did come—she must know that. I'm sure she knows it!

STEPHEN: So then, you have your picture back—

PAT: My picture?

STEPHEN: The one you love so—your picture of yourself. Now your pet illusion is whole again, and all is well, eh?

PAT: I don't know what you're—

STEPHEN: You built your whole life upon an illusion—and it went—and still you want it back—from death, even!

PAT: I don't know what you're talking about.

STEPHEN: Your idea of your own perfection.

PAT: That's not true—

STEPHEN: No?—You came back, yes—but in your own time. A swine? Indeed you are!—But what brought you? How much of it was the self-contempt you felt for having left her?

PAT: None of it.

STEPHEN: —And how much your love of her, your want of her?

PAT: All!

STEPHEN: Which is it you can't live with, now? Which is it that spoils your picture?

PAT: Oh, be still about my picture! You're talking about a spoiled boy, stuffed with what he thought were fine ideals. Fakes, all of them! I've left that boy behind. I've got no picture anymore. I know I'm what I am—myself!

STEPHEN: Then can you face yourself—say good-bye to your last illusion and come through alive?

PAT: Go—will you?

STEPHEN: If you cannot—what else is there for you?

[*A moment. Then*]

PAT [*To himself*]: —Off to Africa.

STEPHEN: Well—?

[PAT *moves toward the garden steps.*]

PAT: Off to—! [*But half-way up the steps, he stops. When he speaks, it is with a fine, saving scorn:*]—One big last shining gesture, eh? Watching myself go by. Another pretty picture: "He died for love." [*He raises his head.*] No!—That's for the weak ones. I stay.

STEPHEN [*A murmur*]: That's right, that's right.

[*He leaves him, and moves painfully toward his corner.*]

PAT: But I want her so. Ann—Ann––

[FELIX *comes in from house.*]

FELIX: Pardon, Monsieur—je regrette que j'avais laissé passer l'heure. Maintenant, il est onze heures moins douze. Je regrette beaucoup, Monsieur. C'est ma faute.

[PAT *does not reply.* FELIX *goes out. A moment, then* ANN'*s voice is heard softly, from the garden:*]

ANN: Pat?

PAT [*A cry of joy*]: *Ann!* [*In an instant he is up the garden steps and out.*] I'll find you this time. Ann!

[STEPHEN *gropes for his chair in the corner and seats himself.*]

STEPHEN: —All right, you. Very well—I am ready. This ends, and that begins.—Oh, so you'd like to end it, would you? All of it, eh? [*He half rises, gasping for breath.*] Well, you can't!—I tell you—you cannot! [*Gasping*] I tell you—!

[*There is a slight shuffling sound, as he slumps into death. A moment. Then* TOM *comes in from the garden with the brandy glass, as* FELIX *enters from the house and crosses the terrace toward him, with three traveling bags.*]

FELIX: Pardon, Monsieur—

[*He goes up the garden steps and out.* HOPE *comes in from the house. She is dressed to leave. She sees* TOM *and goes to him quickly.*]

HOPE: Tom, Tom—

TOM: —I beg your pardon, but have you by any chance seen an old priest called Father—[*Then he recognizes her.*] Why—why, hello, Hope—

HOPE: —Who, did you say?

TOM: Why—I don't know—[*He frowns at the brandy glass.*] I thought I—I had this for someone—who was it? I was taking it to him, to—Lord, *I* don't know—[*He looks at her closer.*]—How are the children?

[LILY *comes in from the house, also dressed for departure.*]

HOPE: —The children—that's good, that is!—Do you realize that that's just what you've been acting like?

TOM [*To himself*]: —Under the piano. Under the—

[ALICE *comes down the stairs from the balcony. She wears a coat and carries a small traveling bag.*]

ALICE: Listen: could anyone tell me what's got into the Rose man?

HOPE: Not Norman, too!

ALICE: —I opened my door into the hall, and there he was, stretched on the floor outside it, fast asleep on a fur rug. [*She looks back over her shoulder.*]—And now he's—

[NORMAN *appears upon the balcony, the fur rug still over his arm.*]

NORMAN [*Heartily*]: Well, everyone—how goes it?

TOM: What's that you've got?

NORMAN: How'd you like to—? [*He stops and frowns at the rug.*] Why, it's a—[*His accent leaves him.*] Damned if I know.

[*He drops it, and cleans his fastidious hands of it.*]

TOM: Was it a bargain?

[NORMAN *looks at him sharply.*]

NORMAN: —Am I right in believing that some pretty funny business went on here tonight?

[*All look troubled, eyeing one another furtively, trying to figure out how much the other remembers, how much one remembers oneself.*]

LILY [*Finally*]: Well, I don't know if you'd call it funny—but suddenly everything seems possible.—It's like beginning all over again.

[ALICE *stretches upon her cushion.*]

ALICE: I hope I didn't miss anything. I had a delicious nap.

LILY: —And did you dream?

ALICE: Dream?—I should say not. I was too dead. [*Another silence. All stare in front of them. Finally* ALICE *speaks again, this time as if from a distance:*] Did I tell you?—Once when I was in England staying with the Potters, they had a—[*Then suddenly, with an air of discovery*]—Why, Norman! That was where I met you, wasn't it?

NORMAN: Yes.

ALICE: —Strange.

[*Again silence. Then*]

TOM: At school the big idea used to be to sneak off in the afternoons and smoke real tobacco in real pipes.—Lord, how big that made us feel.

NORMAN [*After another moment*]: —I often wonder what happened to old Morris Sterner. He gave me my first real job.—Once he told me that—

[*But he relapses into silence, which* LILY *at length breaks.*]

LILY: It's fantastic, this terrace. It just hangs here. Some day it will float off into space, and anchor there, like an island in time.

HOPE: Don't!

ALICE: Don't what?

HOPE: Please, everyone make sense. It must be nearly time to leave.

TOM: Hope—[*She turns to him.*] Would you mind awfully if I don't sail with you?

HOPE: Why?

TOM: I want to go off somewhere by myself for a while. I think at last I've really got a line on something that may be the answer for me.

HOPE [*Unconvinced*]: Yes?

TOM: —In a way it's a kind of faith, in place of the old one—maybe it's the same. Anyhow, I want to work it out.

HOPE: Sweet Tom.

[PAT *and* ANN *are nearing the terrace from the garden.* PAT*'s voice is heard:*]

PAT: There's so much I'd have gone without—

[*They come in, her hand in his, and stand together upon the garden-steps.*]

TOM [*To* HOPE]: —I don't know how long it will take—but if I send for you—

[HOPE *smiles.*]

HOPE: Don't come—

TOM: Don't come.

[*Now everyone is talking in concert:*]

PAT: —Without so many good, quiet things—

TOM: I'm excited about this, Hope.

HOPE: So am I, Tom—if you do it.

PAT [*To* ANN]: I want to sit with the wife I love, and read books, and look at maps—

LILY: You won't believe me when I tell you—

ALICE: What?

LILY: Next year I'm going to play Cordelia in *King Lear*.

PAT: —And fish trout streams with my boys, and take my daughter walking—

HOPE: —What time is it, Norman? Oughtn't we be starting?

NORMAN: I'm not going to Paris.

[ALICE *glances at him in alarm.*]

HOPE: Really!—And who was it who simply had to be home by the tenth for a corporation meeting?

NORMAN: They can meet without me. They can whistle for me. I'll be in Andorra.

PAT [*To* ANN]: —And build a house and mend a fence, and be tired of a good day's work, and sleep—

[*Now they have come down the steps and joined the others.* ALICE *moves toward* NORMAN.]

ALICE: Norman—

NORMAN: What, Alice?

ALICE: I'll miss you.—Take me with you!

[NORMAN *starts forward.*]

NORMAN: You'd come!?

ALICE: Just ask me.

NORMAN: Alice—

ALICE: —Darling.

[*Then*]

NORMAN: *That's* the way to see Andorra!

[ALICE *and* NORMAN *keep on gazing at each other as if they could never look their fill.*]

TOM [*Suddenly*]: Now I know how it happened! [*To* ANN] Where's your father?

[LILY *rises quickly, and stares toward* STEPHEN*'s chair, which conceals him from their view.*]

ANN: He must have gone down to the bastide.—Why?

TOM: Hotel Universe!—*He'll* know.

ANN: What?

TOM: Don't you know the story?

ANN: Oh—you mean about Réné Mayer's house—

TOM: I mean about this house—

ANN: You must be mixed, Tom. This was built in nineteen-twelve by a man from Lyons.

[*A moment.* TOM *gazes at her. Then*]

TOM: Are you sure?

ANN: Oh, yes. Father leased it from him.

[LILY *starts back from* STEPHEN*'s chair with a sudden cry:*]

LILY: Pa!

HOPE: Don't, Lily—please don't again—

LILY: Pat—Pat!

[*He goes to her.*]

PAT: What is it, Lily?

LILY [*A moan*]: —I don't know, I don't know—

ANN: Lily—darling—

LILY: —I feel as if all that held me together had suddenly let go.

[*She begins to cry, softly.*]

ANN: Lily—darling—don't!

LILY: It's all right—I'll be all right—

[FELIX *re-enters from the garden and goes to* PAT.]

FELIX: Pardon, Monsieur—il est onze heure juste, Monsieur.

[HOPE *jumps up.*]

HOPE: Eleven! We've got to fly!

[*They all talk together:*]

ALICE: We'll probably be late at that.

NORMAN: Oh, no—not if we hurry.

TOM: You can make good time on these roads at night.

FELIX [*To* ANN]: Pardon, Mademoiselle, les valises sont dans les voitures.

ANN: —Your bags are all in.

TOM: Where's yours, Pat? Are you ready?

LILY: No! *You've* got to stay! Do you understand that?—You've got to stay!

PAT: Why yes, of course.—I'm not going.

[ANN *glances at him quickly.*]

ANN: Pat!

PAT: I'm staying, Ann.

TOM: Now there's a good idea!

HOPE: I had a hunch Pat was no mountain climber!

NORMAN: That's the stuff, Pat.

[HOPE *goes to* ANN *and kisses her.* ALICE *slips her arm through* NORMAN'*s.*]

HOPE: Good-bye, Ann.

ANN: Good-bye, dear.

TOM: Good-bye, Pat. Take it easy for a while.

PAT: Yes. Good-bye, Tom.

LILY: Hurry, *hurry!*

[TOM *kisses* ANN.]

TOM: Good-bye and thanks, Ann.—Say good-bye to your father for me.

HOPE: Yes.

NORMAN: Yes!

[TOM *frowns.*]

TOM: Say to him, that—

LILY: *Hurry, hurry!*

TOM: —Say good-bye to him.

NORMAN: Do you want to come with us, Tom?

[TOM *turns upon the garden steps.*]

TOM: To Andorra? Why, it sounds like a good idea.

HOPE: No, no! Alone! You've got to go alone!

TOM: But Hope—you know what a friendly soul I am. You know how I need company.

HOPE: [*To the others*]: What can you do with him?

[*They go out.* NORMAN *and* ALICE *mount the steps, calling over their shoulders:*]

NORMAN *and* ALICE: Good-bye! Thanks! Good-bye!

[PAT, ANN *and* LILY *are left.*]

LILY: You two—you're for each other, aren't you?

PAT: I hope so.

ANN: Then we are.

LILY [*to* ANN]: Your father—remember what he said? It does go on. [ANN *looks at her.*] Wherever we may be—breezes from the other fields still blow upon us—

ANN: Why, yes. Why do you—?

LILY: I think that's good to know. God love him. God love you. Good-bye—

[*She mounts the steps, pauses for one brief instant to glance down at* STEPHEN, *then goes out into the garden.* PAT *and* ANN *are left alone.* ANN *touches his cheek.*]

ANN: Dear love.

PAT: I want to make love to you for years. Oh, it's a life, Ann!

ANN: I know, dear—don't I know! [*She murmurs:*]—Thank you, Father.

PAT: Yes—thanks! [*In the distance, far off in the garden, a cock crows hoarsely.* PAT *starts.*] What's that? What time is it?

ANN: Hush, darling, never mind.—It's just an old white rooster—one of Father's pets—his clock he calls him.

PAT: It must be dawn somewhere.

ANN: But of course, dear—always!

PAT: Wherever there is an end, he said—

ANN: —From it the beginning springs.

[*She stares straight in front of her, her apprehension growing in her eyes. Slowly, fearfully, her head turns in the direction of* STEPHEN. *Silence. Then again the cock exults.*]

CURTAIN

THE ANIMAL KINGDOM

THE ANIMAL KINGDOM

was first produced by Gilbert Miller and Leslie Howard
at the Broadhurst Theatre, New York City,
on January 12, 1932.
It was directed by Mr. Miller;
the settings were designed by Aline Bernstein.

CAST

OWEN ARTHUR • G. Albert Smith
RUFUS COLLIER • Frederick Forrester
CECELIA HENRY • Lora Baxter
RICHARD REGAN • William Gargan
TOM COLLIER • Leslie Howard
FRANC SCHMIDT • Betty Lynne
JOE FISK • Harvey Stephens
DAISY SAGE • Frances Fuller
GRACE MACOMBER • Ilka Chase

■ ACTION AND SCENE ■

The action of the play takes place in the course of
about eighteen months, last year and this.
The scenes are as follows:

ACT I

Scene 1—At Tom Collier's, in Connecticut. An evening in April.
Scene 2—At Daisy Sage's, on Thirty-eighth Street.
Later the same evening.

ACT II

Scene 1—At Tom Collier's. An evening in January.
Scene 2—At Daisy Sage's. An afternoon in May.

ACT III

Scene 1—At Tom Collier's. A Sunday morning in October.
Scene 2—At Tom Collier's. Later the same evening.

■ ACT I ■

SCENE I

The library of TOM COLLIER*'s house in the country near New York. About seven o'clock on an April evening, two years ago.*

The library is a fair-sized, comfortable room in a small, partially converted farmhouse, situated in a countryside which is neither fashionable nor suburban. There is an entrance from the hall at Left and one into the dining room through another hall at Back Right. In the center wall at Back, there is a fine old fireplace, framed with pine panelling. The side walls are of white plaster, windows in the one at Right, with bookshelves around them. At Left, a small staircase leads to the upper floor. The furniture, of no particular period, is well chosen and, in the case of chairs and sofa, invitingly comfortable. It is a cheerful room, now filled with the late evening sun.

Upon the sofa, sits OWEN ARTHUR. *In an easy chair, turned away from him, is* RUFUS COLLIER. CECELIA HENRY *is seated in a straight chair beside a table at Right Center.* OWEN *is about thirty-five, well built, well dressed, agreeable-looking.* RUFUS *is in his early fifties, small, slight and gray. He wears silver-rimmed spectacles, which add to his picture of himself as the man of decision.* CECELIA *is twenty-eight, lovely of figure, lovely of face, beautifully cared for, beautifully presented.*

For some moments, all sit staring in front of them, saying nothing. Finally OWEN *clears his throat, waits a moment, and without turning, ventures:*

OWEN: There's quite a fine view from the hill behind the house. [*A silence*]—Or did I tell you that?

RUFUS: Yes.

OWEN: Sorry.

[*Another silence. Then* CECELIA *speaks:*]

CECELIA: You've really never been here before?

RUFUS: I?

CECELIA: Yes.

RUFUS: Never.

CECELIA: It seems a little strange.

RUFUS: I've never been asked before. [*He glances about him.*] What anyone wants with a place at the end of the world like this is beyond me anyhow.

OWEN: I make it in less than an hour, as a rule.

RUFUS: Oh, you come often, do you?

OWEN: Fairly. I find there's nothing like it after a stiff week in Court. I'm a new man since Friday.

RUFUS: You seem to be a fixture with him. I'm surprised he hasn't given you the go-by, as well.

OWEN: I'm too fond of him. I won't allow it.

RUFUS: But you're well-off, you work hard, you live like a gentleman—his natural enemy, I should say.

OWEN: We make few demands on each other. And he knows how I love this place.

RUFUS: But there's nothing *here!* No social life, no—

OWEN: Exactly.

CECELIA: His press is in the Village, isn't it?

RUFUS: Press? What press?

CECELIA: The Bantam Press. [*He stares.*] You know—for books.

RUFUS: Oh, so it's publishing now, is it?

CECELIA: I think it has been, for some time.

RUFUS [*To* OWEN]: How's it going, do you know?

OWEN: Very well. Last year he only lost something like—

RUFUS: —Don't tell me!

[*He rises and goes to the window.*]

CECELIA: You're not awfully fond of your son, are you, Mr. Collier?

[RUFUS *turns to her.*]

RUFUS: Miss—I beg your pardon—you said your name was—?

CECELIA: Henry. Cecelia Henry.

RUFUS: Miss Henry, if you had spent the time and money and effort I have to make that young man realize who he is and what he ought to be doing in the world—how long have you known him?

CECELIA: I'm comparatively new, I'm afraid.

RUFUS [*To* OWEN]: Perhaps, from longer experience, you might enlighten her.

OWEN: I presume what Mr. Collier means is that on ordinary terms, Tom doesn't seem to have got very far.

CECELIA: There's still time, isn't there?

RUFUS: Thirty-one—thirty-two in October—and he's wasted his life from the cradle.

CECELIA: It must have been pathetic to see him wasting it at three.

RUFUS: I assure you, his genius for it showed even then. I send him to Harvard, and he lasts two years there. I send him to Oxford, and he commutes from Paris. I put him in the Bank, and he—[*He sighs profoundly.*]—The world at the feet of that boy, the whole world. And all he's ever done is to run from it.

OWEN: Tom has his own ideas about what he wants to do with his life. [RICHARD REGAN *has come into the room. He is about thirty-two, with the figure of an athlete, red hair, and a genial, ugly Irish face that appears at some time to have been thoroughly mauled. He wears dark trousers and a white linen jacket, and carries a slip of paper in his hand.*]—Yes, Regan?

REGAN: There's a radio message came by phone for him.

OWEN: You can leave it here. I'll tell him.

[REGAN *folds the message and places it upon the table.*]

REGAN: Right. [*He turns and beams upon them.*]—Everything satisfactory?

OWEN: Yes, thanks.

REGAN: Comfortable, Miss?

CECELIA: Quite, thank you.

REGAN: Like a drink, anyone?

RUFUS [*Exasperated*]: No, no! Nothing! We were talking!

REGAN [*With a wave of his hand*]: Go right ahead. Make yourselves to home. He'll be along.

[*He goes out.* CECELIA *laughs.*]

CECELIA: —The butler? But he's charming!

RUFUS: He looks like a prizefighter.

OWEN: He was.

[RUFUS *begins to hover curiously about the radio message, wanting to read it, not quite able to bring himself to.*]

RUFUS: Why did he send me word to come out here tonight? Exceedingly important? Don't let anything interfere?

OWEN: I don't know. I found a message asking me to get Miss Henry at my aunt's in New Canaan, and come back on the run. He had to go to town for something.

RUFUS: Well, I'll tell you what's in my mind—God knows I don't want it there.—That girl he's been living with for the last three years—

[OWEN *glances quickly at* CECELIA.]

OWEN: Just a minute, Sir.

CECELIA: It's all right, Owen.

RUFUS: Good Lord, it's no secret, is it? [*To* CECELIA]—You're not her, are you?

CECELIA: Not that I know of.

RUFUS [*To* OWEN]: Who is she, anyhow? What is she?

OWEN: —An extremely nice girl—hard-working, talented. She draws for the fashion magazines, and very successfully.

RUFUS: Admirable.—Well, I believe he's got me out here to tell me he wants to marry her—or has already.—I've no doubt he'll bring her with him.

OWEN: Seriously—can you see Tom marrying anyone?

RUFUS: I can see her marrying him. It has happened before, and to better men.

[*Again he hovers about the radio message.*]

OWEN: If it was going to them, it would have long before this. Besides, she left for her magazine's Paris office three months ago, for an indefinite stay.

RUFUS: Maybe she's coming back.—In fact, I'm certain that she's why we're here. It offers the perfect opportunity to cut himself off finally and completely from the life he was born to. I'm surprised he has missed it as long as he has. Well—I've stood for his rowdy friendships, I've put up with his idleness, his ill-mannered insolence, his—

[CECELIA *rises and faces him.*]

CECELIA: I'm sorry, Mr. Collier, but I'll have to ask you to let it go at that.

RUFUS: Ah? Why so?

CECELIA: —Because it so happens that *I'm* why we're here.

RUFUS: How's that?

CECELIA: It's me Tom's going to marry, and I've heard enough against him to last me quite a while.

[RUFUS *stares.* OWEN *starts forward.*]

OWEN: —You that Tom's—?!—Good Lord, C, what are you talking about?

CECELIA: Marrying. On May first, to be exact. [*To* RUFUS] He asked you out here to tell you, and, I imagine, to receive your good wishes. [RUFUS *still stares.*]—Thanks so much.

[*She reseats herself,* OWEN *continues to gaze at her, speechless.*]

RUFUS: What did you say your name was? I'm sorry, but I—

CECELIA: Cecelia Henry. My mother was Cecelia Bond, of Baltimore. She married Stephen Henry, also of Baltimore. Except for a few distant cousins, such as Owen here, I'm alone now—poor, but quite respectable. Will it do?

RUFUS: Tom has very little of his own, you know.

CECELIA: It will be ample, thank you.

RUFUS [*After a moment*]: Miss Henry, I'm inclined to like you. I think you have what I call "character."

CECELIA: Really? You're too kind.

RUFUS: You'll need it with him.

CECELIA: I don't agree with you. Tom is the most interesting, most attractive man I've ever known. I consider myself shot with luck. And you make me a little tired with your abuse of him.

RUFUS: —Very loyal.

CECELIA: Not at all. I simply believe in him.—Not in his so-called "past" perhaps—I'm not quite a fool—but certainly in what's to be.

RUFUS: Faith is a beautiful thing.

CECELIA: *I* think so.

RUFUS: Well, if you can make a respectable citizen of Tom Collier at this date, you'll have nothing but praise from me, my dear.

[*He picks up the radio message and draws it through his fingers.*]

CECELIA: It seems not to occur to you that when Tom has someone who really understands him to work and care for—

OWEN: Understands him!

CECELIA: Yes. Completely. [*Again to* RUFUS]—He'll make what you call "a citizen" of himself.

[RUFUS *adjusts his spectacles and reads the message.*]

RUFUS: You think?

CECELIA: I know.—And if what you laughingly refer to as my "faith" is of any use to him—

RUFUS: "Love will conquer all." Yes, yes—of course—[*He sighs and refolds the message.*]—But forgive me a few doubts.

[OWEN *leans forward.*]

OWEN: Oh? How's that, Sir?

RUFUS: "Darling. Am coming back. Arrive on 'Paris' at eight tonight. Much love. Daisy."

[*He looks at* CECELIA. *There is a slight pause. Then*]

CECELIA: Well?

[RUFUS *rises, and regards her intently.*]

RUFUS: —Yes, you seem to be a first-rate girl.

CECELIA: I've heard some rather agreeable things about *you,* now and then. It would be pleasant sometime to—

RUFUS [*Smiling*]: —To see one or two of them? Well, my dear, perhaps some day you shall.—And now if you'll let me have Mr.—er—Mr. Arthur to myself for a moment—[*He moves toward the doorway.*]—There are a few dull but practical facts about—er—about your fiancé, I should like to—[*He turns to* OWEN.]—Would you mind?

[OWEN *moves to follow him.* RUFUS *goes out.*]

CECELIA: Wait a minute, Owen, will you please?

[OWEN *stops and turns.*]

OWEN: Well?

CECELIA: I'm sorry you had to learn about it so—abruptly.

OWEN: It doesn't matter much, does it?

CECELIA: I don't know.

OWEN: Perhaps I was supposed to hear it with little cries of pleasure.

CECELIA: The point is, that I intended to tell you on the way over, but somehow couldn't.

OWEN: I'm touched by your reluctance to deliver the blow.

CECELIA: Don't be nasty, Owen.

OWEN: It was kind of me to bring you together, wasn't it?

CECELIA: An inspiration. I'm sure I'm most grateful.

OWEN: I can't make it out. You aren't in the least the sort of girl I'd expect Tom to be interested in.

[*She laughs.*]

CECELIA: Thanks!

OWEN: You know what I mean.

CECELIA: Perhaps it's the artist in him. You see, he has the charming illusion that I'm a real beauty.

OWEN: —And I can't make *you* out, either.

CECELIA: It's quite simple: I'm in love at last.

OWEN: Have you the remotest idea of what you're letting yourself in for?

CECELIA: I think so.

OWEN: I'm the one friend you and Tom have in common.

CECELIA: —But such a lovely friend, Owen. Don't ever leave me—us.

OWEN: There's not a taste, not an attitude—

CECELIA: Perhaps there will be. Give us time.

OWEN: C—how on earth did it happen?

CECELIA: Very suddenly, very sweetly.—Yesterday. [*He turns away.*] I'm sorry. You asked.

[*A moment. Then*]

OWEN: —I'll see what it is Mr. Collier wants, if you don't mind.

[OWEN *goes out.* CECELIA *looks after him for a moment, then removes her hat, seats herself in a large chair, hidden from the door-*

way, and thoughtfully lights a cigarette. A moment, then TOM COLLIER *appears in the doorway,* REGAN *close behind him.* TOM *is in his early thirties, slim, youthful, with a fine, sensitive, humorous face. He carries several packages in his arms.*]

TOM: Where are they?

REGAN: Well—they *were.*

[CECELIA *rises and turns.*]

CECELIA: Hello, Tom.

TOM [*To* REGAN]: Take my hat. [REGAN *removes it from his head.*] Thanks. Now get out.

REGAN: I just wanted to tell you that—

TOM: Later.

[*He is gazing fondly at* CECELIA.]

REGAN: But there's a—

TOM: Get, will you, Red?

[REGAN *goes out, murmuring:*]

REGAN: —Radio message come for you.

[*But* TOM *scarcely hears him. Suddenly he drops his parcels upon the table, goes to* CECELIA *and takes her in his arms.*]

TOM: Darling, darling—

[*He is about to kiss her, but she averts her head.*]

CECELIA: No. You're late. I'm furious with you.

TOM [*Blankly*]: Late?

[*She looks at him for a moment, then smiles and kisses him lightly.*]

CECELIA: There.—All right?

TOM: Terrible. I've taken up with a thrifty spinster.

CECELIA: It's all you deserve.

[*He laughs.*]

TOM: How do you like it?—I mean the place.

CECELIA: I love it.

TOM: I call it "the house in bad taste."—Look out for taste, C. There's too much of it in the world. [*He goes to the packages on the table.*] See here—what I fetched from town for you.

CECELIA: What are they?

TOM: A celebration: good things to eat and drink.—Where are they? Father? Owen?

CECELIA: In the other room.

TOM: What do you think of Father?

CECELIA: Well—

TOM: Keep a civil tongue in your head.

CECELIA: It may take a little time.

TOM: You can learn to like him and beer together. Mother was the prize: you missed something, there. Father means well, but you have to stand him off. Give him an inch, and he takes you home in his pocket. Did you really say you'd marry me?

[*He slips her arm through his and leads her to a chair.*]

CECELIA: I'm afraid I did.

TOM: Heaven help us both.—Just this one marriage please, darling. I haven't been very good about marriage. I was exposed to a very bad case of it as a baby. We must make a grand go of it.

CECELIA: We shall, never you fear.

[TOM *smiles.* CECELIA *seats herself in the chair,* TOM *upon the arm of it.*]

TOM: —Just do everything I say, and it will be all right.

CECELIA: —With pleasure.

[*He gazes at her.*]

TOM: C, what a marvellous object you are. [*He picks up her hand, looks at it.*] Look at those fine small bones in your wrist.

CECELIA: What about them?

TOM: This—[*He kisses the wrist.*]—You're so cunningly contrived.

CECELIA: What?

TOM: I say, you're put together on the very best principles.

CECELIA: I don't see so many blunders in you either, Thomas.

TOM: No, mine is entirely beauty of soul. Shall I tell you about my

CECELIA [*Softly*]: Put your arms around me, Tom.

soul, C?—With lantern slides?

[*He draws her to him and kisses her. Then*]

TOM: —Oh God, I feel good!

CECILIA [*In a breath*]: —So do I.

TOM: —Let's have all our good things together. [*He turns and calls loudly:*] Red! Oh, Red! [*Then turns again to* CECELIA] That's a very good rule of life, darling: all one's good things together.

CECELIA: Is it, dear?

[REGAN *appears beaming.* TOM *rises from the chair.*]

REGAN: Hello. Not so loud.

TOM: —Glasses with ice, Red, and run all the way.

REGAN: O.K.

[*He goes out.* TOM *calls again:*]

TOM: Owen? Father! [*Then turns and regards* CECELIA *once more*] Oh, my lovely C—you lovely thing, you.

CECELIA: Stop it, Tom. You're really embarrassing me. I feel quite naked.

TOM: That's fine. [*He goes to her and draws two fingers gently across her cheek.*] It's such a fine binding, darling—such a good book. [RUFUS *re-enters, followed by* OWEN.] Hello, Father, hello, Owen—terribly nice you're here. You've met Miss Henry, Father?

RUFUS: I've had that pleasure, yes.

TOM: It *is* a pleasure.—How are the horses?

RUFUS: Do you care?

[TOM *laughs.*]

TOM: Not a bit.

RUFUS: Then why ask?

TOM: Politeness.

RUFUS: You said five o'clock. It's seven.

TOM: Did I? Is it?—Listen—you and Owen—I want to tell you what this is all about.

RUFUS: We know. We've heard.

[TOM *looks to* CECELIA.]

CECELIA: He was abusing you so, I had to tell him.

[TOM *laughs delightedly.*]

TOM: And it didn't discourage you?

CECELIA: On the contrary.

TOM: Stout heart. [*Then, gravely, to* RUFUS] Why, thank you very much, Sir, but I think *I'm* the one to be congratulated. Yes, indeed we are. Yes, I'm sure we shall be. [REGAN *comes in with a tray of glasses filled with ice.*] Oh—er—this is my father, Red.

REGAN: Glad to meet you, Sir.

[RUFUS *bows slightly.* REGAN *undoes one of the packages and produces a bottle of champagne.*]

TOM: —And my fiancée, Miss Henry.

[*Bottle in hand,* REGAN *stares at him, puzzled.*]

REGAN: Your—?

[*Then goes to* CECELIA, *seizes her hand, shakes it warmly and goes out.* CECELIA *laughs.*]

CECELIA: He is priceless!

TOM: A magnificent fellow, Red. We box every morning. I gave him that ear—but you watch, I'll pay for it. [*To* RUFUS] *You* keep pretty fit, don't you, Father?

RUFUS: Quite. Do you mind?

TOM: I'm delighted. My only wonder is that some designing woman doesn't snap you up. Look how C got me. [*To* CECELIA]—Like rolling off a log, wasn't it?

CECELIA: Easier, much.

RUFUS: I keep my defenses well in line.

[TOM *laughs, and turns to* OWEN.]

TOM: Did you hear what he said? [*To* RUFUS]—Millions for defense, eh, Sir?—But not one cent for cab fare. [REGAN *has come in again with the bottle, now opened, and is filling the glasses.*] That's the boy, Red. Pass them, will you? Then get dinner going. I could eat an ox. [REGAN *passes the glasses.* TOM *turns to* CECELIA.] Are you hungry too, Angel?

CECELIA: Simply famished.

TOM: Good. I like a girl who likes her food. Once I said to Daisy—[*He stops, waits a moment, then smiles and raises his glass.*] Well—here's how and why and wherefore—and you know where marriages are made. [*All drink.* REGAN *has a glass of his own, which he downs at a gulp.*]—Speaking of eating, I ran into Jim Winter—you know Jim, Owen—in town today. He wants me to go salmon fishing in Canada in June. I think I'll take him up on it. I've never done it.—It sounds like great sport, eh, Red?

REGAN [*Putting down his glass*]: Did you get your radio, Tom?

TOM: What radio's that?

REGAN: There on the table.

[*He goes out.*]

CECELIA: In June, did you say?

TOM: Yes. It won't be for long. [*He takes a swallow from his glass and puts it down.*] My, what a noble wine. [*He picks up the radio message.*]—I'll be back in three weeks at the outside.

CECELIA: Then we'll be married in July.

TOM [*Turning*]: July! You said May.

CECELIA: Not if you're going straight off on a trip.

[*There is a silence. He regards her soberly.*]

TOM: —That's easy, then. I won't go.

CECELIA: Perhaps you'd better think it over.

TOM: No, darling. I don't have to.

CECELIA: All right, Tom. [*She smiles and raises her glass to him.*]—To May first.

[*All drink.* TOM *opens the radio message, reads it and refolds it carefully. All are watching him. He thinks a moment, frowning, then turns to* OWEN.]

TOM: Owen—would you like to show Father the new bantam cock?

[OWEN *rises and moves toward* RUFUS.]

OWEN: The red one?—Right.—Will you come along, Sir?

[OWEN *goes out.* RUFUS *does not stir.* TOM *goes to him, and slips his arm through his.*]

TOM: You must see him, Father. He's a beauty, that bird. He fights at the drop of a hat. [*He draws him toward the door,* OWEN *following.*] —Even if you don't drop it, he fights. I'm sure he'll be interested to meet you, too, Sir.

[*He withdraws his arm, and* RUFUS *goes out.* TOM *closes the door after him, hesitates a moment, then returns slowly to* CECELIA.]

CECELIA: Don't tell me if you don't want to, Tom.

TOM: But I do. I intended to at the first opportunity anyhow, and— [*He glances at the radio message once again*]—And it seems that suddenly here it is.

[*And puts it in his pocket.*]

CECELIA: Am I to be a good soldier?

TOM: No. There's no need to be.—Though I'm sure you would be, if there were.

CECELIA: Thanks, dear.

TOM: C, for quite a long time I've known—known intimately—a girl who's been very important to me—

CECELIA: Yes?

TOM: —Who always will be very important to me.

CECELIA [*Smiling*]: —That's harder.

TOM: It shouldn't be. Because it has nothing to do with you and me, not possibly.

CECELIA: I'm relieved to hear that.

TOM: In fact, as it stands, I think she'll be glad for us.

CECELIA: I hope she will.

TOM: I'm sure of it.—C, Daisy has done more for me than anyone in this world. She's the best friend I've got. I believe she always will be. I'd hate terribly to lose her. It's been a queer sort of arrangement—no arrangement at all, really. There's never been any idea of marriage between us. It's hard to explain what there has been between us. I don't believe it's ever existed before on land or on sea. Well—

[*He hesitates again.*]

CECELIA: Is she attractive, Tom?

TOM: To me, she is. She's about so high, and made of platinum wire and sand.—You wouldn't like me half so well, if Daisy hadn't knocked some good sense into me.

CECELIA: Well, someone's done a good job.

[TOM *laughs.*]

TOM: I'll tell her that. [*Then seriously*] I sent her a long cable about us this morning. She couldn't have got it, because this—[*He taps his pocket.*] this is from the boat. She lands tonight.

CECELIA: I see.

TOM: I want to be sure that you understand it—understand it both ways. I'd rather not go—terribly deeply into it if you don't mind.

CECELIA: I don't, Tom.

TOM: We've been—everything possible to each other of course, and—

CECELIA: Yes, Tom.

TOM: But at the same time, free as air. There's never been any responsibility to each other involved in it—

CECELIA: I can understand that.

TOM: Can you, C? Because I never could.—Anyhow, that's the way it's been.—We haven't been what you'd call "in love," for quite a long time, now, so—

CECELIA [*Smiling*]: Does she know that?

TOM: She knew it first. Well—I don't know what more there is to say about it, except that there's no reason at all for you to worry, and—you won't, will you?

CECELIA: No, Tom. Not if you tell me I needn't.

TOM: I do.—And finally, that I think she ought to know the—news about us, pretty promptly.

CECELIA: Yes. Probably.

TOM: Is whatever I do about it all right with you?

CECELIA: Absolutely.

TOM: Thanks, C.

CECELIA: There's just one thing I'd like to ask. May I?

TOM: Why of course, darling. What?

CECELIA: Are you quite sure that—? [*She sees* OWEN *and* RUFUS *coming in.*]—Poor Mr. Collier. I'm sure you loathe chickens. I quite agree with you.

RUFUS: —Vicious little beast.

[REGAN *comes in beaming.*]

REGAN: Come on, everyone! Dinner!

TOM: You haven't put the car away, have you?

REGAN: Say, how many hands have I got?

TOM: Don't. I'll need it.

[REGAN *goes out.* TOM *turns to his father.*]

TOM: Father, I'm afraid I'll have to ask you to do the honors at dinner.

RUFUS: The—? Why? How's that?

TOM: I find I've got to go straight back to town.

[*A silence. Then*]

OWEN: But I thought this was to be a celebration.

RUFUS: I had the same impression.

TOM: I'm sorry: it can't be helped.

OWEN: Is it so important to go in just this minute, Tom?

TOM: Yes—unfortunately.

[RUFUS *is eying him shrewdly.*]

RUFUS: Why? What's wrong?

TOM: Nothing at all. It's simply that someone's arriving from Europe. I've missed the landing, as it is. [*To* OWEN]—Someone I've known a long time, and am fond of.

OWEN: Oh, I see.

TOM [*To* RUFUS]: I must—well, the fact is, I must tell her my—my good news.

RUFUS: Now you listen to me—

[TOM *confronts him.*]

TOM: —And it seems to me extremely important that I should do it at once. In fact, I can't do otherwise.

[RUFUS *bursts out:*]

RUFUS: —You have the effrontery, the colossal bad taste, on the night of celebrating your engagement to a fine, trusting, loyal girl, to go from her—your fiancée—to your—to your—

[TOM *smiles.*]

TOM: —The same old difficulty with words, eh, Sir?—Never mind. None of them would apply to Daisy.

RUFUS: It's beyond me. It's the confoundest impertinence I've ever known.

TOM [*Smiling*]: But you see, for all your splendid moral judgments, you know so very little, Sir.

RUFUS: I suppose you know better.—If you leave here tonight—

[TOM'*s smile vanishes.*]

TOM: —Yes. Much better. [*He returns to* CECELIA, *lifts her hand and kisses it lightly.*]—Until tomorrow, my Angel.

[*He nods good night to* OWEN *and* RUFUS, *and goes out.*]

CURTAIN

■ ACT I ■

SCENE II

The sitting room of DAISY SAGE'*s flat, later the same night.*

DAISY'*s flat occupies the top floor of an old house in the Murray Hill section of New York. The sitting room also serves as a workroom for* DAISY. *Victorian in atmosphere, it is light and cheerful and has been decorated and furnished with an original and unerring feeling for the period. There is a fireplace of simple design at Left and above it, a door opening into the bedroom. The entrance from the hall is up Right, and into the pantry, down Right. The sofa and chairs are fine old Victorian pieces, but comfortable in spite of it. There are three large windows in the back wall. Below them stands* DAISY'*s worktable, piled with old magazines and sketches, drawing boards, crayons, pens and pencils.*

Opposite TOM, JOE FISK *is seated. Between them stands* FRANC SCHMIDT, *violin under her chin, playing, and playing well, the concluding measures of a César Franck sonata. She is thirty, hard, rugged—in appearance more of a handsome farm girl than musician.* JOE *is twenty-eight, fine Irish, nervous, intense, attractive.* FRANC *concludes the piece.*

JOE: Good!—You'll get there, Franc, if you work.

[*She returns the violin to its case and seats herself near them. She speaks with a slight German accent.*]

FRANC: —Only I played it much better, much.

TOM: He just wasn't impressed, eh?

FRANC: Oh, yes.—He could book me on the Big Time, he said.

JOE [*Incredulously*]: Vaudeville?

FRANC: —That is, if I would learn to roller-skate.

TOM: He wanted you to play on skates?

FRANC: —A sensation, he said.

[JOE *and* TOM *laugh with delight.* JOE *goes to her, takes her face between his hands and kisses her resoundingly upon the brow.*]

JOE: My darling. My Dutch darling.

[*She brushes him aside.*]

FRANC: Get away.

[JOE *calls in the direction of the bedroom:*]

JOE: Daisy!—Did you hear about Franc and the booking agent? [*He turns to* FRANC.] Where is she?

FRANC: —Probably taking another bath. It will be her third in six hours. That's what Europe does for you.

TOM [*Indicating the pantry*]: —No. She's in there, I think.

JOE [*Incredulously*]: Six hours! Two o'clock—?

FRANC: It's past it.

TOM: Will you two never go home?

JOE [*Calling in the direction of the pantry*]: Daisy! We're going! [*To* TOM *and* FRANC]—And I promised myself tomorrow I'd do a chapter or die.

TOM: How's it coming?

JOE: All right. At least it's begun to move.

TOM: What are you calling it?

JOE: "Easy Rider."

TOM: I like that.

FRANC: But what does it mean?

JOE: Good God, must it mean something? [*Again he calls:*] Daisy!

FRANC: Yes. Your eyes have got smaller. You should get to bed.

TOM: Both of you should—go on, will you?

JOE: Why?

TOM: I want to talk to Daisy.

JOE: Look here, Tom, what *is* on your mind?

TOM: I've got something to tell her.

JOE: News?

TOM: Yes.

JOE: Good news?

TOM: Very.

FRANC: Will she cheer?

TOM: I think so.

FRANC: Tell *us,* Tom!

TOM: No.

JOE: Why not?

TOM: I want to tell Daisy first. [*To* FRANC] You know, I've been thinking: Johnny Bristed might get a concert for you.

FRANC: I don't want it yet. I'm not ready yet.

[*Again* JOE *calls:*]

JOE: Daisy!

[DAISY SAGE *comes in from the pantry. She is twenty-six, slim, lithe, a stripling, but with dignity beyond her years and a rare grace to accompany it. In contrast to* CECELIA'*s lush beauty, she is plain, but there is a certain style of her own, a presence, a manner that defies description. Instantly and lastingly attractive, like no one else one knows; in short "a person," an "original." She wears white pajamas that might as well be a dress, and carries a tray containing coffee and sandwiches.*

DAISY: —And furthermore, I don't believe I like France as much as I say I do. [*She puts down the tray.*]—And I don't for a minute believe that you're leaving.

FRANC: Joe must. So must I.

DAISY: —You stay the night, if you like, Tom. You can have my room. I've got all the work in the world to do before morning.

TOM: Why thanks, Daisy, but—

DAISY: As you like. [*She seats herself, and gives them coffee and sandwiches.*] I had thirty sketches to get through on the boat.—Oh, what lovely intentions.

FRANC: Was it rough?

DAISY: No, but Pilard was on board and we spent hours on end in the smoking room—talk, talk, and more talk.

JOE: He's a fine painter, Pilard.

TOM: He's a good painter.

JOE: Fine, I said.

TOM: —And last week Henry Collins could write. Hold on to your standards, Joe.

JOE: You teach me, will you, Master?

TOM: Collins' life shows in his work. He can't make up his mind whether he wants to be a writer or a man-about-town.

JOE: Why not both?

TOM: —Because, little Joe, his work is the only true mistress a real artist ever had. When he takes on the world he takes on a whore.

FRANC: That goes for all good men, not only artists.

DAISY: —But all good men are, aren't they?—Look at Tom.—You don't have to put marks on paper or dents in stone to qualify, do you?

TOM [*To* JOE]: Yes, and pays for her favors wtih something a lot more precious than twenty dollars left on the mantelpiece.

[JOE *reflects.*]

JOE: *I* had twenty dollars once. Now, when was it?

DAISY: There's a statue in Florence that made me think of you, Tom.

[TOM *laughs.*]

TOM: Me! How?

DAISY: It's a David by Donatello.

TOM: You mean with the curls and the derby hat?

DAISY: That's right!

[TOM *shakes his head.*]

TOM: —No David, me. I'm just the no-account-boy. Ask Father—he'll tell you.—Hand me another sandwich, Joe.

[JOE *gives him one.*]

JOE: No-account, is it?—You've done more for people than any one man I know.

TOM: Why thanks, Joe.—It's not true, of course, but thanks.

JOE: And done it in the damndest, most unassuming way I've ever heard of.

TOM: Oh, go to hell, will you?

JOE [*To* FRANC]: I could name a dozen first-class talents that, if *he* hadn't nosed 'em out, would have—

TOM: Say, are you two going to hang around here all night?

JOE: We haven't seen her either you know.

[FRANC *puts down her cup.*]

FRANC: I must teach you again how to make coffee, darling.

DAISY: Your country's the one, Franc.

FRANC: Ach! There is no more new music in Germany today than there is here.

JOE: I thought there was plenty here.

FRANC: Like what?—If someone goes—[*She hums the opening bar of the "Rhapsody in Blue."*]—at me again, I shall become mad.

[DAISY *gazes at the bulging briefcase on the floor beside the work-table. Her smile fades.*]

DAISY: Oh, that work!—Look at it.

TOM: Is there much of it?

DAISY: At least eight hours.

JOE: I wish we could help.

TOM: —You can. Good night, Joe.

DAISY: —And Briggs was at the dock.

TOM: I didn't get your radio till seven.

DAISY: That didn't matter. Anyhow I hate being met. Anyhow, I tell myself I do. Briggs was frantic. Apparently they've held the presses for two days.

TOM: You're a bad girl.

DAISY: I'm a scoundrel. I swore it would be on his desk at nine. I'll be lucky if I'm through by noon.

[JOE *laughs, and rises.*]

JOE: Urge us to stay once more and we may give in.—Come along, Franc. I'll see you across the hall.

[FRANC *rises and takes up her violin case.*]

FRANC: —It is good to have you back, too, Tom. You are better than all of us, but Daisy. She is better than best. Between you, you stir up our lazy bones, you hold us together, you bind our wounds. You two are the—ach!—my blood is turned to beer.—Auf Wiedersehen. Good night.

[*She goes out.*]

JOE: I'll drop in tomorrow afternoon about five, if I can.

DAISY: Fine. I ought to be up by then.

[*She follows* FRANC *into the hall.*]

JOE [*To* TOM]: Will you be here?

TOM: I'm afraid I'll have to go to the country.

JOE: Shun the country. Things come out of the ground there in spring.

[*He goes out.* TOM *is alone for a moment. Then* DAISY *re-enters.*]

DAISY: —Love them as I do, I thought they'd never go.

TOM: So did I.

[*She puts her arms around him and looks up at him.*]

DAISY: Hello, you dear Tom.

TOM: Hello, Daisy.

[*She kisses him lightly*]

DAISY: Now it seems I haven't been away at all. [*And leaves his arms.*] Oh, it's grand to be back!

TOM: It's grand having you.—Was the trip really all that you hoped it would be?

DAISY: It was better.—If only you'd been along. Oh Tom—the pictures! I got drunk on them every day, twice a day.

TOM: I was sure you would.

DAISY: And at night when the galleries were closed I sat around and dreamed of them.—The silly contempt I always pretended to have for painting—self-protection, of course—the stuff *I* draw.

TOM: But some of it's good.

DAISY: You're right, my boy. Some of it is. [*She goes to the table and picks up a portfolio.*] Look—full—sketches.And not a dress, a hat, a pajama among them. A market wagon—the angle of a doorway—an open trunk. A melon cut in half—three glasses and a corkscrew—all manner of funny objects. Oh Tom, two of the most exciting things have happened to me! Not one—two! [*She moves toward the sofa.*] Come—sit down—

TOM: What are they?

DAISY: I'm bursting with them. [*She makes room for him beside her on the sofa, looks at him lovingly, smiles contentedly, touches his arm.*] Good, this—isn't it?

TOM: But what, Daisy? Did you fall in love with Pilard?

DAISY: Well I should say not! [*She laughs.*] Pilard! [*Then*] What's that? [*From the distance the strains of a violin are heard, playing variations on the scales.*] Oh—Franc. Still working.—Guess what I found in my room when I came in? [*He looks at her questioningly. She laughs.*] —It seems the Swede maid Franc got me doesn't approve of you:— Four shirts, three socks, five ties and a razor, all done up in a great big white handkerchief.

TOM: You'd better go back to colored ones.—Maids, I mean.—

DAISY: —Remember Gladys?

TOM: Remember Hannah?

DAISY: Remember Marietta? [*They laugh together happily. She slips her arm through his, and for a moment drops her head upon his shoulder.*] Oh Tom, God love you.

TOM: God love you, my dear. [*For a moment there is silence except for the sound of* FRANC'*s violin. Then she raises her head and they speak simultaneously:*] Daisy—

DAISY: Darling—[*She laughs.*] What?

TOM: No—you tell me—

DAISY: Well, my heavy sledding ought to be over in a few weeks—by the first of May, anyway. What have you got on the fire—much?

TOM: Yes. A great deal. The fact is—

DAISY [*In a rush*]: —Work night and day until May. Then come to Mexico for a month with Daisy. I'm dying to go. Pilard was full of it. I know it's what I need for a while, because—well, first—oh, I feel like a fool. You mustn't breathe a word of it. [*He shakes his head.*] —Tom, I think I can paint.

TOM: But that's no surprise. I've always thought if only you'd—

DAISY [*Quickly*]: Then you've always been wrong!—It's new. It's since these two months.—I believe that if I work my eyes out, and my fingers to the bone, someday I may paint.—You must be hard with me—no parties—no hell-raising—*work*.—And you mustn't let me show until you know I'm ready to. Is that agreed?

TOM: All right.

DAISY: You have a funny instinct about such things. I count on you.— As for the second thing—[*She hesitates.*]—You know—suddenly I feel shy with you. [*She rises.*] I don't like it. I don't like it a bit.

TOM: We've—it's been a long time.

[DAISY *goes again to the worktable.*]

DAISY: Too long.—Perhaps I'd better wait to tell you the second thing.

TOM: No. Tell me now.

DAISY: Oh, my dear—what's wrong with us? Come here to me. [*He goes to her, takes her hands in his.*] That's better. Now I don't feel it so much. [*But still she looks at him anxiously. Finally she releases her hands, turns and fumbles among her work materials, picks up a pencil.*]—These are German pencils. They can't touch ours. You'd think they could, but they can't. Give me a "Venus-6B," every time. [*She stares fixedly at the pencil for another moment, then puts it down and turns to him.*] You're a free man, Tommy. You always have been, with me. No questions asked. But please, Mexico in May together, because listen—No! Don't look at me. Look the other way—[*He averts his head. She goes on, rapidly.*]—I stayed three days with the Allens at Vevey and they've got the sweetest small boy about two and I got crazy about him and I want one, I want one like the devil. I'm crazy for one, and would you please be good enough to marry me, and—

TOM: Daisy, I—!

DAISY: Oh, it needn't be terribly serious!—It's not a life-sentence—just for a short while, if you like—it'd be such a dirty trick on him, if we didn't.—After I get my stuff through for the June issue—then Mexico for a month—I love you so much, I was a fool ever to think I didn't, and—ah, come on, Tom—be a sport—[*She is breathless.*]—Give me a cigarette—[*But he does not.*]

TOM: Daisy—

DAISY [*Quickly*]: All right. No go. Let's forget about it. What a foul necktie that is. The colors are awful.

TOM: Daisy, I—Oh God, God Almighty—

DAISY: Well, what is it? [*He covers her hand with his.*]—You're going to tell me something terrible.—What is it?

TOM: I'm going to be married.

DAISY [*Incredulously*]: To be—?!

[*Then silence. She averts her head.*]

TOM: Listen to me, darling, listen: you don't really care so much. You can't. It's simply that we—you and I—after all this time, naturally we'd feel—

DAISY: It must have happened pretty quickly.

TOM: It did. A month ago we hadn't even met. It was—

DAISY: You can spare me the details, please. I don't even want to know who she is.

[*He moves away from her.* FRANC'*s violin begins to be heard again.*]

TOM: —Her name is Cecelia Henry.

DAISY: It sounds familiar. I've heard or read that somewhere. Where?—Well, well, will wonders never cease?—If I'd thought you were in a marrying mood, I might have thrown my own—[*She picks up a small, limp hat from the table.*]—could you call it a hat?—in the ring a bit sooner. [*She drops the hat upon the table.*]—Behold, the bridegroom cometh—and no oil for my lamp, as usual.—A foolish virgin, me—well, foolish, anyway.—When's it to be? Soon?

TOM: —About the first of May, we planned.

DAISY: I see.—Of course, in that event Mexico *would* be out, wouldn't it?

TOM: —But I never dreamed you'd—oh God, I feel so awful.

DAISY: Does she know about us?

TOM: Yes.

DAISY: Honest Tom.

TOM: Oh, shut up.

DAISY: Remember me, Tom.

TOM: Oh my dear—as if ever in this world I—[*Suddenly, fearfully*] Daisy!—There's to be no nonsense about not seeing each other as friends again, or any of that, you know—

DAISY: No?

TOM: No. We're grown-up human beings. We're decent and we're civilized. We—

DAISY: But there *will* be that nonsense. Oh yes—there'll be that, all right.—"Cecelia Henry"—Now I know where it was!

[*She picks up a magazine and begins to run through it.*]

TOM: —But I don't understand it. I don't see why we shouldn't. I thought for a long time we'd been out of danger so far as—well, so far as—

[*He cannot finish it, but* DAISY *can.*]

DAISY: —Wanting each other goes?

TOM: But haven't we?

DAISY: Speak for yourself, Tom.

[*He looks at her, waits a moment, then speaks:*]

TOM: —You too, Daisy.—You first, I thought.

DAISY [*Slowly, thoughtfully*]: It's true, that side of it was never so much to us, was it? Not in comparison—not after those first crazy months. But I thought that was natural. I was even glad of it—glad to find it was—other needs that held us together. [*She looks away.*]—Closely —without claims—not a claim—but so closely. [*A moment. Then suddenly, sharply*] Tom—do you have to marry her?

TOM: I want to marry her.

DAISY [*Into the magazine*]: I was just thinking—perhaps you simply want her—want her most awfully.

TOM: It's more than that, much more.

DAISY: I don't see how you can tell quite yet.—For all our big talk, we still belong to the animal kingd—[*She stops and looks closely at a photograph in the magazine.*] Here she is!—Oh, these neat, protected women. I've drawn so many of them, dressed so many more.

TOM: If you knew her—

DAISY: But I don't, you see—[*She holds the magazine at arm's length, gazing at the photograph.*] Such a pretty face—lovely eyes, Tom. She's a prize, my boy. [*She closes the magazine and replaces it upon the table.*]—But look out for that chin.

TOM: Why?

DAISY: Just look out for it. [*She goes to him.*]—Does she love you? *Will* she love you, head over heels, regardless, as I—shall I say "as I once did"? Would you rather?

TOM: Daisy—don't—

DAISY: I hold you dear, Tom—*you* for what you are—just *as* you are. I thought it was my special gift. But maybe she has it too. I hope, I hope—

[*He gropes for her hand, raises it to his lips and kisses it.*]

TOM: There's no one like you—never will be. *I* know that.—But this—it's the damndest thing—I can't tell you—

DAISY: Don't try.—I'll pray for you every night, Tom. I really shall, you know I do that.

TOM: Oh, my sweet dear—

DAISY: Yes—be good enough to remember me kindly, if you will.

[*She returns to the table.*]

TOM [*Wretchedly*]: Oh, don't *talk* that stuff!

[*He goes to the fireplace. She takes up her workboard.*]

DAISY: Now just stand like that a minute, will you? Erect!—Will you stand erect, please?

[*He turns. She looks at him keenly.*]

TOM: What's all this about "remembering"? You sound as if we were—

[*She draws one strong line upon the paper and lets the workboard drop.*]

DAISY: There! That's all I want of you, all I shall keep of you. So good-bye, you Tom Collier.

[*He looks at her, puzzled.*]

TOM: "Good-bye"?—Until when—?

DAISY [*So lightly*]: Doomsday, my darling.

TOM: Daisy, what *are* you talking about!

DAISY: Just that.

[*He advances to her, takes her shoulders in his hands.*]

TOM: Now you listen to me: If you think I'm going to allow two people as important to each other as you and I are, to be separated by any such false, ridiculous notion as this, you're mistaken. Just you try it.

DAISY: Tell me good-bye!

TOM: I'll do nothing of the sort.

DAISY: Yes! You have to.—Sharp, decent, clean—no loose ends between *us* two!

TOM: But it's not decent!—It's soft. It's sentimental. It's the sort of thing you've never had any use for—taught *me* never to.

DAISY: Good-bye!

TOM: I will not say it.

DAISY: Good-bye!

TOM: No.

DAISY: You must!

TOM: You'll never get me to. So give up.

[DAISY *throws back her head and closes her eyes in pain.*]

DAISY: Oh, sweet heaven, what a world! *I* could do better by people than this—

TOM: Daisy dear—listen to me—

DAISY: —And I want you to take those things of yours—you hear? I don't want them hanging around the place, not me.—That new maid had a very fine hunch about us, didn't she?—Packed you all up, yes. Second sight—well, she gets the gate for it, the big Swede.

[*He stands gazing at her.*]

TOM: I don't believe in this. I don't believe in any of it.

[*She indicates the bedroom.*]

DAISY: —Go in and get them, will you? Fetch, Thomas. It's quite a neat, tidy little bundle. You won't be ashamed of it.—But if it stays around—well, I don't quite see myself crying into an old shirt, do you?—I have work to do, my son—a great deal of it. [*He does not move.*] No? Won't fetch?—Then kindly permit me to—[*She moves toward the bedroom.*]—And then you must say good-bye to me—you will, won't you? You've said it so many times, so brightly—Say it this time sadly.—We'll make it an *un*-marriage ceremony, to keep it all quite regular. You must grasp my hand in yours—one splendid gesture—and murmur "Good-bye, my Daisy. Thanks very much. A charming association." [*She goes into the bedroom.*]—And may we never, never meet again so long as we two shall live.You will, won't you?

[*He has been staring fixedly after her. Suddenly he straightens.*]

TOM: —No.

[*He moves swiftly to the hall doorway, picks up his hat and goes out. A moment. Then* DAISY *comes in again, with a small bundle tied up in a large white handkerchief.*]

DAISY: —See?—The wash is back.—Now do as Daisy says, and say—

[*She sees that he has gone. She moves toward the door, stops against the worktable. The bundle droops in her hand, drops upon the table. There she stands, staring at the door. Again,* FRANC*'s violin is heard, playing the scales.*

CURTAIN

■ ACT II ■

SCENE I

At TOM COLLIER'*s. About half-past seven on a Saturday night the following January.*

The living room has undergone a certain change. Small, feminine touches, such as new lamps, cretonne curtains at the windows and slipcovers of the same material on chairs and sofa, have made a woman's room of it.

CECELIA *and* GRACE MACOMBER *are seated near the fireplace having after-dinner coffee.* GRACE *is just over thirty. Without a single feature to remark upon except a slim and well-kept body, she manages, with the aid of coiffeurs, dressmakers and manicurists, to impress one as an attractive woman. She puts down her coffee cup and moves closer to the fire.*

GRACE: My dear, I'm congealed. I can't say I envy you the trip into town.

CECELIA: It's not my idea.

[*She takes up a piece of needlepoint and begins to work upon it.*]

GRACE: But why do you do it? It's so grim.

CECELIA: Tom wants to.

GRACE: Such devotion.

CECELIA: It's her first big concert and he thinks for some reason we ought to be there.

GRACE: Who is she, anyway?

CECELIA: Schmidt, her name is.

[GRACE *laughs.*]

GRACE: My dear! Not really!

CECELIA: Franc Schmidt, at that.—Tom says she's supreme.

GRACE: Oh—she's a friend, then.

CECELIA: She used to be.

GRACE [*With meaning*]: I see.

[CECELIA *smiles.*]

CECELIA: No, Grace. I doubt if you do.

GRACE: I suppose publishers have to hobnob with all sorts of queer people.

CECELIA: We see very few people of any description any more.

GRACE: Don't tell me about the hermit life you live! I think the least you could do would be to come to my Sunday breakfasts now and then. Tomorrow's will be such fun. Do, C.

CECELIA: Perhaps we shall.

GRACE: —Not if you go in tonight.

CECELIA: Perhaps we shan't go in.

GRACE [*Knowingly*]: Ah-ha! [*She looks about her.*]—You know, you could do so much with this house.

CECELIA: —If we weren't so poor.

GRACE: Don't be funny. Your name's Collier, isn't it?

CECELIA: Somehow that doesn't seem to make the difference it might.

GRACE: Well, I think it's brutal the way old Rufus K. hangs onto it.

CECELIA: We seem to manage somehow.

GRACE: I'd take *knives,* my dear, and gouge it out. [*A moment. Then*]—What would he be doing now, for instance? Tom, I mean.

CECELIA: Didn't he say he had letters to write?

[GRACE *seats herself again.*]

GRACE: He's really extraordinary. He defeats me.

[CECELIA *laughs.*]

CECELIA: What's so extraordinary about writing letters?

GRACE: The minute dinner's finished? Before coffee, even?—I guess I'm just not familiar with publishers' eccentricities.

[*Again* CECELIA *laughs.*]

CECELIA: He's a little worried tonight, poor dear.—Some more coffee? [*She gives* GRACE *a second cup.*]—He has a rather difficult ordeal to face.

GRACE: The concert?

CECELIA: No. Discharging Regan.

GRACE: Reg—?

CECELIA: —When, as and if he gets back from his weekly bat in town.

GRACE: You mean that desperate butler? Oh my dear, I'm so glad! He must have embarrassed you to death—But how did you manage to persuade Tom to let him go?

CECELIA: I had nothing to do with it.

GRACE: No? [*She laughs gaily.*] I believe that! [TOM *comes in from the other room with two or three magazines, which he is unwrapping.*] Ah! With us again.

TOM: With you again. [*He looks at his watch.*] Look here, C—hadn't we better be getting under way?

CECELIA: We've got hours. Let's not sit and wait in a stuffy theater.

[*A silence. Then*]

GRACE [*Brightly*]: I read the new book you published last week, Tom.

TOM [*Without interest*]: Yes? What did you think of it?

GRACE: Superlative, my dear. I was simply ravished!

TOM: Well, that's something, isn't it?

[GRACE *laughs.*]

GRACE: —Isn't he beyond words? [*To* TOM] You're the world's funniest man. You couldn't possibly be funnier.

TOM: You don't know me.

GRACE: Oh yes I do! Don't *you* adore it, C? The book, I mean—

CECELIA: I like it very much. [*She glances at* TOM.] In fact I'm afraid it was I who made Tom do it.

TOM: And I'm afraid I still think it's the worst tripe The Bantam ever published.

GRACE: —But my dear! Everyone's simply devouring it!

TOM: There'll be a lot of sickness this winter.

CECELIA: You're so foolish about it, Tom. [*To* GRACE]—He'll make enough on that one book to bring out ten he really cares for.

[TOM *unwraps a second magazine.*]

TOM: I suppose that's the way it works.

CECELIA: Of course it is. It's simply common sense.

TOM: I suppose so.

CECELIA: Besides, I don't care what you say, it really is amusing.

TOM: It's tripe.

GRACE: Isn't there such a thing as having too high a standard?

TOM: No, there's not.

[*She looks at him, startled.*]

CECELIA: What Grace means—

TOM [*More emphatically still*]: No, C. There is not.

CECELIA: All right, darling. [*He looks over one of the magazines. A moment. Then*] Oh—I meant to tell you: your father wants us to dine with him Wednesday, and spend the night.

[GRACE *pricks up her ears.*]

TOM: Get us out of it, won't you?

CECELIA: Again? How can I?

TOM: Oh, say I'm up to my ears in work, or something else he won't believe. Say the old boat is frozen stiff.

GRACE: I could easily send you in, in the closed car. Sammy and I might even join you.

TOM: Thanks. We cannot accept your sacrifice.

GRACE: But this weather—in that *racer!* It couldn't be more sobbing.

TOM: Oh yes it could!

[GRACE *rises.*]

GRACE: Well, I guess I'd better be "barging along," as they say. I'm sure it's getting colder by the minute.

TOM: Yes—I think we'd best bring the brass monkeys in tonight.

[*He returns to his magazine.*]

GRACE: The—? Oh, by the way, do you happen to know a stage director named Prentice Frith?

TOM: You know, I'm awfully afraid I don't?

GRACE: He's supposed to be the absolute top in amateur dramatics.

TOM: I can't imagine how I've missed him.

GRACE: He's coming out especially for my Sunday breakfast tomorrow—

TOM: That's perfectly fine. That's just what Sunday breakfast needs, isn't it?—Of course the coffee must be very hot, as well.

[GRACE *stares.* CECELIA *rises quickly. Finally* GRACE *turns to her.*]

GRACE: Good night, C.

CECELIA: Good night, Grace. Must you really?

GRACE [*Moving toward the hall door*]: Yes. I'm afraid I must.

[*She goes out, followed by* CECELIA. TOM *lights a cigarette, seats himself upon the stairs and continues to glance through the magazine. A door is heard to close in the hall. A moment, then* REGAN *comes in and makes his way quietly, but only fairly steadily, toward the dining-room door. He has almost reached it, when* TOM *turns.*]

TOM: Hi, Red.

REGAN: 'Evening.

TOM: Did you have a good day in town?

REGAN: Fine, thanks.

TOM: Lots of beer?

REGAN: No.

TOM: No?

REGAN: —Ale.

TOM: Why ale?

REGAN: It's quicker.

TOM: It's bitter.

REGAN: It's bitter and quicker.

TOM: You don't seem to be in very good shape.

REGAN: I'm in awful shape.

TOM: You'd better get to bed.

REGAN: —Just where I'm headed.

[*He moves toward the door again.*]

TOM: —See here a minute first, Red—

[*He turns.* TOM *goes to him and confronts him sternly.*]

REGAN: Yes?

[TOM *hesitates. Then*]

TOM: The fact is, that—[*He stops, and concludes.*]—Bring a couple of bottles of beer, will you?

REGAN: Right.

[*He goes out.* TOM *draws a deep breath of smoke, sinks down upon the sofa, and exhales it slowly.* CECELIA *comes in from the hall.*]

CECELIA: You ought to be ashamed, Tom.

TOM: Why?

CECELIA: You were terrible to Grace.

TOM: Why we should be exposed to a woman like that at all is more than I can make out.

CECELIA: She's perfectly kind and friendly.

TOM: She's a silly, idle, empty, destructive woman. And the woods are full of her.

CECELIA: Grace destructive?—She doesn't know enough to be.

TOM: It's pure instinct with her. If she were malicious, that might be interesting.—Come on—it's nearly eight.

CECELIA: She thought you were trying to insult her.

TOM: Do you have to change or are you ready?

CECELIA: It seemed to *me* you were unnecessarily rude.—I have to change.

TOM [*Rising*]: I'll warm up the car.

CECELIA: Now we've simply got to go to her breakfast in the morning.

TOM: Not me.

CECELIA: But you'll have to make *some* gesture toward her.

TOM: I only know one.

CECELIA: Tom—please be serious.

TOM: Darling, I've spent my life trying to get away from her kind of people.

CECELIA: Just what do you call her kind?

TOM: Well—people utterly without stature, without nobility of any sort.

CECELIA: It takes all kinds to make a world, doesn't it?

TOM: Yes—and then what have you got? [*He laughs, takes her face between his hands, and kisses her.*] Go get dressed.

CECELIA: All the same. I insist that if—What did you say to Regan?

TOM: Why, I—[*He stops and smiles.*]—I told him to bring some beer, but I expect he's forgotten it.

CECELIA: Oh, I see.

TOM: —Anyhow, I've been thinking: He never drinks on duty. Why shouldn't he have a right to get slightly mellow on his day off?

CECELIA: "Slightly mellow"!—When he came back last week, he could hardly stand. When I said "Good evening" to him he didn't even answer.

TOM: Maybe he couldn't speak.

CECELIA: Probably not.—I said "Don't forget the furnace, Regan," and all he did was to bow like this, with a foolish grin—so low he nearly toppled over.

TOM: It's pretty hard to gauge a bow under those conditions.

CECELIA: Of course *I* think it's selfish of us to keep him.

TOM: Selfish?

CECELIA: We're certainly depriving him of any chance he ever had to make anything of himself.

TOM: But hang it, C—he broke his hand. He'll never fight again.

CECELIA: I don't mean fighting.

TOM: These are hard times: I don't know what else there is for him.

[CECELIA *shrugs and rises.*]

CECELIA: All right. Do as you like about him. I'll leave it to you.

TOM: —And anyhow, I feel for some reason that Red's good luck for me. He's—I don't know—we understand each other. I'm awfully fond of him.

CECELIA: You must be, to ruin whatever chance in life he might have.

[*A moment. Then*]

TOM: I wouldn't do that, C. You know I wouldn't.

CECELIA: You're doing it, though. What possibly could be more degrading to a man than housework?

TOM: You're making a regular Simon Legree of me. Where's my whip?

CECELIA: No, it's simply that in your delightful, casual way, you've never thought of his side of it.

TOM [*Thoughtfully*]: —I wouldn't do that to Red. I really wouldn't. [*A moment. Then*] Ring for him, will you?

CECELIA: Not me. I have nothing to do with it.

[TOM *stares in front of him for a moment, then goes to a bell in the wall, presses it and returns to the fireplace.*]

TOM: I don't know how I'll tell him.

[*A silence. He ponders it. Then*]

CECELIA: I suppose you feel we really must go into town tonight—

TOM: Why, yes. Why?

CECELIA: She'll play again, won't she?

TOM: I hope so—and often. But the first concert's an occasion, you know.

CECELIA: I suppose all your old friends will be there, en masse.

TOM: Without a doubt. [*Then, to himself*]—All week long I've been trying to tell Red—

CECELIA: —The one you were so fond of—the Daisy something—

TOM: —Daisy Sage.

CECELIA: What's *she* doing now?

TOM: Painting, I believe.

CECELIA: Well?

TOM: I don't know. But I should imagine so.—I haven't seen her.

CECELIA: Don't you see any of them anymore?

TOM: No.

CECELIA: But why not, dearest?

[*A moment. Then*]

TOM: They won't see me.

CECELIA: —Won't see *you!*

TOM: No.—Go on now, please, like a good girl, and get ready. [*She turns, passing her hand over her eyes, and moves toward the stairs.*] What's the matter?

CECELIA: Nothing.

TOM: But dear—what is it?

CECELIA: Just this blasted headache, that's all. I've had it all day.

TOM: What a shame.—The cold air will fix you up.

CECELIA: It's that that gave it to me. I'm—honestly, Tom, I don't think I can face it. Why not telegraph, instead? Best wishes, and all that.

TOM: It wouldn't do.

CECELIA: I'm sure she'd be every bit as glad to have a telegram.

TOM: You don't understand, C. Franc has been working for years for this. She—[REGAN *comes in with bottles of beer and two glasses on a tray.*]—Just put them there, will you? [*He does so, and turns to go.*] —And wait a minute. What's the rush? Stick around.

REGAN: Certainly.

[*He waits, steadying himself in the doorway.* TOM *turns again to* CECELIA.]

TOM: —Sorry, darling, a telegram wouldn't do. I've got to be there. But there's no particular reason why you should come. I can go alone.

CECELIA: I'll come.

TOM: No, you hop into bed with a flock of aspirin. I'll be out again bright and early.

CECELIA: —I'll come, too.

[*She goes out, up the stairs.* TOM *waits a moment, then turns to* REGAN.]

TOM: —Drag up a chair.

[REGAN *brings a chair to the table.*]

REGAN: One more's about all I need. [TOM *opens the beer and fills the glasses.*] This morning if all the bad heads in the world'd been put together in a row, my head would've got up and sneered at the rest of them.

[TOM *laughs and raises his glass.*]

TOM: Here's how.

[REGAN *raises his.*]

REGAN: How. [*He drinks, and beams.*] That's the stuff.

TOM: It builds you up.

REGAN: Yo! [*He takes an old pack of cards from his pocket.*]—Seen this one?

TOM: I don't think so.

[REGAN *holds the pack up before him and releases one card after another with his thumb.*]

REGAN: —Tell me where to stop, and remember the card.

TOM: All right.

REGAN: Got it?

TOM: I've got it.

[REGAN *makes a concealed "pass," shuffles the pack rapidly and hands it to him.*]

REGAN: Where is it?

[TOM *looks through the pack.*]

TOM: Gone, of course.

REGAN: Feel in your pocket.

[TOM *feels in his breast pocket.*]

TOM: Not this time.

REGAN: No? [*He reaches into the pocket, draws out a card and shows it to him.*] That it?

TOM: Marvellous.

[REGAN *gloomily returns the pack to his pocket.*]

REGAN: I paid five dollars for that one. I'll let it go for two ninety-eight.

TOM: Not interested. [*A moment*]—Was it cold in town, today?

The Barry house at Hobe Sound

Barry embowered

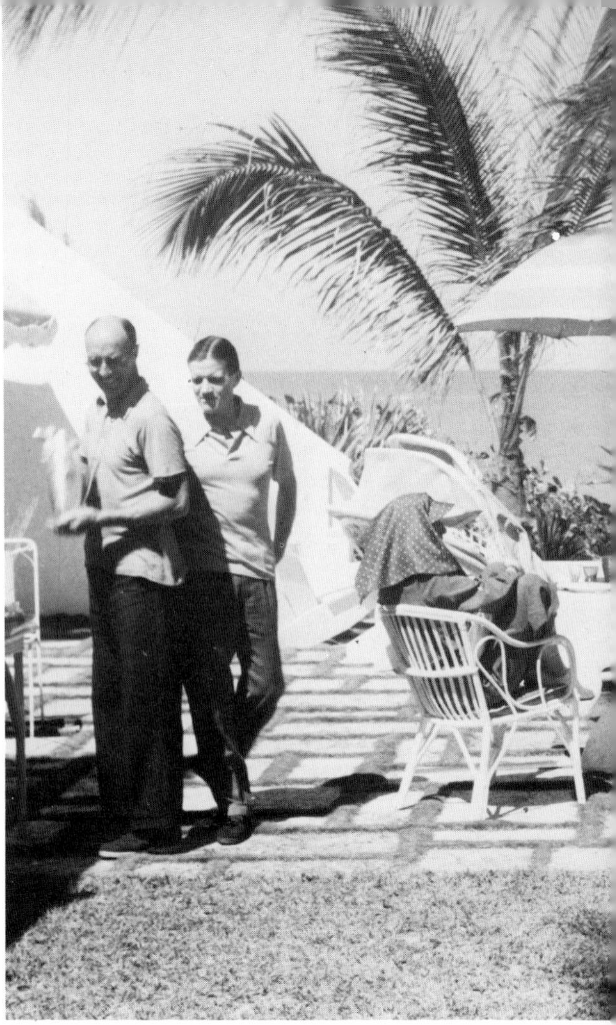

A buffet lunch at the house of Adèle and Robert Lovett at Hobe Sound, during the Second World War. Lovett, an old Yale friend of Barry, at the time this picture was taken had left his lofty position as a partner in the banking firm of Brown Brothers Harriman and was serving as Assistant Secretary of War for Air. He is the man vigorously shaking cocktails. Also present are the James Forrestals and the Barrys.

Barry liked hearing from Bob Lovett, shown here in a portrait by Gardner Cox, that if Barry had wanted to he could have had a successful career in Wall Street.

Ellen and Philip

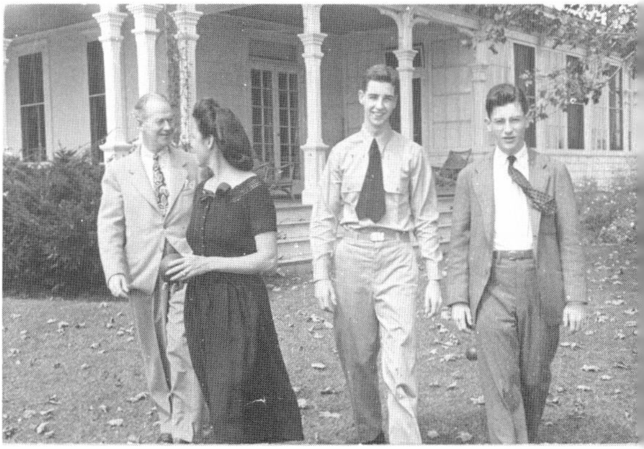

Above, left, on the road with *Without Love,* Detroit, 1942. From left to right, the director, Arthur Hopkins; automobile magnate Edsel Ford; the star of the show, Katharine Hepburn; and the Barrys. *Without Love* was damned by the critics when it reached Broadway, but thanks to Miss Hepburn it had a respectable run. Barry said of his bad notices that they would make it possible for the producers to advertise "A unanimous press on Philip Barry's new play!"

Center, the master of "Still Pond"

Philip and Ellen with their sons, Philip Semple and Jonathan, on a pleasant fall day in East Hampton. Young Philip served in the Navy during the Second World War and Jonathan was at school.

In the forties, the Barrys purchased "Sommariva," in East Hampton. Said to be the first house in town built simply for summer use, it dates back to the early eighteen-seventies. It stands on high ground above the shores of Hook Pond, with, in the distance, a view of the sea. Ellen renamed the property "Still Pond," an echo of a game of her childhood. She reckoned that Philip and she had moved twenty-six times since their marriage and she hoped that they had settled down at last, but no—a few years later, they sold "Still Pond" and took up residence in an apartment in New York.

The Barrys' friend Alexander Brook, engaged in remodeling his studio in Sag Harbor. At the time, he was also painting a portrait of Ellen.

Gerald Murphy and a granddaughter in East Hampton. Murphy was as gifted an amateur architect and interior designer as he was a painter. He turned an old dairy barn in East Hampton into an enchanting house, which he later sold to Buffie Montgomery, who sold it in turn to its present owners, Mary and Alfred de Liagre.

Ellen Barry

Robert Sherwood, S. N. Behrman, and Barry

Barry in the gondola given to him as a birthday present by the Barrys' neighbor Buffie Harkness Montgomery, who owned a house on the opposite shore of Hook Pond

A portrait painted by Ellen Barry as a birthday present to Philip in 1949, the year of his death. He was delighted that she had caught his "fox's eye."

Barry's gravestone in East Hampton

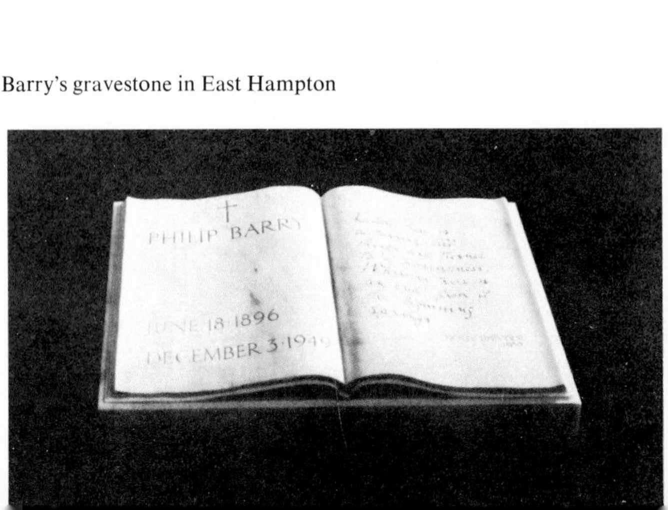

REGAN: —I don't envy those guys selling apples on the corners.

TOM [*Soberly*]: No.—Not much of a job, that.

REGAN: Women's work.

TOM: Pretty tough times, all right.

REGAN: —Some of 'em, by God, are down to selling those white flowers that stink so. [*Again he raises his glass.*] Two hundred for steel!

[*They drink.*]

TOM: I'm feeling the pinch a bit myself.

REGAN: —Say, look here, Tom—

TOM: What?

REGAN: If I—[*But he thinks better of it and concludes.*]—nothing.

[*They finish their glasses.* TOM *refills them.*]

TOM [*Suddenly*]: Red, I might as well tell you straight off—

REGAN: What?

TOM [*After a moment*]: —Nothing.

[*They drink.*]

REGAN: —All goes to show you ought to put something by.

TOM: It certainly does.

REGAN: —Clean up while you're young and close your mitt on it.

TOM: That's it.

[*A silence. Then*]

REGAN: How's your father these days?

TOM: Never better.

[REGAN *shakes his head.*]

REGAN: Tsch-tsch-tsch.

TOM: Red, do you ever think of your future?

REGAN [*Ruefully*]: I guess I'll go to hell, all right. [TOM *laughs.*] Oh—you mean here.—Now that's a funny thing, because listen, Tom—

TOM: What?

REGAN: I've been thinking: maybe I—[*He falters, and cannot go on.*] —Oh, what the hell—

TOM: But what?

[REGAN *holds out his glass.*]

REGAN: Fill her up, will you?

[TOM *refills both glasses.*]

TOM: Not much future in buttling, eh, Red?

REGAN [*With a deprecatory gesture*]: Oh, well—

TOM: I'm—I'm certainly very grateful for all you've done.

REGAN [*Uncomfortably*]: Ah!—Be still, will you?

TOM: I am, though.

REGAN: That's fine, from you.—I'll never forget, when I was—and you—[*He gulps.*] I'll never forget it.

[*He sniffs, and drinks.*]

TOM: Put it there, old man. [*They clasp hands across the table.*] You're a fine fellow.

REGAN: You're the top, boy. I don't know what you'll think of me, when I—

[*Again, he is unable to continue.*]

TOM: When you what?

REGAN: When I—well, what would you say, for instance, if I—[*He looks at him, then looks away.*] Nope, it's no good—

TOM [*Anxiously*]: You're not in trouble, are you?

REGAN: Trouble? Me? What trouble?

[TOM *once more refills the glasses. Then, steeling himself*]

TOM: —Then look here, Regan—

REGAN: Well, Chief?

[TOM *looks at him. The steel melts.*]

TOM: —Good old Red.

[REGAN *raises his glass.*]

REGAN: Tom Collier for President. The People's Choice.

TOM: Listen a minute—

REGAN: Wait! [*He takes another deep draught.*] Tom, I've just got to tell you. I've—I've—[*He grasps for* TOM*'s hand and misses it.*]—Don't hold it against me, Tom, but I'm quitting you. I've took another job.

[TOM *half rises in astonishment.*]

TOM: You've—?!

REGAN: Oh, I know what you'll say!

[TOM *drops into his chair again, and stares.*]

TOM: Holy cats, Red—

REGAN: I couldn't stand it any longer. She don't like my ways. I mean the Missus. I get on her nerves.—Last week Moe Winters told me he wanted to open a country gym and would I run it with him, on the order of Muldoon's, but with a little bar attached and, well, God help me, I give him my word.

TOM: What's there in it for you?

REGAN: Don't put it that way, Tom.

TOM: But I really want to know.

REGAN: Two hundred a month, and a smell at the gate, if any.

TOM: It sounds like a good deal.

REGAN: Ah, the hell with it!—Let's let it go. I'll phone him.

TOM [*Alarmed*]: No! [REGAN! *looks at him.*] When do you start?

REGAN: He wanted me last Wednesday. I've been trying all week to get up the nerve to tell you. But—

TOM: How long will it take you to pack?

[REGAN *grins.*]

REGAN: Well, there's my hat trunk and my shoe trunk, and the trunk for my fancy-dress ball-clothes—

TOM [*Firmly*]: You leave by noon tomorrow, you hear? Not a minute later.

[REGAN*'s grin fades.*]

REGAN: O.K., Chief.—I'm sorry you had to take it this way.

TOM: Don't be a fool. I'm overjoyed for you.

REGAN [*Uncertainly*]: Fact?

TOM: Absolute. [*He raises his glass.*] Here's to the new job.

REGAN: —Take it from me, boy, you're the goods.

TOM: You've got your points, too, you know.

[REGAN *rises, swaying slightly, and raises his glass.*]

REGAN: Anyhow—

[TOM *rises and raises his.*]

TOM: Anyhow.

[*They drain their glasses, put them down and again clasp hands.*]

REGAN: You'll explain to the Missus?

TOM: Of course.

REGAN: Tell her I'm sorry—hope no inconvenience—but—

TOM: I'll explain.

REGAN: So long, Tom.

TOM: Good-bye, Red.

REGAN: So long, Tom.

TOM: Good-bye, Red.

REGAN: I'll give you a ring how it goes.

TOM: Do that.

REGAN: Keep your bib clean.

TOM: I will, old boy.

[*Suddenly* REGAN *sobers, looks at him intently for a long moment, then touches him on the shoulder and says:*]

REGAN: Good luck, Tom.

[*Turns abruptly, and swiftly and steadily goes to the door and out.* TOM *takes a deep breath and seats himself at the table, with his back to the stairs, in utter dejection. He picks up* REGAN*'s pack of cards and moodily glances through it.* CECELIA *comes down the stairs in a lovely negligee. A moment, then she speaks lowly:*]

CECELIA: Tom—

TOM [*Without turning*]: Hello. Ready?

CECELIA: Did you tell him?

TOM: I'll miss that guy. I'll miss having him around.

[*She goes to him.*]

CECELIA: I know, dear. But it's for the best. I'm sure of it.

[TOM *puts down the cards.*]

TOM: I've got a feeling that my luck's going with him.

CECELIA: No, no!—I'm your luck.

[*She draws him into her arms and takes his head against her breast. A moment. Then*]

TOM: You feel good, C.

CECELIA: Do I, dear?

TOM: You haven't any clothes on. Go on—dress—dress quickly—we've got to run.

[*She moves from him toward the stairs, where she turns again.*]

CECELIA: —Come and help me? [*He looks at her for an instant, then goes to her. She turns into his arms. He holds her to him for a moment, then she leans away from him, provocatively.*] No, you'd better not. [*She glances down at the negligee, arms out.*] Look—I came across it in the bottom drawer, and my spine simply melted.—Do you remember it?

[*He picks up the edge of the loose sleeve and kisses it.*]

TOM: —Quebec.

CECELIA: Then you do!—That funny little French hotel—

TOM [*Gazing at her*]: Yes.

CECELIA: —Darling place.—Wasn't it cold that morning?—Frost on the windows an inch thick.—Remember?

TOM: —We couldn't see out—

CECELIA: We didn't want to.

TOM: No one else could see in.

CECELIA: Breakfast before the fire—shivering—Remember—?

TOM: I remember.

CECELIA: We didn't finish it—

TOM: No.

CECELIA [*With a little laugh*]: There was only one way to keep warm.

[*He moves toward her.*]

TOM: Oh C, darling—

[*She retreats, up one step of the stairs.*]

CECELIA: No.—You'll make us late.

TOM: What of it?

CECELIA: It's late already. It's—we might miss the concert altogether.

TOM: What if we do?

CECELIA: Tom, you're the limit! Ten minutes ago you said—[*A moment. Then, in another voice*] Tom—

TOM: Oh yes, darling. What—

CECELIA: You go in alone. I've decided to stay here.

TOM: You've—?

CECELIA: Yes. It's too cold. I'm going to tuck myself into my warm bed, and—you'll need your heavy coat, won't you? It's here—[*She goes into the hall, returning with an overcoat which she leaves upon a chair.*] Good night, love. I'll miss you—[*He is about to take her in his arms, but she retreats, with the same provocative smile and an admonitory gesture.*] No, no!—Good night, dear. Keep warm.

[*He turns from her. She mounts the stairs, turns once, smiles down upon him curiously, and goes out leaving the door open. A moment. Then he takes up his coat, crosses the room, puts out the lights, and is returning to the hall doorway when he hears* CECELIA *singing lowly to herself from upstairs. He stops, listens a moment, then moves slowly to the side table, where he leaves his coat upon a chair and takes up the telephone.*]

TOM: Western Union, please. [*A moment*] Western Union? [*The curtain begins to fall.*] I want to send a telegram.

CURTAIN

■ ACT II ■

SCENE II

At DAISY SAGE*'s. Late afternoon on a fine bright day the following May. The sitting-room is as before, except for the painting materials upon the worktable, and a large easel, turned away from the front, at the window.*

JOE *is seated upon the sofa, smoking.* FRANC *stands at the window, looking out. A moment, then she turns abruptly to* JOE.

FRANC: —But what if *she* doesn't come?

JOE: She'll come.

[FRANC *leaves the window and seats herself, tense, upon a chair near him.*]

FRANC: My nerves are like that.

JOE: Have a cigarette?

FRANC: No.

JOE: It ought to be quite a meeting. Only that once, months ago—think of it.

FRANC: And in a speakeasy!

JOE: —Like old times, though, like a reunion. That is, until *they* came for him.—You know, I think the last thing he wanted to do was to go to that party with them.

FRANC: She is pretty, the wife.—But did you notice? In his top hat, when he put it on, suddenly he looked like only anybody.

JOE: Domestication works fast, when it works.

FRANC: —Well, Daisy has not spoke of him one time since. Never, never will she forgive us this.—Give me a cigarette. What did he say to you?

[*He gives her a cigarette and lights it for her.*]

JOE: He just telephoned that he wanted to see me, said it seemed years. —Your hand's shaking.

FRANC: I know it.—What did you tell him?—Why shouldn't it shake?

JOE: I said I'd be back at five. Then I left a note on the door: "Had to go to Daisy's. Come there."—It wouldn't if you smoked less.

FRANC: At five. [*She looks at her watch.*] Ach, Gott!

JOE: You're getting emotional in your old age, Frankie.

FRANC: —But why did you do it? It was well enough left alone.

JOE: I like Tom, and he sounded pathetic. I imagine he saw her exhibition, and—

FRANC: What makes you think he did?

JOE: He said he was telephoning from the Overton Gallery.—I wonder what he thought of it.

FRANC: What did you?

JOE: I know so damn little about painting.

FRANC: I know less.—But it all seemed to me so fresh—done with such spirit.

JOE: That's it!

FRANC: —Bold—what-you-call-it—un—in—without compromising.

JOE: Yes.—And the real stuff. No fakiness.

FRANC: —Every one of them Daisy. No little Matisses or Picassos.

[*A moment*]

JOE: But Franc—

FRANC [*Nerves again*]: Yes? All right. What?

JOE: What really did you think of them?

[*She shrugs.*]

FRANC: I tell you I am not—what-you-say—competent to judge.

JOE: What did they do to you, Franc?

[*She looks at him sharply, hesitates. Then*]

FRANC: —Nothing. I am sorry. But nothing—

JOE: Nor to me.

[*She grasps his arm.*]

FRANC: —But we must believe in her, Joe!

JOE [*In pain*]: We do, don't we?—Oh Lord, if only all my friends made shirts for a living.

FRANC: Yes. You could say "That is not a good shirt" quite easily.

JOE: This afternoon—after a few minutes we duck out on them, understand?

FRANC: Joe, I don't like it. I am afraid of this. I think it is not wise.

JOE: —If only they'd have one of their good old-time rows. I'll bet he and that wife of his never had a decent scrap in their lives.

FRANC [*Thoughtfully*]: —And still, maybe seeing him, Daisy finds it is all over—finished—cold. Sometimes that is so. I hope for her it will be so.

JOE: Listen, child: it's May, and the trees are in bloom.

FRANC [*Scornfully*]: You should write in German.

JOE: Poor Tom. Poor guy. He's up against it for fair now, Franc.

FRANC: Why now more than usual?

JOE: Well, I ran into Hal Foster today, and—

FRANC: Foster—?—The one who did those stories?

JOE: That's the boy. He's finished a new novel that's even better, they say. Apparently Tom thinks he can grab it for The Bantam, and stage a comeback on the strength of it. A sort of a last straw. He's to meet him this afternoon.

FRANC: Oh, good!

[JOE *shakes his head.*]

JOE: No, not so: Foster told me that hard up as he is, he'd be damned before he'd go with a house that was responsible for "Young Ecstasy" and—

FRANC: But you should have talked to him, Joe!

JOE: I did, till I was blue in the face. He just kept saying "Then how about *you?*" It was no use explaining how Tom thought I'd do better with—[JOE *glances quickly at the door, and rises.*] Look out!

FRANC: Him?

JOE: Yes, or—[DAISY *comes in.*] Oh, hello, Daisy!

[DAISY *pulls off her hat and gloves and looks at them.*]

DAISY: My, you're hearty. [*To* FRANC] What's the matter?

FRANC: With me?

DAISY: Yes. You look queer.

FRANC: I don't like the spring. I don't like May and the trees in bloom.

DAISY: No? Nor do I. I say it's maple syrup, and I say the hell with it. [*She seats herself near them.*] Well, the show's over. It's been a fine week. I've learned a lot about new painters, the so-called Public and the so-called Press.

FRANC: There are no judges of one's work but oneself, Daisy.

DAISY: Then you don't by any chance agree with them?

FRANC: I would sooner sleep with an art critic than agree with him.

DAISY: It's touching the way my friends have rallied round. Stout hearts. Thanks, thanks.—But oh heaven!—If only someone I love and trust would be honest with me!

JOE: And what do you call what we've been?

DAISY: Friendly, Joe, very friendly.

JOE: *I* tell you: let's all get drunk.

DAISY: No thanks. [*For a brief moment she covers her face with her hands, then looks up again.*] It's all right. It's over. Let's talk about something. Who knows anything?

[*A silence.* DAISY*'s head sinks again. Finally* FRANC *ventures:*]

FRANC: Jim and Nancy Peters are going to have a baby.

DAISY [*Absently*]: A boy?

FRANC: I think so.

DAISY: Good for them.

[*Another silence. Then*]

JOE: —Er—Tom Collier rang me up this afternoon.

[*A moment. Then*]

DAISY: Oh? How is he?

JOE: He sounded sunk.

DAISY: That's too bad. [*She cools her wrists. Then, to* FRANC]—You know, it's *hot.*

FRANC: It *is* hot.—Don't be bitter, Daisy.

DAISY: I heard grand things about Nova Scotia yesterday.—Why should I be bitter?

FRANC: You shouldn't.—About what? Where is it?

DAISY: North, way north.—Better! Me!—They say it's beautiful beyond words, and you can live there on oh, so little.

JOE: He said—I mean Tom did—that—

DAISY: Joe, you seem to have an idea that I might be interested in what he'd say—

JOE: Well—

DAISY: But as it happens, I'm not. [*To* FRANC] There are miles of green meadows and a seacoast that's nobody's business. Woods, as well. [*To* JOE]—I suppose he was full of explanations about those choice eggs The Bantam Press has been laying lately.

JOE: No, he didn't mention them. He only said—

DAISY: Why tell *me?* [*To* FRANC] The only out's the swimming. It's too cold. But other things make up for it. [*To* JOE]—He always gets colds in the spring—I suppose his voice was gone entirely—

JOE: It didn't seem to be.

DAISY [*To* FRANC]: It's like Maine, they say. Only better, much.

FRANC: Not too many people?

[DAISY *closes her eyes.*]

DAISY: No people. Gloriously, happily, mercifully, no people. [*The buzzer of the door sounds.*] Joe—will you? [*To* FRANC]—Speaking of no people. [JOE *presses a button to open the door.* DAISY *continues to* FRANC.] Imagine Joe thinking that at this date *I* should give a damn what—

[TOM *comes in with a briefcase in his hand.*]

TOM: Joey! How are you? [*He drops the brief-case upon the work-table.*] Franc!

FRANC: Tom, you look fine.

[*He turns to* DAISY.]

TOM: Hello, Daisy.

DAISY [*So coolly*]: Hello. How have you been?

TOM: In rude health, thanks.—And you?

DAISY: Never better.

TOM: Oh, it's fine to see you! I've been starving for you—all of you.

DAISY: Thanks.

TOM: How's the job?

DAISY: The magazine job?

TOM: Yes.

DAISY: I gave it up last winter.—A trifle—shall we say "quixotic"?—of me?

TOM: Shall we? [*He looks from one to the other of them.*] Listen: I love you three, I love you. [*He takes* FRANC*'s head in his hands and kisses her brow.*] Oh Lord! [*Gives* JOE *a friendly shove*] Lord Almighty—[*Laughs joyfully, seats himself and gazes fondly at them. There is a long silence. Finally*] Holy cats! Talk to me, will you?—Am I a leper? [*Silence. He leans forward.*] Now listen, the lot of you: I've had enough of this nonsense. For months you've been avoiding me like the plague and I won't stand for it. You're important to me and by heaven, I'm going to hang onto your coattails, dog your footsteps, sit on your doorsteps, until you're ready to grant that a man can marry, and go on being a friend. Is that understood?—Well, then: who's seen Sandy Patch?

[*Then, in a rush*]

JOE: I have.

FRANC: So have I.

DAISY: We all have.

TOM: What's he doing?

JOE: A war group in bronze for some town in Texas. He's making them look like sheep.

TOM: Good boy!

DAISY: —Except that they'll probably throw it back at him.

JOE: He'll get paid, though. Sam Frankl sees to that for him now.

TOM: How's your book doing?

JOE: Fair.—Of course nothing like The Bantam's "Indian Summer" or "Young Ecstasy."

TOM: Ouch.
JOE: What the devil made you take them on?
TOM: Money. —Ah, but Joey, I'm reforming! Did you know it?
JOE: In time, I hope.—How?
TOM: Williamson, Warren can have those bright boys now, and welcome.
JOE: It's about where they belong.
TOM: Wait till you see The Bantam's new list.
JOE: I'm waiting.
TOM: —That was certainly a foul format Brandon gave your book.
JOE: The words are there.
TOM: If you can read them. What's the stock they printed it on—paper-towelling?—I hear you're a hit, Franc.
FRANC: It has gone well enough.

[*He looks at* DAISY, *hestitates. Then*]

TOM: I—I saw your exhibition today.
DAISY: Oh really?—Funny I missed you. What did you think of it?
TOM: Well—
DAISY [*Suddenly, eagerly*]: Tell me!
TOM: I don't think you were ready to show yet. How did it happen?
DAISY: Saunders and Munn arranged it.
TOM: Your old editors? The fashion boys?
DAISY: What about it?

[TOM *shakes his head.*]

TOM: Daisy, Daisy.—How were the notices?
DAISY: Appalling.
TOM: I suppose their reasons were all wrong—
DAISY: Of course.—What are yours?

[*A moment. Then*]

TOM: Well, you've been painting less than a year—
DAISY: Yes.
TOM: —And yet you had about thirty canvases to show.

[*Now* DAISY *is well on her mettle.*]

DAISY: Thirty-two.
TOM: It's a lot, Daisy.
DAISY: So you didn't care for any of them.
TOM: Oh yes!—One I loved particularly: the one of the doorstep, with the milk bottles. I'd like to own that one.
DAISY: —Number Seven.—Sorry, it's not for sale.
TOM: Two hundred—?
DAISY: Nope.

TOM: Two-fifty!
DAISY: Nope.
TOM: Seventy-five—
DAISY: Nope.
TOM: Four hundred and one—
DAISY: Nope.
TOM: I wouldn't take it as a gift.
DAISY: That's all right, then.
TOM: Of course your drawing's a marvel. Lord, how that's come along!
DAISY: —Only what?
TOM: Good draughtsmanship's not to be sneezed at, is it?
DAISY: Certainly not. Look at Belcher.
TOM: No—at Goya.
DAISY: Thanks so much.
TOM: Of course it depends on what you want to be. I thought it was a painter.
[FRANC *rises.*]
DAISY: So did I.—Goya painted pretty well, too, I thought.
TOM: In the first year? I doubt it.
DAISY: I wasn't aware it took a definite length of time.
TOM: —And living in cities all your life, you know.
DAISY: Perhaps I'd better hie me to some sylvan dell.
TOM: I don't think it would hurt a bit.
DAISY: —Listen, you: if you can show me a purer cobalt than the winter sky over the East River any afternoon at four—
TOM: That's not the point.
[DAISY'*s voice is higher.*]
DAISY: What is?
TOM: Fever—rush—hysteria—all day, every day.
[DAISY *turns away.*]
DAISY: Oh, go to hell, will you?
[FRANC *moves toward the door.*]
TOM: Sure. When do we start?
FRANC: Come along, Joe.
[JOE *follows her.*]
DAISY: —And leave me with this mossback? This—[*Again she turns upon* TOM.]—So I'm to sit under a parasol and paint tight little cows in streams, am I?
TOM: That's not what I said.
[*Unnoticed by* DAISY, JOE *and* FRANC *have gone out.*]

DAISY: —Something suitable as an overmantel for the Home of Her Dreams, I suppose.

TOM: Now you're being bullheaded.

DAISY [*Turning*]: Bullheaded!—He call *me* bull—[*She sees that* FRANC *and* JOE *are no longer there.*] Oh, you snakes—

TOM [*With a gesture*]: Well—

DAISY: Well? What more, Teacher?

TOM: All I said and all I'm saying is, you can't expect, the first crack out of the box, to—*you've* got to *work,* Daisy.

DAISY: Sweet heaven! What else have I been doing? What have I done but?

TOM: —But differently—with such pains. You're turning out too much, you know it.

[*Suddenly the fight goes out of her.*]

DAISY: Maybe, maybe.—Anything's too much.

TOM: Ah, darling—

DAISY: No!—Don't soften on me. Stay tough!

TOM: I do believe that's it, though. I believe it's the whole story: still hung over from the old job. Pressure, pressure all the time. Still rushing countless sketches through against a magazine's deadline.

[*She looks away from him. Her hand gropes blindly for his and finds it.*]

DAISY: —Anyway, against some deadline—

TOM: Daisy—darling—

DAISY: You're cruel, inhuman. You're a brute.

TOM: Oh Daisy—

DAISY: Thanks for being.

TOM: If you mean it—

DAISY: From my heart—[*She looks at him, smiling now.*] Oh, you skunk—

[*He laughs, relieved.*]

TOM: Worse. Much worse.

DAISY [*Serious again*]: Who but you, Tom? [*She points her finger at him.*] Look: only you and strangers honest with me ever.

[*He draws her down beside him on the sofa.*]

TOM: —The country's the place to work, Daisy. Listen: There's a grand little house about six miles from us. Woods, hills, meadows—you can get it for almost nothing.

DAISY: That's about my price.

TOM: It could easily be painted up. What about a white roof for it?

DAISY: Oh, lovely idea!

TOM: C discovered it. She can find out all about it. I'll tell her who it's for.

[*But at this,* DAISY'*s mood changes.*]

DAISY: Don't dream of it.

TOM: Why not?

DAISY: I've got other places in mind.

TOM: Anyhow, go somewhere.

DAISY: Sure—somewhere.

TOM: You're going to be good, Daisy. Don't think I don't think you're good.

DAISY: I won't. I won't think anything.

TOM: This is a big day for me, do you know it?

DAISY: How?

TOM: Well, I've been seeing the folly of my ways here lately. Poor C—I must have been sweet to live with this past week. She's been grand about it, though.

DAISY: I'm sure she has.

TOM: I—suddenly, for some reason, I saw that I'd got off the track—my track. It was pretty painful—But I'm getting back on, I think.

DAISY: I'm glad, Tom. You must, you know.

TOM: Did you ever hear of a fellow named Hal Foster?

DAISY: No. What does he do?

TOM: Writes. My God, how he writes!—And nobody knows it—not yet—

DAISY: Have you got him?

TOM: I'm getting him. He's done a fine, poisonous short novel that makes Candide look sick. [*In growing excitement*] I'm going to make a grand type-job of it, advertise it all over the place, and sell it at two bucks. I don't care if I lose my shirt on it.—I'm to meet him at six this afternoon, to make arrangements.

DAISY: It must be nearly that now. You'd better go.

TOM: —Daisy.—Have you missed me, Daisy?

DAISY: You? Well, I'll tell you, it's this way: I—

[*But she stops and looks at him, drops her bantering tone, and nods, dumbly.*]

TOM: Much?

[*Again she nods, and adds, under her breath:*]

DAISY: —Skunk, skunk.

TOM: Oh, and I you!—It's a lot of nonsense, this. It's ridiculous.

[*She looks at her watch.*]

DAISY: It *is* six.

TOM: Hell.

DAISY: You'd better run.

TOM: We need each other, we two do.

DAISY: You think?

TOM: Most terribly. I'm convinced of it. There never were such friends as you and me. It's wicked to give that up, to lose anything so fine for no good reason.—Why you, of all people, for a shabby, lowdown question of convention, fit only to be considered by shabby, low-down—

DAISY: Wait a minute!

TOM: A hundred times I'd have given my eyes to see you, to talk to you—

DAISY: Well—here I am—

TOM [*Eagerly*]: Daisy—may I come again?—Just now and then, you know?

DAISY [*After a moment*]: —If you like—just now and then.

TOM: Oh my sweet dear—thanks!

DAISY: But don't say "sweet dear." That belongs to another life, years ago.

TOM: Oh—there are to be rules, are there?

DAISY: One or two. One strict one—

[*She hesitates.*]

TOM: What?

DAISY: Never secret. Never hidden.

TOM: No, no!

DAISY: —Always open, as before.

TOM: But of course, of course!

DAISY: I couldn't go it otherwise.

TOM: Why should a friendship be hidden? What's there to hide?

DAISY: It gets misunderstood.

TOM: It won't, it can't, or the whole world's rotten.

DAISY: It's been pretty ripe for a long time, Tommy.

TOM: "Tommy"! [*He laughs exultantly and draws her into his arms. They stand rocking back and forth, laughing in delight.*] Oh my darling, how grand this is!

DAISY: I see you run to tweeds this season.

TOM: I even have a horse now—practically a county squire.

DAISY: Look out for it.

TOM: Oh, it's tame.

DAISY: I mean going county.

TOM: Never you fear! I wouldn't be let. I'm a terribly queer duck to them.

DAISY: "Lit'ry," I suppose.

TOM: "Very artistic."

DAISY: Are they good and dull?

TOM: Crashing.

DAISY: —And respectable.

TOM: My God, how!

DAISY: *We* aren't respectable.

TOM: Not a bit. Never shall be.

DAISY: For which, praise heaven.

TOM: Heaven, I praise you that Daisy and I are not—Kiss the boy, Daisy.

DAISY: No.—You've got to go.

TOM: Why? Would it take long?

[*She laughs, and pecks his cheek.*]

DAISY: There.

TOM: Ask me am I happy—

DAISY: It's all right, isn't it?

TOM: Magnificent.—All as before.

DAISY: Yes.—But for one thing.

TOM: What?

[*She leaves his arms.*]

DAISY: We aren't in love any more.—Now run. You might miss what's-his-name.

TOM: How about lunch tomorrow?

DAISY: It's fine with me.

TOM: The old place?

DAISY: I'd love it.

TOM: One o'clock?

DAISY: One o'clock.

TOM: —And we'll dine at John Donovan's. He's opened a new place on Forty-eighth Street.

DAISY: Dine?

TOM: Why not?

DAISY: All right.

TOM: The next day's Wednesday, isn't it? I said I'd drive out in the morning to see Pat Atkins. He's been sick again.

DAISY: Poor dear. I'm sorry.

TOM: He's better now.—Come along with me, Daisy.

DAISY: Wednesday? No—Wednesday, I—

TOM: If it's a good day we'll take a picnic. What do you say?

DAISY: I—I guess so.

TOM: Fine!—We'll get back in time to—let's see, can I stay in town Wednesday night? Yes, of course, I can. I want to see that black woman dance.

DAISY: Which one?

TOM: Down on Grand Street.

DAISY: Oh yes, I've heard about her!

TOM: We can look in, anyway.—Thursday I'm at the Press all day. But Friday—

DAISY: Wait a minute, Tom.—You said only now and—

TOM: I'll bring Hal Foster in about four on Friday. Will you be here?

DAISY: I—I think so.

TOM: Good-bye then, darling. Till tomorrow!

DAISY: Good-bye, Tom.

[*He takes her face in his hands, kisses it several times, then her mouth, briefly.*]

TOM: Sweet dear, sweet dear—[*He releases her.*] One o'clock?

DAISY: One o'clock.

[*He goes swiftly to the door, where he turns once more.*]

TOM: —*Ten minutes* to one!

[*He is gone, his footsteps heard upon the stairs. She stands rigid, exalted, her eyes shining. Then she sees his briefcase, left behind upon the worktable. She stares at it for a long time, apprehension growing in her eyes. Then she murmurs "Franc," runs to the door, flings it open and calls in terror:*]

DAISY: Franc!

[*Then returns, puts* TOM's *briefcase upon a chair, then places a work-box upon her table and begins filling it with tools and materials.* FRANC *comes in.*]

FRANC: Daisy?—What is it? Your voice frightened me.

DAISY: Franc, you're the one woman I know who can hold her tongue.

[FRANC *shrugs.*]

FRANC: What is not my business—[*She sees what* DAISY *is doing, and her casual air is replaced by a real anxiety.*] Packing? What's this? What for? You and—? Oh, Daisy, hold on a minute. Wait, Liebchen. Think, are you wise, Daisy—

DAISY: I'm going alone—a long way, for a long time.

FRANC: To that place you said?

DAISY [*A sudden idea*]: Yes!

FRANC: Wait! I come with you—

DAISY: No, I don't want anyone now. Later, maybe.

FRANC: But what is it, dear?

DAISY: I guess I'm running for my life, Franc.

FRANC: —Tom again.

DAISY: —Still.

FRANC: It's no better—

DAISY [*Packing furiously*]: —It's worse.

FRANC: Poor child.

DAISY: No, no! I'm glad.—But I've got to get out.

FRANC: Yes, that is wise.

DAISY: No one's to know where I've gone to.

FRANC: No.

DAISY: No mess—it's to avoid one I'm going.

FRANC: —But compose yourself, Daisy. Be calm.

DAISY: I can't! Look—[*She points to the briefcase.*] He went without it. He'll come back for it. And if I see him again for one more minute I'll die.

FRANC: He loves you, Daisy?

DAISY: I don't know. I don't believe *he* knows. But—[*She looks up from her packing.*] Oh Franc—he's so young!—Did you notice how young he looked?

FRANC: Yes, like a child.

DAISY: All slim and brown and sandy.

FRANC: Quick, Daisy!

DAISY [*Far away*]: He'll always be like that—even when he's old. I know! —And the way he stands—that funny way—stiff—with his feet out—

FRANC: —What they call duck-footed, eh?

DAISY [*Indignantly*]: Not at all. It's a perfectly natural way to stand. It's a fine, strong way to stand.

FRANC: Hurry, darling. Run quick!

DAISY: Yes, yes, I must.

[*She resumes her packing.*]

FRANC: Will you take a trunk?

DAISY: The small one.

FRANC: How do you go—by train?

DAISY: I don't know. Boat, I think.

FRANC: But when? From where?

DAISY: I guess Boston. [*A moment*] Perhaps I'd better see him just once more. Maybe if I can explain to him how impossible it is for us to—

FRANC: No!—And you go to Boston tonight.

DAISY: Yes. Yes, that's right. [FRANC *goes into the bedroom.* DAISY *continues to pack for a moment, then calls:*] Franc!

FRANC: What now?

DAISY: When those things come back from the Gallery, cover them, will you?

FRANC: Yes, dear.

DAISY: —Number Seven—do you hear me, Franc?

FRANC: I hear.

DAISY: Pack Number Seven and send it to him at the Press.

[FRANC *re-enters.*]

FRANC: All right, dear.

DAISY: You're lunching with him tomorrow.

FRANC: So?

DAISY: At the old place, at one o'clock.

FRANC: One o'clock.

DAISY: Franc—

FRANC: Yes, darling?

[DAISY *gathers up some paint tubes.*]

DAISY: When you see him—

FRANC: Yes, darling—

DAISY: Kiss him for me. [*She realizes what she has said, and murmurs:*] Kiss him for me—[*Then hurls a tube into the box, in fury.*] *Kiss* him for me!

[*The buzzer sounds imperatively.* DAISY *starts in alarm.* FRANC *takes her arm.*]

FRANC: Come—and don't speak—

[*She leads her toward the bedroom, stopping to press the button at the fireplace. They go out.* TOM *is heard running up the stairs. He hurries in, calling:*]

TOM: Daisy—? [*There is no answer. He goes to the table, and calls again:*] Daisy!

[*A moment. Then* DAISY'*s voice is heard faintly from the next room:*]

DAISY: Hello—

TOM: I forgot my case. [*He finds it upon the chair and picks it up.*] It's all right. I've got it. [*At the door he turns once more and calls:*] Don't be late tomorrow! Remember! Twelve-thirty!

[*And goes out. Again footsteps are heard upon the stairs, and a door slams below.*]

CURTAIN

■ ACT III ■

SCENE I

At TOM COLLIER*'s, six months later. Ten o'clock of a bright Sunday morning. Alterations have been made, and the old library has become a chaste dining room. Now, at last,* TOM*'s house is* CECELIA*'s house, which is to say, The House in Good Taste.*

The door beside the fireplace at Right opens, through the hall, upon a large new living room. The library furniture has been replaced with a dining-room table, sideboard, serving table and chairs. The large table is set for breakfast and there are various breakfast dishes being kept hot upon the serving table.

CECELIA *and* OWEN *are at breakfast,* CECELIA *seated and* OWEN *standing, napkin in hand, half turned in the direction of the serving table, toward which* GRACE *is moving with a coffee cup.*

GRACE: Oh no, thanks! I love to serve myself. It's so English.

[OWEN *reseats himself.* GRACE *refills her cup and returns to the table with it.* CECELIA *presses a button upon the table.*]

CECELIA: I'll order some more hot.

[OWEN *takes a swallow of water, puts down his napkin and pushes back his chair.*]

OWEN: Well, for the morning after a party, I feel pretty good. Where's the birthday boy?

CECELIA: Still recovering upstairs.

GRACE: He was never more amusing. Honestly, when he did that skit from his new magazine, I thought I couldn't stand it. I was in stitches.

OWEN: —What's happened to the artistic element? Still asleep?

CECELIA: Miss Sage and Fisk insisted upon walking to the station with La Schmidt. It turned out that she had to take an early train.

GRACE: I've never known a musician to make such difficulties about playing.

CECELIA: She's used to her own violin.

GRACE: But is there any differ—? [*Then, thoughtfully*] Yes—I suppose there is.—The Sage is rather a number, isn't she? Do you know she actually spent six months in Tierra del Fuego?

OWEN: Nova Scotia.

GRACE: I mean Nova Scotia.

CECELIA: Yes, I'd heard.

GRACE: The places they go!—C, I wish I knew how you get hold of such interesting people.

CECELIA: I asked them as a particular favor, for Tom's birthday. I insisted on it. It was part of the surprise party.

[GRACE *sighs.*]

GRACE: —They invariably *say* they'll come to me, and then at the last minute something always happens.

CECELIA: —Besides they're very old friends of his. I said he was longing to see them.—I think he really has missed them a little.

OWEN: Clever Cecelia.

CECELIA: Why?

OWEN: Real security at last, eh?

CECELIA: Do you object?

[GRACE *looks at them suspiciously.*]

GRACE: What are you talking about? [*There is no answer. She rises.*] Oh, you subtle people! I wish I were subtle.

[CECELIA *presses the bell again.*]

CECELIA: I wish someone would answer this bell.

[GRACE *looks about her.*]

GRACE: Darling, you *have* done wonders with this house. It's all in such perfect taste, now.

CECELIA: I wish Tom was as enthusiastic about it as you are.

GRACE: Oh, men never like changes.

CECELIA: Unless they think of them themselves.—We're having a charming time about the roof.

OWEN: The roof?

CECELIA: It's got to be fixed—and ever since he came back from Bermuda last winter he's been saying he wanted a white roof—been wanting to whitewash it white.

GRACE: What!?

OWEN [*Simultaneously*]: The roof here?

CECELIA: Yes. They're all white in Bermuda.

OWEN: But this isn't Bermuda.

CECELIA: I've tried to explain that to him.

OWEN [*To* GRACE]: But I don't think I've ever seen a white roof around here, have you?

GRACE: Let me think. [*She thinks, painfully. Then*]—No.

CECELIA: He says, What does that matter? He wants one. He thinks they're pretty. He thinks—[*In sudden irritation*] Oh, he can be exasperating! [*To* OWEN] His father sent him a check for his birthday: he may accept it, he may not.

GRACE: Not accept a *check?*

CECELIA: —Because it's from him.

GRACE: Well, I'm amazed.—A whopper, too, I'll bet.

CECELIA: I don't know. I didn't see it.

OWEN: I thought he'd got over the nonsense about his father.

CECELIA: So did I. Everything has been simply beautiful for months. He's been so pleased with Tom, and the way business has been going. Apparently someone told him about it.

OWEN: Williamson, probably.

CECELIA: —Or Warren. I don't know which.

GRACE: Are they the ones that want to buy The Bantam Press?

CECELIA: —To buy into it, yes.

GRACE: How does Tom feel about that?

[CECELIA *shrugs.*]

OWEN: He's made the price so high they'll have to refuse it.

CECELIA: Not if *you* tell them not to, Owen!

OWEN: I thought I'd explained all that to you.

[*A moment. Then*]

CECELIA: —I suppose I'll have to get the coffee myself. [*She rings again.*] I told Tom that with *him* back, the maids would do nothing.

OWEN: It does seem funny, seeing him around again.

GRACE: I was overcome last night.—How did it happen, C?

CECELIA: The new job didn't pan out. Tom ran into him somewhere and telephoned to ask if he could bring him out for a day or two, he'd been ill. There was nothing to do but say yes. Now, of course, he wants to keep him.

GRACE: Why not—you know—just give him something, and—?

CECELIA: He won't take anything without earning it. Tom swears he'll teach him manners—at least to the extent of calling us "Sir" and "Madam." He said it was the one birthday present he really—[*She sees* REGAN *standing, beaming, in the doorway.*] Oh.

REGAN: Did someone ring?

CECELIA: Several times. Will you bring some hot coffee, please?

REGAN: Sure thing.

[*He takes the coffeepot and goes out with it.*]

[GRACE *laughs.*]

GRACE: Manners!

CECELIA: I'm afraid he's hopeless.

GRACE: You know, I can't get over old Rufus K. actually sending checks. He can be nice, can't he?

CECELIA: Extremely. Did I tell you? He's invited us to spend the winter with him in town.

GRACE: Not in the big house?

CECELIA: Yes.

GRACE: But it's the most unheard-of thing I've ever heard of!

CECELIA: We may not go. Tom's not too keen for that, either.

GRACE: He's mad!—Of course you can persuade him. It will *be such*— [TOM *comes down the stairs, a trifle white and wan.*] Ah! Good morning, host!

TOM: Is it?—How are you, Grace? Hello, Owen. [*He seats himself and eyes the food distrustfully.*] Did Franc get her train?

CECELIA: I imagine so.

TOM: I meant to get up. Where are Joe and Daisy?

CECELIA: They went walking.

[TOM *settles back painfully in his chair.*]

GRACE: Oh come now! It's not as bad as that.

TOM: Lady, you don't know. [*To* CECELIA] Was I dreadful?

CECELIA: You were delightful.

TOM: Oh, don't say that!—That means I put on an act.

GRACE: You were the life of the party.

[TOM *cringes.*]

TOM: Good Grace.

[REGAN *comes in with the coffeepot and a glass of what appears to be milk.*]

REGAN [*Heartily*]: How're'ye, Tom, my boy!

TOM: —'Morning, Red.

[REGAN *puts the coffeepot upon the serving table.* TOM *looks guiltily at* CECELIA, *who turns away.* REGAN *comes beaming from the serving table, the glass in hand.*]

REGAN: Look what Baby brought you—

[TOM *rises and goes to him.*]

TOM: —Just a minute. [*He puts his arm through his, turns him away from the others and low enough to be heard by no one but him, murmurs:*] Look, Red—if you don't mind, I think you'd better be "Regan" from now on, and us "Sir" and "Madam."—You're a pretty good actor.

[REGAN *stiffens into the Perfect Butler.*]

REGAN [*Audibly*]: Right, Sir. H'I knows me place, Sir.

[TOM *laughs, and returns to the table.*]

TOM: Don't lay it on.

REGAN: Oh no, Sir.

[*He offers the glass obsequiously.* TOM *takes it.*]

GRACE: Milk?!

TOM: —Punch. [*He makes a face over it and returns it to* REGAN.] Could you possibly brush the nutmeg off?

REGAN: I think so, Sir.

TOM: Try. Move heaven and earth.

[REGAN *returns to the serving table with the glass and removes the nutmeg.* DAISY *comes in from the hall.*]

GRACE: Oh, hello!

DAISY: Good morning.

CECELIA: How was the walk?

DAISY: Very pleasant, thanks. We went miles. It's a lovely village.

CECELIA: It is nice.

DAISY: Whose house is the pretty white one on the Square?

CECELIA: Near the Post Office? [*To* GRACE] Isn't that Judge Evans's?

GRACE: Yes.

DAISY [*To* TOM]: I hope you remembered to find the new magazine proofs for me.

[TOM *extends some folded proof sheets from his pocket.*]

TOM: Right here.

[DAISY *extends her hand.*]

DAISY: Please—

TOM: If you'd really like to—

DAISY: I should, very much.

[*She takes the proofs and goes to the stairs, where she seats herself upon the bottom step.* REGAN *returns the glass of punch to* TOM.]

TOM: That's better.

[JOE *comes in from the hall.* REGAN *coughs discreetly behind his hand.*]

REGAN [*Not presuming to look directly at his master*]: Beg pardon, Sir—

TOM: Yes?

REGAN: —If I may say so, Sir—it has always seemed to me that life is like a sailboat—

TOM [*Smiling*]: Ah?

REGAN: In good weather, no better ridin' anywhere—but the very deuce, Sir, in a storm, Sir.

[TOM *laughs and waves him away.*]

TOM: Get out!

[REGAN *bows gravely.*]

REGAN: Very good, Sir.

[*And goes out.* CECELIA'*s fixed smile leaves her face. She takes a deep breath.* DAISY *laughs softly,* JOE *loudly.* GRACE *turns to* JOE.]

GRACE: Oh hello!

[JOE *recovers himself and advances into the room.*]

JOE: How are you?

GRACE: Pleasant walk?

JOE: If you like the country.

GRACE: I'll bet you made a good plot, too.

JOE: A good—?

GRACE: I know you writer-men!

DAISY [*From the stairs*]: —Remember your prescription for me, Tom?

TOM: Prescription?

DAISY: "The country's the place to work," you said.

JOE: Something did it for you, Daisy.

TOM: —Daisy herself.—You can spend the night, can't you, Joe?

JOE: It's up to Daisy.

DAISY: I'm not certain, yet. Must we say straight off?

CECELIA: Of course not.—Do, though. We'd so love having you.

TOM: I've got to run over to Greenwich to see one C. B. Williamson, but I'll be back this evening.

JOE: The publisher?

TOM: Yes. Why?

JOE: What have *you* got to do with that old pirate?

[TOM *smiles.*]

TOM: Shh!—It's a secret.

[JOE *stares.*]

JOE: My God!

GRACE: You're coming to my house for Sunday breakfast, you know.

JOE: Thanks, we've had it.

GRACE: Oh, but mine is a very special breakfast!—

JOE [*To* TOM]: —I liked the old Press building better.

TOM: We needed more room.

CECELIA [*To* TOM]: Don't you want some coffee or something?

TOM: This is fine. Will you join me in a milk punch, Daisy?

DAISY: Would you mind awfully if I didn't?

TOM: I'm not sure.

GRACE: Not disapproving, is she?

[DAISY *laughs pleasantly.*]

DAISY: Not in the least.

TOM [*to* JOE]: —You couldn't publish a magazine in that old shack.

JOE: Don't tell me it's that smart.

GRACE: *I* think it's going to be a sensation. I'm practically a collaborator, aren't I, Tom?

[TOM *laughs.*]

TOM: Grace is my reaction agent. She submits to tests.

[DAISY *stares at the proofs.*]

DAISY: Is this all of it?

TOM: —The dummy for the first number.

DAISY: No name yet—

TOM: No.

JOE: —Any Sunday papers, by any chance?

TOM: —In the living room. I'll send for them.

JOE: It's all right. I'll read them there.

[*He goes out.* TOM *looks after him.* GRACE *rises.*]

TOM: Extraordinary fellow, Fisk.

GRACE: My people will be arriving. Who's going to run me home?

[*She holds out her hand to* TOM. *He takes it and rises.*]

TOM: We'll go in Joe's Ford, and shock the village.

GRACE: Divine!

DAISY: Bring it back, Tom.

TOM: You bet.—How about your coming with us?

[DAISY *rises upon the stairs.*]

DAISY: Thanks, but I want to finish this.

TOM: Be sure to like it.

DAISY: I'm afraid I'm no judge.

GRACE: Tom, I've got to tell you: *I* think the idea of a white roof in this country is idiotic.

[*She tucks his hand under her arm and they move toward the door.*]

TOM [*As they go out*]: So do I. It's insane. What ever made you think of it? [DAISY *mounts the stairs and goes out,* CECELIA *watching her.* OWEN *moves toward the living room,* CECELIA*'s low voice stops him.*]

CECELIA: Owen—

OWEN: What, C?

CECELIA: Why did she come?

OWEN: Daisy? I thought you wanted her, for those highly special reasons.

CECELIA: —First she said she couldn't. Then she telephoned back she would.

OWEN: Well?

CECELIA: I believe she came for some special reason of her own.

OWEN: Quite possibly.

CECELIA: What, though?

OWEN: Search me.

CECELIA: Twice last night I caught her watching me in the most curious way. Once when I was with Fisk, once with you.—But you know, I'm not the least bit jealous any more. I'm even inclined to like her.

OWEN: That's big of you.

CECELIA: I suppose Fisk is one of hers, too.

OWEN [*Frowning*]: How do you mean?

CECELIA: Sweet innocent!

OWEN: How's that?

CECELIA: I should think by this time you'd know a promiscuous little—[*She sees his frown deepen, and with a gesture, concludes:*]—Oh, well—

OWEN: You're a strange girl, C.—And a pretty cruel one.

CECELIA: —Not at all. I tell you I don't mind in the least. In fact I really don't see why Tom and she shouldn't be as good friends now as—well, as you and I are.

OWEN: Their history is a little different.

CECELIA: Why? Don't you like our history?

OWEN: What there is of it.—A trifle uneventful, don't you think?—Or shall we simply call it lacking in excitement?

[*A moment. Then*]

CECELIA: —You've been so strange, lately. So remote, Owen.

OWEN: I wasn't aware of it.

CECELIA: —Refusing to help us one bit with Mr. Williamson.

OWEN: But Tom doesn't want to be helped!

CECELIA: I do.

OWEN: C, I've told you. I simply can't do it.

[CECELIA *turns from him coldly.*]

CECELIA: Very well.

OWEN: Certainly, you must realize—

CECELIA: Of course. [*She moves toward the living room.*] Come on—shall we?

OWEN: I've told you a dozen times, I'm counsel for Williamson's, and—

[CECELIA *stops and turns to him.*]

CECELIA: Exactly.—And so they do whatever you tell them to.

OWEN: Tom's price is out of all reason.

CECELIA: Not if they really want it.

OWEN: But hang it, he made it that to stand them off! He doesn't want them to have it.

CECELIA: Tom doesn't know what he wants. [*Coaxing*]—Just one little word to them from you—on the telephone—before he goes over this afternoon—now—before he gets back from Grace's.

OWEN: There's something called legal ethics you seem not to understand, C.

CECELIA: And something called friendship? [*He turns away. A moment. Then she looks at him sideways.*] Owen—[*He gestures "What?"*] "Lacking in excitement," you said.—For you?

OWEN: For you, I meant.

CECELIA: I suppose you're the judge of that, too.

OWEN: I don't know who else.

CECELIA: Of course you couldn't possibly be wrong.

OWEN: Could I?

CECELIA [*Softly*]: —And I'm not a human being at all, of course. [*He advances toward her.*]

OWEN: C—!

CECELIA [*Quickly*]: Do one thing for me: just tell them it *might* be a good thing for them.—It might, mightn't it?

OWEN: But even so, I—don't think I can.

CECELIA: —That it *is* high—admit that—but it might be a good thing. [*He ponders it, frowning.*]—Owen—telephone him—just one little word, Owen—[*He is about to protest again, but is stopped by her even gaze and her hand upon his arm. Finally he nods assent. She breathes:*] You darling—[*He inclines toward her, but she leans away from him. Suddenly he glances up at the staircase. She senses that someone is coming, and begins to talk rapidly, in a different voice:*]—And of course it will be the most marvellous thing for Tom if Williamson agrees. You can imagine what it will mean to him.

OWEN: Yes, of course.

[DAISY *comes down the stairs, the magazine proofs still in hand.*]

CECELIA: His father will be pleased as Punch, too, but the main thing is—[*She looks at* DAISY *in pretended surprise.*] Oh, hello! Owen and I were just talking about The Bantam Press combining with Williamson's. Owen engineered it.

OWEN: Oh no, C. If there's any credit due—

[CECELIA *laughs, and exclaims*:]

CECELIA: Never mind! [*Then again, to* DAISY]—I'm so excited about it, I can hardly speak. [*Then, to* OWEN]—Why, Owen—do you realize?—But you wanted to telephone, didn't you?

OWEN: Why, er—why—yes, yes, I did.

[CECELIA *moves toward the living room.*]

CECELIA: It's in here, now. [*He follows. She speaks over her shoulder to* DAISY:] Coming along?

DAISY: In just a moment.

[OWEN *and* CECELIA *go out, encountering* JOE *coming in.* DAISY *gazes after them.*]

JOE [*To* CECELIA]: I thought I'd get ready for breakfast—lunch—whatever it is.

CECELIA: But you look lovely!

[*She follows* OWEN *out, into the living room.* DAISY *moves to the table, where she sits, staring in front of her, slowly comprehending.* JOE *approaches her, as* REGAN *comes in.*]

JOE [*to* DAISY]: What do you say we—[REGAN *clears his throat portentously.*]—God, Red, get that fixed, will you?

[REGAN *lifts a lemon in two fingers.*]

REGAN: Have you seen this one?

JOE: I had grapefruit.

REGAN: Give me a five-dollar bill. [JOE *finds one for him.* REGAN *folds it and closes his hand upon it.*] Which hand?

JOE: That one. [REGAN *opens* both hands. DAISY *is still staring, wrapt in thought.*] Good!—Only where does the lemon come in?

[REGAN *beckons him nearer, cuts the lemon with a fruit knife, extracts a five-dollar bill from it, shows it to him, picks up a tray, and moves toward the door.*]

REGAN: Thank you, Sir.

[*He goes out with the tray and* JOE*'s five dollars.* JOE *turns to* DAISY *about to speak, but she speaks first:*]

DAISY: Are you packed, Joe?

JOE: Not yet. Why?

DAISY: I want to go.

JOE: What's the rush?

DAISY: I want to get out of this house.

JOE: But why all of a sudden?

DAISY: I want to get out, that's all.

JOE: Tom?

DAISY: Yes.

JOE: Poor devil—

DAISY: Yes.

JOE: Of course he's terribly on the defensive: you can see that.

DAISY [*Dully*]: Can you?

JOE: Of course. He felt us disapproving, and simply gave us the works.

DAISY: Maybe.

JOE: He was awful last night, all right.

DAISY: Go and pack, Joe.

JOE: And what an outfit they were!—I give you Grace Macomber in your Christmas stocking.

DAISY: Thanks.

JOE: I'll even throw her husband in, for good measure.

DAISY: That would be too divine.

JOE: And all those pitiful second-hand opinions of Tom's! What's happened to him? What do you suppose has done it, for God's sake—

DAISY: That's what I came to find out.

JOE: Have you?

DAISY: Yes.

JOE: What?

DAISY: The most pitiful thing that can happen to any man.

JOE: But what?

DAISY: Go and pack, Joe.

JOE: It won't take a minute.—It certainly can't be C. *I* think she's a fine girl, don't you? I talked with her for quite a while last night. She made great sense. I think she's a damned nice, attractive woman. [DAISY *moves away from him.*]

DAISY: So was Delilah.

JOE: Deli—? Oh come on, Daisy!

DAISY: —And bring my bag down with yours.

JOE: But I don't get you at all.

DAISY [*Turning*]: Will you go and pack?

JOE: Honestly, Daisy, you're the damndest girl.

[TOM *comes in from the pantry, a whisky-and-soda in hand.*]

TOM: A drink anyone?

JOE: At this hour? I should say not.

[TOM *seats himself at the end of the table, facing them.*]

TOM: Too bad.

JOE: Besides, we've got to go.

TOM: So soon? Too bad. [*He takes a swallow of his drink, and smiles at them.*] Godspeed—

JOE [*After a moment*]: —There was a fellow once told me drink was in a way to becoming my own personal Hollywood—

TOM: Really? How amusing.

JOE: You, by a strange coincidence.

TOM: Oh not possibly!

JOE: —And it was you, incidentally, who taught me how to drink moderately.

TOM: No mean feat, I'm sure.

JOE [*With a gesture*]: Well, physician—

[TOM *raises his glass again, still smiling.*]

TOM: Similia similibus curantur. Translated, the hair of the dog that—

DAISY: Go get ready, will you, Joe?

[JOE *stares at* TOM *a moment, then mounts the stairs and goes out.*]

TOM: —So solemn—all so solemn. [*He puts down his glass, unfinished.*] I'm sorry you don't like my friends.

DAISY: Your—?

TOM: They are, however.—Did you read the magazine?

DAISY: Most of it.

TOM: Couldn't finish it, eh?

DAISY: No. I didn't care for it.

TOM: Why not?

DAISY: It seemed to me that one oh-so-bright weekly was enough, without more of the same.

TOM: —Not sufficiently solemn. I see.

DAISY: Not half!—And so *cheap,* Tom! Oh, how can you?

[*A moment. Then*]

TOM: You can't please everybody.

DAISY: Never mind. It doesn't matter.

[TOM *drops his cynical tone and speaks genuinely:*]

TOM: Doesn't it, Daisy?

DAISY: Tom, ever since I got home I've heard from all sides how you've changed. I came here to find out if it was true, and if so why.

TOM: Well, is it?

DAISY: Tom—

TOM: And if so why? Why?

DAISY [*A sudden cry*]: Oh, Tom—I pity you with all my heart!

[*He is at her side in an instant, her wrists in his hands.*]

TOM: Pity me! What are you talking about?

DAISY: I came to find out. I've found out. Now I'm going. [*She calls:*] Joe!

TOM: Found out what? Pity me why?

[DAISY *looks down at her wrists.*]

DAISY: Would you mind? [*He releases her. A moment. They gaze at each other. Her eyes soften.*]—And love you, Tom—love you with all my heart, as well. Remember that.

TOM [*Brokenly*]: Daisy, I—[*He recovers himself, and with the recovery the cynical smile returns. He advances, one hand out, his voice coaxing:*] Give us a kiss, Daisy.

[*She takes a step back from him, in horror. Her call is almost a scream:*]

DAISY: Joe! Are you ready?

[JOE*'s voice is heard from the stairs.*]

JOE: Coming!

[JOE *comes down the stairs with the bags.* CECELIA *comes in from the living room.*]

CECELIA: Did someone call? [*She sees the bags.*] Why, what's all this?

DAISY: I'm sorry, but we've got to leave.

CECELIA: But what's happened?

DAISY: I suddenly remembered something. Please don't bother—

CECELIA: But I never heard of such a—

DAISY: I'm terribly sorry, but it can't be helped.

CECELIA: But can't you at least wait until after luncheon?

DAISY: I'm afraid not.

[*She turns to* JOE.]

JOE [*To* CECELIA]: Good-bye. Thanks very much.

CECELIA: Good-bye. I must say it all seems very strange. [*Then to* DAISY]—And when we've so loved having you.

DAISY: You were kind to ask us.

CECELIA: Well, if you insist, I suppose there's no help for it. Good-bye. Do come again when you can really stay.—Your coat's here, isn't it? [*She goes out into the hall.*]

JOE: Give me a ring sometime, Tom.

TOM: Right.

[JOE *looks at* DAISY. *She nods her head in the direction of the door. He goes out.*]

DAISY: Good-bye, Tom.

TOM: —Once I wouldn't say it, would I?

DAISY: Once you wouldn't—

TOM: Well, good-bye.

DAISY: —This time you do—

TOM: Good-bye.

[*She gestures helplessly, turns and goes out. For a moment he is alone. A door is heard to close, then* CECELIA *re-enters.*]

CECELIA: Honestly! If that wasn't the rudest thing! [*He is silent.*]—I presume you agree, don't you?

TOM: I don't know what it was.

[*He stares in front of him, unseeing. She looks at him intently for a moment. Then*]

CECELIA: Well—if we're going to Grace's—

TOM: I'll get my hat.

[*He moves toward the hall. She follows.*]

CURTAIN

■ ACT III ■

SCENE II

At TOM COLLIER'*s. Ten o'clock the same night.*

The dining room is dimly lighted from the hall and living room. There is a small fire burning in the fireplace. Leaves have been removed from the table, which is now at its smallest. Two chairs are at the table, the others against the wall.

REGAN *comes in from the hall with an armful of wood, some of which he places upon the fire, making it burn brighter. This done, he lights a small candle lamp upon the table. Two places have been set and a light supper prepared: a platter of cold meat, a bowl of salad, sandwiches, fruit. There is a champagne glass at each place. A moment, then* CECELIA *calls from upstairs:*

CECELIA: Regan?

REGAN: —Right here, Ma'am.

CECELIA: I thought I heard a car.

REGAN: Yes, Madam.

CECELIA: Is Mr. Collier's supper ready?

REGAN: Yes, Madam.

[*He lights a small lamp on the serving table, pokes the fire again, and goes out into the hall. A moment, then* CECELIA *comes down the stairs, in another charming negligee, this time more severe in cut and somber in color. She examines the table, rearranges a few things and puts out the lamp upon the serving table. Now the room is lit only by the candle lamp and the fire upon the hearth. A door closes in the hall. She turns toward it, calling:*

CECELIA: Tom?

[TOM *comes in.*]

TOM: Hello. [*He looks at the table.*] What's all this?

CECELIA: I thought you might be hungry. I know what you think of Williamson's food. [*He looks at the fire, then around him, curiously.*] What's the matter?

TOM: —Lighted this way, it reminds me of some place.

CECELIA: Where?

TOM: I don't know.

[*His voice is strange, as if speaking from a distance.*]

CECELIA: Do eat something, dear.

[*Again he looks about him, puzzled.*]

TOM: —I came back the long way, over the Pound Ridge road, through Middle Patent.

CECELIA: What made you do that, silly—

TOM: I don't know, I wanted to drive.

[*Now it is her he looks at curiously.*]

CECELIA: Tom—what *is* the matter?

[*He shakes his head, as if to shake something out of it, and laughs shortly.*]

TOM: Sorry!

CECELIA [*Anxiously*]: Everything went all right, didn't it?

TOM: Oh yes, perfectly. [*A moment. Then*] In fact, it's settled.

CECELIA: Not already!

TOM: Yes. They've signed. All I have to do is to dig up a notary in the village and write my name under theirs.

CECELIA: Oh, Tom!

TOM: Are you pleased?

CECELIA: Aren't you?

TOM: I think something's happened to my nervous system. I feel awfully light.

CECELIA: You're famished. Come and sit down and eat—[*She draws him to the table. He seats himself there, and for a moment drops his head in his hands.*]—And tired, too, poor darling.

TOM: No—just light. So awfully light.—Thinking too much.

[*She puts meat and salad upon a plate and sets it before him.*]

CECELIA: Here.

TOM: C—

CECELIA: Yes, dear?

TOM: I think it's time we had a child or two, C.

[*A moment. Then*]

CECELIA: We'll talk about that.

TOM: Yes. We must. [*Another moment*]—The trees along the road stood out like—[*He rubs his eyes and looks up again.*]—like whatever it is trees stand out like.

CECELIA: You've been going much too hard, you know.

TOM: It's good for me. I'm having visions. [*Again he looks around him.*]—What *is* it it reminds me of?

[*She seats herself near him at the table.*]

CECELIA: —Nothing. You're just tired and hungry.

TOM: Please let me have my visions. [REGAN *comes in with a pint of champagne.*] Good evening, Mr. Regan.

REGAN: Good evening, Sir.

TOM: —Those buttons on your coat—you know, they're terribly bright.

REGAN: I'll try to bring 'em down.

TOM: Do. It's essential. Champagne, is it?

CECELIA: I thought you might feel like celebrating.

TOM: Well—

CECELIA: A little wine won't hurt you, Tom.

TOM [*To himself*]: —The little more, and how much it is—[*Rousing himself*]—Fill them, Mr. Regan. [REGAN *looks at him oddly, then fills the glasses.* TOM *raises his and squints at it.*]—Infinite riches, in a little room.

[CECELIA *laughs.*]

CECELIA: You've got the quotes badly.

TOM: Little lamb, who made thee?—Regan—dost thou know who made thee? [*He holds out the glass to him.*]—And a little more, old son. [REGAN *refills the glass and goes out.* TOM *watches him, curiously.*] The discreet withdrawal—I've seen that before, too. [*Looks around him again, then cries, suddenly:*] I know! The Florentine!—A private room at the Florentine.

CECELIA: What's that?

TOM: A kind of a hotel. Flora Conover's place.

CECELIA: It sounds wicked.

TOM: It used to be the best twenty-guinea house in London.

CECELIA: Twenty-guinea? What are you talking about?

TOM: In advance, at that.

[CECELIA *glances at him.*]

CECELIA: Rather expensive, wasn't it?

TOM: But one went to Flora's to celebrate.—And the food was good, the waiter discreet, the wines excellent, the lady most artful.

CECELIA: Tom! How revolting—

TOM: But we must send the boys back happy, you know.

CECELIA: I don't care to hear about it, thank you.

TOM: Very well, my dear.

[*A moment. He stares at his glass. Then*]

CECELIA: Weren't they difficult at all, Tom?
TOM: Who? Williamson's?—Easy.
CECELIA: And you actually got your own terms?
TOM: Except for their right to pass on my selections.
CECELIA: That's probably just a form.
TOM: Probably.
CECELIA: They want to feel they have *some* say.
TOM: That's all.—C, what have you done to your hair?
CECELIA: Why, nothing, why?
TOM: It looks lighter.
CECELIA: It isn't.

[*He gazes at it for a moment longer, then eats a little, disinterestedly.*]

TOM: I quashed the announcement they'd prepared for the papers.
CECELIA: Why? What was it?
TOM: "Williamson, Warren and Company have absorbed The Bantam Press, formerly owned by—"
CECELIA: "Absorbed"!
TOM: Yes. Like a sponge. I quashed it. For "absorbed" read "bought a controlling interest in."
CECELIA: Well—that's more like it.
TOM: —Poor little Bantam.—For "Bantam" read small little, plucked little capon.
CECELIA: Oh, don't, Tom! You know it's a good thing for you—it's a grand thing for you.
TOM: —Increased scope.
CECELIA: Of course.
TOM: —Perfect distribution facilities.
CECELIA: But aren't they?
TOM: Williamson, Warren Books Girdle the Globe. Hear the eagle scream.—Poor little Bantam—peep, peep—
CECELIA: —And I thought you'd be beside yourself for joy.

[*He gazes at her. She is.*]

TOM: C, your eyes are so bright.

[*She laughs shortly.*]

CECELIA: Eat, you. You're seeing things.

[*He looks at his plate.*]

TOM: C—
CECELIA: Yes, dear?
TOM: —Little love is no love.
CECELIA: —Meaning what, precisely?

TOM: It wasn't necessary to lock your door against me last night.

[*A moment. Then*]

CECELIA: But I didn't.—I mean—not against—

TOM: Then why?

CECELIA: I'm—it's just that sometimes I'm afraid, alone at night.

[*He is watching her.*]

TOM: I don't believe you.

[*She laughs nervously.*]

CECELIA: Well, really!

TOM: I don't believe you, C. [*She averts her head.*]—Only I'd like you to know that that isn't necessary, ever.

CECELIA: Very well.

[*Suddenly he reaches for her hand and takes it.*]

TOM: Why was it? Tell me instantly why it was.

CECELIA: Is that an order?

TOM: Tell me.

[*She tries to meet his gaze, but cannot.*]

CECELIA [*With difficulty*]: You mean—why I—why I didn't want you near me—

TOM: Yes.

CECELIA: —And you don't know—

TOM: No.

CECELIA: Well, if you don't, you ought to.

TOM: Tell me, I say.

CECELIA: You'd been so—consistently disagreeable, that's all.

TOM: About what?—Wanting Regan back?

CECELIA: No.

TOM: What, then?

CECELIA: Your father, chiefly. [*She rises and goes to the serving table.*] He telephoned this afternoon. [*A moment*] He wanted to know if you'd got the birthday check. [*Another moment*] I told him that you had, and had tried to call him. [*He turns away.*] Well, I had to say something!

[*She reseats herself at the table with a plate for herself.*]

TOM: I don't know whether to send it back, or just not to cash it.

[*He finds a check among the letters in his pocket, and looks at it, frowning.*]

CECELIA: —Of course, you simply can't allow yourself to show any kind of graciousness toward him.

TOM: No.

CECELIA: —As a way of telling how pleased with you he is, he sends you a small check—and you have the extraordinary bad taste to— [*He holds the check out for her to see. Her eyes widen.*] What!— Good heavens—I don't believe it!

TOM: There it is.

CECELIA: But there isn't that much money in the world!

TOM: In Father's world there is. He feels he can afford it, to get us to come and live with him.

CECELIA: Of course, I don't understand your attitude about that, either.

TOM: Don't you, C?

CECELIA: He knows how inconvenient it is here in winter—and having that great, huge, lovely house in town, it's perfectly sweet and natural of him to—to, well, to ask—

TOM: Yes—you, to preside night after night at his deadly dinners, me to listen eternally to his Delphic advise on what to do and how to live—in short, to allow him to own us. Of course, he's willing to pay. He always is.

CECELIA: Oh, how ridiculous you are, really!—His whole life long he's tried to help you, to do things for you—

TOM: —In order to own me. I tell you I know him.

CECELIA: You're the only child he's got, and he's an old man and a very lonely man. I think it's horrible beyond belief, the way you treat him. How you can be so hard, I don't know.

TOM: Hard!—I'm not hard enough. All my life I've been trying to harden. I was born soft, that's the trouble with me.

CECELIA: You soft!

TOM: Yes. Born it.—And then brought up to refuse to face any truth that was an unpleasant truth, in myself or anyone else—always be the little gentleman, Tommy—charming and agreeable at all costs—give no pain, Tommy.

CECELIA: You seem to have outgrown it nicely.

TOM: Not yet, I haven't. No, not by a long shot. The inclination's still there, all right. Still going strong.

CECELIA: But don't be discouraged.

TOM [*Wearily*]: All right, C.

CECELIA: —It's nothing but your old self-consciousness about money, again. It simply defeats me.—Honestly, has everyone who lives well sold his soul to the devil?

TOM [*Rising*]: "Lives well"!—I'd give my eyes to live well. That's all I want for us.

[*He goes to a chair at the window.*]

CECELIA: Oh—definitions again.—We being so weak, of course, that a little luxury would completely ruin us.

TOM: —Little—little—everything's so little. Add it up, though. [*His head sinks upon his breast.*]—Add it up.

CECELIA: To my way of thinking, if a person can't stand—

TOM: Let's drop it.

CECELIA [*Coldly*]: Very well. We shall.

[*He looks up again.*]

TOM: —Now you've gone from me again—

CECELIA: A lot you care.

TOM: Oh C—my lovely C—Where are you? What's become of you?

CECELIA: There's something you call your damned integrity—

[TOM *rises from his chair.*]

TOM [*Suddenly, sharply*]: That's the word!

[CECELIA *rises also.*]

CECELIA: I see it's no use talking.

[*A silence. He looks at her intently.*]

TOM: —This is what you call "being disagreeable."

CECELIA: Yes. Very.

[*He returns to her.*]

TOM: —But how to be otherwise, when—

CECELIA [*In a burst*]: Possibly by being the fine, kind, generous man you ought to be!

TOM: To Father?

CECELIA: You might begin there.

TOM: —Accept the check with thanks—and go to live with him—

CECELIA: It's only for a few months—and I think to refuse his present would be extremely bad manners—just about in a class with those of your little lady of easy virtue, this morning. If—[*She sees she has gone too far.*] I'm sorry to have said that about her. I didn't mean—

TOM: Never mind. [*A long moment. Then*]—Suppose I should do as you say about Father—

CECELIA: Oh, Tom—do be the darling I know you are!

TOM: Would you like me better?

CECELIA: Much.

TOM: How much?

CECELIA: Oh—very much.

[*He leans forward, watching her, hardly believing it possible.*]

TOM: No locked door, any more?

CECELIA [*Lowly*]: Not one—ever—

TOM: That sounds—most inviting.

[*She smiles.*]

CECELIA: Does it?

[*Again he seats himself at the table.*]

TOM: —And suddenly I'm beginning to see with an awful clearness—

[*He stops.*]

CECELIA [*Smiling*]: What? How stupid you've been?—And what I am to you?

TOM [*After a moment*]: Yes.

CECELIA: —And so you *are* going to be nice again?

TOM: You'll see.

[*Again* CECELIA'*s smile*]

CECELIA: —But how am I to be sure?

TOM: You've told me ways to convince you.

CECELIA: I do hate us not to agree, Tom.

TOM: I know.

[*She brings her chair closer and sits at his side.*]

CECELIA: I want so to feel—I don't know—together again, as we used to be.

[*Once more,* TOM *looks incredulously around him, at the room. Then*]

TOM: You're very pretty, you know—

CECELIA: Why, thank you, Sir.

TOM: —Very exciting, too.

[*His manner has changed. From now on, he is no longer the husband sitting before the fire with his wife, but a host at supper with a pretty girl, whom later he will know better.*]

CECELIA: I don't know whether it's you or the wine speaking.

TOM: —Me.

CECELIA: Shall we have a little more?

TOM: Why not?

[*She presses the button.*]

CECELIA: It's a party, then.

TOM: It's a party.

CECELIA: Sometimes you're so thrilling, Tom.

TOM: You think?

[*A moment. Then*]

CECELIA: Put your arms around me, Tom—

[*He inclines toward her, does not touch her, but looks full into her eyes, searching for something he still cannot believe he will find.*]

TOM: Are they around?

CECELIA [*In a breath*]: Oh—yes—yes—

[REGAN *comes in.*]

TOM: Another small bottle.

[REGAN *goes out.* CECELIA *laughs a little throaty, excited laugh.*]

CECELIA: We shouldn't. You know we shouldn't.

TOM: But we seem to be—

CECELIA: I feel—all at once I feel terribly naughty, somehow—

TOM: I suppose you're the prettiest girl I've ever seen—

CECELIA [*Archly*]: So nice of you to think so, Sir.

TOM: —So very attractive—

CECELIA: I like to be attractive.

TOM: So very seductive—

CECELIA: There, there! That's enough!

[*He has found it. Coldly he salutes it:*]

TOM: You're a strange woman. Your lips drop honeycomb, your mouth is smoother than oil.

CECELIA: Now what are you quoting?

[REGAN *comes in with the wine.*]

TOM: —Give the lady some, waiter. [REGAN *fills* CECELIA*'s glass, then* TOM*'s, without a word.*] You can leave the bottle. [REGAN *places it upon the table, near him.*]—And that will be all. [REGAN *bows and goes out.* CECELIA *raises her glass and smiles invitingly. He raises his, murmuring:*]—To the pleasant ways of life.

[*She drinks. He does not.*]

CECELIA: —Such pleasant ways.

[*She smiles at her glass.*]

TOM: Is it good?

CECELIA: So good.—I'm feeling it a little.

TOM: That's what it's for, eh?

CECELIA: It must be.

TOM: "Champagne, the friend of lovers"—

[*Her face inclines to him, then she averts her head.*]

CECELIA [*Softly*]: No—not yet—

TOM: Artful child.

CECELIA: You think?

TOM: —Lovely, alluring thing—

CECELIA: I like you too, now.

TOM: Pleasant here, isn't it?

CECELIA: So pleasant. [*She refills her glass and finds that his is still full.*] —But you aren't taking any—

TOM: It makes me see almost too clearly.

CECELIA: Take a little more, and everything will get so—lovely and vague and—the way I feel now.

TOM: —A good feeling, is it?

CECELIA [*A whisper*]: Delicious—[*She gropes for his hand, holds it against her breast.*] Oh—Tom—[*He looks at her. She smiles again.*] —One last toast? [*He draws her to her feet, glass in hand.*] But to what—what to?

TOM: You name it.

[*A moment. Then*]

CECELIA: To love—[*She comes against him, steadies her glass in both hands against his breast, bends her head and takes it. He raises his glass, holds it for a moment near his lips, then sets it down, untouched, upon the table. She replaces hers beside it, and murmurs:*] And darling—

TOM: Yes?

CECELIA: You—you *are* going to be an angel about—about things, aren't you?

TOM: You'll see.

CECELIA: Oh, I knew you would!—I'm so happy—[*She smiles, moves slowly toward the stairs, and mounts them, opening the door at the top. There she turns and whispers:*] Don't be long—

[*And goes out.* TOM*'s eyes following her. Then he turns and stares down at the table. Finally his hand finds the bell and presses it. A moment, then* REGAN *enters, in a business suit.*]

TOM: See here, Red, I—

REGAN [*Sharply*]: Never mind! [TOM *looks up.* REGAN *gestures.*] All I mean is—well, I'm out for good, this time.

TOM: Why?

REGAN: I just don't like it here, that's all.

TOM: When do you want to go?

REGAN: As soon as I can.

TOM: Tonight, then.

REGAN: That's all right with me. I'm packed.

TOM: Look in and say good-bye as you're leaving.

REGAN: I'm leaving now.

TOM: Look in, anyhow. [REGAN *turns to go.*]—Have you got a fountain-pen? [REGAN *finds a pen and gives it to him.*]—Don't let me forget to return it. [REGAN *goes out. Slowly, methodically,* TOM *opens the pen, shakes it, spreads the check upon the table and writes upon its back. Then, as carefully, he replaces the top of the pen, picks up the check and waves it back and forth, to dry it.* REGAN *re-enters with a traveling bag.* TOM *returns the pen to him.*]—Here you are. Thanks.

REGAN: Well—good-bye—

TOM: Get into the car.

REGAN: I can walk to the train all right.

TOM: Bring my coat and hat, will you? [REGAN *does not stir.*]—Will you bring my coat and hat, please? [REGAN *puts down his bag and goes into the hall for them.* TOM *folds the check carefully, goes to the fireplace and places it upon the mantelpiece, one corner under a vase.* REGAN *re-enters with his overcoat and hat.* TOM *puts on the hat.* REGAN *holds the coat for him.* TOM *gets into it. He takes a cigarette from the pocket and puts it in his mouth.*]

REGAN: What's the idea?

TOM: —Light, please—[REGAN *holds a match for him.* TOM *pulls on his gloves.*] Now, then—

REGAN: I can walk, I tell you.

TOM: Not at all. We'll drive in.

REGAN: *We* will—?

TOM [*Very gently*]: I'm going back to my wife, Red.

REGAN: To your—?

[*Puzzled,* REGAN *looks toward the lighted doorway at the top of the stairs.*]

TOM: —To my wife, I said.

[REGAN *picks up his bag, and goes out, into the hall.* TOM *looks once around him, draws a deep breath of smoke, exhales it slowly, then turns and follows him.*

CURTAIN

HERE COME THE CLOWNS

HERE COME THE CLOWNS

was first produced by Eddie Dowling
at the Booth Theatre in New York City
on December 7, 1938.
It was directed by Robert Milton;
the setting was designed by John Koenig.

CAST

WALTER	James Hagan
MAJOR ARMSTRONG	Jerry Austin
JOHN DICKINSON	Russell Collins
MA SPEEDY	Ralph Bunker
CONNIE RYAN	Madge Evans
NORA CLANCY	Doris Dudley
VAL GURNEY	Bertram Thorn
DAN CLANCY	Eddie Dowling
JIM MARBLE	Frank Gaby
GERT MARBLE	Hortense Alden
MAX PABST	Leo Chalzel
FREDDIE BALLANTINE	A. H. Van Buren
LEW COOPER	Thomas Palmer
FAY FARREL	Eve March

■ ACTION AND SCENE ■

The play takes place in an American city on a
Saturday night in late March, several years ago.
The action is continuous, beginning at
about eleven o'clock in the Back Room
of Ma Speedy's Café des Artistes,
where it concludes two hours later.
In the intervals between acts
no time is presumed to have elapsed.

■ ACT I ■

MA SPEEDY'*s* CAFÉ DES ARTISTES *is a long, narrow building extending from the corner of Front Street and Vine halfway down the block to the stage alley of James Concannon's Globe Theatre, of which it is a structurally integral part.*

The Back Room is MA SPEEDY'*s special and secret pride. There is a miniature stage, set into the back wall, flanked on either side by a small booth, on the same level. Red curtains, which pull from the side, now partially cover the stage. The booths can be used as dressing rooms when occasion demands, also by pulling curtains across them. The artists are given to trying out new acts here in the presence of their critical fellows and sometimes, when the spirit moves, spontaneous entertainments take place. From the booth at left a small, steep staircase mounts to a narrow balcony which stretches the length of that side of the room and leads into the dance hall which occupies the upstairs front of the building. In addition to the tables in the booths, there are two other tables set on ground level in each corner of the room, and one in the center, facing the stage.*

In the left wall there are two doors, the large one giving access to the restaurant, the smaller swinging one leading directly to pantry and kitchen. Opposite them is the private entrance from the alley, available only to the sacred and special few. It is after the show on a Saturday night in late March and the little lamps on the tables are lighted and the gas log on the alley side aglow, making the room quite cozy and inviting. In the booth at the right sits MAJOR ARMSTRONG, *a copy of the then current "Billboard" propped up before his face. This, and the long, checkered tablecloth almost completely hide him from view. Certainly no one not knowing him could be aware of the cushion upon which he sits.* JOHN DICKINSON, *also alone, occupies the opposite booth. A siphon and glass stand upon the table before him and his head is down upon his folded arms.*

The door from the alley has been cautiously opened not more than six inches. WALTER, *the waiter, stands there looking out, one hand securely grasping the door knob, the other flat on his flank, holding his apron down against the wind which blows up the alley on March nights such as this one. He speaks quietly to the two dim figures who stand in the half light beyond the door.*

WALTER: I'm sorry, ladies. You'll have to go to the front entrance. This is private.

[*A woman's voice, husky, pleasing, replies from outside the door:*]

CONNIE: I know—but it was Mr. Gurney who sent us. He said just to mention his name.

WALTER: I'm sorry, ladies, but Mr. Gurney would have to be with you.

[*Another woman's voice, frail, lighter, is heard:*]

NORA: You know me—I've been here lots of times.

WALTER: All the same, he'd have to be with you.

CONNIE: He'll be along in a minute. He and Mr. Ballantine are just finishing counting up.

WALTER: I'm sorry, but it's the rules. You'll have to wait for him in the front.

NORA: Come along, Connie. I'm all right.

CONNIE: Like fun you are. You need something and you need it quick. [*Then again to the waiter:*] Look, whatever your name is, it's raining. Please, will you?

WALTER: You'll have to go around to the front. Just back down the alley and around. This room is strictly reserved for the artists from the Globe.

CONNIE: But I tell you it was Val Gurney himself, who—

WALTER: No one can come in without their private key or else accompanied.

NORA: Come along, Connie.

CONNIE: But she's sick, I tell you! She's had a shock. She's all in. She needs something. She needs something right away.

WALTER: You must of made a mistake. This is no Speak. We don't serve a thing here. This is Ma Speedy's Café des Artistes, and strictly within the—

CONNIE: Listen! Tell Ma Speedy for me that Connie Ryan, head usher at the Globe, is here with her sister who's had a shock!

WALTER: I'm sorry, ladies. The proprietor is in the front. You'll have to ask there.—And *strictly* within the law. [*He closes the door and waits a moment, his hand still on the knob, until he is sure they have gone. Then he moves to the booth nearest him and inquires cheerfully:*] What'll it be, Major Armstrong?

[*The voice that replies from behind "The Billboard" has its own peculiar quality:*]

THE MAJOR: A bottle of the Canadian ale, if you please.

WALTER: The Molson's?

THE MAJOR: The Molson's.

[WALTER *scratches upon his pad and moves toward the kitchen door. He is about to pass the second booth when the figure within it stirs and speaks:*]

DICKINSON: Wait. [WALTER *stops and turns.* DICKINSON *slowly raises his head and drops both hands upon the table from the elbows. Then he lifts his face, smiling slightly, all like a machine capable of but one motion at a time. There are forty years in the face, every one of them, every day, every minute.*] What's the prodigious rush?

WALTER: No rush, Mr. Dickinson, no rush at all.

DICKINSON: Another double rye.

[WALTER *hesitates an instant.*]

WALTER: Are you sure?

DICKINSON: Certainly I'm sure.

THE MAJOR: —Also a small sandwich. Any kind.

[*He lowers the paper from before his face and the great head with its thin crest of white hair is for the first time visible.*]

WALTER: You know Ma don't want us serving food in here, Major.

[*So far as he can,* THE MAJOR *draws himself erect upon his bench. The patient eyes grow larger under their shaggy brushes. The fine, bony beak of a nose widens slightly with the intake of breath.*]

THE MAJOR: And you know I can't go in there and be stared at. Tell Ma who it's for.

WALTER: If you say so, Major.

THE MAJOR: Any kind but cheese.

WALTER: I'll see what they have on hand.

DICKINSON: And don't be so damned officious.

WALTER: Ma expects us to exercise discretion, in the cases of—

DICKINSON: Exercise it outside.

[WALTER *lowers his head, crosses and pivots through the swinging door. For a moment the two men sit staring out in front of them from their opposite cubicles, without speech. Finally, without turning his head.* THE MAJOR *addresses* DICKINSON*:*]

THE MAJOR: That must have been Clancy's wife at the alley door.

DICKINSON: So I gathered.

THE MAJOR: Then she must have been in the theater when it happened.

DICKINSON: Ask me the three worst weeks in show business—

THE MAJOR: Three—let me see. Are there three?

DICKINSON: Yes: the week before Christmas, Holy Week, and Naomi and her Violin.

THE MAJOR: Very good. Very good indeed.

DICKINSON: —So they combine two of them and wonder what happens to business. They run in a number like Naomi and then tell me I don't know how to handle the publicity. Will you tell me how to get space for a female frog with a fiddle?

THE MAJOR: Will you tell me what we can do about Clancy?

DICKINSON: I wonder what it was that hit that crazy stagehand?

THE MAJOR: Clancy's not crazy, John.

DICKINSON: He gave a good imitation of it, stopping the show that way.

THE MAJOR: It was the last number—and it was only Cooper and Farrel.

DICKINSON: A swell world. A swell job all around.

THE MAJOR: Poor Clancy.

DICKINSON: —But the nerve of the guy, disappearing for a year, nobody knows where the hell to or at, then coming back out of the blue and right on stage in the middle of a turn and asking for someone!—Who, for God's sake?

THE MAJOR: It seems so, doesn't it?

[*The door from the restaurant opens and a short, stout, pink-and-white man comes in, carrying two vases of white carnations. He wears a dinner coat, which drapes gracefully over his curves. He has very small feet and rotates upon them a trifle as he walks. His face is genial and kindly under its crown of wavy, unconvincingly reddish hair, and for all the fact that his features are now somewhat blurred by fat, one can see that he has once been handsome in his way. This is* MA SPEEDY *and he is in an expansive mood. He cries out in his musical voice:*]

SPEEDY: Good evening, John! Good evening, Major!

THE MAJOR: Good evening, Ma.

DICKINSON: Hello, Ma.

[WALTER *comes in with the drinks.* SPEEDY *places the carnations on the tables and stands off to view the effect.*]

SPEEDY: Everything all right?

DICKINSON: Oh, just hunky-dory.

[WALTER *sets a glass, a bottle and a small sandwich before* THE MAJOR.]

SPEEDY: I wanted to see who was here. A couple of ladies just came in the front, and—do you remember our old friend Clancy, the stagehand?

DICKINSON: We certainly do.

SPEEDY: Well, it seems that one of them's his wife. Women and their nerves! I gather he's turned up again—I mean Clancy.

DICKINSON: He certainly has.

SPEEDY: The dance team, Cooper and Farrel—they just told me as they were going upstairs. I've never heard the like. Who do you suppose it is that he's after? Why wouldn't he at least say the name? You don't suppose he'll come wandering in here, do you?

DICKINSON: I doubt it.

SPEEDY: His wife needs a little refreshment, her sister says. Shock.—And I wondered if you'd mind them coming in here for a moment?

DICKINSON: Not me. I'll move in with The Major.

[*He moves from his booth to* THE MAJOR'*s*.]

SPEEDY: I know they won't be long.

DICKINSON: For all me, they can both get stewed to the eyes.

THE MAJOR: Give us the cribbage set, Walter.

WALTER: Cribbage.

DICKINSON: A dollar says I'm going to beat the little pants off you.

THE MAJOR: We'll see about that.

[WALTER *returns with the game*.]

DICKINSON: Privacy, Walter. [WALTER *draws a red curtain partially around the booth, making* THE MAJOR *and* DICKINSON *invisible from the table near the restaurant door, through which* SPEEDY *now calls:*] This way, ladies! Right in here, please! [*He glances about him.*]—Cozy. Where will one find a cozier nook?

[NORA CLANCY *and* CONNIE RYAN *come in from the restaurant.* NORA *is slight and frail, somewhere in her pretty, middle twenties.* CONNIE *is two years older, without* NORA'*s cheap refinement of feature, but curiously vital and attractive. Her half-open coat reveals the blue uniform of a Globe usher. Her low, husky voice is full of strength and self-confidence:*]

CONNIE: Thanks, Mr. Speedy.

NORA: Yes—thanks, I'm sure.

[SPEEDY *draws out chairs for them, flutters over them.*]

SPEEDY: Just sit yourselves doon and order what you like, only no food, please. Food in the front, sandwiches to write home about, a grilled chicken that would break your heart. [NORA *and* CONNIE *seat themselves.* SPEEDY *claps his hands together.*] Walter!—Ask the ladies what they will have, Walter.

WALTER: Yes, ladies?

CONNIE: A beer for me and a double brandy for her.

WALTER: With seltzer?

CONNIE: With plain water.

SPEEDY: Perfect. A perfect prescription for the nerves.—The really good brandy, Walter. [*He looks knowingly at* WALTER, *who marks on his pad, tucks his pencil behind his ear and goes out into the pantry.*] We'll soon get the roses back into those pretty cheeks again!

NORA: Thanks. I guess I could use a couple.

SPEEDY: If anyone who comes in speaks to you, please don't mind. We're all just one big family here.

CONNIE: We won't mind. Come one, come all.

SPEEDY: It's really like a little club, you know—Ma Speedy's little nook for members of the N.V.A.—Artistes for Artistes, you know!

[*He purses his little mouth into an "O" and goes out again into the restaurant, whistling happily.* CONNIE *scrutinizes* NORA *intently.*]

CONNIE: Stop shaking.

NORA: I'm not shaking.

CONNIE: You are and you're a fool, Nora.

NORA: I—I can't help it.

CONNIE: Clancy couldn't have seen you way up there in the balcony. He couldn't possibly have.

NORA: It wasn't that.

CONNIE: Then what was it?

NORA: His voice. He—he acted so crazy.

CONNIE: You think it's Val that he's after, don't you?

NORA: I'm scared, Connie. I'm so scared.

CONNIE: You know he's gentle as a baby. You know he wouldn't lift a finger to you.

NORA: But Val—if he goes after Val—

CONNIE: He doesn't even know it was for Val you walked out on him! He doesn't know it was for anyone, the poor innocent.

NORA: He might of found out some way.

CONNIE: How could he have? He felt town two days after. And that was months ago.

NORA: Someone might of wised him up—some busybody.

CONNIE: Go on—it's nothing but your own guilty conscience.

NORA: It was only while I was with him I had a guilty conscience.

CONNIE [*After a moment*]: There are times I just don't get you at all.

NORA: We're different, that's all. We always have been.

CONNIE: I'll say we have.—But don't kid yourself that if Clancy's gone off his head it wasn't you who did it, because it was.

NORA: It was not! It was not!

CONNIE: All right, all right—calm yourself!—Anyway, I don't believe for a minute that he has.

NORA: He was always half nuts—half the time he didn't make sense at all.

CONNIE: You mean the kind of sense *you* could understand. You never had his imagination.

NORA: Oh my God—"imagination"!

CONNIE: You heard me.

NORA: I know I did. And I know how you've always stuck up for him, regardless.

CONNIE: Why shouldn't I have?—If ever a guy got a dirty deal from life *and* his wife—

NORA: —Why? Lots of people have accidents and lose their jobs and have a kid die on them and—

CONNIE: —*And* his wife, I said.

NORA: Maybe you should of married him instead.

CONNIE: Wha-at? [*She laughs shortly.*] Me marry Clancy? That's a good one. I should've sailed right up to him, I suppose. I should've said, "Mr. Clancy, I know you've got an eye for a pretty face but I'm the girl for you, Mr. Clancy. Plain Connie Ryan, good and dependable."—Yes: I wouldn't've married him if he'd offered himself on a silver platter. Not if he'd come to me on his knees, I wouldn't've. Me married to Clancy! That really *is* to laugh.

NORA: Maybe yes, maybe no. At least you could of plowed through all those foolish books with him and talked big talk till two in the morning on one glass of beer about God knows what. And of course *you'd* never of wanted to go to dances and things.

CONNIE: Listen: I like dances just as much as you do! Clancy likes them too—if he goes with someone who sticks to him and doesn't roll her eyes around like a couple of hoops.

NORA: Tell me one thing: how'd you like to be married to someone who made you feel mean all the time?

CONNIE: Nobody could me.

NORA: —When all you wanted was a little fun every other year or so.

CONNIE: Show me somebody funnier than Dan Clancy when he wanted to be.

NORA: I guess he just didn't want to be, with me: I guess that was it.

CONNIE: *I* never had to wait around for the laughs with him.

NORA: It's just what I'm telling you: *you're* the one who should of—

CONNIE: Here's your drink. [WALTER *swings in from the pantry and up to them with their orders.* CONNIE *fingers her purse.*] How much, Old Willie the Watchdog?

WALTER: Sixty and twenty-five: eighty-five.

CONNIE: He can count.

NORA: Val will settle for them when he comes.

CONNIE [*To* WALTER]: Mr. Gurney is doing the honors. Is that all right?

WALTER: Sure thing. Why not?

[*He moves to the other table and wipes it off, around the vase of white carnations that stands upon it.* NORA *takes a swallow of her drink.*]

NORA: It's strong.

CONNIE: You surprise me.

NORA: —If only I could get him to hate me. If I could just simply get him to hate me.

CONNIE: There's none of it in him—not for anyone.

[NORA *finishes her glass, then sits staring down into it, turning it in her fingers.*]

NORA: I don't know why a fellow like Clancy—a stagehand who never made more than forty-eight a week at the most—I don't know why *he* should be so important, anyway.

[CONNIE *looks at her over her beer.*]

CONNIE: I don't know either. I wonder why he is?

[WALTER *has glanced up with sudden interest at the mention of* CLANCY*'s name.*]

WALTER: Is Clancy back?

CONNIE: He's back.

WALTER: How is he?

CONNIE: Fine. They call him Lucky Dan he gets so many of the breaks.

[*A key is turned in the alley door and* VAL GURNEY *comes in—a jaunty, tricked-out, sharp-featured little man of thirty. He sails his natty hat onto a hook on the wall, adjusts his cuffs and makes directly for the table where* CONNIE *and* NORA *sit, and bends over* NORA*, who brightens at his approach.*]

GURNEY: Well, well. Well, well, well!—I see you're taking your tonic, Baby.

NORA: Hello, Val.

CONNIE: I thought you were so well known here.

GURNEY: You seem to have got in all right.

CONNIE: Just like a couple of pianos through a transom.

GURNEY: Exclusive, is what Ma's is. [*He seats himself with them, takes one of* NORA*'s hands in his and calls across his shoulder to the waiter:*]

Make mine a Scotch highball, Walter m'boy!

[WALTER *continues his polishing.*]

WALTER: One Scotch.

GURNEY [*To* NORA]: Now don't you worry, sweetheart. Nothing's going to happen to you.

NORA: I'm all right now.

GURNEY: There's no way Clancy could've got onto the fact that we've been friends, that I can see.

CONNIE: "Friends!"

GURNEY: Now sister! Don't put your oar in again. Fingers out of other people's pies, sister. Little girls get burned.

CONNIE: You're disgusting. You're just plain disgusting.

GURNEY: And don't try to insult me. I been insulted by experts. [*Then, to* NORA] You get upset too easy, dearie. It couldn't've been me he was looking for. Not old Val—not me. He'd've come right to my little cage in the lobby. Wouldn't he? Wouldn't he of?

NORA: I guess so—yes, I guess so.

CONNIE: And suppose he had?

GURNEY: Suppose not, sister, lest ye be supposed.

CONNIE [*To* NORA]: How you can stand him!

NORA: If you don't like it, you know what you can do.

CONNIE: You said it. [*She pushes her glass away and rises from the table.*]

GURNEY [*To* NORA]: —Clancy don't know a thing, not one thing. Take my word for it. Walter m'boy—another for the lady!

WALTER: One Scotch, one brandy.

[CONNIE *has crossed to the alley door.*]

CONNIE: I suppose it's all right to go *out* this way?

WALTER: Absolutely, lady, absolutely.

CONNIE: Funny, the difference between two sides of a door.

[WALTER *moves toward the pantry.* CONNIE *opens the door. Halfway through it, she stops and listens up the alley, then re-enters, closing the door behind her, and moves swiftly back to the table.* GURNEY *is reassuring* NORA.]

GURNEY: Baby—Baby!

NORA: I'm all right, Val—I'm all right. The only thing that worries me is—oh, to hell with it.

[GURNEY *glances up at* CONNIE.]

GURNEY: What's up? Who asked for an encore?

CONNIE: Get out. Get in there—quick! Get into the front!

NORA: Oh my God, Val.

[NORA *rises,* GURNEY *after her.*]

GURNEY: We'll take our drinks in the front, Walter.

WALTER [*Going out*]: —Isn't allowed.

CONNIE: Go *on!*

NORA: I got to have another drink.

GURNEY [*To* CONNIE]: Will you keep him here?

CONNIE: I don't guarantee anything.

NORA: —I just simply got to.

[GURNEY *pilots* NORA *toward the restaurant door.*]

GURNEY: Listen, Honey, don't worry: there's something on the old hip. And we'll just sit ourselves right down and get outside of a nice welsh rabbit, or what would the lady like?

NORA: No, no—I don't want anything to eat! All I want is—you keep him here, Connie—you hear me?

GURNEY: —Now look, Honey: nobody's going to bust up Val Gurney's Saturday night snack with his own girl, believe you me—Clancy or nobody else. Who does he think he is, anyhow?

[*They go out into the restaurant.* CONNIE *reseats herself at the table with her back to the alley door and pulls her glass toward her. Again a key turns in the lock and a boyish, discontented-looking young woman,* GERT MARBLE, *enters, followed by* JIM MARBLE, *a lanky individual of about forty, and* DAN CLANCY. CLANCY *is probably somewhere in his middle thirties, but with such lines of fatigue in his face, such anxiety in his fearsome eyes as to make any conjecture as to his actual age irrelevant and beside the point. One of* MARBLE'*s arms is about his shoulders as they enter, and in the crook of the other he carries a bulky object in a large canvas bag, like a duffel bag.* MARBLE *is talking very fast.*]

MARBLE: —And Frank's got the makings of a great dramatic artist, see? And he's a personal friend of mine, but what he don't know about business would fill a book, see? And they're trying to sign him for a series of twenty short subjects, so I go to the Grossett office with him, see? [MARBLE *puts the bag on the piano bench.* GERT *lights a cigarette and looks about her, distastefully.* MARBLE *continues to talk without pause.* CLANCY *sits staring out in front of him, barely listening.*] —And Jack Grossett himself, he starts to roll it out.—And—

GERT: *This* dump. Why do we do it?

MARBLE: —And I say, "Talking pictures my eye. Who wants to hear shadows talk?" And he pounds the table and shouts, "They want sound. The public's crying for sound!" "Wrong," I say. "They don't know what they want till we give 'em it." "Just what I say," he says. "And we're going to give 'em sound." [GERT *rises from the table. He turns to her.*]—Where you going, Gert?

GERT: Give me some chips.

MARBLE: What for?

GERT: Food. I'm empty as a drum.

[MARBLE *takes two bills from a roll and gives them to her.*]

MARBLE: Don't be long.

GERT: You bet. [*She passes* CLANCY, *prods him affectionately.*] You're all right, Clancy.

MARBLE [*To* CLANCY]: —Where was I?

CLANCY: What?

MARBLE: I say, where was I?

CLANCY: You were talking.

[GERT *goes out into the restaurant.* MARBLE *settles back again.*]

MARBLE: I remember!—"We are not interested in your opinions, Mr. Marble," he says. "But in the case of your friend Frank here—" "So long as I'm taking care of him," I say, "he's going to stay in vaudeville." "Then he'd better get a new nurse," he says, "because vaudeville is not long for this world."—Can you beat it?

CLANCY: Can you beat it?

[*He shifts his position slightly and looks around him. His eyes fix upon* CONNIE*'s back at the table opposite him.* MARBLE *undoes the strings of the black bag and draws* THE DUMMY *out of it; he folds the bag into a cushion for* THE DUMMY *and places it on the piano bench.*

MARBLE: —There you are, Frank, my friend. Now mind you behave yourself.

[THE DUMMY*'s grotesque mouth flaps open and shut:*]

THE DUMMY: God, how you love to hear yourself talk!

[MARBLE *pushes him in the face.*]

MARBLE: Insect!

[THE DUMMY *collapses face down upon the piano bench.* CLANCY *pronounces the name slowly, directly at* CONNIE*'s back.*]

CLANCY: Connie Ryan.

[CONNIE *raises her head, without turning it.*]

CONNIE: Hello, Dan Clancy. [*Then she turns and eyes him evenly.*] You don't seem too glad to see me.

[CLANCY*'s accent has not breadth enough for a brogue. It is only* *through a faintly musical intonation and an occasional odd locution that his Irish reveals itself.*]

CLANCY: I'm glad to see you.

CONNIE: You look thin.

CLANCY: You ought to see me sideways. How's Nora?

CONNIE: She's all right.

CLANCY: What's she living by? Is she working again?

CONNIE: She is.

CLANCY: There wasn't much she could do.

CONNIE: How have you been?

CLANCY: —She's flighty, you know. Nora's flighty.

CONNIE: You're telling me—who brought her up from a baby?

[THE DUMMY *makes a snoring sound.*]

MARBLE: —Disagreeable little mutt. When will you learn manners?

THE DUMMY: Shut up and let me sleep.

CONNIE [*To* CLANCY]: —Tell me, how's it been going with yourself? I got to wondering about you once or twice, when I had a spare minute or two.

CLANCY: I've been all over the place.

CONNIE: So I heard tell, from the stage of the Globe tonight.

CLANCY: That was a bad thing I did.

CONNIE: Only for Cooper and Farrel—and they're young.

CLANCY: All the same, it was bad and ill-mannered, interrupting the show that way. But I was almost out of my senses, Connie.

CONNIE: And where are you now, would you say?

CLANCY: The sight of you brings me back into 'em. You're the real foul-weather friend, Connie.

CONNIE: You'll turn my head with your compliments.

CLANCY: I'm a queer duck, and there's no denying it.

CONNIE: Who is it you're after, Dan? Who've you been looking for? [CLANCY *looks away.*]—I only thought I might maybe give you a steer.

CLANCY: No, there's no one can do that.

CONNIE: You certainly got all the bum breaks there were.

CLANCY: You have to take what comes.

CONNIE: —What they call "resignation."

CLANCY: They do, and they call it well.

CONNIE: If I were you, I'd get good and sore, believe me I would.

[*Suddenly* CLANCY *flares up.*]

CLANCY: Why should I? God damn it, it's the will of God! [WALTER *comes swinging in from the pantry.* CLANCY *glances at him.*] Hello, Walter.

WALTER: I heard you were back. I'm that glad to see you.

CLANCY: It's good to be back.

WALTER: What'll it be?

MARBLE: Whisky for Clancy, whisky for me.

CLANCY: Thanks, Jim, I don't want it.

MARBLE: How do you know till you've tried?—Who's in the booth there, Walter? Anyone thirsty?

WALTER: It's Mr. Dickinson and The Major.

[MARBLE *sets his mouth and the next instant from the inside of the booth, the yapping of a small dog is heard. The curtain is pulled roughly aside and* DICKINSON *is seen peering under the table.* MARBLE *laughs.*]

MARBLE: Look out—he bites!

[DICKINSON *looks out at him.*]

DICKINSON: Why, you low-life clown. You dirty low-life clown. [*He comes down from the booth.*]—And who's this guy with you, with a face like the coast of Kerry?

CLANCY: Hello, John. [*He takes* DICKINSON*'s hand.*] How are you?

DICKINSON: Drunk—and mean to get drunker. How's it with you?

CLANCY: I'm fine. Why shouldn't I be?

DICKINSON: Well, don't get tough about it. Who's the mystery man you're trailing around theaters and such?

CLANCY: If I told you, you still wouldn't know.

[THE MAJOR *calls from his booth.*]

THE MAJOR: Welcome home to you, Clancy!

CLANCY: Thank you, Major. Welcome to yourself.

DICKINSON: Drinks all around. This is a celebration.

THE MAJOR: Ale for me, if you don't mind.

MARBLE: Two. Gert likes ale.

CONNIE: Three—one for me. That is, if I'm included.

[WALTER *goes out into the pantry.*]

WALTER: —Got 'em.

CLANCY: You are all of you acquainted with Connie Ryan, my wife's sister?

MARBLE: The fair Connie? I know her well. [*Again he bends over* THE DUMMY.] And surely you remember my unpleasant little friend, Frank Frenzy?—Manners, Insect!

[THE DUMMY *sits bolt upright, grinning.*]

THE DUMMY: Hello, Connie! How's tricks?

CONNIE: Hello, Frank! Fine!—How's with you?

THE DUMMY: Couldn't be better. [*He winks broadly.*]—So long as I get my liquor.

[*Again* MARBLE *pushes him in the face but this time he remains upright.*]

CLANCY: —And John Dickinson.

DICKINSON: How are you, Connie?

CONNIE: How-de-do, Mr. Dickinson?

DICKINSON: Wearing the usher's uniform to bed these nights, are you?

CONNIE: I—I came out in a sort of a hurry.

[CLANCY *gestures toward the booth.*]

CLANCY: —Major Armstrong, Miss Connie Ryan.

CONNIE: Very pleased to meet you, I'm sure, Major.

[THE MAJOR *lets himself down from his cushion upon the bench, is lost to view for a moment as he comes under the table, and then emerges again from behind the tablecloth, the cushion under his arm. His tiny form—for now it is seen that* THE MAJOR *is a dwarf —negotiates the two steps to the floor level, and stumps with dignity up to* CONNIE *and offers her a hand.*]

THE MAJOR: The pleasure is mine, Miss Ryan.

CONNIE: I and the rest of the girls've enjoyed your act so much this week.

THE MAJOR: I am sincerely glad.

MARBLE: —Always a favorite with the ladies, eh, Major? Tom Thumb the Second.

THE MAJOR: Do you know, they had General Tom Thumb in wax in Madame Tussaud's Museum in London for many years?

MARBLE: You don't say!

CLANCY: Did they, now!

THE MAJOR: He stood there among other world notables, such as Napoleon and Nelson, and was the object of much interested comment.

[DICKINSON *takes the cushion from him and puts it upon a chair.*]

DICKINSON: Let's all sit. [*He lifts* THE MAJOR *from the floor and places him upon the cushion.*] For God's sake, let us sit upon our bums and tell sad stories of the death of kings.

[*All, with the exception of* CLANCY, *seat themselves, all friends together, a new liveliness in their talk.*]

THE MAJOR: Don't misquote The Bard, John. That's not allowed even to scholars like you.

DICKINSON: Scholars and scholarliness be damned together. Where are the drinks?

MARBLE: You drink too much, see?

DICKINSON: Or not enough—I was never sure. Clancy, I see in your eye that at last you agree with me it's one louse of a world.

CLANCY: It can bite, can't it, John?

THE MAJOR: —"The Best of All Possible Worlds," a book I know says.

DICKINSON: For what? For whom?

MARBLE: I guess we all of us have our troubles.

CLANCY: That's right—and must be resigned to 'em.

DICKINSON: A beautiful virtue, resignation.

CLANCY: That's right.

DICKINSON: Horse feathers.

THE MAJOR: —Of course, the main thing is how we take them. That's where philosophy comes in.

DICKINSON: Where philosophy comes in is where I go out.

CLANCY: If you were as hard as you think you are, John, they'd have split you up long since, and used you for coffin wood.

DICKINSON: I wish they had. It must be the rat holes.

CONNIE: This is a real gay party. This is certainly an evening out. When do the Australian Wood Choppers come on?

[*Again* MARBLE *sets his lips and from above them a falsetto voice is heard singing:*]

THE VOICE: "O dry those tears, And calm those fears. Life is not made for sorrow."

[THE DUMMY *twists his head around and looks up.* CONNIE *exclaims admiringly.*]

CONNIE: It's wonderful the way you do that, Mr. Marble.

MARBLE: I'm a very wonderful fellow.

[CLANCY *glances toward the balcony.*]

CLANCY: What's that other sound I hear, like an orchestra?

[*He moves toward the restaurant.* CONNIE *follows him swiftly.*]

CONNIE: Don't go in there! [*He stops. She explains:*]—They've had music upstairs since the first of the year. They dance there, eleven to one.

[CLANCY *speaks without interest.*]

CLANCY: Do they, now.

CONNIE [*After a moment*]: Dan—

CLANCY: What?

CONNIE: Do something for me?

CLANCY: What?

CONNIE: Will you promise to do it?

CLANCY: I will if I can.

CONNIE: You'll really promise?

CLANCY: If I—

CONNIE: No "if"s!

CLANCY: Then I will.

CONNIE: Come up to the hall and dance a dance with me!

CLANCY: Oh no, Connie—what are you talking about?

CONNIE: You promised.

CLANCY: But I've forgotten how. My feet wouldn't—

CONNIE: You've not! It's not a thing, once known, you forget. It's like swimming or riding a bike—it stays with you. [*She holds out both hands to him.*] Come on—one dance, like in the old days.

CLANCY: God help me, I'll try.

[*She snatches a white carnation from the vase on the table, breaks the stem and fixes the flower in his lapel.*]

CONNIE: There! Now you look more like your old jaunty self!

[CLANCY *gazes down at the flower.*]

CLANCY: That's an odd thing. *He* always used to wear one, didn't he?

CONNIE: Who did?

CLANCY: A man I know. [*Then his eyes look off into the far distance, across years, across waters.*] Carnations—my father used to raise them in the gardens of Roche's Hotel in Glengariff, where he worked. And my mother told me once the white one was the flower of God, God bless her. And we had a lemon tree, too. They grow there, you know. There's a warm current passes the coast. Figs, as well—even a palm now and then. My, how that lemon tree used to smell of a morning! It was glorious. It was like heaven. [*He stops and passes his hand over his face.*]—And still I was always wanting to go to Connemara. I never got there, I don't know why. The good Lord willed it otherwise, I suppose.

THE MAJOR: It was your father who wore the carnations?

CLANCY: No. Never him. They were too dear, and must be kept for the table. But a man I know did—and you know him, too.

[*A moment's silence. Then* CONNIE *laughs lightly and slips her arm through his.*]

CONNIE: You and your lemon tree and carnations! Come along—you're daydreaming! [*She leads him to the stairway.*] Just remember one thing, dancing—they don't whirl about as they did.

[*They mount the stairs.*]

CLANCY: What is it they do, then?

CONNIE: You'll see! It always came natural to you, Dan! Once on the floor, you were like a man inspired.

CLANCY: Me grandfather claimed he introduced the waltz into Ireland. [*They are moving along the balcony now.*]

CONNIE [*Mocking him*]: —Me grandmother claimed she introduced Irish to your grandfather.

CLANCY: The language or the whisky?

CONNIE: Both!—Will you promise to whirl me, Dan?

CLANCY: That I will—like a top on a table!

[*There is a burst of music as they pass through the door and into the dance hall.* MARBLE *glances up, then takes a deep breath and settles down into his chair again. He replaces* THE DUMMY *in the bag and sets the bag upon the floor at his feet.*]

MARBLE: Well, I guess if he can dance—

DICKINSON: —And if he can whistle very loud in the dark.

MARBLE: He's like a man that's been hit over the head, isn't he?

DICKINSON: Well, so he has—and I'd hate to count the times.

[*Unnoticed by them the door on the balcony again opens and a* FIGURE *appears there: a stoutish man of uncertain age, wearing a dark suit of foreign cut. His face is bland, and, in repose, curiously benevolent. What hair he has is cropped short. He comes to the railing and stands there, looking out thoughtfully.* THE MAJOR *reflects:*]

THE MAJOR: It's true: *he* always did wear one.

DICKINSON: Who wore what?

THE MAJOR: I think I know now who it is Clancy wants to see—

DICKINSON: Who?

THE MAJOR: The Old Gentleman himself—the owner of the Globe, James Concannon.

MARBLE: Go on—nobody ever sees Concannon any more.

DICKINSON: —And very few in the past, did they?

THE MAJOR: Clancy did now and then. So did I. I think it's to him he would naturally turn. In fact, I don't believe I've ever known one human being to reverence another as Clancy does James Concannon.

DICKINSON: Concannon, my foot. [*He rises and moves to the little stage.*] I'll bet the dust is deep on that private staircase of his, the old fake. Let's have a look. I even doubt if he's here at all any more.

[*He opens the stage curtains wide.* MARBLE *calls after him:*]

MARBLE: Well, if he isn't, where is he?

DICKINSON: As Jack Grossett down in New York—he might tell you.

Sure—just go right up to the door of Grossett Enterprises and say "How come we don't see Mr. Concannon, since your Mr. Jack went out to get him?" [*He draws aside the spangled curtain which masks the brick wall at the back of the stage, and discloses a small door marked* "MR. CONCANNON. PRIVATE."]—Locked tight. I thought so. Where *is* the old fake? I'd really like to know. Who runs things now, anyway? Don't tell me Ballantine!

THE MAJOR: Mr. Concannon is not a fake, John.—And I think Clancy came back tonight believing he'd be—

[THE FIGURE *on the balcony leans out and inquires in a low, precise voice with a Middle European accent:*]

THE FIGURE: —Or I wonder—I wonder could it be me, simple Max Pabst, for whom that poor, unfortunate fellow has been looking?

[DICKINSON *turns quickly and stares up at him.*]

DICKINSON: The great illusionist again, is it?—Listen: old bag of tricks, say that once more, and I'll—!

THE FIGURE: —So sorry to disturb.

MARBLE: Sit down, John.

[DICKINSON *reseats himself, muttering:*]

DICKINSON: What's he doing here tonight anyway? What's the point of arriving in town two days ahead of time? He doesn't go on until Monday, does he? Who ever heard of an act blowing in on a Saturday? Anyhow, I swear to God I've seen him some place.

[THE FIGURE *on the balcony comes quietly along it to the stairs.* SPEEDY *re-enters from the restaurant, calling back after him:*]

SPEEDY: This way, gentlemen! Right in here, Professor Pabst! [MARBLE *brings a loose deck of cards from his pocket and shows them to* THE MAJOR *who nods. They go to the table in the booth at right of the little stage and begin to deal out cold hands.* DICKINSON *hunches his chair nearer to his table and picks up his drink again.* FREDDIE BALLANTINE *enters, a dapper little middle-aged man in a dinner coat, carrying an umbrella.* SPEEDY *cries out in surprise:*] But where's the Professor?

[BALLANTINE *turns and looks back into the restaurant.* THE FIGURE *coming down the stairs speaks very softly:*]

THE FIGURE: Here I am.

SPEEDY: Gracious! You're just everywhere at once, *you* are!

PABST: A little tour: I like to see things for myself. [*He looks around him.*] Pleasant—how pleasant—a charming setting. Anything could happen here—no?

SPEEDY: —This little nook is my pet, Professor!—*This* is the true Café des Artistes—isn't it, Freddie?

BALLANTINE: Absolutely.

PABST: —And a stage, also?

BALLANTINE: We've absolutely even rehearsed here at times.

[WALTER *re-enters.*]

SPEEDY: But it's chiefly for little informal entertainments—you know—just among ourselves, when the spirit moves us.

[WALTER *places drinks before the cardplayers.*]

DICKINSON: Thanks. It's about time.

SPEEDY [*To* PABST]: Don't you think it's cozy?

PABST: Very.—Full of what-you-call-it—*gemütlichkeit.*

SPEEDY: Oh, I love that word! It's just the word for it!

PABST: Take it—take it for your own.

SPEEDY: *"Gemütlichkeit."*

[*Ballantine draws out chairs at the other table.*]

BALLANTINE: His liquor's all right. I'll grant him that.

SPEEDY: Bring a bottle of the "Perfection," Walter. [*He explains:*] We're serving "Perfection" now. It's really quite good. [*He calls to the other table:*] Hello, fellows!—Got every little thing you want?

MARBLE: Sure thing.

THE MAJOR: Yes, indeed.

DICKINSON: And a couple we don't.

[WALTER *goes out.* SPEEDY *seats himself with* BALLANTINE *and* PABST.]

BALLANTINE: What a night! I never made such a long speech in my life.

PABST: But an explanation to the audience was indicated, was it not?

BALLANTINE: Just let Clancy try something like that again. Just once more.

SPEEDY: Poor Cooper and Farrel. I never heard of such a thing happening. [*He ponders a moment.*] Except once, I remember, at Keith's in Washington, a cat walked on stage right in the middle of my act. It was one of the worst ordeals I've ever gone through. I was in the middle of the Prayer from *La Tosca* and, you know, the House threatened to get quite out of hand.

PABST: I have no doubt.

SPEEDY: Well, sir, you know what I did? I held the top note as long as I could—[*He arches the fingers of one hand upon his bosom and elevates the other hand like a chalice. He throws back his head and in a shrill falsetto sings a line from the aria.*]—I can't get up there any more. Then I let—quite unexpectedly, you know—I let out a long "meaow" [*He demonstrates, and finds his lower register again.*] Well, sir, they loved it! They laughed with me, not at me. They were absolutely mine.

PABST: An inspiration—a most happy inspiration.

SPEEDY: Those were the days. Three years running, I was held over a second week at The Palace. I had a special curtain and drop of my own—a living mass of sequins. Harry Collins made my gowns. I traveled with six trunks and had thirty-two changes. All New York was mad about me. I had a cigar named after me.

PABST: Those must, indeed, have been the days.

BALLANTINE: You should have stuck it out a little longer, Ma.

SPEEDY: I couldn't, Freddie. I simply couldn't. [*To* PABST]—I don't know about in Europe, but here, in some way, the War changed the audience's attitude toward my kind of art. Well, sir, I saw the handwriting on the wall, as they say—so I just bought this little nest and settled down in it. In a way it was a relief: I could eat all I wanted to at last and see all my old friends as they came through and just sit back and let my figure go—and don't you think it's cute?—My little setup here, I mean.

PABST: *Gemütlich.*

SPEEDY: *Ja—ganz gemütlich.* [WALTER *re-enters with drinks from the pantry, and* GERT *from the restaurant.*] That's right, Walter.—Good evening, Gert.

GERT: Hello, Ma.

[*She proceeds to the table in the booth and seats herself with* MARBLE *and* THE MAJOR *as* WALTER *places drinks before* SPEEDY, BALLANTINE *and* PABST.]

SPEEDY: —The wife of the ventriloquist you saw tonight. She assists.

PABST: He was very good.

MARBLE [*To* GERT]: Where've you been all this time?

GERT: I got to talking.—You know the kid I got the fan note from yesterday?

MARBLE: What about her?

GERT: She was in the front—and guess what.

MARBLE: What?

GERT: She's spending next week in Syracuse too—with friends.

[MARBLE *slams down his cards.*]

MARBLE: The hell she is!

GERT: Why? What's the matter?

MARBLE: I'll show you what's the matter. I'll show her, too! See?

GERT: Is he drunk?

THE MAJOR: Would you like a hand?

GERT: Sure. All aces, please. [*She glances contemptuously at* MARBLE. *He picks up his cards again, still watching her under his eyelids. She murmurs:*] Try not to be more of a fool than God made you.

[*The game proceeds.* BALLANTINE *turns to* PABST, *who has been listening attentively to the altercation at the other table.*]

BALLANTINE: You haven't said how you liked the rest of the bill.

PABST: On the whole, very much. Well selected and well arranged. I was particularly interested in the performance of the Irishman who afforded me such a what-you-call-it—good build-up—

BALLANTINE: Clancy.—Yes—some performance! Absolutely!

[DICKINSON *turns in his chair.*]

PABST: I think he is a natural comic.

DICKINSON: Horse feathers.

PABST: I beg your pardon?

DICKINSON: A comic, eh?—That's most discerning of you, I'm sure.

BALLANTINE: Come on over.—I want you to meet the Professor. [DICKINSON *makes his way to them a little too steadily.*]—Professor Max Pabst—Dickinson, our press man.

[PABST *rises and bows stiffly.*]

DICKINSON: How do you do, I'm sure.

BALLANTINE: He'll absolutely want to ask you a few questions for the Monday press.—Sit down, John.

[DICKINSON *and* PABST *seat themselves.* DICKINSON*'s manner is definitely antagonistic.*]

DICKINSON: I must have caught your act somewhere.

PABST: You have traveled much in Europe?

DICKINSON: No. Not any.

PABST: Then it is not possible.

DICKINSON: But you look familiar.

PABST: That is an impression I often give. It is part of my what-you-call—stock in trade.

DICKINSON: —Got the usual advance stuff with you, I suppose.

PABST: Unhappily no.

BALLANTINE: He came on in such a hurry. When La Paloma took sick in Detroit—

DICKINSON: —We were stuck for an Easter Week headliner, sure. But how'd we happen to get such a break as the Professor?

PABST: I was in the Grossett offices in New York when the telegram came about the sudden illness of the Thinking Horse.

DICKINSON: —So you leaped right into La Paloma's shoes, eh?

PABST: On an impulse, I offered myself as substitute.

DICKINSON: There's something phoney about this. Maybe Jack Grossett did oust Concannon out, back there when he thought he'd run vaudeville, north and south, east and west—himself, single-handed. Maybe he's had you here all along. Maybe, in fact, you're the present Concannon.

PABST: An amusing idea, but no.

DICKINSON: You and Ballantine aren't in cahoots, of course?

BALLANTINE: Cahoots! Me?

PABST: "Cahoots"—what is that?

DICKINSON: It's cahoots. Anyhow there's an idea around that it's Concannon our friend Clancy was looking for tonight.

PABST: Really? How very interestin'. I met the old gentleman once or twice in years past. He was most impressive.—He seemed to me a very lonely man—but then who, of any importance, is not?

[BALLANTINE *thrusts a piece of paper at* DICKINSON.]

BALLANTINE: Here's the change in the program copy. You'll absolutely have to check it.

[DICKINSON *takes it and looks it over. At the next table,* MARBLE *leans to* GERT, *speaking lowly.*]

MARBLE: You'll have to head her off. See?

GERT: Who?

MARBLE: Your new Little Number.

GERT: God, what a mug you can be.

[MARBLE*'s hand falls on her arm.*]

MARBLE: You heard me. It's bad enough having to play a split-week like Syracuse, without any of that going on.

GERT: I don't know what you mean.

MARBLE: You heard me!

[SPEEDY *glances at them.* PABST *has already been listening intently.* SPEEDY *calls gaily:*]

SPEEDY: Now, now! No domestic strife, please!

MARBLE: Out! This is a private conversation.

[THE MAJOR *inquires mildly over his cards:*]

THE MAJOR: Are we playing?

GERT [*To* MARBLE]: Behave yourself, you!

[MARBLE *removes his hand and stares at his cards, swearing softly under his breath.*]

MARBLE: What a load I've taken on. God! Will it never end?

GERT: If you can't take it, you know what to do.

THE MAJOR: Please. I can't think.

SPEEDY [*To* PABST]: And they're really the most devoted couple, you know.

PABST: Very interestin', very—

[DICKINSON *puts the paper in his pocket.*]

SPEEDY: Here? You don't mean it!

DICKINSON: Upstairs, I said. Dancing.

PABST: So? I must have missed him.

BALLANTINE: Dancing! Absolutely!

DICKINSON: You know how they do—on volcanoes?

SPEEDY: Oh dear—I don't like this at all!

PABST: He is a natural comic. I hope I may be able to do something for him—something, perhaps, to help him forget his troubles.

DICKINSON: I'm sure he'd appreciate that no end.

PABST: Such a curious search of his—for whom—for what?

DICKINSON: You tell us, Professor.

[PABST *gazes at him for a moment. Then speaks in a brisk, matter-of-fact voice to* SPEEDY:]

PABST: I hope my bag of effects will be safe in the coatroom?

SPEEDY: Don't you worry. No one's ever lost even a hat at Ma Speedy's.

PABST: And that was his wife in the front, with her lover?

SPEEDY: Well, they do say she and Gurney are—of course *he* doesn't *dream*—

[CLANCY'*s voice is heard from the balcony above:*]

CLANCY: This way, Lew! Come along, Fay!

PABST: Shh! *Jetzt kommt er. Er ist punkt.* [*He looks up at the balcony from which a brief blare of music is heard as the door from the dance hall is opened, admitting* CONNIE *and* CLANCY, *who stand there, waiting for their companions.* PABST *smiles in anticipation. He speaks softly:*] Yes, we must see—we must certainly see what we can do for this unfortunate clown.

[CONNIE *and* CLANCY *still wait, and* PABST *watches.*]

CURTAIN

■ ACT II ■

The Same.

The positions are the same as at the end of Act One. The time is immediately after it. The action is continuous.

CONNIE *and* CLANCY *are joined on the balcony by the dance team,* LEW COOPER *and* FAY FARREL, *a slim, youthful and engaging pair, who enter from the dance hall and precede them along the balcony toward the stairs.*

FAY: Honest, I never had such a whirl in my life!

[*All are laughing and seem very merry as they come down the stairway.*]

CLANCY: —And the night at the beach, when we danced in the marathon—you remember, Lew? Fay, do you remember?

FAY: My feet hurt yet, when I think of it.

CONNIE: I've still got the doll we won.

CLANCY: Have you, now!—It was a big doll.

CONNIE: It still is. The fact is, it's grown three or four inches.

LEW: Connie, I could fall for you!

[*And without warning he falls down the last half dozen steps and lies prone on the floor at the bottom.* MA SPEEDY *springs up with an exclamation, then sits down again as* FAY *walks calmly over* LEW.]

SPEEDY: —Now *that's* why I like this place!

[CLANCY *looks down admiringly.*]

CLANCY: I'd give my left arm to be able to do that, Lew.

CONNIE: Only you couldn't without it.

[FAY *moves up to the empty table at the Left.*]

SPEEDY: They're song-and-dance: Cooper and Farrel.—And that's Clancy.

PABST: I know.

[CONNIE *and* CLANCY *step over* LEW'*s still prostrate form.*]

CONNIE: Oh that music, that music!

CLANCY: Wasn't it grand? It went right to my feet.

MARBLE [*To* THE MAJOR]: The boy's better.

THE MAJOR: Much.

[LEW *picks himself up and follows the others to the table, calling to the waiter.*]

LEW: Beer all around, Walter.

WALTER: Four beers—count 'em—four.

[*He goes out again into the pantry.*]

FAY: How long ago was it we all went to the beach together?

CONNIE: Three years Decoration Day.

CLANCY: Where was Nora that night?

CONNIE: She was laid up with a cold—don't you remember?

CLANCY: That's right.

CONNIE: I named the doll after you, Clancy.

CLANCY: Did you, now.

FAY: Fay Jack of the Jack Sisters, I was named after.

LEW: I was named after nobody.

FAY: *You* don't mind, though!

LEW: The hell I don't.—How'd you like to be called something the top dame in an orphan asylum made up for you?

FAY: I wouldn't mind. [*She mocks him, singing:*] "No foolin', who do you love? Who are you thinking of, no foolin'?"

[*At the other table,* DICKINSON *lets his arms down wearily.*]

DICKINSON: If we had numbers for names, someone would try to make 7 stand out over 4.

BALLANTINE: Absolutely!

DICKINSON: 7 grows a beard, and 4 goes to night school.

PABST: Quiet! Quiet, and listen! This is most interestin'.

LEW: You'd more or less like to know who you are though, wouldn't you?

FAY: "No foolin', who do you miss, when it's time to kiss, no foolin'?" [*She stops singing, and replies:*] *I* wouldn't care! Really I wouldn't. [*She cocks her head gaily up at him.*] Are names the reason you won't marry me?

LEW: They might be.—And that ugly mug, of course.

FAY: This guy has been crazy for me for five years, nearly. Ever since we teamed up and developed our act, he has. And still he won't marry me. He won't even sleep with me.

LEW: Nary a wink, so lay off.

[*He leaves the table and moves to the piano bench.*]

CLANCY: He's the deep one, Lew is. You need a long line with Lew.

[LEW *begins to play* FAY'*s song softly upon the piano.* CONNIE *has been shaping her napkin into a cone. She sets it up before her upon the table.*]

CONNIE: Night and day he stands up there on my dresser like this, that doll does. "Dan Clancy," I say to him, "you keep out of trouble. You're always getting into trouble."

CLANCY: *I* must have been named after Daniel in the lion's den.

CONNIE: "If you were troubled with lions," said the King, "you must have brought them yourself."

CLANCY: If my little Angela had been a boy, I was going to name *her* after Michael the Archangel.

FAY: Who? What circuit does he play?

CONNIE: Listen to her!

CLANCY: The Universal! Up the heavens and down again. He's captain of the selfsame troops that defended the throne of God against the assault and battery of the Old Nick, that time there was the trouble.

DICKINSON: "And there was War in Heaven!"

CLANCY: There was that all right—and what a war! My mother told me all about it, over and over. Three hundred years it went on. Of course, their time is not like ours.

CONNIE: Three days, most likely—or else three minutes.

DICKINSON: "Michael and his angels fought against the Dragon. And the great Dragon was cast out into the Earth." [*To* PABST] I thought you looked familiar.

PABST: You are so amusing.

CLANCY: Anyhow, Michael's the fine old bird, and without him God knows where we'd be now.

DICKINSON: And where are we?

CONNIE: And don't be so irreverent, calling him an "old bird."

CLANCY: I'm not. I know The Captain well.—Once in the army—the time I got conked—I thought I saw him. [*He salutes.*]—Maybe I did.

CONNIE: Oh, sure.

FAY: I'll tell you what, Clancy: if Lew ever marries me and we have any kids I'll name the first one "Michael Daniel," after you both.

CLANCY: You can leave out the "Daniel"—or call the next one it.

[*Abruptly* LEW *stops his playing.*]

LEW: Oh, lay off this marrying-and-kids stuff! It's enough to drive a guy crazy!

FAY: Why, Lew—

LEW: —Just lay off it! Talk sense!

FAY: He's been this way all week—some chip on his shoulder for everything and nothing.

LEW: Well, it's been one hell of a week—playing to empty houses—and on the same bill with a flock of midgets. Midgets—God!

[CONNIE *glances in the direction of* THE MAJOR.]

CONNIE: Hush, Lew—

LEW: I don't care. I hate 'em. I hate the sight of 'em. [WALTER *re-enters.*] Hey, come on! Come on with those drinks, will you? I want a drink!

[PABST *leans confidentially toward* DICKINSON *and murmurs:*]

PABST: He does not know who he is, he will not marry—and he dislikes midgets.—Isn't it interestin'?

DICKINSON: No.

[MAJOR ARMSTRONG *lays down his hand.*]

THE MAJOR: I think this is mine.

GERT: You think wrong. Look!

[*She lays down hers.* MARBLE *examines both hands and pushes* GERT'*s back to her impatiently.*]

MARBLE: Your mind's wandering.

GERT: But with three jacks and a pair of—

MARBLE: —And wandering where?

[WALTER *comes up to them and puts a folded note on the table before* GERT.]

WALTER: A young lady in the front asked would I bring this note to you.

[GERT *is about to pick up the note but* MARBLE'*s quick hand reaches it first.*]

GERT: You give that here!

[MARBLE *opens it and reads it, then crumples it up and flings it upon the floor.*]

MARBLE: God! It's sickening. God, it makes me want to vomit.

GERT: Get down on your knees and pick it up and give it to me.

MARBLE: What am I to do with you? How can I keep you off it, you filthy, underhanded little—

[SPEEDY *rises and calls:*]

SPEEDY: Jim—Jim Marble!

MARBLE: What do you want?

[SPEEDY *smiles and shakes his finger at him.*]

SPEEDY: —Please, Jim, for the sake of the rest of us.

[MARBLE *gestures him away.* GERT *rises, finds the note and reads it.* MARBLE *mutters:*]

MARBLE: How is a man supposed to stand it? Tell me, someone—tell me, will you?

[GERT *tucks the note into her bosom, returns to the table and begins unconcernedly to deal out another hand.* PABST *smiles to himself and murmurs:*]

PABST: Perfection. [SPEEDY *slides the bottle toward him, but that is not what he means. He repeats:*] Simple perfection.

BALLANTINE: What?

PABST: —As fine a collection of wretched, unhappy human beings as ever it has been my privilege to behold.

DICKINSON: So what?

PABST: Oh, nothing—nothing at all. The world in miniature—the variety-show *par excellence*—we cannot but regard it with pity. We must not be too amused.

[BALLANTINE *half rises.*]

BALLANTINE: Let's go.

PABST: Oh no—no, I beg of you! I am learning so much.

BALLANTINE: One more drink, then.

SPEEDY: Oh yes—at least! [*He claps his hands together.*] Walter! [WALTER *turns to him.*] Freshen us up, Walter.

BALLANTINE: One—and one only.

[WALTER *nods and goes out into the pantry.* PABST *has turned and is gazing intently at the other table. Finally he calls very softly:*]

PABST: Mr. Clancy? Oh—Mr. Clancy!

CLANCY: Me?

PABST: You—yes. [*He beckons him to them.*] Come—join us for a moment.

CLANCY: Thank you—but it's—it's my friends I'm among here.

PABST: A moment—only for a moment. Come—

[*Reluctantly* CLANCY *rises and moves to the table.*]

DICKINSON: He thinks you're wonderful, Clancy. He wants to marry you.

PABST [*To* BALLANTINE]: Introduce us, please.

BALLANTINE: Dan Clancy—former chief stagehand—meet the great Professor—world-famous Illusionist—fresh from European triumphs —next week's headliner in place of La Paloma, who has the heaves in Detroit.—And maybe you'll tell me what you meant by coming on stage and ruining our show tonight?

CLANCY: Good evening to you, Professor.—I'm sorry about it, Mr. Ballantine. It was impolite and unthinking of me.

BALLANTINE: Haven't we absolutely done everything that could have been done for you?

CLANCY: Mr. Concannon has always been very kind.

BALLANTINE: Mr. Concannon was away. It was me who slipped those extra bills in your envelope.

CLANCY: You were very kind.—And is he returned, as yet?

BALLANTINE: No—at least, I don't think so.

[SPEEDY *glances toward the stage.*]

SPEEDY: That stairway of his hasn't been used since I don't know when. I know, for I looked. I picked the lock.

DICKINSON: There's a rumor around it's the Old Man himself you came back to see, Clancy.

[*At the next table* THE MAJOR *folds his cards into a book and listens. In fact, by now they are all listening.* CLANCY *shakes his head.*]

CLANCY: No, it was not. [*He thinks a moment.*] Mr. Concannon is a great and a noble man and always was. I've never in my life known a better or finer, but—[*And another moment. Then thoughtfully, to himself:*]—And to be sure, he might take that form as well as another, I suppose. But—

PABST: "Form"?

DICKINSON: Who might?

CLANCY: I don't like to say. It's a personal matter between me and him.

MARBLE: What *is* this?

[*There is a silence. At last* PABST *leans toward* CLANCY *and speaks very softly:*]

PABST: Mr. Clancy—[CLANCY *turns to him.*]—Unhappy and luckless Mr. Clancy—is it possible, by some curious chance, that he for whom you have been searching is no less a personage than—

CLANCY: Stop where you are!

PABST: —Than God Himself?

[*Another silence. Then* CLANCY *raises his head proudly.*]

CLANCY: It is!—And what's there curious about it?

CONNIE: Dan! What are you talking about?

SPEEDY: Good gracious!

DICKINSON: —A still hunt for the Almighty! It's marvelous.—Clancy, you certainly fly high.

[CLANCY *wheels on him and demands:*]

CLANCY: And why not? Isn't He everywhere? Is there a nook or a corner where He's not? What's there so strange in going out to find Him? Others have done it, and others will again! [*Once more his head sinks and his wild eyes stare blankly at the floor. He goes on, half to himself:*] I have to find Him! 'Tis a necessary thing to me. I have some things to ask Him which nobody else can answer. I know it is His will that things happen as they do, but I've come to a place where I have to know the reason for certain of them.—And know I will!

PABST: Of course, of course—

MARBLE: It's the damndest thing—

THE MAJOR: Why, Jim?

BALLANTINE: But in a vaudeville house—on a Saturday night! Absolutely!

SPEEDY: Yes—that takes the cake, it certainly takes the—

MARBLE: Why, of all places, did you think He'd pick the Globe for a personal appearance?

CLANCY: I don't know.—I was in Cleveland. I'd been many other places among the poor and the lowly, where they say it's easiest to—where they say He spends much of His time—but nor hide nor hair of Him. I was out walkin' by myself when all of a crack it came over me, like a cat jumped down on my back from a wall: "Tomorrow night at James Concannon's Globe—Holy Saturday night—hurry, me boy, hurry!"—So I came as quick as I could. I don't know how I got here. I don't even remember the—the train, it must have been. It wasn't till near curtain time did I arrive. The sweat was pouring from me, for fear of missing Him—[*His voices rises:*] But I can't have! I can't! I know in my bones He was there!

[*Swiftly* CONNIE *moves to his side.*]

CONNIE: Come along now, Dan. Come along with Connie.

[CLANCY *pulls away from her.*]

CLANCY: Don't treat me as if I was bereft of my senses! I'm not!—I'm sane as the next one, maybe more so. I could be a bit off on my reckoning, of course.—Maybe it was tomorrow night—no, tomorrow's Sunday and the house will be locked fast, and dark.—Or maybe it was somewhere not precisely *in* the Globe, but roundabouts. Maybe it was even—even—[*He glances about him.*]—No, Connie—the night's not over yet.

CONNIE: Will you please to come along, please?

CLANCY: And maybe miss Him entirely?—After all this time render me search null and void?

[PABST *rises and touches his elbow and gently steers him into a chair at the table, then turns and calmly surveys the incredulous faces about him.*]

PABST: This seems not at all as strange to me as it appears to seem to you. A man searches for the Truth and calls it "God"—Why not? It has many names, and as many faces.

CLANCY: —It has one: and that's the name and the face of God!

DICKINSON [*To* PABST]: Maybe you can scare Him up for the poor guy, Professor. Maybe *you* can evoke Him.

PABST: The Truth I can evoke.

DICKINSON: Who says?

PABST: You do not believe me.

DICKINSON: No.

PABST: You would like a demonstration, perhaps?

[*There is a silence. Then*]

DICKINSON: Yes. Strut your stuff.

MARBLE: —And be sure you make it good.

PABST: Very well.—But you must promise not to interfere.—Agreed?

[DICKINSON *gestures assent.* PABST *moves swiftly to the little stage and mounts it.*]

SPEEDY: An entertainment! Oh, good! I did hope there'd be! [*He rises to view the stage. Suddenly he cries out angrily:*] Those drapes! Who touched those drapes?

DICKINSON: I did.

SPEEDY: Well—you shouldn't have!

[PABST *tries the private door, finds it fast, then carefully draws the spangled curtains together again over it.*]

PABST: —And surely if He should choose to reveal Himself, Truth would prepare the way for Him, would it not?

[*He arranges a chair and table at the center of the little stage.* BALLANTINE *rises and picks up his hat and umbrella.*]

BALLANTINE: I've had enough for one week. Good night, all. [*He moves toward the alley door.*] Me, I take Sundays off. I absolutely do my theatergoing on weekdays.

[BALLANTINE *goes out.* PABST *comes forward upon the stage and inquires:*]

PABST: Shall we begin?

FAY: Look, Lew—he's going to do his act!

[*She moves to the piano bench and seats herself beside* LEW.]

PABST: Act?—I have no act. It is you who have the acts. [*He descends the steps and turns to* MARBLE.] Mr. Marble—please—

SPEEDY: But—but aren't *you* going to do *some*thing?

[PABST *smiles his slow, intolerable smile and levels his palms.*]

PABST: I? Oh no—*I* shall merely be master of ceremonies. [*He turns again to* MARBLE.] You are a ventriloquist, I understand.

MARBLE: That's the old rumor about me.

PABST: And this is your wife with you?

MARBLE: Yes, you might call her that.

GERT: Don't turn my head, will you?

PABST: —And you have your little man there in the black bag.

[*A muffled voice is heard from the bag:*]

THE DUMMY: Let me out! Let me out!

PABST: At once, little man. [*To* MARBLE] Your wife assists you?

MARBLE: In black tights: she has a fine figure, they say.

GERT: —And don't fail to tell us everything.

PABST: You will not need an assistant tonight. Take your place on the stage, please.

MARBLE: Listen, Professor: I've played twelve performances this week and I'm weary, see? I'm throatsore and weary.

THE DUMMY [*From the bag*]: Me too! Me too!

PABST [*Without accent*]: This will refresh you both.

DICKINSON: At times your English is better than at others.

PABST: *Danke.* Thank you very much—Well, Mr. Marble?

[MARBLE *rises, draws* THE DUMMY *from the bag and makes his way toward the stage.* SPEEDY *follows him, turns a switch at the side of the stage and lights a spotlight which casts a brilliant circle of light directly upon stage center.* DICKINSON *drags himself to his feet and stands swaying, bracing himself against the table.*]

DICKINSON: Marble's too good for Number One on any bill. I'll do the opener: it's a recitation, very short and to the point. Listen, Clancy—this is for you—[MARBLE *mounts the little stage and arranges himself there on the chair in the circle of light, a whisky glass, a package of cigarettes and an ash tray upon the table beside him, as* DICKINSON *proceeds:*] Once there was a little man like you in County Kerry—and he led a little life—and one day he began to pack a little bag. And *They* said, "Where are you off to? Where are you going?" And *he* said, "I'm packing my bag and I'm going to Connemara." And They said, "You mean, you're going to Connemara, God willing." And he said, "I mean I'm going to Connemara."—So God changed him into a frog and put him in a frog pond and kept him there for seven years. [CONNIE *laughs.*]

CONNIE: What kind of a God would do that to a little man?

DICKINSON: Oh—Clancy's—and yours—and other people's generally.—And then God changed him back again—and what did the little man do? He began at once to pack his little bag.—And They said, "Where are you off to? Where are you going?" And he said, "I'm going to Connemara." And They said, "You *mean,* you're going to Connemara, *God willing,*" And he said, "I mean I'm going to Connemara or back to the frog pond!"

[*He gestures drunkenly toward* CLANCY *and reseats himself.*]

CLANCY: I see what you mean.

DICKINSON: —When you arrive there, send me a postcard.

CLANCY: A postcard?

DICKINSON: A postcard—with the answer.

PABST: Apt—but we must have no more interruptions. [*He turns to* MARBLE, *who now has* THE DUMMY *astride his knee.*] Shall we begin?

MARBLE: Come now, Frank! Speak nicely to the gentleman.

[THE DUMMY *turns to* PABST.]

THE DUMMY: Good evening, Professor.

PABST: Good evening, Frank.

[*He seats himself upon the bench at the foot of the little stage.* THE DUMMY *barks at him:*]

THE DUMMY: "*Mr.* Frenzy" to you, please!

PABST: A thousand pardons.

THE DUMMY: —Make it two thousand.

PABST: Two thousand, then.

THE DUMMY: I'll take it! [THE DUMMY *blinks its eyes and turns its empty face up to* MARBLE.] You seem depressed, Jim. What's the matter?

MARBLE: Me? Depressed?

THE DUMMY: Yeh—down in the mouth. What for?—Has the little witch been acting up again?

MARBLE: The little—? I don't know who you mean, Frank.

THE DUMMY: W-i-t-c-h—"w" as in "butter." She certainly runs you ragged. I don't see how you stand it.

MARBLE: If it's my wife you are referring to—

THE DUMMY: Of course it's your wife! Who else would it be?

MARBLE: I don't care to discuss my domestic affairs.

THE DUMMY: You're going to whether you care to or not.

[GERT *stirs in her chair.*]

GERT: Oh, lay off.

[THE DUMMY'*s head swings in her direction.*]

THE DUMMY: Out! This is a private conversation—What a woman! Just a chippie off the old block, eh, Jim?

MARBLE: To what block do you refer, Frank?

THE DUMMY: Tenth Avenue, between Fourteenth and—

MARBLE: —That's enough!

THE DUMMY: It ought to be.

MARBLE: You'd better learn not to be so outspoken, my friend.

THE DUMMY: Hooey! The trouble with you is you never speak out. You let her get away with murder.

GERT: Oh, he does, does he?—Look out, or there'll be a real one.

MARBLE: I can't allow you to talk this way, Frank.

THE DUMMY: Try and stop me.

MARBLE: What are your views on politics? Do you think the Democrats—?

[*He takes a swallow of his drink.* THE DUMMY *talks through it:*]

THE DUMMY: I don't give a damn about politics! What worries me is the ride that dame's taking you on.

[MARBLE *puts down his glass.*]

MARBLE: My wife and I are very happy together, see?

THE DUMMY: Like fun you are.

MARBLE: She is the soul of loyalty—kind, generous, sweet-tempered—

THE DUMMY: Don't make me laugh.

MARBLE: —Loving and economical. In fact, the perfect helpmeet.

THE DUMMY: "Hellcat," did you say?

GERT: Thanks. That'll be about all!

MARBLE: "Helpmeet" is what I said.

THE DUMMY: Hooey.

MARBLE: I beg your pardon?

THE DUMMY: Hooey! Hooey!

MARBLE: Quiet, Frank—people will hear you.

THE DUMMY: So they'd ought! All this secrecy—that's how she gets away with it. If everyone knew the way she—

[MARBLE *claps a hand over the mouth.*]

MARBLE: Insect!—Quiet, I say!

THE DUMMY: Okay! Okay!

MARBLE: Promise?

THE DUMMY: Hope to die.

[MARBLE *removes his hand.* THE DUMMY *gasps, coughs once, and is quiet for a moment.*]

GERT: Very funny. In fact, a howl. I'll book you.

[MARBLE *lights a cigarette, keeping it in his mouth.*]

MARBLE: You know, Frank, sometimes you're almost as dumb as a man.

THE DUMMY: Yep—and two women.

[MARBLE *offers the cigarette.*]

MARBLE: Would you like a smoke?

THE DUMMY: No thanks. It gets in my eyes.

MARBLE: Too bad.

THE DUMMY: Yep—both of 'em.

MARBLE: Do you care for bridge?

THE DUMMY: Nope.

MARBLE: Why not?

THE DUMMY: I get tired of all the time being the dummy.

SPEEDY: Marvelous! He's as good as Marshall Montgomery.

PABST: —But this is extraneous. I feel the Truth struggling to come through. Something is holding it back—No?

[MARBLE *removes the cigarette from his mouth and puts it out, turning his head to one side with great deliberation as* THE DUMMY *turns in the opposite direction and gazes blankly into space, attemping a whistle that does not quite come off. Finally it inquires disinterestedly:*]

THE DUMMY: Why are you such a liar, Jim?

MARBLE: A liar? Me?

THE DUMMY: Yes.—Why not out with the truth once in a while? It would do you good—her, too.

MARBLE: Truth is pretty dangerous medicine, old boy.

PABST: —But effective—very often effective. [THE DUMMY*'s head swings around toward him.*]—I beg your pardon.

THE DUMMY: I grant your grace. I hope the cat will spit in your face.

PABST: But are we not again departing from our subject?

MARBLE: What subject is he referring to, Frank?

THE DUMMY: You know: that little b-i-t—that little bit of a wife of yours.

[GERT *half rises.*]

GERT: I won't stand it!

THE DUMMY: Then sit it!

MARBLE: I'm afraid I'll have to ask you to mend your language, my friend.

THE DUMMY: She's got her claws in you and she won't let go, will she?

MARBLE: As a matter of fact, she's often told me I can leave any time I like.

GERT: And I tell you again!

THE DUMMY: Then why don't you?

MARBLE: Why—I guess I just don't want to.

THE DUMMY: More hooey—you mean you're too soft-hearted to. You know if you don't watch her like a hawk she'll go straight to hell in a hack—well, why not let her?

MARBLE [*After a moment*]: She was a sweet kid, once.

[*Then* MARBLE*'s face changes, and* THE DUMMY *barks:*]

THE DUMMY: —You mean before the girls came around.

MARBLE: The what?

THE DUMMY: The girls! The girls! The girls!

[GERT *springs up.*]

GERT: What do you mean, you—!

[*The head swings around on her.*]

THE DUMMY: You heard me!—The girls! The little cries—the soft ones—the frilly ones—the girly-girls—

[GERT *advances threateningly.*]

GERT: I'll kill you, you damned little—

THE DUMMY: And what do you call yourself?—What could sink a man lower than to have to live with a woman who—

GERT: I won't stand it! I don't have to listen to such talk! I—I'll—[*She seizes* THE DUMMY *and shakes it violently.*] You—you foul little, lying little—[*She flings it down and makes her way blindly to the restaurant door.*] You'll never see me again! Never in this world—you hear me?

[*She is gone, the door banging closed after her.* MARBLE *picks up the sprawling* DUMMY, *replaces it in its black bag, pulls the strings together, hunches it into the crook of his arm and moves in the direction taken by* GERT. PABST *follows him.*]

PABST: Where are you going?

MARBLE: After her. She'll just sit in there till I come.

PABST: I would not, if I were you.

MARBLE: Why not?

PABST: Is that not just what she wants? Is that not just what you always have done?

CONNIE: But the poor, misguided creature—who else is she to turn to?

SPEEDY: She's got a right to her own life!

DICKINSON: Who says?

[MARBLE *stares at* PABST, *hesitates.* CLANCY *cries out:*]

CLANCY: Go on, Jim! Go on, man!

[MARBLE *turns and gazes at him. Finally he speaks:*]

MARBLE: No.

[*He sinks into a chair at the table, the black bag dropping at his feet.*]

CLANCY: —But she's your own wife!—And she might do some harm to herself.

MARBLE: Let her! Who gives a damn?

CLANCY: That's no thing to say!

PABST: Wise—at last he grows wise.

CLANCY: Wise, me foot! Who's to help her but him?

PABST: Never mind her. The truth has set *him* free!

DICKINSON: The hell it has. It's only moved him into another kind of prison.

MARBLE: Shut up, the lot of you!

THE MAJOR: You shouldn't have done it, Jim.

[PABST *turns blandly to* THE MAJOR.]

PABST: You, also, did not care for the performance?

THE MAJOR: No, I did not.

PABST: Perhaps you and I might give a better one—you think?

[THE MAJOR *stares at him.*]

THE MAJOR: How do you mean?

PABST: You could be *my* little man—no?

THE MAJOR: I don't understand you.

PABST: Would you be so kind as to come on stage with me, please?

THE MAJOR: No. No, thank you.

[PABST *moves closer to him, stands over him.*]

PABST: But I must insist! It is very important to a friend of yours—[*He glances at* CLANCY.]—It is, in fact, essential.

SPEEDY: Oh go on, Major—it's all in fun. Gracious!

THE MAJOR: But I don't see how—

[PABST *holds a hand out to him.*]

PABST: Come—you will soon find out how. It is really as simple as what-you-say—a-b-c.

[*Reluctantly* THE MAJOR *takes the proffered hand and together they move to the rear of the room, mount the shallow steps and are upon the stage.*]

SPEEDY: The long and the short of it! Isn't it sweet?

[PABST *seats himself upon the chair that* MARBLE *had occupied, swings* THE MAJOR *around to him, lifts him up and sets him upon his knee.*]

DICKINSON: Do you see what I see?

SPEEDY: Shh! No comments from the audience.

PABST: Now then! Attention, please—everyone attention!—Good evening, Major.

THE MAJOR: Well, what is it you want to know from me?

PABST: Just a few little things.—Like our friend Clancy, there are small things that puzzle me.

THE MAJOR: Well, what are they?

PABST: We are a little world in ourselves, we vaudeville artists, are we not?

THE MAJOR: In a way, yes.—Yes, I expect we are.

PABST: Our lives are so concentrated: twice a day, six days a week, we must give our all in the brief space of ten minutes.

THE MAJOR: *My* act runs twenty.

PABST: Twenty for the headliners—true. But we are not all headliners. Take our friend Clancy—he is hardly one of us at all—and yet, he, too, is a kind of essence. Wouldn't you say?

THE MAJOR: Yes. Yes, I would. Very much of a one.

PABST: And at present seems to believe that he represents, in his small self, all the essential troubles of the world.

CLANCY: I never said—!

PABST: Move nearer, Mr. Clancy. [*With a downward, sweeping motion of his arm he invites him to them.*] Sit here at our feet, that you may be even more one of us.

[CLANCY *comes forward and seats himself upon the second step of the stage steps.*]

CLANCY: I don't know at all what it is that you're after—

PABST: Only the Truth, Mr. Clancy. The ways there, alas, are not always straight ways. [*He turns again to the* MAJOR, *urging him:*] Tell me about this Clancy. Acquaint me briefly with the facts of his decline and his fall.

CLANCY: That might be private.

PABST: Quiet, please.

[THE MAJOR *speaks woodenly:*]

THE MAJOR: From the beginning, his life has been a hard one. As a boy he knew cold and hunger, and he has known them since.—He never asked for much, and much was never given him.

CLANCY: Don't make me out sorry for myself now—for I'm not!

THE MAJOR: —In fact, the little that he had, at last was taken from him. He lost his little home and he lost his little savings. He lost the sight of one eye.

CLANCY: Well, I never did any crying over myself with either of them. It's not such things alone—

THE MAJOR: —He lost his job—his young brother and his little daughter. That was the worst. He was left with only his beloved wife to mourn all these things that had been so dear to him. Then he woke one fine morning and found that she was gone too.

PABST: His wife? Where to? With whom—a lover?

[CLANCY *springs up.*]

CLANCY: Put up your dukes! You get a poke in the nose for that!

[PABST *holds his hands out to him.*]

PABST: Forgive me—

CLANCY: Then why did you say such a thing?

PABST: I was in error: forgive me.

CLANCY: The poor child left me because she thought she was bad luck for me. She said it to me once: "I bring you bad luck, Dan," she said.

PABST: Of course—of course——

CLANCY: —"Of course" no such thing! She only thought it!

PABST: I understand.

CLANCY: See that you do!—And in the future, mind your tongue.

[PABST *bows his head.* CLANCY *reseats himself.* PABST *turns again to* THE MAJOR.]

PABST: —And his little girl—how hold was she?

THE MAJOR: I don't know precisely. Two—three—

CLANCY: Three years, four months, two days.

PABST: They are sweet at that age.

CLANCY: *She* was!—And she was good, too, and pretty as a picture and full of jokes and laughing. Never a tear out of her, except now and then when her little insides hurt her, with the wind or the like—or when she grew aware of the vast world about her and felt too small in it and needed comforting.

PABST: —A bitter blow to lose her.

CLANCY: It was, that. How it happened, I don't know—or why it ever did. She was always well and strong, for all that she was a seven-months' baby. It started with no more than a little cold—the same as any child might have in changing weather. But it grew and it grew until it was all the way through her and then the doctor could only shake his head and sit and watch her, fighting for breath, beating her little fists in the air.

PABST: What could be sadder?

CLANCY: There's little that could be.—I don't know of anything could, now I think of it.—Angela was all that was ever all my own. My job could be taken any time—the eye is a delicate organ, subject to accidents—my house was never fully paid for—young Timmy, my brother, drank—and my Nora was my wife only so long as she was willing to put up with me. But Angela was all my own.

PABST: Still, all such deprivations mean something—don't you agree, Major? They all have some purpose in the scheme of life.

DICKINSON: Oh, sure, sure—they add zest.

CLANCY: But mean *what?* That's what I want to know! The purpose of 'em!—And I want to know other things!

PABST: Would you wish to have had a child, too, Major?

[THE MAJOR'*s face sets.*]

THE MAJOR: I had one.

[PABST *seems surprised.*]

PABST: Indeed.

THE MAJOR: Yes, I had a son.

PABST: That was long ago—

THE MAJOR: Yes—that was long ago.

PABST [*After a moment*]: And where is he now?

THE MAJOR: I can't say. I don't know.

PABST: Tell us a little, Major. Speak out to us. It will do you good.

[*There is a brief silence. Then* THE MAJOR*'s voice begins, toneless and flat, as if reading faded print aloud:*]

THE MAJOR: Anna and I had wanted a child for years, but we had been afraid. We—

[*He stops again,* PABST *helps him:*]

PABST: She was small, too, I take it.

THE MAJOR: —Smaller even than me. She could walk under my arm. That's the way she came on stage with me: it made a—it made a very good entrance. She was the only grownup I have ever known that I was bigger than. She was a true midget, not a dwarf like me—fine in every part—hands, feet, little wrists and ankles, all perfectly proportioned. She had the bluest eyes ever there were—my, they were blue! She was a treat to see. A reviewer in Savannah once referred to her as "the Vest-pocket Venus" and other papers took it up. Finally we used it in our billing: "Major Armstrong and His Vest-pocket Venus."

PABST: Charming.—And the child?

THE MAJOR: We—we thought that having one would be like shouting from the housetops, "Look! See how these small people have loved! Love is not denied the small in stature if their souls, if their spirits be—" [*Again he stops and swallows. Then he goes on:*]—He was born as a Caesar was, and the medical men in attendance were very interested and very pleased with themselves. He was—all right in every way—like Anna's grandmother—like my father.

SPEEDY: Who'd ever believe such a thing! Gracious!

PABST: But were you not gratified?

THE MAJOR: At first, yes—we were even proud of it. But finally, as he kept growing, it got so that we couldn't sleep at night, wondering, planning, fearing. At four he was as tall as his mother was. At five, he came to here on me. We were—we were like three children together.—But when he was seven, we sent him away.

PABST: —For his own good. An unselfish and noble act.

THE MAJOR: —All I know is, that try as she might my Anna could not endure a world without him. Month by month she dwindled away to nothing and one night she just turned on her pillow and died.

PABST: Dear, dear, how dreadful.

THE MAJOR: It was here, in the Sims' Hotel. I would have followed her, but Mr. Concannon gave me the courage to wait.

PABST: James Concannon?

THE MAJOR: Is there another?

PABST: —And what became of the boy?

THE MAJOR: The people he was with were not good people—they couldn't have been, because he ran away from them. I've never been able to find out where—or anything about him—though I've tried very hard to. [*He looks away.*] He'd be a grown man now. I—I dare-say he'd make a dozen of me. [*He waits an instant, then looks up at* PABST.]—And now may I get down, please?

PABST: One moment. [*He turns to* CLANCY.] Well, Mr. Clancy—?

[CLANCY *looks up. His eyes are dazed again.*]

CLANCY: Who—? Where—? What did you say?

[PABST *turns to the others.*]

PABST: —It appears that our saddened friend does not yet realize that others among us also have our burdens to bear.

CLANCY: Ah, that I do! I do indeed! But what help is that to anyone? [*He turns to* THE MAJOR.] My heart is knotted up into a fist for you, Major.

THE MAJOR: Thank you, Clancy.

[PABST *frowns down upon* CLANCY.]

PABST: Which is the worse—to have the Almighty take a child, or to have to give it away to strangers? To have it safe in heaven—or to have it roam the world, nameless and alone?

CLANCY: The cases are not the same—nor the circumstances! But both are bad, both!

PABST: Which is the better—to have one's wife die, wracked to the bone with grief—or to have her leave one, and live on?

CLANCY: It's not the same—there's no similarity!

[*There is a pause.* PABST *ponders, then turns and speaks suddenly:*]

PABST: You, there—Cooper and Farrel—[*They start in surprise. He adds, softly:*] Would you come a little nearer, please? [LEW *and* FAY *look at each other uncertainly, then rise.*] You, Miss—another step forward—one, two, three! [*Deliberately* FAY *advances three steps, and three only.*] Now, then, little song-and-dance lady—hearing what you have heard, do you still wish to marry?

[FAY *replies stoutly:*]

FAY: Yes. I do.

PABST: And have a child—children?

FAY: Yes. I do!

LEW: Look: what's the idea?

PABST: So young, so brave, so unafraid. Is it not interestin', Major? Is it not interestin', Mr. Clancy? [*They do not reply. He turns to* FAY *again, smiling his smile.*] Pretty as you are, it should be so simple—just to take him by the hand and lead him to the altar—no?

FAY: Maybe it should be, but it's not.

PABST: And why, pray?

FAY: He won't come.

PABST: He must have his reasons.

FAY: I suppose he has. But he keeps them to himself.

PABST: Dear, dear.—Are you quite sure he loves you?

FAY: Yes. Yes, I am.

LEW: What *is* this? Why should you have to tell this old goat what you—

PABST: "Old goat"? That is not nice. That is not nice at all.

LEW [*Advancing*]: Oh, can it! What right have you got to mix in, anyway?

PABST: That's it—closer. Come a little closer.

[LEW *stops abruptly.*]

LEW: I'll stay where I am, thanks.

PABST: But this is impolite of you. It is not in the interests of a varied entertainment. [*He coaxes and smiles, gesturing:*] Come, young man—come—come—

LEW: That'll be all right!

PABST: He is stubborn, little Major. It appears *we* must go to *him.* [*With* THE MAJOR *perched awkwardly against his shoulder he proceeds down the stage steps, advances to* LEW *and stands directly facing him.*] Look at him, little Major. Gaze upon this strange contradiction: a young man in love who will not marry. Talented, well-off, sound in limb and in sinew, and still he will not marry.

LEW: That's my business, isn't it?

PABST: Ah yes—deeply so. Look at him, Major—you are a wise little man—perhaps you can account for this perverse attitude. All that we know of him is that he is a foundling, that he is in love and that he will not marry.—Ah, yes! And one thing more—

LEW: Shut up. Shut up, you!

PABST: —Just one—a certain unaccountable distaste for very small people, like yourself. Look at him closer—consider the brow, the elevated cheekbones. And the eyes—did you ever see eyes so blue in a man's head? Where have you ever seen their like before? [LEW *begins to tremble. His hands close and unclose spasmodically.*] He seems to grow nervous—I wonder why? Of what can he be afraid? [*His voice lowers:*] Little Major—does it not grow more apparent why he will not marry? [*A sudden cry is wrung from* THE MAJOR *and he turns his gaze sharply from the dancer's face. But* PABST *goes on:*] Is it not now somewhat more evident who he is?

[THE MAJOR *struggles in* PABST*'s arms.*]

LEW: You—you fishy, fatheaded slob, you—what the hell do you think you're trying to pull off?

THE MAJOR: Let me go! Let me go!

PABST: —But certainly.

[*He sets him carefully down upon his feet.* THE MAJOR *totters toward the stage, sinks down upon the lowest step and sits there, his head in his hands, his narrow shoulders shaking.* FAY *looks wonderingly from him to* LEW, *then back again.*]

FAY: Oh Lew—

[*Suddenly* LEW *shouts:*]

LEW: He lies! He's not!

[PABST *inquires mildly:*]

PABST: Who is not what? Have I said anything?

LEW: Plenty! But it's not true I'm his—he's my—!—And you know damn well it's not!

PABST: Of course, of course—

LEW: Then why do you make it seem that it is? You, with your oily roundabout way of—your cheap, ten-twenty-thirty trick of piling it up, and then making it sound like it was the McCoy—!

[*He flounders and stops.*]

FAY: Lew—listen, Lew—

LEW: I tell you it's just his rotten idea of being funny! It's a stinking lie, the whole thing, cooked up out of nothing! I'll be damned if I'll hang around and take any more of it! To hell with the lot of you—

[*He storms out into the alley.* CLANCY *drops down upon the step and throws one arm protectingly about* THE MAJOR. FAY *moves to the alley door, where she turns and faces* PABST.]

FAY: I think—I think you're a living horror. God damn you to hell.

[*She goes out.* PABST *sighs, lowers his head and clasps his hands across his front.*]

PABST: Dear, dear. It seems that even the semblance of Truth is not popular.

CLANCY: The "semblance," is it? Then you're admitting yourself it's not so!

PABST: We always have coincidence to contend with.

CONNIE: —And "coincidence," too—it's a grand time to be saying that!

PABST: I regret I have not your command of the language.

CONNIE: And don't be coming at us with that kind of five-act talk! Even if it was a fact, facts aren't the truth always.

PABST: Now there—*there* you have me. That is very astute of you.

DICKINSON: Why should we take all this from you, anyhow?

PABST: Shall I stop where I am, perhaps?

DICKINSON: Hell, no. We've seen nothing yet that any smalltime ham couldn't pull off as well or better.

[PABST *looks at him oddly.*]

PABST: Thank you. Then I shall proceed.

DICKINSON: In the interests of accuracy, it just happens that *I* know who Lew's father is—and where he is.

CLANCY: Then tell him, man, tell him!

DICKINSON: I'd sooner draw and quarter him.

SPEEDY: Is it that bad?

DICKINSON: It's worse.

[PABST *is looking at* DICKINSON *with new interest. He crooks his finger at him and murmurs mockingly:*]

PABST: Ah-ha!

[DICKINSON *gestures him away.*]

CLANCY [*After a moment*]: Anyhow, Major, now you know it's not so, not a bit of it.

THE MAJOR: All I know is that if ever I did find him, it might—it might be like that.

[CLANCY *glances angrily at* PABST.]

CLANCY: You tricky old wretch, you. Lew and Fay were better off as they were—and so was the Major.

PABST: —But advise me seriously, Mr. Clancy—would you not rather your daughter were dead than that she had ever grown up to deny you?

CLANCY: She never would have!

CONNIE: Why should she have? Where's the girl ever had a better man for a father?

CLANCY: And I say again, you shouldn't have done this to the Major. You've not done him good, you've done him ill!

PABST: A matter of opinion.—Would you rather it had been done to you?

CLANCY: There's nothing can be done to me any more! All that could be has been.

PABST: Are you sure?

CLANCY: I am.

PABST: That must console you.

CLANCY: I have other consolations.

PABST: Ah? Such as—

CLANCY: I had a wife who loved me once, and still does maybe. I had a good job to occupy my mind. I had my health and I had a small house with a flower bed behind it. And for a time I had a little girl who was all my own. I had everything!

PABST: Brave memories.

CLANCY: There'll never be braver! They're of a nature to comfort any man alive!—But as for you, I can't for the life of me figure you out. What are you up to with all these cooney tricks, anyhow? Why do you do what you do?

PABST: Perhaps at heart I am a humanitarian.

CONNIE: At what?—I doubt if you've got one.—Come along, Dan, you can sleep at Mrs. Carlson's. She's got an empty bed.

CLANCY: Yes—I'll come—[*He turns again to* PABST.]—Good night to you, old slyboots, and small thanks, if any.

PABST: So—you give up your great search so easily.

CLANCY: You can leave that to me!

PABST: —You hug your "consolations" to you, and settle for a penny in the pound. Most interestin', most.

[DICKINSON *thumps upon the table.*]

DICKINSON: Connemara—to Connemara!

[CLANCY *glances at him, then back to* PABST.]

PABST: No—it is too difficult. The Irish are a soft race, really. The bravery is all in front.

CLANCY: Who says it is?

CONNIE: Dan—here we go, Dan—

CLANCY: No. Wait a bit. [*To* PABST] Who says they are?

PABST: —An Irishman without a cause—is there a sadder sight in the world?

CLANCY: If my cause is a lost one, it's none the less my own, you old crock!

PABST: —One moment, please. [*In the center of the room he deftly arranges two chairs, facing each other. Then he moves quickly to* SPEEDY, *bends and whispers something to him.* SPEEDY *looks at him blankly. Now* PABST *speaks aloud to him:*] Please not to make difficulties. Tell her it is only for a moment. Tell her he has gone—

[SPEEDY *hesitates briefly, then goes to the restaurant door and out.*

CLANCY *seats himself stubbornly in the chair with its back to the door.* CONNIE *advances to him.*]

CONNIE: Well, are you coming or aren't you?

CLANCY: Sit down a bit, Connie.

CONNIE: I will not.

[PABST *approaches them.*]

CLANCY: Why not? Just one little minute, till—

CONNIE: Because that's what he wants us to do! And I'll tell him nothing!

PABST: What is there to tell?

CONNIE: You heard me, didn't you?—Nothing!

PABST: No?—Not one little word to the one man in the whole world you—

CONNIE: —That isn't so! I don't! I don't at all!

PABST: —Don't what? What have I said?

CONNIE: Never mind!—Come on, Dan. I don't like it here. I don't like it a bit. I've got a queer feeling it's—well, what are you looking at me so funny for? [*He is gazing at her, his eyes again dazed, as if he had found something gravely amiss.*] Are you coming or are you not?

CLANCY: What's different about your face, Connie? What's wrong with it?

CONNIE: Nothing that hasn't always been. You don't have to look at it!

CLANCY: *I* know!—Where are your earrings?

CONNIE: I never had earrings.

CLANCY: You did so. Your grandmother pierced your ears with a hot needle when you were small and she set little round gold earrings in them and said you'd never get the rheumatism.

CONNIE: She did no such thing!

CLANCY: You told me she did.

CONNIE: You're thinking of Nora.

[*A moment, then* CLANCY*'s head droops and he murmurs:*]

CLANCY: So I am. So I am.

CONNIE: *I* wouldn't have them on a bet.

CLANCY: They're pretty things.

CONNIE: —Not if I had to die for the lack of them, I wouldn't.

CLANCY: You were always the stubborn one, Connie.

CONNIE: Be that as it may, I—! [*She stops suddenly and gazes in alarm beyond him to the opposite side of the room where* NORA *stands in the doorway,* SPEEDY *behind her.* CONNIE *speaks softly:*]—Take it easy, Dan. You're in for it now, all right.

CURTAIN

■ ACT III ■

The Same.

The positions are the same as at the end of Act Two. The time is immediately after it. The action is continuous.

SPEEDY *is urging* NORA *into the room.*

SPEEDY: Just a little informal entertainment, that's all.

NORA: But why should I be the stooge for a trick man, for God's sake? The gentleman I'm with steps into the washroom for a minute, and—

[CLANCY *straightens abruptly at the sound of her voice, but does not turn.* PABST *holds the chair opposite him out for* NORA.]

PABST: —This way, Madam, if you will be so good.

[*She moves uncertainly past* CLANCY *to the chair.*]

NORA: But what's the point? My friend won't know where I've—[*She turns, sees* CLANCY, *and gasps:*] You! [*She grasps the back of the chair.*] Speedy said you'd gone. He said—

CLANCY: Nora—[*Then suddenly he springs up, crying out joyously:*] Ah, Nora, Nora—you've come back!

[*And moves swiftly toward her.* NORA *draws herself erect against the chair.*]

NORA: I have not! And you stay where you are—keep your distance away from me! [CLANCY *stops in his tracks and gazes at her.*] Go back where you were. [*He does not move.*] I mean it!—Don't you know yet that I mean what I say? [*Dumbly* CLANCY *returns to his chair.* NORA *turns and meets* CONNIE'*s accusing eyes, with dark resentment in her own.*] I suppose it's you I've got to thank for this.

CONNIE: I'd nothing to do with it. I'd've done wonders to keep it off.

[NORA *seats herself with deliberation, faces* CLANCY *squarely and demands:*]

NORA: Well—what do you want?

[CLANCY *can only stare.* DICKINSON *waits a moment, then speaks:*]

DICKINSON: I suppose we just might have the decency to clear out and leave them.

MARBLE: I was thinking that.

THE MAJOR: Yes.

NORA: What for? This is a free-for-all. The more the merrier. [*She turns again to* CLANCY.] Well—get it out, can't you? I left a good plate of eggs for this.

CLANCY: You're changed.
NORA: Only to you, I imagine.
CLANCY: You were never like this.
NORA: I was always like this.
CLANCY: No—you've got hard.
NORA: I was born hard, hard as nails.
CLANCY: I never saw it.
NORA: You weren't let: I took good care of that.
[CLANCY *frowns at her, puzzled.*]
CLANCY: What is it you're saying? What is it you mean?
NORA: You had such a sweet little idea of me, I thought I'd live up to it, that's all.
CLANCY: I don't believe it.
NORA: You never believe anything but what you want to.
CLANCY: And that's not so, either.
NORA: It is, and everything I'll be telling you will be! That's why I'm willing to sit here, to put you straight once and for all—so you'll never trouble me again, ever.
CLANCY: "Trouble" you, did you say?
NORA: That's what I said. You're a blight on me, Dan Clancy, and you always have been.
CLANCY: This can't be you, Nora. Surely it can't.
NORA: But it is.
CLANCY: You who were so good and gentle and loving—
NORA: I know!—I ought to of gone on the stage.
CLANCY: Something's just suddenly come over you. Tell me, so I can—
NORA: Oh, tie it outside! You're a worse fool than I thought you.
[CLANCY *half rises.*]
CLANCY: You mind your tongue, Miss!
NORA: —Irish.—It doesn't scare me. It never did. I was raised on it.
[CLANCY *turns in bewilderment to* CONNIE.]
CLANCY: What's the matter with her, Connie? What is it?
CONNIE: She's had a drink or two, I guess. Dutch courage, I guess.
NORA: You keep your oar out!
CLANCY: But she never touched anything.
NORA: Oh didn't I? And didn't I used to have a fine laugh at you, for not catching on!
CLANCY: You've been bewitched.
[*She leans toward him, elbow on knee, chin on hand, exasperated.*]
NORA: Listen—will you never learn?

CLANCY: Why did you run away from me with never a word? Was it because of all the misfortune that had suddenly come on us—and you thinking you'd brought it?

NORA: That's what you told yourself, is it?

CLANCY: I'm asking you, Nora—and what's more, you're to tell me.

NORA: That was part of it, yes.

CLANCY: What else?

NORA: Because I couldn't stand you!

[*He looks at her aghast.*]

CLANCY: You don't mean that all at once there was no more love in your heart for me—

NORA: I mean there never was any!

[CLANCY *frowns, still unable to comprehend. Again he turns to* CONNIE.]

CLANCY: She's joking.—You hear her, Connie: she's trying to make some kind of a joke.

NORA: Joke, my eye! I'm saying what I mean now, for once—and I mean just that—never ever—never a scrap of love!

[*He looks at her from under his brows.*]

CLANCY: For nearly four years we were man and wife—

NORA: You don't need to tell *me* that!

CLANCY: —You can't fool me, Nora. I have too good a memory.

[*She sees what he means, and laughs shortly.*]

NORA: Oh, I liked that part of it all right. I got round heels, you know.

[CLANCY*'s face sets and his now angered eyes travel her from head to foot and back again. Finally he speaks very softly.*]

CLANCY: —From a dear and a loving and warm-hearted girl, full of grace and delight, something or someone has turned you in no time at all into a cheap, dirty-mouthed little piece. Someone has put a spell on you—who is it?

NORA: So there has to be someone *else,* does there? Listen, you—

CLANCY: Who is it? Tell me who it is. Because I'll render him null and void, so I will!

NORA: Don't be a fool. No one's anything to me but myself, and never has been.

CONNIE: That's nice of you. It's right sweet of you to leave him something.

[CLANCY *looks from one to the other, then rises and goes to* NORA, *stands over her, searching the impudent pretty face for something he wants desperately to find there. At last he speaks:*]

CLANCY: It's not that I don't love and cherish you as I always have, but you anger me. Your unwomanly talk and your vast impertinences and the silly, hollowed-out sound of a laugh that used to be sweet like a string orchestra—it makes me angry.

NORA: So what?

CLANCY: I don't know yet, but you must be made to unlearn your new tricks.

NORA: Oh? By who?

CLANCY: By me!—You fresh, brassy little jape, sitting there on your hard seat with that new chippie look in your shoe-button eyes and that two-for-a-dollar smile round your mouth, you were once my wife, you still are. And I'll have no wife of mine abroad on such behavior, and you can make book on it!

NORA: So what do you plan to do?

CLANCY: You know what I'd like to do this minute?—I'd like to give you one with the flat of me hand that'd send you spinning down the ages.

NORA: —Only you won't.

CLANCY: Don't be so sure, Miss.

NORA: You haven't it in you to. You're the original Mister Softheart, and your hands were made for love pats. [*She rises.*] Well—save 'em for someone else. I'm not taking any. [*She drops a step or two back from him, opens her handbag, peers into a mirror in it, puts powder on her nose, snaps the bag shut and addresses him with a fine air of finality:*] Anything more?—If not, I'll be getting along now.

CLANCY: You will, will you?

NORA: Yes I will.

CLANCY: You'll stay directly where you are! You'll not move a step till I've found out another thing or two.

NORA: You're the thorough one, aren't you? Just a real good house-cleaning.

CLANCY: There's many the dirty chimney I'd like to send the goose down tonight, I can tell you that!

[*She turns to* SPEEDY *with a great show of dignity.*]

NORA: Mr. Speedy, is it customary for ladies to be detained in your place against their wish?

SPEEDY: I never come between husband and wife. I've learned enough for—

[*He stops as the door from the restaurant is opened and* GURNEY *comes in. He is lighting a cigarette and kicks the door to after him.*]

GURNEY: Hello, everybody. How about a round on me? [*Silence greets him. He looks up, puzzled, and snaps his cigarette lighter shut with a flourish as* CLANCY *turns slowly and regards him. He tosses the lighter into the air, catches it again, pockets it and casually advances into the room.*] How are you, Clancy, old man? We've missed you round the Globe. It hasn't been the same place without your daily specialty. How about a small one on me, to celebrate the homecoming?

CLANCY: No thank you.

GURNEY: No?—Then how about—er—your good lady?

CLANCY: She neither.

PABST: —Isn't it interestin'?

GURNEY: Your eye looks fine—damned if I'd know it was any different from the other.

CLANCY: Never mind my eye!

GURNEY: Oh, come on! What's all the gloom about? Lent's over!

CLANCY: I wish you would go.

GURNEY: Thanks for the buggy ride, only I'm staying.

CLANCY: I wish you would kindly leave now.

GURNEY: You're kidding. You know I'm a permanent attraction here. [*He seats himself at* DICKINSON*'s table and slaps his hand down upon it.*] Come on—fill 'em up! [*He fills a glass from the whisky bottle and looks about him.*] What! No music? Where's Piano Mary?

[CLANCY *leans back against the table. Again his eyes have the dazed look in them.*]

CLANCY: Maybe I'm hungry. I don't know when I ate last.

[CONNIE *rises.*]

CONNIE: I'll bring something in for you from the front.

[CLANCY *straightens.*]

CLANCY: No. I don't want it. [*Again he turns and addresses* GURNEY:] I ask you please to move along out of here. I'm talking with my wife.

[GURNEY *squints through his glass at the others.*]

GURNEY: I see: just a private run-through with all the boxes full. Why pick on me?

CLANCY: I don't like you, Val Gurney, and I never did. All I ever owed you was that it was through you that I first met up with Nora. But since she's left me I owe you no more.

GURNEY: Why, Clancy, you surprise me. I thought we were old friends. What's the trouble between you and the Missus?

[CLANCY *looks at* NORA.]

CLANCY: It turns out it was a stray cat I brought home. I buttered her paws, but she stayed only to lick them off, and then strayed again.

GURNEY: You don't say. And I thought you'd be the perfect match.

CLANCY: I remember you said so. [*Suddenly he advances to* NORA *and seizes her wrist.*] Only where did you stray *to?*

NORA: Let go!

CLANCY: I never thought—but I'm thinking now! Who was it?

CONNIE: Go easy, Dan.

NORA: You let me go!

CLANCY: Tell me his name! I'll—!

[NORA *cries out for help.*]

NORA: Val! Val!

[CLANCY *drags her up to him and stares into her face, then thrusts her aside and gazes incredulously at* GURNEY. PABST *whispers something to* SPEEDY, *and unnoticed by the others, they move to the restaurant door and go out.* GURNEY *puts out his cigarette and rises uncertainly.*]

GURNEY: Look here, old man—no need for any rough stuff, you know.

CLANCY: —So it was you.

GURNEY: Never mind about that. The point now is—

CLANCY: Never mind about it?

GURNEY: What I mean is, we can settle everything peacefully, with no hard feelings.

CLANCY: Settle a man's wife running off from him to another man—and one the likes of you?

GURNEY: Let's not get personal, now.

MARBLE: What would you like him to get?

DICKINSON: Yes—*you* tell us, will you?

GURNEY: Keep out, the lot of you! This is between Clancy and me. Am I right, Dan?

CLANCY: It is, that. It is surely.

GURNEY: It could happen to any of us, you know. What a man wants with a woman he can't hold I could never see anyway.

CLANCY: Couldn't you?

GURNEY: No, frankly I couldn't.

CLANCY: And why?

GURNEY: Well, it's—you know—just bad box office. It's bound to flop sooner or later.

CONNIE: Oh, the worm!

[CLANCY *advances.*]

GURNEY: Keep away!—If you so much as touch me, I'll—[*But* CLANCY*'s hand is at the back of his neck now, and has begun to shake him* *slowly, like a sack.* GURNEY *struggles to free himself from the grasp, gasping:*] Let go, you fool! What do you think you're doing?

NORA: Stop it! Stop!

[*But the shaking goes on.*]

GURNEY: You, Speedy—call somebody! What kind of a joint is this?

NORA: Oh, stop it! Stop! Stop!

CONNIE: He had it coming. You both of you had.

[*With one twist of his arm,* CLANCY *sends* GURNEY *crashing against the base of the little stage, where he lies for a moment before he finds his feet again. Finally he rises, pulls himself together, brushes himself off, eyeing* CLANCY *with a look half fear, half hatred. He makes his way to the alley door. His hand fumbles behind him for the door knob, finds it, turns it and holds on to it. Then he spits out his words:*]

GURNEY: You scum. You half-witted moron. Come around and ask me some more questions sometime. Ask me about your kid, for instance. She came pretty quick, didn't she?—Seven months, my foot—six was nearer it! Why else do you think Nora married you, you poor, dumb—

CONNIE: No, no!

[NORA *breaks in frantically:*]

NORA: Don't listen to him! [CLANCY *strides toward* GURNEY *but he is out the door before he can reach him.* NORA *stands shaking with rage, muttering to herself:*] He's lying. He's—

[CLANCY *comes up behind her.*]

CLANCY: Then why did you marry me—and not him? [*He swings her around to him.*] Tell me!

CONNIE: Don't hurt her, Dan!

CLANCY: She'll tell me!—Why?

NORA: He—he wouldn't. However much I asked—however much I—

CLANCY: It was him introduced us, him that brought us together. And from the first sight of you, you knew it was all up with me. And you took me straight off—

NORA: He made me! He kept after me till I—

CLANCY: —You put your head on my shoulder and said, "Let's not wait, Dan. Let's not wait a week even." Do you remember you did?

NORA: You don't know—you don't know—

CLANCY: That was in April—and less than seven months after—on the second day of November—though we'd not looked for it till the first of the year, if that soon—and the doctor said often at seven months if the mother was not as strong as she might be—[*Suddenly his voice catches and he stops. His head drops upon his breast. He murmurs to himself:*]—And I told myself there was no more ill could happen to me! [*He raises his head, his face working. He touches her once, twice, lightly upon the shoulder with two fingers, speaking very gently.*]—You can go along now, Nora. [*He takes her coat from the chair and lays it upon her shoulders, pulling it awkwardly into place.*] There now—there we are. [*The pressure of his hand directs her to the door. He holds it open for her.*] Good-bye now. When I think of the frets and the worries you've had, my heart aches for you, you bad girl, you.—Good-bye, now. Good-bye, Nora—

[*She turns and looks at him. Finally she speaks:*]

NORA: Don't hate me, Dan.

CLANCY: No, Nora—no. [*She goes out and he closes the door after her. He stands there for a moment, then squares his shoulders, comes up to the table where* THE MAJOR *and* DICKINSON *sit and takes the chair left by* MA SPEEDY.] I think I'll have a small drink now, if that's agreeable. [DICKINSON *fills a glass and sets it before him. He drains it at a gulp, puts it down and draws the back of his hand across his mouth.*]—That's what I needed.—"There comes a time," as they say.

DICKINSON: Oh yes, it's a swell world. God's in His Heaven, all right—and He's going to stay there.

[*This time* CLANCY *makes no attempt to refute him. He stares down at the table and his fingers begin to drum on it.* CONNIE *slips into the chair beside him, catches at the hand and holds it flat between her two own, rubbing it back and forth, as if to draw the blood back into it.*]

CONNIE: She was yours, little Angela was. She was all your own. Never have I known a baby to go so for any man. You were the one bright star in her little life. She was just a little fool for you, Dan—no one else even counted with her.

[*He swings around, frees his hand and joyously opens and shuts it between his face and* CONNIE'*s. His eyes are bright with tears, though he is half laughing. He demands of her:*]

CLANCY: D'you remember—? How she—how she used to—? The way she would—?—When I'd come in before supper and she heard my tread on the stairs, how she'd—?

[*He cannot finish.* CONNIE'*s arm goes around his shoulders, contracts briefly and is withdrawn.*]

CONNIE: She was all yours. She was all your own.

[CLANCY *shakes his head slowly.*]

CLANCY: She was not—and Nora never was neither. And all my fine consolations are no more than a heap of angel droppings, as my young brother Tim used to say.

CONNIE: Hush, Dan—

[*Suddenly he strikes his fist upon the table.*]

CLANCY: I'll not! There's too much hushing done! We hush when we should be—! [*He throws back his head and shouts:*]—You up there, why do You send such blank confusion upon the world? What's the earthly good of half the things that happen?—Things that on the face of them are blundering injustices with no sense nor purpose—what's the reason for them? [*He drags himself to his feet and half circles the room.*] Have You not said You'd come when we called You? Then where are You keeping Yourself?—What have You to lose by passing a moment or two with a man of Your own making in such unholy need of You? [*His arm lashes through the air in a peremptory gesture and his voice thunders the command:*] Can You not hear me? Then come to me! Come!

[*There is an expectant moment, as if the others half-believed the command would be obeyed. Then* DICKINSON*'s glass upon the table shatters the silence.*]

DICKINSON: Knock, and it shall be locked in your face. Seek, and you'll go on seeking.

CLANCY: Don't say it. Never say such a thing.

MARBLE: It's a sell, Dan, see?—All we can do is to make the best of it.

THE MAJOR: —That's what I say—the best of it.

CONNIE: It's—it's a long way up to heaven, you know—and it's a long way down.

CLANCY: It's a long time here—that I know, I know that.

DICKINSON: —*Now* do you believe in Him?

CLANCY: I don't know where He keeps Himself.

DICKINSON: Because your only hope is not to, Clancy. Anyone's is.

[CONNIE *goes to* CLANCY *and takes his hand in hers.*]

CONNIE: Don't mind him. Don't mind anything. Come along, now. It's sleep you need, Dan.

CLANCY: It is, it is that.

CONNIE: —And maybe it's a better day tomorrow, you know.

CLANCY: Yesterday was the good day—yesterday a long time ago. [*He stands for a moment, staring dully at the floor, then kicks at it once, as if to remove a worthless object from his path.*] What good is the Truth when you don't know what to do with it?

DICKINSON: Don't tell me it hasn't set *you* free, either.

[CLANCY *moves toward the alley with* CONNIE, *mumbling:*]

CLANCY: Free for what? Free for what?

[*Suddenly, through the spangled curtains at the back of the little stage a light is seen.* CLANCY *stops at the sight of it. Then the curtains are opened quietly, and from the now open private doorway there emerges the figure of an old man in a gray suit. He wears a soft white shirt with a flowing black tie. He has a gray mustache and his head is crowned with a great shock of white hair. He wears spectacles, and although his features are somewhat blurred against the strong light from the staircase behind him, it can be seen that his face is kindly, even benevolent. There is a white carnation in his buttonhole. He comes a few steps forward upon the stage and stands looking down over it, into the room.* THE MAJOR *looks up with a start and catches his breath.*]

THE MAJOR: It's—it's Mr.—!

[*All follow his eyes. When* THE FIGURE *speaks, it is in a thin, musical Irish voice, the accent much broader than* CLANCY'*s.*]

THE FIGURE: Dan Clancy— [CLANCY *turns slowly.* THE FIGURE *smiles down at him, his face growing suddenly almost youthful with the smile.*]—Don't be in such a hurry, Clancy.

CLANCY: Mr. Concannon!—Look, Connie—it's Mr. Concannon!

CONNIE: I—I see it is. [THE MAJOR *slips down from his chair and stands stiffly erect. The venerable* FIGURE *comes forward a little further upon the stage.* CLANCY *exclaims joyfully:*] Well now, well now—this is more like it! Welcome back to you, Sir!

MR. CONCANNON: Thank you, thank you! [*He turns to* THE MAJOR.]—Major Armstrong, good evening.

THE MAJOR: How—how do you do, Sir?

MR. CONCANNON: Much the same, thank you—much the same! And how are you, Clancy?

CLANCY: I'm fine, Sir—just fine!

[MR. CONCANNON *seats himself and indicates the step at his feet.*]

MR. CONCANNON: Sit where I can see you. [CLANCY *seats himself, looking up at him.* SPEEDY *re-enters quietly from the restaurant, resumes his place at the table and watches them with his hand over his mouth, cunning and privy.* MR. CONCANNON *smiles down upon* CLANCY.] What's been the trouble, my boy?

CLANCY: Trouble? [*Then, apologetically*] I'm sorry, Sir, but things in general haven't been going quite as well as they might for me.

MR. CONCANNON: Things in general rarely do for anyone, it seems.

[CONNIE *seats herself with* THE MAJOR *at the other table.*]

CLANCY: They've just about got me down, I'm ashamed to admit.

MR. CONCANNON: You?—I don't believe you, Clancy. We all of us have our bad times, you know. Even I have had mine.

CLANCY: —That devil Jack Grossett—I recollect well. But he couldn't down *you.* Why, you look younger even than when I first saw you, though you must have stretched sixty then.

MR. CONCANNON: Sixty—was I ever that young?

CLANCY: Anyway, it's a real treat to have a sight of you again. Where is it you've been, Sir, if I may ask?

MR. CONCANNON: Oh—to and fro—up and down—all over, you know.

CLANCY: That was me own itinerary, too! And when did you get back, if I may also ask?

MR. CONCANNON: Just tonight.

CLANCY: This very night—and didn't I do the same! [*A moment, then*] And were you at the Globe by any chance, Sir?

MR. CONCANNON: I was there.

CLANCY: I regret deeply I had to make such a holy display of myself.

MR. CONCANNON: You were deeply troubled: I understood that.

CLANCY: I guess there's not much you don't understand.

MR. CONCANNON: I have lived a long time.

[CLANCY *ponders a moment before going on.*]

CLANCY: It's a fair marvel that you happened to come back just tonight. It's a matter of—of vast encouragement to me. [*Then, carefully*] Was there—? Did somebody—? Don't take me amiss, Sir, but was there something special that brought you?—Just precisely on this very night, you know—

[MR. CONCANNON'*s smile comes and goes. Finally, with a little gesture toward* CLANCY, *he speaks:*]

MR. CONCANNON: It's hard to explain. Somehow, I felt impelled to come.

CLANCY: Was it—was it as if—as if a cat jumped down on your back from a wall, maybe?

MR. CONCANNON: Why yes—yes, that expresses it perfectly.

CLANCY: Like me in Cleveland! Then you were—you must have been—! [*He checks himself.*]—And how long will you be staying, if I may ask?

MR. CONCANNON: That depends on you, Dan Clancy. How long do you think you will need me?

[*Suddenly* CLANCY *bounds to his feet with a joyous shout.*]

CLANCY: Oh Glory be, it's the truth then!

MR. CONCANNON: What, my boy?

CLANCY: Mr. Concannon, you're the noblest, godliest man ever I've—

MR. CONCANNON: Oh, come now!

CLANCY: —And the fact is, that all unbeknownst to yourself, you've been sent to answer my questions for me.

CONNIE: Dan—!

MARBLE: Well, for the love of—!

DICKINSON: Oh, let him get it off his chest.

CLANCY: I regret the inconvenience, but surely it's so.

MR. CONCANNON: Questions, you say?

CLANCY: I'm near to bursting with 'em!

MR. CONCANNON: What are they, Clancy?

CLANCY: Well—now I'm put to it I can hardly—[*He pauses.*] Well, you see, I—there've been a number of things—[*And pauses again.*]—But I mustn't speak of myself alone. There are plenty worse off than me. [*And again.*]—Maybe *you* can tell me, Sir—maybe you can tell me why, for all its pretty scenery, the whole earth is full of human misery, of death and tyranny and torture? Wherever I've been, for one contented individual I've found a dozen who suffered and sweat and strained—for what?—To get their backs broken and the hope put out of their eyes. [*In his excitement he rises and, still talking, paces up and down in front of the little stage.*] Even the rich I've seen, leading the life of Riley, have no great look of enjoying it—on the contrary! And even the luckiest ones must die in the end.

MR. CONCANNON: You are afraid of death?

CLANCY: I don't savor the thought of it. Not while I've yet to find the meaning of life—and find it, I can't for the life of me. For from what I can make out, it's an old, old story: the ancients being as full of corruption in their time as the Sixth Ward along River Street is today.

MR. CONCANNON: What else have you to ask?

CLANCY: Well, Sir, to come straight out with it, if it's Good that rules over us, why is it Evil that always seems to have the upper hand?

MR. CONCANNON: Things are not always what they seem.

CLANCY: Begging your pardon, Sir—but that's hardly an answer. I'm well aware that misfortune sometimes makes better men of us, but just as often—in fact, oftener—we're made the worse by it. So what's a man to think?

MR. CONCANNON: The problem of Good and Evil is a difficult one, Clancy. I expect we shall all know the answer one day.

CLANCY: But I'd like to know now—for I'm tough, and the hereafter looks a long way away to me.

MR. CONCANNON [*After a moment*]: There must be the occasions for sin, must there not—that Virtue may hold her lovely head aloft? There must be persecution, must there not—to fortify man's faith in heaven? There must be slavery, must there not—that he may know the priceless boon of freedom?

CLANCY: Maybe there must be, but why must we *stand* 'em? Why can't we fight 'em off the face of the earth?

MR. CONCANNON: Submission: it is the Will of God. All must be left to the Almighty Will.

CLANCY: The same old—

[CONNIE *rises and demands:*]

CONNIE: Why? Why should we be leaving everything to Him, when long ages ago He left it all to us?

[CLANCY *turns and frowns at her.*]

CLANCY: How do you mean He did?

CONNIE: He gave us a will of our own, didn't He? It showed too much faith in us, maybe—but give it He did. How'd you like it taken back again? A man of your build—never able so much as to think or choose for himself—how'd you like that?

CLANCY: I wouldn't.

CONNIE: Well, then!

[CLANCY *swings around slowly and looks at* MR. CONCANNON, *distrust and suspicion growing in his eyes.* MARBLE *speaks to* DICKINSON:]

MARBLE: It seems to me life's nothing but a sleeper jump to death. Why can't we have more wars, and get the whole job over with?

DICKINSON: Wars, yes! And rapes and lynchings—plagues and purges!

SPEEDY: Life's all right. It all depends on how you live it.

[THE MAJOR *looks at him, then stumps up beside* CLANCY *and addresses* MR. CONCANNON *in a shaky, earnest voice:*]

THE MAJOR: Tell me if you will, Sir—tell me His reason for—for creating things like—like me and Ma Speedy. Why are—why are freaks?

[MR. CONCANNON *smiles, not so benevolently this time.*]

MR. CONCANNON: Would you deny Him a sense of humor?

[THE MAJOR *starts back as if struck.*]

THE MAJOR: Oh, don't—please don't—

[CLANCY *springs up angrily.*]

CLANCY: That's no thing to say! What kind of a thing is that to be saying? And every question I've asked you, you've turned off with one of your own. You're not the James Concannon *I* know! Who are you, you old devil?—[*Suddenly he advances up the steps and upon the stage.*] Maybe the old war in Heaven came out the other way—maybe Michael the Archangel lost the fight after all—and to a crafty old rat too smart to let on that he'd won.—So we'd take *his* will as the will of God, eh? [*He plucks the carnation from* MR. CONCANNON*'s buttonhole and flings it away.*] That would explain a lot of things, eh? Holy God, what wouldn't it! [*Deliberately the old gentleman takes off his wig, mustache and glasses, and a familiar face smiles mockingly at* CLANCY. CLANCY *steps back.*] You—?

[SPEEDY *crows delightedly:*]

SPEEDY: The Professor! Isn't he marvelous? He had his little kit in the coatroom and did the whole change in less than—Gentlemen, the Professor!

MARBLE: The Professor, my foot! That was an act, too. Who is it? Is it Jack Grossett himself maybe—here all along?

DICKINSON: Why not? *He* knows this town. He knows it's the Big Time's last stand, or damn near it—and why? James Concannon! Like hell they'd come to *his* Globe, or anyone else's. They'd follow the rest to the picture houses—*he* knows!

CLANCY [*To* PABST]: Me life long I've thought it was Good ruled the world, but from the way you've ruled us here this night—

PABST: How dared you interfere with a show in my theater? How dared you interrupt as smooth a bill as tonight's?

[DICKINSON *rises.*]

DICKINSON: Clancy, you're right. The Devil is God now.

[*He draws his revolver.* SPEEDY *springs up.*]

SPEEDY: Stop that! What do you think you're doing?

DICKINSON [*To* PABST]: Oh you beauty, you beauty, you.—All right, Professor—relax, your act's over. It stank, Professor.

SPEEDY: Stop it, I say!

DICKINSON: Sit down. The guy who doubles for God has got to be good. Otherwise—

[PABST *glances at* CLANCY, *smiles, and beckons to* DICKINSON.]

PABST: Come to the Globe Easter Monday.

DICKINSON: You don't open on Monday. You're canceled—booked out!

[DICKINSON *advances.*]

MARBLE: Easy there, boy.

DICKINSON: I hate the evil bastard. The world'll be better for—

PABST: Closer—come closer—

CONNIE: No, no! Look at him—it's what he wants!

DICKINSON: —And gets.

[*The beckoning hand is still a safe distance from the pistol. Once more* PABST *glances at* CLANCY, *then beckons again.*]

PABST: Closer—closer—a little closer—

DICKINSON: —Sweetheart.

[*He levels the pistol. Suddenly* PABST *cries out:*]

PABST: Help me, Clancy!

CONNIE: Watch out, Dan!

[*But* CLANCY *springs down from the stage toward* DICKINSON *just as the double discharge is heard. He buckles once, straightens again, and stands there, his eyes round with astonishment.*]

CLANCY: Well now, well now—

CONNIE: It was another trick! Dan—are you all right?

CLANCY: For a second I felt as if something hit me, but I feel nothing now. [*He bears down upon* DICKINSON *and knocks the pistol from his hand.*] You!—That's no way to be doing it!

DICKINSON: I tell you the Devil is God! Pabst is Grossett and Grossett, Concannon. And the Devil is God and we do his will!

CLANCY: No—that's as wrong as the other! Oh, I see now it's no will of God things are as they are—no, nor Devil's will neither! It's the will of all them like himself, the world over—men bad by their own choice —and the woods full of 'em!

[*He moves toward the table, sways and braces himself against it.* CONNIE *follows him.*]

CONNIE: Dan! What is it?

CLANCY: Answer? *You* gave me it!—the proud will of Man is my answer! The free will of Man, turned the wrong way. By the grace of God, free to think and choose for himself, was he?—Free to make his own world, eh? The fine job he's made of it! [*He comes around the table laughing joylessly.*]—With pride at the top and despair at the bottom and all manner of misery in the between—turning lies into truth and truth into lies until nobody knows the one from the other—

[*He gropes for a chair and sinks into it.* CONNIE *stands over him anxiously.*]

CONNIE: Dan—what's the matter with you?

[CLANCY*'s face sets and his hand strikes the table.*]

CLANCY: But know we will, know we *will!*—For it's a fine instrument, the free will of man is, and can as easy be turned to Good as to Bad.—Ah, it's the grand thing, is man's will! Whatever it's sunk to, it can rise again. It can rise over anything, anything!

[PABST *is watching him intently.*]

PABST: Except one: Death, my poor clown.

CLANCY: Even that! By the stars, it can live and die and resurrect itself!

PABST: An appropriate sentiment for the day.

[CONNIE *cries out to* PABST*:*]

CONNIE: "Death"! What do you mean by that!

PABST: Look at him.

[DICKINSON *and* MARBLE *move toward* CLANCY.]

DICKINSON: Clancy, for Christ's sake—

MARBLE: You, Speedy—get someone, quick!

CONNIE: Hurry—hurry!

CLANCY: No! Let me be! This is me own affair.

[*But* SPEEDY *has hastened out.* CLANCY*'s head sinks.*]

DICKINSON: Clancy!

[CLANCY *turns his head and smiles sideways at him.*]

CLANCY: Poor John—so glorious drunk, you thought you could rid the world of evil in a blow.

PABST: He is fantastic. He is incredible. [*He moves toward the restaurant door.* MARBLE *moves to stop him.* PABST *gestures peremptorily.*] One side!

[CLANCY *looks up.*]

CLANCY: Let him go. There are bigger birds than him.

[MARBLE *stands aside.* PABST *addresses them all:*]

PABST: I think we may view this as an accident.—That is, unless the change at the Globe is made public. Then I am afraid we shall have to hang Dickinson.

[*He goes out.* CLANCY*'s head lowers again.*]

CONNIE: Dan!

CLANCY: Come here, girl—

[*She comes to the table, drops down into a chair beside him.*]

CONNIE: But *are* you hurt? Tell me!

CLANCY: Just give me a look at you.

CONNIE: But tell me!

CLANCY: Do you know something?

CONNIE: What?

CLANCY: I like it better without.

CONNIE: It?

CLANCY: Your face.

CONNIE: Without what?

CLANCY: The little gold earrings.

CONNIE: But what's that got to do with—? [*Then in spite of herself, she cries out happily:*] Oh, do you, Dan?

CLANCY: I do—and that's the truth—and me last word on the subject.

[*For a moment they gaze at each other, saying nothing.* DICKINSON *begins softly:*]

DICKINSON: Once there was a little man in County Kerry and he began to pack his little bag—

[CLANCY *turns to him. There is a broad smile upon his face, and his eyes are merry.*]

CLANCY: I'll send you the postcard.

[*He makes a half gesture toward* CONNIE, *then slumps forward upon the table.*]

CONNIE: Dan!

[*He does not reply.* THE MAJOR *murmurs:*]

THE MAJOR: The things that happen. Is—is he going to die?

[CLANCY *raises his head once more.*]

CLANCY: Who is not going to?

DICKINSON: —Those who live and die like you, Dan Clancy.

CLANCY: Thank you, John. [*His eyes half close. He draws a deep and satisfied breath.*] I smell the lemon tree. The air's full of it. Good-bye to you all, now.

[*His head sinks slowly.* CONNIE *seizes his hand, clings to it desperately.*]

CONNIE: No, no! I won't let you!—Dear God, don't let him!

CLANCY: Hush, girl. I go of me own will, where I go.

[*His head settles down upon his breast and he is still.*]

CURTAIN

THE PHILA- DELPHIA STORY

THE PHILADELPHIA STORY

was first produced by the Theatre Guild
at the Shubert Theatre, New York City,
on March 28, 1939.
It was directed by Robert B. Sinclair;
the settings and lighting were by Robert Edmond Jones.

CAST

TRACY LORD • Katharine Hepburn
DINAH LORD • Lenore Lonergan
MARGARET LORD • Vera Allen
ALEXANDER LORD • Dan Tobin
THOMAS • Owen Coll
WILLIAM TRACY • Forrest Orr
ELIZABETH IMBRIE • Shirley Booth
MACAULAY CONNOR • Van Heflin
GEORGE KITTREDGE • Frank Fenton
C. K. DEXTER HAVEN • Joseph Cotten
SETH LORD • Nicholas Joy
ELSIE • Lorraine Bate
MAC • Hayden Rorke
MAY • Myrtle Tannahill
EDWARD • Philip Foster

■ ACTION AND SCENES ■

The action of the play takes place in the course of twenty-four hours at the Seth Lords' house in the country near Philadelphia.
The time is late June of the present year.
The scenes are as follows:

ACT I
The sitting room. Late morning, Friday.

ACT II
Scene 1—The porch. Late evening, Friday.
Scene 2—The porch. Early morning, Saturday.

ACT III
The sitting room. Late morning, Saturday.

■ ACT I ■

The sitting room of the Lords' house in the country near Philadelphia is a large, comfortably furnished room of a somewhat faded elegance containing a number of very good Victorian pieces. The entrance from the hall is at Right 2 upstage, down two broad, shallow steps. The entrance into what the family still call "the parlor" is through double doors downstage Right 1. At Left are two glass doors leading to the porch. A writing desk stands between them. There is a large marble fireplace in the back wall with chairs Right and Left of it; a stool in front of it. A grand piano in the corner at up Left. Chairs and a table are at down Left Center, and at down Right Center, a coffee table, an easy chair and a sofa. There is a large and fine portrait over the fireplace and other paintings here and there. A wall cabinet Right of fireplace contains a quantity of bric-a-brac and there is more of it, together with a number of signed photographs in silver frames, upon the tables and piano. A bookcase above doors Right 1. There are also several cardboard boxes strewn about, indicating an approaching wedding.

It is late on a Friday morning in June, an overcast day. DINAH, *who is all of fifteen years old, is stretched out on the sofa reading a set of printers' galley proofs.* TRACY, *a strikingly lovely girl of twenty-four, sits in the chair at Left, a leather writing set upon her knees, scribbling notes. She wears slacks and a blouse.* MARGARET LORD, *their mother, a young and smart forty-seven, comes in from the hall with three more boxes in her arms. She places them upon the table near* TRACY.

MARGARET [*Entering Right 1 with three boxes. Going to back of table Left*] I'm so terribly afraid that some of the cards for these last-minute presents must have got mixed. Look at them, Tracy—perhaps you can tell. [*Puts boxes upper end of table.*]

TRACY: In a minute, Mother. I'm up to my neck in these blank thank-you notes.

DINAH [*Rises*]: This stinks! [*Goes in Center with papers.*]

MARGARET [*Back of table*]: Don't say "stinks," darling. If absolutely necessary, "smells"—but only if absolutely necessary. What is it? [*Crosses to desk—picks up three-page typed list.*]

DINAH [*Going up to piano*]: I found it in Sandy's room. It's something that's going to be in a magazine. It certainly stinks all right.

MARGARET [*At desk*]: Keep out of your brother's things, dear—and his house. [*Crossing down Left, reading:*] Ninety-four for the ceremony, five hundred and six for the reception—I don't know where we'll put them all, if it should rain. [*Looks out Left 1.*]

DINAH [*Crossing down back of table Left*]: It won't rain.

MARGARET [*Crossing below table to chair Left Center; sits*]: Uncle Willie wanted to insure against it with Lloyd's but I wouldn't let him. If I was God and someone bet I wouldn't let it rain, I'd show him fast enough. This second page is solid Cadwalader. Twenty-six.

DINAH [*Back of table*]: That's a lot of Cadwalader.

MARGARET: One, my child, is a lot of Cadwalader.

TRACY: How do you spell omelet?

MARGARET: O-m-m-e-l-e-t.

TRACY: I thought there was another "l."

[DINAH *moves up to and leans on piano, reading proof sheets.*]

MARGARET: The omelet dish from the—? [*Rises.*]

TRACY: You said it was an omelet dish.

MARGARET: It might be for fish.

TRACY: Fish dish? That sounds idiotic. [*Tears up card—starts new letter.*]

MARGARET: I should simply say "Thank you so much for your lovely silver dish."

TRACY [*Taking up card from another box*]: Here's the tag, "Old Dutch Muffin Ear, Circa 1810"—What the—[*Dropping card*] I am simply enchanted with your old Dutch Muffin Ear—with which my husband and I will certainly hear any muffin coming a mile away.

DINAH [*Crossing down back of table*]: Lookit, Tracy: don't you think you've done enough notes for one day? [*Starts to handle things on table.*]

TRACY [*Waving her off*]: Don't disturb me. [*Picking up cards, reads:*] From Cousin Horace Macomber, one pair of game shears, looking like hell. [*Picks up shears.*]

DINAH: He's so awful. What did he send the other time?

TRACY [*Writing "game shears" on the card*]: No one to speak of sent anything the other time.

MARGARET [*In armchair*]: It's such a pity your brother Junius can't be here for your wedding. London's so far away.

DINAH [*Back of table*]: I miss old Junius: you did a good job when you had him, Mother.

MARGARET: The first is always the best. They deteriorate as you go on. [*A look between* DINAH *and* TRACY]

TRACY [*Writes note*]: There was no occasion to send anything the other time.

DINAH [*Reading the proof sheets—crossing to Center*]: This is certainly pretty rooty-tooty all right.

TRACY [*Still writing at table*]: It would scarcely be considered a wedding at all, the other time. When you run off to Maryland on a sudden impulse—as Dexter and I did—

DINAH [*Crossing back behind table Left*]: Ten months is quite long to be married, though. You can have a baby in nine, can't you?

TRACY: I guess, if you put your mind to it.

DINAH: Why didn't you?

TRACY [*Looks up from her writing*]: Mother, don't you think it's time for her nap?

DINAH: I imagine you and George'll have slews of 'em. [*Slouches to Center.*]

TRACY: I hope so, all like you, dear, with the same wild grace.

[DINAH *stops Center and looks at her.* TRACY *rises; picks up box of envelopes and places it on desk.*]

DINAH [*Center*]: Lookit: "the other time"—he's back from wherever he's been.

[TRACY *goes in to back of table Left.*]

MARGARET [*After a glance at* TRACY]: What do you mean?

DINAH: Dexter, of course. I saw his car in front of his house: [*Crossing Right*] the roadster. It must be him.

MARGARET: When? When did you?

DINAH [*At sofa*]: This morning, early, when I was out exercising The Hoofer. [*Sits on sofa Right; puts sheets on coffee table.*]

MARGARET: Why didn't you tell us?

TRACY [*Back of table, near* MARGARET*'s chair*]: I'm not worried, Mother. The only trouble Mr. C. K. Dexter Haven ever gave me was when he married me.—*You* might say the same for one Seth Lord. If you'd just face it squarely as I did—[*Sits on end of table.*]

MARGARET: That will do! I will allow none of you to criticize your father.

TRACY: What are we expected to do when he treats you—

MARGARET: Did you hear me, Tracy?

TRACY [*Rising*]: All right, I give up.

MARGARET [*Softly, and taking* TRACY*'s hand*]: —And in view of this second attempt of yours, it might pay you to remind yourself that neither of us has proved to be a very great success as a wife.

TRACY [*Crossing to behind table*]: We just picked the wrong first husbands, that's all.

MARGARET: That's an extremely vulgar remark.

TRACY: Oh, who cares about either of them any more—[*Crosses back of* MARGARET, *who is in chair Left Center. Crouches to embrace her.*] Golly Moses, I'm going to be happy now.

MARGARET: Darling.

TRACY: Isn't George an angel?

MARGARET: George is an angel.

TRACY: Is he handsome, or is he not?

MARGARET: George is handsome.

TRACY [*Straightens up and picks up boxes from table, also writing-case*]: Suds. I'm a lucky girl. [*Crosses Right upper.*]

DINAH: I like Dexter.

TRACY [*Continuing on her way up Right*]: Really? Why don't you ask him to lunch, or something? [*Goes out Right 2.*]

DINAH [*Looking after her for a moment—rises and crosses to Center*]: She's awfully mean about him, isn't she?

MARGARET: He was rather mean to her, my dear.

DINAH [*Over Left Center at* MARGARET*'s chair*]: Did he really sock her?

MARGARET [*Still comparing lists and letters*]: Don't say "sock," darling. "Strike" is quite an ugly enough word.

DINAH: But did he really?

MARGARET: I'm afraid I don't know the details.

DINAH [*By* MARGARET *at chair Left Center*]: Cruelty and drunkenness, it said.

MARGARET: Dinah!

DINAH: It was right in the papers.

MARGARET: You read too much. You'll spoil your eyes.

DINAH [*Crossing Right to sofa*]: I think it's an awful thing to say about a man. I don't think they like things like that said about them.

MARGARET: I'm sure they don't.

DINAH [*At sofa picks up three proof sheets*]: Father's going to be hopping when he reads all this about himself in that magazine, *Destiny,* when it comes out.

MARGARET: All what? *About whom?* [*Turns to face* DINAH.]

DINAH: Father—that they're going to publish.

MARGARET: Dinah, what *are* you talking about?

DINAH [*Crossing Center with paper*]: It's what they call proof sheets for some article they're going to call "Broadway and Finance," and Father's in it, and so they just sent it on to Sandy—sort of—you know, on approval. [*Crosses Left Center.*]

MARGARET: But the article! What does the article say? [*Takes paper from her.*]

DINAH: Oh, it's partly about Father backing three shows for that dancer—what's her name—Tina Mara—and his early history—and about the stables—and why he's living in New York, instead of with us, any more, and—

MARGARET: Great heaven—what on earth can we do?

DINAH: Couldn't Father sue them for liable?

MARGARET: But it's true—it's all—[*Realizing her error, she glances at* DINAH, *then rises and crosses to Right at coffee table.*] That is, I mean to say—[*Reading sheets*]

DINAH: I don't think the part about Tina Mara is, the way they put it. It's simply full of innundo. [*Sits in armchair Left Center.*]

MARGARET [*Turning*]: Of what?

DINAH: Of innundo. [*Rests elbow on table Left.*] Oh, I do wish something would happen here. Nothing ever possibly in the least ever happens. [*Rises, crossing Right*] Next year can I go to the Conservatory in New York? They teach you to sing and dance and act and everything at once. Can I, Mother?

MARGARET [*Front of sofa, down Right*]: Save your dramatics, Dinah. Oh, why didn't Sandy *tell* me!

DINAH: Mother, why won't Tracy *ask* her own *father* to her *wedding?*

MARGARET [*Crossing over Left to the table—picks up list and three letters which she had left there*]: Your sister has very definite opinions about certain things.

DINAH [*Crosses to Left Center to* MARGARET]: She's sort of—you know—hard, isn't she?

MARGARET: Not hard—none of my children is that, I hope. Tracy sets exceptionally high standards for herself, that's all, and although she lives up to them, other people aren't always quite able to. If your Uncle Willie Tracy comes in, tell him to wait. I want to see him. [*Starts for window Left 1.*]

DINAH [*Follows her to Left*]: Tell me one thing: don't you think it's stinking not at least to *want* Father?

MARGARET [*Turning to her*]: Yes, darling, between ourselves I think it's good and stinking. [*Goes out Left 1.*]

DINAH: And I bet if Dexter knew what she—[DINAH *waits a moment, then goes to the telephone on desk and dials four numbers.*] Hello. May I please speak to Mr. Dexter Haven—what?—Dexter! It's you! [*Then affectedly*] A very great pleasure to have you back. Dinah, you goat, Dinah Lord. What?—You bet!—Lookit, Dexter, Tracy says why don't you come right over for lunch? What? But she told me to ask you.—Listen, though, maybe it would be better if you'd—Hello!—Hello! [*Taps the telephone several times to get operator. Hangs up as* TRACY *enters Right 1 with a large roll of parchment.*]

TRACY [*Entering, crossing to Left*]: Who was that?

DINAH: Wrong number.

[TRACY *moves over Left to back of table.* DINAH *moves to her.*]

TRACY [*Spreads roll of paper out on table*]: Listen, darling, give me a hand with this cockeyed seating arrangement, will you? At least hold it down.—George doesn't want the Grants at the bridal table. [SANDY LORD, *twenty-six, comes in from Right 2.*] He says they're fast. He—

SANDY [*Entering and going down Center*]: Hello, kids.

TRACY [*Rushes up Center to embrace him*]: Sandy!

SANDY: Where's Mother?

[DINAH *crosses Left Center back of armchair.*]

TRACY: She's around. How's New York?—How's Sue?—How's the baby?

SANDY: Blooming. They sent their love, sorry they can't make the wedding. Is there a party tonight, of course?

TRACY: Aunt Geneva's throwing a monster.

SANDY: Boy, am I going to get plastered. [*Crossing to armchair* L. *to* DINAH] Hello, little fellah. [*Makes a boxing pass at her.*]

DINAH: Hello, yourself.

SANDY [*Giving her a flat box*]: This is for you, Mug; get the three race horses into the paddock. It's tough. Work it out.

DINAH: Oh, thanks. [*Remains at Left Center armchair.*]

SANDY [*Turning to* TRACY]: Sue's and my wedding present comes by registered mail, Tracy—and a pretty penny it set me back.

TRACY: You're a bonny boy, Sandy. I love you.

SANDY: Mutual—

[TRACY *goes to Left armchair; looks at toy with* DINAH.]

MARGARET [*Re-enters Left 1. She carries three envelopes and the three proof sheets. As she enters*]: I was wondering about you.

SANDY [*Crosses Left below table—kisses her*]: Give us a kiss.—You look fine.—Imagine this, a *grand*mother. How's everything? [*Goes to front of table.*]

MARGARET [*Left of Left table*]: Absolute chaos.

SANDY [*Front of table Left*]: Just how you like it, eh? Just when you function best!

MARGARET: How's my precious grandchild?

SANDY: Couldn't be better; Sue too. Ten more days in the hospital, and back home they'll be.

MARGARET [*Crossing Right below him to sofa with papers*]: I broke into your house and did up the nursery.

SANDY [*Crossing Center*]: Good girl. Where's George, Tracy?

TRACY [*Sitting on arm of chair Right*]: He's staying in the Gatehouse. He still had business things to clear up and I thought he'd be quieter there.

SANDY [*Crosses below table to Right Center*]: Did he see his picture in *Dime?* Was he sore at the "Former Coal Miner" caption?

MARGARET [*At sofa*]: What about this absurd article about your father and—er—Tina Mara in *Destiny?* Can't it be stopped?

[DINAH *goes in Center.*]

TRACY [*Rises, crossing Right*]: About Father and—let me see! [*Takes article from* MARGARET.]

SANDY: Where'd you get hold of that? [*Tries to take it from her.*]

MARGARET [*Sits sofa*]: Get ready for lunch, Dinah.

DINAH [*Going up Right, sits on step—works at puzzle*]: In a minute. I'm busy.

TRACY [*Reading sheets*]: Oh! The absolute devils—Who publishes *Destiny?* [*Sits on armchair Right.*]

SANDY [*Center*]: Sidney Kidd.—Also *Dime,* also *Spy,* the picture sheet. I worked on *Dime* for two summers, you know that.

TRACY: Stopped? It's got to be! I'll go to him myself.

SANDY [*Center*]: A fat lot of good that would do. You're too much alike. God save us from the strong. [*Crossing to behind armchair Right Center*] I saw Kidd the day before yesterday. It took about three hours, but I finally got through to him.

TRACY: What happened?

SANDY: I think I fixed things.

TRACY: How?

SANDY: That would be telling.

MARGARET: Just so long as your father never hears of it.

SANDY: I had a copy of the piece made, and sent it around to his flat, with a little note saying, "How do you like it?"

TRACY: You are a fellah.

MARGARET: Sandy!

SANDY: Why not? Let him worry a little.

[THOMAS *enters Right 2; comes down steps.*]

TRACY: Let him worry a lot!

SANDY [*Crosses up to him*]: Yes, Thomas?

THOMAS [*At door*]: Mr. Connor and the lady say they will be down directly, sir.

SANDY: Thanks, that's fine. Tell May or Elsie to look after Miss Imbrie, will you?

THOMAS: Very good, sir. [*Goes out Right 2.*]

MARGARET: What's all this?

TRACY: "Mr. Connor and—?"

SANDY [*Takes paper from* TRACY; *crossing Left Center, sits on arm of chair*]: Mike Connor—Macaulay Connor, his name is.—And—er—Elizabeth Imbrie. I'm putting them up for over the wedding. They're quite nice. You'll like them.

TRACY: You asked people to stay in this house without even asking us?

MARGARET: I think it's very queer indeed.

TRACY: I think it's queerer than that—*I* think it's paranoic! [*Rises and crosses Left Center to him.*]

SANDY: Keep your shirt on.—I just sort of drifted into them and we sort of got to talking about what riots weddings are as a rule, and they'd never been to a Philadelphia one, and—

TRACY: You're lying, Sandy.—I can always tell.

SANDY: Now look here, Tracy—

TRACY: Look where? "Elizabeth Imbrie"—I know that name! She's a—wait—damn your eyes, Sandy, she's a photographer!

SANDY: For a fact?

TRACY: For a couple of facts—and a famous one!

SANDY: Well, it might be nice to have some good shots of the wedding.

TRACY: What are they doing here?

SANDY: Just now I suppose they're brushing up and going to the bathroom. [*Rising, Right Center*] They're very interesting people. She's practically an artist, and he's written a couple of books—and—and I thought you liked interesting people.

DINAH [*Rising*]: *I* do.

[SANDY *crosses to Right armchair.* DINAH *is up on step up Right.*]

TRACY: I know—now I know! They're from *Destiny—Destiny* sent them!

MARGARET: *Destiny?*

SANDY [*Sitting in armchair Right*]: You're just a mass of intuition, Tracy.

TRACY: Well, they can go right back again. [*Goes to him.*]

SANDY: No, they can't. Not till they get their story.

TRACY: Story? What story?

SANDY: The Philadelphia story.

MARGARET: And what on earth's that?

SANDY: Well, it seems Kidd has had Connor and Imbrie and a couple of others down here for two months doing the town: I mean writing it up. It's to come out in three parts in the Autumn. "Industrial Philadelphia," "Historical Philadelphia"—and then the third—

TRACY: I'm going to be sick.

SANDY: Yes, dear, "Fashionable Philadelphia."

TRACY: I *am* sick. [*Turns to Center.*]

MARGARET: But why us? Surely there are other families who—

TRACY [*Crossing a bit to Left Center*]: Yes—why not the Drexels or Biddles or the *qu'est-ce que c'est* Cassats?

SANDY [*Seated*]: We go even further back: It's those Quakers.—And of course there's your former marriage and your looks and your general prowess in golf and fox-hunting, with a little big game on the side, and your impending second marriage into the coal fields—

TRACY [*Center*]: Never mind that!

SANDY: I don't, but they do. It's news, darling, news.

MARGARET: Is there no such thing as privacy any more?

TRACY: Only in bed, Mother, and not always there.

SANDY: Anyhow I thought I was licked—and what else could I do?

TRACY: A trade, eh? So we're to let them publish the inside story of my wedding in order to keep Father's wretched little affair quiet!

MARGARET: It's utterly and completely disgusting.

SANDY: It was my suggestion, not Kidd's. I may have been put in the way of making it. I don't know. It's hard to tell with the future President of the United States.

TRACY: What's the writer's name again?

SANDY: Connor, Macaulay Connor. I don't think he likes the assignment any more than we do—the gal either. They were handling the Industrial end.

TRACY [*Crossing to desk to phone—dials four numbers*]: My heart's breaking for them.

MARGARET [*Rises*]: I don't know what the world is coming to. It's an absolute invasion; two strange people tramping through the house, prying and investigating—

TRACY [*At the telephone*]: Maybe we're going through a revolution without knowing it. [*In telephone*] Hello, is Mr. Briggs there?—This is Tracy Lord, Mr. Briggs.—Look, I wonder if you happen to have on hand any books by Macaulay Connor? [SANDY *rises.*] You have!—Could you surely send them out this afternoon?—Thanks, Mr. Briggs, you're sweet. [*Hangs up.* SANDY *goes in Left Center*]—If they've got to have a story, I'll give them a story—I'll give them one they can't get through the mails!

SANDY [*Left Center*]: Oh—oh—I was afraid of this—

TRACY: Who the hell do they think they are, barging in on peaceful people—watching every little mannerism—jotting down notes on how we sit, and stand, and talk, and eat and move—

DINAH [*Crossing down back of sofa*]: Will they do that?

TRACY [*Center*]: —And all in the horrible snide corkscrew English!—Well, if we have to submit to it to save Father's face—which incidentally doesn't deserve it—I'm for giving them a picture of home life that will stand their hair on end.

MARGARET [*Right*]: You will do nothing of the sort, Tracy. [*Sits on sofa.*]

SANDY [*Left, embracing* TRACY]: She thinks she'll be the outrageous Miss Lord. The fact is, she'll probably be Sweetness and Light to the neck.

TRACY: Oh, will I? [*Turns out of his arm, to back of armchair Right.*]

SANDY: You don't know yet what being under the microscope does to people. I felt it a little coming out in the car. It's a funny feeling.

MARGARET: It's odd how self-conscious we've all become over the worldly possessions that once made us so confident.

SANDY [*Center*]: I know; you catch yourself explaining away your dough, the way you would a black eye: you've just run into it in the dark or something.

MARGARET: We shall be ourselves with them; very much ourselves.

DINAH [*Back of sofa*]: But Mother, you want us to create a good impression, don't you?

MARGARET [*To* SANDY]: They don't know that *we* know what they're here for, I hope?

[TRACY *sits on the arm upper end of sofa.*]

SANDY: No; that was understood.

DINAH [*Crossing down lower end of sofa*]: I should think it would look awfully funny to them, Father's not being here for his own daughter's wedding.

TRACY: Would you now?

SANDY: That's all right; I fixed that, too. [*Goes in Right Center back of armchair.*]

TRACY: How do you mean you did?

SANDY: I told Sue to send a telegram before dinner. "Confined to bed with a cold, unable to attend nuptials, oceans of love, Father."

MARGARET: Not just in those words!

SANDY: Not exactly.—It'll come on the telephone and Thomas will take it and you won't have your glasses and he'll read it aloud to you.

MARGARET: Tracy, will you promise to behave like a lady, if only for my sake?

TRACY: I'll do my best, Mrs. Lord. I don't know how good that is.

MARGARET: Go put a dress on.

TRACY: Yes, Mother.

MARGARET [*Rises*]: There are too many legs around here.

TRACY [*Rises*]: Suds! I'll be pure Victorian, all frills and ruffles, conversationally chaste as an egg. [UNCLE WILLIE TRACY, *sixty-two, comes in from the Right 1 door.*] Hello, Uncle Willie. Where did you come from? [*Gets back of table Left for roll of paper.*]

UNCLE WILLIE [*Down Right*]: Your Great-aunt Geneva has requested my absence from the house until dinnertime. Can you give me lunch, Margaret?

MARGARET: But of course! With pleasure—

DINAH: Hello, Uncle Willie—[*She goes up—leaves toy on bookcase and stops behind armchair Right Center.*]

SANDY: How are you, Uncle Willie?

WILLIE: Alexander and Dinah, good morning. [*Crossing Center*] My esteemed wife, the old warhorse, is certainly spreading herself for your party. *I* seriously question the propriety of [TRACY *goes down Center.*] any such display in such times. But she—Why aren't you being married in church, Tracy?

TRACY [*At Left Center chair*]: I like the parlor here so much better. Didn't you think it looked pretty as you came through?

UNCLE WILLIE: That is not the point. The point is that I've sunk thousands in that church, and I'd like to get some use of it.—Give me a glass of sherry, Margaret. [*Goes in Center.*]

[DINAH *goes down* L.C. TRACY *goes to* SANDY, *back of Right Center armchair.*]

MARGARET: Not until lunchtime, my dear.

UNCLE WILLIE: These women.

DINAH [*At Left Center*]: You're really a wicked old man, aren't you?

UNCLE WILLIE [*Points to the porch Left*]: What's that out there?

[DINAH *turns to look. He vigorously pinches her behind.*]

DINAH: Ouch!

[SANDY, *standing at upper end of sofa, is chatting with* TRACY.]

UNCLE WILLIE: Never play with fire, child. [*Looks at the* OTHERS *over Right.*] What's a-lack here? What's a-stirrin'? What's amiss?

SANDY: Uncle Willie, do you know anything about the laws of libel?

UNCLE WILLIE [*Sitting in Right armchair*]: Certainly I know about the laws of libel. Why shouldn't I? I know all about them. In 1916, I, Willie Q. Tracy, successfully defended the *Post,* and George Lorimer personally, against one of the cleverest, one of the subtlest—why? What do you want to say?

SANDY [*Sits on sofa*]: It isn't what *I* want to say—

TRACY [*Breaking in—sits at his feet on floor Center*]: Is it enough if they can simply prove that it is true?

[DINAH *goes back of him; sits on arm of sofa.*]

UNCLE WILLIE [*Turns to* TRACY]: Certainly not! Take me; if I was totally bald and wore a toupee, if I had flat feet, with these damnable metal arches, false teeth, and a case of double—

DINAH: Poor Uncle Willie.

UNCLE WILLIE: I said *"If* I had." [DINAH, *behind him, leans over and gives a derisive laugh through "haw."*]—And if such—[WILLIE *gives her a dirty look*]—facts were presented in the public prints in such a manner as to hold me up to public ridicule, I could collect substantial damages—and would, if it took me all winter.

TRACY [*Rising*]: Suppose the other way around; suppose they printed things that weren't true.

UNCLE WILLIE [*Rising and crossing Center.* TRACY *sits on arm of chair Right Center*]: Suppose they did? Suppose it was erroneously stated, that during my travels as a young man I was married in a native ceremony to a dusky maiden in British Guinea, I doubt if I could collect a cent. [*Looks off up Right 2—clears throat—crossing up.*] Who are these two strange people coming down the hall?

[*The* FAMILY *rises, frozen in their tracks a second.*]

MARGARET [*Rises*]: Oh, good gracious!

[DINAH *goes up to doorway Right 2.*]

TRACY: Come on—out. [*Goes Center, grabs* WILLIE *and leads him to down Right.*]: What was she like, Uncle Willie?

[SANDY *gets in corner up Right near mantel.*]

WILLIE: Who?

TRACY [*Crossing Right*]: British Guinea?

WILLIE [*Crossing Right*]: So very unlike your Aunt Geneva, my dear. [*And they exit Right 1.*]

MARGARET [*Crossing up for* DINAH*—takes hold of her—moves down Right with her*]: Dinah—

DINAH: But, Mother, oughtn't we—?

MARGARET: Sandy can entertain them until we—until we collect ourselves. [*Puts* DINAH *out Right 1.*]

SANDY [*Crossing to* MARGARET *at door Right 1*]: What'll I say?

MARGARET: I wish I could tell you—in a few very well-chosen words. [*She goes out.*]

[SANDY *is alone for a moment; leans against bookcase, Right.* MIKE CONNOR, *thirty, and* LIZ IMBRIE, *twenty-eight, come in from the hall.* LIZ *has a small and important camera hanging from a leather strap around her neck.*]

LIZ [*Enters from Right 2, crossing Left Center*]: —In here?

MIKE [*Entering down Center—gazes about room—notices crystal chandelier*]: He said the sitting room. I suppose that's contrasted to the living room, the ballroom—the drawing room—the morning room the—[*He sees* SANDY.] Oh, hello again. Here you are.

[LIZ *goes over Left to Left of table and sits.*]

SANDY: Here I am. [*Goes Center.*]

MIKE [*Up Center toward mantel*]: It's quite a place.

SANDY [*Crossing up to* MIKE]: It is, isn't it?—I couldn't help overhearing you as you came in. Do you mind if I say something?

MIKE: Not at all. What?

SANDY: Your approach to your job seems definitely antagonistic. I don't think it's fair. I think you ought to give us a break.

MIKE: It's not a job I asked for. [*Goes down Left Center.*]

SANDY [*Up Right Center*]: I know it's not. But in spite of it, and in spite of certain of our regrettable inherited characteristics, we just might be fairly decent. Why not wait and see?

MIKE [*Sits Right of table Left*]: You have quite a style yourself. [SANDY *picks up stool at fireplace, crossing down Center.*]—You're on the *Saturday Evening Post,* did you say?

SANDY: I work for it.

MIKE: Which end?

SANDY: Editorial. [*Sits on stool he brought down.*]

MIKE: I have to tell you, in all honesty, that I'm opposed to everything you represent.

SANDY: *Destiny* is hardly a radical sheet: what is it you're doing—boring from within?

MIKE: —And I'm not a Communist, not by a long shot.

LIZ: Just a small pin feather in the Left Wing. [MIKE *looks at her.*] —Sorry.

SANDY: Jeffersonian Democrat?

MIKE [*Looks at him*]: That's more like it.

SANDY: Have you ever seen his house at Monticello? *It's* quite a place too.

LIZ: Home Team One; Visitors Nothing—[*Rises.*] Is this house very old, Mr. Lord? [*Goes up Left.*]

SANDY: No, there are a very few old ones on the Main Line—The Gatehouse is, of course. Father's grandfather built that for a summer place when they all lived on Rittenhouse Square. Father and Mother did this about 1910—the spring before my brother Junius was born. He's the oldest. You won't meet him, he's in the diplomatic service in London.

MIKE [*To* LIZ]: Wouldn't you know? [*Putting out cigarette on table tray*]

SANDY: *I* worked for Sidney Kidd once. What do you make of him?

MIKE [*After a short pause*]: A brilliant editor, and a very wonderful man. [*Gets cards from his pocket.*]

LIZ: Also, our bread and butter.

SANDY: Sorry to have been rude.

MIKE [*Looking through cards*]: I suppose you're all of you opposed to the Administration?

SANDY: The present one? No—as a matter of fact we're Loyalists.

MIKE [*Has a sheaf of typewritten cards and looks at them*]: Surprise, surprise.—The Research Department didn't give us much data.—Your sister's fiancé—George Kittredge—aged thirty-two.—Since last year General Manager Quaker State Coal, in charge of operation.—Is that right?

SANDY: That's right.—And brilliant at it.

MIKE: So I've heard tell. I seem to have read about him first back in '35 or '36.—Up from the bottom, wasn't he?

[LIZ *sits on arm of Left Center chair.*]

SANDY: Just exactly—and of the mines.

MIKE: Reorganized the entire works?

SANDY: He did.

MIKE: National hero, new model: makes drooping family incomes to revive again. Anthracite, sweet anthracite.—How did your sister happen to meet him?

SANDY: She and I went up a month ago to look things over.

MIKE: I see. And was it instant?

SANDY: Immediate.

MIKE: Good for her.—He must be quite a guy.—Which side of this—er—fine, aboriginal family does she resemble most, would you say?

SANDY [*Looks at him; rises*]: The histories of both are in the library; I'll get them out for you. I'll also see if I can round up some of the Living Members. [*Goes up to door Right 2.*]

LIZ: They don't know about *us*, do they? [*Goes above table.*]

SANDY [*In the doorway stops and turns*]: —Pleasanter not, don't you think?

LIZ: Much.

SANDY: That's what *I* thought—also what Kidd thought. [*Moves a step up.*]

MIKE [*Rising and going near Center*]: Look here, Lord—

SANDY [*Stops*]: Yes—?

MIKE [*Crossing up Center*]: Why don't you throw us out?

SANDY: I hope you'll never know. [*A smile and goes out Right 2.*]

LIZ: Maybe Der Kidder has been up to his little tricks. [*Goes up Left.*]

MIKE [*At mantel*]: If only I could get away from his damned paper—

LIZ: It's Sidney himself you can't get away from, dear. [*Up at piano*]

MIKE: I tried to resign again on the phone this morning.

LIZ [*Touring up Left at piano*]: —Knickknacks—gimcracks—signed photographs! Wouldn't you know you'd have to be rich as the Lords to live in a dump like this? [*Goes to Center. Sees the portrait over the mantel.*] Save me—it's Gilbert Stuart.

MIKE: A what?

LIZ: Catch me, Mike!

MIKE: Faint to the left, will you? [*Crosses down Right to sofa. He returns to the typewritten cards*] "First husband, C. K.—" Can you imagine what a guy named "C. K. Dexter Haven" must be like?

LIZ: "Macaulay Connor" is not such a homespun tag, my pet. [*Goes up Right.*]

MIKE [*Sits on sofa*]: I've been called Mike since I can remember.

LIZ: Well, maybe Dexter is "Ducky" to his friends. [*Goes over Right by steps.*]

MIKE: I wouldn't doubt it.—But I wonder what the "C. K." is for—

LIZ [*Turns upstage—looks at cabinet*]: Maybe it's Pennsylvania Dutch for "William Penn."

MIKE: "C. K. Dexter Haven." God!

LIZ [*Crossing down to upper corner of sofa*]: I knew a plain Joe Smith once. He was only a clerk in a hardware store, but he was an absolute louse.

MIKE: —Also he plays polo. Also designs and races sailboats. "Class" boats, I think they call them. Very upper class, of course.

LIZ: Don't despair. He's out, and Kittredge, man of the people, is in. [*Goes up to mantel.*]

MIKE: From all reports, quite a comer too. Political timber.—Poor fellow, I wonder how he fell for it.

LIZ: I imagine she's a young lady who knows what she wants when she wants it. [*Goes up by piano.*]

MIKE: The young, rich, rapacious American female—there's no other country where she exists.

LIZ [*Comes in Center*]: I'll admit the idea of *her* scares even me.—Would I change places with her, for all her wealth and beauty? Boy! Just ask me. [*Goes up to piano.*]

MIKE: I know how I'm going to begin. [*Leans back on the sofa, closes his eyes, and declaims:* LIZ *goes in Center slowly*] "—So much for Historical Philadelphia, so much for Industrial. Now, Gentle Reader, consider an entire section of American Society which, closely following the English tradition, lives on the land, but in a new sense. It is not the land that provides the living, it is—"

LIZ [*Back of sofa; pats his arm, then crosses Right*]: You're ahead of yourself. Wait till you do your documentation.

MIKE: I'm tired. [*Reclines on sofa, head on upstage end*] Kidd is a slave-driver. I wish I was home in bed. Also I'm hungry. Tell four footmen to call me in time for lunch.

[LIZ *is taking pictures of room off Right 1.*]

DINAH [*Re-enters Left from porch window, the woman of the world. Crossing Center on her toes—hand extended*]: Oh—how do you do?—Friends of Alexander's, are you not?

MIKE [*Rises*]: How do you do?—Why, yes, we—

DINAH [*Crossing Right*]: I am Dinah Lord. My real name is Diana, but my sister changed it.

LIZ: I'm Elizabeth Imbrie—and this is Macaulay Connor. It's awfully nice of—

DINAH [*Goes Right to them—extends an arched hand to each*]: *En-*

chantée de vous voir. [*Shakes hands with* MIKE.] *Enchanté de faire votre connaissance.* [*Shakes hands with* LIZ.]—I spoke French before I spoke English. My early childhood was spent in Paris, where my father worked in a bank—the House of Morgan.

LIZ: Really?

DINAH: *C'est vrai—absolument!* [*Runs up to piano—jumping over stool Center as she goes.*] Can you play the piano? I can. And sing at the same time. Listen—[*Plays and sings*] "Pepper Sauce Woman; Pepper Sauce Woman—"

[*This dialog goes through the song, topping it.*]

LIZ [*Speaks lowly to* MIKE *Down Right*]: What is this?

MIKE: An idiot, probably. They happen in the best of families, especially in the best.

DINAH: —"Oh, what a shame; she has lost her name. Don't know who to blame, walkin' along to Shango Batcheloor." [DINAH *stops singing and continues in a dreamy voice:*] The Bahamas—how well I remember them.—Those perfumed nights—the flowers—the native wines. I was there, once, on a little trip with Leopold Stokowski.

TRACY [*Enters Left 1; stops up at piano. She has changed into a rather demure dress, high in neck and ample in skirt*]: You were there with your governess, after the whooping cough.

[DINAH *gestures airily.* LIZ *goes front of sofa.* MIKE *gets to downstage end.*]

DINAH [*Crossing to* TRACY *and below her to chair Left of table Left*]: —My sister Tracy. Greetings, Sister.

TRACY: Mother wants to see you at once. At once!

DINAH: You've got on my hair ribbon.

TRACY: Your face is still dirty. [DINAH *exits Left 1.* TRACY, *cool, collected and charming, all sweetness and light—crossing down to upper corner of sofa*] It's awfully nice having you here. [*Shakes hands with* LIZ *and* MIKE.] I do hope you'll stay for my wedding.

LIZ: We'd like to very much.

MIKE: In fact, that was our idea.

TRACY: I'm so pleased that it occurred to you. [*Waves them to sit—*ALL *do so together. She in armchair Right Center.* LIZ *and* MIKE *in sofa, together*] The house is in rather a mess, of course. We all have to huddle here, and overflow onto the porch. —I hope your rooms are comfortable.

[MIKE *takes out pack of cigarettes.*]

LIZ: Oh, very, thanks.

TRACY: Anything you want, ask Mary or Elsie [*Passes cigarette box.*] They're magic. What a cunning little camera.

[MIKE *has struck match—sees* TRACY *still holds lighter toward him as she talks to* LIZ*—he slowly bends forward to accept light for cigarette—then blows his match out—she graciously smiles at him.*]

LIZ [*Lights cigarette from* TRACY*'s lighter*]: It's a Contax. I'm afraid I'm rather a nuisance with it.

TRACY: But you couldn't be: I hope you'll take loads. Dear Papá and Mamá aren't allowing any reporters in—that is, except for little Mr. Grace, who does the social news. [*To* MIKE] Can you imagine a grown-up man having to sink so low?

MIKE: It does seem pretty bad.

TRACY: People have always been so kind about letting us live our simple and uneventful little life here unmolested. Of course, after my divorce last year—but I expect that always happens, and is more or less deserved. Dear Papá was quite angry, though, and swore he'd never let another reporter inside the gate. He thought some of their methods were a trifle underhanded.—You're a writer, aren't you, Mr. Connor?

MIKE [*Looks at her*]: In a manner of speaking.

TRACY: Sandy told me. I've sent for your books. "Macaulay Connor"—What's the "Macaulay" for?

MIKE: My father taught English History. I'm "Mike" to my friends.

TRACY: —Of whom you have many, I'm sure. English history has always fascinated me. Cromwell—Bloody Mary, John the Bastard—Where did he teach? I mean your father—

MIKE: In the high school in South Bend, Indiana.

TRACY: "South Bend"! It sounds like dancing, doesn't it? You must have had a most happy childhood there.

MIKE: It was terrific.

TRACY: I'm so glad.

MIKE: I don't mean it that way.

TRACY: I'm so sorry. Why?

MIKE: Largely due to the lack of the wherewithal, I guess.

TRACY: But that doesn't always cause unhappiness, does it?—not if you're the right kind of man. George Kittredge, my fiancé, never had anything either, but he—Are either of you married?

MIKE: No.

LIZ: I—er—that is, no.

TRACY: You mean *you* were, but now you're divorced?

LIZ: Well, the fact is—

TRACY: Suds—you can't mean you're ashamed of it!

LIZ: Of course I'm not ashamed of it.

MIKE [*Is staring at her*]: Wha-at?

LIZ: It was ages ago, when I was a mere kid, in Duluth. [*Flicks ashes in ashtray.*]

MIKE: Good Lord, Liz—you never told me you were—

LIZ: You never asked.

MIKE: I know, but—

LIZ: Joe Smith, Hardware.

MIKE: Liz, you're the damndest girl. [*Rises.*]

LIZ: *I* think I'm sweet. [*Smiles at* TRACY.]

[MIKE *goes to lower end corner of sofa.*]

TRACY: Duluth—that must be a lovely spot. It's west of here, isn't it?

LIZ: Sort of.—But occasionally we get the breezes.

TRACY: Is this your first visit in Philadelphia?

LIZ: Just about.

TRACY: It's a quaint old place, don't you think? I suppose it's affected somewhat by being the only really big city that's near New York.

LIZ: I think that's a very good point to make about it.

TRACY: —Though I suppose you consider us somewhat provincial?

LIZ: Not at all, I assure you.

TRACY: Odd customs, and such. Where the scrapples eat biddle on Sunday. Of course it *is* very old—Philadelphia, I mean, the scrapple is fresh weekly. How old are *you,* Mr. Connor?

MIKE [*Starts for seat—ashes to tray*]: I was thirty last month. [*Sits on sofa again.*]

TRACY: Two books isn't much for a man of thirty. I don't mean to criticize. You probably have other interests outside your work.

MIKE: None.—Unless—[*Looks at* LIZ *and smiles.*]

TRACY: How sweet! Are you living together?

MIKE [*Through the laugh*]: Why—er—no, we're not—

LIZ: That's an odd question, I must say!

TRACY: Why?

LIZ: Well—it just is.

TRACY: I don't see why. I think it's very interesting. [*Leans forward seriously, elbow on knee and chin on hand*] Miss Imbrie—don't you agree that all this marrying and giving in marriage is the damndest gyp that's ever been put over on an unsuspecting public?

MIKE [*To* LIZ]: Can she be human!

TRACY: Please, Mr. Connor!—I asked Miss Imbrie a question.

LIZ: No. As a matter of fact, I don't.

TRACY: Good. Nor do I. That's why I'm putting my chin out for the second time tomorrow. [GEORGE, *off Left, calls "Tracy." She rises.*] Here's the lucky man now. I'll bring him right in and put him on view—a one-man exhibition. [*As she moves over Left and goes off Left*] In here, George!—In here, my dear!

LIZ [*To* MIKE—*rises*]: My God—who's doing the interviewing here? [*Puts out cigarette on table.*]

MIKE [*Rises. Back of sofa to Center*]: She's a lot more than I counted on.

LIZ: Do you suppose she caught on somehow?

MIKE: No. She's just a hellion. [*Has got to Center.*]

LIZ: I'm beginning to feel the size of a pinhead. [*Goes Right Center.*]

MIKE: Don't let her throw you.

LIZ: Do you want to take over?

MIKE: I want to go home.

[TRACY *re-enters with* GEORGE KITTREDGE, *aged thirty-two; brings him to Center.*]

TRACY [*As she crosses*]: Miss Imbrie—Mr. Connor—Mr. Kittredge, my beau.— Friends of Sandy's, George.

GEORGE [*Center*]: Any friend of Sandy's—[*Shakes hands with them.*]

LIZ [*Right Center*]: How do you do?

MIKE [*Center*]: How are you?

GEORGE: Fine as silk, thanks.

LIZ: You certainly look it.

GEORGE: Thanks, I've shaken quite a lot of coal dust from my feet in the last day or two.

TRACY [*Left Center*]: Isn't he beautiful? Isn't it wonderful what a little soap and water will do?

MIKE: Didn't I read a piece about you in *The Nation* a while ago?

GEORGE: Quite a while ago: I've been resting on my laurels since that—and a couple of others.

MIKE: Quite a neat piece of work—anticipating the Guffey Coal Act the way you did.—Or do I remember straight?

GEORGE: Anyone should have foreseen that—I was just lucky.

LIZ: A becoming modesty.

GEORGE: That's nothing to what's yet to be done with Labor relations.

TRACY: You ought to see him with the men—they simply adore him.

GEORGE: Oh—come on, Tracy!

TRACY [*Backing a few steps to Left*]: Oh, but they do! Never in my life will I forget that first night I saw you, all those wonderful faces, and the torchlights, and the way his voice boomed—

GEORGE: You see, I'm really a spellbinder.—That's the way I got her.

TRACY [*Crossing up to* GEORGE]: Except it was me who got you!—I'm going to put these two at the bridal table, in place of the Grants.

GEORGE: That's a good idea.

TRACY [*Crossing to Left, back of table*]: George, it won't rain, will it?—Promise me it won't rain. [*Looking out window*]

GEORGE [*Follows her*]: Tracy, I'll see to that personally.

TRACY: I almost believe you could.

MIKE: I guess this must be love.

GEORGE: Your guess is correct, Mr. Connor.

TRACY: I'm just his faithful Old Dog Tray.

GEORGE: Give me your paw?

TRACY [*She does*]: You've got it.

[GEORGE *takes her hand and kisses it.*]

[MARGARET *enters Right 1, followed by* DINAH. DINAH *remains in doorway.* MARGARET *goes directly to between* LIZ *and* MIKE *in front of sofa, Right.*]

MARGARET [*Shakes hands with* BOTH]: How do you do? We're so happy to have you. Forgive me for not coming in sooner, but things are in such a state. I'd no idea that a simple country wedding could involve so much. [*Crosses to* TRACY *and* TRACY *comes to her. They meet Center and beam.*] My little girl—[SANDY *enters Right 2 and crosses down to table Left near* TRACY. GEORGE *works to Left of table Left.*]—I do hope you'll be comfortable. Those rooms are inclined to be hot in this weather.—Aren't you pretty, my dear! Look at the way she wears her hair, Tracy. Isn't it pretty?

TRACY: Mighty fine.

MARGARET: I do wish my husband might be here to greet you, but we expect him presently. He's been detained in New York on business for that lovely Tina Mara. You know her work?

LIZ: Only vaguely!

MARGARET: So talented—and such a lovely person! But like so many artists—no business head, none whatever. [*Gives* TRACY *a knowing smile.* TRACY *and* SANDY *smile.* SANDY *then smirks.* EDWARD *enters from Right 2. He carries tray with sherry decanter and eight glasses.* THOMAS *follows to serve. They go up Center.*] Good morning, George!

GEORGE: Good morning, Mrs. Lord!

MARGARET: And this is my youngest daughter, Diana—

[DINAH *curtseys.*]

MIKE [*Is working his way behind sofa to down Right*]: I think we've met.

[THOMAS *gives* MARGARET *drink and napkin.*]

MARGARET: Thank you, Thomas.

[DINAH *then works her way across back of sofa to armchair Left Center—stops to get glass of sherry for* SANDY.]

SANDY [*Sitting in armchair Left Center*] Now let's all relax, and throw ourselves into things. Hi, George!

[MARGARET *sits in armchair Right Center.* TRACY *sits stool Center.* GEORGE *works slowly to behind her.*]

GEORGE: Hello, Sandy—Welcome home!

[THOMAS *serves* LIZ. DINAH *serves* SANDY *with sherry.*]

MARGARET: After lunch Sandy must show you some of the sights—the model dairy, and the stables, and the chicken farm—and perhaps there'll be time to run you out to some other places on the Main Line—Devins, Saint Davids, Bryn Mawr, where my daughter Tracy went to college—

[THOMAS *serves* MIKE, *then* THOMAS *goes up for* WILLIE*'s wine.*]

DINAH: 'Til she got bounced out on her—

MARGARET: —Dinah!

UNCLE WILLIE [*Entering Right*]: It's a pretty kettle of fish when a man has to wait two mortal hours—

TRACY [*Rising*]: Papá!—Dear Papá—

UNCLE WILLIE: What's that?

TRACY [*As she rushes over Right to embrace him*]: Didn't the car meet you?

UNCLE WILLIE [*Amazed, but hardly audible*]: The car?

TRACY [*Crossing down Right*]: You Angel—to drop everything and get here in time for lunch—Isn't he, Mamá?

MARGARET: In—indeed he is.

UNCLE WILLIE: I'm not one to jump to conclusions, but—

TRACY: These are our friends, Mr. Connor and Miss Imbrie, Father.—They're here for the wedding.

MIKE: How are you, Mr. Lord?

LIZ: How do you do, Mr. Lord?

UNCLE WILLIE: Dashed fine. How are you?

[*Shakes hands with* MIKE.]

SANDY [*Over Left*]: Hi, Pops!

UNCLE WILLIE [*Crossing in Center*]: —Alexander.

DINAH [*Crossing in Center*]: Welcome back, Daddy!

UNCLE WILLIE: Dinah—Kittredge—[*He turns to* MARGARET *and bows.*] Margaret, my sweet.

[THOMAS *comes down to his Left with a sherry.* UNCLE WILLIE *takes sherry and tosses it off; glass back to* THOMAS, *who, taking stool from Center, goes up to fireplace.*]

TRACY: Mother, don't you think you ought to explain the new arrangement to Father before lunch?

MARGARET [*Taking* WILLIE *by the arm*]: Why—yes—I think I'd best. [*Having* WILLIE *by arm, takes him over Left as* DEXTER *enters. They meet Left 1.*] See here—here is the list now—Seth.

[TRACY *goes up Center.*]

SANDY[*As he sees* DEXTER *enter*]: Holy cats!

MARGARET [*As she sees him enter she turns quickly to look at* TRACY, *then speaks*]: Dexter Haven!

DEXTER [*Down at Left 1 entrance*]: Hello, friends and enemies. I came the short way, across the fields.

MARGARET: Well, this *is* a surprise.

GEORGE [*Up Center*]: I should think it is.

DEXTER: Hello, you sweet thing. [*Taking* MARGARET *by the shoulders and kissing her cheek*]

[MIKE *and* LIZ *cross.*]

MARGARET: Now you go right home at once!

UNCLE WILLIE: Remove yourself, young man!

DEXTER: But I've been invited. [*Going to* WILLIE *and shaking hands*] How are you, sir?

UNCLE WILLIE: No better, no worse. Get along.

DEXTER: Hello, Sandy.

SANDY [*Shaking hands with* DEXTER]: How are you, boy?

DEXTER: Never better. In fact, it's immoral how good I feel.

DINAH [*Works down Center*]: What—what brings you here, Mr. Haven?

DEXTER [*Crossing to her Center*]: Dinah, my angel! [*Kisses her cheek.*] Why, she's turned into a raving beauty! [*Crossing to* TRACY *as* DINAH *goes up Center*] Awfully sweet and thoughtful of you to ask me to lunch, Tray.

TRACY: Not at all.—Extra place, Thomas.

[GEORGE *crosses down Center.*]

THOMAS: Yes, Miss Tracy. [*He and* EDWARD *go out Right 2.*]

TRACY [*Right Center*]: Miss Imbrie—Mr. Connor—my former husband, whose name for the moment escapes me.

DEXTER [*Center*]: How do you do?

MIKE [*Right*]: How do you do? } [*Together*]
LIZ [*Right Center*]: How do you do? }

DEXTER: —Of course I intended to come anyway, but it did make it pleasanter.—Hello, Kittredge.
[*Turns Center.*]

GEORGE: How are you, Haven?

DEXTER [*Peers at him*]: What's the matter? You don't look as well as when I last saw you. [*He pats his arm sympathetically.*] Poor fellow—I know just how you feel. [*He turns to* TRACY; *gazes at her fondly*] Redhead—isn't *she* in the pink, though!—*You* don't look old enough to marry anyone, even for the first time—you never did! She needs trouble to mature her, Kittredge. Give her lots of it.

GEORGE: I'm afraid she can't count on me for that.

DEXTER: No? Too bad.—Sometimes, for your own sake, I think you should have stuck to me longer, Red.

TRACY: I thought it was for life. [*Crossing to* GEORGE—*Left of him—takes his arm*] but the nice Judge gave me a full pardon.

DEXTER: That's the kind of talk I like to hear; no bitterness, no recrimination—just a good quick left to the jaw.

GEORGE: Very funny.

THOMAS [*Appears in the door Right 2*]: Luncheon is served, Madam.

MARGARET: Thank you, Thomas.

UNCLE WILLIE [*Crossing to Center*]: I don't suppose a man ever had a better or finer family. [*Turns and takes* MARGARET'*s arm.*] I wake in the night and say to myself—"Seth, you lucky dog. What have you done to deserve it?" [*Goes up and exits Right 2, taking* MARGARET *along.*]

MARGARET [*As they go*]: And what *have* you?
[*Exits.*]

TRACY [*Crossing to Right*]: Do you mind if I go in with Mr. Connor, Miss Imbrie?

LIZ: Why, not in the least.

SANDY [*Crossing and goes up Right back of couch, takes* LIZ'*s arm.* BOTH *exit*]: Sandy's your boy.

TRACY [*Taking* MIKE'*s arm and up Center*]: —Because I think he's such an interesting man.

GEORGE: Come on, Dinah, I draw you, I guess.

DINAH [*Taking* DEXTER'*s arm also*]: Dexter—

DEXTER [*As they go*]: Isn't snatching one of my girls enough, you cad?

GEORGE [*At the same cue and time as they go up Right*]: You're a very bright fellow, Haven, I'll hire you.

[*He exits.*]

TRACY [*To* MIKE—*going up*]: That's very insulting—but consistently interesting. We must talk more.

MIKE [*Going up*]: No wonder you want to get away from all this.

[*They are* ALL *up near door Right 2 when* SETH *comes into room from Left 1.*]

SETH [*Stopping* MIKE, DEXTER, DINAH, TRACY. OTHERS *have gone*]: I don't know how welcome I am, but after Sandy's note, I thought the least I could do was to—

[DINAH *starts down but is stopped by* TRACY.]

TRACY [*As she restrains* DINAH]: *Uncle Willie!* [*She turns to* OTHERS.] Please go on in, everyone. I want a word with Uncle Willie.

[*They go in*—DEXTER *turning back with a faint smile at* TRACY. *She crosses down Left, facing* SETH.]

SETH: Well, daughter?

TRACY: Well?

SETH: Still Justice, with her shining sword—eh? Who's on the spot?

TRACY: We are; thanks to you—Uncle Willie.

CURTAIN

■ ACT II ■

SCENE I

The porch, which is more like a room than a porch. Entrance from the sitting room at back Right Center and Left Center to the library, through glass doors at stage Left; to garden, down broad stone steps from porch and along gravel path past shrubbery to Left and Right. Open side of porch shielded. At Right is a step down to path; a door [Right] at upper end of this path; a sofa against extreme Right wall. Flower stands Right and Left on porch; a stool Right; table and chairs Center; chaise longue Left. Pots of geraniums, large and small.

Early evening, Friday. The sky has cleared.

AT RISE: MIKE *is in Left Center chair on porch, making additional notes.* LIZ *is seated on steps over Right, reloading her camera.*

LIZ: I may need more film.

MIKE: I may need more paper.

LIZ: There's a cousin Joanna, who's definitely crazy.

MIKE: Who told you?

LIZ: Dinah.

MIKE: Dinah should know.

LIZ: Where is she now? I want some more shots of her, while it's still light.

MIKE: She's out schooling a horse somewhere. It's the horses that get the schooling hereabouts. Did you shoot the old Tycoon milking his cows?

LIZ: Several times. He shot one at me, but he missed.

MIKE: Caption: "Seventy Times Seven Fat Kine Has He." [*Consults his notes.*] "George Kittredge, Important Official, Important Company. Controlling interest owned by Seth Lord."

LIZ: What a coincidence and will wonders never cease?

MIKE: I'm inclined to like Kittredge—I can see how she fell for him. I think he's in a tough spot, with Haven prowling around, though.

LIZ: Is a sinister fellow, Dexter.

MIKE: Is very.—But George is interesting. Get him on coal some time.

LIZ: I'd rather have him on toast.

MIKE [*Rises, crossing Center*]: Answer me honestly, Liz; what right has a girl like Tracy Lord to exist?

LIZ: Politically, socially, or economically?

MIKE [*Crossing in Right to* LIZ]: But what place has she got in the world today? Come the Revolution she'll be the first to go.

LIZ: Sure; right out under the Red General's arm.

MIKE: She's a new one on me. [*Crossing to Left of table Left*] Maybe Philadelphia produces a different brand of monkey.

LIZ [*Looks at him keenly*]: You're a funny one, Mike.

MIKE: Why?

LIZ: Use the name "Wanamaker" in a sentence.

MIKE: I bite.

LIZ: I met a girl this morning. I hate her, but I—

MIKE: I get you, but you're wrong. You couldn't be wronger. [*Crossing Left of table*] Women like that bore the pants off me.

LIZ: For a writer, you use your figures of speech most ineptly. You know, I wish they knew why we were here. They're all such sweet innocents, it makes me feel like—

[WILLIE, *with a red rose, and* SETH *enter from the garden down Right.* LIZ *rises.*]

UNCLE WILLIE: Would you accept this perfect rose, Miss Imbrie?

[MIKE *crosses and sits on chaise down Left.*]

LIZ: Why, thank you, Mr. Lord. It's a beauty. [*Takes it.*]

SETH: Miss Imbrie is amused at something.

LIZ: I'm sorry, Mr. Tracy, but it's so funny, you being uncle and nephew. Could I have a picture of you together? [*Leaves rose on porch.*]

UNCLE WILLIE: Certainly! [*Slips his arm through* SETH'*s*] Now stand up straight, Willie. He *is* younger than I. It was a matter of half sisters marrying stepbrothers.

LIZ [*Front of them, near Center*]: I see. That is, I think I do. [*Snaps a picture.*]

UNCLE WILLIE: No incest, however.

LIZ: Of course not. [*Snaps another.*]

UNCLE WILLIE: There have been other things, however. [*Looks at* SETH] Uncle Willie—I'm thinking of asking that little dancer, Tina Mara, to come down and dance for the wedding guests tomorrow. Do you think it's a good idea?

SETH: Excellent. It might put an end to the ridiculous gossip about you and her. [*Looks between them.*]

UNCLE WILLIE: Is there gossip?

SETH: There seems to be.

UNCLE WILLIE: Is it ridiculous?

[SANDY *comes from the library Left and crosses to above table.*]

SETH: All gossip is ridiculous.

SANDY: Look alive, men! Time to dress!

SETH: Right you are. Thanks, Sandy—[*Goes up into the house Right Center window to Right.*]

[SANDY *follows.* LIZ *picks up rose.*]

UNCLE WILLIE: Miss Imbrie, as a camera fiend, I think I have another interesting subject for you.

LIZ: Will I have time?

UNCLE WILLIE: Time is an illusion. Come with me, please. [*She takes his arm.*] It's part of the old house, a little removed from it.

LIZ: But what?

UNCLE WILLIE: An ancient granite privy, of superb design—a dream of loveliness.

LIZ: —At sunset—idyllic!

[LIZ *follows* UNCLE WILLIE *out Right 1.* MIKE *crosses and picks up cards on Center table as he leaves table, going up Right.* TRACY *enters Left.*]

TRACY [*Crossing to back of Center table*]: Please wait a minute.

MIKE [*Back Right of Center table*]: With pleasure. [*Turns where he is. She goes to him; looks at him wonderingly.*] What's the matter?

TRACY: I've been reading these stories. They're so damned beautiful.

MIKE: You like? Thanks—

TRACY: Why, Connor, they're almost poetry.

MIKE [*Laughs shortly*]: Don't fool yourself; they *are!* [*Goes down Right below chair.*]

TRACY: I can't make you out at all, now.

MIKE: Really? I thought I was easy.

TRACY: So did I, but you're not. [*Crossing down Cent*er] You talk so big and tough—and then you write like this. Which is which?

MIKE: I guess I'm both.

TRACY: No—I believe you put the toughness on, to save your skin.

MIKE: You think?

TRACY: Yes. *I* know a little about that—

MIKE: Do you?

TRACY: Quite a lot. [*They look at each other for a moment. Then* TRACY *laughs a little embarrassedly and glances away.*] It—the book—it was such a complete—hell of a surprise, that's all. [*Goes down Left.*]

MIKE: Yes—it seems you do. [*Sits Right of table.*]

TRACY [*Turns to him*]: What?

MIKE: Know about it.

TRACY [*Down Left Center*]: The one called "With the Rich and Mighty" —I think I liked *it* best.

MIKE: I got that from a Spanish peasant's proverb—"With the Rich and Mighty always a little Patience."

TRACY [*Crossing into Center, sits Left of table*]: Good! Tell me something, will you? When you can do a thing like this how can you possibly do anything else? [*Leaves book on table.*]

MIKE: Such as what?

TRACY: You said after lunch—what was it you said?—"Cheap stuff for expensive magazines."

MIKE: Did I?

TRACY: Yes. You did. You said you spent most of your time that way.

MIKE: Practically all. Why? What about it?

TRACY: I can't understand it. And I like to understand things.

MIKE: You'll never believe it, but there are people in this world who have to earn their living.

TRACY: Of course! But people buy books, don't they?

MIKE: Sure they do! They even read them.

TRACY: Well, then?

MIKE: That one represents two solid years' work. It netted Connor something under six hundred dollars.

TRACY: But that shouldn't *be!*

MIKE: —Only unhappily it is.

[*There is a pause.*]

TRACY: And what about your Miss Imbrie?

MIKE: Miss Imbrie is in somewhat the same fix. She is a born painter, and might be an important one. But Miss Imbrie must eat. Also, she prefers a roof over her head to being constantly out in the rain and snow.

TRACY [*Rising and going down Left a little, then up behind her chair*]: Food and a roof—food and a roof—

MIKE: Those charming essentials.

TRACY [*Turns to him*]: Listen: I've got an idea! [*Crosses to him Center; over the table.*] Listen: I've got the most marvelous little house in Unionville. It's up on a hill, with a view that would knock you silly. I'm never there except in the hunting season, and not much then, and I'd be so happy to know it was of some use to someone. [*Crosses Right, then turns back.*] There's a brook and a small lake, no size really, and a patch of woods, and in any kind of weather, it's the—[*Goes down Center step, looking out front at the sky.*]—And look at that sky now, will you! Suddenly it's clear as clear! It's going to be fine tomorrow! It's going to be fair! Good for you, God! [*Glances down Left 1 and sees someone coming.*] Hell! [*Goes back up onto the porch.*] Someone's coming—someone I don't want to be alone with. Stand by for a couple of minutes. Will you?

MIKE [*Rising*]: Certainly—if you like.

TRACY [*Right Center*]: You *will* think about the house, won't you?

MIKE: Why, it's terribly nice of you, but—

TRACY: Don't think I'd come trouping in every minute because I wouldn't. I'd never come, except when expressly asked to.

MIKE: It isn't that. [*Crosses to Left Center.*]

TRACY [*Follows a step*]: What is it?

MIKE: Well, you see—er—you see the idea of artists having a patron has more or less gone out, and—

TRACY [*Looks at him, hurt*]: I see. [*Pauses a moment.*] That wasn't especially kind of you, Mr. Connor. There's no need to rub our general uselessness in.

MIKE: I'm afraid I don't get you.

TRACY: Don't bother. I'm sorry to have seemed—patronizing.

MIKE: I didn't quite mean—

TRACY: Please don't bother, really.

[MIKE *goes up Left.*]

DEXTER [*Enters from Left 1; carries a small tissue-wrapped picture*]: Hello.

TRACY: Hello, fancy seeing you here. [*She crosses over Right.*]

DEXTER [*Mounts the porch to table Center*]: Orange juice? Certainly! [*Pours and drinks.*]

TRACY: You're sure you don't want something stronger? I'll ring if you like. [*Sits on stool Right.*]

DEXTER: Not now, thanks. This is fine. [*Front of Center table*]

TRACY: Don't tell me you've forsaken your beloved whiskey-and-whiskies—

DEXTER: No, indeed. I've just changed their color, that's all. I go in for the pale pastel shades now. I find they're more becoming. [DEXTER *drinks, facing upstage sees* MIKE.] We met at lunch didn't we?

MIKE [*Crossing down back of chair Left Center*]: Yes, I seem to remember. Connor's my name.

DEXTER: —The writer—of course! Do you drink, Mr. Connor?

MIKE: A little. Why?

DEXTER: Not to excess?

MIKE: Not often.

DEXTER: —And a writer! It's extraordinary. I thought all writers drank to excess, and beat their wives. I expect that at one time I secretly wanted to be a writer. [*He looks up at him and grins. Glances at* TRACY, *drinks, then puts glass on table.*]

TRACY: Dexter, would you mind doing something for me?

DEXTER: Anything, what? [*Puts picture on table Center; goes down Right Center.*]

TRACY: Get the hell out of here.

DEXTER: Oh, no, I couldn't do that. That wouldn't be fair to you. You need me too much.

TRACY [*Seated on stool*]: Would you mind telling me just what it is you're hanging around for? [MIKE *moves toward Left.*] No—please don't go! I'd honestly much prefer it if you wouldn't.
[MIKE *sits on chaise Left.*]

DEXTER [*Crossing to Center below table*]: So should I. Do stay, Mr. Connor. As a writer this ought to be right up your street. [*Turns to* TRACY.]

TRACY: Don't miss a word!

DEXTER: Honestly, you never looked better in your life; you're getting a fine tawny look—

TRACY [*Rises, crossing to Right of table Center*]: Oh, we're going to talk about me, are we? Goody.

DEXTER [*Right*]: —It's astonishing what money can do for people, don't you agree, Mr. Connor? Not too much, you know—just more than enough. Particularly for girls. Look at Tracy. There's never been a blow that hasn't been softened for her. There'll never be one that won't be softened—why, it even changed her shape—she was a dumpy little thing originally.

TRACY: —Only as it happens, I'm not interested in myself, for the moment. What interests me now is what, if any, your real point is, in—

DEXTER: Not interested in yourself! My dear, you're fascinated! You're far and away your favorite person in the world.

TRACY: Dexter, in case you don't know it—I—!

DEXTER [*Crossing in Center*]: Shall I go on—?

TRACY: Oh, yes, please do, by all means—[*Sits Right of table.*]

DEXTER: Of course, she is kindness itself, Mr. Connor—[*Goes Left.*]

TRACY: —Itself, Mr. Connor.

DEXTER [*Left*]: She is generous to a fault—that is, except to other people's faults. For instance, she never had the slightest sympathy toward nor understanding of what used to be known as my deep and gorgeous thirst.

TRACY: That was your problem!

DEXTER [*Turns, crossing into Center, above table*]: It was the problem of a young man in exceptionally high spirits, who drank to slow down that damned engine he'd found nothing yet to do with—I refer to my mind. You took on that problem with me, when you took me—You were no helpmate there, Tracy—you were a scold.

TRACY: It was disgusting. It made you so unattractive.

DEXTER: A weakness—sure. And strength is her religion, Mr. Connor. She is a goddess, without patience for any kind of human imperfection. And when I gradually discovered that my relation to her was expected to be not that of a loving husband and a good companion, but—[*Turns away from her to Left, muttering*] Oh—never mind—

TRACY: Say it!

DEXTER [*Turns to her*]: —But that of a kind of high priest to a virgin goddess, then my drinks grew more frequent and deeper in hue, that's all.

TRACY [*Rises, crossing down Right a bit*]: I never considered you as that, nor myself!

DEXTER: You did without knowing it. [*Crossing to her over Right*] And the night that *you* got drunk on champagne, and climbed out on the roof and stood there naked, with your arms out to the moon, wailing like a banshee—

[MIKE *slides off the chaise and into the room Left.*]

TRACY: I told you I never had the slightest recollection of doing any such thing!

DEXTER: I know; you drew a blank. You wanted to—Mr. Connor, what would you say in the case of—[*Turns and sees* MIKE *gone. Crosses to Left of table Center.*]

TRACY: He's a reporter, incidentally. He's doing us for *Destiny.*

DEXTER [*Sits Left of table*]: Sandy told me. A pity we can't supply photographs of you on the roof.

TRACY [*Crossing to front of table*]: Honestly, the fuss you made over that silly, childish—

DEXTER: It was enormously important, and most revealing. The moon is also a goddess, chaste and virginal.

TRACY: Stop using those foul words! We were married nearly a year, weren't we?

DEXTER: Marriage doesn't change a true case like yours, my dear. It's an affair of the spirit—not of the flesh.

TRACY: Dexter, what are you trying to make me out as?

DEXTER: Tracy, what do you fancy yourself as?

TRACY [*Crossing below table to Left at chaise*]: I don't know that I fancy myself as anything.

DEXTER [*Rises, crossing Left to her*]: When I read you were going to marry Kittredge, I couldn't believe it. How in the world can you even think of it?

TRACY [*Turns on him*]: I love him, that's why! As I never even began to love you. [*Sits on chaise.*]

DEXTER: It may be true, but I doubt it. *I* think it's just a swing from me, and what I represent—but I think it's too violent a swing. That's why I came on. Kittredge is no great tower of strength, you know, Tray. He's just a tower.

TRACY: You've known him how long?—Half a day.

DEXTER: I knew him for two days two years ago, the time I went up to the fields with your father, [*Sits on arm of chair Left of table.*] but half a day would've done, I think.

TRACY: It's just personal, then—

DEXTER: Purely and completely.

TRACY: You couldn't possibly understand him or his qualities. I shouldn't expect you to.

DEXTER: I suppose when you come right down to it, Tray, it just offends my vanity to have anyone who was ever remotely my wife, remarry so obviously beneath her.

TRACY: "Beneath" me! How dare you—any of you—in this day and age use such a—?

DEXTER: I'm talking about difference in mind and imagination. You could marry Mac, the night watchman, and I'd cheer for you.

TRACY [*Rises, crossing in Left Center*]: And what's wrong with George?

DEXTER [*On arm of Left Center chair*]: Nothing—utterly nothing. He's a wizard at his job, and I'm sure he is honest, sober and industrious. He's just not for you.

TRACY: He *is* for me—he's a great man and a good man; already he's of national importance.

DEXTER: Good Lord—you sound like *Destiny* talking. [*Rises.*] Well, whatever he is, you'll have to stick, Tray. He'll give you no out as I did.

TRACY: I won't require one. [*Gets Right Center.*]

DEXTER [*Crossing in front of table Center—leans on it*]: I suppose you'd still be attractive to any man of spirit, though. There's something engaging about it, this virgin goddess business, something more challenging to the male than the more obvious charms.

TRACY: Really?

DEXTER: Oh, yes! We're very vain, you know—"This citadel can and shall be taken—and I'm just the boy to do it."

TRACY [*Over Right*]: You seem quite contemptuous of me, all of a sudden.

DEXTER [*Crossing to her*]: Not of you, Red, never of you. You could be the damndest, finest woman on this earth. If I'm contemptuous of anything, it's of something in you you either can't help, or make no attempt to; your so-called "strength"—your prejudice against weakness—your blank intolerance—

TRACY: Is that all?

DEXTER: That's the gist of it; because you'll never be a first-class woman or a first-class human being, till you have learned to have some regard for human frailty. It's a pity your own foot can't slip a little sometime—but no, your sense of inner divinity won't allow it. The goddess must and shall remain intact.—You know, I think there are more of you around than people realize. You're a special class of American female now—the Married Maidens.—And of Type Philadelphiaensis, you're the absolute tops, my dear.

TRACY: Damn your soul, Dext, if you say another—!

[GEORGE *comes in Left Center from the living room. He looks at them and smiles with a great attempt at good humor.*]

DEXTER: I'm through, Tracy—for the moment I've said my say.

GEORGE [*Crossing in Left Center*]: I suppose I ought to object to this twosome.

DEXTER [*Crossing in Right Center*]: That would be most objectionable. Well, anytime either of you want more advice from me—

GEORGE: When we do, we'll give you a ring, Haven.

DEXTER [*Crossing down Center to Right*]: Do that, will you? You'll find that I have a most sympathetic and understanding ear—[*Turns, facing her*] I left you a little wedding present there on the table, Red—I'm sorry I hadn't any ribbon to tie it up with. [*Goes out Right 1.*]

GEORGE [*Right Center*]: You see—it's no use even attempting to be friendly.

TRACY [*Crossing in Right of table*]: Certainly not. You were a dear to try. Please don't mind him.

DINAH [*Enters Right 1, crossing to Center as she speaks*]: You got taken when you bought that roan. She's parrot-jawed.

TRACY: Get into a tub. You're revolting.

DINAH [*Crossing up Left*]: What's more, she swallows wind by the bucket.

TRACY: Where's Miss Imbrie? Wasn't she with you?

DINAH: No. She's gone to the privy with Uncle Willie. [*Goes out Left Center to Left.*]

TRACY [*Front of table. Picks up the package* DEXTER *left on table*]: It's anyone's guess what ths might be. [*Unwraps the package.*] It's, why —it's a photograph of the "True Love."

GEORGE [*Crossing to her*]: —The?—What's that?

TRACY: A boat he designed—and built, practically. We sailed her up the coast of Maine and back, the summer we were married. My, she was yare.

GEORGE: "Yare"? What does that mean?

TRACY: It means—Oh, what does it mean?—Easy to handle—quick to the helm—fast—bright—everything a boat should be. [*Gazes at the photograph for a moment without speaking, then drops it upon table.*] —And the hell with it. [*Goes up Left.*]

GEORGE: Rather bad taste, I'd say, giving you that.

TRACY: Dexter never concerns himself much with taste.

GEORGE: How'd you ever happen to marry a fellow like that, Tracy?

TRACY: Oh, I don't know—I expect it was kind of a hangover from childhood days. We grew up together, you know.

GEORGE: I see—propinquity.

TRACY [*Crossing in to him Center*]: Oh, George—to get away—! Somehow to feel useful in the world—

GEORGE: Useful?—I'm going to build you an ivory tower with my own two hands.

TRACY: Like fun you are.

GEORGE: You mean you've been in one too long?

TRACY: I mean that, and a lot of things.

GEORGE: I'm going to make a grand life, dear—and you can help, all right.

TRACY: I hope I can.

GEORGE: From now on we'll both stop wasting time on unimportant people.

TRACY [*Beside him*]: That's all right with me.

GEORGE: Our little house on the river up there. I'd like people to consider it an honor to be asked there.

TRACY: Why an honor, especially?

GEORGE: We're going to represent something, Tracy—something straight and sound and fine.—[*Looks off Right.*] And then perhaps young Mr. Haven may be somewhat less condescending.

TRACY [*Looks at him*]: George—you don't really mind him, do you? I mean the fact of him—

GEORGE: The—? I don't see what you mean, Tray.

TRACY [*Crossing Left*]: I mean that—you know—that he ever was—was my lord and master—that we ever were—

GEORGE [*Crosses to her*]: I don't believe he ever was—not really. I don't believe anyone ever was, or ever will be. That's the wonderful thing about you, Tray.

TRACY [*Looks at him, startled*]: What? How—?

GEORGE: You're like some marvelous, distant—[*She sits on chaise.*] Oh, queen, I guess. You're so cool and fine and—and always so much your own. That's the wonderful *you* in you—that no one can ever really possess—that no one can touch, hardly. It's—it's a kind of beautiful purity, Tracy, that's the only word for it.

TRACY [*Now really frightened*]: George—

GEORGE [*Sits on upstage side of chaise*]: Oh, it's grand, Tracy—it's just grand! Everyone feels it about you. It's what I first worshipped you for, Tracy, from afar.

TRACY: George, listen—

GEORGE: First, now, and always! [*Leans toward her.*] Only from a little nearer, now—eh, darling?

TRACY: I don't want to be worshipped! I want to be loved!

GEORGE: You're that, too. You're that, all right.

TRACY: I mean really loved.

GEORGE: But that goes without saying, Tracy.

TRACY: And now it's you—[EDWARD, *carrying a tray with drinks, enters Right Center, followed by* ELSIE. *They come Center.* ELSIE *picks up orange juice tray from table.*] who doesn't see what *I* mean. You can just leave them, Edward. [*Rises.*]

[EDWARD *places tray on Center table.*]

ELSIE [*Reaching for wrapped picture*]: Shall I put this picture with the other presents, Miss Tracy?

TRACY [*Crossing Center to table*]: No—just leave it there, please.

ELSIE: Yes, Miss. [*Exits Right Center.*]

[EDWARD *follows.*]

GEORGE [*Crossing to Center*]: Don't let Miss Imbrie get hold of it.

TRACY [*Right of table, wrapping picture*]: I should say not.

GEORGE [*Crossing in to her*]: I hope they'll soft pedal the first marriage angle.

TRACY: I wish they'd pedal themselves right out of here.

GEORGE: They've got a job to do, and it's an honor, you know, Tracy.

TRACY: What is?

GEORGE: Why—to be done by *Destiny*.

TRACY: Are you joking?

GEORGE: Joking—?

TRACY: But you can't seriously mean that you think—!

GEORGE: I think *Destiny* fills a very definite place, Tracy.

MARGARET [*Enters Left, with* SETH]: George, you aren't dressed!—And Tracy, you're the guest of honor—you mustn't be late.

GEORGE [*Crossing down step and to Left*]: Right on my way, Ma'am! Wait for me, Tracy. I make the Gatehouse in nothing flat, now. [*Exits Left 1.*]

SETH: Does he by any chance ever walk anywhere?

TRACY: When he likes, I expect.

[MARGARET *goes Left to chaise and sits.*]

SETH [*Left Center*]: I have a feeling he's going to take the ring tomorrow and go through center with it.

MARGARET: Seth, you idiot.

TRACY: That's very amusing, I'm sure. [*Over to Right Center*]

SETH [*Crossing in Center*]: Oh, don't take things to heart so, Tracy. You'll wear yourself out.

LIZ [*Entering Right 1*]: I won't be a minute. [*Crosses up to window, Right Center.*]

MARGARET: There's no hurry, Miss Imbrie.

[LIZ *exits Right Center.* TRACY *sits stool Right.*]

SETH [*Back of Center table, stirring cocktails*]: What bothers me at the moment is the spectacle we're all making of ourselves for the benefit of the young man and woman from *Destiny*.

TRACY: Whose fault is it?

SETH: That's beside the point.

MARGARET: Never in my life have I felt so self-conscious. It's all simply dreadful.

SETH: It's worse; it's stupid and childish and completely undignified.

TRACY: So are other things.

SETH: They can publish what they like about me, but—

TRACY [*Rises. Crossing up Center*]: —My idea is, they'll publish nothing about any of us.

SETH: How do you propose to stop them? [*Pours two cocktails.*]

TRACY: I don't quite know yet. [*Sits Right of table.*]

SETH: Well, at present the least we can do is to inform Connor and the camera lady that we are all quite aware of their purpose here. I insist on that.

TRACY: All right! I'll tell them myself.

SETH: I think it will come better from me, don't you—as, at least, titular head of the family? [*Crosses down Left with drink for* MARGARET.]

TRACY [*A moment. Then* TRACY *speaks deliberately, harshly*]: Of course —inasmuch as you let us in for it in the first place.

SETH [*Crossing in Left Center*]: Do keep that note out of your voice, Tracy. It's most unattractive.

TRACY: Oh? How does Miss Mara talk? Or does she purr?

MARGARET: Tracy!

SETH [*Turning to Left*]: It's all right, Margaret.

TRACY: Sweet and low, I suppose. Dulcet. Very ladylike.—You've got a fine right, you have—after the way you've treated Mother—after the way you've treated us all—a magnificent right you've got to come back here in your best country manner and strike attitudes and make stands and criticize my fiancé and give orders and mess things up generally, just as if you'd done—

MARGARET: Stop it instantly, Tracy!

TRACY [*Rises*]: I can't help it. It's sickening.—As if he'd done nothing at all!

MARGARET: It is no concern of yours. If it concerns anyone, it concerns —well, actually, I don't know whom it concerns, except your father.

SETH [*Crossing in Left Center towards* MARGARET]: That's very wise of you, Margaret. What most wives won't seem to realize is that their husband's philandering—particularly the middle-aged kind—has nothing whatever to do with them.

TRACY [*Crossing down a step, Right Center*]: Oh? Then what has it to do with?

SETH [*Crossing in Center and sits Left of table*]: A reluctance to grow old, I think. I suppose the best mainstay a man can have as he gets along in years is a daughter—the right kind of daughter.

TRACY [*Crossing over Right Center*]: That's interesting, to say the least.

SETH: —One who loves him blindly—as no good wife ever should, of course.—One for whom he can do no wrong—

TRACY: How sweet.

SETH: I'm talking seriously about something I've thought out thoroughly. I've had to. I think a devoted young daughter gives a man the illusion that youth is still his.

TRACY: Very important, I suppose.

SETH: Very—and without her, he's inclined to go in search of it again, because it's as precious to him as it is to any woman.—But with a girl of his own full of warmth for him, full of foolish, unquestioning, uncritical affection—

TRACY: —None of which I've got.

SETH: None. You have a good mind, a pretty face and a disciplined body that does what you tell it. You have more wealth than any of us, thanks to one grandfather's name, and another's red hair, and a shameless play for both of them since about age three. In fact—

TRACY: I never! I loved them!

SETH: —In fact, you have everything it takes to make a lovely woman except the one essential—an understanding heart. Without it, you might just as well be made of bronze.

TRACY [*After a moment. Turns front*]: That's an awful thing to say to anyone.

SETH: Indeed it is.

TRACY [*Turns to him*]: So I'm to blame for Tina Mara, am I?

SETH: If any blame attaches, to some extent I expect you are.

TRACY: You coward.

SETH: No.—But better to be one than a prig—and a perennial spinster, however many marriages.

MARGARET: Seth! That's too much.

SETH: I'm afraid it's not enough. [*Rises; crosses Left to* MARGARET] I'm afraid that nothing is.

TRACY [*Is staring at him*]: Wha-what did you say I was?

SETH: Do you want me to repeat it?

MARGARET: Seth—now I understand a great deal that I didn't.

SETH [*Crossing to* MARGARET]: It's all past now, Margaret. It has been for some time. Forgive me. You won't have to again. *I* understand a lot more than I did, as well. [*Pats shoulder. She touches his hand.*]

TRACY: "A prig and a"? You mean—you mean you think *I* think I'm some kind of a virgin goddess or something?

SETH [*Crossing Left Center*]: If your ego wishes to call it that, yes.—Also, you've been talking like a jealous woman.

TRACY [*Right Center*]: "A—"? [*Turns away to Right, her face a study*]

What's the matter with everyone all at once, anyhow? [*Goes to column Right.*]

UNCLE WILLIE [*Comes in from Right 1. Crossing up Center*]: Miss Imbrie preferred dressing, to my company. [*To* SETH] What do you make of that, Uncle Willie?

SETH [*Crossing in Center*]: We're going to drop all this. From now on you're yourself again—and so am I. I shall tell them we know what their tender mission is, and at the first opportunity.

[SANDY *and* DINAH *enter Left Center. He goes to back of table.*]

UNCLE WILLIE [*Crossing back of table*]: It's a pity. It was jolly good fun. Let's have a drink—

SANDY [*Crossing back of table*]: Damme, let's do that. [*Pours cocktails.*]

DINAH [*Crossing down Right Center*]: We're all so completely commonplace. *I* don't see how we interest anyone.

MARGARET [*Rises, crossing to* DINAH *Right Center*]: I think that dress hikes up a little behind.

DINAH: No—it's me that does.

[MARGARET *sits Right of Center table.* SANDY *pours two glasses of champagne.*]

TRACY: You look adorable, Dinah.

DINAH: Oh, thanks, Tracy! Thanks ever so much!

SANDY: A wedding without ushers and bridesmaids. Peace! It's wonderful—

DINAH [*Crossing in to Left of* MARGARET]: *I'm* the bridesmaid!—So can I have a cocktail at last? Can I?

MARGARET: Certainly not.

DINAH: It's a dirty gyp. [*Goes over to chaise and sits.*]

SANDY: Tracy? [*Goes to her with cocktail. She shakes her head*]: Champagne, instead?

TRACY: No, thanks.

SANDY: Excuse, please. I forgot, you never. [*Puts drink down on table.*]

UNCLE WILLIE: Never? The girl's demented.

TRACY: —But prigs don't.

UNCLE WILLIE: What's that?

TRACY: Nor spinsters.

SANDY: We don't get you.

TRACY: Nor goddesses, virgin or otherwise.

[MIKE *and* LIZ, *dressed for dinner, enter from Left Center.* SANDY *greets them as they come down Left Center.* LIZ *goes down Left.* MIKE *stays up Left.*]

SANDY [*To* WILLIE]: —Not completely: just a borderline case. Hello, you were quick. [*Goes down Right.*]

[TRACY*, over Right, noticing nothing, stares upstage.*]

UNCLE WILLIE: Miss Imbrie, you are a dream of loveliness. A cocktail or champagne?

LIZ [*Down Left*]: Thanks, champagne. I've never had enough.

[SETH *offers her his seat. She declines. He sits.*]

SANDY [*Right*]: You will tonight.

[WILLIE *gives them each a glass.*]

MIKE [*Up Left*]: Champagne flew. [*To* WILLIE] Mr. Lord—er—that is to say—

SETH [*Simultaneously*]: Mr. Connor—oh—excuse me—

MIKE [*To* WILLIE]: Mr. Lord, Miss Imbrie and I have something on our minds—

UNCLE WILLIE [*Back of Center table*]: That's splendid; just the place for it. What?

MIKE: Well—er—it's rather hard to explain—it's—er—about the reason we're here and so forth.

SETH: I think perhaps there's something I ought to explain too—

MIKE: But did you ever hear of a man named Sidney Kidd—

[THOMAS*, the butler, enters Left with a tray and note and comes to foot of chaise.*]

SETH: —And did you ever hear of a man named Seth—er—? What is it, Thomas?

THOMAS: They've just phoned a telegram, Mr. Lord—

UNCLE WILLIE: Give it here.

THOMAS: It's for Mrs. Lord, Mr. Tracy.

[LIZ *and* MIKE *look.*]

UNCLE WILLIE: Then why didn't you say so?

THOMAS: Mrs. Lord and Miss Lord, that is.

MARGARET: Read it, Thomas. I haven't my glasses.

SANDY [*Right Center*]: Hey! Wait a minute!

MARGARET: Read it, Thomas.

THOMAS [*Left*]: "Most frightfully sorry will not be able to get down for the wedding as am confined to my bed with everything wrong. Baby better. It was only gas. Love, Father." Is there any answer, Madam?

MARGARET: No, Thomas—none in this world.

[THOMAS *goes out Left.*]

LIZ [*To* WILLIE]: He got a little mixed up, didn't he?

UNCLE WILLIE: A common mistake.

SETH: Now do you understand, Mr. Connor?

MIKE: I think we do.

LIZ: It's wonderful. Lord only knows where we go from here.

SANDY: To Aunt Geneva's!—Come on, everybody.

DINAH [*Rising from chair—upstage end*]: My first party, and about time.

UNCLE WILLIE [*Going to* LIZ, *over her shoulder, speaks*]: Who'll come in my little car with me?

MARGARET [*Cutting in and separating him from* LIZ]: Seth and Dinah and I.—Sandy, will you bring Miss Imbrie and Mr. Connor?

SANDY [*Gets up Center. Crossing to* LIZ]: Like a shot.

DINAH: The evening is pregnant with possibilities.

MARGARET [*Takes her gently by shoulders and ushers her out door Left*]: "Full of" is better dear.

[SETH *goes to door Left.* WILLIE *starts to cross Left but hesitates long enough in passing to pinch* LIZ *behind, then goes out innocently.*]

LIZ [*Jumps forward slightly*]: Ouch!

[SETH, *who had been on his way out Left, stops; comes to* LIZ.]

SETH: What was it?

LIZ: N-nothing. [SETH *goes out. She turns to* SANDY *on her Right.*] You know, I felt exactly as if I'd been pinched.

SANDY: Don't think you weren't. [*They both go out Left.*]

[MIKE *crosses down Center; sees* TRACY*; doesn't intend to follow.*]

MIKE: Aren't you coming?

TRACY [*Down Right*]: I'll follow along with George.

MIKE: What's the matter with you, Tracy? [*Below table*]

TRACY: You tell *me,* will you?

MIKE [*Looks at her intently*]: Damn if I know. I'd like to.

TRACY [*Smiles uncertainly*]: Well, if you happen to find out—

MIKE: —I'll tell you. Sure.

TRACY: —And remember, Mike—"With the Rich and Mighty"—

MIKE: "Always a little Patience"—Yes, Highness. I will.

TRACY: Do that. Please do—

[*He goes out Left. She stands for a second, then comes to table, pours a glass of champagne and drinks. Starts to pour a second.*

CURTAIN

■ ACT II ■

SCENE II

The porch. About half-past five on Saturday morning. It is going to be a clear day, and throughout the scene the light increases. MAC, *the night watchman, about thirty, crosses the path from Left 1 to Right 1, smoking a pipe and swinging a lighted lantern. He goes out Right.* SANDY *enters Right Center from the house. He is carrying a tray with two bottles of champagne, one already opened, a pitcher of milk, and glasses. He is followed by* TRACY. *Both are in evening dress.*

SANDY [*At back of table*]: The question is, can we get away with it?

TRACY [*Crossing Left of him*]: You've got to get away with it! You must, Sandy!

SANDY: Me? It's your idea, not mine.

TRACY [*Gets glass champagne*]: What difference does that make? [*Back of table Center*]

SANDY: You get the ideas and I do all the work.

TRACY: Sandy!

SANDY: Okay. [*Goes to chair Right of table.*]

TRACY: What you don't already know about the great Sidney Kidd, you can certainly fill in from Mike's ravings tonight.

SANDY [*Sits*]: I used to have that *Dime* lingo down pretty pat.

TRACY [*Crossing Right of him—kneels at his knee*]: It's a chance to write a beauty; you know it is.

SANDY: Then I swap it with Kidd for Connor's piece on us—and where am I?

TRACY: You'll have the satisfaction of knowing you saved the lot of us single-handed.

SANDY: And if he won't swap?

TRACY: I'm not worried about that.

SANDY: I suppose there's a fair chance the *Post* would go for it.

TRACY: Of course! You can't possibly lose. Quick—they'll be here! How long will it take you? [*Rises and drinks.*]

SANDY [*Rises*]: Three thousand words—all night—what there's left of it. [*Looks at his watch.*] Holy cats! You get to bed.

TRACY [*Right Center*]: Have you got a typewriter?

SANDY [*Right Center*]: My old Corona is upstairs, I think.

TRACY: Make it smoke.

SANDY: You bet.

TRACY: Suds. I can't stand it. You won't fall asleep?

SANDY: I've drunk nothing but black coffee since Connor began his lecture.

TRACY: "Sidney Kidd—his habits—his habitat and how to hunt him."

SANDY: Poor Connor! It must have been bottled up in him for years.

TRACY: Waiter, another bottle.

SANDY [*Crossing Left Center and turning*]: No. I've got enough for three articles now. Profile—fullface—

TRACY [*Crossing below table*]: —Also rear elevation.—Mike and Liz—they mustn't suspect, Sandy.

SANDY: Oh no—oh my, no!

TRACY [*Pours drink*]: They have simply stepped in their own chewing gum.—I suppose Kidd has one of those private numbers the rich and the mighty hide behind in New York. [*Gets Right Center.*]

SANDY: I'll dig it out of Liz and give him a buzz.

TRACY [*Right of table*]: What will you say?

SANDY: I'll be brief, bluff, belligerent. [TRACY *laughs; pours herself a glass of champagne.*] Hey—lay off that!

TRACY: Why?

SANDY [*Front of table*]: You are already in wine, sister.

TRACY: Me? You lie. It never affects me, not in the slightest.

SANDY: That's because you never take it.

TRACY: Even if I did, it wouldn't.

SANDY: Don't say that: it's unlucky. [*Shakes his head over her.*] I have seen people fly in the face of Pommery before.

TRACY [*Crossing down over Right; sits on steps*]: I've just got a good head, I guess.

SANDY [*Crossing down with her*]: Don't say it, don't say it!

TRACY: Sandy, you fool—

SANDY: George will spank.

TRACY: I could spank George for the way he behaved.

SANDY [*Sits*]: He had a right to be sore. You and Connor were gone for two hours, at least.

TRACY: You were along.

SANDY: All the same, tongues were wagging like tails. George said—

TRACY: George wanted to leave sharp at twelve—how could we?

SANDY: They need a lot of sleep, those big fellows.

TRACY: They must.—Then at one, with Father and Mother and Dinah. —Then at two, then at three—every hour on the hour. We fought like wolves in the car coming home.

SANDY: I hope you explained.

TRACY: Certainly not. He should have known. He was extremely rude. You'd have thought I had been out with Dexter [*A pause*]—I wonder where Dext was? I half expected him to—I don't like the look behind Dexter's eyes, Sandy. It makes me sad.

SANDY: Don't be sad, Tracy. [*His arms about her shoulder*]

TRACY: Oh, Sandy, if you knew how I envy you and Sue that darling fat creature you've just produced—

SANDY: You'll probably have four or five of your own any day now.

TRACY: Six! Oh, I hope—I do hope—I hope I'm good for something besides knocking out golf balls and putting horses over fences.

SANDY: You're good for my money any day.

TRACY: Thanks! [*Rises, crossing Center.*] Was I really mean to George, I wonder? I don't want to be.

SANDY: You're in an odd mood, little fellah. What's amiss—what's afoot?

TRACY [*Down on ground Center*]: I guess it's just that—a lot of things I always thought were terribly important I find now are—and the other way around—and—oh, what the hell. [*Goes up step and to table with glass.*]

SANDY [*Rises—crossing up to her at table*]: I don't think I'd spend much more time with Connor tonight, if I were you.

TRACY [*Left of table*]: Why not?

SANDY [*Front of table*]: Writers with wine sauce intoxicate little girls.

TRACY [*Laughs uncertainly. Sits on front of table*] They sort of do, don't they?—He fascinates me. He's so violent, Sandy.

SANDY [*Sits Right of her*]: He's fallen, Tray. I could hear him bump.

TRACY [*Rises*]: Mind your own beeswax, old Nosey Parker.

SANDY: Get thee to bed.

[*She reaches for glass—he takes it from her hand.*]

TRACY: No!

SANDY [*He puts glass down*]: —Before you have to be carried.

TRACY: No! No! No! [*Throws up her arms and head back; crosses over Right.*] I feel too delicious! Sandy, I feel just elegant. [*Cocks her head, listening up Right.*] Is that my bedroom telephone?

SANDY: Now you're hearing things.

TRACY: It couldn't be anyone but George. I *was* sort of swinish to him. Perhaps I'd better— [*Starts up Right*] As for you—get to work, you dog. Stop leaning on your shovel. [*She sees* MIKE *coming into the porch from Left. He is in fine fettle. Goes Center, back of table. Pours champagne.* SANDY *goes Right.*]

MIKE: Listen! Now I'm really under way. Miss not an inflection.

TRACY: Is it Connor the poet, or Connor the conspirator?

MIKE: Both! [*Pours himself a glass of wine*] "No lightweight is balding, battlebrowed Sidney Kidd, no mean displacement, his: for windy bias, bicarbonate." [*Drinks the wine; looks at the glass.*] That is funny stuff. I'm used to whiskey. Whiskey is a clap on the back. Champagne, entwining arms.

TRACY [*Crossing Left, back of* MIKE]: That's pretty. It it poetry? [*On arm of chair Left of table*]

MIKE: *Dime* will tell.

SANDY: "None before him but Writer Wolfgang Goethe has known all about all. Gigantic was Goethe's output, bigger already is Kidd's. Sample from his own pen: 'Pittsburgh is a gentle city.' "

TRACY: Sidney is a gentle man.

[MIKE *and* TRACY *look at each other.*]

MIKE: Potent, able, beady-eyed scion of great wealth in Quakertown, why don't you do a piece on our great and good friend?

SANDY [*Right*]: On Kidd?

MIKE [*Center*]: On none other.

SANDY: Nimble scrivener, it's an idea.

TRACY: Brilliant. I wish *I'd* thought of it.

MIKE: Baby Giant Tycooness.

TRACY: But would it not be a low, dirty deed?

MIKE: *He'd* print a scandal about his best friend: he's said he would.

SANDY: Who is his best friend?

MIKE: I guess Santa Claus. [*Crossing Left*] What is this mist before my eyes?

TRACY [*Rises and goes to Left of table*]: *I* tell you what: let's all have a quick swim to brighten us up. Go get Liz, Sandy. [*Takes off her bracelet and two rings and leaves them on table.*]

SANDY: Not me; it's too cold this early.

TRACY: It's the best hour of the day! Dexter and I always swam after parties.

MIKE [*Over Left Center*]: I haven't got any bathing suit.

TRACY: But we won't need any! It's just ourselves.

[*Turns to him and after a short pause he goes back of table—pours two drinks of champagne.*]

MIKE: Let's dip into this instead. [*Pours more champagne.*]

TRACY [*After a brief pause, to* SANDY]: No takers.—Get Liz anyway, Sandy.

SANDY: If she's not in bed—Or even if she is. [*Goes out Right Center.*]

TRACY [*Looking at* MIKE]: That was an odd thing you just did—

MIKE: Me? [*Crosses down front of Right chair with drink.*]

TRACY [*In front of table*]: You. For a moment you made me—self-conscious.

MIKE: How? About what?

TRACY: Never mind. [*Raises her glass.*] Hello, you.

MIKE [*Raises his*]: Hello.

TRACY: You look fine.

MIKE: I *feel* fine.

TRACY: Quite a fellah.

MIKE: They say.

[*They drink.*]

TRACY: Did you enjoy the party?

MIKE: Sure. The prettiest sight in this fine, pretty world is the Privileged Class enjoying its privileges. [*Drinks.*]

TRACY [*Crossing down lower stage Left*]: —Also somewhat of a snob.

MIKE: How do you mean?

TRACY: I'm wondering.

MIKE [*Leaves glass on table*]: Consider, Gentle Reader, they toil not, neither do they spin.

TRACY: Oh, yes, they do! They spin in circles. [*Spins and sits on floor over Left.*]

MIKE [*Crosses down to her*]: Nicely put. "Awash with champagne was Mrs. Willie Q. Tracy [born Geneva Biddle]'s stately pleasure dome on a hilltop in smart Radnor, P.A. on a Saturday night late in June; the eve of her great-niece's—" [*Sits beside her*] —Tracy, you can't marry that guy. [*She leaves glass on floor near foot of chaise.*]

TRACY: George?—I'm going to. Why not?

MIKE: I don't know; I'd have thought I'd be for it, but somehow you just don't seem to match up.

TRACY: Then the fault's with me.

MIKE: Maybe so; all the same you can't do it.

TRACY [*Rising*]: No? Come around about noon tomorrow—I mean today. [*Goes Center.*]

MIKE [*Rises; after a pause*]: Tracy—

TRACY: Yes, Mr. Connor?

MIKE: How do you mean, I'm "a snob"?

TRACY: You're the worst kind there is: an intellectual snob. You've made up your mind awfully young, it seems to me.

MIKE [*Crossing to her, Center*]: Thirty's about time to make up your mind.—And I'm nothing of the sort, not Mr. Connor.

TRACY: The time to make up your mind about people is never. Yes, you are—and a complete one.

MIKE: You're quite a girl.

TRACY: You think?

MIKE: I know.

TRACY: Thank you, Professor. I don't think I'm exceptional.

MIKE: You are, though.

TRACY: I know any number like me. You ought to get around more.

MIKE: In the Upper Clahss? No thanks.

TRACY: You're just a mass of prejudices, aren't you? You're so much thought and so little feeling, Professor. [*Goes Right.*]

MIKE: Oh, I am, am I?

TRACY: Yes, you am, are you! [*Stops and turns on him.*] Your damned intolerance furiates me. I mean *in*furiates me. I should think, of all people, a writer would need tolerance. The fact is, you'll never—you can't be a first-rate writer or a first-rate human being until you learn to have some small regard for— [*Suddenly she stops. Her eyes widen, remembering. She turns from him.*] Aren't the geraniums pretty, Professor? [*Crossing extreme Right*] Is it not a handsome day that begins?

MIKE [*Gets up on upper platform*]: Lay off that "Professor."

TRACY: Yes, Professor. [*Up on platform*]

MIKE [*Right Center*]: You've got all the arrogance of your class, all right, haven't you?

TRACY [*Right*]: Holy suds, what have "classes" to do with it?

MIKE: Quite a lot.

TRACY: Why? What do they matter—except for the people in them? George comes from the so-called "lower" class, Dexter comes from the upper. Well?

MIKE: Well?

TRACY: —Though there's a great deal to be said for Dexter—and don't forget it! [*Goes Center.*]

MIKE: I'll try not to.

TRACY [*Crossing above table to over Left for glass*]: Mac, the night watchman, is a prince among men and Joey, the stable boy, is a rat. Uncle Hugh is a saint. Uncle Willie's a pincher. [*Picks up glass.*]

MIKE: So what?

TRACY [*Crossing to table—pours*]: There aren't any rules about human beings, that's all!—You're teaching me things, Professor; this is new to me. Thanks, I am beholden to you. [*Pours drink.*]

MIKE [*Watching her*]: Not at all.

TRACY [*Gets below table*]: "Upper" and "lower," my eye! I'll take the lower, thanks. [*Starts to drink.*]

MIKE [*Over Right*]:—If you can't get a drawing room.

TRACY [*Stops drinking and holds. Turns*]: What do you mean by that?

MIKE [*Crossing in Right*]: My mistake.

TRACY: Decidedly.

MIKE [*Crossing a bit Right*]: Okay.

TRACY: You're insulting.

MIKE [*Near post*]: I'm sorry.

TRACY [*Leaning on table*]: Oh, don't apologize!

MIKE [*At Right post*]: Who the hell's apologizing?

TRACY [*Puts glass on table*]: I never knew such a man.

MIKE: You wouldn't be likely to, dear—not from where *you* sit.

TRACY: Talk about arrogance! [*Turning up at table*]

MIKE [*Weakening*]: Tracy— [*Crossing in Center, over her shoulder*]

TRACY: What do you want?

MIKE: You're wonderful.

TRACY [*She horse laughs; her back to him*]: Professor—may I go out?

MIKE: Class is dismissed. [*She moves Left.*] Miss Lord [*She stands still.*] will please wait.

TRACY: Miss Lord is privileged. [*Turns and meets his gaze. Goes to him.*]

MIKE: There's magnificence in you, Tracy. I'm telling you.

TRACY: I'm—! [*A moment. Crossing below him to Right*] Now I'm getting self-conscious again. I—it's funny— [*Another moment. Then*] Mike, let's— [*Turns to him.*]

MIKE: What?

TRACY [*Turns front and to Right*]: I—I don't know—go up, I guess. It's late.

MIKE: —A magnificence that comes out of your eyes, that's in your voice, in the way you stand there, in the way you walk. You're lit from within, bright, bright, bright. There are fires banked down in you, hearth fires and holocausts—

TRACY [*Turns to him*]: You—-I don't seem to you—made of bronze, then—

MIKE [*Step to her*]: You're made of flesh and blood—that's the blank, unholy surprise of it. You're the golden girl, Tracy, full of love and warmth and delight—What the hell's this? You've got tears in your eyes.

TRACY [*Right Center*]: Shut up, shut up!—Oh, Mike—keep talking—keep talking! *Talk,* will you?

MIKE: I've stopped.

[*For a long moment they look at each other. Then* TRACY *speaks, deliberately, harshly.*]

TRACY: Why? Has your mind taken hold again, dear Professor?

MIKE: You think so?

TRACY [*Crossing Right*]: Yes, Professor.

MIKE: A good thing, don't you agree?

TRACY [*Leaning against post Right*]: No, Professor.

MIKE: Drop that Professor—you hear me?

TRACY: Yes, Professor.

MIKE [*Slowly crossing in to her over Right*]: That's really all I am to you, is it?

TRACY: Of course, Professor.

MIKE: Are you sure?

TRACY [*Looks up at him*]: Why, why, yes—yes, of course, Profess—[*His kiss stops the word. The kiss is taken and returned. After it she exclaims softly:*] Golly. [*She gazes at him wonderingly, then raises her face to receive another. Then she stands in his arms, her cheek against his breast, amazement in her eyes.*] Golly Moses.

MIKE: Tracy dear—

TRACY: Mr. Connor—Mr. Connor—

MIKE: Let me tell you something—

TRACY: No, don't—All of a sudden I've got the shakes.

MIKE: I have, too.

TRACY: What *is* it?

MIKE: It must be something like love.

TRACY: No, no! It mustn't be. It can't—

MIKE: Why? Would it be inconvenient?

TRACY: Terribly. Anyway, it isn't. I know it's not. Oh, Mike, I'm a bad girl—

MIKE: Not you.

TRACY: We're out of our minds.

MIKE: —Right into our hearts.

TRACY: That ought to have music.

MIKE: It has, hasn't it?—Tracy, you lovely—[*Starts to kiss. She breaks embrace.*]

[*She hears something; looks quickly toward the door Left.*]

TRACY [*Crossing Center, looking Left*]: They're coming.

MIKE: The hell—

TRACY [*Turns to him*]: It's—it's not far to the pool. It's only over the lawn, in the birch grove—it'll be lovely now.

MIKE [*Holds his arm out*]: Come on—

TRACY: Oh, it's as—it's as if my insteps—were melting away.—What is it? Have I—have I got feet of clay, or something?

MIKE: —Quick! Here they are—[*He takes her hand and hurries her down the steps.*]

TRACY: I—I feel so small all at once.

MIKE: You're immense—you're tremendous.

TRACY: Not me—oh, not me! Put me in your pocket, Mike—

[*They are gone—off Right 1.*]

LIZ [*Off Left*]: You give those back!

[*A moment, then* SANDY *comes quickly in Left from the house, a sheaf of small photographs in his hand. He is followed by* LIZ, *in pajamas and wrapper.*]

SANDY: Look, Tracy—[*Sees that the porch is empty.*]

LIZ [*Crossing down Left Center*]: May I have them, please?

SANDY: Did Kidd *know* you took these shots of him?

LIZ [*Crossing below to Right*]: Some of them.

SANDY: Sit down. Have a drink.

LIZ: I should say not. A drink would be redundant, tautological, and a mistake. [*Wearily she drops into chair Right of table and eyes the pitcher on the table.*] Is that milk?

SANDY [*Goes back of table*]: That is milk.

LIZ: Gimme. Milk I will accept. [*He pours and gives her a glass.*] I met this cow this afternoon. Nice Bossy.

SANDY: Let me keep just these three shots.

LIZ: What for?

SANDY: A low purpose.

LIZ: Sufficiently low?

SANDY: Nefarious.

LIZ: You won't reproduce them?

SANDY: Nope.

LIZ: Nor cause them to be reproduced?

SANDY: Honest.

LIZ: In any way, shape or manner, without permission?

SANDY: So help me, Sidney Kidd.

LIZ: Amen.

SANDY: What's his private number?

LIZ: You mean his private number or his sacred private number?

SANDY: The one by the bed and the bathtub.

LIZ: Regent 4-1416—[*Settles lower in the chair.* SANDY *goes to the telephone off Right Center.*] I won't tell you. [*He dials one number.*] Is Mr. Kittredge pure gold, Lord?

SANDY [*Coming in doorway—but goes back into room again*]: We must never doubt that, Missy.

LIZ [*Sleepily*]: *Lèse-majesté*—excuse it, please.

SANDY [*Comes in to doorway*]: Regent 4-1416 New York. Wayne—22-23. [*To* LIZ]—And Mr. Connor—what of him?

LIZ: Percentage of base metal. Alloy.

SANDY: So.

LIZ: —Which imparts a certain shape and firmness.

SANDY [*In doorway*]: Hello?—Mr. Kidd? This is Alexander Lord.

LIZ [*Listens intently. Calling*]: I know nothing about this.

SANDY [*In doorway*]: No, I'm in Philadelphia.—Yes, I know it is. It's early here, too. Look, Mr. Kidd, I think you'd better get over here as fast as you can. What?—I'm sorry to have to tell you, sir, but Connor has had an accident—yes, pretty bad—he had a pretty bad fall. —No, it's his heart we're worried about now.—Yes, I'm afraid so: He keeps talking about you, calling you names—I mean calling your name.—How's that?—No, the eleven o'clock's time enough. We don't expect him to regain consciousness much before then.

LIZ: His only hope is to get fired—I know it is.

SANDY: Sorry, Miss Imbrie's sleeping. Shock.—[*Crossing into room*] The newspapers? No, they don't know a thing about it. I understand. What? I said I understood, didn't I?—Twelve twenty North Philadelphia—I'll have you met. [*Hangs up—puts the phones in place—enters porch.*] He wants no publicity. [*Goes down Right.*]

LIZ [*Has suppressed her broadening grin. She stirs lazily in her chair and inquires*]: Who was that?

SANDY: God.

[*She looks toward the garden path.* DEXTER *whistles off Right.*]

LIZ: Do I hear someone?

SANDY [*Looks—crossing down Right*]: It's Mac, the night watchman. —Liz—you're in love with Connor, aren't you?

LIZ: People ask the oddest questions.

[DEXTER, *whistling, enters Right 1, smoking cigarette.*]

SANDY: Why don't you marry him?

LIZ: I can't hear you.

SANDY: I say, why don't you—? [DEXTER *comes along the path and stops at the steps Right.*] Hello, here's an early one!

DEXTER: Hello. I saw quite a full day ahead, and got myself up. [*He seats himself on step Right.*]—A good party?

SANDY: Fine.

DEXTER: Good.

LIZ [*Rises*]: —And sufficient. Hell or high water, I'm going to bed. [*Gets up Right and starts Left to back of table.*]

SANDY [*Crossing up Right*]: Why don't you, Liz—*you* know—what I asked?

LIZ [*Back of table*]: He's still got a lot to learn, and I don't want to get in his way yet a while. Okay?

SANDY: Okay.—Risky, though. Suppose another girl came along in the meantime?

LIZ [*Up Left Center at door*]: Oh, I'd just scratch her eyes out, I guess. —That is, unless she was going to marry someone else the next day. [*In doorway*]

SANDY: You're a good number, Liz.

LIZ: No, I just photograph well. [*Goes out Left Center.*]

DEXTER [*Over Right*]: Complications?

SANDY [*Back of table, looking at pictures he brought on*]: There might be.

DEXTER: Where are they?

SANDY: Who?

DEXTER: The complications.

SANDY: They went up—at least I hope and pray that they did.

DEXTER: Well, well.

SANDY [*Moves toward the door Left*]: Make yourself comfortable, Dext. I've got a little blackmailing to do. [SANDY *goes out Left.*]

[*A pause as* DEXTER *smokes. He sees someone coming Left 1. Rises and stamps out cigarette.* GEORGE *comes up the Left 1 path and mounts the porch. He is still in evening clothes.*]

GEORGE [*Entering*]: What are you doing here?

DEXTER [*Crossing Center*]: Oh, I'm a friend of the family's—just dropped in for a chat.

GEORGE: Don't try to be funny. I asked you a question.

DEXTER: I might ask you the same one.

GEORGE: I telephoned Tracy and her phone didn't answer.

DEXTER: I didn't telephone. I just came right over.

GEORGE: I was worried, so I—

DEXTER: Yes, I was worried, too.

GEORGE: About what?

DEXTER [*Crossing Left, face to face with George*]: What do you think of this Connor—or do you?

GEORGE: What about him?

DEXTER: I just wondered.

GEORGE: Listen: if you're trying to insinuate some—

DEXTER: My dear fellow, I wouldn't dream of it! I was only—[*Goes up to table—sees jewelry.*]

GEORGE: Who's that I hear? [*Goes to Right; looks off.*]

DEXTER [*He finds the ring and bracelet upon the table. He glances quickly in the direction of the swimming pool, then pockets them*]: Look, Kittredge: I advise you to go to bed.

GEORGE [*Crossing Center*]: Oh, you do, do you?

DEXTER [*Above* GEORGE]: Yes. I strongly urge you to do so at once.

GEORGE [*Crossing Left, facing upstage*]: I'm staying right here.

DEXTER [*Looks at him*]: You're making a mistake. Somehow I don't think you'll understand.

GEORGE: You'd better leave that to—! I hear someone walking—[*Looks off up Right.*]

DEXTER: Yes?—Must be Mac. [*Crossing to Right, he calls out:*] It's all right, Mac—it's only us! [*Turns to* GEORGE*—comes down to him.*] Come on—I'll walk along with you.

GEORGE [*Crossing up on porch at table*]: I'm staying right here—so are you.

DEXTER: All right, then: take the works, and may God be with you. [*Retires to over Left.*]

[*Finally* MIKE *appears from Right 1, comes to Right corner of the porch, carrying* TRACY *in his arms.* BOTH *are in bathrobes and slippers and there is a jumble of clothes, his and hers, slung over* MIKE*'s shoulder. He stops with her for a moment at the top of the steps. She stirs in his arms, speaks lowly, as if from a long way away. As they enter* DEXTER *crosses below table to up Right.* GEORGE *goes above to Right; confronts* MIKE.]

TRACY: Take me upstairs, Mike—

MIKE: Yes, dear. Here we go.

GEORGE [*Up Center*]: What the—!

DEXTER [*Comes swiftly in between him and* MIKE]: Easy, old boy! [*To* MIKE] She's not hurt?

MIKE: No. She's just—

TRACY [*Murmurs dreamily*]: Not wounded, Sire—but dead.

GEORGE: She—she hasn't any clothes on!

TRACY [*Into* MIKE*'s shoulder*]: Not a stitch—it's delicious.

MIKE [*Speaks lowly*]: It seems the minute she hit the water, the wine—

DEXTER [*Glances at* GEORGE, *who can only stare*]: A likely story, Connor.

MIKE: What did you say?

DEXTER: I said, a likely story!

MIKE: Listen: if—!

DEXTER: You'll come down again directly?

MIKE: Yes, if you want.

DEXTER: I want.

TRACY [*Lifts her head limply and looks at them*]: Hello, Dexter. Hello, George. [*Crooks her head around and looks vaguely up at* MIKE.] Hello, Mike.

[DEXTER *goes and opens drapery Right Center.* MIKE *starts to take her off.*]

DEXTER: The second door on the right at the top of the stairs. Mind you don't wake Dinah.

[MIKE *moves toward the door with* TRACY.]

TRACY: My feet are of clay—made of clay—did you know it? [*Drops her head again and tightens her arms around* MIKE*'s neck.*] Goo' nigh' —sleep well, little man.

[MIKE *carries her out, past* DEXTER.]

DEXTER [*Calling off*]: Look out for Dinah. [*Crossing to front of table—sits on it*] How *are* the mighty fallen! [GEORGE *goes below to Right.*] —But if I know Tracy—and I know her very well—she'll remember very little of this. For the second time in her life, she may draw quite a tidy blank.—Of course she may worry, though—

GEORGE: Good God!

DEXTER [*Turns on him swiftly. On edge of table*]: You believe it, then?

GEORGE: Believe what?

DEXTER: The—er—the implications, of what you've seen, let's say.

GEORGE [*Crossing in a bit*]: What else is there to believe?

DEXTER: Why, I suppose that's entirely up to you.

GEORGE: I've got eyes, and I've got imagination, haven't I?

DEXTER: I don't know. Have you?

GEORGE [*Crossing in Right Center*]: So you pretend not to believe it—

DEXTER: Yes, I pretend not to.

GEORGE: Then you don't know women. [*Goes in Center to* DEXTER.]

DEXTER: Possibly not.

GEORGE: You're a blind fool!

DEXTER: Oh, quite possibly!

GEORGE [*Crossing below him to up Left!*]: —God!

DEXTER [*Studies him*]: You won't be too hard on her, will you?

GEORGE: I'll make up my own mind what I'll be!

DEXTER: But we're all only human, you know. [*Goes Left and up Center.*]

GEORGE: You—all of you—with your damned sophisticated ideas!

DEXTER [*Up Center, back of table*]: Isn't it hell?

[MIKE *comes swiftly through the Right Center door and up to* DEXTER.]

MIKE: Well?

GEORGE [*Crossing up and over Right*]: Why, you lowdown—!

DEXTER [*Quickly*]: The lady is my wife, Mr. Connor. [*His upper cut to* MIKE*'s jaw sends him across the porch and to the floor down Right.*]

GEORGE: You!—What right have—? [*Goes over Right.*]

DEXTER: —A husband's, till tomorrow, Kittredge.

GEORGE: I'll make up my mind, all right! [*He turns and storms out Left 1.*]

DEXTER [*Bends over* MIKE. *After* GEORGE *is gone*]: Okay, old man?

MIKE [*Sits up, nursing his chin*]: Listen: if you think—!

DEXTER: I know—I'm sorry. But I thought I'd better hit you before he did. [MAC, *the night watchman, comes along the garden path, Right 1.*] Hello, Mac. How are you? [*Rises.*]

MAC: Hello, Dexter! Anything wrong?

DEXTER: Not a thing, Mac.—Just as quiet as a church.

MAC: Who is it? [*Looks at* MIKE, *who turns to face him*] Hell!—I thought it might be Kittredge.

DEXTER: We can't have everything, Mac.

[MAC *continues along the path to Left 1.*]

CURTAIN

■ ACT III ■

The sitting room. Late morning. Saturday. The room is full of bright noonday sun and there are flowers everywhere.

AT RISE: WILLIE, *in a morning coat, fancy waistcoat and ascot, stands in the Center of the room, facing* THOMAS. WILLIE *is demanding impatiently.*

THOMAS [*Right*]: I am trying to think, Mr. Tracy.

UNCLE WILLIE: Well? Well?

THOMAS: She wakened late, sir, and had a tray in her room. I believe May and Elsie are just now dressing her.

UNCLE WILLIE: It's not the bride I'm asking about—it's her sister.

THOMAS: I haven't seen Miss Dinah since breakfast, sir. She came down rather early.

UNCLE WILLIE: Is there anything wrong with her?

THOMAS: I did notice that she seemed a trifle silent, took only one egg and neglected to finish her cereal. The hot cakes and bacon, however, went much as usual.

UNCLE WILLIE: She was telephoning me like a mad woman before I was out of my tub. [DINAH, *in blue jeans, slides in from Left 1 and up behind him.*] I expected at least two bodies, hacked beyond recognition, the house stiff police, and—[DINAH *touches his coattail. He starts and turns.*] Good God, child—don't do that! I drank champagne last night.

DINAH: Hello, Uncle Willie.

UNCLE WILLIE: *Why* must I come on ahead of your Aunt Geneva? Why must I waste not one minute? What's amiss? What's about? Speak up! Don't stand there with your big eyes—[DINAH *nudges him, pointing toward* THOMAS.] like a stuffed owl.

[DINAH *glances significantly at* THOMAS.]

THOMAS: Is there anything else, sir? If not—

UNCLE WILLIE: Thanks, Thomas, nothing.

[THOMAS *goes out Right 2.* DINAH *pulls at* WILLIE*'s coattail, drawing him to the armchair Left Center.*]

DINAH: Come over here—and speak very low. Nobody's allowed in this room this morning but Tracy—and speak terribly low. [*Puts him in chair.*]

UNCLE WILLIE: What the Sam Hill for? What's alack? What's afoot?

DINAH: I had no one to turn to but you, Uncle Willie.

UNCLE WILLIE: People are always turning to me. I wish they'd stop.

DINAH: It's desperate. It's about Tracy. [*Goes below table to Left and kneels in armchair; leans over table to* WILLIE.]

UNCLE WILLIE: Tracy? What's she up to now? Tracy this, and Tracy that. Upstairs and downstairs and in my lady's chamber.

DINAH: How did you know?

UNCLE WILLIE: Know what?

DINAH: It seems to me you know just about everything.

UNCLE WILLIE: I have a fund of information accumulated through the years. I am old, seasoned, and full of instruction. But there are gaps in my knowledge. Ask me about falconry, say, or ballistics, and you will get nowhere.

DINAH: I meant more about people and—and sin.

UNCLE WILLIE: I know only that they are inseparable. I also know that the one consolation for being old is the realization that, however you live, you will never die young.—Get to the point, child. What do you want of me?

DINAH: Advice.

UNCLE WILLIE: On what subject or subjects?

DINAH: Well, [*Crossing back of table*] lookit; you don't like George, do you?

UNCLE WILLIE: Kittredge? I deplore him.

DINAH [*Between his armchair and table*]: And you'd like it if Tracy didn't go ahead and have married him after all—or would you?

UNCLE WILLIE: Where do you go to school?

DINAH: I don't yet. I'm going some place next fall.

UNCLE WILLIE: And high time.—Like it? I would cheer. I would raise my voice in song.

DINAH: Well, I think I know a way to stop her from, but I need advice on how.

UNCLE WILLIE: Proceed, child—proceed cautiously.

DINAH: Well, suppose she all of a sudden developed an illikit passion for someone—

UNCLE WILLIE: Can you arrange it?

DINAH: It doesn't need to be. It is already.

UNCLE WILLIE: Ah? Since when?

DINAH: Last night—and well into the morning.

UNCLE WILLIE: You surprise me, Dinah.

DINAH: Imagine what *I* was—and just imagine what *George* would be.

UNCLE WILLIE: And—er—the object of this—er—illikit passion—

DINAH: Let him be nameless. [WILLIE *is exasperated.*]—Only tell me, should I tell George?—It's getting late.

[*Unnoticed by them,* DEXTER *has come in Left 2 and remains up by piano.*]

UNCLE WILLIE: Maybe he'll want to marry her anyway.

DINAH: But she can't. If she marries anyone, it's got to be Mr. Connor!

UNCLE WILLIE: Connor? Why Connor?

DINAH: She's just got to, that's all.

DEXTER [*Crossing to Center*]: Why, Dinah? What makes you think she should?

DINAH [*Looks at him, appalled. Follows to Center, Left of* DEXTER]: Dexter—

DEXTER: Isn't that a pretty big order to swing at this late date?

DINAH: I—I didn't say anything. What did *I* say?

DEXTER: Of course, you might talk it over with her.—But maybe you have.

DINAH: Certainly not. I haven't!

UNCLE WILLIE: Apparently the little cherub has seen or heard something.

DEXTER: That's Dexter's own Dinah.

UNCLE WILLIE: I must say *you* show a certain amount of cheek, walking in here on this, of all mornings.

DEXTER: Tracy just did a very sweet thing: she telephoned and asked me what to do for a feeling of fright accompanied by headache.

DINAH: I should think it would be bad luck for a first husband to see the bride before the wedding.

DEXTER [*Crossing, sits on arm of chair Right Center*]: That's what I figured.—Why all this about Connor, Dinah? Did the party give you bad dreams?

DINAH: It wasn't any dream.

DEXTER: I wouldn't be too sure. Once you've gone to bed it's pretty hard to tell, isn't it?

DINAH: Is it?

DEXTER: You bet your hat it is. It's practically impossible.

DINAH: I thought it was Sandy's typewriter woke me up.

[TRACY *comes in from the hall, Right 2, in the dress in which she is to be married. She has a leather-strapped wrist watch in her hand.* DEXTER *rises and goes up above sofa.* DINAH *to back of* WILLIE'*s chair, Left.*]

TRACY [*Crossing down Right end of sofa*]: Hello! Isn't it a fine day, though! Is everyone fine? That's fine! [*Crossing uncertainly Center of sofa. Sits.*] My, I'm hearty.

DEXTER: How are you otherwise? [*Down to upper corner of sofa*]

TRACY: I don't know what's the matter with me. I must have had too much sun yesterday.

DEXTER: It's awfully easy to get too much.

TRACY: My eyes don't open properly. [*Picks up silver cigarette box from coffee table; looks at eyes.*] Please go home, Dext.

DEXTER: Not till we get those eyes open. [*Sits on sofa beside her.*]

TRACY: Uncle Willie, good morning.

UNCLE WILLIE [*Leaning forward*]: That remains to be seen.

TRACY: Aren't you here early?

UNCLE WILLIE: Weddings get me out like nothing else.

DINAH: It's nearly half-past twelve. [*Goes Right; sits armchair Right Center.*]

TRACY: It can't be!

DINAH: Maybe it can't, but it is.

TRACY: Where—where's Mother?

DINAH [*Rises*]: Do you want her?

TRACY: No, I just wondered.

DINAH [*Reseats herself*]: She's talking with the orchestra, and Father with the minister, and—

TRACY: Doctor Parsons—already?

DINAH: —And Miss Imbrie's gone with her camera to shoot the horses, and Sandy's in his room and—and Mr. Connor, he hasn't come down yet.

DEXTER: And it's Saturday.

TRACY: Thanks loads. It's nice to have things accounted for. [*Passes the hand with the wrist watch over her eyes, then looks at the watch.*] —Only I wonder what this might be?

DEXTER: It looks terribly like a wrist watch.

TRACY: But whose? I found it in my room. I nearly stepped on it.

DINAH: Getting out of bed?

TRACY: Yes. Why?

DINAH [*Knowingly*]: I just wondered. [*Rises and crosses behind* WILLIE'*s chair, Left Center.*]

TRACY [*Puts the watch on the table before her*]: There's another mystery, Uncle Willie.

UNCLE WILLIE: Mysteries irritate me.

TRACY: I was robbed at your house last night.

UNCLE WILLIE: You don't say.

TRACY: Yes—my bracelet and my engagement ring are missing everywhere.

UNCLE WILLIE: Probably someone's house guest from New York.

[TRACY *nods agreement.*]

DEXTER [*Brings them from his pocket*]: Here you are.

TRACY [*Stares at them, then at him*]: —But weren't at the party!

DEXTER: Wasn't I?

TRACY: Were you?

DEXTER: Don't tell me you don't remember!

TRACY: I—I do now, sort of—but there were such a lot of people.

[DEXTER *gives jewels to her.* TRACY *puts them on table.*]

DEXTER [*Rises, crossing up behind Right armchair*]: You should have taken a quick swim to shake them off. There's nothing like a swim after a late night.

TRACY: —A swim. [*And her eyes grow rounder.*]

DEXTER [*Laughs*]: There! Now they're open!

DINAH [*Crossing a bit to Center*]: That was just the beginning—and it was no dream.

DEXTER [*Glances at her, crossing to* WILLIE]: Don't you think, sir, that if you and I went to the pantry at this point—you know: speaking of eye-openers?

UNCLE WILLIE [*Rises and precedes him toward the porch Left 1*]: The only sane remark I've heard this morning. I know a formula that is said to pop the pennies off the eyelids of dead Irishmen. [*Exits Left 1.*]

DEXTER [*Over Left; stops at table*]: Oh, Dinah—if conversation drags, you might tell Tracy your dream. [*Exits Left 1.*]

TRACY: What did he say?

DINAH [*Center*]: Oh, nothing. [*Crossing in front of sofa. Puts arm on* TRACY'*s shoulder.*] Tray—I hate you to get married and go away.

TRACY: I'll miss you, darling. I'll miss all of you.

DINAH: We'll miss you, too.—It—it isn't like when you married Dexter, and just moved down the road a ways.

TRACY: I'll come back often. It's only Wilkes-Barre.

DINAH: It gripes me.

TRACY: Baby.

[*There is another silence. Finally* DINAH *speaks.*]

DINAH [*Sits on upper arm of sofa*]: You know I did have the funniest dream about you last night.

TRACY: Did you? What was it?

DINAH: It was terribly interesting, and—and awfully scarey, sort of—

TRACY [*Rises; a step forward*]: Do you like my dress, Dinah?

DINAH: Yes, ever so much.

TRACY [*Rises too quickly, wavers a moment, steadies herself, then moves to the Left 1 door*]: It feels awfully heavy.—You'd better rush and get ready yourself. [*Goes Center to Left.*]

[MARGARET *enters Right 1.*]

DINAH: You know me: I don't take a minute.

[*Violins off Right tune up.*]

MARGARET: Turn around, Tracy. [TRACY *turns.*] Yes, it looks lovely. [*Goes to Center.*]

TRACY [*Left*]: What's that—that scratching sound I hear?

MARGARET [*Center*]: The orchestra tuning. Yes—[*Crossing up Right*] I'm glad we decided against the blue one. Where's your father? You know, I feel completely impersonal about all this. I can't quite grasp it. Get dressed, Dinah. [*Goes out into the hall. Right 2.*]

TRACY [*Over Left blinks into the sunlight from Left 1*]: That sun is certainly bright all right, isn't it?

DINAH: It was up awfully early.

TRACY: Was it?

DINAH [*Crossing Left Center*]: Unless I dreamed that, too.—It's supposed to be the longest day of the year or something, isn't it?

TRACY: I wouldn't doubt it for a minute.

DINAH: It was all certainly pretty rooty-tooty. [*Sits Right of table Left.*]

TRACY: What was?

DINAH: My dream.

TRACY [*Crossing below table to Center*]: Dinah, you'll have to learn sooner or later that no one is interested in anyone else's dreams. [*Goes to above armchair Right and back of sofa.*]

DINAH: —I thought I got up and went over to the window and looked out across the lawn. And guess what I thought I saw coming over out of the woods?

TRACY [*Back of sofa, then crossing down Right*]: I haven't the faintest idea. A skunk?

DINAH: Well, sort of.—It was Mr. Connor.

TRACY: Mr. Connor? [*At lower end of sofa*]

DINAH: Yes—with his both arms full of something. And guess what it turned out to be?

TRACY: What?

DINAH: You—and some clothes. [TRACY *turns slowly and looks at her.*] Wasn't it funny? It was sort of like as if you were coming from the pool—

TRACY [*Closes her eyes*]: The pool.—I'm going crazy. I'm standing here solidly on my own two hands going crazy.—And then what? [*Goes below sofa to Right Center.*]

DINAH: Then I thought I heard something outside in the hall, and I went and opened my door a crack and there he was, still coming along with you, puffing like a steam engine. His wind can't be very good.

TRACY: And then what?—[*Goes in Center.*]

DINAH: And you were sort of crooning—

TRACY: I never crooned in my life!

DINAH: I guess it just sort of sounded like you were. Then he—guess what?

TRACY: I—couldn't possibly.

DINAH: Then he just sailed right into your room with you and—and that scared me so, that I just flew back to bed—or thought I did—and pulled the covers up over my head and layed there shaking and thinking; if *that's* the way it is, why doesn't she marry him instead of old George? And then I must have fallen even faster asleep, because the next thing I knew it was eight o'clock and the typewriter still going.

TRACY: Sandy—typewriter—

DINAH [*Rises; kneels in chair*]: So in a minute I got up and went to your door and peeked in, to make sure you were all right—and guess what?

TRACY [*Agonized*]: What?

DINAH: You were. He was gone by then.

TRACY: Gone? Of course he was gone—he was never there!

DINAH: I know, Tracy.

TRACY: Well! I should certainly hope you did! [*Goes over Right to armchair; sits.*]

DINAH [*Rises, following* TRACY]: I'm certainly glad I do, because if I didn't and if in a little while I heard Doctor Parsons saying, "If anyone knows any just cause or reason why these two should not be united in holy matrimony"—*I* just wouldn't know what to do.—And it was all only a dream. [*Goes up Center slowly to stool.*]

TRACY: Naturally!

DINAH: I know. Dexter said so, straight off.—But isn't it funny, though—

TRACY [*Half turning*]: Dexter!

DINAH [*Crossing down Center to Left of* TRACY]: Yes.—He said—

TRACY [*Grabbing* DINAH'*s arm*]: You told Dexter all that?

DINAH: Not a word. Not one single word.—But you know how quick he is.

TRACY: Dinah Lord—you little fiend; how can you—?

SETH [*Enters from the hall Right 2. Back of sofa*]: Tracy, the next time you marry, choose a different Man of God, will you? This one wears me out. [*Goes to the Right 1 door; looks in.*] Good heavens!—Dinah! Get into your clothes! You look like a tramp.

[*Is about to go out again Right 2.* TRACY'*s voice stops him.*]

DINAH: I'm going.

[*Goes up to corner Right.*]

TRACY: Father.

SETH [*Turns to her. Crossing down Center*]: Yes, Tracy?

TRACY: I'm glad you came back. I'm glad you're here.

SETH: Thank you, child.

TRACY: I'm sorry—I'm truly sorry I'm a disappointment to you.

SETH: I never said that, daughter—and I never will. [*Looks at her for a moment, touches her arm, then turns abruptly and goes out Right 2.*] Where's your mother? Where's George?

MIKE [*Comes in from the porch Left 1. Crossing in front of table Left, puts out cigarette*]: Good morning.

TRACY: Oh, hello!

MIKE: I was taking the air. I like it, but it doesn't like me.—Hello, Dinah.

DINAH [*Step toward him to armchair Left Center*]: How do you do?

TRACY [*Right Center*]: Did—did you have a good sleep?

MIKE [*Crossing in Center to* TRACY]: Wonderful. How about you?

TRACY: Marvelous. Have you ever seen a handsomer day?

MIKE: Never. What did it set you back?

[DINAH *moves down Center.*]

TRACY: I got it for nothing, for being a good girl.

MIKE: Good.

[*There is a brief silence. They look at* DINAH. *Finally:*]

DINAH [*Crossing below sofa to door Right 1*]: I'm going, don't worry.

TRACY: Why should you?

DINAH [*Over Right at lower end of sofa; turns to them*]: I guess you must have things you wish to discuss.

TRACY: "Things to—"? What are you talking about?

DINAH: Only remember, it's getting late. [*Gingerly she opens the Right 1 door a crack, and peers in.*] Some of them are in already. My, they look solemn. [*Closes door, and moves toward the hall up Right 2.*]

I'll be ready when you are.
[*Exits Right 2.*]

TRACY [*Crossing Left*]: She's always trying to make situations. [*Front of table.* MIKE *arm of Right Center chair; laughs.*] —How's your work coming—are you doing us up brown?

MIKE: I've—somehow I've lost my angle.

TRACY: How do you mean, Mike?

MIKE: I've just got so damn tolerant all at once, I doubt if I'll ever be able to write another line.

TRACY [*Laughs*]: You are a fellah, Mike.

MIKE: Or the mug of this world: I don't know.

TRACY: When you're at work you ought to be doing, you'll soon see that tolerance—What's the matter with your chin?

MIKE: Does it show?

TRACY: A little. What happened?

MIKE: I guess I just stuck it out too far.

TRACY: —Into a door, in the dark?

MIKE: That's it. [*Rises, crossing in Left.*] Are you—are *you* all right, Tracy?

TRACY: Me? Of course! Why shouldn't I be?

MIKE: That was a flock of wine we put away.

TRACY [*Crossing below him to armchair Right Center*]: I never felt better in my life.

MIKE: That's fine. That's just daisy.

TRACY [*Sits in armchair Right Center*]: I—I guess we're lucky both to have such good heads.

MIKE: Yes, I guess. [*Goes to near her.*]

TRACY: It must be awful for people who—you know—get up and make speeches or—or try to start a fight—or, you know—misbehave in general.

MIKE: It certainly must.

TRACY: It must be—some sort of hidden weakness coming out.

MIKE: Weakness? I'm not so sure of that. [*Chuckles.*]

TRACY [*She imitates him. Rises, crossing Center to Left*]: Anyhow, I had a simply wonderful evening. I hope you enjoyed it too.

MIKE [*Right Center*]: I enjoyed the last part of it.

TRACY [*Turns to him*]: Really? Why?—why especially the last?

MIKE: Are you asking me, Tracy?

TRACY [*Front of armchair Left Center*]: Oh, you mean the swim!—We did swim, and so forth, didn't we?

MIKE: We swam, and so forth.

TRACY [*Turns to him suddenly. At table Left Center*]: Mike—

MIKE [*Beside her*]: You darling, darling girl—

TRACY: Mike!

MIKE: What can I say to you? Tell me, darling—

TRACY [*Crossing below him to upper corner of sofa*]: Not anything—don't say anything. And especially not "Darling."

MIKE: Never in this world will I ever forget you.

TRACY: —Not anything, I said.

MIKE [*Crossing in back of armchair Right Center to her*]: You're going to go through with it, then—

TRACY: Through with what?

MIKE: The wedding.

TRACY: Why—why shouldn't I?

MIKE: Well, you see, I've made a funny discovery: that in spite of the fact that someone's up from the bottom, he may be quite a heel. And that even though someone else's born to the purple, he still may be quite a guy.—Hell, I'm only saying what you said last night!

TRACY: I said a lot of things last night, it seems. [*Goes down.*]

MIKE [*After a moment*]: All right, no dice. But understand: also no regrets about last night.

TRACY [*Backs away to Right*]: Why should I have?

MIKE [*Crossing below sofa to her*]: That's it! That's the stuff; you're wonderful. You're aces, Tracy.

TRACY [*Backing away from him to lower corner sofa*]: You don't know what I mean! I'm asking you—tell me straight out—tell me the reason why I should have any—[*But she cannot finish. Her head drops.*] No—don't—[*Goes Center.*] Just tell me—what time is it?

MIKE [*Glancing at his wrist*]: What's happened to my wrist watch?

TRACY [*Stops, frozen; speaks without turning*]: Why? Is it broken?

MIKE [*Front of sofa*]: It's gone. I've lost it somewhere.

TRACY [*Left Center. After a moment*]: I can't tell you how extremely sorry I am to hear that. [*Goes to table.*]

MIKE: Oh, well—I'd always just as soon not know the time.

TRACY [*Her back to him*]: There on the table—

MIKE: —What is? [*Goes to the coffee table; finds the watch.*] Well, for the love of—! Who found it? I'll give a reward, or something. [*Straps the watch on his wrist.*]

TRACY: I don't think any reward will be expected.

DEXTER [*Comes in Left 1, cocktail glass in hand*]: Now, then! This medicine indicated in cases of—[*Stops at the sight of* MIKE.] Hello, Connor. How are you?

MIKE [*At sofa, crossing Left Center*]: About as you'd think.—Is that for me?

DEXTER [*Over Left*]: For Tracy.—Why? Would you like one?

MIKE [*Crossing to Left*]: I would sell my grandmother for a drink—and you know how I love my grandmother.

[TRACY *goes up front of sofa.*]

DEXTER: Uncle Willie's around in the pantry, doing weird and wonderful things. Just say I said, One of the same.

MIKE [*Moves toward the porch and below table to Left 1*]: Is it all right if I say Two?

DEXTER: That's between you and your grandmother. [MIKE *exits Left 1.*]—And find Liz! [TRACY *sits armchair Right Center.* DEXTER *goes to* TRACY *with the drink.*] Doctor's orders, Tray.

TRACY: What is it?

DEXTER: Just the juice of a few flowers.

TRACY [*Takes the glass and looks at it. Drinks*]: Peppermint—

DEXTER: —White.—And one other simple ingredient. It's called a stinger. It removes the sting.

TRACY [*Sets the glass down on coffee table and looks away*]: Oh, Dext—don't say that!

DEXTER: Why not, Tray?

TRACY: —Nothing will—nothing ever can. [*Rises.*] Oh, Dexter—I've done the most terrible thing to you!

DEXTER [*At her chair. After a moment*]: To *me,* did you say? [TRACY *nods vigorously.*] I doubt that, Red. I doubt it very much.

TRACY: You don't know, you don't know!

DEXTER: Well, maybe I shouldn't.

TRACY: You've got to—you must! I couldn't stand it, if you didn't! Oh, Dext—what am I going to do?

DEXTER: —But why to *me,* darling? [TRACY *looks at him.*] Where do I come into it any more? [*Still* TRACY *looks.*] Aren't you confusing me with someone else?—A fellow named Kittredge, or something?

TRACY [*Front of armchair Right Center*]: George—

DEXTER: That's right; George Kittredge. A splendid chap—very high morals—very broad shoulders—

TRACY [*Crossing to the telephone Left*]: I've got to tell him.

DEXTER [*Follows her*]: Tell him what?

TRACY: I've got to tell him. [*Dials a number.*]

DEXTER [*Goes above table to Right of her*]: But if he's got any brain at all, he'll have realized by this time what a fool he made of himself, when he—

TRACY: —When he what? [*To the telephone.* DEXTER *goes up Center and over to Right, back of sofa.*] Hello? Hello, George—this is Tracy. Look—I don't care whether it's bad luck or not, but I've got to see you for a minute before the wedding.—What, *what* note? I didn't get any note.—When? Well, why didn't someone tell me?—Right. Come on the run. [*Replaces the telephone, goes up to mantel to a wall bell and rings it.*] He sent a note over at ten o'clock.

DEXTER: I told you he'd come to his senses.

TRACY: Was—was he here, too?

DEXTER: Sure.

TRACY [*Crossing down Center*]: My God—why didn't you sell tickets?

DEXTER [*Crossing over Right, gets glass from table; gives it to her*]: Finish your drink.

TRACY [*Taking drink*]: Will it help?

DEXTER: There's always the hope.

[EDWARD *comes into the hall doorway, Right 2.*]

EDWARD: You rang, Miss?

TRACY [*Crossing to Center above* DEXTER]: Isn't there a note for me from Mr. Kittredge somewhere?

[DEXTER *gets Left Center.*]

EDWARD: I believe it was put on the hall table upstairs. Mrs. Lord said not to disturb you.

TRACY: I'd like to have it, if I may.

EDWARD: Very well, Miss. [*Exits Right 2.*]

TRACY [*Finishes her drink. Right Center. Gives* DEXTER *glass*]: Say something, Dext—anything.

DEXTER: No—you do.

TRACY: Oh, Dext—I'm wicked! [*Crossing Left*] I'm such an unholy mess of a girl.

DEXTER: That's no good. That's not even conversation.

TRACY: But never in all my life—not if I live to be one hundred—will I ever forget the way you tried to—to stand me on my feet again this morning.

DEXTER [*Crossing front of table Left*]: You—you're in grand shape. Tell me: what did you think of my wedding present? I like my presents at least to be acknowledged.

TRACY [*Turns to him*]: It was beautiful and sweet, Dext.

DEXTER: She was quite a boat, the "True Love."

TRACY: Was, and is.

DEXTER: She had the same initials as yours—did you ever realize that?

TRACY: No, I never did. [*Sits in chair Left of table.*]

DEXTER [*Puts glass down*]: Nor did I, till I last saw her.—Funny we missed it. My, she was yare. [*Leans over table to her.*]

TRACY: She was yare, all right. [*A moment*] *I* wasn't, was I?

DEXTER: Wasn't what?

TRACY: Yare.

DEXTER [*Laughs shortly*]: Not very. [*Sits in chair Right of table.*]—You were good at the brightwork, though. I'll never forget you down on your knees on the deck every morning, with your little can of polish.

TRACY: I wouldn't let even you help, would I?

DEXTER: Not even me.

TRACY: I made her shine.—Where is she now?

DEXTER: In the yard at Seven Hundred Acre, getting gone over. I'm going to sell her to Rufe Watriss at Oyster Bay.

TRACY: You're going to sell the "True Love"?

DEXTER: Why not?

TRACY: For money?

DEXTER: He wired an offer yesterday.

TRACY: —To *that* fat old rum pot?

DEXTER: What the hell does it matter?

TRACY: She's too clean, she's too yare.

DEXTER: I know—but when you're through with a boat, you're—[*Looks at her.*] That is, of course, unless *you* want her. [TRACY *is silent.*] Of course she's good for nothing but racing—and only really comfortable for two people—and not so damned so, for them. So I naturally thought—But of course, if *you* should want her—

TRACY: No—I don't want her.

DEXTER: I'm going to design another for myself, along a little more practical lines.

TRACY: Are you?

DEXTER: I started on the drawings a couple of weeks ago.

TRACY: What will you call her?

DEXTER: I thought the "True Love II."—What do you think?

TRACY [*After a moment*]: Dexter, if you call any boat that, I promise you I'll blow you and it right out of the water! [*Rises.*]

DEXTER: I know it's not very imaginative, but—[*Rises.*]

TRACY [*Crossing in to Right Center to armchair*]: Just try it, that's all!

[*Moves away from him.*] *I'll* tell you what you can call it, if you like—

DEXTER: What?

TRACY: In fond remembrance of me—

DEXTER: What?

TRACY: The "Easy Virtue."

DEXTER [*Crossing to her Right*]: Tray, I'll be damned if I'll have you thinking such things of yourself!

TRACY: What would you like me to think?

DEXTER: I don't know. But I do know that virtue, so-called, is no matter of a single misstep or two.

TRACY: You don't think so?

DEXTER: I know so. It's something inherent, it's something regardless of anything.

TRACY: Like fun it is.

DEXTER: You're wrong. The occasional misdeeds are often as good for a person as—as the more persistent virtues.—That is, if the person is there. Maybe you haven't committed enough, Tray. Maybe this is your coming-of-age.

TRACY [*Crossing to Left*]: I don't know.—Oh, I don't know anything any more!

DEXTER: That sounds very hopeful. That's just fine, Tray.

[*Enter* EDWARD, *Right 2, with note on salver.*]

TRACY [*Over Left*]: Oh, be still, you! [*Turns.* EDWARD *comes back to table Left with note and gives it to her.*] Thanks, Edward.

EDWARD: They are practically all in, Miss—and quite a number standing in the back. [MIKE *and* LIZ *come in Left 2.*] All our best wishes, Miss.

[LIZ *crosses down Left, back of Left Center armchair.* MIKE *back of Left table.*]

TRACY: Thanks, Edward. Thanks, very much.

LIZ: —And all ours, Tracy.

[EDWARD *goes up Right Center.*]

TRACY: Thank you, thank everybody. [*Opens note.*]

[SANDY *rushes in Right 2 and goes to her, Left.* EDWARD *goes out Right 2.*]

SANDY: Tray—he's here! He's arrived!

TRACY: Who has?

SANDY: Kidd—Sidney Kidd.

TRACY: What for? What does *he* want?

LIZ: May I scream?

MIKE: What the—!

TRACY: Oh, now I remember.

SANDY: Well, I should hope you would. I haven't been to bed at all. I gave him the profile. He's reading it now. I couldn't stand the suspense, so I—

MIKE: Profile, did you say? What profile?

SANDY [*Crossing to* MIKE—*back of table*]: The Kidd himself, complete with photographs. Do you want to see a copy?

MIKE: Holy Saint Rose of South Bend!

SANDY: —Offered in exchange for yours of us. I've told him what a help you'd both been to me.

LIZ [*Left*]: I don't think you'll find it so hard to resign now, Mike. Me neither.

MIKE [*Left back of table*]: That's all right with me.

LIZ: Belts will be worn tighter this winter.

SANDY: I'll see how he's bearing up. [*Moves up to door Right 2.* DR. PARSONS *enters Right 2.*] Good morning, Doctor Parsons. How's everything?

DR. PARSONS: Where is your sister? [*Goes down back of sofa.* SANDY *points to her and goes out Right 2.* TRACY *is reading the note.*] Tracy? Tracy!

TRACY [*Looks up, startled*]: Yes?

[*He smiles, and beckons engagingly.*]

DEXTER [*Upstage corner of sofa*]: One minute, Doctor Parsons, Mr. Kittredge is on his way.

[DR. PARSONS *smiles again, and goes out into the living room, Right 1.*]

DEXTER [*Turns to* TRACY]: I'm afraid it's the deadline, Tracy.

TRACY [*Center*]: So is this. Listen—"My dear Tracy: Your conduct last night was so shocking to my ideals of womanhood that my attitude toward you and the prospects of a happy and useful life together has changed materially. Your, to me, totally unexpected breach of common decency, not to mention the moral aspect—"

GEORGE [*Comes in from the porch, Left 1*]: Tracy!

TRACY: Hello, George.

GEORGE: Tracy—all these people!

[*Goes Center.*]

TRACY: It's only a letter from a friend. They're my friends, too. "—not to mention the moral aspect, certainly entitles me to a full explanation, before going through with our proposed marriage. In the light of day, I am sure that you will agree with me. Otherwise, with profound regrets and all best wishes, yours very sincerely—" [*Folds the note and returns it to its envelope.*] Yes, George, I quite agree with you—in the light of day or the dark of night, for richer, for poorer, for better, for worse, in sickness, and in health—and thank you so very much for your good wishes at this time.

GEORGE [*Center*]: That's all you've got to say?

TRACY [*Right Center*]: What else? I wish for your sake, as well as mine, I had an explanation. But unfortunately I've none. You'd better just say "good riddance," George.

GEORGE: It isn't easy, you know.

TRACY: I don't see why.

LIZ [*Crossing down Left to* MIKE]: Say something, Stupid.

MIKE [*Down Left in front of chair*]: Wait a minute.

GEORGE: You'll grant I had a right to be angry, and very angry.

TRACY: You certainly had, you certainly have.

GEORGE: "For your sake, as well," you said—

TRACY: Yes—it would be nice to know.

LIZ [*To* MIKE]: Will you say something?

MIKE: Wait!

[*Goes in Left Center, front of table.*]

LIZ: What for?

MIKE: Enough rope.

GEORGE: —On the very eve of your wedding, an affair with another man—

TRACY: I told you I agreed, George—[*Crossing Left below him to near chair Left Center*] and I tell you again, good riddance to me.

GEORGE: That's for me to decide.

TRACY: Well, I wish you would a—a—little more quickly.

MIKE: Look, Kittredge—

TRACY: If there was some way to make you see that—that regardless of it—or even because of it—I'm—somehow I feel more of a person, George.

GEORGE: That's a little difficult to understand.

TRACY: Yes, I can see that it would be.

[*Sits Left Center armchair.*]

DEXTER: Not necessarily.

GEORGE: You keep out of it!

DEXTER: You forget: I am out of it.

[*Sits on sofa.*]

MIKE [*Front of table Left*]: Kittredge, it just might interest you to know that the so-called "affair" consisted of exacly two kisses and one rather late swim.

TRACY: Thanks, Mike, but there's no need to—

MIKE [*To* TRACY]: All of which I thoroughly enjoyed, and the memory of which I wouldn't part with for anything.

TRACY: It's no use, Mike.

MIKE: —After which, I accompanied her to her room, deposited her on her bed, and promptly returned to you two on the porch—as you will doubtless remember.

DEXTER: Doubtless without a doubt.

GEORGE: You mean to say that was all there was to it?

MIKE: I do.

[GEORGE *ponders.*]

TRACY [*Is looking at* MIKE *in astonishment. Suddenly she rises and demands of him*]: Why? Was I so damned unattractive—so distant, so forbidding or something, that—?

GEORGE: This is fine talk, too!

TRACY: I'm asking a question!

MIKE [*Softens*]: You were extremely attractive—and as for distant and forbidding, on the contrary. But you were also somewhat the worse—or the better—for wine, and there are rules about that, damn it.

TRACY: Thank you, Mike. I think men are wonderful.

LIZ [*Down Left*]: The little dears.

GEORGE [*Center*]: Well, that's a relief, I'll admit. Still—

TRACY [*Turns to Center*]: Why? Where's the difference? If my wonderful, marvelous, beautiful virtue is still intact, it's no thanks to me, I assure you.

GEORGE: I don't think—

TRACY: —It's purely by courtesy of the gentleman from South Bend.

LIZ: Local papers, please copy.

GEORGE: I fail to see the humor in this situation, Miss Imbrie.

LIZ: I appreciate that. It was a little hard for me too, at first—

TRACY: Oh, Liz—

[*Goes down Left to* LIZ.]

LIZ: It's all right, Tracy. We all go a little haywire at times—and if we don't, maybe we ought to.

TRACY: Liz.

LIZ: You see, Mr. Kittredge, it wasn't Tracy at all. It was another girl: a Miss Pommery, '26.

GEORGE: You'd had too much to drink—

TRACY [*Crossing to him Center*]: That seems to be the consensus of opinion.

GEORGE: Will you promise me never to touch the stuff again?

TRACY [*Looks at him; speaks slowly*]: No, George, I don't believe I will. There are certain things about that other girl I rather like.

GEORGE: But a man expects his wife to—

TRACY: —To behave herself. Naturally.

DEXTER: To behave herself naturally. [GEORGE *glances*.] Sorry.

GEORGE [*To* TRACY]: But if it hadn't been for the drink last night, all this might not have happened.

TRACY: But apparently nothing did. What made you think it had?

GEORGE: It didn't take much imagination, I can tell you that.

TRACY: Not much, perhaps—but just of a certain kind.

GEORGE: It seems *you* didn't think any too well of yourself.

TRACY: That's the odd thing, George: [*Crossing Right in front of armchair*] somehow I'd have hoped you'd think better of me than I did.

GEORGE: I'm not going to quibble, Tracy: all the evidence was there.

TRACY: And I was guilty straight off—that is, until I was proved innocent.

GEORGE: Well?

DEXTER: Downright un-American, if you ask me.

GEORGE: No one is asking you!

SANDY [*Comes in Right 2, consternation on his face. Remains on doorstep*]: Listen—he's read it—and holy cats, guess what?

LIZ: What?

SANDY: He loves it! He says it's brilliant—He wants it for *Destiny!*

MIKE: I give up.

GEORGE: Who wants what?

LIZ: Sidney Kidd; Sidney Kidd.

GEORGE [*Pleased and astonished*]: Sidney Kidd is here himself?!

SANDY: Big as life, and twice as handsome. Boy, is this wedding a National affair now!

[*Exits Right 2.*]

GEORGE [*After a moment*]: It's extremely kind and thoughtful of him. [*Another moment. Then*] Come on, Tracy—it must be late. Let's let bygones be bygones—what do you say?

TRACY [*Right Center*]: Yes—and good-bye, George.

GEORGE: I don't understand you.

TRACY: Please—good-bye.

GEORGE [*Center*]: But what on earth—?

LIZ: I imagine she means that your explanation is inadequate.

GEORGE: Look here, Tracy—

TRACY: You're too good for me, George. You're a hundred times too good.

GEORGE: I never said I—

TRACY: And I'd make you most unhappy, most—[*Crosses Right corner of sofa.*] That is, I'd do my best to.

GEORGE: Well, if that's the way you want it—

TRACY: That's the way it is.

GEORGE [*Looks at her*]: All right. Possibly it's just as well.
[*Starts up Right.*]

DEXTER: I thought you'd eventually think so.

GEORGE [*Confronts him from back of sofa*]: I've got a feeling you've had more to do with this than anyone.

DEXTER: A novel and interesting idea, I'm sure.

GEORGE: You and your whole rotten class.

DEXTER: Oh, class my—! [*But he stops himself.*]

MIKE [*Crossing in Center. Sits on arm of chair Left Center*]: Funny—I heard a truck driver say that yesterday—only with a short "a."

GEORGE: Listen, you're all on your way out—the lot of you—and don't think you aren't.—Yes, and good riddance. [*He goes out Right 2.*]

MIKE: There goes George—
[*Orchestra plays "Oh Promise Me."*]

TRACY [*Rushes over to door Right 1; looks off*]: Oh, my sainted aunt—that welter of faces! [*Closes door, and returns to up Center.* MAY, *the housemaid, appears Right 2 with* TRACY'*s hat and gloves.*] What in the name of all that's holy am I to do?

MAY [*Crossing to Center*]: You forgot your hat, Miss Tracy. [*Gives them to her and exits Right 2.*]

TRACY: Oh, God—Oh, dear God—have mercy on Tracy!

MIKE [*Rises*]: Tracy—

TRACY: Yes, Mike?

MIKE [*Crossing in Center to* TRACY]: Forget the license!

TRACY: License?

DEXTER: I've got an old one here, that we never used, Maryland being quicker—

MIKE: Forget it! [To TRACY] Old Parson Parsons—he's never seen Kittredge, has he? Nor have most of the others. I got you into this, I'll get you out.—Will you marry me, Tracy?

TRACY [*A pause*]: No, Mike.—Thanks, but no. [*Goes Left. Puts hat in chair Left Center.*]

MIKE: But listen, I've never asked a girl to marry me before in my life!—I've avoided it!—You've got me all confused—why not—?

TRACY [*Left Center*]: —Because I don't think Liz would like it—and I'm not sure that you would—and I'm even a little doubtful about myself. But—I'm beholden to you, Mike, I'm most beholden.

MIKE [*Center*]: They're in there! They're waiting!

LIZ [*Front of Left chair*]: Don't get too conventional all at once, will you?—There'll be a reaction.

MIKE: Liz—[*Goes Left.*]

LIZ: I count on you sustaining the mood.

DEXTER [*Rising*]: It'll be all right, Tracy: you've been got out of jams before.

TRACY [*Between corner of sofa and Right armchair*]: Been *got out* of them, did you say?

DEXTER: That's what I said, Tracy. Don't worry [MARGARET *and* SETH *enter from Right 2*] you always are. [*Rises; goes up corner of sofa.*]

MARGARET [*At upper corner of sofa*]: Tracy, we met George in the hall—it's all right, dear, your father will make a very simple announcement.

SETH [*Back of Right armchair*]: Is there anything special you want me to say?

TRACY: No! I'll say it, whatever it is.—I won't be got out of anything more, thanks. [*She moves to the door Right 1.*]

[WILLIE *and* DINAH *enters Right 2. He goes Left Center. She goes to* SETH.]

UNCLE WILLIE: What's alack? What's amiss?

MARGARET [*Crossing to* SETH]: Oh, this just can't be happening—it can't.

[TRACY *reaches door Right 1.* MIKE *crosses Right to sofa beside* DEXTER.]

TRACY [*Having thrown the doors open*]: I'm—I'm—hello! Good morning.—I'm—that is to say—I'm terribly sorry to have kept you waiting, but—but there's been a little hitch in the proceedings. I've made a terrible fool of myself—which isn't unusual—and my fiancé—my fiancé—[*She stops.*]

MARGARET: Seth!

SETH: Wait, my dear.

TRACY: —my fiancé, that was, that is—he thinks we'd better call it a day, and I quite agree with him.—Dexter—Dexter—what the hell next?

DEXTER: "Two years ago you were invited to a wedding in this house and I did you out of it by eloping to Maryland—" [*Rushes over to* MARGARET.]

TRACY: "Two years ago you were invited to a wedding in this house and I did you out of it by eloping to Maryland—" Dexter, Dexter, where are you?

DEXTER [*To* MARGARET]: May I? Just as a loan? [*Takes ring from her finger; goes to* MIKE.] Here, put this in your vest pocket.

MIKE: But I haven't got a vest.

DEXTER: Then hold it in your hand. [*Rejoins* TRACY.]

DEXTER [*To* TRACY]: "Which was very bad manners—"

TRACY: "Which was very bad manners—"

DEXTER: "But I hope to make it up to you by going through with it now, as originally planned."

TRACY: "But I hope to make it up to you by—by going—" —by going beautifully through with it now—as originally and—most beautifully —planned. Because there's something awfully nice about a wedding— I don't know—they're gay, and attractive—and I've always wanted one—

DEXTER [*Rushes to* MIKE]: I'd like you to be my best man, if you will, because I think you're one hell of a guy, Mike.

MIKE: I'd be honored. C. K.

UNCLE WILLIE: Ladies, follow me; no rushing, please.

[LIZ *and* MARGARET *go out with him, Right 2.* WILLIE *goes last.*]

DEXTER: "So if you'll just keep your seats a minute—"

TRACY: "So if you'll just keep your seats a minute—"

DEXTER: That's all.

TRACY: "That's all!" [*Murmurs off Right 1. And she closes the living-room doors; turns to* DEXTER, *down Right.*] Dexter—are you sure?

DEXTER: Not in the least; but I'll risk it—will you?

TRACY: You bet!—And you didn't do it just to soften the blow?

DEXTER: No, Tray.

TRACY: Nor to save my face?

DEXTER: It's a nice little face.

TRACY: Oh—I'll be yare now—I'll promise to be yare!

DEXTER: Be whatever you like, you're my Redhead.—All set?

TRACY: All set!—Oh, how did this ever happen? [*Running Left Center—gets hat from chair, goes Left, looking in mirror, puts on hat.*]

SETH: Don't inquire.—Go on, Dinah: tell Mr. Dutton to start the music.

DINAH [*Going up*]: I did it—I did it all! [*Exits Right 2.*]

[DEXTER *and* MIKE *go to door Right 2.*]

SETH: Daughter—

TRACY [*Crossing over to* SETH, *Center*]: I love you, Father.

SETH: And I love you, daughter.

TRACY: Never in my life have I been so full of love before—

[*Music: "Wedding March"*]

DEXTER: See you soon, Red!

TRACY: See you soon, Dext! [DEXTER *and* MIKE *exit Right 2.*] How do I look?

SETH: Like a queen—like a goddess.

TRACY: Do you know how I feel?

SETH: How?

TRACY: Like a human—like a human being!

SETH: —And is that all right?

TRACY [*She takes his arm. They slowly start down Right Center towards door Right 1*]: All right? Oh, Father, it's Heaven!

[*Music swells.*]

CURTAIN

SECOND THRESHOLD

The play that follows is the manuscript of *Second Threshold* as it existed when Barry died on December 3, 1949. He also left notes for a rewriting of Act II, Scene 3, including a lengthy speech for Josiah. In the year that followed before the actual production of the play, the playwright Robert Sherwood, a close friend of Barry's, revised *Second Threshold* extensively. Barry's unrevised version is printed here for the first time. The characters known in the Sherwood version as Bolton were originally called "Brook"; the name was changed when Clive Brook was chosen to play the leading role.

SECOND THRESHOLD

was first produced by Alfred de Liagre, Jr.,
at the Morosco Theatre, New York City,
on January 2, 1951.
It was directed by Mr. de Liagre;
the setting and lighting were by Donald Oenslager.

CAST

TOBY WELLS • Hugh Reilly
MALLOY • Gordon Richards
MIRANDA BROOK • Margaret Phillips
JOSIAH BROOK • Clive Brook
THANKFUL MATHER • Betsy von Furstenberg
JOCK BROOK • Frederick Bradlee

■ ACTION AND SCENES ■

The action of the play takes place in the library of Josiah Brook's house on West Tenth Street, New York City, in the course of three days, late last July. The scenes are as follows:

ACT I

Scene 1—The library, Saturday night.

Scene 2—The same, Sunday noon.

ACT II

Scene 1—The library, Sunday afternoon.

Scene 2—The same, Sunday night.

Scene 3—The same, Monday afternoon.

■ ACT I ■

The library of Josiah Brook's house on West Tenth Street, New York City, is a moderately large, well-proportioned room in the rear of the house, looking out over a small garden through tall window-doors giving onto an ironwork balcony, the room itself being on the second floor.

The main entrance is through double doors from the hall at Back Right, through which a portion of the stairway leading to the upper floors may be seen. There is a handsome old fireplace in the back wall, centered between the hall entrance and the left wall, where the windows are. There is also a single door, usually kept closed, in the right wall, leading into a sitting room on the street side of the house. Bookshelves run from floor to ceiling but are broken by a gun cabinet containing a number of shotguns and rifles on one side of the fireplace and a cabinet of bibelots on the other.

The decoration and furnishings of the room are largely Victorian but not entirely so, there being an occasional good English or French piece to save it from being too rigidly period. It is, on the whole, a comfortable, handsome, livable room which has been put away for the summer, rug removed, chairs and sofa slipcovered, chandelier and the two or three paintings covered with tarlatan. There is a tray with a thermos-carafe of milk and a plate of sandwiches on a table between the windows. The time is late last July, Saturday night, a little after midnight.

At rise, TOBY WELLS *stands at the side of the doorway into the hall, listening intently, head cocked downward in the direction of the stairs. He is in his mid-twenties, spare, rangy, with a humorous, likable face, not at all handsome. He is coatless, with necktie awry and shirtsleeves rolled up. He waits silently, motionlessly for what seems a long time, then moves backward a little into the room and waits again.* MALLOY, *a small, wiry, bright-eyed, white-haired man of sixty-five, comes along the hall from downstairs, a suitcase in each hand and a smaller one under one arm. He wears dark trousers and a black alpaca coat. He has almost passed the doorway on his way upstairs when* TOBY'S *quiet voice stops him:*

TOBY: Malloy.

[MALLOY *turns and regards him.*]

MALLOY: I thought surely you'd be left by this time.

TOBY: Is it Miss Brook?

MALLOY: It is. She's stopped in the kitchen to speak to Mrs. Malloy.

TOBY: She's alone?

MALLOY: She is.

TOBY: You didn't say I was here—

MALLOY: Not thinking you were not, I did not.

TOBY: Go on up. But quietly. I expect he's asleep.

MALLOY: That I'll believe when I see it.

[*He goes out, along the hall.* TOBY *waits a moment, then crosses the room to a chair near the open window, pulling down his shirt-sleeves and adjusting his tie as he goes. He picks up his jacket from the chair and has it half-on when he thinks better of it. He drops the jacket to the floor, takes off his tie, opens his collar, rolls up his sleeves again and seats himself in an easy chair with his feet over the side of it. He picks up a newspaper, opens it, lowers it, peers over toward the doorway, then quickly raises it again.* MIRANDA BROOK *appears in the hall.* TOBY *snaps the newspaper. She stops and looks into the room. He lowers the paper slowly, folds and discards it and rises, beckoning her in as he did* MALLOY, *speaking softly:*]

TOBY: Would you mind for a minute?

[MIRANDA *hesitates, then advances into the room. She is twenty-four, strikingly lovely in spite of, or perhaps in some degree because of, a certain coolness and detachment proceeding from an ever-present sense of the serious problems, world and otherwise, which confront her. She looks Toby up and down calmly and thoroughly before speaking. Then*]

MIRANDA: Do I know you?

TOBY: There was a time.

MIRANDA: Oh? When was that?

TOBY: Quite a few years ago.

MIRANDA: My memory's not what it was.—You seem reasonably at home here.

TOBY: It's hot.

MIRANDA: I won't argue that one. [*She finds the sandwiches and milk.*] Food—heaven!

TOBY: I've been dropping in pretty regularly to see your father, my father being off on his vacation.

MIRANDA: Do I have to guess or will you tell me?

TOBY: I'm by name of Toby Wells.

MIRANDA: The summer at Christmas Cove! Doctor Wells's little boy!

TOBY: Hell, woman, I was shoving seventeen.

MIRANDA: You were minute.

TOBY: I shot up fast, once I started.

MIRANDA: A crew cut and an absolute darling. You used to bring me things: bunches of field flowers and pails of clams. What is it you've grown up into? Also an M.D.?

TOBY: It's in the family.—Congratulations on your own B.A. Bennington lets out late. Just today, wasn't it?

MIRANDA: Just. What with my travels hither and yon with Father, I was a little slow coming by it, I'm afraid.

TOBY: What did you major in?

MIRANDA: Psychology.

TOBY: Hot dog.

MIRANDA: Applied. Field work in the Psychiatric Ward at Massachusetts General.

TOBY: No less! They're supposed to know their stuff there.

MIRANDA: They do. So do I.

TOBY: I also gather that further congratulations may be in order.

MIRANDA: You mean on my engagement? Thanks, they are. I'm sailing Monday—day after tomorrow—heavens! We're being married soon after I land—August second, I think Matthew said. Isn't it nice?

TOBY: God how. But I thought weddings usually took place chez Bride.

MIRANDA: Oh, he's much too busy with his newspapers. [*She slaps the napkin down upon the tray.*] There! I feel better. That motor trip's a brute at night. [MALLOY *stops in the doorway on his way down.*] Bless you, Malloy. The collation was a great idea.

MALLOY: The Missus's, Miss.

MIRANDA: Thank her for me. And please say we'll be down for breakfast about nine—my little houseguest and I, I mean: Miss Mather.

MALLOY: On the back terrace maybe, if it's a good morning?

MIRANDA: That's another great idea. I gave her a key and she can hist her own bag, so no need to wait up. Good night, you angel.

MALLOY: Good night, Miss Miranda.

[*He goes out.* MIRANDA *turns to Toby.*]

MIRANDA: I'm carting my fiancé's stepniece or something off to London with me. She's a darling child, twenty or thereabouts. Completely natural—you know, the real norm: Thankful Mather—isn't that Boston for you? She's something. Have a meal before we sail and see for yourself.

TOBY: Love to.

MIRANDA: Well, good night. It's been terribly nice seeing you again. Do drop in at any time. And give my best remembrances to your father, won't you?

TOBY: Where do you think you're going?

MIRANDA: Now?

TOBY: Now.

MIRANDA: To see mine, before I fold for the night.—Though I'm feeling none too tenderly toward him, I may say. Not showing for my graduation, indeed! I can understand about Mother and Jock, but Father's always been so—oh well, what the hell!

[*She moves toward the door.*]

TOBY: Sit down.

MIRANDA: I beg your pardon?

TOBY: I said, sit down. The hope is he's asleep.

[MIRANDA *stops, speaks without turning:*]

MIRANDA: How do you mean "the hope is"?

TOBY: He hasn't been getting much lately.

MIRANDA: You mean on account of me—of my engagement?

TOBY: I suppose so—among other things.

MIRANDA: What other things?

TOBY: Sit down and we'll discuss it.

[*She hesitates a moment, then seats herself facing him.*]

MIRANDA: Yes, dear Doctor?

TOBY: And you can drop the Diplomatic Usage. This isn't Washington nor London nor even Copenhagen. It's West Tenth Street, New York, and midsummer and nobody's in town. But nobody.

MIRANDA: Do you happen to know where my mother is?

TOBY: The address and number are there on the pad on the desk. She called earlier.

MIRANDA: Nice of her.—I *have* wondered a little at Father. As a rule he hates the city in summer. Well? What's it all about, if any?

TOBY: We medical men do not always regard insomnia as being invariably innocuous.

MIRANDA: What a statement!

TOBY: Your father's not in good shape, hasn't been in some time. My father's worried. So am I. So should you be—that is, if you give a damn.

MIRANDA: "If I—"! Whom do you think you're talking to?

TOBY: To the highly intellectual daughter of an even more highly so father. The big trouble with you big intellectuals is that all your personal reactions—do people still call you Mandy?

MIRANDA: No. They do not.—You mean said reactions are also intellectual?

TOBY: That's what I mean.

MIRANDA: You must have led a very sheltered life.

TOBY: Sure. Cotton-wool. Sterilized. Born with a tongue depressor in my mouth.

MIRANDA: Just what do you figure is wrong with my father?

TOBY: Hard to say, exactly. But my father says that most men worth their salt—whatever their jobs—big-shot international lawyer like him or just plain groceryman on the corner—when they get to a certain age, they're apt to hit a pretty awkward problem.

MIRANDA: The wilting of the brave male plumage?

TOBY: Ahead of me.—Didn't I tell you?

MIRANDA: Sorry.

TOBY: *He* says they're likely to hit a blank spot—a very blank spot—where they pull up short and say, "Well, here I am. But where the hell am I? Where do I go from here?"

MIRANDA: Or "What do I settle for" maybe?

TOBY: That's the point.—And of course it's the big boys in, or once in high places, who get smacked the hardest—the so-called public figures like your old man, who've already accomplished just about all there is to—and find it's dust and ashes in the mouth, and so forth. Not an uncommon malady—not at all an—

MIRANDA: And what are you prescribing for dust and ashes these days?

TOBY: It's one of the ones we haven't licked yet.—Not sulphur and molasses, anyway.

MIRANDA [*After a moment*]: Naturally, stepping down from—from any kind of eminence requires adjustment. Especially when you're as tired as he must be.

TOBY: Tired! My God, this is a case of real exhaustion.—And then of course you had to pile it on.

MIRANDA: Who? Pile what on?

TOBY: All of you. And plenty. Two years ago your mother divorced him without so much as a—you want me to give it to you blow by blow?

MIRANDA: His brother Andy's death—

TOBY: Let's say the circumstances attending it.

MIRANDA: His son Jock flunking out of law school—

TOBY: The Law's not just a profession to him: it's an art.

MIRANDA: I'll talk to Jock: it's on the agenda.—His own law partners not wanting him back.

TOBY: Two-faced bastards.

MIRANDA: He was always too big for that outfit, anyway.—Then finally me, I suppose—

TOBY: How would any man feel about a daughter who's been as close to him as you've been, looping it off to England to marry some bird two years older than he is?

MIRANDA: We met Matthew together on the last mission to London. They got on very well. He seemed to like him.

TOBY: How did he like his newspapers?

MIRANDA: I didn't ask.

TOBY: How do you like them?

MIRANDA: It's the paper shortage, you fool! [*Then*] Sorry.

TOBY: Don't be. I welcome the unintellectual response.

[*A brief pause. Then*]

MIRANDA: My only agreement with Father was that I'd consult him before marrying anyone. I've done that by letter and by telephone. And if he wants to be pigheaded about it, that's his lookout.

TOBY: You silly girl. Don't you see he's got no outlook left?

MIRANDA: No. I don't. He has plenty to occupy him and always has had.

TOBY: I once heard about his going to work at age twelve: adds up to quite a long stint, don't you think?

MIRANDA: He thrives on work. And now that he has his memoirs in hand—

TOBY: —Like a certain man in New Hampshire, since deceased?

[MIRANDA *turns on him.*]

MIRANDA: What do you mean?!

TOBY: I grant you there's small chance of one Josiah Brook taking any such way out. But the fact is, he hasn't written a line in four months or more.

MIRANDA: What's he been doing, then?

TOBY: Oh—sitting—and thinking—and reading—and eating a little at odd times—and sleeping a little at odder—and in the evenings playing Russian Bank and listening to records with me—

MIRANDA: You seem very devoted to him.

TOBY: I just happen to think he's all hell on wheels, that's all.

MIRANDA: I think rather well of him myself. So do a number of his countrymen, I expect.

TOBY: But the man's alone, Miranda. All alone. Everyone near him's quit on him.

MIRANDA: That isn't so, it's not in the least so!

TOBY: I don't know what you'd call it, then.

MIRANDA: I was committed to that house party Christmas. And on his birthday, I—

TOBY: Oh, sure, sure!

MIRANDA: Anyway, he's made it increasingly clear that he wanted to be by himself. Even after the accident, he insisted I shouldn't come on from college.

TOBY: Which accident?

MIRANDA: You know—last March—when he crashed that little chartered plane. I know it wasn't serious, but—look: do you suppose there might have been a concussion or something?

TOBY: They went over him like a dog for ticks: nothing but a sprained wrist, minor abrasions and contusions. It was miraculous. They say the ship was a wreck.

MIRANDA: He's such a good pilot. I never quite knew how it happened.

TOBY: Just wanted to take the air, he said—and came in too low.

MIRANDA: He knows better than that. I've been with him when he's gone up again and circled three or four times before landing.

TOBY: I suppose we all get careless.

MIRANDA: Not Father.—Look: if by all of this you mean—

TOBY: All I mean is that a first-rate man is in a first-rate jam, and that someone who loves him ought to stand by and see him through it.

MIRANDA: —Me.

TOBY: You. Damn it, it's a duty—and it ought to be a pleasant one.

MIRANDA: But I can't! It's impossible.

TOBY: Of course, maybe your brother—

MIRANDA: Don't be foolish: Jock's just a kid of twenty-three.

TOBY: How old are you?

MIRANDA: Twenty-four. But the one year doesn't signify.

TOBY: I understand.

MIRANDA: Besides, he's signed up at that damned summer theatre for all season, I expect.

TOBY: Tough.—And there's no sort of an old friend, close enough, wise enough to—?

MIRANDA: —Russell Evans and he were classmates. He's in town during the weeks, I suppose. And for weekends there must be any number of—heavens, he has a host of friends. Or had—

TOBY: Foul weather ones never did grow on trees, I guess.

MIRANDA: I shouldn't think New York need be too bad in summer. There's the theatre and movies and the Stadium Concerts and—

TOBY: Look: you're awfully bright, but there's something you don't seem to get: it's one week to August, and he hasn't stirred out of this house and its two-by-four garden since exactly May thirtieth.

MIRANDA: That long? Really?

TOBY: Really.—Decoration Day, when he drove himself down the Island to Amagansett, with you know what results.

MIRANDA: No. I'm afraid I don't.

TOBY: Ask him.

MIRANDA: I'm asking you. What results?

TOBY: Possibly he may not want people to—anyhow, *it* also turned out not to be serious. But in the meantime—

MIRANDA: You mean to say he literally just sits here?

TOBY: Oh, I expect there's some plain and fancy pacing done in the small hours.

MIRANDA: —What I used to call the Caged-Lion Department! one big job finished, the next not yet on. I've felt it a little myself at times. I went everywhere with him, you know—that is, practically. Even before Mother left him—of course *she* couldn't go with, being both seasick and airsick—chiefly homesick, I always suspected. I was useful, too! I'll say that for myself. Secretary, hostess, valet, courier. And I do know that caged-lion feeling, believe me. I know Father, too; he'll pull out of it.

TOBY: Only this time it's not a cage. It's a vacuum.

MIRANDA: Whatever it is, he'll pull out of it.

TOBY: Not without help of a very special sort.

MIRANDA: You don't know him as I do.

TOBY: God give me patience.

MIRANDA: You think maybe a psychiatrist?

TOBY: Catch him putting himself within reach of any such. Anyway, he could out-psych anyone I ever heard of with both hands tied behind him and a potato in his mouth.

MIRANDA: But if it's really as bad as you say it is—

TOBY: Really bad's what it may get to be, my girl.

MIRANDA: How? Why? What's the outlook?

TOBY: Have you ever seen an actual Grade A Depression—at the Massachusetts General, say?

MIRANDA: Yes. Several.

TOBY: Not very pretty, are they?

MIRANDA: No.

TOBY: —Not yet, luckily. Just possibly headed that way.

MIRANDA: But that's awful! He can't be—he mustn't!

TOBY: Then do something. For your special information, it seems to be less of a medical problem than a human one.

MIRANDA [*After a moment*]: *I* know! I'll get him to come abroad with me. I'll make him come!

TOBY: Fat chance. He's seen all he wants of Europe for a while.

MIRANDA: I—I might stay on a few days, and fly instead.

TOBY: It's a three months' job at the very least. Six would be nearer it.

MIRANDA: But I can't! Matthew's mother is old. Also, she's ill. She's just hanging on until—I simply can't!

TOBY: It's up to you, of course.

MIRANDA: It's not! It's up to Father! If he just plain only wouldn't be so damn stubborn.

TOBY: —Or you and your own little plans so damned definite.

MIRANDA: Listen! I've been furious with him about Matthew and me and still am. Also, he should have taken me to Germany with him and he knows it. But I don't see why, after we talk it out, he shouldn't be willing to go to England with me now. Matthew went through every single proper motion. He wrote first, and got no reply. Then he cabled. Then he called from London, and—

TOBY: —I know: I was up in his study with him when the call came through.

MIRANDA: Wha—what did he say?

TOBY: Usual exchange of greetings, and so forth. No heads broken. Then a silence, during which I suppose your hand was being duly spoken for. Then the reply.

MIRANDA: Please tell me.

TOBY: "I congratulate you on being so well-off in such times and I am not questioning your journalistic or administrative genius. I happen, however, to have looked up the date of your birth and I am obliged to tell you that I am not offering my daughter for adoption."

MIRANDA: Oh, the—he dared to—! [*Then*] I knew I'd have a great deal to say to Father. Apparently I have more than I'd figured on.

TOBY: Go to it. It might stir up interest. I've often thought that if people would be really honest and outspoken with themselves and each other, there'd be a lot less need for the psychiatrists' tender offices. [*He gathers up his coat and tie and moves toward the hall.*] You see, he's just not interested in anything any more. He's just the man who had everything—once. [*He pauses in the doorway.*] Do I hear someone?

MIRANDA: Probably Thankful, in from her party.

TOBY: No, it's from upstairs. Well—[*He smiles and gestures.*] Good night, Mandy.

MIRANDA: Then it must be—! Please wait just one minute, will you? [*He moves back into the room, putting on his jacket. She explains:*] It's—it's just that I don't want to be alone with him straight off. I've got to think.

TOBY: Ever try feeling, instead?

MIRANDA: All right, all right! But I'll tell you here and now: I've learned enough to know that—that hysterical cases are often better treated with a firm hand than—than—

TOBY: —With gloves?

MIRANDA: Yes.

TOBY: I don't think you'll find him hysterical. On the contrary.

MIRANDA: I was using the word in its professional sense.

TOBY: Oh, I beg your pardon, Doctor. I do indeed. [JOSIAH BROOK *comes in from the hall.*] Now look, sir—you're supposed to have turned in. [JOSIAH, *whatever the "certain age," is built like an athlete, one in good trim, and looks younger than his years. He is a man who has borne many responsibilities, much success and many disappointments and seems to have been bent down by none of them, at least exteriorly. There is, however, in both manner and speech, a detachment and a distance that suggest a deliberate self-removal from further future involvements, big or little. He wears bedroom slippers and, over his pajamas, a dark wrapper. He moves directly to the desk.*]

JOSIAH: I turned out again. Also, I seem to have run out of— [*He takes a package of cigarettes from a box on the desk, opens it carefully, glances up, sees* MIRANDA.] Oh, it's you. Greetings and so forth. How are you?

MIRANDA: Fine, thanks. How are you?

JOSIAH: Never better.

MIRANDA: That's fine.

JOSIAH: So you did get here.
MIRANDA: So I did.
JOSIAH: With a purpose to gather up last belongings, I suppose.
MIRANDA: That was the main idea.
JOSIAH: Mrs. Malloy will be anxious to help.
MIRANDA: I was counting on same.
JOSIAH: Cigarette?
MIRANDA: Thanks, I've given them up.
JOSIAH: Admirable.
MIRANDA: That depends on how you look at it.
JOSIAH: So much does. [*He glances from her to* TOBY *and back.*] You two know each other? Yes. Of course.
MIRANDA: Of yore.
JOSIAH: A good summer, that one in Christmas Cove.
TOBY: I'll say. Not a care in this world that a Band-Aid wouldn't fix.
JOSIAH: They catch up with you, cares and so forth.
TOBY: Do they not!
JOSIAH: Nothing like the American summer.
MIRANDA: In town?
JOSIAH: Anywhere. Particularly in England.—Very pretty outfit you're wearing.
MIRANDA: Thanks. Always grateful for notice.
JOSIAH: Very becoming. [*To Toby*] Don't you agree?
TOBY: Anything but a surgical gown, I'm a wild man.

[*He moves toward the hall.* JOSIAH *continues to regard* MIRANDA *coolly and impersonally.*]

JOSIAH: Real style comes from the inside, I've always claimed.
MIRANDA: Yes, I remember that being dunned into me quite young.
JOSIAH: So I expect you'll keep it, even in England.
MIRANDA: Just what is this you've suddenly got against England?
JOSIAH: Only an occasional Englishman.
MIRANDA: O.K. I asked for it.

[*Now* TOBY *has gone.*]

JOSIAH: Departing when?
MIRANDA: Monday at four. The twenty-fifth. The "America."
JOSIAH: You and I usually flew, didn't we?
MIRANDA: We were in even more of a hurry.

[JOSIAH *turns toward the hall and calls out Left:*]

JOSIAH: Toby? Come in tomorrow, if you like!

[TOBY'S *voice is heard from downstairs:*]

TOBY: How's around lunchtime?

JOSIAH: Fine with me!

TOBY: It's a date!

[JOSIAH *turns again to* MIRANDA.]

JOSIAH: A nice boy.

MIRANDA: Would you say?

JOSIAH: I'm fond of his father.

MIRANDA: I once was of mine.

JOSIAH [*With no apparent emotion*]: Oh, for heaven's sake go on your way, Miranda. Pick up your things and move on, my dear.

MIRANDA: I figure to. [*A moment, then*] Incidentally, I think you've been horrible about Matthew and me. What's possibly wrong with him?

JOSIAH: He begins by being years too old for you.

MIRANDA: I've never cared for younger men: you know that.

JOSIAH: What you've never cared for is men who haven't yet arrived. You've been exposed to too many celebrities. You've caught the current American woman's disease: celebrities.

MIRANDA: I'll try to live out my natural span with it.

JOSIAH: Just how much do you care for him himself?

MIRANDA: Matthew?—More than I ever thought I could for anyone. He fascinates me: his mind, his looks, his manner, his whole approach to life.

JOSIAH: It's still not enough.

MIRANDA: For me it is, and more than.

JOSIAH: You're a rare girl, Miranda. For you it ought to be rapture and total beauty.

MIRANDA: I'm not the starry-eyed type: you know that also.

JOSIAH: No, I'm not sure I do. And if you're not, more's the pity.

MIRANDA: Why?—Sooner or later they fall on their faces. I've no intention of ever falling on mine.

JOSIAH: Look ahead ten years.

MIRANDA: Make it twenty. I adore being with him and I'm certain we're going to have a grand life together.

JOSIAH: You can still pretty well tell a man by his work. The newspapers aren't even vicious. They're trash.

MIRANDA: He's more or less left them to the staff, up till now. He means to do differently.

JOSIAH: With your help?

[*She smiles disarmingly.*]

MIRANDA: There's been talk of it.

JOSIAH: My chief fear for you is that you're by way of missing life altogether.

MIRANDA: How so?

JOSIAH: The way I've missed mine, let's say.

MIRANDA: But you've had a wonderful one! Good heavens, when you stop to—

JOSIAH: —Not for my money, I haven't. And I think I know why, too—

MIRANDA: Oh? Why—

JOSIAH: Because of always deliberately planning everything out beforehand.

MIRANDA: What's wrong with that?

JOSIAH: Somehow you lose the impact—of life itself, I mean.

MIRANDA [*After a moment*]: You've always treated me as—as a mind, haven't you? Never just as a loving daughter.

JOSIAH: I don't wonder you object to that.

MIRANDA: But the point is I don't. I think it's what's given me what strength of character I have.

JOSIAH: Mentally, very advanced, I'll admit. But emotionally still in the egg.

MIRANDA: Oh, to hell with emotion. It's sloppy and messy and to my mind—

JOSIAH: —To your mind. What about to your heart?

[*Again her smile*]

MIRANDA: A stout, muscular organ, useful for pumping blood. What about yours?

JOSIAH: I'll grant you it seems not to—lift, as it once did.

MIRANDA: Good. Better function. Won't throw the rhythm out.

[*He looks at her for a moment. Then*]

JOSIAH: Just what is it you're after now? The parental blessing on the holy union?

MIRANDA: It would be nice. I think I should treasure it.

JOSIAH: Well, it's not forthcoming. It is not vouchsafed.

MIRANDA: On occasion you can be a real stinker, can't you?

JOSIAH: It's been said of me.

MIRANDA: I'm afraid you've begun to take the times you live in personally, Father. It's not good for you. You're thinner than you were, you know.

JOSIAH: I can only trust it's becoming.

MIRANDA: Look: did you eat any dinner, for instance?

JOSIAH: As it happens, I had a late tea.

MIRANDA: How very British. [*She puts the plate of sandwiches before him and pours a glass of milk from the carafe.*] I want you to eat and drink this right here and now.

JOSIAH: What for?

MIRANDA: Sustenance—and because I say so.

[*A moment, then he takes a bite of a sandwich, washes it down, stares at the plate.*]

JOSIAH: It reminds me.

MIRANDA: Me too. You used to take some looking after in the past, in the food department.

[*He looks from the plate to her, then around him.*]

JOSIAH: Other places, other nations, other ends of days.

MIRANDA: Conferences, conferences— "Thank the Lord they've left at last," you'd say.

JOSIAH: "The Wops"!

MIRANDA: "The Frogs"!

JOSIAH: "The Bolshies"!

MIRANDA: We had great times together.

JOSIAH: We did that.

MIRANDA: Eat up—and tell me how the new work's coming.

JOSIAH: What work?

MIRANDA: You've answered me. [*A moment. Then*] Do you really feel so awful, Father?

JOSIAH: About what?

MIRANDA: Oh—you know—everything, I guess.

JOSIAH: Well, I don't feel so good. Who does?

MIRANDA: It's never been quite the same without Mother, has it?

JOSIAH: Let's not discuss your mother.

MIRANDA: She was born gay and fun-loving. Not even a war could change that.

JOSIAH: No one wanted it changed.

MIRANDA: Once she told me that the real reason she'd left you was that you'd become so permanently remote and—and solemn, she said.

JOSIAH: What I'd become, I'd become of necessity: at last more occupied with a job than with her and home and fireside. She didn't care for that.

[*Another moment. Then*]

MIRANDA: And does a brother really miss a brother so terribly?

[*He looks away, murmurs:*]

JOSIAH: Andy—

MIRANDA: That horrible creature they fought over—Clover O'Neil—I read in some column that she's in town from San Francisco.

JOSIAH: Nice for the San Franciscans.

MIRANDA: It still rankles, doesn't it?

JOSIAH: Rankles is as good a word as any.

MIRANDA: But what I mean is, mightn't it help to talk to her—get the whole story first-hand, I mean?—Oh, I know, I know! But if you had someone with you—me or Russell Evans, say—

JOSIAH: Drop it, Miranda.—Incidentally, before you sail I wish you and Jock would go down to the bank to see Evans.

MIRANDA: Why, particularly?

JOSIAH: Because you both have your own money now—have had for some time—and you ought to discuss certain grim facts with him.

MIRANDA: Our own—? You mean instead of the allowances?

JOSIAH: That's right. I've made a formal settlement, as they call it, on each of you. It's no fortune, but the income ought to be enough to feed and clothe and shelter you—that is, if your tastes aren't too—Oh well—talk to Russell.

MIRANDA: I'm sure I'm very grateful. But—

JOSIAH: —Also, I've got rid of the place in the country and have put this one on the market, being quite certain that all of us are pretty well through with them both. Prices are still up, and it seemed—

[MIRANDA *has been watching him closely.*]

MIRANDA: "His house in order"?

[*He laughs shortly.*]

JOSIAH: Yes, in a way!—Or you might call it a gradual shedding of responsibilities—you know—with the purpose to regain the unbent shoulders, the elastic step.

MIRANDA: I'll take your gracious gift when I have that withheld blessing, Father.

JOSIAH: The cash is already in the bank in your name, I'm afraid.

MIRANDA: It can sit there.

[JOSIAH *rises.*]

JOSIAH: As you like, of course.

[*She also rises. They confront each other.*]

MIRANDA: That's how I like!

JOSIAH: It's a little on the late side. You must be tired after your trip. Incidentally, congratulations on your Graduation. And now shall we say good night?

MIRANDA: My God, the manner is positively Continental! Matthew Atwater's a country lout by comparison.

JOSIAH: I think I've had enough of this, Miranda.

MIRANDA: I've never known such an appalling change in a man. What on earth has come over you?

JOSIAH: Possibly a desire for a somewhat different life than the one I've been leading.

MIRANDA: I wouldn't dream of interfering with any of your plans, of course—

JOSIAH: I doubt if at this point anyone would be allowed to.

MIRANDA: I'm expecting a young friend here with me until we sail together on Monday. If you'd prefer us to move to a hotel—

JOSIAH: Not at all. You're both quite welcome to stay as long as you like.

MIRANDA: There may also be other friends I may want to be seeing.

JOSIAH: Welcome as well. Just warn me in time, so that I can keep clear of them.

MIRANDA: You know—I've got a theory about you.

JOSIAH: Theory?

MIRANDA: About why you're in the state you are.

JOSIAH: I wasn't aware I was, but as always, theories interest me. [*She waits a moment, then speaks in a sudden rush:*]

MIRANDA: It may not be Mother or Uncle Andy's tragic end or disappointment in Jock or the brush-off from your law firm or disgust with the world in general, including me, or a combination of all of them. It—it—

[*She stops to catch her breath.*]

JOSIAH: Quite a list. Odd I never stopped to add up.

MIRANDA: —But my theory is, it may not be mental at all! It might easily be physical. You've been overworked and underexercised and literally taking no care of yourself for years, and I wish the minute Doctor Wells gets back from wherever he is, you'd go into the hospital for a complete checkup. Also, it's perfectly possible that you didn't get out of that accident as lightly as you thought.

JOSIAH: How can you get out more lightly than to have a red-faced Bonacker lobsterman haul you out by the seat of your swimming pants?

[*She stares at him, puzzled.*]

MIRANDA: Lobsterman? Out of what?

JOSIAH: The water, of course.

MIRANDA: The—which water?

JOSIAH: Gardiner's Bay. It was still cold, and as a swimmer I hadn't the staying powers I thought I had.

MIRANDA: I—I was meaning the time you crashed the plane.

[*Now she is watching him closely.*]

JOSIAH: Oh that—that was just bad judgment. The last was plain stupidity.

MIRANDA: Decoration Day, when you went down to Amagansett—

JOSIAH: Yes. Then I did write you about it? I wasn't sure. [*Again his short laugh*] No, child. No ill effects from either. Physically still intact. Mentally a bit confused, maybe—as who isn't these days, with any realization at all of how the world is wagging? Of his own incapability of making it wag otherwise?

MIRANDA: —Then that's it.

JOSIAH: What's what?

MIRANDA: You think you're through.

JOSIAH: Me? Through? Josiah Brook? At his age? Why, my dear, I feel young as a pup and chipper as a cricket.

MIRANDA: You're lying in your teeth, Father.

JOSIAH: Which I still have—and don't you forget it! Yes, and can show them, too!

MIRANDA: Tell me, Father. You always could.

[*He looks at her steadily for a moment, then speaks.*]

JOSIAH: Maybe it's a little like—I don't know—casting off from all you've had and taking your bearings from new stars you can scarcely see. Does that sound too romantic?

MIRANDA: It sounds lonely.

JOSIAH: Oh, I don't know! I expect there are compensations. In fact, the law of compensation is the only natural law I've ever fully credited. It's the single—Who's this?

[*A girl of twenty has come quietly a little way into the room from the hall. She wears an evening dress, carries a light wrap over her arm and is very pretty, with wide, unsmiling eyes and a single expression, one of somewhat puzzled intentness. This is* THANKFUL MATHER, *in the delectable flesh. What goes on in her head no one knows: what she has to say proceeds from elsewhere.*]

MIRANDA [*Still watching* JOSIAH]: Hello, Thankful. How was the party? As usual?

THANKFUL: Hello, Sweetie.—Good. But I'm bushed. I'm beat.

MIRANDA: This is my father.—Thankful Mather, Father. Matthew's stepniece from Boston.—That's right, isn't it?

THANKFUL: I know it sounds silly.

JOSIAH: How do you do, Miss Mather?

THANKFUL: How do you do? What's it like to be parent to such a Brain?

JOSIAH: Frightening.

THANKFUL: I'd perish.—I'm really flattened, Miranda. They dance so differently down here, particularly Princeton men. I'm really all wore out. Pity me.

JOSIAH: How in heaven's name old are you?

THANKFUL: I'll be twenty-one next month. No: I needn't lie about it: who am I fooling? I'll be twenty. Why?

JOSIAH: Just the difficulty of believing you're completely all wore out. It generally comes later. Good night to you both.

[MIRANDA, *still preoccupied, moves to him, kisses him briefly on the cheek.*]

MIRANDA: Good night, Father.

JOSIAH: Good night, Daughter. Sleep well.

MIRANDA: You too.

JOSIAH: I shouldn't be at all surprised. [*He moves toward the hall, turns and points a finger at Thankful.*] And you, sweet innocent! [THANKFUL *starts slightly.*]

THANKFUL: Me? Oh I always! [*Again his short laugh, as he goes out.* THANKFUL *takes a deep breath and lets it go.*] Goodness, what an attractive man.

MIRANDA: You think?

THANKFUL: And knows it, I expect. They usually.

MIRANDA: No—No, I dont' think he does at all. And that may be part of it.

THANKFUL: Part of what?

MIRANDA: It's so awful. I've got to think it out. I must.

THANKFUL: What is? What must you? Do you like this cape? They come in several weights, but I like this. It's lighter than the heavier ones. [*She lets the cape droop and passes a hand over her eyes.*] Goodness! I'm still a soupçon dizzy.

MIRANDA [*Scarcely having heard her*]: Have you been drinking things?

THANKFUL: Only ginger ale. Dreggy. But I'm drunk, I guess. I seem to get drunk on nothing, when they dance so differently.

MIRANDA: Um.

THANKFUL: Principally I'm sleepy. If you don't mind I think I'll hit the sack.—I'm sorry something's awful for you.

MIRANDA: One flight up. Straight ahead. The big room and turn right into the little room.

THANKFUL: You're sweet to have me and I do appreciate—why, Miranda Brook—look at you!

MIRANDA: What about me?

THANKFUL: Your eyes. Of course, I can't imagine *you* crying about anything. But—

MIRANDA: Cry! I haven't cried since I was five.

THANKFUL: I do, once in a. Sometimes they just, you know, bust loose. I only meant your eyes look funny—stary, sort of.

MIRANDA: Go to bed, Thanks.

THANKFUL: I always let 'em rip. It feels good after, sometimes even during. [*She half turns, then turns back again.*] I only meant if there's anything I might do to help—?

MIRANDA: There's nothing anyone at all—Unless—unless maybe—[*She lowers her head, murmurs:*] "Check against the normal."

THANKFUL: What'd you say?

MIRANDA: I said "Check against the normal." It's something I've been taught.

THANKFUL: I've been taught things, too. But I guess I just don't retain. [*Suddenly* MIRANDA *takes her by the shoulders and gazes at her intently.*]

MIRANDA: Look, you: you're about as normal a living, breathing, delicious little animal as they come, aren't you? [*She shakes her a little.*] Answer me! Aren't you?

THANKFUL: I—I guess I'm not bright enough to be anything else.—Thanks for the "delicious," though.

[MIRANDA *drops her arms, stands away from her.*]

MIRANDA: What would you do if someone—if suddenly you discovered that someone who—who was terribly dear to you was in terrible danger?

THANKFUL: Why, I—I think I'd try to do something about it right away. Wouldn't you?

MIRANDA: Yes. Yes, I think I would. [*She turns away.*] But if you felt so horribly helpless and alone!

THANKFUL: There're always people. That's the nice thing about people. So at least I'd try to, you know, form a rescue party or something. [MIRANDA *looks back to her quickly. She explains:*] You know: like when you're skiing or something and someone gets lost?

MIRANDA: Thank you, Thanks.

[*She goes to the desk, searches the papers on it.*]

THANKFUL [*Suddenly*]: Not—not *him?!*

MIRANDA: Him.

[*She finds what she wants, dials the telephone.*]

THANKFUL: You mean someone is—he's got an enemy or something?

MIRANDA: About the worst there is, I'd say. [*To the telephone*] Bedford Village 517.

THANKFUL: You mean a Public Enemy?

MIRANDA: Go to bed, Thanks. [*Then, to the telephone*] Algonquin 4-0616. That's right.

THANKFUL: But can't you have him app—what they call "apprehended"?

MIRANDA: We can do our best to.

THANKFUL: Honestly, Miranda, I mean it: if I can help even in the littlest way—

MIRANDA: You might. So might several people. It's something that's got to be very carefully thought out.—Oh, if only I could get Mother and him together again! Divorce is nonsense for those two.—If he'd care enough about Jock to talk up the law and law school, get him really excited about it.—If he'd meet up just once with this Clover O'Neil job and let off some steam. If—if something could make him see that Matthew and I are—oh, if he just could be made not to *evade* life! Is that too much to ask? Is—? [*Then, to the telephone*] —Mother? Yes. Yes, about an hour ago. One second, will you? [*She turns again to* THANKFUL.] Please go to bed. Chances are I'll be up before you're asleep.

[THANKFUL *gathers up her wrap.*]

THANKFUL: I go right off to. But if you shake me a little—

MIRANDA: I promise, if I need to. Good night, Thanks.

THANKFUL: 'Night, Miranda. [*She glances about her apprehensively and murmurs:*] Goodness!

[*She goes out.* MIRANDA *returns to the telephone.*]

MIRANDA: Mother?—Yes. Yes, I realize it. Import—? Well, naturally I wouldn't, if it wasn't.—Listen: do you happen to know if Russell Evans is in town, or if he isn't, where I might—? Mother! Could you simply tell me whether—? Good!—And is there any other address for Jock except that silly straw-hat playhouse? I mean where I could maybe get him now on the telephone?—Mother! Will you first of all please to tell me—! Thanks, thanks very much. [*She notes a number on a pad.*] Yes. Right! I've got it. [*Her voice lowers. She attempts to control it, but it begins to shake a ltitle.*] And look, my dear: what's particularly important is that you yourself get into town by twelve tomorrow morning.—Damn it, Mother, I don't care! Sunday or not, hot or not, you must!—What?—All I can tell you now, is that it's of the utmost.—Come directly to the house.—Yes, of course he's here. That's just the point.—No—but he may be, and very. —I tell you I can't say any more until I see you! [*A longer silence. Then her voice hardens:*] O.K. Yes. Do make the effort. Sometimes it's worth it.—Just one thing: I promise you I'll hate you all my life unless you do. I mean that exactly and precisely. What's more, I think you'll hate yourself—and that you could never stand. That would be really inconvenient. [*Then it breaks.*] Oh, good night, darling—and oh please do come! [*She replaces the telephone. Her head goes down and her shoulders begin to shake and she sobs to herself:*] And oh God, dear God—how I hate the ones who blubber!

[*She takes deep breaths to control her tears, straightens slowly and reaches for the telephone again. She brings it to her ear, dials a number and waits.*]

CURTAIN

■ ACT I ■

SCENE II

The library, about half-past twelve the following noon, Sunday. The room is the same but seems much brighter and pleasanter: both windows are open and the midday sunlight is strong outside.

SUSAN BROOK *and* RUSSELL EVANS *sit very erect upon their chairs.* JOCK BROOK *is half reclining upon the sofa, his hands clasped behind his head, staring at the ceiling. All look tense and expectant.* SUSAN *is a young, slim and smart forty-eight, attractively turned out in a dark linen street dress and a small, becoming hat.* RUSSELL *is older, graying slightly, but probably handsomer than when he was younger. He wears a gray flannel suit which sits well on him.* JOCK *is twenty-three, with a sensitive, humorous face and his father's rangy frame. He wears flannels and a jacket. There is a long silence. Then*

SUSAN: I can't stand it a moment longer. Where are they? [*Another silence. She goes on:*] I didn't close an eye until three. I woke sharp at ten, gulped down my coffee and hurtled into town like a jack-rabbit.

JOCK: Lucky some farmer lad didn't wing you.

SUSAN: Sit up straight, Jock. Don't loll.

JOCK [*Without stirring*]: Yes, Mother.

SUSAN: It's shocking these days how even reasonably well-built young girls tend to—

JOCK: I know: posture is everything.

SUSAN: Not quite. But you needn't all of you look so consistently spineless.

JOCK: I'll get the word around.

RUSSELL: Posture aside, Jock—

JOCK: —Yes, Mr. Evans?

RUSSELL: Just how, with your brains and your background, did you happen to flunk out of law school?

JOCK: It's not called that in First Year. The proper expression is "get dropped."—I don't know. I guess maybe my little heart just wasn't in it.

SUSAN: Where was it, then?

JOCK: Couldn't say, really couldn't. Failed to inquire.

SUSAN: Have you by any chance got a girl?

JOCK: Mother, by some amazing chance I have four girls, all exquisitely lolly.

[SUSAN *laughs in spite of herself.*]

SUSAN: Jock, I love you.

JOCK: Likewise, pal. You're the smartest little old lady I've seen round here in a mule's age.

SUSAN: Thank you. Only I repeat: *why* are we here?

[RUSSELL *looks at his watch.*]

RUSSELL: Malloy said Jo was out, but that she wouldn't be long—Miranda, I mean.

SUSAN: She sounded so really alarming. She practically put a curse on me, if I failed to come in.

RUSSELL: I'm not positive, but I think she threatened my life.

JOCK: Sounded quite manic to this baby also.

RUSSELL: It must mean trouble of some sort.

[*He has moved to the window, where he stands looking down into the garden.*]

JOCK: It better.

RUSSELL: Look here a minute, Sue.

[SUSAN *goes to his side, follows his gaze.*]

JOCK: Lucky I'm not in this week's show. Lucky for me, that is. Sad for the poor yokels sitting out front, of course.

SUSAN [*To* RUSSELL]: But it's unheard of!

RUSSELL: Apparently to Malloy and him, that's what's known as being "out."

SUSAN: Pottering in the garden—and he used to call everything petunias! I call it pathetic.

[MIRANDA *has come in with a vase of flowers in each hand, cool and pretty in a summer dress.*]

MIRANDA: That's the word, Mother. That's easily the word.

SUSAN: Miranda, tell us instantly—

MIRANDA: —Hello, Jock. Glad to see you.

JOCK: Hi, Sweet Girl Graduate. It makes hot, n'est-pas?

MIRANDA: Horriblement. Hello, Russell. Thanks for coming.

RUSSELL: Not at all, my dear. Only—

[MIRANDA *places the flowers, pats them into better arrangement, glances from him to* SUSAN.]

MIRANDA: You know, it's funny.—You look fine, Russ. You both do—handsome as ever, which is handsome.—Yes, it's very funny.

SUSAN: What is? Oh, this is so aggravating—

MIRANDA: I remember, as quite a small girl, coming into the big room in the country one afternoon, and there you two were—

SUSAN: Were what? I don't understand you.

JOCK: Elaborate, Mandy.

MIRANDA: Mother was sitting in the big chair with gnarled legs—I mean the chair's—and he was standing so upright behind her—

RUSSELL: A very upright chap, old Evans.—So therefore?

MIRANDA: And I had the same definite sense that the air was trembling all around you.—It must have been the heat then, as well.

RUSSELL: Yes—it most assuredly must have been.

SUSAN: How ridiculous you can be!

[MIRANDA *gives the final touches to the flowers.*]

MIRANDA: Can't I just?—There, that looks better: less like a tomb—though of course they have flowers, too. If Father's determined to stay on here, we must get these gloomy dustcovers off.

SUSAN: Miranda, we've been waiting hours for you. So if you'll kindly—

MIRANDA: Not hours, Mother. Not quite hours.

RUSSELL: I actually haven't a great deal of time, myself.

MIRANDA: At the moment, it's not going to take much. When you've heard, I think you'll devote what is necessary. Please, everyone—sit, will you?

[SUSAN *and* RUSSELL *seat themselves facing her.*]

RUSSELL: The sorry fact is, I have a lunch engagement with another sordid banker at one.

MIRANDA: I understand that Father's given Jock and me some money.

[JOCK *sits bolt upright.*]

RUSSELL: He told you?

MIRANDA: He did.

JOCK: Well, well! Astonish your friends with your ability to play the flute.

RUSSELL: It's quite a nice little nest egg for each of you.

MIRANDA: I'm not taking mine, at the moment.

RUSSELL: No?

JOCK: I'd like mine sunny-side up, please.

MIRANDA: The question is, why did he do it just at this point?

RUSSELL: Why, I suppose because he's fond of you. And of course taxwise it's—

MIRANDA: —Has he done anything else in that line?

RUSSELL: Well, just in the bosom of the family, late in May he did cash in all his holdings except the Governments, and—

MIRANDA: I knew it!

RUSSELL: He didn't say why. But as it turned out—marketwise, that is—

SUSAN: "Marketwise" "taxwise"! Are we here to talk investments?

MIRANDA: No. We are not.

RUSSELL: Then come on, child, come on!

MIRANDA: I have terribly bad news for you. In fact, I don't know how it could very well be worse.

[*A moment's silence. Then*]

SUSAN: Your father?

MIRANDA: Yes. Yes, of course.

JOCK: You mean he's got some—oh, damn it!—some kind of illness or something?

MIRANDA: You could call it that. Yes, you certainly could.

SUSAN: Miranda—

MIRANDA: I had quite a long session with Doctor Wells's son last night and another longer one with Father himself afterward. Between them, I learned quite a lot.

RUSSELL: Don't break the news to bits, Miranda.

[*She turns and confronts him:*]

MIRANDA: All right, I won't. It's just this: as things stand, I doubt very much if Father has more than a month or two to live.

SUSAN: Oh, my dear! Russell—did you hear what she said?

RUSSELL: I heard.

JOCK: What the—! Why, he's always been fit as a—! [*He kicks his heel at the floor.*] Some life, ain't it? Yeah—

RUSSELL: Does he know?

MIRANDA: He—[*Tears start into her eyes. She swallows, gives a single, short, bitter laugh*] Oh, sure, sure! He knows, all right. [*She moves away from them, exclaims exasperatedly*] Damn it! Will I kindly stop this?

SUSAN: It's so dreadful. I simply can't grasp—oh, the poor darling—after all he's been through.

MIRANDA: You do admit it's been plenty, then.

RUSSELL: Don't take that tone with your mother.—"As things stand," you said. What does that mean?

MIRANDA: It means we've got to do something, do something!

SUSAN: But surely Doctor Wells—isn't everything possible being done?

MIRANDA: Oh, you just don't understand—

RUSSELL: You're not making it easy for us to. What's wrong with him? In one breath you say "a month or two," and then—

MIRANDA: —Give me a minute. [*A brief pause. Then she turns to them, once more in control.*] Look, Mother—Russell—Jock: if there's anything in this world Father cares about any more, we four here now are the closest to it. Now that Uncle Andy's gone, we're the only living—

[JOCK *rises abruptly.*]

JOCK: You're still stalling. Speak your piece, kid.

SUSAN: It's incredible, all of it.

MIRANDA: I know—but you've got to believe me, you've all simply got to! I had it dumped in my lap last night and I've thought it out from every possible angle: Father's desperately ill—not in his body, but in his mind. He believes he's completely washed up, finished, through. Life and living mean utterly nothing to him: he's had enough, and more than. He knows his number's up, because he himself's put it up.

RUSSELL: Nonsense.

[MIRANDA *turns upon him.*]

MIRANDA: We might manage without you, if you don't care enough!

RUSSELL: See here, my dear girl: Jo Brook and I were friends before you ever—

MIRANDA: —He arranges his affairs, turns everything into cash, makes provision for Jock and me—and how much do *you* see? Twice he comes within *that* of death—and it never occurs to anyone that it well may have been by his own humble plan and intention!

JOCK: The plane crash and—and the other time?

MIRANDA: Yes, yes! Of course!

JOCK: He just might be accident-prone.

MIRANDA: What do you know about "accident-prone"?

JOCK: I read a little here and there.

MIRANDA: I do more than just read. I've spent considerable time among pitifully unhappy people, and I think by now I recognize the clearly suicidal when I see it.

SUSAN: Oh, don't say it!

MIRANDA: I'm sorry, Mother, but there it is.

JOCK: You're quite a conclusion-jumper, you know.

MIRANDA: Lucky someone is.

RUSSELL: And always very persuasive, too.

MIRANDA: I've never felt that having a mind is anything to be ashamed of. It's about all we do have to distinguish us from the animals.

JOCK: Maybe that's why I like animals.

SUSAN: It's not a time to be funny, Jock.

JOCK: I'm just trying to get ahold of this.

MIRANDA: Two tries already—and knowing Father, I'm certain he's not apt to fumble it a third time.—Oh, it'll look like an accident—sure! He'll see to that very carefully, for all our sakes.

SUSAN: I simply cannot absorb it. Even if he told me himself—

MIRANDA: Father? He's likely to, isn't he?

SUSAN: What is it you want us to do, Miranda?

MIRANDA: Even if I were wrong about it—which I'm certain I'm not—my plan couldn't but make him a little happier—and just that little might be enough. What it comes down to is this: with all possible interest in living gone, the one hope is somehow to restore it for him.

RUSSELL: If the salt has lost its savor, wherewith shall it then be salted?

MIRANDA: That's up to us!

JOCK: Speaking of salt, don't kid yourself any buttering-up can be done. Not with Father. That's been tried various places on this so-called globe.

MIRANDA: Don't I know! I was there.

RUSSELL: Perhaps if I went to Washington—at least telephoned—telegraphed—

MIRANDA: Don't think it's another big job he wants. Far from it.

RUSSELL: What, then?

MIRANDA: I don't think he knows—but I believe I do. I believe if he could simply be made to feel useful again—not to his country this time—but just useful and necessary to a few simple human beings like ourselves, people close to him, it might—you know—take him out of himself and get him over the hump.

JOCK: That almost makes sense. Only how?

MIRANDA: In the one way that would keep him from suspecting what we're up to!—You, Russ—for all your smooth manner and politesse, you're in trouble, deep trouble. You must be. You're at the age for it.

RUSSELL: I beg your pardon?

SUSAN: How do you mean "the age"? Russell's barely—

MIRANDA: The bigwig who made our commencement address said we were standing on the threshold of life—

RUSSELL: Don't they always?

MIRANDA: I suppose. But last night, talking to Toby and Father, I got to thinking that there's a second one for most people later on—threshold, I mean—and one very much harder to take in one's stride. And he's there and you're there—and you, Mother! Your pretty looks and sweet laugh don't fool me; you're in shreds at the prospect.

SUSAN: How absurd. I'm one of the most contented—

MIRANDA: Like fun you are, like very thin fun, Mother.—And sometimes when I look at Jock—still at his first one like me—and think of things, my heart just breaks for him.

JOCK: Lay off.—Anyhow, what's this got to do with—?

MIRANDA: —Everything! Father was one of the greatest troubleshooters of his time. "Snafu, is it? Get Brook. Send Brook." The nose for trouble must still be there, waiting for something to make it twitch. All I'm asking is that the four of us be honest—above all, be honest with ourselves—take our deepest, darkest troubles to him in the greatest, biggest way, and dump them in *his* lap and see what happens. We four, and one more person.

RUSSELL: It's an idea. There might be something in it.

SUSAN: They do say confession is good for the soul.

MIRANDA: My theory is, it's equally good for the father-confessor.

JOCK: "One more person," you said. Who would that be?

MIRANDA: Uncle Andy's girl. Clover O'Neil.

RUSSELL: What!

MIRANDA: Luckily, it happens she's in town.

SUSAN: But Miranda, certainly you're not going to—!

MIRANDA: But I am. I'm very curious about Clover O'Neil.

SUSAN: But we know all about her!

MIRANDA: Do we? All *I* know is that there's one wound of Father's that's never even begun to heal.

[JOCK *looks toward the balcony, speaks warningly:*]

JOCK: Take it easy, kids.

SUSAN: A creature of that sort—how can she possibly—?

MIRANDA: Mother, whatever she is, how do you think she must feel—with one good man dead for her and another locked up for life?

SUSAN: —No conscience at all, I'm sure.

MIRANDA: Nobody's that lucky.

JOCK: Easy, I say!

RUSSELL: It's Josiah, Sue.

[SUSAN *goes on in a different voice:*]

SUSAN: I got my angelic hair-dresser to come to the hotel on a Sunday. I thought I'd kill two birds. But I could be back around teatime, say.

[JOSIAH *appears in the balcony window, looking back down over his shoulder.*]

MIRANDA: Do plan to be, Mother—preferably with every hair in place. You too, Russ.—Oh, hello, Father. How's life in the open? How does your garden grow?

JOSIAH: Those balcony steps are a bit rickety.

RUSSELL [*Heartily*]: As what isn't these days, eh, old boy?

[JOSIAH *comes a step or two into the room, smoking a cigarette. He is in flannels and shirtsleeves, an old jacket over his arm.*]

JOSIAH: They do say that here and there in the Bronx they devote the backyards to raising marijuana. Not at all a bad idea.—Susan—Russell—Jock—how are you?

RUSSELL: Never better. I got an early start for a lunch appointment on the Square, and thought I'd stop by.

JOSIAH: Nice of you. Nice to have seen you.

[*He moves toward the hall.*]

SUSAN: —And I thought I'd combine Miranda with the hairdresser.

JOSIAH: Her fiancé may object to that.

JOCK: Mandy asked us all for lunch.

JOSIAH: Good. She told me she was expecting people, but didn't say who. I hope Mrs. Malloy does you well.

RUSSELL: Unfortunately I can't stay. But I wondered if I might drop in later—you know—just for a chat. I need advice, Jo.

[JOSIAH *stops and turns.*]

JOSIAH: Oh? About what?

RUSSELL: Oh, just this and that.

JOSIAH: This address always finds me.

SUSAN: I must say you look wonderfully well, Jo, considering.

JOSIAH: Considering what? I'm always well, barring accidents.

[*A moment's pause. Then* JOCK *ventures:*]

JOCK: Look, sir: the reason *I'm* here is—

JOSIAH: —I suppose a little matter of a little extra money?

[JOCK *grins.*]

JOCK: No, for once. I've just heard my Dad's made me quite a present.

JOSIAH: Not that old skinflint!

JOCK: And I wanted to thank him. Also—

JOSIAH: I wouldn't worry about it.

JOCK: Okay, I won't.—Only also I'm in a kind of a jam, Father.

JOSIAH: That's not unusual, is it?

JOCK: I know. But this time—

JOSIAH: Talk to your mother and Russell about it. Get some use out of your godfather. So few do.

JOCK: Only I thought maybe *you* could suggest—

JOSIAH: Not possibly. I'm not anxious to take on anyone else's troubles, being at last so blissfully free of my own. [*Then, to* MIRANDA] What have you done to *your* hair?

MIRANDA: Nothing. I did wash it this morning.

JOSIAH: That seems to me something, rather than nothing.

MIRANDA: I yield the point.

JOCK: I'm hungry. When do we eat?

MIRANDA: As soon as Toby and Thankful arrive. You'll love the little creature, Jock. She hasn't a brain in her head.

JOCK: Anything else anywhere?

JOSIAH: Considerable.—Which reminds me to say the country seems to agree with you, Susan.

RUSSELL: Doesn't it, just?

SUSAN: Thank you both, I'm sure.

JOSIAH: Don't thank us. Thank Him who made it—Him from whom all blessings flow.—Only God! Why do women wear hats?

SUSAN: I'll take it off, if you like.

JOSIAH: Don't think of it. A purely rhetorical question.

[SUSAN *rises abruptly.*]

SUSAN: See here, Josiah Brook!

JOSIAH: Yes?

[*She turns away.*]

SUSAN: Never mind.

JOSIAH: The sad truth of it is, I couldn't less, my dear.

MIRANDA [*After a moment*]: Isn't that rather rude, Father?

JOSIAH: Perhaps. I'm afraid I've forgotten my manners, dwelling so long among the savage tribes.

JOCK: What tribes would those be?

JOSIAH: Oh, you know, human beings generally.

JOCK: *I* think they're pretty swell, most of them.

JOSIAH: Keep your innocence, my boy: a priceless possession.

RUSSELL: Ten to one.—As for me, I've got to get going.

JOSIAH: Nice to have seen you.

RUSSELL: You said that.

JOSIAH: Did I? Then that makes it doubly nice.

RUSSELL: Damn it, Jo, if you want to live like a hermit—!

JOSIAH: —Make it a hermit crab.

RUSSELL: By God, that's just what I make it!

JOSIAH: By God, then you've hit the nail on the head.

RUSSELL: Sue—Miranda—Jock—I may see you later. [*Then to* JOSIAH] Because I'm stopping in again around five, regardless.

JOSIAH: Do that, by all means. Then it will be thrice nice.

[RUSSELL *moves toward the hall.*]

RUSSELL: The new manner's damned unbecoming, Jo—and don't let anyone tell you otherwise.

JOSIAH: Oh, I shan't! Not on any account.

RUSSELL: God!

[*He goes out.* JOSIAH *shakes his head and chuckles.*]

JOSIAH: The friends of one's youth—how they do hang on! [*He moves toward the hall.*] Forgive me my unalloyed bastardy, all of you.

MIRANDA: Only what if we don't?

JOSIAH: I should be saddened indeed.

MIRANDA: Where are you going?

JOSIAH: Back to my cave.

SUSAN: Jo—

[*He stops and turns.*]

JOSIAH: Yes?

SUSAN: Please wait.

JOSIAH: Well?

SUSAN: What is it? What's come over you?

[JOSIAH *speaks lightly:*]

JOSIAH: Oh—just a shadow—the shadow of a doubt or two!

[JOCK *glances to the others. Then*]

JOCK: Fear me we don't get that one, Dad.

JOSIAH: The aim is to confuse.

SUSAN: How can you stand it, all alone here in the summer?

[*He lights another cigarette.*]

JOSIAH: I seem to survive, do I not?

SUSAN: But you must have some plans—what are your plans?

JOSIAH: To stay precisely where I am for a while. Later on, I figure on a little trip.

MIRANDA: Not to England with me, by any chance?

JOSIAH: By no chance.—Arizona, to hunt. It's tentative: it depends on whether Nelson, my old guide, still exists and I can find him. Good of you to be interested.

JOCK: A hunting party, is it—

JOSIAH: Not a party. Just Nelson and myself. I like it better that way.

SUSAN: You mean alone?

JOSIAH: Nelson and I understand each other. It would be nice to get a mountain lion before I die, don't you think? *I* do.

SUSAN: Before you—?

[*Again the chuckle*]

JOSIAH: Now Susan—even you'll admit I'm getting on!—And years ago the old boy promised that if sometime I'd come without a crowd of roistering friends, he and I without fail would—[*He stops as* THANKFUL *and* TOBY *come in.*] Hello, Toby. You made it.

TOBY: Good morning, sir. Sure: I just packed three moribunds in dry ice and left them.

[JOSIAH *fixes* THANKFUL *with an eye.*]

JOSIAH: Now here's one who doesn't.

THANKFUL: Doesn't what?

JOSIAH: Wear a hat. [*She stares at him. He waves it away.*] Unimportant. Dismiss it.

THANKFUL: But I never! I wouldn't be found dead in one. [*Her hand goes to her lips. She glances at* MIRANDA *in dismay.*] Oh!—I—I'm sorry.

MIRANDA: My mother and my brother Jock. Thankful Mather, Mother.

SUSAN: How do you do, Miss Mather?

THANKFUL: How do you do, Mrs.—er—

[SUSAN *smiles.*]

SUSAN: —Still Brook.

THANKFUL: I'm glad. He's divine. I adore him.—Hello, Jock.

JOCK: It's a date.

SUSAN: How are your father and mother, Toby, and where are they?

TOBY: Fine, thanks.—Still by the sea, the beautiful sea. Hi, Jocko.

JOCK: Haven't seen you in a coon's age, boy.

TOBY: Goddam, let's correct that. [*He slips his arm through* THANKFUL'*s.*] I found this little Emergency, adroop on your doorstep and took her down the street and put a cocktail in her.

THANKFUL: Two. He's the funniest man.

JOCK: Competition, is there? Good! I thrive on it.

THANKFUL: He said the funniest thing. "I rarely drink in the middle of the hay," he said. [*To* JOSIAH] Don't you think that's funny?

JOSIAH: Moderately.

THANKFUL: I think it's funny.

[MALLOY *comes into the doorway.*]

MALLOY: A lady waiting in a taxi for you, Miss Miranda. A Mrs. O'Neil.

MIRANDA: I'll be right down.

[JOSIAH *turns and looks fixedly at* MIRANDA.]

MALLOY: And lunch at anytime now, sir—madam. Just a little buffet on the terrace.

SUSAN: Thank you, Malloy.

TOBY [*To* MALLOY]: Did you get them open all right?

MALLOY: It's not a trick that once known you forget.

[*He goes out.*]

JOCK: Why? What got stuck?

TOBY: I brought Mandy some clams.

MIRANDA: Sweet. It takes me back.—Where are the field flowers?

TOBY: Where are the fields in this muggy dump?

JOSIAH: [*To* MIRANDA]: "O'Neil"—?

MIRANDA: Clover O'Neil.

JOSIAH: Fancy that.

MIRANDA: I'm lunching at the Brevoort with her. I asked her here, but she won't.

JOSIAH: Commendable of her. And particularly so of you to—make contact, shall we say. [*He moves toward the hall.*] Till later, friends of my youth.

SUSAN: But Jo—at least *you're* lunching with us!

JOSIAH: Thanks: I had some parsley in the garden.

[*He goes out.* JOCK *looks after him.*]

JOCK: Still a glint of the old spark now and then: is that hopeful?

SUSAN: But it's not going to be easy, not at all easy.

MIRANDA: I never figured it would. At least he's being exposed to some kind of life again. That's a beginning.

JOCK: But Arizona—hunting—alone: by crikey, *that* ain't so good, is it?

MIRANDA: Now are you convinced?

SUSAN: I—suddenly I'm freezing.

TOBY: What's it all about? Not my patient, by any chance—

MIRANDA: In the winter, your patient crashed a plane. In the spring, he was hauled out of Gardiner's Bay. For the autumn, he plans a shooting trip in the West. What's the prognosis, Doctor?

TOBY: I see what you mean. But according to what I've gathered, he's not that way at all.

MIRANDA: Perhaps when you're older and wiser, little man.

TOBY [*To Jock*]: I like everyone in this family except your sister.

JOCK: She's a tough baby: takes knowing.

TOBY [*To* MIRANDA]: My father says that while a little learning is a dangerous thing, a little psychiatry is plain disaster.

MIRANDA: We'll have to risk it.

THANKFUL [*Big eyes wide*]: You—you can't actually mean you actually think he's actually con—contemplating—?

MIRANDA: If you'll keep that pretty little trap shut, yes, I'm afraid we do.

THANKFUL: Gracious.

[SUSAN *moves toward the windows.*]

SUSAN: But a meal is waiting, as meals often are. Come—we'll go this way.

[JOCK *follows with* THANKFUL.]

THANKFUL: —But when life's so good!

JOCK: I tell you, kid: just you demonstrate that, will you?

THANKFUL: I—I'll try! Honest I will. I'm already too demonstrative.

JOCK: Honest, I believe you could.

[*They go out.* TOBY *stands watching* MIRANDA.]

MIRANDA: Anything, anything to take him out of himself!—I just wish I knew what tack *I'm* to take.

TOBY: Now I catch on.—Fantastic, of course, but anyhow it's action.

MIRANDA: Of which you're a man of which, or not?

TOBY: Yes. Under the circumstances, I guess I'd say I am.

MIRANDA: Splendid. Then join the rest of us and heave-ho. [*She glances at her watch.*] Lady in taxi—damn her hide, let her cool a bit. [*Then goes to a small mirror and begins to comb her hair hastily.*] "Clover"—I wonder how she came to be called Clover.

TOBY: Born in a field of it, maybe.

MIRANDA: Lives in one, anyway.—Or did till today.

TOBY: "Miranda."—Were you born in a tempest?

MIRANDA: I must ask.—What stumps me is how she got to be as well known as she's always been.

TOBY: My father once talked to a couple of admirals: San Francisco in wartime: rich, a widow, good looks, a pretty house, fine victuals, a real gift for living—what they called "an original." So be warned.

MIRANDA: Thanks loads. Forewarned is forearmed, they do say. Also two-fisted, I hope.

TOBY: I've been thinking: suppose *I* was in some low bar and *your* name came up and someone said of you what what's-his-name-Tom Foster—did of her: "Oh yes: quite a number. Who's she sleeping with now?"—Do you know what I'd do?

[MIRANDA *turns, finds her gloves and handbag.*]

MIRANDA: *Sam* Foster.—What Uncle Andy did to him I should expect: socko.

TOBY: And get myself knocked down and killed for my pains? And have the poor dope sent up for life for an accident? No: I'd simply say "Tut-tut," that's what I'd say. Just "tut-tut. Loose talk. Naughty. Mustn't."

MIRANDA: —And live to fight another day. Possibly more sensible.—Well—see you after lunch, maybe. Sorry I can't partake of the clams. They don't keep, do they?

TOBY: Awhile—if they keep their little traps shut.

MIRANDA: You think maybe I'm inclined to talk too much—as well as think too much?

TOBY: There's a painless way of stopping both.

MIRANDA: Oh? How—[*In one quick motion, he takes her face in his hands and kisses her. She stands off from him, eyes blazing.*] Why! Why, you—

TOBY: Us men of action—who can resist us?

MIRANDA: You—you animal!

[*He points a finger at her.*]

TOBY: Vegetable—mineral—intellectual.

[*She seizes a book, brandishes it.*]

MIRANDA: Get out of here, or I'll—damn you, I'll demolish you! I'll—

TOBY: —Tut-tut. Such a display! [*He backs toward the balcony, grinning.*] Welcome back to the human race, Mandy.

[*He goes out.* MIRANDA *drops the book on a chair. Her head lowers thoughtfully. She murmurs to herself:*]

MIRANDA: It's an idea—[*Then raises it high again, moves swiftly to the hall and goes out*]—It's a thought!

CURTAIN

■ ACT II ■

SCENE I

The scene is the same, a little before six the same afternoon. The summer light through the windows is still of a volume to keep the room bright. Dustcovers and tarlatan have been removed from furniture, chandelier and pictures. A stepladder stands near the hall door to indicate that the work has just been completed. The room is livelier in its new guise.

At rise, the telephone has already been ringing for several moments. It rings again. JOSIAH, *comfortable with a book in an easy chair, with his back to the windows, disregards it. It stops.* JOSIAH *stretches, hooks a toe around a lighter chair facing him, draws it toward him, puts his feet up on it, turns a page and continues reading. He is now wearing a light summer suit.* MALLOY *comes in from the hall.*

MALLOY: I rang here from downstairs, but—

JOSIAH: Yes, I know. Please don't do it to me, Malloy.

MALLOY: But it's the Department again, sir. They seem most insistent.

[JOSIAH *resignedly folds his book.*]

JOSIAH: Are they still on?

MALLOY: They are.

[JOSIAH *rises and moves to the desk.*]

JOSIAH: How did they get the new number? Is there no—

[MALLOY *rolls up a piece of tarlatan hanging from the stepladder.*]

MALLOY: —Ah, they have ways and means—unscrupulous as always.

JOSIAH [*To the telephone*] Hello. Yes? Yes, that's right, speaking. Put him on. [*Then to* MALLOY]: Hang up in the pantry.—And nothing more, nothing—unless really urgent.

MALLOY: If I could rightly judge what you would consider—

JOSIAH: Just say Sorry, unavailable. Take messages, if any.

MALLOY: Yes, sir.—I thought you might like to know that the Madam and Mr. Evans have been walking up and down across the street for the past half hour in close conversation.

JOSIAH: There's no law against that.

MALLOY: It's only that me and the Missus have somehow got the impression that something's afoot, and—

[*He stops as* JOSIAH *returns to the telephone.*]

JOSIAH: How are you, old man?—Fine, thanks. Couldn't be better. Good to hear yours, too. How's it with the world? [*There is a pause.* MALLOY *goes out, with the stepladder.* JOSIAH *holds the telephone a little away from his ear, smiles slightly. Then*] Such language! But who shall blame you? Don't say you weren't warned.—I see.—I see. Yes, the fact is he called me from London an hour ago. No—purely social—asked me to stay with them over Miranda's wedding. Had to regret.—What? God, again?—No, I haven't any opinion on that one, honestly haven't. What?—Oh, just taking it easy.—Excellent.—Like a baby. How's that? [*Another silence, then drily*] Well, I'll tell you: just get the Good Lord to create another variety of human being—or better still, begin all over again with our friend the dog, say.—Honestly, I tell you I'm out of it, completely out!—What's that? Why? What's on your mind? [*A briefer silence, then*] Oh no, I couldn't even consider it. Honored and all that, but I can't, not possibly.—Oh—"personal reasons"—doesn't that still cover it?—What?—But of course! That's different. When? You come here. Just the two of us. Like to very much. Oh seven-thirty—eight. Right! Week from tomorrow. Set! Thanks for calling. God bless you, if He's still operating. Good-bye, old boy.

[*He replaces the telephone, looks at it, puzzled, for a moment, picks up two opened telegrams from the desk, glances at them briefly, drops them and returns to his chair and his book. A moment, then* THANKFUL *comes quietly in from the balcony and up behind his chair. She puts her hands lightly over his eyes and demands:*]

THANKFUL: Guess who?—I mean whom.

JOSIAH: Good Lord, I thought this trick had gone out with—[*her hands tighten over his eyes. He grunts*]: Trixie Friganza?

THANKFUL: Nope.

JOSIAH: Carrie Chapman Catt.

THANKFUL: Wrong again.

JOSIAH: Margaret Rose, you get right back to the palace!

[*She laughs, removes her hands and in a quick movement swings around the end of his chair and seats herself facing him on the arm of it.*]

THANKFUL: Aren't you *funny*.

JOSIAH: You think?

THANKFUL: Well, I certainly do!

JOSIAH: Well, that's certainly fine.

[*She gazes at him intently, her face about a foot from his, to his growing discomfort.*]

THANKFUL: You know something?

JOSIAH: Less every day. But what have you in mind?

THANKFUL: I just can't make you out.

JOSIAH: I can't tell you how sorry I am.

THANKFUL: You aren't either, you aren't sorry at all.

JOSIAH: No?

THANKFUL: No. You're just saying that.

JOSIAH: I'm afraid I'll have to admit it. My small talk has a way of becoming microscopically so. Where's Jock? Where's Miranda? Where's—?

THANKFUL: —And now you're trying to change the subject.

JOSIAH: I'm a trifle confused: just what is the subject?

THANKFUL: You. You are.

JOSIAH: We'll get nowhere on that one. It's a sleeveless errand.

THANKFUL: Sleeveless?

JOSIAH: You know—like a sweater.

THANKFUL: All right: I give up.

JOSIAH: That's a good girl.—And go sit over there, will you?

THANKFUL: Why?

JOSIAH: It will be less congested.

THANKFUL: In a minute.—You know something else?

JOSIAH: Off-hand, no.

THANKFUL: You wouldn't.

JOSIAH: Then that's that. So if you'll be young and spry enough to remove your—

THANKFUL: What you wouldn't know is that you're most terrifically attractive.

[*He laughs uncomfortably.*]

JOSIAH: Why, thank you very much, I'm sure!

THANKFUL: Don't bother.

JOSIAH: Very well, I won't.—But will you kindly tell me—no, never mind.—Look: that chair is yawning for you.

THANKFUL: —Tell you what?

JOSIAH [*After a moment's reflection*]: Just why and what is this apparently mad current rush of young girls toward—I shall put it mercifully—toward somewhat older men?

THANKFUL: You think there's one on—a rush, I mean?

JOSIAH: I've observed it in various quarters, even in my own family. Of course, I've also observed that the men are usually either well-off or well-known. Not that I qualify in any such—

THANKFUL: —Well, don't you think either one's more attractive than having curly hair or a seven-handicap at The Myopia or The Meadowbrook?

JOSIAH: I am merely asking for information, merely seeking enlightenment.

[*She gets up, stands over him and demands:*]

THANKFUL: Don't you admit it's being a little more advanced on girls' parts than on men's, who just keep on always being attracted to pretty girls just because they're pretty?

JOSIAH: Yes—yes, if pressed, I'm bound to say I do.

THANKFUL: Anyhow, *I* don't *like* curly hair or golf either.

JOSIAH: Flash the news to the Associated Press.

THANKFUL: What does that mean?

JOSIAH: It's known as a quip. Forgive it.

THANKFUL: Anyhow, you do think I'm pretty, don't you?

JOSIAH: Why yes. Extravagantly. Do you mind?

THANKFUL: Not a bit.—And therefore attractive?

JOSIAH: That, my dear child, is none of your business.

THANKFUL [*In a breath*]: Anyhow, I just want you to get it into your thick skull that the world's just full of girls like me and for all you know they might any number of them be ready to be just crazy about you—and it's fun—within certain limits, of course—and so why don't you do something about it? That is, unless you're dead on your feet, which would be silly at your age, don't you think?

[JOSIAH *rises and gazes at her, appalled.*]

JOSIAH: Will you kindly inform me, who or what on earth put you up to—?

THANKFUL: I made you a simple suggestion.

JOSIAH: I—if you don't mind, I—I'm afraid I'll have to take a—a rain check, as they say.

THANKFUL: That's all right, so long as you don't miss the game entirely. I'm not necessarily referring to myself. [JOSIAH *gestures and seats himself at the desk.* JOCK *comes in from the hall.*] Hello, Sweetie. You look nice and cool and clean. How d'you manage?

JOCK: Oh, I just stood under a hydrant with some of the other kids.

THANKFUL: I've got to take me a bath myself. I'm revolting. [*She moves toward the hall, stops and turns to* JOSIAH.] Just remember what I told you, won't you?

JOSIAH: Till my dying day.

[*She stares first, in alarm, then smiles and goes out.* JOCK *grins.*]

JOCK: A little heart-to-heart?

JOSIAH: Jock, I want to warn you there's a maniac loose in this house—and I'd rather not say what kind of a one.

JOCK: Thankful? She's harmless. You just don't understand women.

JOSIAH: I sincerely trust you're right.

JOCK [*After a moment*]: There's quite a little you don't understand, Dad.

JOSIAH: Oh? Such as—

JOCK: Me, for instance.

JOSIAH: Who am I to attempt to plumb your profundities?

JOCK: There you go again.

JOSIAH: Do I? Where—

JOCK: Blocking off what you don't want to hear, with the well-known sarcasm.

JOSIAH: I'm no great admirer of sarcasm. I must have changed.

JOCK: Don't think you haven't. You know what?

JOSIAH: What?

JOCK: Well, if I have any sense of humor, I must have got it from you. Granted?

JOSIAH: "Sense of—"! My God, don't use that trite expression!—Also, the most overrated characteristic that ever—

JOCK: —I'm young. I don't mind being trite.—Well? Granted? Did I? From you?

JOSIAH: I'd like to think so. Of course, your mother—

JOCK: Mother's witty at times but doesn't have the real thing. Granted?

JOSIAH: What *is* this, anyhow?

JOCK: It's just that I think the real trouble with you is that you've lost your own.

JOSIAH: Why, you—!

JOCK: Smacko! Right on the nose.

JOSIAH: So there's trouble with me, is there?

JOCK: Sure. Plenty. Has been since about two years ago, when you first began to lose your sense of it. Now it's gone—but good.

JOSIAH: I've always considered the so-called sense of humor to be really a sense of proportion—the real saving grace.

JOCK: Me too. Not just for laughs: for keeping a proper slant on life, on people, on yourself. That's what I mean.

JOSIAH: —A fairly serious accusation to make.
JOCK: No accusation: just a little tip.
JOSIAH: Any chance of recovering one that's lost, do you think?
JOCK: Well, if anyone can, you're the guy to do it.
JOSIAH: Thanks. I'll give it some thought.
JOCK: Give it all you've got. It's worth it to you, Dad.
JOSIAH: You may be right, you little bastard.
JOCK: Father! Don't say such things against yourself!
[JOSIAH *laughs. A moment's silence. Then*]
JOSIAH: You've had something on your mind for quite a time now—
JOCK: You aren't kidding.
JOSIAH: On a dozen occasions you've been about to bring it up, and then sidestepped it.
JOCK: Or been blocked.
JOSIAH: Perhaps I have too high a respect for you to attempt to pry out something not readily forthcoming.
[JOCK *glances at him quickly.*]
JOCK: I'd like to think it's that.
JOSIAH: Go right ahead: think it and believe it.
JOCK: Thanks. Very genial.
JOSIAH: What's on your mind, Jock? Is it bad?
JOCK: *You'll* think so.
JOSIAH: How do you know?
JOCK: I know you.
JOSIAH: Allow me to wonder how well.—Well? Come on with it!
JOCK: It's—it isn't easy.
JOSIAH: Could anyone help?
JOCK: I wish to God someone could.
JOSIAH: May I have a shot at it?
JOCK: Shoot.
JOSIAH [*After a moment*]: It's not a girl. And it's not money.
JOCK: Nope. I can handle those departments.
JOSIAH: It's no kind of what-they-call "disgrace."
JOCK: Shouldn't be. But damn it—!
JOSIAH: You weren't the only one dropped from your class. There were twenty others.
JOCK: Twenty-two.
JOSIAH: There are other law schools probably as good or better, apart from the snob-value.
JOCK: I know.

JOSIAH: It's no crime to have to repeat a year.

JOCK: I know. But—but damn it, I—!

[*Again he bogs down.*]

JOSIAH: —But damn it, the fact is you want nothing at all to do with the law. [JOCK *looks away.* JOSIAH *continues grimly:*] You have no desire whatsoever to continue in the glorious tradition of your father and two grandfathers. [JOCK *is silent.* JOSIAH *adds:*] Sarcasm. [JOCK *smiles faintly.*]

JOCK: Noted.

JOSIAH: What you want is to do something quite different with your life.

JOCK: That's it.

JOSIAH: —Something quite irregular, as they say.

JOCK: You've said it.

JOSIAH: Well, that's as far as I go. Take over.

JOCK: Look, Dad: it began in school—then later more so in college —but in the Navy it really hit me. Maybe I'm just a show-off—

JOSIAH: I hadn't noticed it.

JOCK: I've had some bad times thinking that, I can tell you.—But the fact is, I'm only happy when my feet are going and I'm singing and cracking jokes and when—when other people are enjoying it. Oh God, how good I feel then! I feel—you know—of some use in the world.

JOSIAH: That's quite a feeling, however you come by it.

JOCK: Boy—is it not!—And look: I write my own stuff and a lot of it's quite funny and original. The voice is only fair, but it's true and the timing's the nuts. And I can dance like a fool.

JOSIAH: Anything like as well as—as Astaire or Kelly, would you say?

JOCK: Not yet, but give me time! [*He looks away. His voice lowers:*] Well—there it is, I guess.

JOSIAH: You want to be a song-and-dance man—an entertainer—a comedian.

JOCK: Whatever you want to call it, I don't want to be anything else.

JOSIAH: You'd have to be good. It's almost like being a poet, you know: you can't be just pretty good.

JOCK: Don't I know!

JOSIAH: You'd have to work your head off for months—years—get knocked around—one disappointment after another—

JOCK: And God, am I willing!

[JOSIAH *rises abruptly.*]

JOSIAH: Then why in hell are you ashamed of it?

[MIRANDA *comes in.* JOCK *rises and shouts back:*]

JOCK: Who the hell said I was?

[MIRANDA *turns to go out again.* JOSIAH *calls:*]

JOSIAH: No! I'd like you to hear this. [*She approaches them, stands waiting.*] Your brother seems to want to devote his life to giving people pleasure.

MIRANDA [*After a moment*]: Quite an ambition.

JOSIAH: For myself, I'd like to say that I consider it a very high one.

JOCK: You mean you for cat's sake don't mind?

JOSIAH: Didn't you for cat's sake hear what I said? [*Then, to* MIRANDA] Well?

MIRANDA: But—but I thought if ever you seriously talked about the law together—

JOSIAH: We have. It's out. And properly. This replaces it. [*He scowls at* JOCK.] But if I catch him ruining his voice and wind chain-smoking and throwing drinks into him—

JOCK: It's only when I'm around you that I get nervous.

JOSIAH [*Roaring*]: Then stay away from me!

JOCK: Yes, sir.

JOSIAH [*In another voice*]: Go up to my study and look in the corner of the bottom bookshelf on the left for a canvas-bound manuscript with a red string around it.

JOCK: Why? What is it?

JOSIAH: My junior year I wrote the book for the Hasty Pudding Show, and—

JOCK: —You lie! You never!

JOSIAH: And I want an opinion: I want to know if it's still funny.

MIRANDA: Was it then?

JOSIAH: It was hilarious.

JOCK: Dad, you know for all your dotage, you ought to stick around for quite a while yet. You're good for people.

JOSIAH: Go do as I say. I'll be right there.

JOCK: Okay, Mandy. You're up.

MIRANDA: A hoofer. Just a low-class hoofer.

[*With some difficulty* JOSIAH *has gone into an old-fashioned dance routine and is singing out:*]

JOSIAH: "Although I'm rarely in the money,
It is really rather funny
How I always seem to land upon my feet."

[*Which he does, with emphasis.* JOCK *picks up the dance step with considerably greater facility, moves past* MIRANDA *toward the door and demands of her:*]

JOCK: See? Heredity. The genes. You cannot beat the genes.

MIRANDA: Heredity, hell. It's obviously the environment.

JOCK: The Genes, the Freds, the Jocks: Kelly to Astaire to Brook!

[*He dances out.* JOSIAH *concludes his song:*]

JOSIAH: "When out strolling with my Honey
On a day that's bright and sunny,
I invariably tell her she's a treat!"

[*He stops, wipes his brow and inquires of* MIRANDA*:*] Funny?

MIRANDA [*Solemnly*]: Father, it's a riot.

JOSIAH: Maybe it was the straw hat I wore.

MIRANDA: A boater?

JOSIAH: With an exceptionally broad brim.—Ah, youth, youth!

[MIRANDA *seats herself.*]

MIRANDA: I've just been busily recapturing some of mine.

JOSIAH: Oh? How so?

MIRANDA: On the terrace of the Brevoort. With Toby. He was fresh enough to barge into my lunch date with Clover. [*She waits a moment.* JOSIAH *does not speak.*] We've been drinking white wine and seltzer. "Gesprichts," they call them. And don't think they don't make you.

JOSIAH: Sprechen?

MIRANDA: Jawohl.—I think he's quite a dear, don't you?

JOSIAH: It's a word I'm reluctant to apply to my own sex.

MIRANDA: —Sex.

[*She has murmured it dreamily.* JOSIAH *glances at her.*]

JOSIAH: What about it?

MIRANDA: Oh—nothing—

JOSIAH: You have a peculiar look on your face.

[*She sighs and looks away.*]

MIRANDA: It will wear off in time, I expect.

JOSIAH: Time for what?

MIRANDA: Oh—my wedding.

JOSIAH: Miranda, I'd appreciate a little clarification on—

MIRANDA: —Don't tell me you're interested! The man without interest in practically anything—

JOSIAH: Who said I—? I am merely inquiring what kind of a bug—

[*She shakes her head firmly.*]

MIRANDA: No bug, Father, nor germ nor virus. Purely psychological—and sound psychology at that.

JOSIAH: Wine and soda, plus the heat.

MIRANDA: I had two and didn't even finish the second. And it was cool there—oh so deliciously cool! I'll have to admit I'm a little disturbed, though.

JOSIAH: Too bad. The disturbed wards are full-up these days. Ask Toby.

MIRANDA: How did you know it was about Toby?

JOSIAH: How did I know about Jock and his fix? I'm a very canny fellow, at times.

MIRANDA: What's he told you?

JOSIAH: Toby? Not a thing. I'm simply a trained observer with a very good memory—at least one that goes back as far as Christmas Cove.

MIRANDA: It's quite normal, I'm sure. It must be related to the essential Id and its desire to preserve its sphere of activity. Knowing that in a few days I'll be married-up for life, I—

JOSIAH: Yes?

MIRANDA: Well, don't stare at me! Isn't it just as natural for a girl to want one as for a man?

JOSIAH: Want one what?

MIRANDA: One last fling, I suppose you'd call it.

[*There is a silence. Then* JOSIAH *speaks quietly:*]

JOSIAH: I don't think I'd try any such, Daughter.

MIRANDA: Why?

JOSIAH: Not if I were you.

MIRANDA: Why not?

JOSIAH: Not on that young man.

MIRANDA: But where's the harm?

JOSIAH: Not if you want your hair left on your head, my dear.

[MIRANDA *laughs.*]

MIRANDA: So you think I might be the one to suffer!

JOSIAH: If there's any suffering to be done, I should fondly hope so.

MIRANDA: That's nice of you.

JOSIAH: Because, as you must realize, the whole idea is both contemptible and immoral.

MIRANDA: Honestly, of all the high-minded stands to take about anything so ridiculously—!

JOSIAH: —Also, I'd give any such persons as Clover O'Neil a very wide berth.

MIRANDA: At last you've brought her up.

JOSIAH: Brought her up?

MIRANDA: I knew you would. Obviously, there you *are* interested.

JOSIAH: My interest in the O'Neil is entirely confined to the distance she keeps from all of us.

MIRANDA: You'd feel differently if ever you saw her.

JOSIAH: Which, thank God, is most unlikely.

MIRANDA: Three times she wrote to you.

JOSIAH: Did she? I lost count.

MIRANDA: She's amazing-looking. Really breathtaking. Nearer thirty than forty, you'd say.

JOSIAH: *I'd* say the devil is kind to his own.

MIRANDA: You're fair about everyone else, why not her? We had a long talk, very honest, very open. She has an odd point of view.

JOSIAH: I'll admit that odd points of view sometimes interest me.

MIRANDA: Well, hers is extremely odd—about you, that is to say.

JOSIAH: Me?

MIRANDA: Yes: I'm afraid she doesn't think much of you.

JOSIAH: Good!

MIRANDA: Maybe you'd prefer to skip it—

JOSIAH: Not at all. I'd like to know.

MIRANDA [*After a moment*]: I suppose you've actually a right to.

JOSIAH: *I* should suppose I had.

MIRANDA: Of course, it's all mixed up with her feelings about Andy. She was only very fond of him, it seems—no more.

JOSIAH: I shouldn't have imagined her capable of even that.

MIRANDA: I think maybe we've misjudged her—you and me and all of us. She insists Andy knew exactly how she felt, and I believe her. And as for her being capable of real feeling—although I certainly didn't tell her so—I should call her attitude toward you decidedly ambivalent.

JOSIAH: I never quite understood that word.

MIRANDA: Mixed love and hate: heavy portions of each.

JOSIAH: Love? Hate? O'Neil for me?

MIRANDA: To anyone with the special knowledge, definitely and distinctly. Of course, she thinks it's all hate: they mostly do.

JOSIAH: They?

MIRANDA: The ambivalents. You see, you were a kind of obsession with Andy: he'd apparently always sung your praises to the skies. And I think she'd got an odd image of you: Andy's charm, which wasn't enough for her, plus your strength—and it's strength she goes for, I gather. One thing: she believes we're all frightened to death of you. [*He laughs shortly.*]

JOSIAH: Yes! I've noticed that.

MIRANDA: She believes that for all his so-called wild ways, Andy was just a sweet, appealing, fundamentally very conventional boy.

JOSIAH: Andrew Brook was thirty-two years of age when he died.

MIRANDA: All the same—

JOSIAH: Rot! Nonsense! San Francisco malarkey!

MIRANDA: You asked me.

JOSIAH: Any more gems?

MIRANDA [*Slowly now*]: Yes: that you always expected too much of him. That he grew up in your shadow, always feeling inadequate. That that was why he was forever asserting himself—in the drinking, the flying, the general big talk. And finally—

[*She stops, looks away.*]

JOSIAH: —In the fight over her precious honor?

MIRANDA: I guess yes.

JOSIAH: In short, that I was responsible for his death.

MIRANDA: According to her, to quite an extent. Of course, you have to realize that blamed as she's been, she sees things in a somewhat distorted light, and would be inclined to pass the buck.

JOSIAH: Is that all?

MIRANDA: Just about.

JOSIAH: All right—what else?

MIRANDA: Isn't that enough?

JOSIAH: What else!

[MIRANDA *speaks with difficulty:*]

MIRANDA: —That while there is no doubt at all about your success as —as a public man, she said, there's equally none as—as to your—

[*Again she cannot go on.*]

JOSIAH: Say it!

MIRANDA: —Your failure as a human being.

[*There is a silence. Then* JOSIAH *speaks quietly:*]

JOSIAH: And is that news, do you think?

MIRANDA: Oh, Father—

JOSIAH: —To me, do you think?

MIRANDA: Father—please—you mustn't for a minute—

JOSIAH: Any other evidence offered?

MIRANDA: Mother leaving you—Jock—me—us all leaving you, she said.

JOSIAH: Good, good! The woman has a case.

MIRANDA: Naturally she's been upset. Naturally she'd try to think—

JOSIAH: Tell me what *you* think, Miranda.

MIRANDA: Well, of course to me, it's simply beyond—

JOSIAH: —Honestly what you think.

[*Their eyes meet. Then*]

MIRANDA: I think—I think there's something in it, Father.

JOSIAH: That's my girl.

[*His head lowers. She moves to him swiftly.*]

MIRANDA: Oh but my dear, my dear—don't you see? If it should be so, it's all the more reason why now—the great thing, the wonderful thing is that you're still young enough—wise, strong enough—to have another crack at it—to go at life and living in another way—from—from a different starting point!

JOSIAH: Less personally ambitious? Less—intellectual, maybe?

MIRANDA: Yes! Me too!—And what a chance! How much finer and more exciting!

JOSIAH: As a challenge?

MIRANDA: Yes, yes! You've never refused one yet.

JOSIAH: One thing I'd like to know: why suddenly today should everyone rush at me with—?

[*He stops, as* TOBY *wanders in from the hall.* MIRANDA *waits a moment before speaking:*]

MIRANDA: —Toby. Well, that was quick.

TOBY: I ran all the way.

MIRANDA: If that's a new shirt, you'd never know it.

TOBY: Sixth Avenue. It's all in the way you wear them.

[*She goes to him, passes her hand lightly down his cheek.*]

MIRANDA: Also a shave! You look sweet. [*She slips her arm through his and turns them both toward* JOSIAH.] How do we present, Father?

JOSIAH: Just remember what I said, my girl. [*He moves toward the hall.*] And if and when Russell comes, ring my room, will you?

[*He goes out.* MIRANDA *moves from* TOBY, *stands staring at the floor. She murmurs:*]

MIRANDA: Shock therapy.

TOBY: What say?

MIRANDA: I've just administered a treatment. I hope it wasn't too stiff. Jock rather throws me: that went all wrong. But something wonderful's going to happen, Toby—something to make up for everything.

TOBY: I'm all ears.

MIRANDA: Mother's going to come back to Father.

TOBY: You've arranged that, have you?

MIRANDA: Not exactly. But I just know it. It's my feminine intuition.

TOBY: If it was, I'd believe you. But I'm afraid it's only your female reasoning process.—You know, it's a shame about you as a girl—

MIRANDA: As a—? What do you mean?

TOBY: Because you could be such a one, if you'd ever stop using your head.

MIRANDA: Oh? Like Thankful, I suppose—

TOBY: Don't underrate Thankful. Never underrate the power of a headless woman.

MIRANDA: I suppose you're annoyed at my using you too.

TOBY: Always glad to be useful. I just didn't know I was being.

MIRANDA: It's only to give him another something but himself to concern himself with.

TOBY: Bad English. Describe the article.

MIRANDA: Just an impression that I'm by way of having a last—you know—whooping it up a bit with a childhood beau.

TOBY: Me?

MIRANDA: Sorry—there was no one else around. And he likes you, doesn't want you hurt. It'll worry him.

TOBY: I see.

MIRANDA: Anything, anything that will help to—! Please don't mind, will you, Toby?

[*A moment. Then* TOBY *grins.*]

TOBY: Hell, no. I'll go right along with you.

MIRANDA: Thanks. It won't require much activity on your part.

TOBY: But little thoughts may occur.

MIRANDA: Oh, there's so desperately little time, Toby!

TOBY: However, I thought you were all for being honest.

MIRANDA: For the others, yes. But for me, I think it's better to be just a trifle dis.

TOBY: Okay. You be dis, and I'll be dese, dose, dat. [*He catches her hands and draws her to him*] Mandy, I gotta big yen fer yuh, Babe. Smootch!

[MIRANDA *laughs and releases herself.*]

MIRANDA: Stop it, you fool! If you're going to be that way again—[SUSAN *and* RUSSELL *come in from the hall.*] Oh, hello—[*She goes to the desk, presses a bell.*] Father wanted to know the minute you arrived.

RUSSELL: Well, this is the minute.

[*He goes to the table, mixes himself a drink.* MIRANDA *holds out a hand to* TOBY.]

MIRANDA: We'll leave you alone. Come along, precious lamb. [*She moves toward the balcony with him, turns at the window to* SUSAN.] Remember, Mother: honest—utterly and completely honest.

RUSSELL: Will you kindly leave that to us?

MIRANDA: Dear Russ—as if you could ever be anything else!

[*She and* TOBY *go out.* SUSAN *draws a deep breath.*]

SUSAN: I'm just plain terrified. What are we going to do? Or say?

RUSSELL: We've been all over it. Just let it come naturally.—Incidentally, I forgot to tell you I made a few calls after lunch, including Washington and London. Also sent a wire or two.

SUSAN: I hope you didn't overdo it.

RUSSELL: I could use a little trust in my judgment, my dear.

SUSAN: Russ!—I only meant that he mustn't by any chance suspect that we suspect that he—[*She stops as* JOSIAH *re-enters, then speaks gaily:*] Good evening, Mr. Brook. You have callers again.

JOSIAH: So I am led to observe.

RUSSELL: Gracious sort of fellow—makes you feel really welcome.

JOSIAH: Have a drink.

RUSSELL: Having it.

JOSIAH [*To* SUSAN]: Tea?

SUSAN: Had it.

[JOSIAH *seats himself. There is a pause. Then*]

JOSIAH: Obviously you both have something you want to say: why not say it and get it over with?

[*A moment.* RUSSELL *clears his throat. Then*]

RUSSELL: Jo, the three of us were once very important to each other—

SUSAN: —Once, and for a long time. I—we—

[*She flounders, stops.* JOSIAH *looks at her a moment, then speaks suddenly:*]

JOSIAH: I never quite knew why you left me, you know. Does that help?

[SUSAN *looks away.*]

SUSAN: Yes. That helps.—Though I did think I made it reasonably plain to you.

JOSIAH: The implication was that you couldn't stand living with me any longer.

SUSAN: Please remember that once I had said that in anger, I was given small chance to explain.

JOSIAH: The bare statement seemed ample at the time.

SUSAN: Always the proud man: incline the head, fold the toga and withdraw.

JOSIAH: Do you know anything more humiliating than to be informed that one's wife—

SUSAN: —Suppose I'd said it was for another man?

JOSIAH: That would have been less so, infinitely.

SUSAN: Really?

JOSIAH: But of course!—I might have wanted to strangle him, but knowing how people get overtaken by their emotions, at least I'd have understood.

SUSAN: That's very interesting. And would you still want to strangle him?

JOSIAH: Not at this date, my dear.

RUSSELL: Now do you see what fools two people can be?

SUSAN: I'm beginning to. [*She thinks a moment. Then*] Jo, I left you because I couldn't go on living with you and the quaint sense of guilt I had from being in love with someone else.

JOSIAH: What did you say?

SUSAN: Just that.—Of course it's quite possible that I wouldn't have fallen in love if world problems, et cetera, hadn't changed you from a charming, delightful, most amusing human being into—

JOSIAH: Thank you.

SUSAN: —Into such a grim old sobersides. Also there was the little matter of myself, my growing insecurity, my fading charms, and so forth.

JOSIAH: Fading? You look fine to me.

SUSAN: Thank *you.*—But just that, Jo.

JOSIAH: Well, where is he? Why haven't you married him?

SUSAN: Because of our enormous respect and affection for you—you do have great powers for commanding such, my dear—because we just couldn't, as they say—oh, what do they say?

RUSSELL: —Couldn't deliver the blow—destroy the faith—administer what's generally considered the final humiliation.

JOSIAH: Well, for heaven's sweet sake! You and Russ?

RUSSELL: You never remotely suspected?

JOSIAH: Not for a minute—a second!

RUSSELL: Of course, we were remarkably well-behaved.

SUSAN: And himself, of course, was much too busy, much too preoccupied with the affairs of the world.

JOSIAH: But I call *this* the affair of the world! It's superb—by God, it's downright magnificent.

SUSAN: Russell and I have never really had an affair, Jo. You mustn't get a wrong impression.

JOSIAH: Then what have you had? What is it?

SUSAN: A—just a romantic attachment, you might say.

RUSSELL: Rather prim and proper people, really.—At least she is.

JOSIAH: Honorable, honorable—

RUSSELL: Damn your eyes, it's been almost a religion to us!

JOSIAH: You absolute idiots.

SUSAN: I beg your pardon?

RUSSELL: You see? What did I tell you?

SUSAN: You really think that's what we are and were and have been—?

JOSIAH: But of course I do! Good Lord, think of the time you've wasted!—And you're so perfectly suited, so absolutely matched—and the luck of it, happening again at your time of life!—Sue, you wretch to have let me worry about you the way I have.

SUSAN: Worry? About me?

JOSIAH: You! Of all women to be adrift in the world without a man! Sue, the darling. Sue, the delicious. Sue the distracted, if left alone for one hour—

SUSAN: I just may have learned to—to value my independence.

JOSIAH: I doubt it, I sincerely doubt it.—And never once letting on! What a pair!

SUSAN: In all fairness, Russell was for telling you from the first. I just couldn't.

JOSIAH: But what you could and did do was the lowest and meanest trick you could play on a man: to give him deliberately to think he was too confounded boring for a lively woman any longer to abide. [SUSAN *rises indignantly*.]

SUSAN: I never!

JOSIAH: No? What else?—Insecure about yourself, did you say—what do you think that did to me?—Well, I'm not one to cherish a grudge. Russ—[*He goes to him, shakes his hand firmly, then turns to* SUSAN.] Sue, my witless angel—[*He grasps her hand also, pumps it.*] You've not only lifted a great burden of concern from me, you've restored a certain confidence a man never likes to lose at any age. God bless you both: sweet innocents, gallant, devoted and misguided friends!—Now get out of here and get married promptly—or by God, I'll start some nasty rumors about you.

[RUSSELL *turns on him furiously*.]

RUSSELL: Well, of all the complete—!

JOSIAH: That's it, boy! That's the stuff! You've thought the best of me for much too long. Now, for the love of heaven, think the worst. Go on—bestir yourselves. Life is real, life is earnest, life is also mercilessly short.

[RUSSELL *stands glaring at him*.]

RUSSELL: Susan?

SUSAN: You go ahead, Russ. I want a final word with Miranda. I'll—I'll meet you at your flat.

RUSSELL: Well, don't be so damned arch about it.

SUSAN: Arch?—If there's one thing I'm never—

JOSIAH: Now, now!

RUSSELL: Just tell me one thing in his presence: who was right from the beginning?

SUSAN: You were. But that doesn't make—

RUSSELL: That's all I wanted to hear.

[*He turns and marches out.* JOSIAH *calls after him:*]

JOSIAH: Sorry about the delay, old man, terribly sorry! I'll send her right along! [*He turns again to* SUSAN.] Wonderful fellow. A little stiff, but you can get that out of him. Great happiness in store for you both, my dear.

SUSAN: He *is* sweet, isn't he?

JOSIAH: A dear—a perfect dear!

SUSAN: But Jo—about you—about yourself—

JOSIAH: Fine—fine—immense!

SUSAN: Funny—I have a sudden sense that all the overjoyment's not so much for Russ and me, as for at last having found a way to be finally rid of the two of us.

JOSIAH: Don't talk nonsense. I can take Russ or leave him, mostly the latter. But as for my erstwhile Susan, I'll always think of her fondly and with—

SUSAN: You swear it?

JOSIAH: Most solemnly.

[*She links her arms around his neck, gazes at him.*]

SUSAN: You know, I'm shameless: given my choice now, I don't know which I'd take.

JOSIAH: Behave yourself, Susan.

[*She lifts her face to his and kisses him.* MIRANDA *re-enters from the balcony.*]

MIRANDA: Jock and Toby are now discussing Thankful as a wife and mother. They—[*She stops in her tracks.*] Oh, my darlings!

[JOSIAH *disengages himself.*]

JOSIAH: News, Miranda: your mother's going to marry Russell.

MIRANDA: Mother and Russell! But that's not at all what I—

JOSIAH: —What you what? Give her a hug and a kiss or I'll smack you.

[*A moment, then* MIRANDA *goes to* SUSAN *and kisses her.*]

MIRANDA: Every best of course, darling.

SUSAN: Thank you, my dear. Is your own—I mean, is your wedding dress in your—?

MIRANDA: On the bed. Go on up. I'll be there in a minute.

[SUSAN *moves toward the door, speaking over her shoulder to Josiah.*]

SUSAN: Good night, you monster.

JOSIAH: Good night, Jezebel.

SUSAN: Watch out for me—I'm tricky!

[*She laughs and goes out.* MIRANDA *waits an instant. Then*]

MIRANDA: But we simply can't allow it!

JOSIAH: How are we going to stop it? And why should we?

MIRANDA: I—I'll—! [*She turns swiftly and goes out, nearly colliding with* TOBY *coming in.*] Oh—sorry—

[TOBY *stands aside to let her pass.*]

TOBY: One crowded hour with thee, dear heart, one day of bliss—[*She is gone.* TOBY *moves to* JOSIAH.] Snitched from Malloy for you, sir: two telegrams and a book by special messenger. [*He glances at the wrapping of the book.*] Holy cats—look from who! I thought we were all good Protestants here.

JOSIAH: Thank you. [*He fumbles the telegrams open, murmuring:*] Very odd day. Very odd behavior all around. Something peculiar that I can't quite put my finger on. Maybe you—[*He reads one telegram, then the other.*] By God, it's insane! It'll be flowers next. All coming at me as if I were on my deathbed.

[*He tosses the telegrams onto the desk, rips the cover from the book, stares at it.* TOBY *grins.*]

TOBY: You've made it. You'll have to lie in it.

JOSIAH: What's that you say?

TOBY: Maybe you're thought to be critical, sir. Sometimes the cooling one is the last to realize.

JOSIAH: I'm afraid I don't—

[TOBY'*s grin broadens.*]

TOBY: Very dangerous, going shooting way out West. Particularly after a couple of such near ones—you know: those horrid little accidents.

JOSIAH: Well, for the love of God!

TOBY: Did I say something?

JOSIAH: So that's what they're up to with all their great solicitude! People! You mean to tell me they have some quaint idea that I'm planning to do myself in?

TOBY: I'm a stranger in these parts myself, sir.

JOSIAH: Never mind—I have ways of finding out! Of all the—it's an outrage! It's the most humiliating, most insulting—*I'll* teach them to jump to conclusions this way!

TOBY: Yes *sir!*

JOSIAH: I'll put a scare into them that will—! Toby, I haven't had a great deal of enjoyment out of life these past years. Here lately I've been laying low, looking deep, trying to get a line on myself. The nearest I've come to it is a bewildered sense that for a long time I've been living in a plaster cast of my own making—adding a thin little layer by layer day by day. If I don't break out of it soon, I'll damn well suffocate.

TOBY: Has happened, sir. My father says it's all in the attitude.—We had a grand old colored cook once. He asked her if something would be too much trouble. She said "Laws, no! Ah jes wears life lak a loose garment."

JOSIAH: That's it! That's the stuff: From now on, by all that's holy—[*After a moment*] Go tell Miranda and her mother I'm talking rather queerly, will you?

TOBY: Glad to.—I don't know whether you've noticed, but I'm nuts about your daughter, sir.

JOSIAH: My daughter is an overeducated moron!

[TOBY *moves toward the hall.*]

TOBY: I guess maybe that's why I'm how I am about her.

[*He goes out.* JOSIAH *takes off his coat, throws it on a chair, rolls up his sleeves. He goes to the gun cabinet, takes out a gun-cleaning kit, places it on a table beside a chair, returns to the cabinet, takes two cartridges from a box, replaces the box, lifts a double-barrelled shotgun from the rack, loads it, returns to the chair, seats himself with it between his knees, opens the cleaning kit and begins to prepare the implements. He has just soaked a swab in oil and is affixing it to a rod when* SUSAN *and* MIRANDA *appear in the doorway,* TOBY *behind them.* SUSAN *stops, transfixed, then cries out in horror:*]

SUSAN: Josiah!

[JOSIAH *looks up and inquires mildly:*]

JOSIAH: Yes, my dear?

[MIRANDA *moves to him with deliberate lack of haste.*]

SUSAN: Wha-what are you up to?

JOSIAH: They need it, after the damp summer. And I enjoy it. Lots of things I enjoy. Ah jes wears mah life lak a loose garment.

[SUSAN *hides her face, exclaims:*]

SUSAN: Oh—oh—too far—I knew it!

TOBY: I think it'll be all right, Mrs. Brook.

[*Very gently* MIRANDA *takes the gun from* JOSIAH *and weighs it in her hands.*]

MIRANDA: Is it the twelve-gauge or the twenty?

[*She sights it out of the window.*]

JOSIAH: The twelve.—Careful there!

[*She lowers the gun.*]

MIRANDA: Why? [*She breaks the gun and the two shells snap out of it.*] Father—for heaven's sake!

JOSIAH: I always keep them loaded. Haven't I often told you? It's safer. Then you know.

MIRANDA: Oh yes: now I remember.

JOSIAH: Give it here.

[MIRANDA *gives the gun to him. He proceeds with the cleaning.*]

MIRANDA: You need something heavier for mountain lion, don't you?

JOSIAH: Of course.—And a rifle: the thirty-thirty.

MIRANDA: I see.

JOSIAH: Do you know where to reach Clover O'Neil right now?

MIRANDA: Why yes, I think so. Why?

JOSIAH: Please call her for me and say I'd like her to dine with me uptown and will stop for her at eight promptly.

SUSAN: You—? Dine with—? I won't allow it!

MIRANDA [*Simultaneously*]: But Father! She's leaving for the Coast tomorrow, and most likely has a—

JOSIAH: —All the more reason. Say it's of the utmost importance and the breaking of any prior engagement is clearly indicated. [MIRANDA *stares. Suddenly he shouts:*] Well? Have you forgotten how to get things done for me?

[MIRANDA *goes to the desk.* TOBY *turns to* JOSIAH.]

TOBY: Wouldn't care to have us join you, maybe?

JOSIAH: Certainly. Later on. After dinner. Also Jock and Thankful. Somewhere with music.

TOBY: There must be some such place in New York.

[MIRANDA *dials a number and turns to* JOSIAH.]

MIRANDA: Now that you're at it, how about including Mother and Russ?

SUSAN: But I promised Russ I'd—

JOSIAH [*Simultaneously*]: No. Let's keep it young and sprightly.

[*He returns to the gun, begins humming to himself.*]

MIRANDA: Hello? I'd like to speak to Mrs. O'Neil, please.—Miss Brook.

[*Suddenly* JOSIAH *breaks into song:*]

JOSIAH:

"Although I'm rarely in the money,
It is really rather funny
How I always seem to land upon my feet."

[*Both feet pound the floor.* THANKFUL *comes in, followed by* JOCK. JOSIAH *interrupts his song:*] Hello, my darling. How pretty you look!

THANKFUL: Do I? Thank you, darling. You too.

JOSIAH: Then come and kiss me, sweet-and-twenty, Youth's a stuff will not endure.

[*He holds out his arms to her.* SHE *moves toward him, then stops.*]

THANKFUL: But sweetie—such a lot of people. [*She smiles upon him.*] Rain check?

JOSIAH: Rain check.

[*He drops his arms, returns to his gun.* JOCK *stands agaze.*]

SUSAN: Well, really!

MIRANDA: Clover? This is Miranda. Father wants to know—

JOCK: What cooks, Dad? Preparations for Mandy's wedding?

[*Again* JOSIAH *takes up his song:*]

JOSIAH:

"Oh I'm the strictly out-for-fun boy,
The look-out-for-Number-One boy,
The saving grace of humor I possess."

[*The song and* MIRANDA*'s telephone conversation go on simultaneously as* JOCK *and* SUSAN *stare and* THANKFUL *beams.*]

MIRANDA: —Whether you can have dinner with him—he's awfully urgent about it—and then we'll all join up later some place and—But break it! That's simple, and this is extremely—My dear, I tell you it's essential!

JOSIAH:

"Though I'm canny, cute and wily,
I still lead the life of Riley,
With a weather-eye out for damsels in distress—
Yes, yes!
Any dam-dam-double-dam damsel in distress!"

[*He looks up at them and declaims:*] "How now, Usumeasane! Is it not brave to be a king? Is it not passing brave to be a king and ride in triumph through Persepolis?"

CURTAIN

■ ACT II ■

SCENE II

The Library, about one o'clock the same night. The room is empty and dimly lighted by the one small lamp on the desk. The curtains at the windows are pulled. Here and there about the room there are a dozen small white pots of white geraniums, in full bloom. More light comes from the hall.

At rise, there is silence for a moment, then feet are heard coming up the stairs and THANKFUL *passes swiftly along the hall, followed instantly by* TOBY, *who catches her hand, jerks her to a stop and draws her just inside the room. Her hair is around her shoulders. She stands with her back to the wall, one foot up against it, pinioned there by* TOBY'*s arm across her shoulder.*

THANKFUL: I—I want to go to bed. I'm sleepy.

TOBY: Plenty of sleep later.

THANKFUL: Never enough for me.

TOBY: You also want to help *him,* don't you?

THANKFUL: Oh, you know how I!

TOBY: He asked me to arrange it: personal request. [*She looks inquiring*]—Better not to know till the time comes. It won't mean anything, except to the others. But you're on no account to let on to anyone—understand?

THANKFUL: Yes. But—

TOBY: But, but, but!—All you have to do is—how many ways do you know how to say Yes?

THANKFUL: I—I'm afraid too many.

TOBY: That's fine, that's just daisy. That's all there is to it. Just be the yea sayer.

THANKFUL: Whatever he says to me, I—?

TOBY: You answer yes. But vary it. Make it real. Put your heart into it. Shouldn't be hard for you. You've got a big one.

THANKFUL: But no brain?

TOBY: You know, sometimes I wonder.

[*Suddenly she ducks her head and lets her hair fall over her face, practically into his face.*]

THANKFUL: Want to feel some silk?

[TOBY *passes his hand over the lovely stuff.*]

TOBY: I'll take the whole bolt. Wrap 'er up, honey.

[JOCK *comes in from the hall, switches the rest of the lamps on from the doorway.*]

JOCK: What are you doing with my girl?

TOBY: The night is made for love and laughter. [*He moves from her.*] Not back yet?

JOCK: Dad? Nope. Not a sign. Must have taken her home by way of Harlem.—Say, she's something, isn't she?

TOBY: Yea.

[THANKFUL *wanders to the sofa.*]

THANKFUL: She's everything I'd ever like to be in all my life.

JOCK: You just be yourself, Thanks. That'll do real nice. [*He joins her on the sofa, turns to* TOBY.] Look: Miranda's on the pantry phone, talking to London.

TOBY: Sure enough?

JOCK: Don't you want to break it up?

TOBY: You know I'd never dream of that.

[*He moves swiftly to the hall and out.* THANKFUL *stares in front of her.*]

JOCK: What's the matter, little fellah?

THANKFUL: I'm sad.

JOCK: Don't be.

THANKFUL: I can't help it. London's miles, and I'm practically there.

JOCK: You'll be back.

THANKFUL: I wish I was all married up and settled down right here.

JOCK: Fact?

THANKFUL: With six babies.

JOCK: Six?

THANKFUL: Yes. I think they're almost the nicest pets there are, don't you?

JOCK: Six is a lot of pets. [*A moment. Then*] Wasn't Father a howl with that goldfish act?

THANKFUL: You know something, Jock?

JOCK: What?

THANKFUL: I'm not nearly so worried about him as I was.

JOCK: How's that?

THANKFUL: From something that happened there in that night club.

JOCK: The jokes? And the trick with the dime and the wineglass? I'll admit he seemed—but it's just all part of the swan song, Mandy says.

THANKFUL: This had nothing to do with any swan. It was when I—I sort of accidentally touched his foot with mine under the table, and—[*She rubs her knee reflectively.*]—And—well, I just want to say *I* don't think your father's anywhere near dead!
[JOCK *laughs.*]

JOCK: Brazen little—of course, if you want to ask for trouble!

THANKFUL: I was sabotaged to the quick.

JOCK: All men are beasts, especially when kicked into being.

THANKFUL: —I'm still sad.—To think that by noon tomorrow we'll be bounding on the main.

JOCK: Noon today.—I'll miss you like a ton of bricks, Thanks.

THANKFUL: I'll move mountains and molehills to get back by September.

JOCK: By then we certainly ought to know how serious we are.

THANKFUL: I certainly wouldn't want to be a millstone around the neck of your career.

JOCK: You wouldn't. You couldn't. I've told you how, if I could simply train a stooge—I mean a partner—who'd—[MIRANDA *comes in, followed by* TOBY.] How's His Nibs, Mandy? Just having morning tea in bed?

MIRANDA: He seemed so far away. [*She seats herself, gazes vacantly in front of her. One can almost see the self-assurance go out of her and the bewilderment and apprehension take its place*] All I hope is that I made him understand.

TOBY: All that clattering of mine in the icebox. I'm—

MIRANDA: —It didn't matter. Thankful, I'm sorrier than I can say, but I just can't leave things here the way they are. You'll have to sail alone tomorrow.

THANKFUL: Oh dear. I knew it.

MIRANDA: I'll follow by air when I can, if I can. I swear I'll make it up to you somehow.

THANKFUL: I don't need any making up to for.

JOCK [*To* MIRANDA]: I thought Father was in great shape. Dinner with the O'Neil seemed to have worked wonders.

MIRANDA: Don't you know real desperation when you see it, Jock?

JOCK: No. I guess I don't. I did think they might both be a little bit squiffed.

MIRANDA: Not in the least. Not possibly. Father never. Not even in Russia. It was different, so different! Oh, I know I've been every kind of a fool: first Mother and Russ, then bringing him and Clover, with their awful sense of guilt, together.—But what are we going to do? What *are* we? He's right at the end of his rope, I can tell. *You* don't believe that because you don't want to. Well—do you suppose it's something *I* want to?

[*There is a silence. Then* JOCK *speaks gently.*]

JOCK: A little hard to say. Without knowing it, it just might be. [*She turns and stares at him.*] What I mean is, he's been blocking your—international alliance and so forth, hasn't he?—Nice, direct way to remove the obstruction.

THANKFUL: Gracious!

MIRANDA: That's all I needed to hear, Jock.

TOBY: You're talking through your hat, boy.

JOCK: You think?

TOBY: I know.

MIRANDA: Thanks, Toby. Thanks very much, I'm sure.

TOBY: Not at all. Merely a comment.

[JOSIAH *comes in from the hall, very bright, very brisk.*]

JOSIAH: What, what, what! Still up? Still conscious?

TOBY: Just.

JOSIAH: What of the morrow, Toby?

TOBY: I called my landlady. There was a wire from my father. He's due back at noon. Which means I get my month off now.

JOSIAH: Splendid! Why not ship aboard with the girls?

TOBY: There's a little question of the fare.

JOSIAH: Forget it. I know the Captain. Book third, and enjoy first-class privileges.

TOBY: Of first-class privileges, I am capable of great enjoyment.

JOSIAH: Just let me know before sailing time. Thankful's plans, of course, are subject to—[*He takes a small box from his pocket and presents it to her.*]—For you, Thankful.

THANKFUL: Yes—?

JOSIAH: From a lovely lady, with her congratulations.

THANKFUL: A little gold four-leaf clover!

JOSIAH: She keeps a stock on hand, for special persons.

JOCK: Congratulations on what?

JOSIAH: Chiefly for being herself, she said. [*There is a silence. He stands gazing at them for a moment, then speaks:*] All so mortally young. Can it be that I hanker after youth? In my lifetime, I wanted four children: two boys, two girls. I was not vouchsafed them. How do you do?

[*And turns away abruptly. They exchange glances. Then*]

MIRANDA: Malloy left a message: Mother called three times: eleven-forty, twelve-fifteen, one o'clock.

JOSIAH: Sweet of her to send me all these white geraniums.

MIRANDA: She—she must have remembered how you love them.

JOSIAH: All living, breathing plants. Leaf and branch, root and stem, pushing up, pushing up.—So unfunereal. [*Suddenly he wheels upon* JOCK.] What did you say?

JOCK: Me? Not a thing.

[JOSIAH *takes a gold cigarette case from his pocket, looks at it.*]

JOSIAH: Jock, you've often admired this cigarette-case—

JOCK: —Sure have.

JOSIAH: I'd like you to have it.

JOCK: But—but Dad—

[JOSIAH *hands it to him.*]

JOSIAH: Think nothing of it.

JOCK: I'll think a great deal of it.

[JOSIAH *leans back against the desk, folds his arms, gazes into space. Finally he speaks:*]

JOSIAH: Once, as a young man, I made the trip down the Saguenay River in Canada. The guidebook said, "This voyage is made over seemingly bottomless waters, between the twin cliffs of Eternity and Trinity—"

MIRANDA: Really? That's quite lovely.

JOSIAH: It added, cynically and lamely, "which rise on either side to a height of nearly two thousand feet." I can't tell you how the statement depressed me. Beauty once more destroyed by the factual, majesty made piddling by definition, life to the letter—brutal, intolerable—appalling, appalling—how do we endure it? [*Suddenly he moves to the windows.*] Who closed these curtains? Aways—always let in the air! Curtains—walls—fences! Ceilings—roofs—clouds—thunderheads! Ceiling zero—sub-zero—grounded—grounded—[*He yanks the curtain cord. The curtains swing open, but the long cord breaks and dangles from his hand.*] What! Again?—Malloy—where's Malloy?

MIRANDA: A-asleep, I expect.

JOSIAH: —A little sleep, a little slumber, a little folding of the hands in sleep.

[*He stands staring at the cord.* JOCK *speaks softly to* MIRANDA*:*]

JOCK: I take back what I said.

MIRANDA: I wish to heaven you hadn't to.

TOBY: Heaven's where the heart is, and mine is in the highlands.

[JOSIAH *wheels on him.*]

JOSIAH: What? What say?

TOBY: Nothing—just maundering, sir.

[JOSIAH *picks up a pair of long scissors from the desk, looks at them reflectively, then snips the brass weight from the end of the cord, advances to the center of the room, sinks down and sits cross-legged among them, twisting the cord in his hands.*]

JOSIAH: When I was a boy of twelve, there was a skipper of a fishing smack in Georgian Bay who taught me sailor knots. That was some time ago. I wonder do I still remember?—Also Jock, get out that first scrapbook, will you? There are snapshots of that old German Benz I bought and put in shape.—God, the joy I took in that car! How old was I then? It was the second year I was married, the year I won my first big case. Me at the wheel, little Miranda on the seat beside me. See if you can find it.—Thankful? Come here, my dear—sit by my side.

THANKFUL: Yes?

JOSIAH: —Yes. Toby—?

TOBY: Sir?

JOSIAH: If you please—a cushion for her little bottom.

TOBY: Catch—

JOSIAH: Caught! Hook, line and sinker. Lock, stock and barrel. Aber, Crombie and Fitch. [*He reaches up for her hand and draws her down to the cushion at his side.*] Comfortable, pretty one?

THANKFUL: Ever so.

JOSIAH: If not, consult my lawyers: Weary, Stale, Flat and Unprofitable.

[JOCK *gives him an opened album.*]

JOCK: Here you are. Pretty rakish in that two-way visored cap.

JOSIAH: Ah, the little beauty!—Not you, Miranda. You were a plain baby: the car. You were my ewe lamb but it was the apple of my eye.

MIRANDA: I—I'm jealous.

[*He shows the picture to* THANKFUL.]

THANKFUL: Divine. But you look positively unformed.

JOSIAH: —You know, I wouldn't care if I never saw another radish.—You like me better as I am now?

THANKFUL: No comparison.

[*He gives her a brief hug.*]

JOSIAH: That's my girl. [*and removes the snapshot from the album.*] I wanted it to show Clover. She starts out for the Coast tomorrow in a ten-year-old Bentley she picked up in Syosset. Reconditioned, of course. Speed on the road's another enthusiasm we share.

THANKFUL: Now I'm jealous too.

[JOSIAH *again begins twisting at the cord.*]

JOSIAH: Flying can't touch it: there just aren't the hazards.—Never be jealous—anyone of anything. I knew a man once who was married to a jealous wife for more than twenty years. Not just of other women, but of his time, his thoughts, even of his work. The aim was to domesticate—to reduce him to the status of a tame cat by the fire. It nearly did for him. It did do for the marriage. [*He holds out a knot for* THANKFUL *to see.*] This is a simple double hitch.

THANKFUL: Is it? Of course if you say so—

JOSIAH: I do and with considerable conviction.

JOCK: Is Clover's Bentley an open job?

JOSIAH: What they used to call a phaeton. All motor: four-and-a-half litre. It still ought to do a hundred and ten. We're giving it a road test in the morning, to make sure all the bugs are out.

JOCK: Early?

JOSIAH: Fairly. Ladybug, ladybug, fly away—

JOCK: —Where?

JOSIAH: I thought the Merritt Parkway.

JOCK: Front wheels raked?

JOSIAH: I expect so.

JOCK: Right-hand drive?

JOSIAH: As original: unconverted.

JOCK: Roll over in one of those and you're through.

JOSIAH: The aim is to remain on the road, and upright. [*To* THANKFUL] Tell me—you liked Clover, too?

THANKFUL: I think she's delicious. She seems to make everything around her sort of gay.—And still she's—you know—reposeful: doesn't at all lack languor.—Yes. I liked her.

JOSIAH: You have another trait in common.

THANKFUL: Yes? I mean do we?

JOSIAH: Yes. You're a true innocent. So is she.

[MIRANDA *laughs briefly.*]

MIRANDA: Innocent—that one!

JOSIAH: *An* innocent, I said. Noun, not adjective. It's a state of being. They are rare in this world the true innocents—born without original sin, I expect—at least without the sense of guilt that rides the rest of us. Whatever their age, they never grow old. They live and breathe youth and impart it to others. They are the life givers.—This is called a bowline-on-a-bight.

[*He unties the knot and begins on another.*]

MIRANDA: It was something but life she gave Uncle Andy.

JOSIAH: No. I'm aware now that Andy died of his years. He was born old. He belonged in an earlier century. He was an anachronism. He was a romantic—it was his own heroics that finally brought him down. Now I know why I felt so oddly relieved when he died—

MIRANDA: Relieved! Do you know what you're saying?

JOSIAH: I do indeed—and no longer ashamed of it! One must belong to the times: live them, write them, paint them: he never did. God help him if he'd lived longer: every year would have been one worse for him. He would not learn, he could not learn. All he could do was to dwell in the past, enraged at the present, full of fear of the future. Poor boy—poor old man—but I'm glad he died when he did, as he did, with a gesture.

MIRANDA: Aren't you—aren't you protesting too much, Father?

JOSIAH: My dear girl, there are times when your smattering of—! No! And all I am *not* glad about is the man unjustly in prison for his death.

MIRANDA: I give up. It beats me.

JOSIAH: For me, it does quite the opposite. [*He looks at the new knot in his hands.*]—Whereas *this* one—now what would this be?

JOCK: Look, Dad—that's no sailor's knot.

JOSIAH: No?

JOCK: No.

[*He takes it from him, examines it.*]

JOSIAH: What would you call it then?

JOCK: Looks more like a hangman's noose to me.

JOSIAH: Really? How odd. How very odd. What could I have had in mind? Sam Foster? Or another person or persons more truly responsible?

[JOCK *crams the cord into his pocket.*]

JOCK: I don't know. Look: it's late. Hadn't we all better hit the hay?

JOSIAH: Now? Why, the night's young!—I seem to have heard that somewhere—[*He leans back on his hands and gazes at the ceiling.*] O there's a woman like a dewdrop, she's so purer than the purest.—Youth—youth—what is there more precious?

JOCK: What is so rare as a day in June?

THANKFUL: I knew *that* one: a Chinaman with whiskers.

JOSIAH: —He was wrong, the man who said of youth that no one knows its value until he's too old to enjoy it. The great, the astonishing thing about it is that it may be enjoyed twice: once through one's own, later—and better—through that of another. [*He rises and faces them.*] Jock—Miranda—I have news for you. Steel yourselves.

JOCK: Oh? What's that?

JOSIAH: Let's turn somersaults, let's swim out to the raft, let's go crabbing, let's have an ice-cream soda: the hermit has emerged from his cave, the monk from his cell: centurion though he be, your father has a girl.

[*There is a silence. Then*]

JOCK: Dad, I grant you she's a knockout. But you certainly work fast.

JOSIAH: Time is of the essence.—And very soon, if all goes as expected—

MIRANDA: —A girl! She's thirty-eight if she's a day!

JOSIAH: Thirty-eight? Thankful?

[*Then*]

MIRANDA: Thankful!

JOCK: What the living—?

JOSIAH: —Living, yes! Breathing, laughing, loving—and my own! [*He reaches for* THANKFUL*'s hand, draws her to her feet beside him.*] True, my darling—?

THANKFUL: Yes.

JOCK: You actually mean to say you and Father—?

THANKFUL: Yes! Yes, I do!

MIRANDA: But it's insane! You must realize he's old enough to—to—

[*She falters and stops.*]

JOSIAH: —Isn't that a little odd, coming from you?

MIRANDA: If you're referring to Matthew and me, there's a difference!

JOSIAH: In age, I know. But otherwise?

MIRANDA: I'm not Thankful.

JOSIAH: True—true, you're not. [*He laughs and turns to* THANKFUL.] That would be a little awkward, wouldn't it, dear?

THANKFUL: It certainly would.

[*He puts his hands on her shoulders and turns her toward him.*]

JOSIAH: You *are* quite sure of your—feelings?

THANKFUL: You know I am.

JOSIAH: Certain that you care enough?

THANKFUL: More than!

MIRANDA: Look here, Father—

JOSIAH: Would you deny me it, Miranda? One last—

MIRANDA: —You needn't throw that in my teeth! This is beyond anything I ever—Thankful, you mean to say you can stand there and deliberately tell me that you and Father—?

[THANKFUL *strikes a defiant attitude.*]

THANKFUL: Yes! A thousand times yes!

JOCK: There's just one thing I'd like to know—No—never mind.

MIRANDA: I give up twice.

TOBY: I guess you and Atwater have more or less set the pace, Miranda.

THANKFUL: She and Uncle Matthew have nothing to do with it. I know my own mind—yes, and nobody think I haven't got one, either!

JOSIAH: It's all right if we decide tomorrow as to whether you sail to tell him in person, or—?

THANKFUL: —Anything you say.

JOSIAH: No, my dear—anything you do. Sleep on it, Sweet. You've been through a lot today.

THANKFUL: I—I *am* terribly sort of sleepy, really. I'm really comparatively entirely pooped . . .

[*He raises her face and kisses her gently.*]

JOSIAH: Good night, good night—and may heaven's brightest angels watch over thee.

THANKFUL: Thee too.

[*She pats his cheek lightly, smiles, turns and moves toward the hall passing* TOBY, *who murmurs:*]

TOBY: Duse.

THANKFUL: What?

TOBY: Dese-a, dos-a, dat-a.

THANKFUL: You're crazy.

[*She proceeds on her way.* JOSIAH *calls after her:*]

JOSIAH: Till the morning then, my darling?

[*She turns in the doorway and flings out a hand toward him.*]

THANKFUL: Oh, yes! Yes, yes!

[*She goes out. There is a moment's silence. Then*]

TOBY: May I offer my congratulations, sir?

JOSIAH: Thank you, Toby.—Miranda?

MIRANDA: You—you honestly think it's fair to her?

JOSIAH: That's something one can never be sure of, my dear. A short spell as an old man's darling may be a rewarding experience. Who knows but that she may speak kindly of me, when I am one with Nineveh and Tyre? [*He chuckles, then turns to* JOCK.] Well, Jock—you don't seem to have much to say.

JOCK: It's a little hard for me to get my mind around. You see, I had quite a sneaker for her myself.

JOSIAH: Sorry, son. I didn't know.

JOCK: Anyhow, it'll be nice having her in the family.

JOSIAH: I'm glad you haven't lost your sense of humor.

JOCK: Oh, go climb a tree, will you? [*He takes the cord from his pocket and tosses it to him.*]—And you might take this with you! [JOSIAH *laughs, drops the noose on a table.* JOCK *goes out, exclaiming:*] Women! You can have the lot of them.—*And* six babies!

MIRANDA [*After a moment*]: I—I do want you to know that I'm for anything that will make you happy, Father.

JOSIAH: Thank you, Daughter. That's good to hear. [*The telephone rings. He goes to it.*] I must admit that life had become very dull for me. But they do say that even a stopped clock is right twice a day. [*Then, to the telephone*] Yes? Hello?—Oh—Susan.—Yes, but I thought it was a little late to call you back. Very grateful to you for the floral display. They're very pretty. What? A street-cart? How like old times! All the lovelier.—What?—But of course—go right ahead. [*Another moment, then more slowly*] Oh, I'm sorry. I am sorry. I thought you and he completely—really? How distressing.—No, the fact is I have an early appointment that will keep me until—expecting you both for late breakfast, you know, before Miranda's sailing. [TOBY *glances at* MIRANDA. *She gestures him to silence.*] I see. Perhaps if you could give me some inkling now—[*Again he listens, then speaks gravely:*] I see.—But of course you may have misunderstood him.—I say it may all be in your imagination. [*He listens further, begins to smile.*] I tell you what, dear: I'm wide awake as an owl and you sound the same. I'll hop in the car and come uptown directly. We'll have a meeting of the minds.—Absolutely!—The Fifty-eighth Street side? Good. What's your room number?—Got it. Fifteen minutes, not more. [*He hangs up and turns to* MIRANDA.] Are the keys in your car?

MIRANDA: On the hall table.

JOSIAH: Leave word for Malloy to call me at six, will you?

MIRANDA: That doesn't give you much sleep.

JOSIAH: We're a long time asleep, child!

MIRANDA: What's wrong with Mother?

JOSIAH: A number of things. But the present one is, she thinks she's discovered that Russell prefers his bachelorhood.

MIRANDA: *I* think she's discovered that she prefers you.

JOSIAH: Now wouldn't that be embarrassing? Wouldn't that be the—? [*He fingers his necktie.*] Bow ties irritate Susan. Perhaps I'd better change to one. [*He moves to* MIRANDA, *takes her by the shoulders, gazes solemnly into her eyes.*] Miranda, since Thankful—how shall I say it?—Well, I understand much better than I did. And I want you to know that you're the finest and most rewarding daughter a man ever had. [*He kisses her upon the brow.*] Bless you, child—and bless anyone you choose to cast your lot with, including Matthew Atwater. —Breakfast at ten sharp.

[*He goes swiftly out. There is a brief silence. Then* MIRANDA *gasps.*]

MIRANDA: I'm scared!

TOBY: What for? What of?

MIRANDA: Oh Toby, I'm scared pink! He's never been so—so final. And giving me his blessing!

TOBY: But isn't that nice to have for a girl?

MIRANDA: You don't understand!—Oh, if only I'd waited. If I hadn't bullheadedly rushed things. That old guide in Arizona—maybe he's old and wise. Maybe he'd have talked him out of it. Maybe he's guide, philosopher and friend. He'll never in this world marry Thankful—he has too much dignity.—Or has he, now?—Yes, the most—the worst he'll do is make a monkey out of her and then himself. There was a little Danish countess once, but she had a husband. Oh—and then his conscience! Oh Toby—instead of preventing it, I—I think I've hastened it!

TOBY: What?

MIRANDA: The end.

TOBY: Funny—right now I'd say he has a better than average expectancy.

MIRANDA: You don't know—you just don't know! Oh, didn't he have enough troubles, without my—? And now Mother—Thankful—Clover—Russell and Jock, too—

TOBY: Quite a busy life—all at once: may keep him interested.

MIRANDA: I tell you he's desperate! You heard the way he talked—it wasn't sane—oh, it just broke my heart—it was so utterly distracted.

TOBY: I thought that suddenly he was saying what came to mind. That's good. I'd prescribe that.

MIRANDA: —Toby—you missed the point! You did! How could you?—And that damned fast car in the morning—whatever they say, they both do feel responsible for Uncle Andy. And you don't realize what a part expiation plays. Anyhow, they're both so damned reckless—anything could happen—I'm so scared that something will. Oh, I'm a wreck myself, I'm just a wreck—[*Suddenly she puts both arms around him and her head against his chest.*] Let me do this for a moment, will you?

TOBY: Go right ahead.

MIRANDA: You know—just friendlywise.

TOBY: Friendly, certainly. But as to wise—

MIRANDA: Don't get any false ideas. You won't, will you?

TOBY: Hell no. Not me.

MIRANDA: Understand—if you were just a post, I'd cling to you.

TOBY: O.K., I'm a post—hitch thou onto me.

MIRANDA: I've balled everything up so terribly. I feel so awful.

TOBY: You're wrong. You feel good.

MIRANDA: Don't make jokes.

TOBY: It's no joke.

MIRANDA: I'm so tired. All last night I just thrashed around.

TOBY: One whole night? Desperate.—Hypo, Nurse. Repeat if necessary.

[*Now his arms are lightly around her and they are rocking slightly to and fro.*]

MIRANDA: Toby, I don't like myself any more. Not for a damn, I don't.

TOBY: Maybe I like you enough for two.

MIRANDA: Somebody better—somebody, please—I wish I was dead. I'm tired—Oh Toby, I'm tired—

TOBY: You've just got brain strain. Sit here—[*He draws her to the sofa. She sits stiffly upright beside him.*] No: that only aggravates it. The perpendicular is known to increase tension. Whereas the horizontal—[*He leans back into a corner of the sofa and draws her head down upon his shoulder.*] Feet up. Swing 'em around, Nurse! Come, come—where did you train? [MIRANDA*'s head works more comfortably into his shoulder.*] That's it. That's the stuff. This isn't sex, Madam, it's medicine.

[*Her voice becomes drowsier.*]

MIRANDA: Make no mistake—about that—just you—make no mistake.

TOBY: Not me. Not T. H. Wells, M.D.—good friend and wise physician. —Big body-and-fender man.

MIRANDA: You *are* a good friend, Toby. Always be my friend, please.

TOBY: Sure thing. Now do as the nice doctor says. Take deep breaths. Close your eyes. Above all, shut your mouth.

MIRANDA: I guess—I just don't want any of you—throwing yourselves away on a pretty little nitwit like Thankful. Although I *am* fond of her—remember that.

TOBY: You certainly couldn't possibly be jealous of her—

MIRANDA: —Should say not.

TOBY: Is she descended from Cotton Mather, do you suppose?

MIRANDA: —Shouldn't be surprised.

TOBY: I think *he* might be.

MIRANDA: If life just wouldn't be so complicated.—It didn't used to be.—Remember the autumn day we went—cranberrying at Christmas Cove.

TOBY: I remember.

MIRANDA: And I—got stuck in the bog—and you were right there—with both arms to hoist me out?—You were pretty fresh even in those days.

TOBY: Hell, woman, in those days I *was* fresh! Now, most likely, I'd just let you sink.

MIRANDA: Sink, sank, sunk.—I'm sunk now, Toby, I'm so sunk.—You would not.—You'd no such thing.—You'd help me. You'd always help me.

TOBY: Only maybe.

MIRANDA: Though why anyone wants to marry me—any such—ignoramus—me—I don't know—

TOBY: It's certainly a mystery to me, too. Of course you can never tell about Englishmen.

[*She lifts a limp hand.*]

MIRANDA: See my pretty ring.

TOBY: Window glass.

MIRANDA: It was his great-grandmother's.

TOBY: She went around breaking windows at her age?

MIRANDA: I'm going to be—good wife—Matthew, Toby.

TOBY: Go right ahead.

MIRANDA: He was so sweet on—telephone—tonight—so understanding. And I had—most wonderful letter—him this morning. He write like—he writes the way he talks—he does do both so brilliantly—so eq-eqloquently—

TOBY: While you're at it, why not have a go at Churchill?

MIRANDA: Isn't he married?

TOBY: Anyhow, when it comes second-husband time, give a thought to home folks, Mandy.

[*She yawns*]

MIRANDA: Don't be silly. You're being silly.—But you're nice. I like you. I do like you. I like you better than me. [*and settles her head still deeper into his shoulder.*] Tell me a story, Toby—

TOBY: What about?

MIRANDA [*Now a small girl, half asleep, fading fast*] Anything—just a story. You're an animal—tell me—animal story—

[*A moment. Then* TOBY *begins:*]

TOBY: Remember how I told you that after that first accident, we went over your father like a dog for ticks?

MIRANDA: I remember—

TOBY: —Well, once upon a time—about eight o'clock this morning—a young woman, aged twenty-five, was admitted to the—hospital for observation. Rapid pulse, temperature one-o-one and two-fifths, respiration normal, but with a most beautiful and extensive rash. Measles and scarlet fever ruled out: both present in childhood. Upon routine questioning, the patient was determined to be from the south shore of Long Island and the possessor of two small, long-haired dogs, pets, of the Skye-terrier breed. These animals she cared for herself, exercising great pains to remove ticks twice daily, it being full tick season in that area. She had not worn gloves nor employed any mechanical aids. It was a clear and truly magnificent case of Rocky Mountain spotted fever, formerly, in humans very often fatal, certainly of a very high mortality. But happily we now—and really just now—possess an antibiotic of remarkable efficacy called Aureomycin. And in a comparatively short time the woman will be discharged completely cured and, we hope, somewhat wiser about the always dangerous occupation of removing ticks from any animal barehanded. Wonderful stuff, these new drugs. But in many cases, if I had to choose between them and the will to live, I'd take the old original. And what do you think of that, for instance? [*There is no answer.*] I say, what do you think of—? [*And still no answer. He cocks his head at her.*] You mean you don't think a thing? [*She is silent, sleeping peacefully. He grins, speaks softly*] That's fine. All the same, it's nice we have both.—All the same, that rash wasn't pretty.—You're so pretty. Darling, if you ever have pups, promise me you'll be awfully careful with them, won't you?

[JOSIAH *comes a step into the room from the hall. He now wears a jaunty bow tie. He glances at the semirecumbent pair and gestures questioningly to* TOBY. TOBY *raises his hand and makes the thumb-and-forefinger "O" gesture in return.* JOSIAH *smiles, fixes a geranium flower in his buttonhole, turns in the doorway, returns the same gesture to* TOBY, *and goes out.*]

CURTAIN

■ ACT II ■

SCENE III

The library, a little before ten the following morning, Monday, a bright day. The windows are open, as is the door to the front room. THANKFUL *is standing against the wall in much the same position as at the beginning of the preceding scene, only now it is* JOCK *who pinions her there. He is half-dressed, still without coat or necktie, and in bedroom slippers. A moment, then*

JOCK: Well?

THANKFUL: I'm hungry. I want my breakfast.

JOCK: We're all having it together at ten. You can wait ten minutes.

THANKFUL: I don't know.

JOCK: —Just tell me that there's nothing in it.

THANKFUL: In what?

JOCK: In what—in what!—In you and Father, of course.

THANKFUL: How can I answer questions and finish packing, with my tum right flat against my back?

JOCK: Packing.—Then it's settled. You *are* going.

THANKFUL: Yes.

JOCK: Miranda too?

THANKFUL: I haven't seen her yet. She was up and out—I don't know where—before you—you sailed in.

JOCK: Listen: I paced the floor half the night—didn't you hear me pacing?

THANKFUL: I didn't hear anything.

JOCK: Well, I did. And I arrived at certain conclusions.

THANKFUL [*A wail*]: Jock—I'm hungry!

JOCK: Answer what I ask and I'll see that you get something.

THANKFUL: Just tea and toast and orange juice—then I don't care *when* I have breakfast!

JOCK: I decided there'd been something screwy about—

THANKFUL: —Did you?

JOCK: See? You know there was!

THANKFUL: I didn't say that.

JOCK: I figured what I'd been seeing was a pretty good act put on—

THANKFUL: —Well, you did say if you could train up a partner— [*Her hand flies to her mouth.*]

JOCK: You admit it!

THANKFUL: I do not, I do not!

JOCK: You were in cahoots with Dad.

THANKFUL: I was no such thing. I don't even know what it means. "Cahoots."

JOCK: With someone, then. [*Suddenly he snaps his fingers and points.*] Toby!

THANKFUL: Don't do that. It makes my insides jump. [*She attempts to snap her own fingers.*] I never could. I can't whistle either. I'm useless. [*She smiles winningly at him.*] Do you think I'm useless?

JOCK: —Which means that *he* knows and Father knows.—Yes, and that you know too!

THANKFUL: I never really thought he would.

JOCK: Why not?

THANKFUL: —Not after I knew him, that is. And I think that's sort of something I'd know about someone.

JOCK: What makes Miranda, then?

THANKFUL: I suppose much as we love him, she loves him ten times more. It's like having your own pet sick: you get scared.

JOCK: That leaves Mother and Russell: they seemed to believe it all right.

THANKFUL: That's Miranda again. She could convince anyone of anything, at least for a while. She convinced me first semester I ought to take Eurythmics.

[MALLOY *comes in from the hall with letters on a tray.*]

MALLOY: You asked me to let you know when your father—

JOCK: —Where is he?

MALLOY: I told him that Mr. Evans had been walking the garden for some time—how that man walks! So he went to—[*He glances down into the garden.*] No. They must have come inside. Mr. Evans looked quite tense.

[JOCK *takes* THANKFUL*'s hand and draws her quickly toward the balcony.*]

JOCK: Come on—this way! Clear for them!

THANKFUL: But I—

JOCK: Food, child. [THANKFUL *accelerates her pace.* JOCK *calls back over his shoulder:*] Clear, Malloy!

MALLOY: All in good time. All in good time. [JOCK *and* THANKFUL *go out.* MALLOY *arranges the letters on the desk.* JOSIAH *and* RUSSELL *come in from the hall.* MALLOY *moves toward the hall.*] Morning mail on the desk, sir.

JOSIAH: Thank you, Malloy.

MALLOY: I'll be doing your bags now.

JOSIAH: No great rush. You know what I'll be wanting to take?

MALLOY: I think so. If I'm in any doubt—

JOSIAH: —Yes. Do that.

[MALLOY *goes out.* JOSIAH *moves to the desk, seats himself there.* RUSSELL *follows him halfway across the room and stands confronting him.*]

RUSSELL: Susan ought to be here. She said she'd come early.

JOSIAH: You've talked to her this morning?

RUSSELL: A little before nine. Miranda was with her then. She said they'd both—

[JOSIAH *speaks mildly, glancing at the mail.*]

JOSIAH: —I'm afraid I can't take the blame for your entire lack of enlightenment. And it's hardly my fault if you give her the impression that you prefer your single blessedness.

RUSSELL: That's not the case, and you know it!

JOSIAH: No, I really don't. Actually your singleness *is* pretty damned blessed, isn't it?

RUSSELL: Never mind that!

JOSIAH: But it appears I'm obliged to mind it. By you. By Susan.—Though why it should be my responsibility—

RUSSELL: You went to Susan's hotel late last night.

JOSIAH: So I did.

RUSSELL: Are we friends or are we not?

JOSIAH: I thought so.

RUSSELL: It was a deliberately unfriendly thing to do.

[MIRANDA *has come in. She turns to go out.*]

MIRANDA: —Sorry.

JOSIAH: Sit down, my dear, sit down.

RUSSELL: Yes, by all means.

[MIRANDA *drops into a chair near the door, sits there.*]

MIRANDA: Mother had to stop for something for the country. She—

[RUSSELL *turns to* JOSIAH.]

RUSSELL: —You were there with her for some time.

JOSIAH: An hour—a little more—who knows? Time passes quickly with Sue. We talked. There was nothing you or your client could remotely take exception to.

RUSSELL: Except that now she says she's considering remarrying you.

JOSIAH: Really? I'm not sure I'm averse to it. Would you be?
MIRANDA: What about Thankful?
JOSIAH: I'm thinking perhaps I ought to retire in favor of Jock.
MIRANDA: I'm not sure he can make it.
JOSIAH: An unpleasant thought has occurred: that her attraction to me is mainly due to the fact that I'm just a block off the old chip.
MIRANDA: I wouldn't count on that.
JOSIAH: *Are* you averse, Russ?—I mean, of course, except for the immunities and privileges of your ecstatic bachelorhood.
RUSSELL: To hell with my bachelorhood!
JOSIAH: I hope you're not saying that lightly: it's a very precious thing. I must also advise Jock to that effect.—No family cares—no responsibilities: I'm inclined to envy you.
RUSSELL: Are you indeed?
JOSIAH: Yes. In a way, it may have been what I was trying to get back to: the vantage point for another crack at life—but this time free, clear, unobstructed.
RUSSELL: All right, you're there. Go to it.
JOSIAH: I don't know.
MIRANDA: I think I've learned a lot about life these last two days.
JOSIAH: Good!
MIRANDA: I think it's an unholy mess.
JOSIAH: Always an open question, wide open.
MIRANDA: All the same, Father, if this is a real defection of Russell's, I'd be careful.
JOSIAH: Of what?
MIRANDA: Mother. Knowing your weakness for the lady-in-distress, she just might be using it to get at you.
JOSIAH: Really, Miranda, I'm sure your mother—
MIRANDA: —Wouldn't she though! I told you I'd been discovering—
JOSIAH: Mind your tongue, my dear.
MIRANDA: Yes—you've made a rule for yourself: never a word against her, haven't you?
JOSIAH: There aren't any. The only failing she might have is a certain essential you know—a kind of duplicity. But to offset it she possesses great decorum, and a debonair quality that rarely deserts her.
MIRANDA: Never—so long as she gets her own way.
JOSIAH: Miranda—
MIRANDA: I remember once, when I was little, she deliberately put jam

on my face before the tea guests came. She thought it went with the pinafore and would make for amusement.

JOSIAH: I consider that charming.

MIRANDA: I don't.—And not being the jam-faced type, I wiped it off and she was livid with me.

RUSSELL: That's a curious grudge to hold.

MIRANDA: There were other things.

JOSIAH: You're talking nonsense, Miranda. Your mother is a wonderful woman.

MIRANDA: Fearful and wonderful.

JOSIAH: —In fact, about the best that comes. So if she should really want to marry me again—

RUSSELL: —But she doesn't!

JOSIAH: I'd do a great deal for you, Russ. But it's only fair to warn you I'd be unwilling to re-establish the old setup. I think it would serve no useful purpose.

RUSSELL: There never was any "setup" as you call it. Didn't we make that clear yesterday?

JOSIAH: You attempted to.

RUSSELL: Damn your eyes, Jo.

MIRANDA: And damn yours, you old bore, with your—

JOSIAH: Stop it, Miranda.

MIRANDA: Why should I? He's been around our necks for years.—All the charm and romance and none of the responsibility. The ever-welcome, wherever we might be—and always the right little, tight little bachelor flat to retire to when—

JOSIAH: That's enough! [MIRANDA *inclines her head. He turns again to* RUSSELL.] All that concerns us now is the fact that Susan has expressed a wish. And, as you well know, I've never been able to refuse her anything, including a divorce.

RUSSELL: Ask yourself *why* she wants to remarry you—or says she does —the real reason for it—? To save you—

JOSIAH: From—from what?

RUSSELL: Yourself. And of all the—

MIRANDA: Look here! That's going—!

RUSSELL: —You keep out!—And of all the lowdown advantages to take of a woman, the threat you're making is about the lowest.

[JOSIAH *slowly lets himself down upon the chair behind the desk, affecting to look the beaten man.*]

JOSIAH: Threat—?

RUSSELL: You heard me! [*He turns upon* MIRANDA.] And so did you!

[JOSIAH *looks away, speaks in a small voice:*]

JOSIAH: How did you know, Russ?

RUSSELL: Never mind how I knew!

JOSIAH: —And Susan too. Miranda and Jock. How completely humiliating—

MIRANDA: Father—darling—

JOSIAH: —Awful—it's awful.

RUSSELL: It certainly is!—A man of your standing, your value, your intellectual power—damn it—your common sense and moral courage—to admit defeat at your age—at any age! It's about as contemptible a—

[MIRANDA *wheels upon him.*]

MIRANDA: —Who the hell do you think you're talking to? And what about?—Cares, duties, responsibilities—you've never had any, except for your own and other people's money. My father's a great man and he's done great work. He's made his own way since the beginning. —And everyone close to him has let him down. And life's piled up on him to a point where it's—it's insupportable. He hasn't any fear and —and now no personal obligations beyond—beyond not making a mess of it, which he never would.—If he's had enough, why shouldn't he have the right to call the turn? Why shouldn't it be his to say when?

RUSSELL: Because it never is! Not if he's a man. He can't *do* it to himself. It's not standing up to things. It's downright cowardly.

[MIRANDA *goes to* JOSIAH, *puts an arm around his shoulder, rests her head on his.*]

MIRANDA: You can do what you like with your life, Father. It's all your own. But I'm telling you one thing now: you do that with it and I'll do the same with my own—at once! And that's a promise! [*Tears fill her eyes and her shoulders begin to shake.*] And I won't want to at all—it will be hard for me—because for all the awful things about it and all the jams I get in, I love living, I just love it—and oh, if you only would again—because I love you too—and I couldn't stand your going that way, and me not having been able—and I'm so crazy about Toby I don't know where I'm at and—all the same, I'd do it! I would, I would!—I promise, promise, promise!—Hear me?

JOSIAH: I hear you, Daughter.

RUSSELL: He can't—he mustn't—he won't, Miranda.

[JOSIAH *rises, an arm around* MIRANDA.]

JOSIAH: Russell—

RUSSELL: What?

JOSIAH: You're right. I won't.

RUSSELL: Oh, thank God.

[MIRANDA *raises her face.*]

MIRANDA: You mean it?

JOSIAH: I mean it.

MIRANDA: Oh—oh—

[*She clings to him.* SUSAN *and* JOCK *come in from the hall,* SUSAN *with a small package.* TOBY *follows them.*]

SUSAN: I found the most charming little thing in a shop on—[*She stops and stares at them.*] But what is it?

JOSIAH: Good morning, Toby.—Susan, Miranda, Jock, Russell—it seems it was discovered, erroneously or otherwise, that I may have had certain dishonorable intentions on myself. It's true that life had more or less lost its savor for me. It's equally true that, among you, somehow you have restored it—for which, my love and thanks.—I've had plenty of trouble, as the sparks fly upward—and may have a lot more. In fact, as a result of it, I may die before my time—at eighty-two or five, say—but I hereby engage in your presence most solemnly that it will never be by my own hand.

JOCK: Get it, Toby?

TOBY: I get it.

RUSSELL: We count on you, Jo.

JOSIAH: Well you may, Russell. At least in that particular.

SUSAN: Oh, I'm so relieved! Of course it does change certain things.

JOSIAH: —I'm well aware of that, my dear. For instance, I think I talked you two into marrying each other.—I've talked a lot of people into a lot of things my life long, including myself. I don't think well of the practice.—And I don't believe either of you want to marry anyone—particularly Susan.

RUSSELL: Now look here—

SUSAN [*Simultaneously*]: Well, I must say!

JOSIAH: Sue, I have a base suspicion that you cooked up the whole idea of Russ and his single blessedness because you so thoroughly enjoy your own. Could I be right?

RUSSELL: Susan—

SUSAN: I'm afraid in a way he is. I'm afraid I must admit that I was rather content with things as they were.

[SUSAN *goes to* MIRANDA, *kisses her briefly.*]

SUSAN: Darling, we *would* see you off, but you know what even the smell of a boat does to me.

MIRANDA: Yes, Mother.

[JOCK *turns abruptly and goes out.*]

SUSAN: Happiness, dear.

MIRANDA: Yes, Mother.—And to you.

[SUSAN *and* RUSSELL *move toward the hall. At the door* SUSAN *stops and glances briefly about the room.*]

SUSAN: I did like this house.

[*They go out. A moment, then*]

MIRANDA: Funny—nothing came out as I intended.—But what the hell!

JOSIAH: What the heaven!—You're the angel that troubled the waters, Miranda.

TOBY: —And got its own little feet a little wet in so doing.

MIRANDA: I hate you.

TOBY: I know.

MIRANDA: Toby—you do understand that I have to go over and tell him myself?

TOBY: Certainly.

MIRANDA: I'll miss you so.

TOBY: I'm coming along, Mandy.

MIRANDA: You're—!

TOBY: —In a bunk in the ship's doctor's cabin, thanks to your father.

MIRANDA: Oh, Father! [*Then*] I don't deserve any of this, but—you're perfectly certain you're going to be all right?

JOSIAH: —Let's even consider that there was a mistake made: that I was just loafing along—and resolving a few personal problems—and catching up on my reading.—And the accidents purely accidental. How about it? All willing?

[TOBY *glances at* MIRANDA, *who suddenly looks crestfallen, then back to* JOSIAH.]

TOBY: That would be a little difficult, sir. You were pretty low in your mind. You weren't in good shape at all. You know how to put down a plane. You know how far you can swim. In public life you're celebrated for—what's the word?—prudence. O.K.—why the sudden recklessness? Whether you knew it yourself or not, you may easily have been headed for—and incidentally, who besides yourself did you want to hurt?

MIRANDA: Toby!

TOBY: Elementary.

JOSIAH: Toby, you rascal.

[TOBY *grins at him.*]

TOBY: Yes, sir.

[MALLOY *comes in from the hall.*]

MIRANDA: Oh, if only you were coming with us!

JOSIAH: It would be nice. But I'm going in the opposite direction. [*He glances at his watch.*] And pretty promptly.

[MALLOY *is moving about putting the room in order.*]

MALLOY: Bags in the car as instructed, sir. And breakfast on the table—if Mr. Jock and the little Miss are leaving any of it.

JOSIAH: Thank you, Malloy. I've had mine. [*To* MIRANDA]—California—to get a man there out of prison.

MIRANDA: Calif—? You mean Uncle Andy's—you mean Sam Foster? [JOSIAH *nods firmly.*] But—

JOSIAH: —You forget what a good lawyer I once was.

MIRANDA: —But that's criminal law!

JOSIAH: I've always had a secret hankering for it. And it seems to me that in these happy halcyon days, it and international are very much the same.

MALLOY: It's an odd-looking car, the one out front, I must say. But a fine-looking lady at the wheel.

JOSIAH: Isn't she?

MALLOY: A pleasant smile.—She's not come in. She said she'd wait. [*He moves toward the hall, stops a moment, looking straight ahead.*] It was curious, how she said it: "I don't mind waiting," she said. "I've been waiting a long time."

[*He goes out, shaking his head.* MIRANDA *moves swiftly to* JOSIAH.]

MIRANDA: Father!

JOSIAH: Daughter!

MIRANDA: Are you going to marry her?

JOSIAH: How do I know? That's one of the good things about life: it's so unexpected.

[*She leans up and kisses him.*]

MIRANDA: Then let's have at it?

JOSIAH: Let's have at it!

[*The curtain begins to fall. She holds out her hand behind her in* TOBY'*s direction.*]

MIRANDA: Come what will?

JOSIAH: Come what may!

[MIRANDA *moves slowly toward* TOBY, *hand out ready to be taken, still looking back at* JOSIAH.]

CURTAIN